# THE CONTEMPORARY WORLD

Since 1850

*Western Society: Institutions and Ideals*

McGRAW-HILL BOOK COMPANY  *New York   St. Louis   San Francisco
Toronto   London   Sydney*

*Melvin Cherno*

*Associate Professor of History, Oakland University*

VOLUME IV

# THE CONTEMPORARY WORLD

Since 1850

*THE CONTEMPORARY WORLD Since 1850, Volume IV*

*The following articles or selections have been reprinted in this volume with the permission of
the publishers:*

Selection from PHYSICS AND PHILOSOPHY by W. Heisenberg. Copyright © 1958 by
Werner Heisenberg. Reprinted by permission of Harper & Row, Publishers.

Selection from THE BROTHERS KARAMAZOV by F. Dostoevski, translated by D. Magarshack. Penguin Books, 1958.

Selection from THE MYTH OF SISYPHUS AND OTHER ESSAYS by Albert Camus, translated by Justin O'Brien. Alfred A. Knopf, Inc., 1926.

Selection from HONEST TO GOD by John A. T. Robinson. © SCM Press Ltd., 1963. Published U. S. A. by the Westminster Press, 1963.

Selection from L'ARGENT by Charles Peguy. Editions Gallimard, 1932.

Selection from THE ECONOMIC CONSEQUENCES OF THE PEACE by John Maynard
Keynes. Copyright 1920 by Harcourt, Brace & World, Inc.; renewed 1948 by Lydia Lapakova
Keynes.

Selection from WHAT IS BACK OF THE WAR by Albert J. Beveridge. Copyright 1915
by the Bobbs-Merrill Co., Inc. Renewed 1942 by Mrs. Catherine Spencer Beveridge. Reprinted
by permission of the publisher, The Bobbs-Merrill Co., Inc.

Selection from Lenin, SELECTED WORKS, Vols. II and VII, Lawrence & Wishart, Ltd.,
London, 1936 and 1937.

"Ignatio Silone," pp. 83–94, 99–112, from THE GOD THAT FAILED, edited by Richard
Crossman. Copyright 1949 by Ignatio Silone. Reprinted by permission of Harper & Row,
Publishers.

Selection from MEIN KAMPF by Adolf Hitler, Manheim translation. Houghton Mifflin Co.,
New York, 1943.

Selection from THE ORIGINS OF TOTALITARIANISM, copyright 1951, 1958 by Hannah
Arendt. Reprinted by permission of Harcourt, Brace & World, Inc.

Selection from THE ORGANIZATION MAN by William H. Whyte, Jr. Simon & Schuster,
Inc. 1956.

Selection from THE HIDDEN PERSUADERS by Vance Packard. Copyright © 1957 by Vance
Packard. Used by permission of David McKay Co., Inc.

Selection from THE DECLINE OF THE WEST, Volume I, by Oswald Spengler. Copyright
1926 by Alfred A. Knopf, Inc.

Selection from THE REVOLT OF THE MASSES by Jose Ortega y Gasset. Copyright 1932
by W. W. Norton & Co., Inc., renewed 1960 by Teresa Carey.

Selection from THE FUTURE AS HISTORY by Robert L. Heilbroner, pp. 175–209. Copyright © 1960 by Robert L. Heilbroner. Reprinted by permission of Harper & Row, Publishers.

"Post-civilization" by Kenneth Boulding, from SEEDS OF LIBERATION, edited by Paul
Goodman. Reprinted with permission of the publisher, George Braziller, Inc., and *Liberation*
magazine.

*To MARIAN WILSON, friend, critic, and secretary extraordinary*

# *Preface*

This anthology grew out of a college freshman course in Western
Institutions and Social Ideas taught by a staff that used original sources
as materials for discussion and analysis. To keep a discussion course stimulating and exciting to teacher and student alike, we found ourselves
supplementing existing anthologies with new documents. This anthology
is the logical end product of these efforts. On the basis of our experience in
discussing original documents in an introductory course, we determined
that three principles should characterize our anthology.

*First,* we asked that an anthology have a range sufficient to allow real
flexibility. A useful anthology should permit the revamping of a course
from year to year, if only to prevent the instructors from going stale.
In theory, our four volumes at well over one million words could
include enough selections to supply a two-year discussion course meeting
four days a week. Attractive as some of us might find such a prospect,
most Western civilization courses meet for a single academic year
and, at that, for one or two weekly discussion sessions. We would expect
most courses to use less than half of the anthologized documents in any
one year. Consequently, this anthology should provide every instructor
(or staff) with ample leeway to assign material to fit his particular students.

Our arrangement of the readings within each of the four volumes is
topical as well as chronological. Although we have grouped together
documents that are likely to be discussed together (or that provide a
common pool from which to choose one reading) and have put them in
what seems to us a sensible sequence, our organization in no way impinges
upon the freedom of the instructor to rearrange as he sees fit.

*Second,* we felt that a useful anthology should have definite limits and
a point of view; otherwise flexibility might dissolve into chaos. Our
limits are explicit: we selected documents either to portray ideas about
Western society or to illustrate Western political, economic, religious,
or other institutions. We did not seek to present historical events as such,
leaving this task to a text or to the discretion of the instructor. By focusing on institutions and social ideas, we excluded "pure" philosophy (such
as linguistic analysis) and "pure" science (such as the Quantum Theory)
on the one hand, and literature and art for their own sakes on the other.
Selections from Chaucer's *Canterbury Tales* and Dostoevski's *The Brothers
Karamazov* appear in this collection because in our judgment they illustrate certain values and institutions better than other available documents. It is in any case obvious that with the availability of primary
works in paperback, an instructor who so wishes can easily pick supple-
mentary literary works. By focusing on the West, we have deliberately

excluded documents from cultures like the Byzantine or Islamic that are related, yet raise complex questions of affiliations best handled in text or lecture.

*Third,* we relied on our classroom experience for selecting documents that by their content and format lend themselves to fruitful and interesting discussion. By choosing selections of from ten to twenty pages, we have been able to include many documents in full and others in excerpts substantial enough to permit the author's line of argument and point of view to emerge. Athough almost every conceivable type of document—from philosophical treatise to personal diary—is represented, we have been sparing in the use of legal and constitutional texts that tend to appeal to professional historians, but are too technical for undergraduate discussion. In making our selections, we have tried neither to draw up a catalogue of familiar names nor to stock a museum of esoterica. We have tried to find and edit the most interesting and significant documents that illustrate major ideological and institutional trends. Some two dozen documents have been specially translated into English for this anthology. Our guidelines throughout have been significance, intrinsic interest, and discussability.

Our introductions preceding the documents attempt to provide just enough background to permit intelligent reading, without prejudging issues by means of capsule summaries or leading questions. They make no claim to provide continuity or depth. We consider it more constructive to suggest to the student—in the short introductory essay following the Table of Contents—the kinds of questions by which he can learn to come to grips with original sources for himself.

From its half-conscious inception to its final form, this four-volume anthology has been a collective venture on the part of three historians and one philosopher. Not only did all the editors participate in the detailed planning of each volume, but each of us has contributed selections and introductions to each of the four volumes. Our overriding concern has been to produce a collection of readings that would be interesting, unhackneyed, and enjoyable to use. We can only hope that we have succeeded.

*Melvin Cherno*

*Peter H. Amann*
*Richard J. Burke, Jr.*
*Gerald M. Straka*

# Contents

## III  IMPRESSIONS OF AN AGE

## IV  MASS SOCIETY IN CRISIS: SINCE 1914

## V  RETROSPECT AND PROSPECT

# On Reading
# Original Sources

A generation ago the historian Carl Becker shocked an after-dinner audience with a speech entitled, "Every Man His Own Historian." His audience was made up of members of the American Historical Association who had come to honor and hear their newly elected president. Yet Becker upset their mental equilibrium—and their digestion—by suggesting that history was not some secret art to be passed on to a cloistered initiate who would emerge years later from behind ivy walls with eyesight impaired and a Ph.D. to his name. Becker's point was that man's attempt to make sense of his own past was a natural and universal concern; that since no two men were alike, every man had to deal with the past—to be his own historian—in terms meaningful to himself. Yet Becker did not imply that all men were equally qualified for the task. Though the past is always seen through human eyes—by someone with interests, predilections, prejudices, and blind spots—there is nonetheless something like 20/20 vision in history as opposed to the myopia that results from lack of training. There are *some* tricks to the trade, and they can be learned.

One of the aims of any course using an anthology such as this is to provide you with some critical insight into the unavoidable job of being your own historian. All your life you will have to come to terms with the past, whether it be yesterday's personal encounter or the international roulette wheel stopping at your number. Even most family arguments boil down to historical controversy.

In dealing with the readings in this anthology, your first objective should be to master the technique of being your own *competent* historian. Here you are asked to make sense of a cultural tradition by analyzing documents illustrating different aspects of that tradition. The variety of documents that you will face is enormous. They may be roughly classified as follows:

1 History, biography, autobiography
2 Letters, journals, memoirs
3 Philosophical and scientific treatises
4 Speeches, sermons, manifestoes, public debates
5 Articles in periodicals
6 Essays, dialogues, poetry
7 Legal and constitutional documents
8 Diplomatic reports

You may best begin your analysis by following some rather basic considerations. Every one of these documents may be studied from various perspectives: each will have (1) an author, (2) a social and cultural context, (3) a purpose or function, (4) a subject matter, (5) a structure and method, and (6) relationship with and affiliations to other documents. You can make each of these "dimensions" of a document a focus for analysis, either by yourself or in class discussion. Each is a *direction* in which you can strike out; each suggests a *question* or a cluster of questions that you can raise about the document. If you learn to ask these questions habitually while reading, you are well on your way toward a critical understanding of history, even in its more difficult social and intellectual aspects.

*Dimension 1: The Author.*   You may read a document as an expression of the author's point of view. A presidential message to Congress, for instance, is an expression of presidential policy on a given problem or problems. You may raise the question of the author's background, of his values and biases. In most cases this is a straightforward enough question. Sometimes this may be a crucial question, although at other times it is of minor importance or even altogether irrelevant.

*Dimension 2: The Historical Context.*   You may read a document as reflecting the social and cultural milieu out of which it comes. When a Chinese leader makes a statement of national policy, for example, to what extent do his ideas and the way in which he puts them reflect the historical experience of China on the one hand, of the Chinese Communist movement on the other? This kind of question is related to the previous one, yet it is broader: it involves the ideas and values held during whole historical eras. You should learn to move back and forth between textbook and documents, evaluating the textbook interpretations of the Protestant Reformation or of the Industrial Revolution in terms of generalizations you have drawn from your original readings for each period.

*Dimension 3: The Purpose.*   Not all documents aim simply to tell the truth, the whole truth, and nothing but the truth. Many of them, through the use of rhetorical devices, are designed to win a case, whether in an actual court, in formal debate, or in a wider forum of opinion. Many are pitched to a special audience to get some particular point across, for instance, a speech of Adolf Hitler's addressing a Nazi party rally. Some are justifications of actions already taken, others exhortations for the future. Clearly, all written documents are intelligible only in terms of the purpose or function they intended to serve and of the audience they attempted to reach.

*Dimension 4: The Subject Matter.*   This may be the obvious question, yet it may not always be easy to answer. What is the reading about? You should practice summarizing documents in your own words and as briefly as possible, particularly when this is difficult to do. You may have to summarize ideas that have been advanced or to characterize institutions that have been described or exemplified. In historical or biographical narratives, subject matter is normally central. What were the ancient Germans like? What sort of man was Leonardo da Vinci? What was the structure of the ancient Roman Republic? What was life like at the court of Louis XIV of France?

*Dimension 5: Structure and Method.* This is the *internal* dimension. How does a document hang together? What is the relation of the parts to the whole? *How* does the President present his case for certain legislation to Congress? In a straightforward historical narrative or a list of grievances, these internal relationships may be very simple; in a philosophical treatise or in a tragedy the internal structure may be very complex and artful. If a document presents an *argument,* then the question of its validity is perfectly in order, as is the question of the truth of its premises.

*Dimension 6: Relationships to Other Documents.* In this broad category fall all the questions about the influence of earlier writers on later ones and about similarities, contrasts, "climates of opinion," and traditions. How does the foreign policy statement of our Chinese Communist leader compare with earlier such announcements? With announced Russian Communist aims, recent and in Lenin's day? With the way non-Communist countries justify and announce their policy? Does our Chinese Communist seem to follow the guidelines for holding on to power suggested by Machiavelli in the sixteenth century? You may consider a given document as an effect of earlier developments and as a cause of subsequent ones. It may be combined with others of its own period to form a trend. It may be grouped in countless ways. As editors, we have already done some grouping by dividing the readings into four volumes and by choosing an arrangement within the volumes that is partly topical. Your instructor, by assigning some readings and not others, will have made yet another such grouping.

All this may seem very abstract and remote, until you really get down to cases. Take, as an example, the Declaration of Independence of July 4, 1776 (see Vol. III, pages 327–330). This document is at least vaguely familiar to most Americans, yet it reveals its full significance—as well as a nest of controversial issues—only when analyzed in terms of the six dimensions that have been suggested.

The Declaration of Independence was drafted chiefly by Thomas Jefferson, revised by a committee that included Benjamin Franklin and John Adams, and signed by all fifty-six delegates to the Second Continental Congress, the representatives of the "Thirteen" United States of America. Who, then, was its *author?* Does it really represent the views of all the inhabitants of those thirteen states? A majority of them? How were the delegates elected?

The social and cultural *context* of the document was the eighteenth-century Enlightenment, with its appeal to "self-evident truths" characteristic of that period's buoyant confidence in the power of human reason to apprehend objective fact. Could such an appeal carry any force today, after modern psychology has revealed the numberless ways in which we all deceive ourselves and after the history of modern wars and totalitarian regimes has demonstrated the folly of calling man the "rational animal"?

The *purpose* of the Declaration, as we are told explicitly, is to justify the revolution of the thirteen colonies against their mother country. But what is "justification"? Is it only a convenient cover-up for what they had undertaken? Was it an attempt to win support from other countries, perhaps from France?

As for its *subject matter,* most of it seems to be about the actions of "the present

King of Great Britain." (This is puzzling in itself, for did not the Glorious Revolution of 1688–1689 establish the supremacy of Parliament over the King?) On closer examination, however, these actions all have one thing in common: they are allegedly violations of the "rights" of the colonists. With this as a clue, we see that the opening and closing sections of the document also deal with the concept of rights.

This leads to a consideration of the *structure* of the Declaration of Independence, which proves to be that of a "hypothetical syllogism": *if* any government fails to protect the rights of its citizens to life, liberty, and the pursuit of happiness, *then* such a government forfeits all claim to their allegiance; the English government *has* failed to protect our rights (the long list of grievances is intended to prove this) ; *therefore* we owe the English government no allegiance. This is Jefferson's argument reduced to its essentials. In form it is a logical argument: if $x$ is true, then $y$ is true; but $x$ *is* true: therefore $y$ is true. If its premises are also true—and this is quite another question—then its conclusion must be accepted. But what are these premises? How can we tell whether they are true?

Finally, the Declaration of Independence reveals the strong *influence* of John Locke's Second Treatise of Civil Government (see Vol. III, pages 44–64), and in turn the Declaration of Independence had an undoubted *effect* on the great French Revolution that broke out only thirteen years later. Did the Declaration also serve as the basis for the United States Constitution, or was that latter document founded on different philosophical premises? Did the Declaration establish political democracy? Did it have anything to say about capitalism? Have the principles set forth in the Declaration played any part in the current wave of colonial wars of independence in Africa and Asia?

Not all these dimensions are equally important in every document. Even so, you would do well to cultivate the habit of asking yourself all six questions about every document you encounter, before deciding which are the most significant in each particular case. In time this becomes second nature, yet to do this is to cultivate the critical faculty that is an essential part of an educated man.

*THE CONTEMPORARY WORLD*

Since 1850

*Part One*

# Intellectual Currents

# ୶ LECTURES ON THE PHILOSOPHY OF HISTORY

*Georg Wilhelm Friedrich Hegel*

*Georg Wilhelm Friedrich Hegel (1770–1831) was the author of the most comprehensive and influential system of philosophy in modern times. Very much a part of the Napoleonic era, his writings nevertheless are closely related to trends in our own time—nationalism, fascism, communism, even our emphasis on the social sciences.*

*Hegel wrote books on theology, logic, metaphysics, natural science, politics, ethics, and law. After his death four more books were compiled from his famous lectures at the University of Berlin on religion, art, the history of philosophy, and "philosophical history." It is from the last of these compilations that the following selection is taken.*

*All this was not simply fearsome erudition. These bodies of knowledge were carefully organized, not only internally but each in relation to the others, so that they formed a unified whole. The idea which ties them all together is* development, *or change taking place according to a definite law. Everything in nature is developing, including man, and therefore including human society and the human mind itself. Only with a philosophical method as dynamic and flexible as reality itself can we hope to catch reality on the wing, avoiding cold abstractions and irrelevant formalism.*

*Hegel's philosophy is usually called "absolute idealism," but no two words can begin to convey the breadth and complexity of his thought. He was convinced that he had not only incorporated within his system the main points of all the great thinkers since the ancient Greeks, but that he had also anticipated all the possible objections to this system and refuted them within the system itself. It was designed to be a grand synthesis in which everything of value in human civilization finds its proper place and can thus be properly appreciated and understood.*

*Hegel, as a contemporary of Goethe and Schiller, Beethoven and Schubert, may be considered a romantic philosopher. He found logic divorced from life, and he tried to reconcile them by injecting life into logic. By "reason" he meant not dry analysis but the vital process of thinking that leads from a problem to its solution and on to another problem. His great discovery was that nature and society acted as if they too were thinking. Everything seemed to be governed by a vast plan, as Christian theologians had been saying all along (Hegel spent his early years in a seminary); but for him this plan was internal rather than*

3

*external, flowing from the tendency of all things to develop according to their own inner laws. This conception, a brilliant combination of Aristotle, Saint Augustine, and modern Enlightenment, offered something to everyone. And, in fact, nearly everyone was influenced by it, each emphasizing those aspects of it which he found most congenial.*

*Hegel was a supporter of the Prussian monarchy, but he had also written favorably of the French Revolution and Napoleon; both had come about through necessary laws of development, so each was right for its time and place. He was hailed by Christians for having rescued religion from the materialists and by atheists for having spoken of spiritual matters in purely human terms. Marx and Engels acknowledged him as their mentor and as a forerunner of communism, but so did Mussolini with his fascism and John Dewey with his liberalism.*

*This selection is taken from Hegel's* Lectures on the Philosophy of History, *edited by E. Gans in 1837. By the phrase "philosophy of history" Hegel meant simply the demonstration that history is governed by laws of development, a concept which has exerted a decisive influence on modern European thinking about man and society. His view of history as determined by vast impersonal forces rather than by outstanding individuals and events is the starting point for all modern work in this area.*

. . . The most general definition that can be given, is, that the Philosophy of History means nothing but the *thoughtful consideration of it.* Thought is, indeed, essential to humanity. It is this that distinguishes us from the brutes. In sensation, cognition, and intellection; in our instincts and volitions, as far as they are truly human, Thought is an invariable element. To insist upon Thought in this connection with history may, however, appear unsatisfactory. In this science it would seem as if Thought must be subordinate to what is given, to the realities of fact; that this is its basis and guide: while Philosophy dwells in the region of self-produced ideas, without reference to actuality. Approaching history thus prepossessed, Speculation might be expected to treat it as a mere passive material; and, so far from leaving it in its native truth, to force it into conformity with a tyrannous idea, and to construe it, as the phrase is *"à priori."* But as it is the business of history simply to adopt into its records what is and has been, actual occurrences and transactions; and since it remains true to its character in proportion as it strictly adheres to its data, we seem to have in Philosophy, a process diametrically opposed to that of the historiographer. This contradiction, and the charge consequently brought against speculation, shall be explained and confuted. We

G. W. F. Hegel, *Lectures on the Philosophy of History,* trans. J. Sibree (New York: Dover Publications, Inc., 1956), pp. 8–10, 13–15, 27–33, 38–40, 45–46, 52–53, 73–75, 78–79.

do not, however, propose to correct the innumerable special misrepresentations, trite or novel, that are current respecting the aims, the interests, and the modes of treating history, and its relation to Philosophy.

The only Thought which Philosophy brings with it to the contemplation of History, is the simple conception of *Reason;* that Reason is the Sovereign of the World; that the history of the world, therefore, presents us with a rational process. This conviction and intuition is a hypothesis in the domain of history as such. In that of Philosophy it is no hypothesis. It is there proved by speculative cognition, that Reason—and this term may here suffice us, without investigating the relation sustained by the Universe to the Divine Being—is *Substance,* as well as *Infinite Power;* its own *Infinite Material* underlying all the natural and spiritual life which it originates, as also the *Infinite Form*—that which sets this Material in motion. On the one hand, Reason is the *substance* of the Universe; viz., that by which and in which all reality has its being and subsistence. On the other hand, it is the *Infinite Energy* of the Universe; since Reason is not so powerless as to be incapable of producing anything but a mere ideal, a mere intention—having its place outside reality, nobody knows where; something separate and abstract, in the heads of certain human beings. It is *the infinite complex of things,* their entire Essence and Truth. It is its own material which it commits to its own Active Energy to work up; not needing, as finite action does, the conditions of an external material of given means from which it may obtain its support, and the objects of its activity. It supplies its own nourishment, and is the object of its own operations. While it is exclusively its own basis of existence, and absolute final aim, it is also the energizing power realizing this aim; developing it not only in the phenomena of the Natural, but also of the Spiritual Universe—the History of the World. That this "Idea" or "Reason" is the *True,* the *Eternal,* the absolutely *powerful* essence; that it reveals itself in the World, and that in that World nothing else is revealed but this and its honor and glory—is the thesis which, as we have said, has been proved in Philosophy, and is here regarded as demonstrated.

In those of my hearers who are not acquainted with Philosophy, I may fairly presume, at least, the existence of a *belief* in Reason, a desire, a thirst for acquaintance with it, in entering upon this course of Lectures. It is, in fact, the wish for rational insight, not the ambition to amass a mere heap of acquirements, that should be presupposed in every case as possessing the mind of the learner in the study of science. If the clear idea of Reason is not already developed in our minds, in beginning the study of Universal History, we should at least have the firm, unconquerable faith that Reason *does* exist there; and that the World of intelligence and conscious volition is not abandoned to chance, but must show itself in the light of the self-cognizant Idea. Yet I am not obliged to make any such preliminary demand upon your faith. What I have said thus provisionally, and what I shall have further to say, is, even in reference to *our* branch of science, not to be regarded as hypothetical, but as a summary view of the whole; the *result of the investigation* we are about to pursue; a result which happens to be known to *me,* because I have traversed the entire field. It is only an inference from the history of the World, that its development has been a rational process; that the history in question has constituted the rational necessary course of the World-Spirit—that Spirit whose nature is always one and the same, but which unfolds this its one nature in the phenomena of the World's existence. This must, as before stated, present itself as the ultimate *result* of History. But we have to take the latter as it is. We must proceed historically—empirically. . . .

The science of which we have to treat, proposes itself to furnish the proof (not indeed of the abstract *Truth* of the doctrine, but) of its correctness as compared with facts. The truth, then, that a Providence (that of God) presides over the events of the World—consorts with the proposition in question; for *Divine* Providence is Wisdom, endowed with an infinite Power, which realizes its aim, viz., the absolute rational design of the World. Reason is Thought conditioning itself with perfect freedom. But a difference—rather a contradiction—will manifest itself, between this belief and our principle, just as was the case in reference to the demand made by Socrates in the case of Anaxagoras's dictum. For that belief is similarly indefinite; it is what is called a belief in a general Providence, and is not followed out into definite application, or displayed in its bearing on the grand total—the entire course of human history. But to *explain* History is to depict the passions of mankind, the genius, the active powers, that play their part on the great stage; and the providentially determined process which these exhibit, constitutes what is generally called the "plan" of Providence. Yet it is this very plan which is supposed to be concealed from our view: which it is deemed presumption, even to wish to recognize. The ignorance of Anaxagoras, as to how intelligence reveals itself in actual existence, was ingenuous. Neither in his consciousness, nor in that of Greece at large, had that thought been farther expanded. He had not attained the power to apply his general principle to the concrete, so as to deduce the latter from the former. It was Socrates who took the first step in comprehending the union of the Concrete with the Universal. Anaxagoras, then, did not take up a *hostile* position toward such an application. The common belief in Providence *does;* at least it opposes the use of the principle on the large scale, and denies the possibility of discerning the plan of Providence. In isolated cases this plan is supposed to be manifest. Pious persons are encouraged to recognize in particular circumstances, something more than mere chance; to acknowledge the guiding hand of God; *e.g.,* when help has unexpectedly come to an individual in great perplexity and need. But these instances of providential design are of a limited kind, and concern the accomplishment of nothing more than the desires of the individual in question. But in the history of the World, the *Individuals* we have to do with are *Peoples;* Totalities that are States. We cannot, therefore, be satisfied with what we may call this "peddling" view of Providence, to which the belief alluded to limits itself. Equally unsatisfactory is the merely abstract, undefined belief in a Providence, when that belief is not brought to bear upon the details of the process which it conducts. On the contrary our earnest endeavor must be directed to the recognition of the ways of Providence, the means it uses, and the historical phenomena in which it manifests itself; and we must show their connection with the general principle above mentioned. But in noticing the recognition of the plan of Divine Providence generally, I have implicitly touched upon a prominent question of the day; viz., that of the possibility of knowing God: or rather—since public opinion has ceased to allow it to be a matter of *question*—the *doctrine* that it is impossible to know God. In direct contravention of what is commanded in holy Scripture as the highest duty—that we should not merely love, but *know* God—the prevalent dogma involves the denial of what is there said; viz., that it is the Spirit (der Geist) that leads into Truth, knows all things, penetrates even into the deep things of the Godhead. While the Divine Being is thus placed beyond our knowledge, and outside the limit of all human things, we have the convenient license of wandering as far as we list, in the direction of our own fancies. We are freed from the obligation to refer our knowledge to the Divine and True. On the other hand, the vanity and egotism which characterize it, find, in this false position, ample justification; and the pious modesty which puts far from it the knowledge of God, can well estimate how much furtherance thereby accrues to its own wayward and vain strivings. I have been unwilling to leave out of sight the connection between our thesis—that Reason governs and has governed the World—and the question of the possibility of a knowledge of God, chiefly that I might not lose the opportunity of mentioning the imputation against Philosophy of being shy of noticing religious truths, or of having occasion to be so; in which is insinuated the suspicion that it has anything but a clear conscience in the presence of these truths. So far from this being the case, the fact is, that in recent times Philosophy has been obliged to defend the domain of religion against the attacks of several theological systems. In the Christian religion God has revealed Himself—that is, he has given us to understand what He is; so that He is no longer a concealed or secret existence. And this possibility of knowing Him, thus afforded us, renders such knowledge a duty. God wishes no narrow-hearted souls or empty heads for his children; but those whose spirit is of itself indeed, poor, but rich in the knowledge of Him; and who regard this knowledge of God as the only valuable possession. That development of the thinking spirit, which has resulted from the revelation of the Divine Being as its original basis, must ultimately advance to the *intellectual* comprehension of what was presented in the first instance, to *feeling* and *imagination*. The time must eventually come for understanding that rich product of active Reason, which the History of the World offers to us. It was for awhile the fashion to profess admiration for the wisdom of God, as displayed in animals, plants, and isolated occurrences. But, if it be allowed that Providence manifests itself in such objects and forms of existence, why not also in Universal History? This is deemed too great a matter to be thus regarded. But Divine Wisdom, *i.e.,* Reason, is one and the same in the great as in the little; and we must not imagine God to be too weak to exercise his wisdom on the grand scale. Our intellectual striving aims at realizing the conviction that what was *intended* by eternal wisdom, is actually *accomplished* in the domain of existent, active Spirit, as well as in that of mere Nature. Our mode of treating the subject is, in this aspect, a Theodicæa—a justification of the ways of God—which Leibnitz attempted metaphysically, in his method, *i.e.,* in indefinite abstract categories—so that the ill that is found in the World may be comprehended, and the thinking Spirit reconciled with the fact of the existence of evil. . . .

I will endeavor to make what has been said more vivid and clear by examples.

The building of a house is, in the first instance, a subjective aim and design. On the other hand we have, as means, the several substances required for the work—Iron, Wood, Stones. The elements are made use of in working up this material: fire to melt the iron, wind to blow the fire, water to set wheels in motion, in order to cut the wood, etc. The result is, that the wind, which has helped to build the house, is shut out by the house; so also are the violence of rains and floods, and the destructive powers of fire, so far as the house is made fireproof. The stones and beams obey the law of gravity—press downward—and so high walls are carried up. Thus the elements are made use of in accordance with their nature, and yet to co-operate for a product, by which their operation is limited. Thus the passions of men are gratified; they develop themselves and their aims in accordance with their natural tendencies, and build up the edifice of human society; thus fortifying a position for Right and Order *against themselves.*

The connection of events above indicated, involves also the fact, that in history an additional result is commonly produced by human actions beyond that which they aim at and obtain—that which they immediately recognize and desire. They gratify their own interest; but something further is thereby accomplished, latent in the actions in question, though not present to their consciousness, and not included in their design. An analogous example is offered in the case of a man who, from a feeling of revenge —perhaps not an unjust one, but produced by injury on the other's part—burns that other man's house. A connection is immediately established between the deed itself and a train of circumstances not directly included in it, taken abstractedly. In itself it consisted in merely presenting a small flame to a small portion of a beam. Events not involved in that simple act follow of themselves. The part of the beam which was set fire to is connected with its remote portions; the beam itself is united with the woodwork of the house generally, and this with other houses; so that a wide conflagration ensues, which destroys the goods and chattels of many other persons besides his against whom the act of revenge was first directed; perhaps even costs not a few men their lives. This lay neither in the deed abstractedly, nor in the design of the man who committed it. But the action has a further general bearing. In the design of the doer it was only revenge executed against an individual in the destruction of his property, but it is moreover a crime, and that involves punishment also. This may not have been present to the mind of the perpetrator, still less in .his intention; but his deed itself, the general principles it calls into play, its substantial content entails it. By this example I wish only to impress on you the consideration, that in a simple act, something further may be implicated than lies in the intention and consciousness of the agent. The example before us involves, however, this additional consideration, that the substance of the act, consequently we may say the act itself recoils, upon the perpetrator—reacts upon him with destructive tendency. This union of the two extremes —the embodiment of a general idea in the form of direct reality, and the elevation of a specialty into connection with universal truth—is brought to pass, at first sight, under the conditions of an utter diversity of nature between the two, and an indifference of the one extreme towards the other. The aims which the agents set before them are limited and special; but it must be remarked that the agents themselves are intelligent thinking beings. The purport of their desires is interwoven with *general, essential* considerations of justice, good, duty, etc.; for mere desire—volition in its rough and savage forms—falls not within the scene and sphere of Universal History. Those general considerations, which form at the same time a norm for directing aims and actions, have a determinate purport; for such an abstraction as "good for its own sake," has no place in living reality. If men are to act, they must not only intend the Good, but must have decided for themselves whether this or that particular thing is a Good. What special course of action, however, is good or not, is determined, as regards the ordinary contingencies of private life, by the laws and customs of a State;

and here no great difficulty is presented. Each individual has his position; he knows
on the whole what a just, honorable course of conduct is. As to ordinary, private relations, the assertion that it is difficult to choose the right and good—the regarding it
as the mark of an exalted morality to find difficulties and raise scruples on that score—
may be set down to an evil or perverse will, which seeks to evade duties not in themselves of a perplexing nature; or, at any rate, to an idly reflective habit of mind—
where a feeble will affords no sufficient exercise to the faculties—leaving them therefore to find occupation within themselves, and to expend themselves on moral self-
adulation.

It is quite otherwise with the comprehensive relations that History has to do with.
In this sphere are presented those momentous collisions between existing, acknowledged duties, laws, and rights, and those contingencies which are adverse to this fixed
system; which assail and even destroy its foundations and existence; whose tenor may
nevertheless seem good—on the large scale advantageous—yes, even indispensable
and necessary. These contingencies realize themselves in History: they involve a general
principle of a different order from that on which depends the *permanence* of a people
or a State. This principle is an essential phase in the development of the *creating* Idea,
of Truth striving and urging towards [consciousness of] itself. Historical men—
*World-Historical Individuals*—are those in whose aims such a general principle lies.

Cæsar, in danger of losing a position, not perhaps at that time of superiority, yet
at least of equality with the others who were at the head of the State, and of succumbing to those who were just on the point of becoming his enemies—belongs essentially
to this category. These enemies—who were at the same time pursuing *their* personal
aims—had the form of the constitution, and the power conferred by an appearance
of justice, on their side. Cæsar was contending for the maintenance of his position,
honor, and safety; and, since the power of his opponents included the sovereignty
over the provinces of the Roman Empire, his victory secured for him the conquest of
that entire Empire; and he thus became—though leaving the form of the constitution
—the Autocrat of the State. That which secured for him the execution of a design,
which in the first instance was of negative import—the Autocracy of Rome—was,
however, at the same time an independently necessary feature in the history of Rome
and of the world. It was not, then, his private gain merely, but an unconscious impulse that occasioned the accomplishment of that for which the time was ripe. Such are
all great historical men—whose own particular aims involve those large issues which
are the will of the World-Spirit. They may be called Heroes, inasmuch as they have
derived their purposes and their vocation, not from the calm, regular course of things,
sanctioned by the existing order; but from a concealed fount—one which has not attained to phenomenal, present existence—from that inner Spirit, still hidden beneath
the surface, which, impinging on the outer world as on a shell, bursts it in pieces, because it is another kernel than that which belonged to the shell in question. They are
men, therefore, who appear to draw the impulse of their life from themselves; and
whose deeds have produced a condition of things and a complex of historical relations
which appear to be only *their* interest, and *their* work.

Such individuals had no consciousness of the general Idea they were unfolding,
while prosecuting those aims of theirs; on the contrary, they were practical, political
men. But at the same time they were thinking men, who had an insight into the re-

quirements of the time—*what was ripe for development*. This was the very Truth for their age, for their world; the species next in order, so to speak, and which was already formed in the womb of time. It was theirs to know this nascent principle; the necessary, directly sequent step in progress, which their world was to take; to make this their aim, and to expend their energy in promoting it. World-historical men—the Heroes of an epoch—must, therefore, be recognized as its clear-sighted ones; *their* deeds, *their* words are the best of that time. Great men have formed purposes to satisfy themselves, not others. Whatever prudent designs and counsels they might have learned from others, would be the more limited and inconsistent features in their career; for it was they who best understood affairs; from whom *others* learned, and approved, or at least acquiesced in—their policy. For that Spirit which had taken this fresh step in history is the inmost soul of all individuals; but in a state of unconsciousness which the great men in question aroused. Their fellows, therefore, follow these soul-leaders; for they feel the irresistible power of their own inner Spirit thus embodied. If we go on to cast a look at the fate of these World-Historical persons, whose vocation it was to be the agents of the World-Spirit—we shall find it to have been no happy one. They attained no calm enjoyment; their whole life was labor and trouble; their whole nature was nought else but their master-passion. When their object is attained they fall off like empty hulls from the kernel. They die early, like Alexander; they are murdered, like Cæsar; transported to St. Helena, like Napoleon. This fearful consolation—that historical men have not enjoyed what is called happiness, and of which only private life (and this may be passed under very various external circumstances) is capable—this consolation those may draw from history, who stand in need of it; and it is craved by Envy—vexed at what is great and transcendant—striving, therefore, to depreciate it, and to find some flaw in it. Thus in modern times it has been demonstrated *ad nauseam* that princes are generally unhappy on their thrones; in consideration of which the possession of a throne is tolerated, and men acquiesce in the fact that not themselves but the personages in question are its occupants. The Free Man, we may observe, is not envious, but gladly recognizes what is great and exalted, and rejoices that it exists.

It is in the light of those common elements which constitute the interest and therefore the passions of individuals, that these historical men are to be regarded. They are *great* men, because they willed and accomplished something great; not a mere fancy, a mere intention, but that which met the case and fell in with the needs of the age. This mode of considering them also excludes the so-called "psychological" view, which—serving the purpose of envy most effectually—contrives so to refer all actions to the heart—to bring them under such a subjective aspect—as that their authors appear to have done everything under the impulse of some passion, mean or grand—some *morbid craving*—and on account of these passions and cravings to have been not moral men. Alexander of Macedon partly subdued Greece, and then Asia; therefore he was possessed by a *morbid craving* for conquest. He is alleged to have acted from a craving for fame, for conquest; and the proof that these were the impelling motives is that he did that which resulted in fame. What pedagogue has not demonstrated of Alexander the Great—of Julius Cæsar—that they were instigated by such passions, and were consequently immoral men?—whence the conclusion immediately follows that he, the pedagogue, is a better man than they, because he has not such passions;

a proof of which lies in the fact that he does not conquer Asia—vanquish Darius and Porus—but while he enjoys life himself, lets others enjoy it too. These psychologists are particularly fond of contemplating those peculiarities of great historical figures which appertain to them as private persons. Man must eat and drink; he sustains relations to friends and acquaintances; he has passing impulses and ebullitions of temper. "No man is a hero to his *valet-de-chambre*," is a well-known proverb; I have added—and Goethe repeated it ten years later—"but not because the former is no hero, but because the latter is a valet." He takes off the hero's boots, assists him to bed, knows that he prefers champagne, etc. Historical personages waited upon in historical literature by such psychological valets, come poorly off; they are brought down by these their attendants to a level with—or rather a few degrees below the level of —the morality of such exquisite discerners of spirits. The Thersites of Homer who abuses the kings is a standing figure for all times. Blows—that is beating with a solid cudgel—he does not get in every age, as in the Homeric one; but his envy, his egotism, is the thorn which he has to carry in his flesh; and the undying worm that gnaws him is the tormenting consideration that his excellent views and vituperations remain absolutely without result in the world. But our satisfaction at the fate of Thersitism also, may have its sinister side.

A World-historical individual is not so unwise as to indulge a variety of wishes to divide his regards. He is devoted to the One Aim, regardless of all else. It is even possible that such men may treat other great, even sacred interests, inconsiderately; conduct which is indeed obnoxious to moral reprehension. But so mighty a form must trample down many an innocent flower—crush to pieces many an object in its path.

The special interest of passion is thus inseparable from the active development of a general principle: for it is from the special and determinate and from its negation, that the Universal results. Particularity contends with its like, and some loss is involved in the issue. *It* is not the general idea that is implicated in opposition and combat, and that is exposed to danger. It remains in the background, untouched and uninjured. This may be called the *cunning of reason*—that it sets the passions to work for itself, while that which develops its existence through such impulsion pays the penalty, and suffers loss. For it is *phenomenal* being that is so treated, and of this, part is of no value, part is positive and real. The particular is for the most part of too trifling value as compared with the general: individuals are sacrificed and abandoned. The Idea pays the penalty of determinate existence and of corruptibility, not from itself, but from the passions of individuals. . . .

We have spoken of *means;* but in the carrying out of a subjective, limited aim, we have also to take into consideration the element of a *material,* either already present or which has to be procured. Thus the question would arise: What is the material in which the Ideal of Reason is wrought out? The primary answer would be —Personality itself—human desires—Subjectivity generally. In human knowledge and volition, as its material element, Reason attains positive existence. We have considered subjective volition where it has an object which is the truth and essence of a reality, viz., where it constitutes a great world-historical passion. As a subjective will, occupied with limited passions, it is dependent, and can gratify its desires only within the limits of this dependence. But the subjective will has also a substantial life—a reality—in which it moves in the region of *essential* being, and has the essential itself as the object of its existence. This essential being is the union of the *subjective* with the *rational* Will: it is the moral Whole, the *State,* which is that form of reality in which the individual has and enjoys his freedom; but on the condition of his recognizing, believing in, and willing that which is common to the Whole. And this must not be understood as if the subjective will of the social unit attained its gratification and enjoyment through that common Will; as if this were a means provided for its benefit; as if the individual, in his relations to other individuals, thus limited his freedom, in order that this universal limitation—the mutual constraint of all— might secure a small space of liberty for each. Rather, we affirm, are Law, Morality, Government, and they alone, the positive reality and completion of Freedom. Freedom of a low and limited order, is mere caprice; which finds its exercise in the sphere of particular and limited desires.

Subjective volition—Passion—is that which sets men in activity, that which effects "practical" realization. The Idea is the inner spring of action; the State is the actually existing, realized moral life. For it is the Unity of the universal, essential Will, with that of the individual; and this is "Morality." The Individual living in this unity has a moral life; possesses a value that consists in this substantiality alone. Sophocles in his Antigone, says, "The divine commands are not of yesterday, nor of to-day; no, they have an infinite existence, and no one could say whence they came." The laws of morality are not accidental, but are the essentially Rational. It is the very object of the State that what is essential in the practical activity of men, and in their dispositions, should be duly recognized; that it should have a manifest existence, and maintain its position. It is the absolute interest of Reason that this moral Whole should exist; and herein lies the justification and merit of heroes who have founded states—however rude these may have been. In the history of the World, only those peoples can come under our notice which form a state. For it must be understood that this latter is the realization of Freedom, *i.e.* of the absolute final aim, and that it exists for its own sake. It must further be understood that all the worth which the human being possesses—all spiritual reality, he possesses only through the State. For his spiritual reality consists in this, that his own essence—Reason—is objectively present to him, that it possesses objective immediate existence for him. Thus only is he fully conscious; thus only is he a partaker of morality—of a just and moral social and political life. For Truth is the Unity of the universal and subjective Will; and the Universal is to be found in the State, in its laws, its universal and rational arrangements. The State is the Divine Idea as it exists on Earth. We have in it, therefore, the object of History in a more definite shape than before; that in which Freedom obtains objectivity, and lives in the enjoyment of this objectivity. For Law is the objectivity of Spirit; volition in its true form. Only that will which obeys law, is free; for it obeys itself—it is independent and so free. When the State or our country constitutes a community of existence; when the subjective will of man submits to laws—the contradiction between Liberty and Necessity vanishes. The Rational has necessary existence, as being the reality and substance of things, and we are free in recognizing it as law, and following it as the substance of our own being. The objective and the subjective will are then reconciled, and present one identical homogeneous whole. For the morality (*Sittlichkeit*) of the State is not of that ethical (*moralische*) reflective kind, in which one's own conviction bears sway; this latter is rather the peculiarity of the modern time, while the true antique morality is based on the principle of abiding by one's duty [to the state at large]. An Athenian citizen did what was required of him, as it were from instinct: but if I reflect on the object of my activity, I must have the consciousness that my will has been called into exercise. But morality is Duty—substantial Right—a "*second* nature" as it has been justly called; for the *first* nature of man is his primary merely animal existence. . . .

The inquiry into the best constitution is frequently treated as if not only the theory were an affair of subjective independent conviction, but as if the introduction of a constitution recognized as the best—or as superior to others—could be the result of a resolve adopted in this theoretical manner; as if the form of a constitution were a matter of free choice, determined by nothing else but reflection. Of this artless fashion was that deliberation—not indeed of the Persian *people*, but of the Persian *grandees*, who had conspired to overthrow the pseudo-Smerdis and the Magi, after their undertaking had succeeded, and when there was no scion of the royal family living—as to what constitution they should introduce into Persia; and Herodotus gives an equally naïve account of this deliberation.

In the present day, the Constitution of a country and people is not represented as so entirely dependent on free and deliberate choice. The fundamental but abstractly (and therefore imperfectly) entertained conception of Freedom, has resulted in the Republic being very generally regarded—in *theory*—as the only just and true political constitution. Many even, who occupy elevated official positions under monarchical constitutions—so far from being opposed to this idea—are actually its supporters; only they see that such a constitution, though the best, cannot be realized under all circumstances; and that—while men are what they are—we must be satisfied with less freedom; the monarchical constitution—under the given circumstances, and the present moral condition of the people—being even regarded as the most advantageous. In this view also, the necessity of a particular constitution is made to depend on the condition of the people in such a way as if the latter were non-essential and accidental. This representation is founded on the distinction which the reflective understanding makes between an idea and the corresponding reality; holding to an abstract and consequently untrue idea; not grasping it in its completeness, or—which is virtually, though not in point of form, the same—not taking a concrete view of a people and a state. We shall have to show further on, that the constitution adopted by a people makes one substance—one spirit—with its religion, its art and philosophy, or, at least, with its conceptions and thoughts—its culture generally; not to expatiate upon the additional influences, *ab extrâ*, of climate, of neighbors, of its place in the World. A State is an individual totality, of which you cannot select any particular side, although a supremely important one, such as its political constitution; and deliberate and decide respecting it in that isolated form. Not only is that constitution most intimately connected with and dependent on those other spiritual forces; but the form of the entire moral and intellectual individuality —comprising all the forces it embodies—is only a step in the development of the grand Whole—with its place preappointed in the process; a fact which gives the highest sanction to the constitution in question, and establishes its absolute necessity. —The origin of a state involves imperious lordship on the one hand, instinctive submission on the other. But even obedience—lordly power, and the fear inspired by a ruler—in itself implies some degree of voluntary connection. Even in barbarous states this is the case; it is not the isolated will of individuals that prevails; individual pretensions are relinquished, and the general will is the essential bond of political union. This unity of the general and the particular is the Idea itself, manifesting itself as a *state*, and which subsequently undergoes further development within itself. The abstract yet necessitated process in the development of truly independent states is as follows:—They begin with regal power, whether of patriarchal or military origin. In the next phase, particularity and individuality assert themselves in the form of Aristocracy and Democracy. Lastly, we have the subjection of these separate interests to a single power; but which can be absolutely none other than one outside of which those spheres have an independent position, viz., the Monarchical. Two phases of royalty, therefore, must be distinguished—a primary and a secondary one. This process is necessitated, so that the form of government assigned to a particular stage of development *must* present itself: it is therefore no matter of choice, but is that form which is adapted to the spirit of the people. . . .

Summing up what has been said of the State, we find that we have been led to call its vital principle, as actuating the individuals who compose it—Morality. The State, its laws, its arrangements, constitute the rights of its members; its natural features, its mountains, air, and waters, are *their* country, their fatherland, their outward material property; the history of this State, *their* deeds; what their ancestors have produced, belongs to them and lives in their memory. All is their possession, just as they are possessed by it; for it constitutes their existence, their being.

Their imagination is occupied with the ideas thus presented, while the adoption of these laws, and of a fatherland so conditioned is the expression of their will. It is this matured totality which thus constitutes *one* Being, the spirit of *one* People. To it the individual members belong; each unit is the Son of his Nation, and at the same time—in as far as the State to which he belongs is undergoing development—the Son of his Age. None remains behind it, still less advances beyond it. This spiritual Being (the Spirit of his Time) is his; he is a representative of it; it is that in which he originated, and in which he lives. Among the Athenians the word Athens had a double import; suggesting primarily, a complex of political institutions, but no less, in the second place, that Goddess who represented the Spirit of the People and its unity.

This Spirit of a People is a *determinate* and particular Spirit, and is, as just stated, further modified by the degree of its historical development. This Spirit, then, constitutes the basis and substance of those other forms of a nation's consciousness, which have been noticed. For Spirit in its self-consciousness must become an object of contemplation to itself, and objectivity involves, in the first instance, the rise of differences which make up a total of distinct spheres of objective spirit; in the same way as the Soul exists only as the complex of its faculties, which in their form of concentration in a simple unity produce that Soul. It is thus *One Individuality* which, presented in its essence as God, is honored and enjoyed in *Religion;* which is exhibited as an object of sensuous contemplation in *Art;* and is apprehended as an intellectual conception, in *Philosophy.* In virtue of the original identity of their essence, purport, and object, these various forms are inseparably united with the Spirit of the State. Only in connection with this particular religion, can this particular political constitution exist; just as in such or such a State, such or such a Philosophy or order of Art.

The remark next in order is, that each particular National genius is to be treated as only One Individual in the process of Universal History. For that history is the exhibition of the divine, absolute development of Spirit in its highest forms—that gradation by which it attains its truth and consciousness of itself. The forms which these grades of progress assume are the characteristic "National Spirits" of History; the peculiar tenor of their moral life, of their Government, their Art, Religion, and Science. To realize these grades is the boundless impulse of the World-Spirit—the goal of its irresistible urging; for this division into organic members, and the full development of each, is its Idea.—Universal History is exclusively occupied with showing how Spirit comes to a recognition and adoption of the Truth: the dawn of knowledge appears; it begins to discover salient principles, and at last it arrives at full consciousness. . . .

The very essence of Spirit is activity; it realizes its potentiality—makes itself its own deed, its own work—and thus it becomes an object to itself; contemplates itself as an objective existence. Thus is it with the Spirit of a people: it is a Spirit having strictly defined characteristics, which erects itself into an objective world, that exists and persists in a particular religious form of worship, customs, constitution, and political laws—in the whole complex of its institutions—in the events and transactions that make up its history. That is its work—that is what this particular Nation *is*. Nations are what their deeds are. Every Englishman will say: We are the men who navigate the ocean, and have the commerce of the world; to whom the East Indies belong and their riches; who have a parliament, juries, etc.—The relation of the individual to that Spirit is that he appropriates to himself this substantial existence; that it becomes his character and capability, enabling him to have a definite place in the world—to be *something*. For he finds the being of the people to which he belongs an already established, firm world—objectively present to him—with which he has to incorporate himself. In this its work, therefore—its world—the Spirit of the people enjoys its existence and finds its satisfaction.—A Nation is moral—virtuous—vigorous—while it is engaged in realizing its grand objects, and defends its work against external violence during the process of giving to its purposes an objective existence. The contradiction between its potential, subjective being—its inner aim and life—and its *actual* being is removed; it has attained full reality, has itself objectively present to it. But this having been attained, the activity displayed by the Spirit of the people in question is no longer needed; it has its desire. The Nation can still accomplish much in war and peace at home and abroad; but the living substantial soul itself may be said to have ceased its activity. The essential, supreme interest has consequently vanished from its life, for interest is present only where there is opposition. The Nation lives the same kind of life as the individual when passing from maturity to old age—in the enjoyment of itself—in the satisfaction of being exactly what it desired and was able to attain. Although its imagination might have transcended that limit, it nevertheless abandoned any such aspirations as objects of *actual endeavor*, if the real world was less than favorable to their attainment—and restricted its aim by the conditions thus imposed. This mere *customary life* (the watch wound up and going on of itself) is that which brings on natural death. Custom is activity without opposition, for which there remains only a formal duration; in which the fulness and zest that originally characterized the aim of life are out of the question—a merely external sensuous existence which has ceased to throw itself enthusiastically into its object. Thus perish individuals, thus perish peoples by a natural death; and though the latter may continue in being, it is an existence without intellect or vitality; having no need of its institutions, because the need for them is satisfied—a political nullity and tedium. In order that a truly universal interest may arise, the Spirit of a People must advance to the adoption of some new purpose; but whence can this new purpose originate? It would be a higher, more comprehensive conception of itself—a transcending of its principle—but this very act would involve a principle of a new order, a new National Spirit. . . .

The result of this process is then that Spirit, in rendering itself objective and making this its being an object of thought, on the one hand destroys the determinate form of its being, on the other hand gains a comprehension of the universal element which it involves, and thereby gives a new form to its inherent principle. In virtue of this, the substantial character of the National Spirit has been altered—that is, its principle has risen into another, and in fact a higher principle.

It is of the highest importance in apprehending and comprehending History to have and to understand the thought involved in this transition. The individual traverses as a unity various grades of development, and remains the same individual; in like manner also does a people, till the Spirit which it embodies reaches the grade of universality. In this point lies the fundamental, the Ideal necessity of transition. This is the soul—the essential consideration—of the philosophical comprehension of History.

Spirit is essentially the result of its own activity: its activity is the transcending of immediate, simple, unreflected existence—the negation of that existence, and the returning into itself. We may compare it with the seed; for with this the plant begins, yet it is also the result of the plant's entire life. But the weak side of life is exhibited in the fact that the commencement and the result are disjoined from each other. Thus also is it in the life of individuals and peoples. The life of a people ripens a certain fruit; its activity aims at the complete manifestation of the principle which it embodies. But this fruit does not fall back into the bosom of the people that produced and matured it; on the contrary, it becomes a poison-draught to it. That poison-draught it cannot let alone, for it has an insatiable thirst for it: the taste of the draught is its annihilation, though at the same time the rise of a new principle.

We have already discussed the final aim of this progression. The principles of the successive phases of Spirit that animate the Nations in a necessitated gradation, are themselves only steps in the development of the one universal Spirit, which through them elevates and completes itself to a self-comprehending *totality*.

While we are thus concerned exclusively with the Idea of Spirit, and in the History of the World regard everything as only its manifestation, we have, in traversing the past—however extensive its periods—only to do with what is *present;* for philosophy, as occupying itself with the True, has to do with the *eternally present.* Nothing in the past is lost for it, for the Idea is ever present; Spirit is immortal; with it there is no past, no future, but an essential *now.* This necessarily implies that the present form of

Spirit comprehends within it all earlier steps. These have indeed unfolded themselves in succession independently; but what Spirit is it has always been essentially; distinctions are only the development of this essential nature. The life of the ever present Spirit is a circle of progressive embodiments, which looked at in one aspect still exist beside each other, and only as looked at from another point of view appear as past. The grades which Spirit seems to have left behind it, it still possesses in the depths of its present.

## ᴥᔆ THE ESSENCE OF CHRISTIANITY

*Ludwig Feuerbach*

> *Among the followers of the philosopher Hegel—the Young Hegelians —Ludwig Feuerbach (1804–1872) probably had both the greatest contemporary acclaim and the most influence. In his own day Feuerbach contributed to the intellectual background of the German revolution of 1848, as well as impressing the youthful Karl Marx and Friedrich Engels. Among later writers whose ideas give evidence of his influence are Sigmund Freud, Friedrich Nietzsche (and his predecessor Max Stirner), Martin Buber, and the theologians of the so-called "God is dead" movement.*
>
> *Deeply religious as a youth in southern Germany, Feuerbach planned to enter the ministry. As a result of his university experience (he was especially enthusiastic about Hegel's lectures at the University of Berlin), his interests turned to philosophy. His religious faith suffered a decline, but concern for religious and ethical problems continued to preoccupy him throughout his life. His first published work was a radically outspoken critique of the concept of the immortality of the soul (*Thoughts on Death and Immortality, *1830) which cost him his position in the German university world. After retiring to a small Franconian village, his home for the major portion of his life, he further crystallized his philosophical and religious ideas in a number of books and articles, published mainly in the early 1840s.*
>
> *Feuerbach was troubled by the intellectual effect of both traditional Christianity and current tendencies in philosophy. In each case, he felt, sensual human existence was subordinated to an abstract concept; the danger was the same whether it was the Hegelian Absolute or the Christian God to which man sacrificed himself. What we needed, he believed, was anthropology—concern for man—rather than theology.*

*Unlike the more common atheist who is content to* reject, *Feuerbach insisted on a* positive *approach toward religion, that is, a sympathetic investigation of the human psychological facts which lead men to establish these supernatural conceptions.*

*Our selection is taken from* The Essence of Christianity *(1841), a work very widely read in the mid-nineteenth century by, among others, Marx and Engels, Russian radicals, and the English novelist George Eliot (Marian Evans), who translated this edition.*

[*Chapter I, Section 2, "The Essence of Religion Considered Generally," from the Introduction, Which Lays Down Feuerbach's Basic Premises.*]   Such as are a man's thoughts and dispositions, such is his God; so much worth as a man has, so much and no more has his God. Consciousness of God is self-consciousness, knowledge of God is self-knowledge. By his God thou knowest the man, and by the man his God; the two are identical. Whatever is God to a man, that is his heart and soul; and conversely, God is the manifested inward nature, the expressed self of a man,—religion the solemn unveiling of a man's hidden treasures, the revelation of his intimate thoughts, the open confession of his love-secrets. But when religion—consciousness of God—is designated as the self-consciousness of man, this is not to be understood as affirming that the religious man is directly aware of this identity; for, on the contrary, ignorance of it is fundamental to the peculiar nature of religion. . . . The antithesis of divine and human is altogether illusory. . . . The divine being is nothing else than the human being, or, rather, the human nature purified, freed from the limits of the individual man, made objective—i.e., contemplated and revered as another, a distinct being. All the attributes of the divine nature are, therefore, attributes of the human nature. . . .

That which is to man the self-existent, the highest being, to which he can conceive nothing higher—that is to him the Divine Being. . . . Not the attribute of the divinity, but the divineness or deity of the attribute, is the first true Divine Being. Thus what theology and philosophy have held to be God, the Absolute, the Infinite, is not God; but that which they have held not to be God is God: namely, the attribute, the quality, whatever has reality. Hence he alone is the true atheist to whom the predicates of the Divine Being,—for example, love, wisdom, justice,—are nothing; not he to whom merely the subject of these predicates is nothing. And in no wise is the negation of the subject necessarily also a negation of the predicates considered in themselves. These have an intrinsic, independent reality; they force their recognition upon man by their very nature; they are self-evident truths to him; they prove, they attest themselves. It does not follow that goodness, justice, wisdom, are chimaeras because the existence of God is a chimaera, nor truths because this is a truth. The

Ludwig Feuerbach, *The Essence of Christianity*, trans. Marian Evans (2d ed.; London, 1854), pp. 12–13, 17, 21–22, 140–146, 263, 266–275.

idea of God is dependent on the idea of justice, of benevolence; a God who is not benevolent, not just, not wise, is no God; but the converse does not hold. The fact is not that a quality is divine because God has it, but that God has it because it is in itself divine: because without it God would be a defective being. Justice, wisdom, in general every quality which constitutes the divinity of God, is determined and known by itself independently, but the idea of God is determined by the qualities which have thus been previously judged to be worthy of the divine nature; only in the case in which I identify God and justice, in which I think of God immediately as the reality of the idea of justice, is the idea of God self-determined. But if God as a subject is the determined, while the quality, the predicate, is the determining, then in truth the rank of the godhead is due not to the subject, but to the predicate.

[*Chapter XV, "The Mystery of the Christian Christ, or the Personal God," from Part One, "The True or Anthropological Essence of Religion," in Which Feuerbach Tries to Show the Human Basis of the Various Christian Dogmas.*] The fundamental dogmas of Christianity are realised wishes of the heart;—the essence of Christianity is the essence of human feeling. . . . The highest law of feeling is the immediate unity of will and deed, of wishing and reality. This law is fulfilled by the Redeemer. . . . The Redeemer, the Mediator, the God-man, in opposition to the moral spontaneity of the natural or rationalistic man, satisfies immediately the inward moral wants and wishes, since he dispenses man on his own side from any intermediate activity. . . . Thou desirest to win, to deserve happiness. Thou desirest to make God favorable to thee, to appease his anger, to be at peace with thy conscience. But this peace exists already; this peace is the Mediator, the God-man. . . .

The ancients said that if virtue could become visible, its beauty would win and inspire all hearts. The Christians were so happy as to see even this wish fullfilled. The heathens had an unwritten, the Jews a written law; the Christians had a model— a visible, personal living law, a law made flesh. Hence the joyfulness especially of the primitive Christians, hence the glory of Christianity that it alone contains and bestows the power to resist sin. And this glory is not to be denied it. Only, it is to be observed that the power of the exemplar of virtue is not so much the power of virtue as the power of example in general; just as the power of religious music is not the power of religion, but the power of music; and that therefore, though the image of virtue has virtuous actions as its consequences, these actions are destitute of the dispositions and motives of virtue. But this simple and true sense of the redeeming and reconciling power of example in distinction from the power of law by no means expresses the full religious significance of the Christian redemption and reconciliation. In this everything reduces itself to the personal power of that miraculous intermediate being who is neither God alone nor man alone, but a man who is also a God, and a God who is also man, and who can therefore only be comprehended in connection with the significance of miracle. In this, the miraculous Redeemer is nothing else than the realised wish of feeling to be free from the laws of morality, i.e., from the conditions to which virtue is united in the natural course of things; the realised wish to be freed from moral evils instantaneously, immediately, by a stroke of magic, that is, in an absolutely subjective, agreeable way. . . .

In Christ feeling is first perfectly certain of itself, and assured beyond doubt of the truth and divinity of its own nature; for Christ denies nothing to feeling; he fulfils all its prayers. In God the soul is still silent as to what affects it most closely,—it only sighs; but in Christ it speaks out fully; here it has no longer any reserves. To him who only sighs, wishes are still attended with disquietude; he rather complains that what he wishes is not, than openly, positively declares what he wishes; he is still in doubt whether his wishes have the force of law. But in Christ all anxiety of the soul vanishes; he is the sighing soul passed into a song of triumph over its complete satisfaction; he is the joyful certainty of feeling that its wishes hidden in God have truth and reality, the actual victory over death, over all the powers of the world and Nature, the resurrection no longer merely hoped for, but already accomplished; he is the heart released from all oppressive limits, from all sufferings,—the soul in perfect blessedness, the Godhead made visible.

To see God is the highest wish, the highest triumph of the heart. Christ is this wish, this triumph, fulfilled. God, as an object of thought only, i.e., God as God, is always a remote being; the relation to him is an abstract one, like that relation of friendship in which we stand to a man who is distant from us, and personally unknown to us. However his works, the proofs of love which he gives us, may make his nature present to us, there always remains an unfilled void,—the heart is unsatisfied, we long to see him. So long as we have not met a being face to face, we are always in doubt whether he be really such as we imagine him; actual presence alone gives final confidence, perfect repose. Christ is God known personally; Christ, therefore, is the blessed certainty that God is what the soul desires and needs him to be. God, as the object of prayer, is indeed already a human being, since he sympathises with human misery, grants human wishes; but still he is not yet an object to the religious consciousness as a real man. Hence, only in Christ is the last wish of religion realised, the mystery of religious feelings solved:—solved however in the language of imagery proper to religion, for what God is in essence, that Christ is in actual appearance. So far the Christian religion may justly be called the absolute religion. That God, who in himself is nothing else than the nature of man, should also have a real existence as such, should be as man an object to the consciousness—this is the goal of religion; and this the Christian religion has attained in the incarnation of God, which is by no means a transitory act, for Christ remains man even after his ascension,—man in heart and man in form, only that his body is no longer an earthly one, liable to suffering.

The incarnations of the Deity with the Orientals—the Hindoos, for example—have no such intense meaning as the Christian incarnation; just because they happen often they become indifferent, they lose their value. The manhood of God is his personality; the proposition, God is a personal being, means: God is a human being, God is a man. Personality is an abstraction, which has reality only in an actual man. The idea which lies at the foundation of the incarnations of God is therefore infinitely better conveyed by one incarnation, one personality. Where God appears in several persons successively, these personalities are evanescent. What is required is a permanent, an exclusive personality. Where there are many incarnations, room is given for innumerable others: the imagination is not restrained; and even those incarnations which are already real pass into the category of the merely possible and conceivable, into the category of fancies or of mere appearances. But where one personality is exclusively believed in and contemplated, this at once impresses with the power of an historical personality; imagination is done away with, the freedom to imagine others is renounced. This one personality presses on me the belief in its reality.

[*Chapter XXVI, "The Contradiction of Faith and Love," the Final Chapter of Part Two, "The False or Theological Essence of Religion," in Which the Author Shows the Distortions of Christianity Caused by its Transferring True Ideals from Man to God.*] Although the deeds opposed to love which mark Christian religious history are in accordance with Christianity, and its antagonists are therefore right in imputing to it the horrible actions resulting from dogmatic creeds; those deeds nevertheless at the same time contradict Christianity, because Christianity is not only a religion of faith, but of love also,—pledges us not only to faith, but to love. Uncharitable actions, hatred of heretics, at once accord and clash with Christianity? how is that possible? Perfectly Christianity sanctions both the actions that spring out of love, and the actions that spring from faith without love. If Christianity had made love only its law, its adherents would be right,—the horrors of Christian religious history could not be imputed to it; if it had made faith only its law, the reproaches of its antagonists would be unconditionally, unrestrictedly true. But Christianity has not made love free; it has not raised itself to the height of accepting love as absolute. And it has not given this freedom, nay, cannot give it, because it is a religion,—and hence subjects love to the dominion of faith. Love is only the exoteric, faith the esoteric doctrine of Christianity; love is only the *morality*, faith the *religion* of the Christian religion.

. . . The idea of love was by no means first introduced into the consciousness of mankind with and by Christianity,—is by no means peculiarly Christian. The horrors of the Roman Empire present themselves with striking significance in company with the appearance of this idea. The empire of policy which united men after a manner corresponding with its own idea, was coming to its necessary end. Political unity is a unity of force. The despotism of Rome must turn in upon itself, destroy itself. But it was precisely through this catastrophe of political existence that man released himself entirely from the heart-stifling toils of politics. In the place of Rome appeared the idea of humanity; to the idea of dominion succeeded the idea of love. . . . Christianity was a peculiar manifestation of these human tendencies;—a popular, consequently a religious, and certainly a most intense manifestation of this new principle of love. That which elsewhere made itself apparent in the process of culture, expressed itself here as religious feeling, as a matter of faith. Christianity thus reduced a general unity to a particular one, it made love collateral to faith; and by this means it placed itself in contradiction with universal love. The unity was not referred to its true origin. National differences indeed disappeared; but in their place difference of faith, the opposition of Christian and un-Christian, more vehement than a national antagonism, and also more malignant, made its appearance in history.

All love founded on a special historical phenomenon contradicts, as has been said, the nature of love, which endures no limits, which triumphs over all particularity. Man is to be loved for man's sake. Man is an object of love because he is an end in himself, because he is a rational and loving being. This is the law of the species, the law of the intelligence. Love should be immediate, undetermined by anything else than its object;—nay, only as such is it love. But if I interpose between my fellow-man and myself the idea of an individuality, in whom the idea of the species is supposed to be already realised, I annihilate the very soul of love, I disturb the unity by the idea of a third external to us; for in that case my fellow-man is an object of love to me only on account of his resemblance or relation to this model, not for his own sake. . . . Love is the subjective reality of the species, as reason is its objective reality. In love, in reason, the need of an intermediate person disappears. Christ is nothing but an image, under which the unity of the species has impressed itself on the popular consciousness. Christ loved men: he wished to bless and unite them all without distinction of sex, age, rank, or nationality. Christ is the love of mankind to itself embodied in an image or contemplated as a person, but a person who (we mean, of course, as a religious object) has only the significance of an image, who is only ideal. . . . But love, as has been said, is nothing else than the active proof, the realisation of the unity of the race, through the medium of the moral disposition. The species is not an abstraction; it exists in feeling, in the moral sentiment, in the energy of love. It is the species which infuses love into me. A loving heart is the heart of the species throbbing in the individual. Thus Christ, as the consciousness of love, is the consciousness of the species. We are all one in Christ. Christ is the consciousness of our identity. He therefore who loves man for the sake of man, who rises to the love of the species, to universal love, adequate to the nature of the species, he is a Christian, is Christ himself. Thus, where there arises the consciousness of the species as a species, the idea of humanity as a whole, Christ disappears, without, however, his true nature disappearing; for he was the substitute for the consciousness of the species, the image under which it was made present to the people, and became the law of the popular life.

[*Chapter XXVII, "Concluding Application," in Which He Tries to Show the Way to a Positive Philosophy of Humanitarianism ("Anthropology") through a Rejection of Theism.*] In the contradiction between Faith and Love which has just been exhibited, we see the practical, palpable ground of necessity that we should raise ourselves above Christianity, above the peculiar standpoint of all religion. We have shown that the substance and object of religion is altogether human: we have shown that divine wisdom is human wisdom; that the secret of theology is anthropology; that the absolute mind is the so-called finite subjective mind. But religion is not conscious that its elements are human; on the contrary, it places itself in opposition to the human, or at least it does not admit that its elements are human. The necessary turning-point of history is therefore the open confession, that the consciousness of God is nothing else than the consciousness of the species; that man can and should raise himself only above the limits of his individuality, and not above the laws, the positive essential conditions of his species; that there is no other essence which man can think, dream of, imagine, feel, believe in, wish for, love and adore as the *absolute,* than the essence of human nature itself.

Our relation to religion is therefore not a merely negative, but a critical one; we only separate the true from the false;—though we grant that the truth thus separated from falsehood is a new truth, essentially different from the old. Religion is the first form of self-consciousness. But that which in religion holds the first place—namely,

God—is, as we have shown, in itself and according to truth, the second, for it is only the nature of man regarded objectively; and that which to religion is the second —namely, man—must therefore be constituted and declared the first. Love to man must be no derivative love; it must be original. If human nature is the highest nature to man, then practically also the highest and first law must be the love of man to man. *Homo homini Deus est:*—this is the axis on which revolves the history of the world. The relations of child and parent, of husband and wife, of brother and friend— in general, of man to man—in short, all the moral relations are *per se* religious. Life as a whole is, in its essential, substantial relations, throughout of a divine nature. Its religious consecration is not first conferred by the blessing of the priest. . . . All moral relations [are] . . . enjoyed in a moral spirit, [only] when they are regarded as sacred in themselves. . . . Let friendship be sacred to thee, property sacred, marriage sacred,—sacred the well-being of every man; but let them be sacred *in and by themselves.*

In Christianity the moral laws are regarded as the commandments of God; morality is even made the criterion of piety; but ethics have nevertheless a subordinate rank, they have not in themselves a religious significance. This belongs only to faith. Above morality hovers God, as a being distinct from man, a being to whom the best is due, while the remnants only fall to the share of man. All those dispositions which ought to be devoted to life, to man—all the best powers of humanity, are lavished on the being who wants nothing. The real cause is converted into an impersonal means, a merely conceptional, imaginary cause usurps the place of the true one. Man thanks God for those benefits which have been rendered to him even at the cost of sacrifice by his fellow-man. The gratitude which he expresses to his benefactor is only ostensible: it is paid, not to him, but to God. He is thankful, grateful to God, but unthankful to man. Thus is the moral sentiment subverted into religion! Thus does man sacrifice man to God! The bloody human sacrifice is in fact only a rude, material expression of the inmost secret of religion. Where bloody human sacrifices are offered to God, such sacrifices are regarded as the highest thing, physical existence as the chief good. For this reason life is sacrificed to God, and it is so on extraordinary occasions; the supposition being that this is the way to show him the greatest honour. If Christianity no longer, at least in our day, offers bloody sacrifices to its God, this arises, to say nothing of other reasons, from the fact that physical existence is no longer regarded as the highest good. Hence the soul, the emotions are now offered to God, because these are held to be something higher. But the common case is, that in religion man sacrifices some duty towards man—such as that of respecting the life of his fellow, of being grateful to him—to a religious obligation,—sacrifices his relation to man to his relation to God. . . .

God is jealous of man; religion is jealous of morality; it sucks away the best forces of morality; it renders to man only the things that are man's but to God the things that are God's; and to him is rendered true, living emotion,—the heart. When in times in which peculiar sanctity was attached to religion, we find marriage, property, and civil law respected, this has not its foundation in religion, but in the original, natural sense of morality and right, to which the true social relations are sacred *as such.* He to whom the Right is not holy for its own sake will never be made to feel it sacred by religion. Property did not become sacred because it was regarded as a divine institution, but it was regarded as a divine institution because it was felt to be in itself sacred. Love is not holy because it is a predicate of God, but it is a predicate of God because it is in itself divine. . . . Wherever morality is based on theology, wherever the right is made dependent on divine authority, the most immoral, unjust, infamous things can be justified and established. . . .

To place anything in God, or to derive anything from God, is nothing more than to withdraw it from the test of reason, to institute it as indubitable, unassailable, sacred, without rendering an account *why*. Hence self-delusion, if not wicked, insidious design, is at the root of all efforts to establish morality, right, on theology. Where we are in earnest about the right we need no incitement or support from above. We need no Christian rule of political right: we need only one which is rational, just, human. The right, the true, the good, has always its ground of sacredness in itself, in its quality. Where man is in earnest about ethics, they have in themselves the validity of a divine power. If morality has no foundation in itself, there is no inherent necessity for morality; morality is then surrendered to the groundless arbitrariness of religion. Thus the work of the self-conscious reason in relation to religion is simply to destroy an illusion:—an illusion, however, which is by no means indifferent, but which, on the contrary, is profoundly injurious in its effect on mankind; which deprives man as well of the power of real life as of the genuine sense of truth and virtue; for even love, in itself the deepest, truest emotion, becomes by means of religiousness merely ostensible, illusory, since religious love gives itself to man only for God's sake, so that it is given only in appearance to man, but in reality to God. And we need only, as we have shown, invert the religious relations—regard that as an end which religion supposes to be a means—exalt that into the primary which in religion is subordinate, the accessory, the condition,—at once we have destroyed the illusion, and the unclouded light of truth streams in upon us.

# Dialectical Materialism

*Karl Marx was born in 1818 in Trier in Rhenish Prussia. He was brought up to follow his father as a lawyer but took his degrees instead in philosophy and history, eventually taking a doctorate at the University of Jena. Unwilling to teach under the severely reactionary Prussian university system, he began a long journalistic career both to earn a living and to promulgate, when possible, the socialistic theories he was fast developing under the influence of his numerous contacts among European radicals. He left the Rhineland after his newspaper was shut down by the government in 1843, moved to Paris, and edited a paper for German exiles until 1845 when Louis Philippe's government requested him to leave. He then went on to Brussels, another newspaper, and involvement in the radical workingmen's Communist League. The*

*revolutions of 1848, which injected hope into the hearts of all who
bore the red flag of labor protest, encouraged Marx to return to Germany
where, for a brief moment, it appeared the radicals would gain control.
He and Friedrich Engels had by then written the famous* Manifesto of
the Communist Party *during their time in Belgium. As it did for other
radicals, 1849 marked a turning point in Marx's life: the successful
reaction drove him to England. He remained there until his death in
1883, dividing his time among writing newspaper reports for the* New
York Tribune *as special correspondent, researching into economic history
in the British Museum for his great work* Das Kapital *(Volume I
appeared in 1867), and founding the short-lived International
Workingmen's Association, usually called the First International
(1864–1876).*

*Friedrich Engels, two years Marx's junior, came from a similar if more
affluent middle-class Rhenish background. He was sent by his father
to manage a branch of the family's cotton business in Manchester,
England, and assumed the curious double role of industrial capitalist plus
patron-collaborator-revolutionary-associate to Marx until he retired from
business in 1869. Engels' early masterpiece,* The Condition of the
Working Class in England *(1845), secured for him an independent
reputation among radicals. He subordinated his own talents and linked
his star with Marx's, and together they produced the* Manifesto; *later
Engels completed the remaining volumes of* Das Kapital, *using Marx's
notes. He had already written a larger work in 1878,* Dühring's
Revolution in Science, *from which three chapters were almost immediately
excerpted and published under the title* Socialism: Utopian and
Scientific; *it became the classical philosophical statement of Marxism.
Engels died in 1895. His ashes were symbolically scattered in the sea:
no nation could then claim his remains, for his cause—the workers'—was
international.*

*The work of Marx and Engels is both a conscious synthesis of
nineteenth-century philosophies and an unconscious reflection of dominant
intellectual trends. Marx himself admitted that Hegel and Feuerbach
were conscious influences, Hegel providing the ingredient of the dialectic
progression of conflict and accommodation in historical change and
Feuerbach the belief that this progression operated in the material, not
the so-called spiritual, realm. Marx was under the spell of the "cult" of
scientism and relished the distinction that his theory of class warfare,
as opposed to those proposed by the wishful-thinking Utopians, was
scientifically demonstrable and thus must inevitably be fulfilled. He also
accepted forms of economic analysis already established by Adam Smith
(the concept of division of labor and the theory that labor is the source*

*of wealth) and David Ricardo (the theory of business cycles), though*
*of course he arrived at different conclusions. Finally, Marx belongs to*
*the large group of intellectuals (Darwin, Comte, and Spencer, to name*
*a few) who were reevaluating natural and social changes as manifestations*
*of evolution; his general theory of historical change is a theory of social*
*evolution based on the principle of the survival of the fittest.*

## ◄§ MANIFESTO OF THE COMMUNIST PARTY

*Karl Marx and Friedrich Engels*

A spectre is haunting Europe—the spectre of Communism. All the powers of old Europe have entered into a holy alliance to exorcise this spectre: Pope and Czar, Metternich and Guizot, French Radicals and German police-spies.

Where is the party in opposition that has not been decried as communistic by its opponents in power? Where the Opposition that has not hurled back the branding reproach of Communism, against the more advanced opposition parties, as well as against its reactionary adversaries?

Two things result from this fact:

I   Communism is already acknowledged by all European powers to be itself a power.

II   It is high time that Communists should openly, in the face of the whole world, publish their views, their aims, their tendencies, and meet this nursery tale of the spectre of Communism with a manifesto of the party itself.

To this end, Communists of various nationalities have assembled in London, and sketched the following manifesto, to be published in the English, French, German, Italian, Flemish and Danish languages.

### 1. BOURGEOIS AND PROLETARIANS

The history of all hitherto existing society is the history of class struggles.

Freeman and slave, patrician and plebeian, lord and serf, guild-master and journeyman, in a word, oppressor and oppressed, stood in constant opposition to one another, carried on an uninterrupted, now hidden, now open fight, a fight that each time ended, either in a revolutionary reconstitution of society at large, or in the common ruin of the contending classes.

In the earlier epochs of history, we find almost everywhere a complicated arrangement of society into various orders, a manifold gradation of social rank. In ancient

Karl Marx and Friedrich Engels, *Manifesto of the Communist Party* (New York: International Publishers Company, Inc., n.d.), authorized English trans., pp. 8–21.

Rome we have patricians, knights, plebeians, slaves; in the Middle Ages, feudal lords, vassals, guild-masters, journeymen, apprentices, serfs; in almost all of these classes, again, subordinate gradations.

The modern bourgeois society that has sprouted from the ruins of feudal society, has not done away with class antagonisms. It has but established new classes, new conditions of oppression, new forms of struggle in place of the old ones.

Our epoch, the epoch of the bourgeoisie, possesses, however, this distinctive feature: It has simplified the class antagonisms. Society as a whole is more and more splitting up into two great hostile camps, into two great classes directly facing each other—bourgeoisie and proletariat.

From the serfs of the Middle Ages sprang the chartered burghers of the earliest towns. From these burgesses the first elements of the bourgeoisie were developed.

The discovery of America, the rounding of the Cape, opened up fresh ground for the rising bourgeoisie. The East-Indian and Chinese markets, the colonisation of America, trade with the colonies, the increase in the means of exchange and in commodities generally, gave to commerce, to navigation, to industry, an impulse never before known, and thereby, to the revolutionary element in the tottering feudal society, a rapid development.

The feudal system of industry, in which industrial production was monopolised by closed guilds, now no longer sufficed for the growing wants of the new markets. The manufacturing system took its place. The guild-masters were pushed aside by the manufacturing middle class; division of labour between the different corporate guilds vanished in the face of division of labour in each single workshop.

Meantime the markets kept ever growing, the demand ever rising. Even manufacture no longer sufficed. Thereupon, steam and machinery revolutionised industrial production. The place of manufacture was taken by the giant, modern industry, the place of the industrial middle class, by industrial millionaires, the leaders of whole industrial armies, the modern bourgeois.

Modern industry has established the world market, for which the discovery of America paved the way. This market has given an immense development to commerce, to navigation, to communication by land. This development has, in its turn, reacted on the extension of industry; and in proportion as industry, commerce, navigation, railways extended, in the same proportion the bourgeoisie developed, increased its capital, and pushed into the background every class handed down from the Middle Ages.

We see, therefore, how the modern bourgeoisie is itself the product of a long course of development, of a series of revolutions in the modes of production and of exchange.

Each step in the development of the bourgeoisie was accompanied by a corresponding political advance of that class. An oppressed class under the sway of the feudal nobility, it became an armed and self-governing association in the mediæval commune; here independent urban republic (as in Italy and Germany), there taxable "third estate" of the monarchy (as in France) ; afterwards, in the period of manufacture proper, serving either the semi-feudal or the absolute monarchy as a counterpoise against the nobility, and, in fact, corner-stone of the great monarchies in general— the bourgeoisie has at last, since the establishment of modern industry and of the world market, conquered for itself, in the modern representative state, exclusive political sway. The executive of the modern state is but a committee for managing the common affairs of the whole bourgeoisie.

The bourgeoisie has played a most revolutionary rôle in history.

The bourgeoisie, wherever it has got the upper hand, has put an end to all feudal, patriarchal, idyllic relations. It has pitilessly torn asunder the motley feudal ties that bound man to his "natural superiors," and has left no other bond between man and man than naked self-interest, than callous "cash payment." It has drowned the most heavenly ecstasies of religious fervour, of chivalrous enthusiasm, of philistine sentimentalism, in the icy water of egotistical calculation. It has resolved worth into exchange value, and in place of the numberless indefeasible chartered freedoms, has set up that single, unconscionable freedom—Free Trade. In one word, for exploitation, veiled by religious and political illusions, it has substituted naked, shameless, direct, brutal exploitation.

The bourgeoisie has stripped of its halo every occupation hitherto honoured and looked up to with reverent awe. It has converted the physician, the lawyer, the priest, the poet, the man of science, into its paid wage-labourers.

The bourgeoisie has torn away from the family its sentimental veil, and has reduced the family relation to a mere money relation.

The bourgeoisie has disclosed how it came to pass that the brutal display of vigour in the Middle Ages, which reactionaries so much admire, found its fitting complement in the most slothful indolence. It has been the first to show what man's activity can bring about. It has accomplished wonders far surpassing Egyptian pyramids, Roman aqueducts, and Gothic cathedrals; it has conducted expeditions that put in the shade all former migrations of nations and crusades.

The bourgeoisie cannot exist without constantly revolutionising the instruments of production, and thereby the relations of production, and with them the whole relations of society. Conservation of the old modes of production in unaltered form, was, on the contrary, the first condition of existence for all earlier industrial classes. Constant revolutionising of production, uninterrupted disturbance of all social conditions, everlasting uncertainty and agitation distinguish the bourgeois epoch from all earlier ones. All fixed, fast-frozen relations, with their train of ancient and venerable prejudices and opinions, are swept away, all new-formed ones become antiquated before they can ossify. All that is solid melts into air, all that is holy is profaned, and man is at last compelled to face with sober senses his real conditions of life and his relations with his kind.

The need of a constantly expanding market for its products chases the bourgeoisie over the whole surface of the globe. It must nestle everywhere, settle everywhere, establish connections everywhere.

The bourgeoisie has through its exploitation of the world market given a cosmopolitan character to production and consumption in every country. To the great chagrin of reactionaries, it has drawn from under the feet of industry the national ground on which it stood. All old-established national industries have been destroyed or are daily being destroyed. They are dislodged by new industries, whose introduction becomes a life and death question for all civilised nations, by industries that no longer work up indigenous raw material, but raw material drawn from the remotest zones; industries whose products are consumed, not only at home, but in every quarter of the globe. In place of the old wants, satisfied by the production of the country, we find new wants, requiring for their satisfaction the products of distant lands and climes. In place of the old local and national seclusion and self-sufficiency, we have intercourse in every direction, universal inter-dependence of nations. And as in material, so also in intellectual production. The intellectual creations of individual nations become common property. National one-sidedness and narrow-mindedness become more and more impossible, and from the numerous national and local literatures there arises a world literature.

The bourgeoisie, by the rapid improvement of all instruments of production, by the immensely facilitated means of communication, draws all nations, even the most barbarian, into civilisation. The cheap prices of its commodities are the heavy artillery with which it batters down all Chinese walls, with which it forces the barbarians' intensely obstinate hatred of foreigners to capitulate. It compels all nations, on pain of extinction, to adopt the bourgeois mode of production; it compels them to introduce what it calls civilisation into their midst, *i.e.*, to become bourgeois themselves. In a word, it creates a world after its own image.

The bourgeoisie has subjected the country to the rule of the towns. It has created enormous cities, has greatly increased the urban population as compared with the rural, and has thus rescued a considerable part of the population from the idiocy of rural life. Just as it has made the country dependent on the towns, so it has made barbarian and semi-barbarian countries dependent on the civilised ones, nations of peasants on nations of bourgeois, the East on the West.

More and more the bourgeoisie keeps doing away with the scattered state of the population, of the means of production, and of property. It has agglomerated population, centralised means of production, and has concentrated property in a few hands. The necessary consequence of this was political centralisation. Independent, or but loosely connected provinces, with separate interests, laws, governments and systems of taxation, became lumped together into one nation, with one government, one code of laws, one national class interest, one frontier and one customs tariff.

The bourgeoisie, during its rule of scarce one hundred years, has created more massive and more colossal productive forces than have all preceding generations together. Subjection of nature's forces to man, machinery, application of chemistry to industry and agriculture, steam-navigation, railways, electric telegraphs, clearing of whole continents for cultivation, canalisation of rivers, whole populations conjured out of the ground—what earlier century had even a presentiment that such productive forces slumbered in the lap of social labour?

We see then that the means of production and of exchange, which served as the foundation for the growth of the bourgeoisie, were generated in feudal society. At a certain stage in the development of these means of production and of exchange, the conditions under which feudal society produced and exchanged, the feudal organisation of agriculture and manufacturing industry, in a word, the feudal relations of property became no longer compatible with the already developed productive forces; they became so many fetters. They had to be burst asunder; they were burst asunder.

Into their place stepped free competition, accompanied by a social and political constitution adapted to it, and by the economic and political sway of the bourgeois class.

A similar movement is going on before our own eyes. Modern bourgeois society with its relations of production, of exchange and of property, a society that has conjured up such gigantic means of production and of exchange, is like the sorcerer who is no longer able to control the powers of the nether world whom he has called up by his spells. For many a decade past the history of industry and commerce is but the history of the revolt of modern productive forces against modern conditions of production, against the property relations that are the conditions for the existence of the bourgeoisie and of its rule. It is enough to mention the commercial crises that by their periodical return put the existence of the entire bourgeois society on trial, each time more threateningly. In these crises a great part not only of the existing products, but also of the previously created productive forces, are periodically destroyed. In these crises there breaks out an epidemic that, in all earlier epochs, would have seemed an absurdity—the epidemic of over-production. Society suddenly finds itself put back into a state of momentary barbarism; it appears as if a famine, a universal war of devastation had cut off the supply of every means of subsistence; industry and commerce seem to be destroyed. And why? Because there is too much civilisation, too much means of subsistence, too much industry, too much commerce. The productive forces at the disposal of society no longer tend to further the development of the conditions of bourgeois property; on the contrary, they have become too powerful for these conditions, by which they are fettered, and no sooner do they overcome these fetters than they bring disorder into the whole of bourgeois society, endanger the existence of bourgeois property. The conditions of bourgeois society are too narrow to comprise the wealth created by them. And how does the bourgeoisie get over these crises? On the one hand by enforced destruction of a mass of productive forces; on the other, by the conquest of new markets, and by the more thorough exploitation of the old ones. That is to say, by paving the way for more extensive and more destructive crises, and by diminishing the means whereby crises are prevented.

The weapons with which the bourgeoisie felled feudalism to the ground are now turned against the bourgeoisie itself.

But not only has the bourgeoisie forged the weapons that bring death to itself; it has also called into existence the men who are to wield those weapons—the modern working class—the proletarians.

In proportion as the bourgeoisie, i.e., capital, is developed, in the same proportion is the proletariat, the modern working class, developed—a class of labourers, who live only so long as they find work, and who find work only so long as their labour increases capital. These labourers, who must sell themselves piecemeal, are a commodity, like every other article of commerce, and are consequently exposed to all the vicissitudes of competition, to all the fluctuations of the market.

Owing to the extensive use of machinery and to division of labour, the work of the proletarians has lost all individual character, and, consequently, all charm for the workman. He becomes an appendage of the machine, and it is only the most simple, most monotonous, and most easily acquired knack, that is required of him. Hence, the cost of production of a workman is restricted, almost entirely, to the means of subsistence that he requires for his maintenance, and for the propagation of his race. But the price of a commodity, and therefore also of labour, is equal to its cost of production. In proportion, therefore, as the repulsiveness of the work increases, the wage decreases. Nay more, in proportion as the use of machinery and division of labour increases, in the same proportion the burden of toil also increases, whether by prolongation of the working hours, by increase of the work exacted in a given time, or by increased speed of the machinery, etc.

Modern industry has converted the little workshop of the patriarchal master into the great factory of the industrial capitalist. Masses of labourers, crowded into the factory, are organised like soldiers. As privates of the industrial army they are placed under the command of a perfect hierarchy of officers and sergeants. Not only are they slaves of the bourgeois class, and of the bourgeois state; they are daily and hourly enslaved by the machine, by the over-looker, and, above all, by the individual bourgeois manufacturer himself. The more openly this despotism proclaims gain to be its end and aim, the more petty, the more hateful and the more embittering it is.

The less the skill and exertion of strength implied in manual labour, in other words, the more modern industry develops, the more is the labour of men superseded by that of women. Differences of age and sex have no longer any distinctive social validity for the working class. All are instruments of labour, more or less expensive to use, according to their age and sex.

No sooner has the labourer received his wages in cash, for the moment escaping exploitation by the manufacturer, than he is set upon by the other portions of the bourgeoisie, the landlord, the shopkeeper, the pawnbroker, etc.

The lower strata of the middle class—the small tradespeople, shopkeepers, and retired tradesmen generally, the handicraftsmen and peasants—all these sink gradually into the proletariat, partly because their diminutive capital does not suffice for the scale on which modern industry is carried on, and is swamped in the competition with the large capitalists, partly because their specialised skill is rendered worthless by new methods of production. Thus the proletariat is recruited from all classes of the population.

The proletariat goes through various stages of development. With its birth begins its struggle with the bourgeoisie. At first the contest is carried on by individual labourers, then by the work people of a factory, then by the operatives of one trade, in one locality, against the individual bourgeois who directly exploits them. They direct their attacks not against the bourgeois conditions of production, but against the instruments of production themselves; they destroy imported wares that compete with their labour, they smash machinery to pieces, they set factories ablaze, they seek to restore by force the vanished status of the workman of the Middle Ages.

At this stage the labourers still form an incoherent mass scattered over the whole country, and broken up by their mutual competition. If anywhere they unite to form more compact bodies, this is not yet the consequence of their own active union, but of the union of the bourgeoisie, which class, in order to attain its own political ends, is compelled to set the whole proletariat in motion, and is moreover still able to do so for a time. At this stage, therefore, the proletarians do not fight their enemies, but the enemies of their enemies, the remnants of absolute monarchy, the landowners, the non-industrial bourgeois, the petty bourgeoisie. Thus the whole historical movement is concentrated in the hands of the bourgeoisie; every victory so obtained is a victory for the bourgeoisie.

But with the development of industry the proletariat not only increases in number; it becomes concentrated in greater masses, its strength grows, and it feels that strength more. The various interests and conditions of life within the ranks of the proletariat are more and more equalised, in proportion as machinery obliterates all distinctions of labour, and nearly everywhere reduces wages to the same low level. The growing competition among the bourgeois, and the resulting commercial crises, make the wages of the workers ever more fluctuating. The unceasing improvement of machinery, ever more rapidly developing, makes their livelihood more and more precarious; the collisions between individual workmen and individual bourgeois take more and more the character of collisions between two classes. Thereupon the workers begin to form combinations (trade unions) against the bourgeoisie; they club together in order to keep up the rate of wages; they found permanent associations in order to make provision beforehand for these occasional revolts. Here and there the contest breaks out into riots.

Now and then the workers are victorious, but only for a time. The real fruit of their battles lies, not in the immediate result, but in the ever expanding union of the workers. This union is furthered by the improved means of communication which are created by modern industry, and which place the workers of different localities in contact with one another. It was just this contact that was needed to centralise the numerous local struggles, all of the same character, into one national struggle between classes. But every class struggle is a political struggle. And that union, to attain which the burghers of the Middle Ages, with their miserable highways, required centuries, the modern proletarians, thanks to railways, achieve in a few years.

This organisation of the proletarians into a class, and consequently into a political party, is continually being upset again by the competition between the workers themselves. But it ever rises up again, stronger, firmer, mightier. It compels legislative recognition of particular interests of the workers, by taking advantage of the divisions among the bourgoisie itself. Thus the ten-hour bill in England was carried.

Altogether, collisions between the classes of the old society further the course of development of the proletariat in many ways. The bourgeoisie finds itself involved in a constant battle. At first with the aristocracy; later on, with those portions of the bourgeoisie itself whose interests have become antagonistic to the progress of industry; at all times with the bourgeoisie of foreign countries. In all these battles it sees itself compelled to appeal to the proletariat, to ask for its help, and thus, to drag it into the political arena. The bourgeoisie itself, therefore, supplies the proletariat with its own elements of political and general education, in other words, it furnishes the proletariat with weapons for fighting the bourgeoisie.

Further, as we have already seen, entire sections of the ruling classes are, by the advance of industry, precipitated into the proletariat, or are at least threatened in their conditions of existence. These also supply the proletariat with fresh elements of enlightenment and progress.

Finally, in times when the class struggle nears the decisive hour, the process of dissolution going on within the ruling class, in fact within the whole range of old society, assumes such a violent, glaring character, that a small section of the ruling class cuts itself adrift, and joins the revolutionary class, the class that holds the future in its hands. Just as, therefore, at an earlier period, a section of the nobility went over to the bourgeoisie, so now a portion of the bourgeoisie goes over to the proletariat, and in particular, a portion of the bourgeois ideologies, who have raised themselves to the level of comprehending theoretically the historical movement as a whole.

Of all the classes that stand face to face with the bourgeoisie today, the proletariat alone is a really revolutionary class. The other classes decay and finally disappear in the face of modern industry; the proletariat is its special and essential product.

The lower middle class, the small manufacturer, the shopkeeper, the artisan, the peasant, all these fight against the bourgeoisie, to save from extinction their existence as fractions of the middle class. They are therefore not revolutionary, but conservative. Nay more, they are reactionary, for they try to roll back the wheel of history. If by chance they are revolutionary, they are so only in view of their impending transfer into the proletariat; they thus defend not their present, but their future interests; they desert their own standpoint to adopt that of the proletariat.

The "dangerous class," the social scum (*Lumpenproletariat*), that passively rotting mass thrown off by the lowest layers of old society, may, here and there, be swept into the movement by a proletarian revolution; its conditions of life, however, prepare it far more for the part of a bribed tool of reactionary intrigue.

The social conditions of the old society no longer exist for the proletariat. The proletarian is without property; his relation to his wife and children has no longer anything in common with the bourgeois family relations; modern industrial labour, modern subjection to capital, the same in England as in France, in America as in Germany, has stripped him of every trace of national character. Law, morality, religion, are to him so many bourgeois prejudices, behind which lurk in ambush just as many bourgeois interests.

All the preceding classes that got the upper hand, sought to fortify their already acquired status by subjecting society at large to their conditions of appropriation. The proletarians cannot become masters of the productive forces of society, except by abolishing their own previous mode of appropriation, and thereby also every other previous mode of appropriation. They have nothing of their own to secure and to fortify; their mission is to destroy all previous securities for, and insurances of, individual property.

All previous historical movements were movements of minorities, or in the interest of minorities. The proletarian movement is the self-conscious, independent movement of the immense majority, in the interest of the immense majority. The proletariat, the lowest stratum of our present society, cannot stir, cannot raise itself up, without the whole superincumbent strata of official society being sprung into the air.

Though not in substance, yet in form, the struggle of the proletariat with the bourgeoisie is at first a national struggle. The proletariat of each country must, of course, first of all settle matters with its own bourgeoisie.

In depicting the most general phases of the development of the proletariat, we traced the more or less veiled civil war, raging within existing society, up to the point where that war breaks out into open revolution, and where the violent overthrow of the bourgeoisie lays the foundation for the sway of the proletariat.

Hitherto, every form of society has been based, as we have already seen, on the antagonism of oppressing and oppressed classes. But in order to oppress a class, certain conditions must be assured to it under which it can, at least, continue its slavish existence. The serf, in the period of serfdom, raised himself to membership in the commune, just as the petty bourgeois, under the yoke of feudal absolutism, managed to develop into a bourgeois. The modern labourer, on the contrary, instead of rising with the progress of industry, sinks deeper and deeper below the conditions of existence of his own class. He becomes a pauper, and pauperism develops more rapidly than population and wealth. And here it becomes evident, that the bourgeoisie is unfit any longer to be the ruling class in society, and to impose its conditions of existence upon society as an over-riding law. It is unfit to rule because it is incompetent to assure an existence to its slave within his slavery, because it cannot help letting him sink into such a state, that it has to feed him, instead of being fed by him. Society can no longer live under this bourgeoisie, in other words, its existence is no longer compatible with society.

The essential condition for the existence and sway of the bourgeois class, is the formation and augmentation of capital; the condition for capital is wage-labour. Wage-labour rests exclusively on competition between the labourers. The advance of industry, whose involuntary promoter is the bourgeoisie, replaces the isolation of the labourers, due to competition, by their revolutionary combination, due to association. The development of modern industry, therefore, cuts from under its feet the very foundation on which the bourgeoisie produces and appropriates products. What the bourgeoisie therefore produces, above all, are its own grave-diggers. Its fall and the victory of the proletariat are equally inevitable.

## ✎§ SOCIALISM: UTOPIAN AND SCIENTIFIC

*Friedrich Engels*

### III

The materialist conception of history starts from the proposition that the production of the means to support human life and, next to production, the exchange of things produced, is the basis of all social structure; that in every society that has appeared in history, the manner in which wealth is distributed and society divided into classes or orders, is dependent upon what is produced, how it is produced, and how the products are exchanged. From this point of view the final causes of all social changes and political revolutions are to be sought, not in men's brains, not in man's better insight into eternal truth and justice, but in changes in the modes of production and exchange. They are to be sought, not in the *philosophy*, but in the *economics* of each particular epoch. The growing perception that existing social institutions are unreasonable and unjust, that reason has become unreason, and right wrong, is only proof

Friedrich Engels, *Socialism: Utopian and Scientific,* trans. H. Hotz (New York: Charles Scribner's Sons, 1892), pp. 45–87.

that in the modes of production and exchange changes have silently taken place, with which the social order, adapted to earlier economic conditions, is no longer in keeping. From this it also follows that the means of getting rid of the incongruities that have been brought to light, must also be present, in a more or less developed condition, within the changed modes of production themselves. These means are not to be invented by deduction from fundamental principles, but are to be discovered in the stubborn facts of the existing system of production.

What is, then, the position of modern Socialism in this connexion?

The present structure of society—this is now pretty generally conceded—is the creation of the ruling class of to-day, of the bourgeoisie. The mode of production peculiar to the bourgeoisie, known, since Marx, as the capitalist mode of production, was incompatible with the feudal system, with the privileges it conferred upon individuals, entire social ranks and local corporations, as well as with the hereditary ties of subordination which constituted the framework of its social organisation. The bourgeoisie broke up the feudal system and built upon its ruins the capitalist order of society, the kingdom of free competition, of personal liberty, of the equality, before the law, of all commodity owners, of all the rest of the capitalist blessings. Thenceforward the capitalist mode of production could develop in freedom. Since steam, machinery, and the making of machines by machinery transformed the older manufacture into modern industry, the productive forces evolved under the guidance of the bourgeoisie developed with a rapidity and in a degree unheard of before. But just as the older manufacture, in its time, and handicraft, becoming more developed under its influence, had come into collision with the feudal trammels of the guilds, so now modern industry, in its more complete development, comes into collision with the bounds within which the capitalistic mode of production holds it confined. The new productive forces have already outgrown the capitalistic mode of using them. And this conflict between productive forces and modes of production is not a conflict engendered in the mind of man, like that between original sin and divine justice. It exists, in fact, objectively, outside us, independently of the will and actions even of the men that have brought it on. Modern Socialism is nothing but the reflex, in thought, of this conflict in fact; its ideal reflection in the minds, first, of the class directly suffering under it, the working-class.

Now, in what does this conflict consist?

Before capitalistic production, i.e., in the Middle Ages, the system of petty industry obtained generally, based upon the private property of the labourers in their means of production; in the country, the agriculture of the small peasant, freeman or serf; in the towns, the handicrafts organised in guilds. The instruments of labour —land, agricultural implements, the workshop, the tool—were the instruments of labour of single individuals, adapted for the use of one worker, and, therefore, of necessity, small, dwarfish, circumscribed. But, for this very reason they belonged, as a rule, to the producer himself. To concentrate these scattered, limited means of production, to enlarge them, to turn them into the powerful levers of production of the present day—this was precisely the historic rôle of capitalist production and of its upholder, the bourgeoisie. In the fourth section of "Capital" Marx has explained in detail, how since the fifteenth century this has been historically worked out through the three phases of simple co-operation, manufacture, and modern industry. But the bourgeoisie, as is also shown there, could not transform these puny means of production into mighty productive forces, without transforming them, at the same time, from means of production of the individual into *social* means of production only workable by a collectivity of men. The spinning-wheel, the handloom, the blacksmith's hammer, were replaced by the spinning-machine, the power-loom, the steam-hammer; the individual workshop, by the factory implying the co-operation of hundreds and thousands of workmen. In like manner, production itself changed from a series of individual into a series of social acts, and the products from individual to social products. The yarn, the cloth, the metal articles that now came out of the factory were the joint product of many workers, through whose hands they had successively to pass before they were ready. No one person could say of them: "I made that; this is *my* product."

But where, in a given society, the fundamental form of production is that spontaneous division of labour which creeps in gradually and not upon any preconceived plan, there the products take on the form of *commodities,* whose mutual exchange, buying and selling, enable the individual producers to satisfy their manifold wants. And this was the case in the Middle Ages. The peasant, *e.g.,* sold to the artisan agricultural products and bought from him the products of handicraft. Into this society of individual producers, of commodity-producers, the new mode of production thrust itself. In the midst of the old division of labour, grown up spontaneously and upon *no definite plan,* which had governed the whole of society, now arose division of labour upon *a definite plan,* as organised in the factory; side by side with *individual* production appeared *social* production. The products of both were sold in the same market, and, therefore, at prices at least approximately equal. But organisation upon a definite plan was stronger than spontaneous division of labour. The factories working with the combined social forces of a collectivity of individuals produced their commodities far more cheaply than the individual small producers. Individual production succumbed in one department after another. Socialised production revolutionised all the old methods of production. But its revolutionary character was, at the same time, so little recognised, that it was, on the contrary, introduced as a means of increasing and developing the production of commodities. When it arose, it found ready-made, and made liberal use of, certain machinery for the production and exchange of commodities; merchants' capital, handicraft, wage-labour. Socialised production thus introducing itself as a new form of the production of commodities, it was a matter of course that under it the old forms of appropriation remained in full swing, and were applied to its products as well.

In the mediæval stage of evolution of the production of commodities, the question as to the owner of the product of labour could not arise. The individual producer, as a rule, had, from raw material belonging to himself, and generally his own handiwork, produced it with his own tools, by the labour of his own hands or of his family. There was no need for him to appropriate the new product. It belonged wholly to him, as a matter of course. His property in the product was, therefore, based *upon his own labour.* Even where external help was used, this was, as a rule, of little importance, and very generally was compensated by something other than wages. The apprentices and journeymen of the guilds worked less for board and wages than for education, in order that they might become master craftsmen themselves.

Then came the concentration of the means of production and of the producers in large workshops and manufactories, their transformation into actual socialised means of production and socialised producers. But the socialised producers and means of production and their products were still treated, after this change, just as they had been before, *i.e.,* as the means of production and the products of individuals. Hitherto, the owner of the instruments of labour had himself appropriated the product, because, as a rule, it was his own product and the assistance of others was the exception. Now the owner of the instruments of labour always appropriated to himself the product, although it was no longer *his* product but exclusively the product of the *labour of others.* Thus, the products now produced socially were not appropriated by those who had actually set in motion the means of production and actually produced the commodities, but by the *capitalists.* The means of production, and production itself, had become in essence socialised. But they were subjected to a form of appropriation which presupposes the private production of individuals, under which, therefore, every one owns his own product and brings it to market. The mode of production is subjected to this form of appropriation, although it abolishes the conditions upon which the latter rests.

This contradiction, which gives to the new mode of production its capitalistic character, *contains the germ of the whole of the social antagonisms of to-day.* The greater the mastery obtained by the new mode of production over all important fields of production and in all manufacturing countries, the more it reduced individual production to an insignificant residuum, *the more clearly was brought out the incompatibility of socialised production with capitalistic appropriation.*

The first capitalists found, as we have said, alongside of other forms of labour, wage-labour ready-made for them on the market. But it was exceptional, complementary, accessory, transitory wage-labour. The agricultural labourer, though, upon occasion, he hired himself out by the day, had a few acres of his own land on which he could at all events live at a pinch. The guilds were so organised that the journeyman of to-day became the master of to-morrow. But all this changed, as soon as the means of production became socialised and concentrated in the hands of capitalists. The means of production, as well as the product, of the individual producer became more and more worthless; there was nothing left for him but to turn wage-worker under the capitalist. Wage-labour, aforetime the exception and accessory, now became the rule and basis of all production; aforetime complementary, it now became the sole remaining function of the worker. The wage-worker for a time became a wage-worker for life. The number of these permanent wage-workers was further enormously increased by the breaking-up of the feudal system that occurred at the same time, by the disbanding of the retainers of the feudal lords, the eviction of the peasants from their homesteads, etc. The separation was made complete between the means of production concentrated in the hands of the capitalists on the one side, and the producers, possessing nothing but their labour-power, on the other. *The contradiction between socialised production and capitalistic appropriation manifested itself as the antagonism of proletariat and bourgeoisie.*

We have seen that the capitalistic mode of production thrust its way into a society of commodity-producers, of individual producers, whose social bond was the exchange of their products. But every society, based upon the production of commodities, has this peculiarity: that the producers have lost control over their own social inter-relations. Each man produces for himself with such means of production as he may happen to have, and for such exchange as he may require to satisfy his remaining wants. No one knows how much of his particular article is coming on the market, nor how much of it will be wanted. No one knows whether his individual product will meet an actual demand, whether he will be able to make good his cost of produc-tion or even to sell his commodity at all. Anarchy reigns in socialised production.

But the production of commodities, like every other form of production, has its peculiar, inherent laws inseparable from it; and these laws work, despite anarchy, in and through anarchy. They reveal themselves in the only persistent form of social inter-relations, *i.e.*, in exchange, and here they affect the individual producers as compulsory laws of competition. They are, at first, unknown to these producers themselves, and have to be discovered by them gradually and as the result of experi-ence. They work themselves out, therefore, independently of the producers, and in antagonism to them, as inexorable natural laws of their particular form of production. The product governs the producers.

In mediæval society, especially in the earliest centuries, production was essentially directed towards satisfying the wants of the individual. It satisfied, in the main, only the wants of the producer and his family. Where relations of personal dependence existed, as in the country, it also helped to satisfy the wants of the feudal lord. In all this there was, therefore, no exchange; the products, consequently, did not assume the character of commodities. The family of the peasant produced almost everything they wanted: clothes and furniture, as well as means of subsistence. Only when it began to produce more than was sufficient to supply its own wants and the payments in kind to the feudal lord, only then did it also produce commodities. This surplus, thrown into socialised exchange and offered for sale, became commodities.

The artisans of the towns, it is true, had from the first to produce for exchange. But they, also, themselves supplied the greatest part of their own individual wants. They had gardens and plots of land. They turned their cattle out into the communal forest, which, also, yielded them timber and firing. The women spun flax, wool, and so forth. Production for the purpose of exchange, production of commodities, was only in its infancy. Hence, exchange was restricted, the market narrow, the methods of production stable; there was local exclusiveness without, local unity within; the mark in the country, in the town, the guild.

But with the extension of the production of commodities, and especially with the introduction of the capitalist mode of production, the laws of commodity-production, hitherto latent, came into action more openly and with greater force. The old bonds were loosened, the old exclusive limits broken through, the producers were more and more turned into independent, isolated producers of commodities. It became apparent that the production of society at large was ruled by absence of plan, by accident, by anarchy; and this anarchy grew to greater and greater height. But the chief means by aid of which the capitalist mode of production intensified this anarchy of socialised production, was the exact opposite of anarchy. It was the increasing organisation of production, upon a social basis, in every individual productive establishment. By this, the old, peaceful, stable condition of things was ended. Wherever this organisation of production was introduced into a branch of industry, it brooked no other method of production by its side. The field of labour became a battle-ground. The great geo-graphical discoveries, and the colonisation following upon them, multiplied markets and quickened the transformation of handicraft into manufacture. The war did not simply break out between the individual producers of particular localities. The local struggles begat in their turn national conflicts, the commercial wars of the seventeenth and the eighteenth centuries.

Finally, modern industry and the opening of the world-market made the struggle universal, and at the same time gave it an unheard-of virulence. Advantages in natural or artificial conditions of production now decide the existence or non-existence of individual capitalists, as well as of whole industries and countries. He that falls is remorselessly cast aside. It is the Darwinian struggle of the individual for existence transferred from Nature to society with intensified violence. The conditions of ex-istence natural to the animal appear as the final term of human development. The contradiction between socialised production and capitalistic appropriation now pre-sents itself as *an antagonism between the organisation of production in the individual workshop and the anarchy of production in society generally.*

The capitalistic mode of production moves in these two forms of the antagonism immanent to it from its very origin. It is never able to get out of that "vicious circle," which Fourier had already discovered. What Fourier could not, indeed, see in his time is, that this circle is gradually narrowing; that the movement becomes more and more a spiral, and must come to an end, like the movement of the planets, by collision with the centre. It is the compelling force of anarchy in the production of society at large that more and more completely turns the great majority of men into prole-tarians; and it is the masses of the proletariat again who will finally put an end to anarchy in production. It is the compelling force of anarchy in social production that turns the limitless perfectibility of machinery under modern industry into a compul-sory law by which every individual industrial capitalist must perfect his machinery more and more, under penalty of ruin.

But the perfecting of machinery is the making human labour superfluous. If the introduction and increase of machinery means the displacement of millions of manual, by a few machine, workers, improvement in machinery means the displacement of more and more of the machine-workers themselves. It means, in the last instance, the production of a number of available wage-workers in excess of the average needs of capital, the formation of a complete industrial reserve army, as I called it in 1845, available at the times when industry is working at high pressure, to be cast out upon the street when the inevitable crash comes, a constant dead weight upon the limbs of the working-class in its struggle for existence with capital, a regulator for the keep-ing of wages down to the low level that suits the interests of capital. Thus it comes about, to quote Marx, that machinery becomes the most powerful weapon in the war of capital against the working-class; that the instruments of labour constantly tear the means of subsistence out of the hands of the labourer; that the very product of the worker is turned into an instrument for his subjugation. Thus it comes about that the economising of the instruments of labour becomes at the same time, from the outset, the most reckless waste of labour-power, and robbery based upon the normal conditions under which labour functions; that machinery, "the most powerful instru-ment for shortening labour-time, becomes the most unfailing means for placing every moment of the labourer's time and that of his family at the disposal of the capitalist for the purpose of expanding the value of his capital." Thus it comes about that over-work of some becomes the preliminary condition for the idleness of others, and that modern industry, which hunts after new consumers over the whole world, forces the consumption of the masses at home down to a starvation minimum, and in doing thus destroys its own home market. "The law that always equilibrates the relative surplus population, or industrial reserve army, to the extent and energy of accumulation, this law rivets the labourer to capital more firmly than the wedges of Vulcan did Prometheus to the rock. It establishes an accumulation of misery, corresponding with accumulation of capital. Accumulation of wealth at one pole is, therefore, at the same time, accumulation of misery, agony of toil, slavery, ignorance, brutality, mental degradation, at the opposite pole, *i.e.* on the side of the class that produces *its own product in the form of capital"* (Marx). And to expect any other division of the products from the capitalistic mode of production is the same as expecting the electrodes of a battery not to decompose acidulated water, not to liberate oxygen at the positive, hydrogen at the negative pole, so long as they are connected with the battery.

We have seen that the ever-increasing perfectibility of modern machinery is, by the anarchy of social production, turned into a compulsory law that forces the individual industrial capitalist always to improve his machinery, always to increase its productive force. The bare possibility of extending the field of production is transformed for him into a similar compulsory law. The enormous expansive force of modern industry, compared with which that of gases is mere child's play, appears to us now as a *necessity* for expansion, both qualitative and quantitative, that laughs at all resistance. Such resistance is offered by consumption, by sales, by the markets for the products of modern industry. But the capacity for extension, extensive and intensive, of the markets is primarily governed by quite different laws, that work much less energetically. The extension of the markets cannot keep pace with the extension of production. The collision becomes inevitable, and as this cannot produce any real solution so long as it does not break in pieces the capitalist mode of production, the collisions become periodic. Capitalist production has begotten another "vicious circle."

As a matter of fact, since 1825, when the first general crisis broke out, the whole industrial and commercial world, production and exchange among all civilised peoples and their more or less barbaric hangers-on, are thrown out of joint about once every ten years. Commerce is at a standstill, the markets are glutted, products accumulate, as multitudinous as they are unsaleable, hard cash disappears, credit vanishes, factories are closed, the mass of the workers are in want of the means of subsistence, because they have produced too much of the means of subsistence; bankruptcy follows upon bankruptcy, execution upon execution. The stagnation lasts for years; productive forces and products are wasted and destroyed wholesale, until the accumulated mass of commodities finally filter off, more or less depreciated in value, until production and exchange gradually begin to move again. Little by little the pace quickens. It becomes a trot. The industrial trot breaks into a canter, the canter in turn grows into the headlong gallop of a perfect steeplechase of industry, commercial credit, and speculation, which finally, after breakneck leaps, ends where it began—in the ditch of a crisis. And so over and over again. We have now, since the year 1825, gone through this five times, and at the present moment (1877) we are going through it for the sixth time. And the character of these crises is so clearly defined that Fourier hit all of them off, when he described the first as *"crise pléthorique,"* a crisis from plethora.

In these crises, the contradiction between socialised production and capitalist appropriation ends in a violent explosion. The circulation of commodities is, for the time being, stopped. Money, the means of circulation, becomes a hindrance to circulation. All the laws of production and circulation of commodities are turned upside down. The economic collision has reached its apogee. *The mode of production is in rebellion against the mode of exchange.*

The fact that the socialised organisation of production within the factory has developed so far that it has become incompatible with the anarchy of production in society, which exists side by side with and dominates it, is brought home to the capitalists themselves by the violent concentration of capital that occurs during crises, through the ruin of many large, and a still greater number of small, capitalists. The whole mechanism of the capitalist mode of production breaks down under the pressure of the productive forces, its own creations. It is no longer able to turn all this mass of means of production into capital. They lie fallow, and for that very reason the industrial reserve army must also lie fallow. Means of production, means of subsistence, available labourers, all the elements of production and of general wealth, are present in abundance. But "abundance becomes the source of distress and want" (Fourier), because it is the very thing that prevents the transformation of the means of production and subsistence into capital. For in capitalistic society the means of production can only function when they have undergone a preliminary transformation into capital, into the means of exploiting human labour-power. The necessity of this transformation into capital of the means of production and subsistence stands like a ghost between these and the workers. It alone prevents the coming together of the material and personal levers of production; it alone forbids the means of production to function, the workers to work and live. On the one hand, therefore, the capitalistic mode of production stands convicted of its own incapacity to further direct these productive forces. On the other, these productive forces themselves, with increasing energy, press forward to the removal of the existing contradiction, to the abolition of their quality as capital, to the *practical recognition of their character as social productive forces.*

This rebellion of the production forces, as they grow more and more powerful, against their quality as capital, this stronger and stronger command that their social character shall be recognised, forces the capitalist class itself to treat them more and more as social productive forces, so far as this is possible under capitalist conditions. The period of industrial high pressure, with its unbounded inflation of credit, not less than the crash itself, by the collapse of great capitalist establishments, tends to bring about that form of the socialisation of great masses of means of production, which we meet with in the different kinds of joint-stock companies. Many of these means of production and of distribution are, from the outset, so colossal, that, like the railroads, they exclude all other forms of capitalistic exploitation. At a further stage of evolution this form also becomes insufficient. The producers on a large scale in a particular branch of industry in a particular country unite in a "Trust," a union for the purpose of regulating production. They determine the total amount to be produced, parcel it out among themselves, and thus enforce the selling price fixed beforehand. But trusts of this kind, as soon as business becomes bad, are generally liable to break up, and, on this very account, compel a yet greater concentration of association. The whole of the particular industry is turned into one gigantic joint-stock company; internal competition gives place to the internal monopoly of this one company. This has happened in 1890 with the English *alkali* production, which is now, after the fusion of 48 large works, in the hands of one company, conducted upon a single plan, and with a capital of £6,000,000.

In the trusts, freedom of competition changes into its very opposite—into monopoly; and the production without any definite plan of capitalistic society capitulates to the production upon a definite plan of the invading socialistic society. Certainly this is so far still to the benefit and advantage of the capitalists. But in this case the exploitation is so palpable that it must break down. No nation will put up with production conducted by trusts, with so barefaced an exploitation of the community by a small band of dividend-mongers.

In any case, with trusts or without, the official representative of capitalist society—the State—will ultimately have to undertake the direction of production. This necessity for conversion into State-property is felt first in the great institutions for intercourse and communication—the post-office, the telegraphs, the railways.

If the crises demonstrate the incapacity of the bourgeoisie for managing any longer modern productive forces, the transformation of the great establishments for production and distribution into joint-stock companies, trusts, and State property, show how unnecessary the bourgeoisie are for that purpose. All the social functions of the capitalist are now performed by salaried employees. The capitalist has no further social function than that of pocketing dividends, tearing off coupons, and gambling on the Stock Exchange, where the different capitalists despoil one another of their capital. At first the capitalistic mode of production forces out the workers. Now it forces out the capitalists, and reduces them, just as it reduced the workers, to the ranks of the surplus population, although not immediately into those of the industrial reserve army.

But the transformation, either into joint-stock companies and trusts, or into State-ownership, does not do away with the capitalistic nature of the productive forces. In the joint-stock companies and trusts this is obvious. And the modern State, again, is only the organisation that bourgeois society takes on in order to support the external conditions of the capitalist mode of production against the encroachments, as well of the workers as of individual capitalists. The modern State, no matter what its form, is essentially a capitalist machine, the state of the capitalists, the ideal personification of the total national capital. The more it proceeds to the taking over of productive forces, the more does it actually become the national capitalist, the more citizens does it exploit. The workers remain wage-workers—proletarians. The capitalist relation is not done away with. It is rather brought to a head. But, brought to a head, it topples over. State-ownership of the productive forces is not the solution of the conflict, but concealed within it are the technical conditions that form the elements of that solution.

This solution can only consist in the practical recognition of the social nature of the modern forces of production, and therefore in the harmonising the modes of production, appropriation, and exchange with the socialised character of the means of production. And this can only come about by society openly and directly taking possession of the productive forces which have outgrown all control except that of society as a whole. The social character of the means of production and of the products to-day reacts against the producers, periodically disrupts all production and exchange, acts only like a law of Nature working blindly, forcibly, destructively. But with the taking over by society of the productive forces, the social character of the means of production and of the products will be utilised by the producers with a perfect understanding of its nature, and instead of being a source of disturbance and periodical collapse, will become the most powerful lever of production itself.

Active social foces work exactly like natural forces: blindly, forcibly, destructively, so long as we do not understand, and reckon with, them. But when once we understand them, when once we grasp their action, their direction, their effects, it depends only upon ourselves to subject them more and more to our own will, and by means of them to reach our own ends. And this holds quite especially of the mighty productive forces of to-day. As long as we obstinately refuse to understand the nature and the character of these social means of action—and this understanding goes against the grain of the capitalist mode of production and its defenders—so long these forces are at work in spite of us, in opposition to us, so long they master us, as we have shown above in detail.

But when once their nature is understood, they can, in the hands of the producers working together, be transformed from master demons into willing servants. The difference is as that between the destructive force of electricity in the lightning of the storm, and electricity under command in the telegraph and the voltaic arc; the difference between a conflagration, and fire working in the service of man. With this recognition at last of the real nature of the productive forces of to-day, the social anarchy of production gives place to a social regulation of production upon a definite plan, according to the needs of the community and of each individual. Then the capitalist mode of appropriation, in which the product enslaves first the producer and then the appropriator, is replaced by the mode of appropriation of the products that is based upon the nature of the modern means of production; upon the one hand, direct social appropriation, as means to the maintenance and extension of production —on the other, direct individual appropriation, as means of subsistence and of enjoyment.

Whilst the capitalist mode of production more and more completely transforms the great majority of the population into proletarians, it creates the power which, under penalty of its own destruction, is forced to accomplish this revolution. Whilst it forces on, more and more, the transformation of the vast means of production, already socialised, into State property, it shows itself the way to accomplishing this revolution. *The proletariat seizes political power and turns the means of production into State property.*

But, in doing this, it abolishes itself as proletariat, abolishes all class distinctions and class antagonisms, abolishes also the State as State. Society thus far, based upon class antagonisms, had need of the State. That is, of an organisation of the particular class which was *pro tempore* the exploiting class, an organisation for the purpose of preventing any interference from without with the existing conditions of production, and therefore, especially, for the purpose of forcibly keeping the exploited classes in the condition of oppression corresponding with the given mode of production (slavery, serfdom, wage-labour). The State was the official representative of society as a whole; the gathering of it together into a visible embodiment. But it was this only in so far as it was the State of that class which itself represented, for the time being, society as a whole; in ancient times, the State of slave-owning citizens; in the middle ages, the feudal lords; in our own time, the bourgeoisie. When at last it becomes the real representative of the whole of society, it renders itself unnecessary. As soon as there is no longer any social class to be held in subjection; as soon as class rule, and the individual struggle for existence based upon our present anarchy in production, with the collisions and excesses arising from these, are removed, nothing more remains to be repressed, and a special repressive force, a State, is no longer necessary. The first act by virtue of which the State really constitutes itself the representative of the whole of society—the taking possession of the means of production in the name of society—this is, at the same time, its last independent act as a State. State interference in social relations becomes, in one domain after another, superfluous, and then dies out of itself; the government of persons is replaced by the administration of things, and by the conduct of processes of production. The State is not "abolished." *It dies out.* This gives the measure of the value of the phrase "a free State," both as to its justifiable use at times by agitators, and as to its ultimate scientific insufficiency; and also of the demands of the so-called anarchists for the abolition of the State out of hand.

Since the historical appearance of the capitalist mode of production, the appropriation by society of all the means of production has often been dreamed of, more or less vaguely, by individuals, as well as by sects, as the ideal of the future. But it could become possible, could become a historical necessity, only when the actual conditions for its realisation were there. Like every other social advance, it becomes practicable, not by men understanding that the existence of classes is in contradiction to justice, equality, etc., not by the mere willingness to abolish these classes, but by virtue of certain new economic conditions. The separation of society into an exploiting and an exploited class, a ruling and an oppressed class, was the necessary consequence of the deficient and restricted development of production in former times. So long as the total social labour only yields a produce which but slightly exceeds that barely necessary for the existence of all; so long, therefore, as labour engages all or almost all the time of the great majority of the members of society—so long, of necessity, this society is divided into classes. Side by side with the great majority, exclusively bond slaves to labour, arises a class freed from directly productive labour, which looks after the general affairs of society; the direction of labour, State business, law, science, art, etc. It is, therefore, the law of division of labour that lies at the basis of the division into classes. But this does not prevent this division into classes from being carried out by means of violence and robbery, trickery and fraud. It does not prevent the ruling class, once having the upper hand, from consolidating its power at the expense of the working-class, from turning their social leadership into an intensified exploitation of the masses.

But if, upon this showing, division into classes has a certain historical justification, it has this only for a given period, only under given social conditions. It was based upon the insufficiency of production. It will be swept away by the complete development of modern productive forces. And, in fact, the abolition of classes in society presupposes a degree of historical evolution, at which the existence, not simply of this or that particular ruling class, but of any ruling class at all, and, therefore, the existence of class distinction itself has become an obsolete anachronism. It presupposes, therefore, the development of production carried out to a degree at which appropriation of the means of production and of the products, and, with this, of political domination, of the monopoly of culture, and of intellectual leadership by a particular class of society, has become not only superfluous, but economically, politically, intellectually a hindrance to development.

This point is now reached. Their political and intellectual bankruptcy is scarcely any longer a secret to the bourgeoisie themselves. Their economic bankruptcy recurs regularly every ten years. In every crisis, society is suffocated beneath the weight of its own productive forces and products, which it cannot use, and stands helpless, face to face with the absurd contradiction that the producers have nothing to consume, because consumers are wanting. The expansive force of the means of production bursts the bonds that the capitalist mode of production had imposed upon them. Their deliverance from these bonds is the one precondition for an unbroken, constantly-accelerated development of the productive forces, and therewith for a practically unlimited increase of production itself. Nor is this all. The socialised appropriation of the means of production does away, not only with the present artificial restrictions upon production, but also with the positive waste and devastation of productive forces and products that are at the present time the inevitable concomitants of production, and that reach their height in the crises. Further, it sets free for the community at large a mass of means of production and of products, by doing away with the senseless extravagance of the ruling classes of to-day; and their political representatives. The possibility of securing for every member of society, by means of socialised production, an existence not only fully sufficient materially, and becoming day by day more full, but an existence guaranteeing to all the free development and exercise of their physical and mental faculties—this possibility is now for the first time here, but *it is here.*

With the seizing of the means of production by society, production of commodities is done away with, and, simultaneously, the mastery of the product over the producer. Anarchy in social production is replaced by systematic, definite organisation. The struggle for individual existence disappears. Then for the first time, man, in a certain sense, is finally marked off from the rest of the animal kingdom, and emerges from mere animal conditions of existence into really human ones. The whole sphere of the conditions of life which environ man, and which have hitherto ruled man, now comes under the dominion and control of man, who for the first time becomes the real, conscious lord of Nature, because he has now become master of his own social organisation. The laws of his own social action, hitherto standing face to face with man as laws of Nature foreign to, and dominating, him, will then be used with full understanding, and so mastered by him. Man's own social organisation, hitherto confronting him as a necessity imposed by Nature and history, now becomes the result of his own free action. The extraneous objective forces that have hitherto governed history, pass under the control of man himself. Only from that time will man himself, more and more consciously, make his own history—only from that time will the social causes set in movement by him have, in the main and in a constantly growing measure, the results intended by him. It is the ascent of man from the kingdom of necessity to the kingdom of freedom.

Let us briefly sum up our sketch of historical evolution.

I. *Mediæval Society*    Individual production on a small scale. Means of production adapted for individual use; hence primitive, ungainly, petty, dwarfed in action. Production for immediate consumption, either of the producer himself or of his feudal lord. Only where an excess of production over this consumption occurs is such excess offered for sale, enters into exchange. Production of commodities, therefore, only in its infancy. But already it contains within itself, in embryo, *anarchy in the production of society at large.*

II. *Capitalist Revolution*    Transformation of industry, at first by means of simple cooperation and manufacture. Concentration of the means of production, hitherto scattered, into great workshops. As a consequence, their transformation from individual to social means of production—a transformation which does not, on the whole, affect the form of exchange. The old forms of appropriation remain in force. The capitalist appears. In his capacity as owner of the means of production, he also appropriates the products and turns them into commodities. Production has become a *social* act. Exchange and appropriation continue to be *individual* acts, the acts of individuals. *The social product is appropriated by the individual capitalist.* Fundamental contradiction, whence arise all the contradictions in which our present day society moves, and which modern industry brings to light.

A    Severance of the producer from the means of production. Condemnation of the worker to wage-labour for life. *Antagonism between the proletariat and the bourgeosie.*

B    Growing predominance and increasing effectiveness of the laws governing the production of commodities. Unbridled competition. *Contradiction between socialised organisation in the individual factory and social anarchy in production as a whole.*

C    On the one hand, perfecting of machinery, made by competition compulsory for each individual manufacturer, and complemented by a constantly growing displacement of labourers. *Industrial reserve-army.* On the other hand, unlimited extension of production, also compulsory under competition, for every manufacturer. On both sides, unheard of development of productive forces, excess of supply over demand, over-production, glutting of the markets, crises every ten years, the vicious circle: excess here, of means of production and products—excess there, of labourers, without employment and without means of existence. But these two levers of production and of social well-being are unable to work together, because the capitalist form of production prevents the productive forces from working and the products from circulating, unless they are first turned into capital—which their very superabundance prevents. The contradiction has grown into an absurdity. *The mode of production rises in rebellion against the form of exchange.* The bourgeoisie are convicted of incapacity further to manage their own social productive forces.

D    Partial recognition of the social character of the productive forces forced upon the capitalists themselves. Taking over of the great institutions for production and communication, first by joint-stock companies, later on by trusts, then by the State. The bourgeoisie demonstrated to be a superfluous class. All its social functions are now performed by salaried employees.

III. *Proletarian Revolution*    Solution of the contradictions. The proletariat seizes the public power, and by means of this transforms the socialised means of production, slipping from the hands of the bourgeoisie, into public property. By this act, the proletariat frees the means of production from the character of capital they have thus far borne, and gives their socialised character complete freedom to work itself out. Socialised production upon a predetermined plan becomes henceforth possible. The development of production makes the existence of different classes of society thenceforth an anachronism. In proportion as anarchy in social production vanishes, the political authority of the State dies out. Man, at last the master of his own form of social organisation, becomes at the same time the lord over Nature, his own master —free.

To accomplish this act of universal emancipation is the historical mission of the modern proletariat. To thoroughly comprehend the historical conditions and thus the very nature of this act, to impart to the now oppressed proletarian class a full knowledge of the conditions and of the meaning of the momentous act it is called upon to accomplish, this is the task of the theoretical expression of the proletarian movement, scientific Socialism.

## ⤳ THE POSITIVE PHILOSOPHY

*Auguste Comte*

*In 1667 Bishop Thomas Sprat had noted that the founding of the Royal Society of London for Improving Natural Knowledge meant the establishment of a new and more fruitful form of association among men (see Vol. III, pages 117–128). But it was not until the advent of Henri de Saint-Simon (1760–1825) and his disciple Auguste Comte (1798–1857) that a serious attempt was made to reform society at large along scientific lines.*

*Comte coined the word "positivism" for the scientific attitude, as he understood it, which avoids theological or metaphysical speculation about the nature of reality and instead confines itself to describing the regular relationships among phenomena. He differed from earlier positivists of the Enlightenment in insisting that the crowning science was not mathematics or physics but "sociology"—the study of human groups. This new science, he thought, would supply sound generalizations about the true "Supreme Being"—Mankind—to replace the outdated dogmas of religion, and its practitioners would become the priests of a new Religion of Humanity. Comte knew that most men crave authority to rule them and rituals to appeal to their imaginations. He proposed to turn over secular authority to captains of industry, while an international hierarchy of sociologists —culminating in Comte himself—would administer "sacraments" in honor of a new calendar of "saints": benefactors of humanity like Galileo, Descartes, and Newton. In his later years, Comte turned increasingly for support to two groups which in any case had little to lose in his proposed reorganization of society: proletarians and women. Here too his influence was decisive; both Karl Marx and John Stuart Mill, despite serious reservations, admitted that they derived important ideas from him. Comte was an unbalanced enthusiast, perhaps even mentally ill; nevertheless, a surprising number of modern trends trace their origin to his voluminous works.*

*The following selection is the introductory chapter of his* System of Positive Philosophy, *published in French in six volumes between 1830 and 1842 and "freely translated and condensed" into two volumes by Harriet Martineau in 1853. Although these are not Comte's exact words, there can be no doubt that they are his ideas. Miss Martineau's condensation became an important book in its own right throughout the English-speaking world.*

. . . In order to understand the true value and character of the Positive Philosophy, we must take a brief general view of the progressive course of the human mind, regarded as a whole; for no conception can be understood otherwise than through its history.

From the study of the development of human intelligence, in all directions, and through all times, the discovery arises of a great fundamental law, to which it is necessarily subject, and which has a solid foundation of proof, both in the facts of our organization and in our historical experience. The law is this:—that each of our leading conceptions,—each branch of our knowledge,—passes successively through three different theoretical conditions: the Theological, or fictitious; the Metaphysical, or abstract; and the Scientific, or positive. In other words, the human mind, by its nature, employs in its progress three methods of philosophizing, the character of which is essentially different, and even radically opposed: viz., the theological method, the metaphysical, and the positive. Hence arise three philosophies, or general systems

*The Positive Philosophy of Auguste Comte,* **trans. and condensed by Harriet Martineau** (2 vols.; New York: D. Appleton & Company, Inc., 1853), I, 1–17.

of conceptions on the aggregate of phenomena, each of which excludes the others. The first is the necessary point of departure of the human understanding; and the third is its fixed and definitive state. The second is merely a state of transition.

In the theological state, the human mind, seeking the essential nature of beings, the first and final causes (the origin and purpose) of all effects,—in short, Absolute knowledge,—supposes all phenomena to be produced by the immediate action of supernatural beings.

In the metaphysical state, which is only a modification of the first, the mind supposes, instead of supernatural beings, abstract forces, veritable entities (that is, personified abstractions) inherent in all beings, and capable of producing all phenomena. What is called the explanation of phenomena is, in this stage, a mere reference of each to its proper entity.

In the final, the positive state, the mind has given over the vain search after Absolute notions, the origin and destination of the universe, and the causes of phenomena, and applies itself to the study of their laws,—that is, their invariable relations of succession and resemblance. Reasoning and observation, duly combined, are the means of this knowledge. What is now understood when we speak of an explanation of facts is simply the establishment of a connection between single phenomena and some general facts, the number of which continually diminishes with the progress of science.

The Theological system arrived at the highest perfection of which it is capable when it substituted the providential action of a single Being for the varied operations of the numerous divinities which had been before imagined. In the same way, in the last stage of the Metaphysical system, men substitute one great entity (Nature) as the cause of all phenomena, instead of the multitude of entities at first supposed. In the same way, again, the ultimate perfection of the Positive system would be (if such perfection could be hoped for) to represent all phenomena as particular aspects of a single general fact;—such as Gravitation, for instance.

The importance of the working of this general law will be established hereafter. At present, it must suffice to point out some of the grounds of it.

There is no science which, having attained the positive stage, does not bear marks of having passed through the others. Some time since it was (whatever it might be) composed, as we can now perceive, of metaphysical abstractions; and, further back in the course of time, it took its form from theological conceptions. We shall have only too much occasion to see, as we proceed, that our most advanced sciences still bear very evident marks of the two earlier periods through which they have passed.

The progress of the individual mind is not only an illustration, but an indirect evidence of that of the general mind. The point of departure of the individual and of the race being the same, the phases of the mind of a man correspond to the epochs of the mind of the race. Now, each of us is aware, if he looks back upon his own history, that he was a theologian in his childhood, a metaphysician in his youth, and a natural philosopher in his manhood. All men who are up to their age can verify this for themselves.

Besides the observation of facts, we have theoretical reasons in support of this law.

The most important of these reasons arises from the necessity that always exists for some theory to which to refer our facts, combined with the clear impossibility that, at the outset of human knowledge, men could have formed theories out of the observation of facts. All good intellects have repeated, since Bacon's time, that there can be no real knowledge but that which is based on observed facts. This is incontestable, in our present advanced stage; but, if we look back to the primitive stage of human knowledge, we shall see that it must have been otherwise then. If it is true that every theory must be based upon observed facts, it is equally true that facts cannot be observed without the guidance of some theory. Without such guidance, our facts would be desultory and fruitless; we could not retain them: for the most part we could not even perceive them.

Thus, between the necessity of observing facts in order to form a theory, and having a theory in order to observe facts, the human mind would have been entangled in a vicious circle, but for the natural opening afforded by Theological conceptions. This is the fundamental reason for the theological character of the primitive philosophy. This necessity is confirmed by the perfect suitability of the theological philosophy to the earliest researches of the human mind. It is remarkable that the most inaccessible questions,—those of the nature of beings, and the origin and purpose of phenomena,—should be the first to occur in a primitive state, while those which are really within our reach are regarded as almost unworthy of serious study. The reason is evident enough:—that experience alone can teach us the measure of our powers; and if men had not begun by an exaggerated estimate of what they can do, they would never have done all that they are capable of. Our organization requires this. At such a period there could have been no reception of a positive philosophy, whose function is to discover the laws of phenomena, and whose leading characteristic it is to regard as interdicted to human reason those sublime mysteries which theology explains, even to their minutest details, with the most attractive facility. It is just so under a practical view of the nature of the researches with which men first occupied themselves. Such inquiries offered the powerful charm of unlimited empire over the external world,— a world destined wholly for our use, and involved in every way with our existence. The theological philosophy, presenting this view, administered exactly the stimulus necessary to incite the human mind to the irksome labour without which it could make no progress. We can now scarcely conceive of such a state of things, our reason having become sufficiently mature to enter upon laborious scientific researches, without needing any such stimulus as wrought upon the imaginations of astrologers and alchemists. We have motive enough in the hope of discovering the laws of phenomena, with a view to the confirmation or rejection of a theory. But it could not be so in the earliest days; and it is to the chimeras of astrology and alchemy that we owe the long series of observations and experiments on which our positive science is based. Kepler felt this on behalf of astronomy, and Berthollet on behalf of chemistry. Thus was a spontaneous philosophy, the theological, the only possible beginning, method, and provisional system, out of which the Positive philosophy could grow. It is easy, after this, to perceive how Metaphysical methods and doctrines must have afforded the means of transition from the one to the other.

The human understanding, slow in its advance, could not step at once from the theological into the positive philosophy. The two are so radically opposed, that an intermediate system of conceptions has been necessary to render the transition possible. It is only in doing this, that Metaphysical conceptions have any utility whatever.

In contemplating phenomena, men substitute for supernatural direction a corresponding entity. This entity may have been supposed to be derived from the supernatural action: but it is more easily lost sight of, leaving attention free for the facts themselves, till, at length, metaphysical agents have ceased to be anything more than the abstract names of phenomena. It is not easy to say by what other process than this our minds could have passed from supernatural considerations to natural; from the theological system to the positive.

The Law of human development being thus established, let us consider what is the proper nature of the Positive Philosophy.

As we have seen, the first characteristic of the Positive Philosophy is that it regards all phenomena as subjected to invariable natural *Laws*. Our business is,—seeing how vain is any research into what are called *Causes*, whether first or final,—to pursue an accurate discovery of these Laws, with a view to reducing them to the smallest possible number. By speculating upon causes, we could solve no difficulty about origin and purpose. Our real business is to analyse accurately the circumstances of phenomena, and to connect them by the natural relations of succession and resemblance. The best illustration of this is in the case of the doctrine of Gravitation. We say that the general phenomena of the universe are *explained* by it, because it connects under one head the whole immense variety of astronomical facts; exhibiting the constant tendency of atoms towards each other in direct proportion to their masses, and in inverse proportion to the squares of their distances; whilst the general fact itself is a mere extension of one which is perfectly familiar to us, and which we therefore say that we know;—the weight of bodies on the surface of the earth. As to what weight and attraction are, we have nothing to do with that, for it is not a matter of knowledge at all. Theologians and metaphysicians may imagine and refine about such questions; but positive philosophy rejects them. When any attempt has been made to explain them, it has ended only in saying that attraction is universal weight, and that weight is terrestrial attraction: that is, that the two orders of phenomena are identical; which is the point from which the question set out. Again, M. Fourier, in his fine series of researches on Heat, has given us all the most important and precise laws of the phenomena of heat, and many large and new truths, without once inquiring into its nature, as his predecessors had done when they disputed about calorific matter and the action of an universal ether. In treating his subject in the Positive method, he finds inexhaustible material for all his activity of research, without betaking himself to insoluble questions.

Before ascertaining the stage which the Positive Philosophy has reached, we must bear in mind that the different kinds of our knowledge have passed through the three stages of progress at different rates, and have not therefore arrived at the same time. The rate of advance depends on the nature of the knowledge in question, so distinctly that, as we shall see hereafter, this consideration constitutes an accessory to the fundamental law of progress. Any kind of knowledge reaches the positive stage early in proportion to its generality, simplicity, and independence of other departments. Astronomical science, which is above all made up of facts that are general, simple, and independent of other sciences, arrived first; then terrestrial Physics; then Chemistry; and, at length, Physiology.

It is difficult to assign any precise date to this revolution in science. It may be said, like everything else, to have been always going on; and especially since the labours of Aristotle and the school of Alexandria; and then from the introduction of natural science into the West of Europe by the Arabs. But, if we must fix upon some marked period, to serve as a rallying point, it must be that,—about two centuries ago,—when the human mind was astir under the precepts of Bacon, the conceptions of Descartes, and the discoveries of Galileo. Then it was that the spirit of the Positive philosophy rose up in opposition to that of the superstitious and scholastic systems which had hitherto obscured the true character of all science. Since that date, the progress of the Positive philosophy, and the decline of the other two, have been so marked that no rational mind now doubts that the revolution is destined to go on to its completion,— every branch of knowledge being, sooner or later, brought within the operation of Positive philosophy. This is not yet the case. Some are still lying outside: and not till they are brought in will the Positive philosophy possess that character of universality which is necessary to its definitive constitution.

In mentioning just now the four principal categories of phenomena,—astronomical, physical, chemical, and physiological,—there was an omission which will have been noticed. Nothing was said of Social phenomena. Though involved with the physiological, Social phenomena demand a distinct classification, both on account of their importance and of their difficulty. They are the most individual, the most complicated, the most dependent on all others; and therefore they must be the latest,—even if they had no special obstacle to encounter. This branch of science has not hitherto entered into the domain of Positive philosophy. Theological and metaphysical methods, exploded in other departments, are as yet exclusively applied, both in the way of inquiry and discussion, in all treatment of Social subjects, though the best minds are heartily weary of eternal disputes about divine right and the sovereignty of the people. This is the great, while it is evidently the only gap which has to be filled, to constitute, solid and entire, the Positive Philosophy. Now that the human mind has grasped celestial and terrestrial physics,—mechanical and chemical; organic physics, both vegetable and animal,—there remains one science, to fill up the series of sciences of observation,—Social physics. This is what men have now most need of: and this it is the principal aim of the present work to establish.

It would be absurd to pretend to offer this new science at once in a complete state. Others, less new, are in very unequal conditions of forwardness. But the same character of positivity which is impressed on all the others will be shown to belong to this. This once done, the philosophical system of the moderns will be in fact complete, as there will then be no phenomenon which does not naturally enter into some one of the five great categories. All our fundamental conceptions having become homogeneous, the Positive state will be fully established. It can never again change its character, though it will be for ever in course of development by additions of new knowledge. Having acquired the character of universality which has hitherto been the only advantage resting with the two preceding systems, it will supersede them by its natural superiority, and leave to them only an historical existence.

We have stated the special aim of this work. Its secondary and general aim is this:—to review what has been effected in the Sciences, in order to show that they are not radically separate, but all branches from the same trunk. If we had confined ourselves to the first and special object of the work, we should have produced merely a study of Social physics: whereas, in introducing the second and general, we offer a study of Positive philosophy, passing in review all the positive sciences already formed.

The purpose of this work is not to give an account of the Natural Sciences. Besides that it would be endless, and that it would require a scientific preparation such as no one man possesses, it would be apart from our object, which is to go through a course of not Positive Science, but Positive Philosophy. We have only to consider each fundamental science in its relation to the whole positive system, and to the spirit which characterizes it; that is, with regard to its methods and its chief results.

The two aims, though distinct, are inseparable; for, on the one hand, there can be no positive philosophy without a basis of social science, without which it could not be all-comprehensive; and, on the other hand, we could not pursue Social science without having been prepared by the study of phenomena less complicated than those of society, and furnished with a knowledge of laws and anterior facts which have a bearing upon social science. Though the fundamental sciences are not all equally interesting to ordinary minds, there is no one of them that can be neglected in an inquiry like the present; and, in the eye of philosophy, all are of equal value to human welfare. Even those which appear the least interesting have their own value, either on account of the perfection of their methods, or as being the necessary basis of all the others.

Lest it should be supposed that our course will lead us into a wilderness of such special studies as are at present the bane of a true positive philosophy, we will briefly advert to the existing prevalence of such special pursuit. In the primitive state of human knowledge there is no regular division of intellectual labour. Every student cultivates all the sciences. As knowledge accrues, the sciences part off; and students devote themselves each to some one branch. It is owing to this division of employment, and concentration of whole minds upon a single department, that science has made so prodigious an advance in modern times; and the perfection of this division is one of the most important characteristics of the Positive philosophy. But, while admitting all the merits of this change, we cannot be blind to the eminent disadvantages which arise from the limitation of minds to a particular study. It is inevitable that each should be possessed with exclusive notions, and be therefore incapable of the general superiority of ancient students, who actually owed that general superiority to the inferiority of their knowledge. We must consider whether the evil can be avoided without losing the good of the modern arrangement; for the evil is becoming urgent. We all acknowledge that the divisions established for the convenience of scientific pursuit are radically artificial; and yet there are very few who can embrace in idea the whole of any one science: each science moreover being itself only a part of a great whole. Almost every one is busy about his own particular section, without much thought about its relation to the general system of positive knowledge. We must not be blind to the evil, nor slow in seeking a remedy. We must not forget that this is the weak side of the positive philosophy, by which it may yet be attacked, with some hope of success, by the adherents of the theological and metaphysical systems. As to the remedy, it certainly does not lie in a return to the ancient confusion of pursuits, which would be mere retrogression, if it were possible, which it is not. It lies in perfecting the division of employments itself,—in carrying it one degree higher,—in constituting one more specialty from the study of scientific generalities.

Let us have a new class of students, suitably prepared, whose business it shall be to take the respective sciences as they are, determine the spirit of each, ascertain their relations and mutual connection, and reduce their respective principles to the smallest number of general principles, in conformity with the fundamental rules of the Positive Method. At the same time, let other students be prepared for their special pursuit by an education which recognizes the whole scope of positive science, so as to profit by the labours of the students of generalities, and so as to correct reciprocally, under that guidance, the results obtained by each. We see some approach already to this arrangement. Once established, there would be nothing to apprehend from any extent of division of employments. When we once have a class of learned men, at the disposal of all others, whose business it shall be to connect each new discovery with the general system, we may dismiss all fear of the great whole being lost sight of in the pursuit of the details of knowledge. The organization of scientific research will then be complete; and it will henceforth have occasion only to extend its development, and not to change its character. After all, the formation of such a new class as is proposed would be merely an extension of the principle which has created all the classes we have. While science was narrow, there was only one class: as it expanded, more were instituted. With a further advance a fresh need arises, and this new class will be the result.

The general spirit of a course of Positive Philosophy having been thus set forth, we must now glance at the chief advantages which may be derived, on behalf of human progression, from the study of it. Of these advantages, four may be especially pointed out.

I   The study of the Positive Philosophy affords the only rational means of exhibiting the logical laws of the human mind, which have hitherto been sought by unfit methods. To explain what is meant by this, we may refer to a saying of M. de Blainville, in his work on Comparative Anatomy, that every active, and especially every living being, may be regarded under two relations—the Statical and the Dynamical; that is, under conditions or in action. It is clear that all considerations range themselves under the one or the other of these heads. Let us apply this classification to the intellectual functions.

If we regard these functions under their Statical aspect—that is, if we consider the conditions under which they exist—we must determine the organic circumstances of the case, which inquiry involves it with anatomy and physiology. If we look at the Dynamic aspect, we have to study simply the exercise and results of the intellectual powers of the human race, which is neither more nor less than the general object of the Positive Philosophy. In short, looking at all scientific theories as so many great logical facts, it is only by the thorough observation of these facts that we can arrive at the knowledge of logical laws. These being the only means of knowledge of intellectual phenomena, the illusory psychology, which is the last phase of theology, is excluded. It pretends to accomplish the discovery of the laws of the human mind by contemplating it in itself; that is, by separating it from causes and effects. Such an attempt, made in defiance of the physiological study of our intellectual organs, and of the observation of rational methods of procedure, cannot succeed at this time of day.

The Positive Philosophy, which has been rising since the time of Bacon, has now secured such a preponderance, that the metaphysicians themselves profess to ground their pretended science on an observation of facts. They talk of external and internal facts, and say that their business is with the latter. This is much like saying that vision is explained by luminous objects painting their images upon the retina. To this the physiologists reply that another eye would be needed to see the image. In the same manner, the mind may observe all phenomena but its own. It may be said that a man's intellect may observe his passions, the seat of the reason being somewhat apart from that of the emotions in the brain; but there can be nothing like scientific observation of the passions, except from without, as the stir of the emotions disturbs the observing faculties more or less. It is yet more out of the question to make an intellectual observation of intellectual processes. The observing and observed organ are here the same, and its action cannot be pure and natural. In order to observe, your intellect must pause from activity; yet it is this very activity that you want to observe. If you cannot effect the pause, you cannot observe: if you do effect it, there is nothing to observe. The results of such a method are in proportion to its absurdity. After two thousand years of psychological pursuit, no one proposition is established to the satisfaction of its followers. They are divided, to this day, into a multitude of schools, still disputing about the very elements of their doctrine. This interior observation gives birth to almost as many theories as there are observers. We ask in vain for any one discovery, great or small, which has been made under this method. The psychologists have done some good in keeping up the activity of our understandings, when there was no better work for our faculties to do; and they may have added something to our stock of knowledge. If they have done so, it is by practising the Positive method—by observing the progress of the human mind in the light of science; that is, by ceasing, for the moment, to be psychologists.

The view just given in relation to logical Science becomes yet more striking when we consider the logical Art.

The Positive Method can be judged of only in action. It cannot be looked at by itself, apart from the work on which it is employed. At all events, such a contemplation would be only a dead study, which could produce nothing in the mind which loses time upon it. We may talk for ever about the method, and state it in terms very wisely, without knowing half so much about it as the man who has once put it in practice upon a single particular of actual research, even without any philosophical intention. Thus it is that psychologists, by dint of reading the precepts of Bacon and the discourses of Descartes, have mistaken their own dreams for science.

Without saying whether it will ever be possible to establish à priori a true method of investigation, independent of a philosophical study of the sciences, it is clear that the thing has never been done yet, and that we are not capable of doing it now. We cannot as yet explain the great logical procedures, apart from their applications. If we ever do, it will remain as necessary then as now to form good intellectual habits by studying the regular application of the scientific methods which we shall have attained.

This, then, is the first great result of the Positive Philosophy—the manifestation by experiment of the laws which rule the Intellect in the investigation of truth; and, as a consequence the knowledge of the general rules suitable for that object.

II  The second effect of the Positive Philosophy, an effect not less important and far more urgently wanted, will be to regenerate Education.

The best minds are agreed that our European education, still essentially theological, metaphysical, and literary, must be superseded by a Positive training, conformable to our time and needs. Even the governments of our day have shared, where they have not originated, the attempts to establish positive instruction; and this is a striking indication of the prevalent sense of what is wanted. While encouraging such endeavours to the utmost, we must not however conceal from ourselves that everything yet done is inadequate to the object. The present exclusive speciality of our pursuits, and the consequent isolation of the sciences, spoil our teaching. If any student desires to form an idea of natural philosophy as a whole, he is compelled to go through each department as it is now taught, as if he were to be only an astronomer, or only a chemist; so that, be his intellect what it may, his training must remain very imperfect. And yet his object requires that he should obtain general positive conceptions of all the classes of natural phenomena. It is such an aggregate of conceptions, whether on a great or on a small scale, which must henceforth be the permanent basis of all human combinations. It will constitute the mind of future generations. In order to achieve this regeneration of our intellectual system, it is necessary that the sciences, considered as branches from one trunk, should yield us, as a whole, their chief methods and their most important results. The specialities of science can be pursued by those whose vocation lies in that direction. They are indispensable; and they are not likely to be neglected; but they can never of themselves renovate our system of Education; and, to be of their full use, they must rest upon the basis of that general instruction which is a direct result of the Positive Philosophy.

**III**   The same special study of scientific generalities must also aid the progress of the respective positive sciences: and this constitutes our third head of advantages.

The divisions which we establish between the sciences are, though not arbitrary, essentially artificial. The subject of our researches is one: we divide it for our convenience, in order to deal the more easily with its difficulties. But it sometimes happens—and especially with the most important doctrines of each science—that we need what we cannot obtain under the present isolation of the sciences,—a combination of several special points of view; and for want of this, very important problems wait for their solution much longer than they otherwise need do. To go back into the past for an example: Descartes' grand conception with regard to analytical geometry is a discovery which has changed the whole aspect of mathematical science, and yielded the germ of all future progress; and it issued from the union of two sciences which had always before been separately regarded and pursued. The case of pending questions is yet more impressive; as, for instance, in Chemistry, the doctrine of Definite Proportions. Without entering upon the discussion of the fundamental principle of this theory, we may say with assurance that, in order to determine it—in order to determine whether it is a law of nature that atoms should necessarily combine in fixed numbers,—it will be indispensable that the chemical point of view should be united with the physiological. The failure of the theory with regard to organic bodies indicates that the cause of this immense exception must be investigated; and such an inquiry belongs as much to physiology as to chemistry. Again, it is as yet undecided whether azote is a simple or a compound body. It was concluded by almost all chemists that azote is a simple body; the illustrious Berzelius hesitated, on purely chemical considerations; but he was also influenced by the physiological observation that animals which receive no azote in their food have as much of it in their tissues as carnivorous animals. From this we see how physiology must unite with chemistry to inform us whether azote is simple or compound, and to institute a new series of researches upon the relation between the composition of living bodies and their mode of alimentation.

Such is the advantage which, in the third place, we shall owe to Positive philosophy—the elucidation of the respective sciences by their combination. In the fourth place

**IV**   The Positive Philosophy offers the only solid basis for that Social Reorganization which must succeed the critical condition in which the most civilized nations are now living.

It cannot be necessary to prove to anybody who reads this work that Ideas govern the world, or throw it into chaos; in other words, that all social mechanism rests upon Opinions. The great political and moral crisis that societies are now undergoing is shown by a rigid analysis to arise out of intellectual anarchy. While stability in fundamental maxims is the first condition of genuine social order, we are suffering under an utter disagreement which may be called universal. Till a certain number of general ideas can be acknowledged as a rallying-point of social doctrine, the nations will remain in a revolutionary state, whatever palliatives may be devised; and their institutions can be only provisional. But whenever the necessary agreement on first principles can be obtained, appropriate institutions will issue from them, without shock or resistance; for the causes of disorder will have been arrested by the mere fact of the agreement. It is in this direction that those must look who desire a natural and regular, a normal state of society.

Now, the existing disorder is abundantly accounted for by the existence, all at once, of three incompatible philosophies,—the theological, the metaphysical, and the positive. Any one of these might alone secure some sort of social order; but while the three co-exist, it is impossible for us to understand one another upon any essential point whatever. If this is true, we have only to ascertain which of the philosophies must, in the nature of things, prevail; and, this ascertained, every man, whatever may have been his former views, cannot but concur in its triumph. The problem once recognized cannot remain long unsolved; for all considerations whatever point to the Positive Philosophy as the one destined to prevail. It alone has been advancing during a course of centuries, throughout which the others have been declining. The fact is incontestable. Some may deplore it, but none can destroy it, nor therefore neglect it but under penalty of being betrayed by illusory speculations. This general revolution of the human mind is nearly accomplished. We have only to complete the Positive Philosophy by bringing Social phenomena within its comprehension, and afterwards consolidating the whole into one body of homogeneous doctrine. The marked preference which almost all minds, from the highest to the commonest, accord to positive knowledge over vague and mystical conceptions, is a pledge of what the reception of this philosophy will be when it has acquired the only quality that it now wants—a character of due generality. When it has become complete, its supremacy will take place spontaneously, and will re-establish order throughout society. There is, at present, no conflict but between the theological and the metaphysical philosophies. They are contending for the task of reorganizing society; but it is a work too mighty for either of them. The positive philosophy has hitherto intervened only to examine both, and both are abundantly discredited by the process. It is time now to be doing something more effective, without wasting our forces in needless controversy. It is time to complete the vast intellectual operation begun by Bacon, Descartes, and Galileo, by constructing the system of general ideas which must henceforth prevail among the human race. This is the way to put an end to the revolutionary crisis which is tormenting the civilized nations of the world.

Leaving these four points of advantage, we must attend one precautionary reflection.

Because it is proposed to consolidate the whole of our acquired knowledge into one body of homogeneous doctrine, it must not be supposed that we are going to study this vast variety as proceeding from a single principle, and as subjected to a single law. There is something so chimerical in attempts at universal explanation by a single law, that it may be as well to secure this Work at once from any imputation of the kind, though its development will show how undeserved such an imputation would be. Our intellectual resources are too narrow, and the universe is too complex, to leave any hope that it will ever be within our power to carry scientific perfection to its last degree of simplicity. Moreover, it appears as if the value of such an attainment, supposing it possible, were greatly overrated. The only way, for instance, in which we could achieve the business, would be by connecting all natural phenomena with the most general law we know,—which is that of Gravitation, by which astronomical phenomena are already connected with a portion of terrestrial physics. Laplace has indicated that chemical phenomena may be regarded as simple atomic effects of the Newtonian attraction, modified by the form and mutual position of the atoms. But supposing this view proveable (which it cannot be while we are without data about the constitution of bodies), the difficulty of its application would doubtless be found so great that we must still maintain the existing division between astronomy and chemistry, with the difference that we now regard as natural that division which we should then call artificial. Laplace himself presented his idea only as a philosophic device, incapable of exercising any useful influence over the progress of chemical science. Moreover, supposing this insuperable difficulty overcome, we should be no nearer to scientific unity, since we then should still have to connect the whole of physiological phenomena with the same law, which certainly would not be the least difficult part of the enterprise. Yet, all things considered, the hypothesis we have glanced at would be the most favourable to the desired unity.

The consideration of all phenomena as referable to a single origin is by no means necessary to the systematic formation of science, any more than to the realization of the great and happy consequences that we anticipate from the positive philosophy. The only necessary unity is that of Method, which is already in great part established. As for the doctrine, it need not be *one*; it is enough that it should be *homogeneous*. It is, then, under the double aspect of unity of method and homogeneousness of doctrine that we shall consider the different classes of positive theories in this work. While pursuing the philosophical aim of all science, the lessening of the number of general laws requisite for the explanation of natural phenomena, we shall regard as presumptuous every attempt, in all future time, to reduce them rigorously to one.

Having thus endeavoured to determine the spirit and influence of the Positive

Philosophy, and to mark the goal of our labours, we have now to proceed to the exposition of the system; that is, to the determination of the universal, or encyclopædic order, which must regulate the different classes of natural phenomena, and consequently the corresponding positive sciences.

# ৶§ THE DESCENT OF MAN

### *Charles Darwin*

*Charles Darwin (1809–1882) did not invent the concept of evolution. As early as 1754, in his* Discourse on the Origin of Inequality, *Rousseau had maintained that the proper approach to the understanding of human nature was an evolutionary one (see Vol. III, pages 157–168). In the late eighteenth and early nineteenth centuries, virtually every important theorist of society viewed it as the outcome of a gradual process, in conscious opposition to the static theories of earlier periods. In biology, too, the concept was already fundamental: Jean-Baptiste Lamarck (1744–1829) had based his entire system on it; in Germany Goethe and in England Erasmus Darwin, the grandfather of Charles, had given it wide publicity. The philosophies of Hegel, Comte, and Marx—all represented in this volume—were worked out on evolutionary principles before Darwin's* Origin of Species *was published in 1859.*

*Nor was Darwin the first to speak of "survival of the fittest." The phrase had already been used by Herbert Spencer to describe his own theory, which was akin to Lamarck's; and, as Darwin himself acknowledged, the idea goes back to Malthus's* Essay on Population *(1798).*

*Why, then, is Darwin's name invariably linked with the theory of evolution? And why is he universally considered the greatest scientist of the nineteenth century and among the greatest of all time? The answer to both questions is that other people had thought of evolution, but Darwin proved it. That is, he amassed so much evidence of so many different kinds that, in his own words, "he who is not content to look, like a savage, at the phenomena of nature as disconnected" could no longer doubt that all the species of plants and animals had developed gradually, primarily (although not exclusively) by the twin mechanisms of random variation and natural selection.*

*The novelty in Darwin's theory of evolution lay in its simplicity. All the previous theories, both biological and philosophical, had been forced to postulate some inner cosmic thrust or tendency to account for the emergence of new forms. Darwin saw that Charles Lyell's* Principles of Geology *(1830–1833), with its demonstration that the earth must be millions of years old, made such a postulate unnecessary; even the small changes visible in each generation would accumulate, given that much time, and one need only account for the disappearance of intermediate forms rather than the appearance of new ones. This was easy, at least in principle, since Malthus had already pointed out that every natural species produces more offspring than can possibly survive. Darwin's theory thus had a mechanical, automatic character that rendered superfluous any appeal to a Designer or Architect of nature.*

*But even more startling in its implications was what Darwin's theory had to say about man. In 1871 he published a second great book,* The Descent of Man, *in which many of these implications were made explicit. The following selection is drawn from this book, rather than from its better known forerunner, because it seems to raise issues which are even more fundamental. For example, even today many people dismiss Darwin's theory as applying only to forms of life other than man or at most to man's body but not his soul or his mind. As his argument in this concluding chapter shows, that position simply will not do: all the evidence Darwin adduces points to the evolution of man's mind as well as his body, of everything in and about man, on precisely the same principles. One hundred years later, the evidence is still mounting.*

CHAPTER XXI. GENERAL SUMMARY AND CONCLUSION

A brief summary will be sufficient to recall to the reader's mind the more salient points in this work. Many of the views which have been advanced are highly speculative, and some no doubt will prove erroneous; but I have in every case given the reasons which have led me to one view rather than to another. It seemed worth while to try how far the principle of evolution would throw light on some of the more complex problems in the natural history of man. False facts are highly injurious to the progress of science, for they often endure long; but false views, if supported by some evidence, do little harm, for every one takes a salutary pleasure in proving their falseness; and when this is done, one path towards error is closed and the road to truth is often at the same time opened.

The main conclusion here arrived at, and now held by many naturalists who are well competent to form a sound judgment, is that man is descended from some less highly

Charles Darwin, *The Descent of Man, and Selection in Relation to Sex* (Rev. ed.; New York: D. Appleton & Company, Inc., 1878), pp. 606–619.

organised form. The grounds upon which this conclusion rests will never be shaken, for the close similarity between man and the lower animals in embryonic development, as well as in innumerable points of structure and constitution, both of high and of the most trifling importance,—the rudiments which he retains, and the abnormal reversions to which he is occasionally liable,—are facts which cannot be disputed. They have long been known, but until recently they told us nothing with respect to the origin of man. Now when viewed by the light of our knowledge of the whole organic world, their meaning is unmistakable. The great principle of evolution stands up clear and firm, when these groups of facts are considered in connection with others, such as the mutual affinities of the members of the same group, their geographical distribution in past and present times, and their geological succession. It is incredible that all these facts should speak falsely. He who is not content to look, like a savage, at the phenomena of nature as disconnected, cannot any longer believe that man is the work of a separate act of creation. He will be forced to admit that the close resemblance of the embryo of man to that, for instance, of a dog—the construction of his skull, limbs and whole frame on the same plan with that of other mammals, independently of the uses to which the parts may be put—the occasional re-appearance of various structures, for instance of several muscles, which man does not normally possess, but which are common to the Quadrumana—and a crowd of analogous facts—all point in the plainest manner to the conclusion that man is the co-descendant with other mammals of a common progenitor.

We have seen that man incessantly presents individual differences in all parts of his body and in his mental faculties. These differences or variations seem to be induced by the same general causes, an dto obey the same laws as with the lower animals. In both cases similar laws of inheritance prevail. Man tends to increase at a greater rate than his means of subsistence; consequently he is occasionally subjected to a severe struggle for existence, and natural selection will have effected whatever lies within its scope. A succession of strongly-marked variations of a similar nature is by no means requisite; slight fluctuating differences in the individual suffice for the work of natural selection; not that we have any reason to suppose that in the same species, all parts of the organisation tend to vary to the same degree. We may feel assured that the inherited effects of the long-continued use or disuse of parts will have done much in the same direction with natural selection. Modifications formerly of importance, though no longer of any special use, are long-inherited. When one part is modified, other parts change through the principle of correlation, of which we have instances in many curious cases of correlated monstrosities. Something may be attributed to the direct and definite action of the surrounding conditions of life, such as abundant food, heat or moisture; and lastly, many characters of slight physiological importance, some indeed of considerable importance, have been gained through sexual selection.

No doubt man, as well as every other animal, presents structures, which seem to our limited knowledge, not to be now of any service to him, nor to have been so formerly, either for the general conditions of life, or in the relations of one sex to the other. Such structures cannot be accounted for by any form of selection, or by the inherited effects of the use and disuse of parts. We know, however, that many strange and strongly-marked peculiarities of structure occasionally appear in our domesticated productions, and if their unknown causes were to act more uniformly, they would probably become common to all the individuals of the species. We may hope hereafter to understand something about the causes of such occasional modifications, especially through the study of monstrosities: hence the labours of experimentalists, such as those of M. Camille Dareste, are full of promise for the future. In general we can only say that the cause of each slight variation and of each monstrosity lies much more in the constitution of the organism, than in the nature of the surrounding conditions; though new and changed conditions certainly play an important part in exciting organic changes of many kinds.

Through the means just specified, aided perhaps by others as yet undiscovered, man has been raised to his present state. But since he attained to the rank of manhood, he has diverged into distinct races, or as they may be more fitly called, subspecies. Some of these, such as the Negro and European, are so distinct that, if specimens had been brought to a naturalist without any further information, they would undoubtedly have been considered by him as good and true species. Nevertheless all the races agree in so many unimportant details of structure and in so many mental peculiarities, that these can be accounted for only by inheritance from a common progenitor; and a progenitor thus characterised would probably deserve to rank as man.

It must not be supposed that the divergence of each race from the other races, and of all from a common stock, can be traced back to any one pair of progenitors. On the contrary, at every stage in the process of modification, all the individuals which were in any way better fitted for their conditions of life, though in different degrees, would have survived in greater numbers than the less well-fitted. The process would have been like that followed by man, when he does not intentionally select particular individuals, but breeds from all the superior individuals, and neglects the inferior. He thus slowly but surely modifies his stock, and unconsciously forms a new strain. So with respect to modifications acquired independently of selection, and due to variations arising from the nature of the organism and the action of the surrounding conditions, or from changed habits of life, no single pair will have been modified much more than the other pairs inhabiting the same country, for all will have been continually blended through free intercrossing.

By considering the embryological structure of man,—the homologies which he presents with the lower animals,—the rudiments which he retains,—and the reversions to which he is liable, we can partly recall in imagination the former condition of our early progenitors; and can approximately place them in their proper place in the zoological series. We thus learn that man is descended from a hairy, tailed quadruped, probably aboreal in its habits, and an inhabitant of the Old World. This creature, if its whole structure had been examined by a naturalist, would have been classed amongst the Quadrumana, as surely as the still more ancient progenitor of the Old and New World monkeys. The Quadrumana and all the higher mammals are probably derived from an ancient marsupial animal, and this through a long line of diversified forms, from some amphibian-like creature, and this again from some fish-like animal. In the dim obscurity of the past we can see that the early progenitor of all the Vertebrata must have been an aquatic animal, provided with branchiæ with the two sexes united in the same individual, and with the most important organs of the body (such as the brain and heart) imperfectly or not at all developed. This animal seems to have been more like the larvæ of the existing marine Ascidians than any other known form.

The high standard of our intellectual powers and moral disposition is the greatest difficulty which presents itself, after we have been driven to this conclusion on the origin of man. But every one who admits the principle of evolution, must see that the mental powers of the higher animals, which are the same in kind with those of man, though so different in degree, are capable of advancement. Thus the interval between the mental powers of one of the higher apes and of a fish, or between those of an ant and scale-insect, is immense; yet their development does not offer any special difficulty; for with our domesticated animals, the mental faculties are certainly variable, and the variations are inherited. No one doubts that they are of the utmost importance to animals in a state of nature. Therefore the conditions are favourable for their development through natural selection. The same conclusion may be extended to man; the intellect must have been all-important to him, even at a very remote period, as enabling him to invent and use language, to make weapons, tools, traps, &c., whereby with the aid of his social habits, he long ago became the most dominant of all living creatures.

A great stride in the development of the intellect will have followed, as soon as the half-art and half-instinct of language came into use; for the continued use of language will have reacted on the brain and produced an inherited effect; and this again will have reacted on the improvement of language. As Mr. Chauncey Wright has well remarked, the largeness of the brain in man relatively to his body, compared with the lower animals, may be attributed in chief part to the early use of some simple form of language,—that wonderful engine which affixes signs to all sorts of objects and qualities, and excites trains of thought which would never arise from the mere impression of the senses, or if they did arise could not be followed out. The higher intellectual powers of man, such as those of ratiocination, abstraction, self-consciousness, &c., probably follow from the continued improvement and exercise of the other mental faculties.

The development of the moral qualities is a more interesting problem. The foundation lies in the social instincts, including under this term the family ties. These instincts are highly complex and in the case of the lower animals give special tendencies towards certain definite actions; but the more important elements are love, and the distinct emotion of sympathy. Animals endowed with the social instincts take pleasure in one another's company, warn one another of danger, defend and aid one another in many ways. These instincts do not extend to all the individuals of the species but only to those of the same community. As they are highly beneficial to the species, they have in all probability been acquired through natural selection.

A moral being is one who is capable of reflecting on his past actions and their motives—of approving of some and disapproving of others; and the fact that man is the one being who certainly deserves this designation, is the greatest of all distinctions between him and the lower animals. But in the fourth chapter I have endeavoured to shew that the moral sense follows, firstly, from the enduring and ever-present nature of the social instincts; secondly, from man's appreciation of the approbation and disapprobation of his fellows; and thirdly, from the high activity of his mental faculties, with past impressions extremely vivid; and in these latter respects he differs from the lower animals. Owing to this condition of mind, man cannot avoid looking both backwards and forwards, and comparing past impressions. Hence after some temporary desire or passion has mastered his social instincts, he reflects and compares the now weakened impression of such past impulses with the ever-present social instincts; and he then feels that sense of dissatisfaction which all unsatisfied instincts leave behind them, he therefore resolves to act differently for the future,—and this is conscience. Any instinct, permanently stronger or more enduring than another, gives rise to a feeling which we express by saying that it ought to be obeyed. A pointer dog, if able to reflect on his past conduct, would say to himself, I ought (as indeed we say of him) to have pointed at that hare and not have yielded to the passing temptation of hunting it.

Social animals are impelled partly by a wish to aid the members of their community in a general manner, but more commonly to perform certain definite actions. Man is impelled by the same general wish to aid his fellows; but has few or no special instincts. He differs also from the lower animals in the power of expressing his desires by words, which thus become a guide to the aid required and bestowed. The motive to give aid is likewise much modified in man: it no longer consists solely of a blind instinctive impulse, but is much influenced by the praise or blame of his fellows. The appreciation and the bestowal of praise and blame both rest on sympathy; and this emotion, as we have seen, is one of the most important elements of the social instincts. Sympathy, though gained as an instinct, is also much strengthened by exercise or habit. As all men desire their own happiness, praise or blame is bestowed on actions and motives, according as they lead to this end; and as happiness is an essential part of the general good, the greatest-happiness principle indirectly serves as a nearly safe standard of right and wrong. As the reasoning powers advance and experience is gained, the remoter effects of certain lines of conduct on the character of the individual, and on the general good, are perceived; and then the self-regarding virtues come within the scope of public opinion, and receive praise, and their opposites blame. But with the less civilised nations reason often errs, and many bad customs and base superstitions come within the same scope, and are then esteemed as high virtues, and their breach as heavy crimes.

The moral faculties are generally and justly esteemed as of higher value than the intellectual powers. But we should bear in mind that the activity of the mind in vividly recalling past impressions is one of the fundamental though secondary bases of conscience. This affords the strongest argument for educating and stimulating in all possible ways the intellectual faculties of every human being. No doubt a man with a torpid mind, if his social affections and sympathies are well developed, will be led to good actions, and may have a fairly sensitive conscience. But whatever renders the imagination more vivid and strengthens the habit of recalling and comparing past impressions, will make the conscience more sensitive, and may even somewhat compensate for weak social affections and sympathies.

The moral nature of man has reached its present standard, partly through the advancement of his reasoning powers and consequently of a just public opinion, but especially from his sympathies having been rendered more tender and widely diffused through the effects of habit, example, instruction, and reflection. It is not improbable that after long practice virtuous tendencies may be inherited. With the more civilised races, the conviction of the existence of an all-seeing Deity has had a potent influence on the advance of morality. Ultimately man does not accept the praise or blame of his fellows as his sole guide, though few escape this influence, but his habitual convictions, controlled by reason, afford him the safest rule. His conscience then becomes the supreme judge and monitor. Nevertheless the first foundation or origin of the moral sense lies in the social instincts, including sympathy; and these instincts no doubt were primarily gained, as in the case of the lower animals, through natural selection.

The belief in God has often been advanced as not only the greatest, but the most complete of all the distinctions between man and the lower animals. It is however impossible, as we have seen, to maintain that this belief is innate or instinctive in man. On the other hand a belief in all-pervading spiritual agencies seems to be universal; and apparently follows from a considerable advance in man's reason, and from a still greater advance in his faculties of imagination, curiosity and wonder. I am aware that the assumed instinctive belief in God has been used by many persons as an argument for His existence. But this is a rash argument, as we should thus be compelled to believe in the existence of many cruel and malignant spirits, only a little more powerful than man; for the belief in them is far more general than in a beneficent Deity. The idea of a universal and beneficent Creator does not seem to arise in the mind of man, until he has been elevated by long-continued culture.

He who believes in the advancement of man from some low organised form, will naturally ask how does this bear on the belief in the immortality of the soul. The barbarous races of man, as Sir J. Lubbock has shewn, possess no clear belief of this kind; but arguments derived from the primeval beliefs of savages are, as we have just seen, of little or no avail. Few persons feel any anxiety from the impossibility of determining at what precise period in the development of the individual, from the first trace of a minute germinal vesicle, man becomes an immortal being; and there is no greater cause for anxiety because the period cannot possibly be determined in the gradually ascending organic scale.

I am aware that the conclusions arrived at in this work will be denounced by some as highly irreligious; but he who denounces them is bound to shew why it is more irreligious to explain the origin of man as a distinct species by descent from some lower form, through the laws of variation and natural selection, than to explain the birth of the individual through the laws of ordinary reproduction. The birth both of the species and of the individual are equally parts of that grand sequence of events, which our minds refuse to accept as the result of blind chance. The understanding revolts at such a conclusion, whether or not we are able to believe that every slight variation of structure,—the union of each pair in marriage,—the dissemination of each seed,—and other such events, have all been ordained for some special purpose.

Sexual selection has been treated at great length in this work; for, as I have attempted to shew, it has played an important part in the history of the organic world. I am aware that much remains doubtful, but I have endeavoured to give a fair view of the whole case. In the lower divisions of the animal kingdom, sexual selection seems to have done nothing: such animals are often affixed for life to the same spot, or have the sexes combined in the same individual, or what is still more important, their perceptive and intellectual faculties are not sufficiently advanced to allow of the feelings of love and jealousy, or of the exertion of choice. When, however, we come to the Arthropoda and Vertebrata, even to the lowest classes in these two great Sub-Kingdoms, sexual selection has effected much.

In the several great classes of the animal kingdom,—in mammals, birds, reptiles, fishes, insects, and even crustaceans,—the differences between the sexes follow nearly the same rules. The males are almost always the wooers; and they alone are armed with special weapons for fighting with their rivals. They are generally stronger and larger than the females, and are endowed with the requisite qualities of courage and pugnacity. They are provided, either exclusively or in a much higher degree than the females, with organs for vocal or instrumental music, and with odoriferous glands. They are ornamented with infinitely diversified appendages, and with the most brilliant or conspicuous colours; often arranged in elegant patterns, whilst the females are unadorned. When the sexes differ in more important structures, it is the male which is provided with special sense-organs for discovering the female, with locomotive organs for reaching her, and often with prehensile organs for holding her. These various structures for charming or securing the female are often developed in the male during only part of the year, namely the breeding-season. They have in many cases been more or less transferred to the females; and in the latter case they often appear in her as mere rudiments. They are lost or never gained by the males after emasculation. Generally they are not developed in the male during early youth, but appear a short time before the age for reproduction. Hence in most cases the young of both sexes resemble each other; and the female somewhat resembles her young offspring throughout life. In almost every great class a few anomalous cases occur, where there has been an almost complete transposition of the characters proper to the two sexes; the females assuming characters which properly belong to the males. This surprising uniformity in the laws regulating the differences between the sexes in so many and such widely separated classes, is intelligible if we admit the action of one common cause, namely sexual selection.

Sexual selection depends on the success of certain individuals over others of the same sex, in relation to the propagation of the species; whilst natural selection depends on the success of both sexes, at all ages, in relation to the general conditions of life. The sexual struggle is of two kinds; in the one it is between the individuals of the same sex, generally the males, in order to drive away or kill their rivals, the females remaining passive; whilst in the other, the struggle is likewise between the individuals of the same sex, in order to excite or charm those of the opposite sex, generally the females, which no longer remain passive, but select the more agreeable partners. This latter kind of selection is closely analogous to that which man unintentionally, yet effectually, brings to bear on his domesticated productions, when he preserves during a long period the most pleasing or useful individuals, without any wish to modify the breed.

The laws of inheritance determine whether characters gained through sexual selection by either sex shall be transmitted to the same sex, or to both; as well as the age at which they shall be developed. It appears that variations arising late in life are commonly transmitted to one and the same sex. Variability is the necessary basis for the action of selection, and is wholly independent of it. It follows from this, that variations of the same general nature have often been taken advantage of and accumulated through sexual selection in relation to the propagation of the species, as well as through natural selection in relation to the general purposes of life. Hence secondary sexual characters, when equally transmitted to both sexes can be distinguished from ordinary specific characters only by the light of analogy. The modifications acquired through sexual selection are often so strongly pronounced that the two sexes have frequently been ranked as distinct species, or even as distinct genera. Such strongly-marked differences must be in some manner highly important; and we know that they have been acquired in some instances at the cost not only of inconvenience, but of exposure to actual danger.

The belief in the power of sexual selection rests chiefly on the following considerations. Certain characters are confined to one sex; and this alone renders it probable that in most cases they are connected with the act of reproduction. In innumerable instances these characters are fully developed only at maturity, and often during only a part of the year, which is always the breeding-season. The males (passing over a few exceptional cases) are the more active in courtship; they are the better armed, and are rendered the more attractive in various ways. It is to be especially observed that the males display their attractions with elaborate care in the presence of the females; and that they rarely or never display them excepting during the season of love. It is incredible that all this should be purposeless. Lastly we have distinct evidence with some quadrupeds and birds, that the individuals of one sex are capable of feeling a strong antipathy or preference for certain individuals of the other sex.

Bearing in mind these facts, and the marked results of man's unconscious selection, when applied to domesticated animals and cultivated plants, it seems to me almost certain that if the individuals of one sex were during a long series of generations to prefer pairing with certain individuals of the other sex, characterised in some peculiar manner, the offspring would slowly but surely become modified in this same manner. I have not attempted to conceal that, excepting when the males are more numerous than the females, or when polygamy prevails, it is doubtful how the more attractive males succeed in leaving a larger number of offspring to inherit their superiority in ornaments or other charms than the less attractive males; but I have shewn that this would probably follow from the females,—especially the more vigorous ones, which would be the first to breed,—preferring not only the more attractive but at the same time the more vigorous and victorious males.

Although we have some positive evidence that birds appreciate bright and beautiful objects, as with the bower-birds of Australia, and although they certainly appreciate the power of song, yet I fully admit that it is astonishing that the females of many birds and some mammals should be endowed with sufficient taste to appreciate ornaments, which we have reason to attribute to sexual selection; and this is even more astonishing in the case of reptiles, fish, and insects. But we really know little about the minds of the lower animals. It cannot be supposed, for instance, that male birds of paradise or peacocks should take such pains in erecting, spreading, and vibrating their beautiful plumes before the females for no purpose. We should remember the fact given on excellent authority in a former chapter, that several peahens, when debarred from an admired male, remained widows during a whole season rather than pair with another bird.

Nevertheless I know of no fact in natural history more wonderful than that the female Argus pheasant should appreciate the exquisite shading of the ball-and-socket ornaments and the elegant patterns on the wing-feathers of the male. He who thinks that the male was created as he now exists must admit that the great plumes, which prevent the wings from being used for flight, and which are displayed during courtship and at no other time in a manner quite peculiar to this one species, were given to him as an ornament. If so, he must likewise admit that the female was created and endowed with the capacity of appreciating such ornaments. I differ only in the conviction that the male Argus pheasant acquired his beauty gradually, through the preference of the females during many generations for the more highly ornamented males; the æsthetic capacity of the females having been advanced through exercise or habit, just as our own taste is gradually improved. In the male through the fortunate chance of a few feathers being left unchanged, we can distinctly trace how simple spots with a little fulvous shading on one side may have been developed by small steps into the wonderful ball-and-socket ornaments; and it is probable that they were actually thus developed.

Everyone who admits the principle of evolution, and yet feels great difficulty in admitting that female mammals, birds, reptiles, and fish, could have acquired the high taste implied by the beauty of the males, and which generally coincides with our own standard, should reflect that the nerve-cells of the brain in the highest as well as in the lowest members of the Vertebrate series, are derived from those of the common progenitor of this great Kingdom. For we can thus see how it has come to pass that certain mental faculties, in various and widely distinct groups of animals, have been developed in nearly the same manner and to nearly the same degree.

The reader who has taken the trouble to go through the several chapters devoted to sexual selection, will be able to judge how far the conclusions at which I have arrived are supported by sufficient evidence. If he accepts these conclusions he may, I think, safely extend them to mankind; but it would be superfluous here to repeat what I have so lately said on the manner in which sexual selection apparently has acted on man, both on the male and female side, causing the two sexes to differ in body and mind, in the several races to differ from each other in various characters, as well as from their ancient and lowly-organised progenitors.

He who admits the principle of sexual selection will be led to the remarkable conclusion that the nervous system not only regulates most of the existing functions of the body, but has indirectly influenced the progressive development of various bodily structures and of certain mental qualities. Courage, pugnacity, perseverance, strength and size of body, weapons of all kinds, musical organs, both vocal and instrumental, bright colours and ornamental appendages, have all been indirectly gained by the one sex or the other, through the exertion of choice, the influence of love and jealousy, and the appreciation of the beautiful in sound, colour or form; and these powers of the mind manifestly depend on the development of the brain.

Man scans with scrupulous care the character and pedigree of his horses, cattle, and dogs before he matches them; but when he comes to his own marriage he rarely, or never, takes any such care. He is impelled by nearly the same motives as the lower animals, when they are left to their own free choice, though he is in so far superior to them that he highly values mental charms and virtues. On the other hand he is strongly attracted by mere wealth or rank. Yet he might by selection do something not only for the bodily constitution and frame of his offspring, but for their intellectual and moral qualities. Both sexes ought to refrain from marriage if they are in any marked degree inferior in body or mind; but such hopes are Utopian and will never be even partially realised until the laws of inheritance are thoroughly known. Everyone does good service, who aids towards this end. When the principles of breeding and inheritance are better understood, we shall not hear ignorant members of our legislature rejecting with scorn a plan for ascertaining whether or not consanguineous marriages are injurious to man.

The advancement of the welfare of mankind is a most intricate problem: all ought to refrain from marriage who cannot avoid abject poverty for their children; for poverty is not only a great evil, but tends to its own increase by leading to recklessness in marriage. On the other hand, as Mr. Galton has remarked, if the prudent avoid marriage, whilst the reckless marry, the inferior members tend to supplant the better members of society. Man, like every other animal, has no doubt advanced to his present high condition through a struggle for existence consequent on his rapid multiplication; and if he is to advance still higher, it is to be feared that he must remain subject to a severe struggle. Otherwise he would sink into indolence, and the more gifted men would not be more successful in the battle of life than the less gifted. Hence our natural rate of increase, though leading to many and obvious evils, must not be greatly diminished by any means. There should be open competition for all men; and the most able should not be prevented by laws or customs from succeeding best and rearing the largest number of offspring. Important as the struggle for existence has been and even still is, yet as far as the highest part of man's nature is concerned there are other agencies more important. For the more qualities are advanced, either directly or indirectly, much more through the effects of habit, the reasoning powers, instruction, religion, &c., than through natural selection; though to this latter agency may be safely attributed the social instincts, which afforded the basis for the development of the moral sense.

The main conclusion arrived at in this work, namely that man is descended from some lowly organised form, will, I regret to think, be highly distasteful to many. But there can hardly be a doubt that we are descended from barbarians. The astonishment which I felt on first seeing a party of Feugians on a wild and broken shore will never be forgotten by me, for the reflection at once rushed into my mind— such were our ancestors. These men were absolutely naked and bedaubed with paint, their long hair was tangled, their mouths frothed with excitement, and their expression was wild, startled, and distrustful. They possessed hardly any arts, and like wild animals lived on what they could catch; they had no government, and were merciless to every one not of their own small tribe. He who has seen a savage in his native land will not feel much shame, if forced to acknowledge that the blood of some more humble creature flows in his veins. For my own part I would as soon be descended from that heroic little monkey, who braved his dreaded enemy in order to save the life of his keeper, or from that old baboon, who descending from the mountains, carried away in triumph his young comrade from a crowd of astonished dogs—as from a savage who delights to torture his enemies, offers up bloody sacrifices, practises infanticide without remorse, treats his wives like slaves, knows no decency, and is haunted by the grossest superstitions.

Man may be excused for feeling some pride at having risen, though not through his own exertions, to the very summit of the organic scale; and the fact of his having thus risen, instead of having been aboriginally placed there, may give him hope for a still higher destiny in the distant future. But we are not here concerned with hopes or fears, only with the truth as far as our reason permits us to discover it; and I have given the evidence to the best of my ability. We must, however, acknowledge, as it seems to me, that man with all his noble qualities, with sympathy which feels for the most debased, with benevolence which extends not only to other men but to the humblest living creature, with his god-like intellect which has penetrated into the movements and constitution of the solar system—with all these exalted powers —Man still bears in his bodily frame the indelible stamp of his lowly origin.

# ⋙ ESSAY ON THE INEQUALITY OF HUMAN RACES

*Arthur de Gobineau*

*Count Arthur de Gobineau (1816–1882) was a French nobleman who served his country for many years as a diplomat and man of letters. As an aristocrat in an increasingly democratic world, his reaction was diametrically opposed to that of his friend Alexis de Tocqueville (see pages 163–172). He was convinced that civilization itself was declining, not only in Europe but everywhere, and he decided that it was due to "the mixing of the races." In the Middle Ages, Europe had risen from barbarism through the efforts of the Teutons, the western branch of the Aryans from central Asia. The physical and moral superiority of these people could be seen clearly in a Charlemagne or a Barbarossa. But military and political success had led to wealth and commerce and inevitably to fusion with other races, bringing the degeneration in the modern bourgeoisie so painfully obvious to him. Gobineau had read widely in the history and literature of the East as well as the West, and what he read seemed to confirm his hypothesis: some human races are innately superior in their ability to acquire culture but only as long as they keep themselves from contamination by inferior blood. In 1853, six years before Darwin's* Origin of Species, *Gobineau brought out the first volume of his* Essay on the Inequality of Human Races *in which he claimed to have discovered the "law" that would explain scientifically the rise and fall of civilizations.*

*It should be obvious that Gobineau's book was more literary than scientific, at least as these terms would be used today. His concept of race was biological rather than cultural, however, and his language had an air of scientific detachment. The book was a great success, especially with the decaying aristocracy and the bohemians in revolt against bourgeois respectability. In Richard Wagner's circle in Bayreuth, Germany, Gobineau was much read and admired. One member of the group, an Englishman named Houston Stewart Chamberlain, was inspired to write (in German) another racist book,* The Foundations of the Nineteenth Century *(1899), which in turn influenced Hitler and the Nazis. Thus did a Frenchman and an Englishman supply the doctrine which, although long discredited as science, became the ideology of a third nation, Germany, and even today refuses to die.*

## CHAPTER XI. PERMANENCE OF TYPES

. . . Each race is convinced that its progenitor had precisely the characteristics which now distinguish it. This is the only point upon which their traditions perfectly agree. The white races represent to themselves an Adam and Eve, whom Blumenbach would at once have pronounced Caucasians; the Mohammedan negroes, on the contrary, believe the first pair to have been black; these being created in God's own image, it follows that the Supreme Being, and also the angels, are of the same color, and the prophet himself was certainly too greatly favored by his Sender to display a pale skin to his disciples.

Unfortunately, modern science has as yet found no clue to this maze of opinions. No admissible theory has been advanced which affords the least light upon the subject, and, in all probability, the various types differ as much from their common progenitor—if they possess one—as they do among themselves. The causes of these deviations are exceedingly difficult to ascertain. The believers in the unity of origin pretend to find them, as I remarked before, in various local circumstances, such as climate, habits, &c. It is impossible to coincide with such an opinion, for, although these circumstances have always existed, they have not, within historical times, produced such alterations in the races which were exposed to their influence as to make it even probable that they were the causes of so vast and radical a dissimilarity as we now see before us. Suppose two tribes, not yet departed from the primitive type, to inhabit, one an alpine region in the interior of a continent, the other some isolated

*The Moral and Intellectual Diversity of Races,* trans. H. Hotz (Philadelphia: J. B. Lippincott Company, 1856), pp. 340–346, 369–383 *passim,* 414–423, 439–454.

isle in the immensity of the ocean. Their atmospheric and alimentary conditions would, of course, be totally different. If we further suppose one of these tribes to be abundantly provided with nourishment, and the other possessing but precarious means of subsistence; one to inhabit a cold latitude, and the other to be exposed to the action of a tropical sun; it seems to me that we have accumulated the most essential local contrasts. Allowing these physical causes to operate a sufficient lapse of time, the two groups would, no doubt, ultimately assume certain peculiar characteristics, by which they might be distinguished from each other. But no imaginable length of time could bring about any essential, organic change of conformation; and as a proof of this assertion, I would point to the populations of opposite portions of the globe, living under physical conditions the most widely different, who, nevertheless, present a perfect resemblance of type.

The Hottentots so strongly resemble the inhabitants of the Celestial Empire, that it has even been supposed, though without good reasons, that they were originally a Chinese colony. A great similarity exists between the ancient Etruscans, whose portraits have come down to us, and the Araucanians of South America. The features and outlines of the Cherokees seem to be perfectly identical with those of several Italian populations, the Calabrians, for instance. The inhabitants of Auvergne, especially the female portion, much more nearly resemble in physiognomy several Indian tribes of North America than any European nation. Thus we see that in very different climes, and under conditions of life so very dissimilar, nature can reproduce the same forms. The peculiar characteristics which now distinguish the different types cannot, therefore, be the effects of local circumstances such as now exist.

Though it is impossible to ascertain what physical changes different branches of the human family may have undergone anterior to the historic epoch, yet we have the best proofs that since then, no race has changed its peculiar characteristics. The historic epoch comprises about one half of the time during which our earth is supposed to have been inhabited, and there are several nations whom we can trace up to the verge of ante-historic ages; yet we find that the races then known have remained the same to our days, even though they ceased to inhabit the same localities, and consequently were no longer exposed to the influence of the same external conditions.

Witness the Arabs. As they are represented on the monuments of Egypt, so we find them at present, not only in the arid deserts of their native land, but in the fertile regions and moist climate of Malabar, Coromandel, and the islands of the Indian Ocean. We find them again, though more mixed, on the northern coasts of Africa, and, although many centuries have elapsed since their invasion, traces of Arab blood are still discernible in some portions of Roussillon, Languedoc, and Spain.

Next to the Arabs I would instance the Jews. They have emigrated to countries in every respect the most dissimilar to Palestine, and have not even preserved their ancient habits of life. Yet their type has always remained peculiar and the same in every latitude and under every physical condition. The warlike Rechabites in the deserts of Arabia present to us the same features as our own peaceable Jews. I had occasion not long since to examine a Polish Jew. The cut of his face, and especially his eyes, perfectly betrayed his origin. This inhabitant of a northern zone, whose direct ancestors for several generations had lived among the snows and ice of an inhospitable clime, seemed to have been tanned but the day before, by the ardent rays of a Syrian sun. The same Shemitic face which the Egyptian artist represented some four thousand or more years ago, we recognize daily around us; and its principal and really characteristic features are equally strikingly preserved under the most diverse climatic circumstances. But the resemblance is not confined to the face only, it extends to the conformation of the limbs and the nature of the temperament. German Jews are generally smaller and more slender in stature than the European nations among whom they have lived for centuries; and the age of puberty arrives earlier with them than with their compatriots of another race. . . .

## CHAPTER XII. CLASSIFICATION OF RACES

In the investigation of the moral and intellectual diversities of races, there is no difficulty so great as an accurate classification. I am disposed to think a separation into three great groups sufficient for all practical purposes. These groups I shall call primary varieties, not in the sense of distinct creations, but as offering obvious and well-defined distinguishing characteristics. I would designate them respectively by the terms white, yellow, and black. I am aware of the inaccuracy of these appellations, because the complexion is not always the distinctive feature of these groups: other and more important physiological traits must be taken into consideration. But as I have not the right to invent new names, and am, therefore, compelled to select among those already in use, I have chosen these because, though by no means correct, they seemed preferable to others borrowed from geography or history, and not so apt as the latter to add to the confusion which already sufficiently perplexes the investigator of this subject. To obviate any misconception here and hereafter, I wish it to be distinctly understood that by "white" races I mean those usually comprised under the name of Caucasian, Shemitic, Japhetic; by "black," the Hamitic, African, etc.; by "yellow," the Altaic, Mongolian, Finnic, and Tartar. These I consider to be the three categories under which all races of the human family can be placed. . . .

It is obvious that each of these groups comprises races very dissimilar among themselves, each of which, besides the general characteristics belonging to the whole group, possesses others peculiar to itself. Thus, in the group of black races we find marked distinctions: the tribes with prognathous skull and woolly hair, the low-caste Hindoos of Kamaoun and of Dekhan, the Pelagian negroes of Polynesia, etc. In the yellow group, the Tungusians, Mongols, Chinese, etc. There is every reason to believe that these subvarieties are coeval; that is, the same causes which produced one, produced at the same time all the others.

It is, moreover, extremely difficult to determine the typical character of each variety. In the white, and also in the yellow group, the mixture of the sub-varieties is so great, that it is impossible to fix upon the type. In the black group, the type is perhaps discernible; at least, it is preserved in its greatest purity.

To ascertain the relative purity or mixture of a race, a criterion has been adopted by many, who consider it infallible: this is resemblance of face, form, constitution, etc. It is supposed that the purer a race has preserved itself, the greater must be the exterior resemblances of all the individuals composing it. On the contrary, considerable and varied intermixtures would produce an infinite diversity of appearance among individuals. This fact is incontestable, and of great value in ethnological science, but I do not think it quite so reliable as some suppose. . . .

We find this spectacle among the great civilized nations of Europe, especially in their capitals and seaports. In these great vortexes of humanity, every possible variety of our species has been absorbed. Negro, Chinese, Tartar, Hottentot, Indian, Malay, and all the minor varieties produced by their mixture, have contributed their contingent to the population of our large cities. Since the Roman domination, this amalgamation has continually increased, and is still increasing in proportion as our inventions bring in closer proximity the various portions of the globe. It affects all classes to some extent, but more especially the lowest. Among them you may see every type of the human family more or less represented. In London, Paris, Cadiz, Constantinople, in any of the greater marts and thoroughfares of the world, the lower strata of the *native* population exhibit every possible variety, from the prognathous skull to the pyramidal: you shall find one man with hair as crisp as a negro's; another, with the eyes of an ancient German, or the oblique ones of a Chinese; a third, with a thoroughly Shemitic countenance; yet all three may be close relations, and would be greatly surprised were they told that any but the purest white blood flows in their veins. In these vast gathering places of humanity, if you could take the first comer—a native of the place—and ascend his genealogical tree to any height, you would probably be amazed at the strange ancestry at the top.

It may now be asked whether, for all the various races of which I have spoken, there is but one standard of beauty, or whether each has one of its own. Helvetius, in his *De l'Esprit,* maintains that the idea of beauty is purely conventional and variable. This assertion found many advocates in its time, but it is at present superseded by the more philosophical theory that the conception of the beautiful is an absolute and invariable idea, and can never have a merely optional application. Believing the latter view to be correct, I do not hesitate to compare the various races of man in point of beauty, and to establish a regular scale of gradation. Thus, if we compare the various races, from the ungainly appearance of the Pelagian or Pecherai up to the noble proportions of a Charlemagne, the expressive regularity of features of a Napoleon, or the majestic countenance of a Louis XIV., we shall find in the lowest on the scale a sort of rudimentary development of the beauty which attracts us in the highest; and in proportion to the perfectness of that development, the races rise in the scale of beauty. Taking the white race as the standard of beauty, we perceive all the others more or less receding from that model. There is, then, an inequality in point of beauty among the various races of men, and this inequality is permanent and indelible.

The next question to be decided is, whether there is also an inequality in point of physical strength. It cannot be denied that the American Indians and the Hindoos are greatly inferior to us in this respect. Of the Australians, the same may safely be asserted. Even the negroes possess less muscular vigor. It is necessary, however, to distinguish between purely muscular force—that which exerts itself suddenly at a given moment—and the force of resistance or capacity for endurance. The degree of the former is measured by its intensity, that of the other by its duration. Of the two, the latter is the typical—the standard by which to judge of the capabilities of races. Great muscular strength is found among races notoriously weak. Among the lowest of the negro tribes, for instance, it would not be difficult to find individuals that could match an experienced European wrestler or English boxer. This is equally true of the Lascars and Malays. But we must take the masses, and judge according to the amount of long-continued, persevering toil and fatigue they are capable of. In this respect, the white races are undoubtedly entitled to pre-eminence.

But there are differences, again, among the white races, both in beauty and in strength, which even the extensive ethnical mixture, that European nations present, has not entirely obliterated. The Italians are handsomer than the French and the Spaniards, and still more so than the Swiss and Germans. The English also present a high degree of corporeal beauty; the Sclavonian nations a comparatively humble one.

In muscular power, the English rank far above all other European nations; but the French and Spaniards are greatly superior in power of endurance: they suffer less from fatigue, from privations, and the rigors and changes of climate. . . .


CHAPTER XIV. MUTUAL RELATIONS OF DIFFERENT MODES
OF INTELLECTUAL CULTURE

Had it been the will of the Creator to endow all the branches of the human family with equal intellectual capacities, what a glorious tableau would history not unfold before us. All being equally intelligent, equally aware of their true interests, equally capable of triumphing over obstacles, a number of simultaneous and flourishing civilizations would have gladdened every portion of the inhabited globe. While the most ancient Sanscrit nations covered Northern India with harvests, cities, palaces, and temples; and the plains of the Tigris and Euphrates shook under the trampling of Nimrod's cavalry and chariots, the prognathous tribes of Africa would have formed and developed a social system, sagaciously constructed, and productive of brilliant results.

Some luckless tribes, whose lot fortune had cast in inhospitable climes, burning sands, or glacial regions, mountain gorges, or cheerless steppes swept by the piercing winds of the north, would have been compelled to a longer and severer struggle against such unpropitious circumstances, than more fortunate nations. But being not inferior in intelligence and sagacity, they would not have been long in discovering the means of bettering their condition. Like the Icelanders, the Danes, and Norwegians, they would have forced the reluctant soil to afford them sustenance; if inhabitants of mountainous regions, they would, like the Swiss, have enjoyed the advantages of a pastoral life, or like the Cashmerians, resorted to manufacturing industry. But if their geographical situation had been so unfavorable as to admit of no resource, they would have reflected that the world was large, contained many a pleasant valley and fertile plain, where they might seek the fruits of intelligent activity, which their stepmotherly native land refused them.

Thus all the nations of the earth would have been equally enlightened, equally prosperous; some by the commerce of maritime cities, others by productive agriculture in inland regions, or successful industry in barren and Alpine districts. Though they might not exempt themselves from the misfortunes to which the imperfections of human nature give rise—transitory dissensions, civil wars, seditions, etc.—their individual interests would soon have led them to invent some system of relative equiponderance. As the differences in their civilizations resulted merely from fortuitous circumstances, and not from innate inequalities, a mutual interchange would soon have assimilated them in all essential points. Nothing could then prevent a universal confederation, that dream of so many centuries; and the inhabitants of the most distant parts of the globe would have been as members of one great cosmopolite people.

Let us contrast this fantastic picture with the reality. The first nations worthy of the name, owed their formation to an instinct of aggregation, which the barbarous tribes near them not only did not feel then, but never afterward. These nations spread beyond their original boundaries, and forced others to submit to their power. But the conquered neither adopted nor understood the principles of the civilization imposed upon them. Nor has the force of example been of avail to those in whom innate capacity was wanting. The native populations of the Spanish peninsula, and of Transalpine and Ligurian Gaul, saw Phoenicians, Greeks, and Carthaginians, successively establish flourishing cities on their coasts, without feeling the least incitement to imitate the manners or forms of government of these prosperous merchants.

What a glorious spectacle do not the Indians of North America witness at this moment. They have before their eyes a great and prosperous nation, eminent for the successful practical application of modern theories and sciences to political and social forms, as well as to industrial art. The superiority of this foreign race, which has so firmly established itself upon his former patrimony, is evident to the red man. He sees their magnificent cities, their thousands of vessels upon the once silent rivers, their successful agriculture; he knows that even his own rude wants, the blanket with which he covers himself, the weapon with which he slays his game, the ardent spirits he has learned to love so well, can be supplied only by the stranger. The last feeble hope to see his native soil delivered from the presence of the conqueror's race, has long since vanished from his breast; he feels that the land of his fathers is not his own. Yet he stubbornly refuses to enter the pale of this civilization which invites him, solicits him, tries to entice him with superior advantages and comforts. He prefers to retreat from solitude to solitude, deeper and deeper into the primitive forest. He is doomed to perish, and he knows it; but a mysterious power retains him under the yoke of his invincible repugnances, and while he admires the strength and superiority of the whites, his conscience, his whole nature, revolts at the idea of assimilating to them. He cannot forget or smother the instincts of his race. . . .

But not only savages, even nations of a higher rank in the intellectual scale are incapable of adopting a foreign civilization. We have already alluded to the failure of the English in India and of the Dutch in Java, in trying to import their own ideas into their foreign dependencies. French philanthropy is at this moment gaining the same experience in the new French possession of Algeria. There can be no stronger or more conclusive proof of the various endowments of different races.

If we had no other argument in proof of the innate imparity of races than the actual condition of certain barbarous tribes, and the supposition that they had always been in that condition, and, consequently, always would be, we should expose ourselves to serious objections. For many barbarous nations preserve traces of former cultivation and refinement. There are some tribes, very degraded in every other respect, who yet possess traditional regulations respecting the marriage celebration, the forms of justice and the division of inheritances, which evidently are remnants of a higher state of society, though the rites have long since lost all meaning. Many of the Indian tribes who wander over the tracts once occupied by the Alleghanian race, may be cited as instances of this kind. The natives of the Marian Islands, and many other savages, practise mechanically certain processes of manufacture, the invention of which presupposes a degree of ingenuity and knowledge utterly at variance with their present stupidity and ignorance. To avoid hasty and erroneous conclusions concerning this seeming decadence, there are several circumstances to be taken into consideration.

Let us suppose a savage population to fall within the sphere of activity of a proximate, but superior race. In that case they may gradually learn to conform externally to the civilization of their masters, and acquire the technicalities of their arts and inventions. Should the dominant race disappear either by expulsion or absorption, the civilization would expire, but some of its outward forms might be retained and perpetuated. A certain degree of mechanical skill might survive the scientific principles upon which it was based. In other words, practice might long continue after the theory was lost. History furnishes us a number of examples in support of this assertion. . . .

The preceding observations will, I think, suffice to show that the traces of civilization among a barbarous tribe are not a necessary proof that this tribe itself has ever been really civilized. It may either have lived under the domination of a superior but consanguineous race, or living in its vicinity, have, in an humble and feeble degree, profited by its lessons. This result, however, is possible only when there exists between the superior and the inferior race a certain ethnical affinity; that is to say, when the former is either a noble branch of the same stock, or ennobled by intermixture with another. When the disparity between races is too great and too decided, and there is no intermediate link to connect them, the contact is always fatal to the inferior race, as is abundantly proved by the disappearance of the aborigines of North America and Polynesia. . . .

## CHAPTER XV. MORAL AND INTELLECTUAL CHARACTERISTICS OF THE THREE GREAT VARIETIES

In the preceding pages, I have endeavored to show that, though there are both scientific and religious reasons for not believing in a plurality of origins of our species, the various branches of the human family are distinguished by permanent and irradicable differences, both mentally and physically. They are unequal in intellectual capacity, in personal beauty, and in physical strength. Again I repeat, that in coming to this conclusion, I have totally eschewed the method which is, unfortunately for the cause of science, too often resorted to by ethnologists, and which, to say the least of it, is simply ridiculous. The discussion has not rested upon the moral and intellectual worth of isolated individuals.

With regard to moral worth, I have proved that all men, to whatever race they may belong, are capable of receiving the lights of true religion, and of sufficiently appreciating that blessing to work out their own salvation. With regard to intellectual capacity, I emphatically protest against that mode of arguing which consists in saying, "every negro is a dunce;" because, by the same logic, I should be compelled to admit that "every white man is intelligent;" and I shall take good care to commit no such absurdity.

I shall not even wait for the vindicators of the absolute equality of all races, to adduce to me such and such a passage in some missionary's or navigator's journal, wherefrom it appears that some Yolof has become a skilful carpenter, that some Hottentot has made an excellent domestic, that some Caffre plays well on the violin, or that some Bambarra has made very respectable progress in arithmetic.

I am prepared to admit—and to admit without proof—anything of that sort, however remarkable, that may be related of the most degraded savages. I have already denied the excessive stupidity, the incurable idiocy of even the lowest on the scale of humanity. Nay, I go further than my opponents, and am not in the least disposed to doubt that, among the chiefs of the rude negroes of Africa, there could be found a considerable number of active and vigorous minds, greatly surpassing in fertility of ideas and mental resources, the average of our peasantry, and even of some of our middle classes. But the unfairness of deductions based upon a comparison of the most intelligent blacks and the least intelligent whites, must be obvious to every candid mind.

Once for all, such arguments seem to me unworthy of real science, and I do not wish to place myself upon so narrow and unsafe a ground. If Mungo Park, or the brothers Lander, have given to some negro a certificate of superior intelligence, who will assure us that another traveller, meeting the same individual, would not have arrived at a diametrically opposite conclusion concerning him? Let us leave such puerilities, and compare, not the individuals, but the masses. When we shall have clearly established of what the latter are capable, by what tendencies they are characterized, and by what limits their intellectual activity and development are circumscribed, whether, since the beginning of the historic epoch, they have acted upon, or been acted upon by other groups—when we shall have clearly established these points, we may then descend to details, and, perhaps, one day be able to decide why the greatest minds of one group are inferior to the most brilliant geniuses of another, in what respects the vulgar herds of all types assimilate, and in what others they differ, and why. But this difficult and delicate task cannot be accomplished until the relative position of the whole mass of each race shall have been nicely, and, so to say, mathematically defined. I do not know whether we may hope ever to arrive at results of such incontestable clearness and precision, as to be able to no longer trust solely to general facts, but to embrace the various shades of intelligence in each group, to define and class the inferior strata of every population and their influence on the activity of the whole. Were it possible thus to divide each group into certain strata, and compare these with the corresponding strata of every other: the most gifted of the dominant with the most gifted of the dominated races, and so on downwards, the superiority of some in capacity, energy, and activity would be self-demonstrated.

After having mentioned the facts which prove the inequality of various branches of the human family, and having laid down the method by which that proof should be established, I arrived at the conclusion that the whole of our species is divisible into three great groups, which I call primary varieties, in order to distinguish them from others formed by intermixture. It now remains for me to assign to each of these groups the principal characteristics by which it is distinguished from the others.

The dark races are the lowest on the scale. The shape of the pelvis has a character of animalism, which is imprinted on the individuals of that race ere their birth, and seems to portend their destiny. The circle of intellectual development of that group is more contracted than that of either of the two others.

If the negro's narrow and receding forehead seems to mark him as inferior in reasoning capacity, other portions of his cranium as decidedly point to faculties of an humbler, but not the less powerful character. He has energies of a not despicable order, and which sometimes display themselves with an intensity truly formidable. He is capable of violent passions, and passionate attachments. Some of his senses have an acuteness unknown to the other races: the sense of taste, and that of smell, for instance.

But it is precisely this development of the animal faculties that stamps the negro with the mark of inferiority to other races. I said that his sense of taste was acute; it is by no means fastidious. Every sort of food is welcome to his palate; none disgusts him; there is no flesh nor fowl too vile to find a place in his stomach. So it is with regard to odor. His sense of smell might rather be called greedy than acute. He easily accommodates himself to the most repulsive.

To these traits he joins a childish instability of humor. His feelings are intense, but not enduring. His grief is as transitory as it is poignant, and he rapidly passes from it to extreme gayety. He is seldom vindictive—his anger is violent, but soon appeased. It might almost be said that this variability of sentiments annihilates for him the existence of both virtue and vice. The very ardency to which his sensibilities are aroused, implies a speedy subsidence; the intensity of his desire, a prompt gratification, easily forgotten. He does not cling to life with the tenacity of the whites. But moderately careful of his own, he easily sacrifices that of others, and kills, though not absolutely bloodthirsty, without much provocation or subsequent remorse. Under intense suffering, he exhibits a moral cowardice which readily seeks refuge in death, or in a sort of monstrous impassivity.

With regard to his moral capacities, it may be stated that he is susceptible, in an eminent degree, of religious emotions; but unless assisted by the light of the Gospel, his religious sentiments are of a decidedly sensual character.

Having demonstrated the little intellectual and strongly sensual character of the black variety, as the type of which I have taken the negro of Western Africa, I shall now proceed to examine the moral and intellectual characteristics of the second in the scale—the yellow.

This seems to form a complete antithesis to the former. In them, the skull, instead of being thrown backward, projects. The forehead is large, often jutting out, and of respectable height. The facial conformation is somewhat triangular, but neither chin nor nose has the rude, animalish development that characterizes the negro. A tendency to obesity is not precisely a specific feature, but it is more often met with among the yellow races than among any others. In muscular vigor, in intensity of feelings and desires, they are greatly inferior to the black. They are supple and agile, but not strong. They have a decided taste for sensual pleasures, but their sensuality is less violent, and, if I may so call it, more vicious than the negro's, and less quickly appeased. They place a somewhat greater value upon human life than the negro does, but they are more cruel for the sake of cruelty. They are as gluttonous as the negro, but more fastidious in their choice of viands, as is proved by the immoderate attention bestowed on the culinary art among the more civilized of these races. In other words, the yellow races are less impulsive than the black. Their will is characterized by obstinacy rather than energetic violence; their anger is vindictive rather than clamorous; their cruelty more studied than passionate; their sensuality more refinedly vicious than absorbing. They are, therefore, seldom prone to extremes. In morals, as in intellect, they display a mediocrity: they are given to grovelling vices rather than to dark crimes; when virtuous, they are so oftener from a sense of practical usefulness than from exalted sentiments. In regard to intellectual capacity, they easily understand whatever is not very profound, nor very sublime; they have a keen appreciation of the useful and practical, a great love of quiet and order, and even a certain conception of a slight modicum of personal or municipal liberty. The yellow races are practical people in the narrowest sense of the word. They have little scope of imagination, and therefore invent but little: for great inventions, even the most exclusively utilitarian, require a high degree of the imaginative faculty. But they easily understand and adopt whatever is of practical utility. The *summum bonum* of their desires and aspirations is to pass smoothly and quietly through life.

It is apparent from this sketch, that they are superior to the blacks in aptitude and intellectual capacity. A theorist who would form some model society, might wish such a population to form the substratum upon which to erect his structure; but a society, composed entirely of such elements, would display neither great stamina nor capacity for anything great and exalted.

We are now arrived at the third and last of the "primary" varieties—the white. Among them we find great physical vigor and capacity of endurance; an intensity of will and desire, but which is balanced and governed by the intellectual faculties. Great things are undertaken, but not blindly, not without a full appreciation of the obstacles to be overcome, and with a systematic effort to overcome them. The utilitarian tendency is strong, but is united with a powerful imaginative faculty, which elevates, ennobles, idealizes it. Hence, the power of invention; while the negro can merely imitate, the Chinese only utilize, to a certain extent, the practical results attained by the white, the latter is continually adding new ones to those already gained. His capacity for combination of ideas leads him perpetually to construct new facts from the fragments of the old; hurries him along through a series of unceasing modifications and changes. He has as keen a sense of order as the man of the yellow race, but not, like him, from love of repose and inertia, but from a desire to protect and preserve his acquisitions. At the same time, he has an ardent love of liberty, which is often carried to an extreme; an instinctive aversion to the trammels of that rigidly formalistic organization under which the Chinese vegetates with luxurious ease; and he as indignantly rejects the haughty despotism which alone proves a sufficient restraint for the black races.

The white man is also characterized by a singular love of life. Perhaps it is because he knows better how to make use of it than other races, that he attaches to it a greater value and spares it more both in himself and in others. In the extreme of his cruelty, he is conscious of his excesses; a sentiment which it may well be doubted whether it exist among the blacks. Yet though he loves life better than other races, he has discovered a number of reasons for sacrificing it or laying it down without murmur. His valor, his bravery, are not brute, unthinking passions, not the result of callousness or impassivity: they spring from exalted, though often erroneous, sentiments, the principal of which is expressed by the word "honor." This feeling, under a variety of names and applications, has formed the mainspring of action of most of the white races since the beginning of historical times. It accommodates itself to every mode of existence, to every walk of life. It is as puissant in the pulpit and at the martyr's stake, as on the field of battle; in the most peaceful and humble pursuits of life as in the highest and most stirring. It were impossible to define all the ideas which this word comprises; they are better felt than expressed. But this feeling—we might call it instinctive—is unknown to the yellow, and unknown to the black races: while in the white it quickens every noble sentiment— the sense of justice, liberty, patriotism, love, religion—it has no name in the language, no place in the hearts, of other races. This I consider as the principal reason of the superiority of our branch of the human family over all others; because even in the lowest, the most debased of our race, we generally find some spark of this redeeming trait, and however misapplied it may often be, and certainly is, it prevents us, even in our deepest errors, from falling so fearfully low as the others. The extent of moral abasement in which we find so many of the yellow and black races is absolutely impossible even to the very refuse of our society. The latter may equal, nay, surpass them in crime; but even they would shudder at that hideous abyss of corrosive vices, which opens before the friend of humanity on a closer study of these races.

Before concluding this picture, I would add that the immense superiority of the white races in all that regards the intellectual faculties, is joined to an inferiority as strikingly marked, in the intensity of sensations. Though his whole structure is more vigorous, the white man is less gifted in regard to the perfection of the senses than either the black or the yellow, and therefore less solicited and less absorbed by animal gratifications.

# ⤷ FOLKWAYS

### William Graham Sumner

> The most devastating implication of Darwin's theory of evolution was
> not that the Book of Genesis may not be literally true nor even that
> man and ape are in a sense cousins. As Darwin himself had emphasized
> in The Descent of Man (see pages 63–65), man's moral and religious ideas
> must ultimately be traced to their origins in animal instincts and, like
> everything about us, accounted for in terms of natural selection. At a
> time when the comparative study of societies was just taking shape, this
> idea was not slow in having its impact. Investigators into the world's
> amazing variety of customs, men like Lewis Morgan (1818–1881) and
> Edward B. Tylor (1832–1917), began interpreting them not as noble
> or barbaric but as more or less useful ways of coping with particular
> environments.
>
> This approach found its most influential spokesman, at least in America,
> in William Graham Sumner (1840–1910). Ordained an Episcopal
> minister in 1869, Sumner brought a prophetic zeal to his espousal of
> Social Darwinism. From 1872 to 1909, as the most popular professor
> in the history of Yale University and the author of many brilliant books
> and articles, he exercised an enormous influence on an entire generation
> of Americans. A spellbinding lecturer, he inveighed against protective
> tariffs, trade unions, and socialism as measures promoting the survival
> of the unfit at the expense of the others, thus weakening the society
> as a whole.
>
> In later years Sumner's interests broadened from economics to sociology,
> and in 1906 he brought out the best known of all his writings, from
> which the following selections are taken. Its full title is Folkways: A
> Study of the Sociological Importance of Usages, Manners, Customs,
> Mores, and Morals. The tough-minded realism of this book, reminiscent
> of Hobbes or Machiavelli but firmly based on Darwin, represents an
> attitude toward morals and religion which is characteristic of modern
> social science and which is shared by many who would reject Sumner's
> earlier laissez-faire doctrines.

*1. Definition and Mode of Origin of the Folkways.*  If we put together all that we
have learned from anthropology and ethnography about primitive men and primitive society, we perceive that the first task of life is to live. Men begin with acts,

William Graham Sumner, *Folkways* (New York: Dover Publications, Inc., reprint of 1906
ed.), pp. 2–4, 16–18, 28–30, 48–51, 58–59, 65–66, 418–419, 540–541.

not with thoughts. Every moment brings necessities which must be satisfied at once. Need was the first experience, and it was followed at once by a blundering effort to satisfy it. It is generally taken for granted that men inherited some guiding instincts from their beast ancestry, and it may be true, although it has never been proved. If there were such inheritances, they controlled and aided the first efforts to satisfy needs. Analogy makes it easy to assume that the ways of beasts had produced channels of habit and predisposition along which dexterities and other psychophysical activities would run easily. Experiments with newborn animals show that in the absence of any experience of the relation of means to ends, efforts to satisfy needs are clumsy and blundering. The method is that of trial and failure, which produces repeated pain, loss, and disappointments. Nevertheless, it is a method of rude experiment and selection. The earliest efforts of men were of this kind. Need was the impelling force. Pleasure and pain, on the one side and the other, were the rude constraints which defined the line on which efforts must proceed. The ability to distinguish between pleasure and pain is the only psychical power which is to be assumed. Thus ways of doing things were selected, which were expedient. They answered the purpose better than other ways, or with less toil and pain. Along the course on which efforts were compelled to go, habit, routine, and skill were developed. The struggle to maintain existence was carried on, not individually, but in groups. Each profited by the other's experience; hence there was concurrence towards that which proved to be most expedient. All at last adopted the same way for the same purpose; hence the ways turned into customs and became mass phenomena. Instincts were developed in connection with them. In this way folkways arise. The young learn them by tradition, imitation, and authority. The folkways, at a time, provide for all the needs of life then and there. They are uniform, universal in the group, imperative, and invariable. As time goes on, the folkways become more and more arbitrary, positive, and imperative. If asked why they act in a certain way in certain cases, primitive people always answer that it is because they and their ancestors always have done so. A sanction also arises from ghost fear. The ghosts of ancestors would be angry if the living should change the ancient folkways.

*2. The Folkways are a Societal Force.*    The operation by which folkways are produced consists in the frequent repetition of petty acts, often by great numbers acting in concert or, at least, acting in the same way when face to face with the same need. The immediate motive is interest. It produces habit in the individual and custom in the group. It is, therefore, in the highest degree original and primitive. By habit and custom it exerts a strain on every individual within its range; therefore it rises to a societal force to which great classes of societal phenomena are due. Its earliest stages, its course, and laws may be studied; also its influence on individuals and their reaction on it. It is our present purpose so to study it. We have to recognize it as one of the chief forces by which a society is made to be what it is. Out of the unconscious experiment which every repetition of the ways includes, there issues pleasure or pain, and then, so far as the men are capable of reflection, convictions that the ways are conducive to societal welfare. These two experiences are not the same. The most uncivilized men, both in the food quest and in war, do things which are painful, but which have been found to be expedient. Perhaps these cases teach the sense of social welfare better than those which are pleasurable and favorable to welfare. The former cases call for some intelligent reflection on experience. When this conviction as to the relation to welfare is added to the folkways they are converted into mores, and, by virtue of the philosophical and ethical element added to them, they win utility and importance and become the source of the science and the art of living.

3. *Folkways Are Made Unconsciously.* It is of the first importance to notice that, from the first acts by which men try to satisfy needs, each act stands by itself, and looks no further than the immediate satisfaction. From recurrent needs arise habits for the individual and customs for the group, but these results are consequences which were never conscious, and never foreseen or intended. They are not noticed until they have long existed, and it is still longer before they are appreciated. Another long time must pass, and a higher stage of mental development must be reached, before they can be used as a basis from which to deduce rules for meeting, in the future, problems whose pressure can be foreseen. The folkways, therefore, are not creations of human purpose and wit. They are like products of natural forces which men unconsciously set in operation, or they are like the instinctive ways of animals, which are developed out of experience, which reach a final form of maximum adaptation to an interest, which are handed down by tradition and admit of no exception or variation, yet change to meet new conditions, still within the same limited methods, and without rational reflection or purpose. From this it results that all the life of human beings, in all ages and stages of culture, is primarily controlled by a vast mass of folkways handed down from the earliest existence of the race, having the nature of the ways of other animals, only the topmost layers of which are subject to change and control, and have been somewhat modified by human philosophy, ethics, and religion, or by other acts of intelligent reflection. We are told of savages that "It is difficult to exhaust the customs and small ceremonial usages of a savage people. Custom regulates the whole of a man's actions,—his bathing, washing, cutting his hair, eating, drinking, and fasting. From his cradle to his grave he is the slave of ancient usage. In his life there is nothing free, nothing original, nothing spontaneous, no progress towards a higher and better life, and no attempt to improve his condition, mentally, morally, or spiritually." All men act in this way with only a little wider margin of voluntary variation. . . .

21. *The Struggle for Existence and the Competition of Life; Antagonistic Coöperation.* The struggle for existence must be carried on under life conditions and in connection with the competition of life. The life conditions consist in variable elements of the environment, the supply of materials necessary to support life, the difficulty of exploiting them, the state of the arts, and the circumstances of physiography, climate, meteorology, etc., which favor life or the contrary. The struggle for existence is a process in which an individual and nature are the parties. The individual is engaged in a process by which he wins from his environment what he needs to support his existence. In the competition of life the parties are men and other organisms. The men strive with each other, or with the flora and fauna with which they are associated. The competition of life is the rivalry, antagonism, and mutual displacement in which the indi-

vidual is involved with other organisms by his efforts to carry on the struggle for existence for himself. It is, therefore, the competition of life which is the societal element, and which produces societal organization. The number present and in competition is another of the life conditions. At a time and place the life conditions are the same for a number of human beings who are present, and the problems of life policy are the same. This is another reason why the attempts to satisfy interest become mass phenomena and result in folkways. The individual and social elements are always in interplay with each other if there are a number present. If one is trying to carry on the struggle for existence with nature, the fact that others are doing the same in the same environment is an essential condition for him. Then arises an alternative. He and the others may so interfere with each other that all shall fail, or they may combine, and by coöperation raise their efforts against nature to a higher power. This latter method is industrial organization. The crisis which produces it is constantly renewed, and men are forced to raise the organization to greater complexity and more comprehensive power, without limit. Interests are the relations of action and reaction between the individual and the life conditions, through which relations the evolution of the individual is produced. That evolution, so long as it goes on prosperously, is well living, and it results in the self-realization of the individual, for we may think of each one as capable of fulfilling some career and attaining to some character and state of power by the developing of predispositions which he possesses. It would be an error, however, to suppose that all nature is a chaos of warfare and competition. Combination and coöperation are so fundamentally necessary that even very low life forms are found in symbiosis for mutual dependence and assistance. A combination can exist where each of its members would perish. Competition and combination are two forms of life association which alternate through the whole organic and superorganic domains. The neglect of this fact leads to many socialistic fallacies. Combination is of the essence of organization, and organization is the great device for increased power by a number of unequal and dissimilar units brought into association for a common purpose. McGee says of the desert of Papagueria, in southwestern Arizona, that "a large part of the plants and animals of the desert dwell together in harmony and mutual helpfulness [which he shows in detail]; for their energies are directed not so much against one another as against the rigorous environmental conditions growing out of dearth of water. This communality does not involve loss of individuality, . . . indeed the plants and animals are characterized by an individuality greater than that displayed in regions in which perpetuity of the species depends less closely on the persistence of individuals." Hence he speaks of the "solidarity of life" in the desert. "The saguaro is a monstrosity in fact as well as in appearance,—a product of miscegenation between plant and animal, probably depending for its form of life history, if not for its very existence, on its commensals." The Seri protect pelicans from themselves by a partial taboo, which is not understood. It seems that they could not respect a breeding time, or establish a closed season, yet they have such an appetite for the birds and their eggs that they would speedily exterminate them if there were no restraint. This combination has been well called antagonistic coöperation. It consists in the combination of two persons or groups to satisfy a great common interest while minor antagonisms of interest which exist between them are suppressed. The plants and animals of the desert are rivals for what water there is, but they combine as if with an intelligent purpose to attain to a maximum of life under the conditions. There are many cases of animals who coöperate in the same way. Our farmers put crows and robins under a protective taboo because the birds destroy insects. The birds also destroy grain and fruits, but this is tolerated on account of their services. Madame Pommerol says of the inhabitants of Sahara that the people of the towns and the nomads are enemies by caste and race, but allies in interest. The nomads need refuge and shelter. The townspeople need messengers and transportation. Hence ties of contract, quarrels, fights, raids, vengeances, and reconciliations for the sake of common enterprises of plunder. Antagonistic coöperation is the most productive form of combination in high civilization. It is a high action of the reason to overlook lesser antagonisms in order to work together for great interests. Political parties are constantly forced to do it. In the art of the statesman it is a constant policy. The difference between great parties and factions in any parliamentary system is of the first importance; that difference consists in the fact that parties can suppress minor differences, and combine for what they think most essential to public welfare, while factions divide and subdivide on petty differences. Inasmuch as the suppression of minor differences means a suppression of the emotional element, while the other policy encourages the narrow issues in regard to which feeling is always most intense, the former policy allows far less play to feeling and passion. . . .

*31. The Folkways Are "Right." Rights; Morals.*   The folkways are the "right" ways to satisfy all interests, because they are traditional, and exist in fact. They extend over the whole of life. There is a right way to catch game, to win a wife, to make one's self appear, to cure disease, to honor ghosts, to treat comrades or strangers, to behave when a child is born, on the warpath, in council, and so on in all cases which can arise. The ways are defined on the negative side, that is, by taboos. The "right" way is the way which the ancestors used and which has been handed down. The tradition is its own warrant. It is not held subject to verification by experience. The notion of right is in the folkways. It is not outside of them, of independent origin, and brought to them to test them. In the folkways, whatever is, is right. This is because they are traditional, and therefore contain in themselves the authority of the ancestral ghosts. When we come to the folkways we are at the end of our analysis. The notion of right and ought is the same in regard to all the folkways, but the degree of it varies with the importance of the interest at stake. The obligation of conformable and coöperative action is far greater under ghost fear and war than in other matters, and the social sanctions are severer, because group interests are supposed to be at stake. Some usages contain only a slight element of right and ought. It may well be believed that notions of right and duty, and of social welfare, were first developed in connection with ghost fear and other-worldliness, and therefore that, in that field also, folkways were first raised to mores. "Rights" are the rules of mutual give and take in the competition of life which are imposed on comrades in the in-group, in order that the peace may prevail there which is essential to the group strength. Therefore rights can never be "natural" or "God-given," or absolute in any sense. The morality of a group at a time is the sum of the taboos and prescriptions in the folkways by which right conduct is defined. Therefore morals can never be intuitive. They are historical, institutional, and empirical.

World philosophy, life policy, right, rights, and morality are all products of the folkways. They are reflections on, and generalizations from, the experience of pleasure and pain which is won in efforts to carry on the struggle for existence under actual life conditions. The generalizations are very crude and vague in their germinal forms. They are all embodied in folklore, and all our philosophy and science have been developed out of them.

*32. The Folkways are "True."*   The folkways are necessarily "true" with respect to some world philosophy. Pain forced men to think. The ills of life imposed reflection and taught forethought. Mental processes were irksome and were not undertaken until painful experience made them unavoidable. With great unanimity all over the globe primitive men followed the same line of thought. The dead were believed to live on as ghosts in another world just like this one. The ghosts had just the same needs, tastes, passions, etc., as the living men had had. These transcendental notions were the beginning of the mental outfit of mankind. They are articles of faith, not rational convictions. The living had duties to the ghosts, and the ghosts had rights; they also had power to enforce their rights. It behooved the living therefore to learn how to deal with ghosts. Here we have a complete world philosophy and a life policy deduced from it. When pain, loss, and ill were experienced and the question was provoked, Who did this to us? the world philosophy furnished the answer. When the painful experience forced the question, Why are the ghosts angry and what must we do to appease them? the "right" answer was the one which fitted into the philosophy of ghost fear. All acts were therefore constrained and trained into the forms of the world philosophy by ghost fear, ancestral authority, taboos, and habit. The habits and customs created a practical philosophy of welfare, and they confirmed and developed the religious theories of goblinism. . . .

*55. Organization of the Masses.*   Masses of men who are on a substantial equality with each other never can be anything but hopeless savages. The eighteenth-century notion that men in a state of nature were all equal is wrong-side up. Men who were equal would be in a state of nature such as was imagined. They could not form a society. They would be forced to scatter and wander, at most two or three together. They never could advance in the arts of civilization. The popular belief that out of some such horde there has come by the spontaneous development of innate forces all the civilization which we possess is entirely unfounded. Masses of men who are approximately equal are in time exterminated or enslaved. Only when enslaved or subjugated are some of them carried up with their conquerors by organization and discipline (negroes and Indians amongst us). A horde in which the only differences are those of age and sex is not capable of maintaining existence. It fights because only by conquering or being conquered can it endure. When it is subjugated and disciplined it consists of workers to belabor the ground for others, or tax payers to fill a treasury from which others may spend, or food for gunpowder, or voting material for demagogues. It is an object of exploitation. At one moment, in spite of its aggregate muscle, it is helpless and imbecile; the next moment it is swept away into folly and mischief by a suggestion or an impulse. Organization, leadership, and discipline are indispens-able to any beneficial action by masses of men. If we ignore this fact, we see the machine and the boss evolved out of the situation which we create.

*56. Institutions of Civil Liberty.*   Institutions also must be produced which will hold the activities of society in channels of order, deliberation, peace, regulated antagonism of interests, and justice, according to the mores of the time. These institutions put an end to exploitation and bring interests into harmony under civil liberty. But where do the institutions come from? The masses have never made them. They are produced out of the mores by the selection of the leading men and classes who get control of the collective power of the society and direct it to the activities which will (as they think) serve the interests which they regard as most important. If changes in life conditions occur, the interests to be served change. Great inventions and discoveries, the opening of new continents, new methods of agriculture and commerce, the intro-duction of money and financial devices, improved state organization, increase the economic power of the society and the force at the disposal of the state. Industrial interests displace military and monarchical interests as the ones which the state chiefly aims to serve, not because of any tide of "progress," but because industrialism gives greater and more varied satisfactions to the rulers. The increase of *power* is the primary condition. The classes strive with each other for the new power. Peace is necessary, for without peace none of them can enjoy power. Compromise, adjustment of interests, antagonistic coöperation, harmony, are produced, and institutions are the regulative processes and apparatus by which warfare is replaced by system. The historical process has been full of error, folly, selfishness, violence, and craft. It is so still. The point which is now important for us is that the masses have never car-ried on the struggles and processes by which civilized society has been made into an arena, within which exploitation of man by man is to some extent repressed, and where individual self-realization has a large scope, under the institutions of civil liberty. It is the historical and selected classes which have done this, often enough without intending or foreseeing the results of actions which they inaugurated with quite other, perhaps selfish, class purposes in view. A society is a whole made up of parts. All the parts have a legitimate share in the acts and sufferings of the society. All the parts contribute to the life and work of the society. We inherit all the conse-quences of all their acts. Some of the consequences are good and some are bad. It is utterly impossible to name the classes which have done useful work and made bene-ficial sacrifices only, and the other classes which have been idle burdens and mischief makers only. All that has been done has been done by all. It is evident that no other view than this can be rational and true, for one reason because the will and intention of the men of to-day in what they do has so little to do with the consequences to-morrow of what they do. The notion that religion, or marriage, or property, or monarchy, as we have inherited them, can be proved evil, or worthy of condemnation and contempt on account of the selfishness and violence interwoven with their history, is one of the idlest of all the vagaries of the social philosophers.

*57. The Common Man.*   Every civilized society has to carry below the lowest sections of the masses a dead weight of ignorance, poverty, crime, and disease. Every such society has, in the great central section of the masses, a great body which is neutral in all the policy of society. It lives by routine and tradition. It is not brutal, but it is shallow, narrow-minded, and prejudiced. Nevertheless it is harmless. It lacks initiative and cannot give an impulse for good or bad. It produces few criminals. It can sometimes be moved by appeals to its fixed ideas and prejudices. It is affected in its mores by contagion from the classes above it. The work of "popularization" consists in bringing about this contagion. The middle section is formed around the mathematical mean of the society, or around the mathematical mode, if the distribution of the subdivisions is not symmetrical. The man on the mode is the "common man," the "average man," or the "man in the street." Between him and the democratic political institutions—the pulpit, the newspapers, and the public library—there is a constant reaction by which mores are modified and preserved. The aim of all the institutions and literature in a modern state is to please him. His aim is to get out of them what suits him. The yellow newspapers thrive and displace all the others because he likes them. The trashy novels pay well because his wife and daughters like them. The advertisements in the popular magazines are addressed to him. They show what he wants. The "funny items" are adjusted to his sense of humor. Hence all these things are symptoms. They show what he "believes in," and they strengthen his prejudices. If all art, literature, legislation, and political power are to be cast at his feet, it makes some difference who and what he is. His section of society determines the mores of the whole. . . .

65. *What is Goodness or Badness of the Mores.*    It is most important to notice that, for the people of a time and place, their own mores are always good, or rather that for them there can be no question of the goodness or badness of their mores. The reason is because the standards of good and right are in the mores. If the life conditions change, the traditional folkways may produce pain and loss, or fail to produce the same good as formerly. Then the loss of comfort and ease brings doubt into the judgment of welfare (causing doubt of the pleasure of the gods, or of war power, or of health), and thus disturbs the unconscious philosophy of the mores. Then a later time will pass judgment on the mores. Another society may also pass judgment on the mores. In our literary and historical study of the mores we want to get from them their educational value, which consists in the stimulus or warning as to what is, in its effects, societally good or bad. This may lead us to reject or neglect a phenomenon like infanticide, slavery, or witchcraft, as an old "abuse" and "evil," or to pass by the crusades as a folly which cannot recur. Such a course would be a great error. Everything in the mores of a time and place must be regarded as justified with regard to that time and place. "Good" mores are those which are well adapted to the situation. "Bad" mores are those which are not so adapted. The mores are not so stereotyped and changeless as might appear, because they are forever moving towards more complete adaptation to conditions and interests, and also towards more complete adjustment to each other. People in mass have never made or kept up a custom in order to hurt their own interests. They have made innumerable errors as to what their interests were and how to satisfy them, but they have always aimed to serve their interests as well as they could. This gives the standpoint for the student of the mores. All things in them come before him on the same plane. They all bring instruction and warning. They all have the same relation to power and welfare. The mistakes in them are com-

ponent parts of them. We do not study them in order to approve some of them and condemn others. They are all equally worthy of attention from the fact that they existed and were used. The chief object of study in them is their adjustment to interests, their relation to welfare, and their coördination in a harmonious system of life policy. For the men of the time there are no "bad" mores. What is traditional and current is the standard of what ought to be. The masses never raise any question about such things. If a few raise doubts and questions, this proves that the folkways have already begun to lose firmness and the regulative element in the mores has begun to lose authority. This indicates that the folkways are on their way to a new adjustment. The extreme of folly, wickedness, and absurdity in the mores is witch persecutions, but the best men of the seventeenth century had no doubt that witches existed, and that they ought to be burned. The religion, statecraft, jurisprudence, philosophy, and social system of that age all contributed to maintain that belief. It was rather a culmination than a contradiction of the current faiths and convictions, just as the dogma that all men are equal and that one ought to have as much political power in the state as another was the culmination of the political dogmatism and social philosophy of the nineteenth century. Hence our judgments of the good or evil consequences of folkways are to be kept separate from our study of the historical phenomena of them, and of their strength and the reasons for it. The judgments have their place in plans and doctrines for the future, not in a retrospect. . . .

72. *Might and Right.*    Modern civilized states of the best form are often called jural states because the concept of rights enters so largely into all their constitutions and regulations. Our political philosophy centers around that concept, and all our social discussions fall into the form of propositions and disputes about rights. The history of the dogma of rights has been such that rights have been believed to be self-evident and self-existent, and as having prevailed especially in primitive society. Rights are also regarded as the opposite of force. These notions only prove the antagonism between our mores and those of earlier generations. In fact, it is a characteristic of our mores that the form of our thinking about all points of political philosophy is set for us by the concept of rights. Nothing but might has ever made right, and if we include in might (as we ought to) elections and the decisions of courts, nothing but might makes right now. We must distinguish between the anterior and the posterior view of the matter in question. If we are about to take some action, and are debating the right of it, the might which can be brought to support one view of it has nothing to do with the right of it. If a thing has been done and is established by force (that is, no force can reverse it), it is right in the only sense we know, and rights will follow from it which are not vitiated at all by the force in it. There would be no security at all for right if this were not so. We find men and parties protesting, declaiming, complaining of what is done, and which they say is not "right," but only force. An election decides that those shall have power who will execute an act of policy. The defeated party denounces the wrong and wickedness of the act. It is done. It may be a war, a conquest, a spoliation; every one must help to do it by paying taxes and doing military service or other duty which may be demanded of him. The decision of a lawsuit leaves one party protesting and complaining. He always speaks of "right" and "rights." He is forced to acquiesce. The result is right in the only sense

which is real and true. It is more to the purpose to note that an indefinite series of consequences follow, and that they create or condition rights which are real and just. Many persons now argue against property that it began in force and therefore has no existence in right and justice. They might say the same of marriage or religion. Some do say the same of the state. The war of the United States with Mexico in 1845 is now generally regarded as unjustified. That cannot affect the rights of all kinds which have been contracted in the territory then ceded by Mexico or under the status created on the land obtained by the treaty of peace with that country. The whole history of mankind is a series of acts which are open to doubt, dispute, and criticism, as to their right and justice, but all subsequent history has been forced to take up the consequences of those acts and go on. The disputants about "rights" often lose sight of the fact that the world has to go on day by day and dispute must end. It always ends in force. The end always leaves some complaining in terms of right and rights. They are overborne by force of some kind. Therefore might has made all the right which ever has existed or exists now. If it is proposed to reverse, reform, or change anything which ever was done because we now think that it was wrong, that is a new question and a new case, in which the anterior view alone is in place. It is for the new and future cases that we study historical cases and form judgments on them which will enable us to act more wisely. If we recognize the great extent to which force now enters into all which happens in society, we shall cease to be shocked to learn the extent to which it has been active in the entire history of civilization. The habit of using jural concepts, which is now so characteristic of our mores, leads us into vague and impossible dreams of social affairs, in which metaphysical concepts are supposed to realize themselves, or are assumed to be real. . . .

*439. Meaning of "Immoral."*   When, therefore, the ethnographers apply condemnatory or depreciatory adjectives to the people whom they study, they beg the most important question which we want to investigate; that is, What are standards, codes, and ideas of chastity, decency, propriety, modesty, etc., and whence do they arise? The ethnographical facts contain the answer to this question, but in order to reach it we want a colorless report of the facts. We shall find proof that "immoral" never means anything but contrary to the mores of the time and place. Therefore the mores and the morality may move together, and there is no permanent or universal standard by which right and truth in regard to these matters can be established and different folkways compared and criticised. Only experience produces judgments of the expediency of some usages. For instance, ancient peoples thought pederasty was harmless and trivial. It has been well proved to be corrupting both to individual and social vigor, and harmful to interests, both individual and collective. Cannibalism, polygamy, incest, harlotry, and other primitive customs have been discarded by a very wide and, in the case of some of them, unanimous judgment that they harmful. On the other hand, in the *Avesta* spermatorrhea is a crime punished by stripes. The most civilized peoples also maintain, by virtue of their superior position in the arts of life, that they have attained to higher and better judgments and that they may judge the customs of others from their own standpoint. For three or four centuries they have called their own customs "Christian," and have thus claimed for them a religious authority and sanction which they do not possess by any connection with the principles of Christianity. Now, however, the adjective seems to be losing its force. The Japanese regard nudity with indifference, but they use dress to conceal the contour of the human form while we use it to enhance, in many ways, the attraction. "Christian" mores have been enforced by the best breechloaders and ironclads, but the Japanese now seem ready to bring superiority in those matters to support their mores. It is now a known and recognized fact that our missionaries have unintentionally and unwittingly done great harm to nature people by inducing them to wear clothes as one of the first details of civilized influence. In the usages of nature peoples there is no correlation at all between dress and sentiments of chastity, modesty, decency, and propriety. . . .

*593. Religion and the Mores.* Religion never has been an independent force acting from outside creatively to mold the mores or the ideas of men. Evidently such an idea is the extreme form of the world philosophy in which another (spiritual) world is conceived of as impinging upon this one from "above," to give it laws and guidance. The mores grow out of the life as a whole. They change with the life conditions, density of population, and life experience. Then they become strange or hostile to traditional religion. In our own experience our mores have reached views about ritual practices, polygamy, slavery, celibacy, etc., which are strange or hostile to those in the Bible. Since the sixteenth century we have reconstructed our religion to fit our modern ideas and mores. Every religious reform in history has come about in this way. All religious doctrines and ritual acts are held immutable by strong interests and notions of religious duty. Therefore they fall out of consistency with the mores, which are in constant change, being acted on by all the observation or experience of life. Sacral harlotry is a case, the ethical horror of which is very great and very obvious to us, of old religious ideas and customs preserved by the religion into times of greatly changed moral (i.e. of the mores) and social codes. . . .

## THE ORIGIN AND DEVELOPMENT OF PSYCHOANALYSIS

*Sigmund Freud*

*The last hundred years have seen a revolution in man's way of thinking about himself. Gradually human nature has been brought within the scope of scientific inquiry, and man has learned to study his own processes—including even his deepest thoughts and aspirations—with the same detachment as he would those of a rock formation or an ant colony.*

*This increased knowledge is due to the work of many investigators in fields ranging from physiology to cultural anthropology. But the greatest contribution is generally conceded to be that of Sigmund Freud (1856–1939), the founder of psychoanalysis. Psychoanalysis is both a theory of the development and dynamics of the mind and a technique for treating the mentally ill. More accurately, it is a set of theories and a set of techniques, all derived ultimately from Freud. The validity of much of this material is still a matter of dispute among psychologists and psychiatrists, but Freud's basic discoveries, summarized in the following selection, are widely accepted.*

The Origin and Development of Psychoanalysis *is the title given by Freud to five lectures delivered at Clark University in 1909. He had been invited to the United States to explain his theories after the first International Congress of Psychoanalysis, held in Vienna in 1908, had revealed a growing interest—especially among physicians dealing with nervous disorders—in his work. Freud had begun as a specialist in diseases of the nervous system among children, such as aphasia and cerebral palsy. Gradually he had become convinced of the need for a psychological approach to such diseases, using first hypnosis and then a method of his own called "free association." For years he had worked with his patients in Vienna, attracting little but ridicule from the scientific community. Now at last he was coming into his own.*

*Freud's Clark Lectures were very well received in America. The following year (1910) he established the International Psychoanalytic Association, which has held biennial meetings ever since, and began editing a journal to publish the findings of its members. From 1915 to 1917, at the University of Vienna, he gave a brilliant series of twenty-eight lectures on three main psychoanalytic topics: neuroses, the interpretation of dreams, and the psychopathology of everyday life. These lectures, published in 1924 under the title* A General Introduction to Psychoanalysis, *established his reputation on a firm basis. They still form by far the best summary of his principal ideas.*

*Even after they were accepted by most psychologists, Freud's theories, particularly his ideas about sexuality, met fierce resistance from the general public. This resistance never surprised Freud: to him it was merely the unwillingness of the conscious mind to accept unpleasant or threatening material. He was also not surprised by the barbarism displayed on both sides during World War I. As he put it, each of us, normal and abnormal alike, lives on the rim of a "seething volcano" of repressed desires. But the war, and the social upheavals that followed it, may have been what led him to broaden his interests. In* The Future of an Illusion *(1927),* Civilization and Its Discontents *(1929), and* Moses and Monotheism *(1939), he used his psychoanalytic findings to illuminate the nature of religion, morality, and the basic issues of man's existence.*

*In 1938, when Freud was eighty-two, the Nazis invaded Austria. Freud was a Jew. His books were publicly burned and his passport confiscated,*

*and the old man—who had been suffering from a painful cancer for
sixteen years—escaped from his beloved Vienna by paying a large ransom,
only to die a year later in England. The world was to be dumbfounded
by the horrors of Nazi concentration camps, revealed only after World
War II was over. Freud himself, perhaps, would not have been surprised.*

. . . My point of departure was not, like that of Janet, laboratory researches, but attempts at therapy. Above everything else, it was practical needs that urged me on. The cathartic treatment, as Breuer had made use of it, presupposed that the patient should be put in deep hypnosis, for only in hypnosis was available the knowledge of his pathogenic associations, which were unknown to him in his normal state. Now hypnosis, as a fanciful, and so to speak, mystical, aid, I soon came to dislike; and when I discovered that, in spite of all my efforts, I could not hypnotize by any means all of my patients, I resolved to give up hypnotism and to make the cathartic method independent of it.

Since I could not alter the psychic state of most of my patients at my wish, I directed my efforts to working with them in their normal state. This seems at first sight to be a particularly senseless and aimless undertaking. The problem was this: to find out something from the patient that the doctor did not know and the patient himself did not know. How could one hope to make such a method succeed? The memory of a very noteworthy and instructive proceeding came to my aid, which I had seen in Bernheim's clinic at Nancy. Bernheim showed us that persons put in a condition of hypnotic somnambulism, and subjected to all sorts of experiences, had only apparently lost the memory of those somnambulic experiences, and that their memory of them could be awakened even in the normal state. If he asked them about their experiences during somnambulism, they said at first that they did not remember, but if he persisted, urged, assured them that they did know, then every time the forgotten memory came back.

Accordingly I did this with my patients. When I had reached in my procedure with them a point at which they declared that they knew nothing more, I would assure them that they did know, that they must just tell it out, and I would venture the assertion that the memory which would emerge at the moment that I laid my hand on the patient's forehead would be the right one. In this way I succeeded, without hypnosis, in learning from the patient all that was necessary for a construction of the connection between the forgotten pathogenic scenes and the symptoms which they had left behind. This was a troublesome and in its length an exhausting proceeding, and did not lend itself to a finished technique. But I did not give it up without drawing definite conclusions from the data which I had gained. I had substantiated the fact that the forgotten memories were not lost. They were in the possession of the patient, ready to emerge and form associations with his other mental content, but

Sigmund Freud, *The Origin and Development of Psychoanalysis* (Chicago: Gateway Editions, Henry Regnery Company, 1955), pp. 19–23, 27–28, 33–44, 46–49, 51–54, 56–62, 64–68.

hindered from becoming conscious, and forced to remain in the unconscious by some sort of a force. The existence of this force could be assumed with certainty, for in attempting to drag up the unconscious memories into the consciousness of the patient, in opposition to this force, one got the sensation of his own personal effort striving to overcome it. One could get an idea of this force, which maintained the pathological situation, from the resistance of the patient.

It is on this idea of *resistance* that I based my theory of the psychic processes of hystericals. It had been found that in order to cure the patient it was necessary that this force should be overcome. Now with the mechanism of the cure as a starting point, quite a definite theory could be constructed. These same forces, which in the present situation as resistances opposed the emergence of the forgotten ideas into consciousness, must themselves have caused the forgetting, and repressed from consciousness the pathogenic experiences. I called this hypothetical process "repression" and considered that it was proved by the undeniable existence of resistance.

But now the question arose: what were those forces, and what were the conditions of this repression, in which we were now able to recognize the pathogenic mechanism of hysteria? A comparative study of the pathogenic situations, which the cathartic treatment has made possible, allows us to answer this question. In all those experiences, it had happened that a wish had been aroused, which was in sharp opposition to the other desires of the individual, and was not capable of being reconciled with the ethical, æsthetic and personal pretensions of the patient's personality. There had been a short conflict, and the end of this inner struggle was the repression of the idea which presented itself to consciousness as the bearer of this irreconcilable wish. This was, then, repressed from consciousness and forgotten. The incompatibility of the idea in question with the "ego" of the patient was the motive of the repression, the ethical and other pretensions of the individual were the repressing forces. The presence of the incompatible wish, or the duration of the conflict, had given rise to a high degree of mental pain; this pain was avoided by the repression. This latter process is evidently in such a case a device for the protection of the personality. . . .

We come to the conclusion, from working with hysterical patients and other neurotics, that they have not fully succeeded in repressing the idea to which the incompatible wish is attached. They have, indeed, driven it out of consciousness and out of memory, and apparently saved themselves a great amount of psychic pain, *but in the unconscious the suppressed wish still exists,* only waiting for its chance to become active, and finally succeeds in sending into consciousness, instead of the repressed idea, a disguised and unrecognizable surrogate-creation, to which the same painful sensations associate themselves that the patient thought he was rid of through his repression. This surrogate of the suppressed idea—the symptom—is secure against further attacks from the defenses of the ego, and instead of a short conflict there originates now a permanent suffering. We can observe in the symptom, besides the tokens of its disguise, a remnant of traceable similarity with the originally repressed idea; the way in which the surrogate is built up can be discovered during the psychoanalytic treatment of the patient, and for his cure the symptom must be traced back over the same route to the repressed idea. If this repressed material is once more made part of the conscious mental functions—a process which supposes the overcoming of considerable resistance—the psychic conflict which then arises, the same which the patient wished to avoid, is made capable of a happier termination, under the guidance of the physician, than is offered by repression. There are several possible suitable decisions which can bring conflict and neurosis to a happy end; in particular cases the attempt may be made to combine several of these. Either the personality of the patient may be convinced that he has been wrong in rejecting the pathogenic wish, and he may be made to accept it either wholly or in part; or this wish may itself be directed to a higher goal which is free from objection, by what is called sublimation; or the rejection may be recognized as rightly motivated, and the automatic and therefore insufficient mechanism of repression be reinforced by the higher, more characteristically human mental faculties: one succeeds in mastering his wishes by conscious thought. . . .

Ladies and Gentlemen, it is very useful to designate a group of ideas which belong together and have a common emotive tone, according to the custom of the Zurich school (Bleuler, Jung and others), as a "complex." So we can say that if we set out from the last memories of the patient to look for a repressed complex, we have every prospect of discovering it, if only the patient will communicate to us a sufficient number of the ideas which come into his head. So we let the patient speak along any line that he desires, and cling to the hypothesis that nothing can occur to him except what has some indirect bearing on the complex that we are seeking. If this method of discovering the repressed complexes seems too circumstantial, I can at least assure you that it is the only available one.

In practicing this technique, one is further bothered by the fact that the patient often stops, is at a standstill, and considers that he has nothing to say; nothing occurs to him. If this were really the case and the patient were right, our procedure would again be proven inapplicable. Closer observation shows that such an absence of ideas never really occurs, and that it only appears to when the patient holds back or rejects the idea which he perceives, under the influence of the resistance, which disguises itself as critical judgment of the value of the idea. The patient can be protected from this if he is warned in advance of this circumstance, and told to take no account of the critical attitude. He must say anything that comes into his mind, fully laying aside such critical choice, even though he may think it is unessential, irrelevant, nonsensical, especially when the idea is one which is unpleasant to dwell on. By following this prescription we secure the material which sets us on the track of the repressed complex.

These irruptive ideas, which the patient himself values little, if he is under the influence of the resistance and not that of the physician, are for the psychologist like the ore, which by simple methods of interpretation he reduces from its crude state to valuable metal. If one desires to gain in a short time a preliminary knowledge of the patient's repressed complexes, without going into the question of their arrangement and association experiments, as Jung and his pupils have perfected them. This procedure is to the psychologist what qualitative analysis is to the chemist; it may be dispensed with in the therapy of neurotic patients, but is indispensable in the investigations of the psychoses, which have been begun by the Zurich school with such valuable results.

This method of work with whatever comes into the patient's head when he submits to psychoanalytic treatment, is not the only technical means at our disposal for the widening of consciousness. Two other methods of procedure serve the same purpose, the interpretation of his dreams and the evaluation of acts which he bungles or does without intending to. . . .

Interpretation of dreams is in fact the *via regia** to the interpretation of the unconscious, the surest ground of psychoanalysis and a field in which every worker must win his convictions and gain his education. If I were asked how one could become a psychoanalyst, I should answer, through the study of his own dreams. With great tact all opponents of the psychoanalytic theory have so far either evaded any criticism of the *Traumdeutung*† or have attempted to pass over it with the most superficial objections. If, on the contrary, you will undertake the solution of the problems of dream life, the novelties which psychoanalysis present to your thoughts will no longer be difficulties.

You must remember that our nightly dream productions show the greatest outer similarity and inner relationship to the creations of the insane, but on the other hand are compatible with full health during waking life. It does not sound at all absurd to say that whoever regards these normal sense illusions, these delusions and alterations of character as matter for amazement instead of understanding, has not the least prospect of understanding the abnormal creations of diseased mental states in any other than the lay sense. You may with confidence place in this lay group all the psychiatrists of today. Follow me now on a brief excursion through the field of dream problems.

In our waking state we usually treat dreams with as little consideration as the patient treats the irruptive ideas which the psychoanalyst demands from him. It is evident that we reject them, for we forget them quickly and completely. The slight valuation which we place on them is based, with those dreams that are not confused and nonsensical, on the feeling that they are foreign to our personality, and, with other dreams on their evident absurdity and senselessness. Our rejection derives support from the unrestrained shamelessness and the immoral longings which are obvious in many dreams. Antiquity, as we know, did not share this light valuation of dreams. The lower classes of our people today stick close to the value which they set on dreams; they, however, expect from them, as did the ancients, the revelation of the future. I confess that I see no need to adopt mystical hypotheses to fill out the gaps in our present knowledge, and so I have never been able to find anything that supported the hypothesis of the prophetic nature of dreams. Many other things, which are wonderful enough, can be said about them.

And first, not all dreams are so foreign to the character of the dreamer, are incomprehensible and confused. If you will undertake to consider the dreams of young children from the age of a year and a half on, you will find them quite simple and easy to interpret. The young child always dreams of the fulfillment of wishes which were aroused in him the day before and were not satisfied. You need no art of interpretation to discover this simple solution, you only need to inquire into the experiences of the child on the day before (the "dream day"). Now it would certainly be a most satisfactory solution of the dream-riddle, if the dreams of adults, too, were the same

* [Royal road. (*Ed.*)]

† [Theory of dream interpretation. (*Ed.*)]

as those of children, fulfillments of wishes which had been aroused in them during the dream day. This is actually the fact; the difficulties which stand in the way of this solution can be removed step by step by a thorough analysis of the dream.

There is, first of all, the most weighty objection, that the dreams of adults generally have an incomprehensible content, which shows wish-fulfillment least of anything. The answer is this: these dreams have undergone a process of disguise, the psychic content which underlies them was originally meant for quite different verbal expression. You must differentiate between the *manifest dream-content,* which we remember in the morning only confusedly, and with difficulty clothe in words which seem arbitrary, and the *latent dream-thoughts,* whose presence in the unconscious we must assume. This distortion of the dream is the same process which has been revealed to you in the investigations of the creations (*symptoms*) of hysterical subjects; it points to the fact that the same opposition of psychic forces has its share in the creation of dreams as in the creation of symptoms.

The manifest dream-content is the disguised surrogate for the unconscious dream thoughts, and this disguising is the work of the defensive forces of the ego, of the resistances. These prevent the repressed wishes from entering consciousness during the waking life, and even in the relaxation of sleep they are still strong enough to force them to hide themselves by a sort of masquerading. The dreamer, then, knows just as little the sense of his dream as the hysterical knows the relation and significance of his symptoms. That there are latent dream-thoughts and that between them and the manifest dream-content there exists the relation just described—of this you may convince yourselves by the analysis of dreams, a procedure the technique of which is exactly that of psychoanalysis. You must abstract entirely from the apparent connection of the elements in the manifest dream and seek for the irruptive ideas which arise through free association, according to the psychoanalytic laws, from each separate dream element. From this material the latent dream thoughts may be discovered, exactly as one divines the concealed complexes of the patient from the fancies connected with his symptoms and memories. From the latent dream thoughts which you will find in this way, you will see at once how thoroughly justified one is in interpreting the dreams of adults by the same rubrics as those of children. What is now substituted for the manifest dream-content is the real sense of the dream, is always clearly comprehensible, associated with the impressions of the day before, and appears as the fulfilling of an unsatisfied wish. The manifest dream, which we remember after waking, may then be described as a *disguised* fulfillment of *repressed* wishes.

It is also possible by a sort of synthesis to get some insight into the process which has brought about the disguise of the unconscious dream thoughts as the manifest dream-content. We call this process "dream-work." This deserves our fullest theoretical interest, since here as nowhere else can we study the unsuspected psychic processes which are existent in the unconscious, or, to express it more exactly, *between* two such separate systems as the conscious and the unconscious. Among these newly discovered psychic processes, two, condensation and displacement or transvaluation, change of psychic accent, stand out most prominently. Dream work is a special case of the reaction of different mental groupings on each other, and as such is the consequence of psychic fission. In all essential points it seems identical with the work of disguise, which changes the repressed complex in the case of failing repression into symptoms.

You will furthermore discover by the analysis of dreams, most convincingly your own, the unsuspected importance of the rôle which impressions and experiences from early childhood exert on the development of men. In the dream life the child, as it were, continues his existence in the man, with a retention of all his traits and wishes, including those which he was obliged to allow to fall into disuse in his later years. With irresistible might it will be impressed on you by what processes of development, of repression, sublimation and reaction there arises out of the child, with its peculiar gifts and tendencies, the so-called normal man, the bearer and partly the victim of our painfully acquired civilization. I will also direct your attention to the fact that we have discovered from the analysis of dreams that the unconscious makes use of a sort of symbolism, especially in the presentation of sexual complexes. This symbolism in part varies with the individual, but in part is of a typical nature, and seems to be identical with the symbolism which we suppose to lie behind our myths and legends. It is not impossible that these later creations of the people may find their explanation from the study of dreams.

Finally, I must remind you that you must not be led astray by the objection that the occurrence of anxiety-dreams, contradicts our idea of the dream as a wish-fulfillment. Apart from the consideration that anxiety-dreams also require interpretation before judgment can be passed on them, one can say quite generally that the anxiety does not depend in such a simple way on the dream content as one might suppose without more knowledge of the facts, and more attention to the conditions of neurotic anxiety. Anxiety is one of the ways in which the ego relieves itself of repressed wishes which have become too strong and so is easy to explain in the dream, if the dream has gone too far towards the fulfilling of the objectionable wish.

You see that the investigation of dreams was justified by the conclusions which it has given us concerning things otherwise hard to understand. But we came to it in connection with the psychoanalytic treatment of neurotics. From what has been said you can easily understand how the interpretation of dreams, if it is not made too difficult by the resistance of the patient, can lead to a knowledge of the patient's concealed and repressed wishes and the complexes which he is nourishing. I may now pass to that group of everyday mental phenomena whose study has become a technical help for psychoanalysis.

These are the bungling of acts among normal men as well as among neurotics, to which no significance is ordinarily attached; the forgetting of things which one is supposed to know and at other times really does know (for example the temporary forgetting of proper names); mistakes in speaking, which occur so frequently; analogous mistakes in writing and in reading, the automatic execution of purposive acts in wrong situations and the loss or breaking of objects, etc. These trifles, for which no one has ever sought a psychological determination, which have passed unchallenged as chance experiences, as consequences of absent-mindedness, inattention and similar conditions. Here, too, are included the acts and gestures executed without being noticed by the subject, to say nothing of the fact that he attaches no psychic importance to them; as playing and trifling with objects, humming melodies, handling one's person and clothing and the like.

These little things, the bungling of acts, like the symptomatic and chance acts are not so entirely without meaning as is generally supposed by a sort of tacit agreement.

They have a meaning, generally easy and sure to interpret from the situation in which they occur, and it can be demonstrated that they either express impulses and purposes which are repressed, hidden if possible from the consciousness of the individual, or that they spring from exactly the same sort of repressed wishes and complexes which we have learned to know already as the creators of symptoms and dreams.

It follows that they deserve the rank of symptoms, and their observation, like that of dreams, can lead to the discovery of the hidden complexes of the psychic life. With their help one will usually betray the most intimate of his secrets. If these occur so easily and commonly among people in health, with whom repression has on the whole succeeded fairly well, this is due to their insignificance and their inconspicuous nature. But they can lay claim to high theoretic value, for they prove the existence of repression and surrogate creations even under the conditions of health. You have already noticed that the psychoanalyst is distinguished by an especially strong belief in the determination of the psychic life. For him there is in the expression of the psyche nothing trifling, nothing arbitrary and lawless, he expects everywhere a widespread motivation, where customarily such claims are not made; more than that, he is even prepared to find a manifold motivation of these psychic expressions, while our supposedly inborn causal need is satisfied with a single psychic cause.

Now keeping in mind the means which we possess for the discovery of the hidden, forgotten, repressed things in the soul life: the study of the irruptive ideas called up by free association, the patient's dreams, and his bungled and symptomatic acts; and adding to these the evaluation of other phenomena which emerge during the psychoanalytic treatment, on which I shall later make a few remarks under the heading of "transfer," you will come with me to the conclusion that our technique is already sufficiently efficacious for the solution of the problem of how to introduce the pathogenic psychic material into consciousness, and so to do away with the suffering brought on by the creation of surrogate symptoms.

The fact that by such therapeutic endeavors our knowledge of the mental life of the normal and the abnormal is widened and deepened, can of course only be regarded as an especial attraction and superiority of this method. . . .

Ladies and Gentlemen: At this point you will be asking what the technique which I have described has taught us of the nature of the pathogenic complexes and repressed wishes of neurotics.

One thing in particular: psychoanalytic investigations trace back the symptoms of disease with really surprising regularity to impressions from the sexual life, show us that the pathogenic wishes are of the nature of erotic impulse-components, and necessitate the assumption that to disturbances of the erotic sphere must be ascribed the greatest significance among the etiological factors of the disease. This holds of both sexes.

I know that this assertion will not willingly be credited. Even those investigators who gladly follow my psychological labors, are inclined to think that I overestimate the etiological share of the sexual moments. They ask me why other mental excitations should not lead to the phenomena of repression and surrogate-creation which I have described. I can give them this answer; that I do not know why they should not do this, I have no objection to their doing it, but experience shows that they do not possess such a significance, and that they merely support the effect of the sexual moments, without being able to supplant them. . . .

Now to proceed with the communication of our results. It is true that in another series of cases psychoanalysis at first traces the symptoms back not to the sexual, but to banal traumatic experiences. But the distinction loses its significance through other circumstances. The work of analysis which is necessary for the thorough explanation and complete cure of a case of sickness does not stop in any case with the experience of the time of onset of the disease, but in every case it goes back to the adolescence and the early childhood of the patient. Here only do we hit upon the impressions and circumstances which determine the later sickness. Only the childhood experiences can give the explanation for the sensitivity to later traumata and only when these memory traces, which almost always are forgotten, are discovered and made conscious, is the power developed to banish the symptoms. We arrive here at the same conclusion as in the investigation of dreams—that it is the incompatible, repressed wishes of childhood which lend their power to the creation of symptoms. Without these the reactions upon later traumata discharge normally. But we must consider these mighty wishes of childhood very generally as sexual in nature.

Now I can at any rate be sure of your astonishment. Is there an infantile sexuality? you will ask. Is childhood not rather that period of life which is distinguished by the lack of the sexual impulse? No, gentlemen, it is not at all true that the sexual impulse enters into the child at puberty, as the devils in the gospel entered into the swine. The child has his sexual impulses and activities from the beginning, he brings them with him into the world, and from these the so-called normal sexuality of adults emerges by a significant development through manifold stages. It is not very difficult to observe the expressions of this childish sexual activity; it needs rather a certain art to overlook them or to fail to interpret them. . . .

Lay aside your doubts and let us evaluate the infantile sexuality of the earliest years. The sexual impulse of the child manifests itself as a very complex one, it permits of an analysis into many components, which spring from different sources. It is entirely disconnected from the function of reproduction which it is later to serve. It permits the child to gain different sorts of pleasure sensations, which we include, by the analogues and connections which they show, under the term sexual pleasures. The great source of infantile sexual pleasure is the auto-excitation of certain particularly sensitive parts of the body; besides the genitals are included the rectum and the opening of the urinary canal, and also the skin and other sensory surfaces. Since in this first phase of child sexual life the satisfaction is found on the child's own body and has nothing to do with any other object, we call this phase after a word coined by Havelock Ellis, that of "auto-eroticism." The parts of the body significant in giving sexual pleasure we call "erogenous zones." The thumb-sucking or passionate sucking of very young children is a good example of such an auto-erotic satisfaction of an erogenous zone. The first scientific observer of this phenomenon, a specialist in children's diseases in Budapest by the name of Lindner, interpreted these rightly as sexual satisfaction and described exhaustively their transformation into other and higher forms of sexual gratification. Another sexual satisfaction of this time of life is the excitation of the genitals by masturbation, which has such a great significance for later life and, in the case of many individuals, is never fully overcome. Besides this and other auto-erotic manifestations we see very early in the child the impulse-components of *sexual pleasure,* or, as we may say, of the *libido,* which presupposes a second person as its object. These impulses appear in opposed pairs, as active and passive. The most important representatives of this group are the pleasure in inflicting pain (sadism) and its passive exhibition-pleasure. From the first of these later pairs splits off the curiosity for knowledge, as from the latter impulse toward artistic and theatrical representation. Other sexual manifestations of the child can already be regarded from the viewpoint of object-choice, in which the second person plays the prominent part. The significance of this was primarily based upon motives of the impulse of self-preservation. The difference between the sexes plays, however, in the child no very great rôle. One may attribute to every child, without wronging him, a bit of the homosexual disposition.

The sexual life of the child, rich, but dissociated, in which each single impulse goes about the business of arousing pleasure independently of every other, is later correlated and organized in two general directions, so that by the close of puberty the definite sexual character of the individual is practically finally determined. The single impulses subordinate themselves to the overlordship of the genital zone, so that the whole sexual life is taken over into the service of procreation, and their gratification is now significant only so far as they help to prepare and promote the true sexual act. On the other hand, object-choice prevails over auto-eroticism, so that now in the sexual life all components of the sexual impulse are satisfied in the loved person. But not all the original impulse-components are given a share in the final shaping of the sexual life. Even before the advent of puberty certain impulses have undergone the most energetic repression under the impulse of education, and mental forces like shame, disgust and morality are developed, which, like sentinels, keep the repressed wishes in subjection. When there comes, in puberty, the high tide of sexual desire it finds dams in this creation of reactions and resistances. These guide the outflow into the so-called normal channels, and make it impossible to revivify the impulses which have undergone repression. . . .

Now we turn again to the sexual development of the child. We still have much to say here, since we have given more attention to the somatic than to the mental expressions of the sexual life. The primitive object-choice of the child, which is derived from his need of help, demands our further interest. It first attaches to all persons to whom he is accustomed, but soon these give way in favor of his parents. The relation of the child to his parents is, as both direct observation of the child and later analytic investigation of adults agree, not at all free from elements of sexual accessory-excitation. The child takes both parents, and especially one, as an object of his erotic wishes. Usually he follows in this the stimulus given by his parents, whose tenderness has very clearly the character of a sex manifestation, though inhibited so far as its goal is concerned. As a rule, the father prefers the daughter, the mother the son; the child reacts to this situation, since, as son, he wishes himself in the place of his father, as daughter, in the place of the mother. The feelings awakened in these relations between parents and children, and, as a resultant of them, those among the children in relation to each other, are not only positively of a tender, but negatively of an inimical sort. The complex built up in this way is destined to quick repression, but it still exerts a great and lasting effect from the unconscious. We must express the opinion that this with its ramifications presents the *nuclear complex* of every neurosis, and so we are prepared to meet with it in a not less effectual way in the other fields of mental life. The myth of King Oedipus, who kills his father and wins his mother as a wife is only the slightly altered presentation of the infantile wish, rejected later by the opposing barriers of incest. Shakespeare's tale of Hamlet rests on the same basis of an incest complex, though better concealed. At the time when the child is still ruled by the still unrepressed nuclear complex, there begins a very significant part of his mental activity which serves sexual interest. He begins to investigate the question of where children come from and guesses more than adults imagine of the true relations by deduction from the signs which he sees. Usually his interest in this investigation is awakened by the threat to his welfare through the birth of another child in the family, in whom at first he sees only a rival. Under the influence of the partial impulses which are active in him he arrives at a number of "infantile sexual theories," as that the same male genitals belong to both sexes, that children are conceived by eating and born through the opening of the intestine, and that sexual intercourse is to be regarded as an inimical act, a sort of overpowering.

But just the unfinished nature of his sexual constitution and the gaps in his knowledge brought about by the hidden condition of the feminine sexual canal, cause the infant investigator to discontinue his work as a failure. The facts of this childish investigation itself as well as the infant sex theories created by it are of determinative significance in the building of the child's character, and in the content of his later neuroses.

It is unavoidable and quite normal that the child should make his parents the objects of his first object-choice. But his *libido* must not remain fixed on these first chosen objects, but must take them merely as a prototype and transfer from these to other persons in the time of definite object-choice. The breaking loose of the child from his parents is thus a problem impossible to escape if the social virtue of the young individual is not to be impaired. During the time that the repressive activity is making its choice among the partial sexual impulses and later, when the influence of the parents, which in the most essential way has furnished the material for these repressions, is lessened, great problems fall to the work of education, which at present certainly does not always solve them in the most intelligent and economic way. . . .

The deeper you penetrate into the pathogenic of neurotic diseases, the more the connection of neuroses with other products of human mentality, even the most valuable, will be revealed to you. You will be reminded that we men, with the high claims of our civilization and under the pressure of our repressions, find reality generally quite unsatisfactory and so keep up a life of fancy in which we love to compensate for what is lacking in the sphere of reality by the production of wish-fulfillments. In these phantasies is often contained very much of the particular constitutional essence of personality and of its tendencies, repressed in real life. The energetic and successful man is he who succeeds by dint of labor in transforming his wish fancies into reality. Where this is not successful in consequence of the resistance of the outer world and the weakness of the individual, there begins the turning away from reality. The individual takes refuge in his satisfying world of fancy. Under certain conditions it still remains possible for him to find another connecting link between these fancies and reality, instead of permanently becoming a stranger to it through the regression into the infantile. If the individual who is displeased with reality is in possession of that *artistic talent* which is still a psychological riddle, he can transform his fancies into artistic creations. So he escapes the fate of a neurosis and wins back his connection with reality by this round-about way. Where this opposition to the real world exists, but this valuable talent fails or proves insufficient, it is unavoidable that the *libido,* following the origin of the fancies, succeeds by means of regression in revivifying the infantile wishes and so producing a neurosis. The neurosis takes, in our time, the place of the cloister, in which were accustomed to take refuge all those whom life had undeceived or who felt themselves too weak for life. Let me give at this point the main result at which we have arrived by the psychoanalytic investigation of neurotics, namely, that neuroses have no peculiar psychic content of their own, which is not also to be found in healthy states; or, as C. G. Jung has expressed it, neurotics fall ill of the same complexes with which we sound people struggle. It depends on quantitative relationships, on the relations of the forces wrestling with each other, whether the struggle leads to health, to a neurosis, or to compensatory over-functioning. . . .

Ladies and Gentlemen, I am of the opinion that there are, on the intellectual side, two hindrances to acknowledging the value of the psychoanalytic viewpoint: first, the fact that we are not accustomed to reckon with a strict determination of mental life, which holds without exception, and, second, the lack of knowledge of the peculiarities through which unconscious mental processes differ from these conscious ones with which we are familiar. One of the most widespread resistances against the work of psychoanalysis with patients as with persons in health reduces to the latter of the two moments. One is afraid of doing harm by psychoanalysis, one is anxious about calling up into consciousness the repressed sexual impulses of the patient, as though there were danger that they could overpower the higher ethical strivings and rob him of his cultural acquisitions. One can see that the patient has sore places in his soul life, but one is afraid to touch them, lest his suffering be increased. We may use this analogy. It is, of course, better not to touch diseased places when one can only cause pain. But we know that the surgeon does not refrain from the investigation and reinvestigation of the seat of illness, if his invasion has as its aim the restoration of lasting health. Nobody thinks of blaming him for the unavoidable difficulties of the investigation or the phenomena of reaction from the operation, if these only accomplish their purpose, and gain for the patient a final cure by temporarily making his condition worse. The case is similar in psychoanalysis; it can lay claim to the same things as surgery; the increase of pain which takes place in the patient during the treatment is very much less than that which the surgeon imposes upon him, and especially negligible in comparison with the pains of serious illness. But the consequence which is feared, that of a disturbance of the cultural character by the impulse which has been freed from repression, is wholly impossible. In relation to this anxiety we must consider what our experiences have taught us with certainty, that the somatic and mental power of a wish, if once its repression has not succeeded, is incomparably stronger when it is unconscious than when it is conscious, so that by being made conscious it can only be weakened. The unconscious wish cannot be influenced, is free from all strivings in the contrary direction, while the conscious is inhibited by those wishes which are also conscious and which strive against it. The work of psychoanalysis accordingly presents a better substitute, in the service of the highest and most valuable cultural strivings, for the repression which has failed.

Now what is the fate of the wishes which have become free by psychoanalysis, by what means shall they be made harmless for the life of the individual? There are several ways. The general consequence is, that the wish is consumed during the work by the correct mental activity of those better tendencies which are opposed to it. The repression is supplanted by a condemnation carried through with the best means at one's disposal. This is possible, since for the most part we have to abolish only the effects of earlier development stages of the ego. The individual for his part only repressed the useless impulse, because at that time he was himself still incompletely organized and weak; in his present maturity and strength he can, perhaps, conquer without injury to himself that which is inimical to him. A second issue of the work of psychoanalysis may be that the revealed unconscious impulses can now arrive at those useful applications which, in the case of undisturbed developments, they would have found earlier. The extirpation of the infantile wishes is not at all the ideal aim of development. The neurotic has lost, by his repressions, many sources of mental energy whose contingents would have been very valuable for his character building and his life activities. We know a far more purposive process of development, to so-called *sublimation*, by which the energy of infantile wish-excitations is not secluded, but remains capable of application, while for the particular excitations, instead of becoming useless, a higher, eventually no longer sexual, goal is set up. The components of the sexual instinct are especially distinguished by such a capacity for the sublimation and exchange of their sexual goal for one more remote and socially more valuable. To the contributions of the energy won in such a way for the functions of our mental life we probably owe the highest cultural consequences. A repression taking place at an early period excludes the sublimation of the repressed impulse; after the removal of the repression the way to sublimation is again free.

We must not neglect, also, to glance at the third of the possible issues. A certain part of the suppressed libidinous excitation has a right to direct satisfaction and ought to find it in life. The claims of our civilization make life too hard for the greater part of humanity, and so further the aversion to reality and the origin of neuroses, without producing an excess of cultural gain by this excess of sexual repression. We ought not to go so far as to fully neglect the original animal part of our nature, we ought not to forget that the happiness of individuals cannot be dispensed with as one of the aims of our culture. The plasticity of the sexual-components, manifest in their capacity for sublimation, may cause a great temptation to accomplish greater culture-effects by a more and more far reaching sublimation. But just as little as with our machines we expect to change more than a certain fraction of the applied heat into useful mechanical work, just as little ought we to strive to separate the sexual impulse in its whole extent of energy from its peculiar goal. This cannot succeed, and if the narrowing of sexuality is pushed too far it will have all the evil effects of a robbery. . . .

# ✑ PHYSICS AND PHILOSOPHY

*Werner Heisenberg*

> *In 1905 a brilliant young German physicist named Albert Einstein*
> *ushered in a revolution in science, announcing a new quantum theory of*
> *light and a relativity theory of mass and energy. In the succeeding years,*
> *other epoch-making discoveries followed. Einstein (1879–1955) was*
> *joined by Niels Bohr (1885–1962), Erwin Schrödinger (b. 1887), and*
> *Werner Heisenberg (b. 1901); and terms like "photoelectric effect,"*
> *"Fitzgerald contraction," and "indeterminacy principle" became symbols*
> *of a bewildering new body of knowledge, too complex for any but*
> *physicists to understand. It was an unprecedented situation. Intellectuals,*
> *as always, began speculating as to the wider human significance of the*
> *new theories; but this time the physicists themselves solemnly declared*
> *that they had been misunderstood, that the inferences being drawn did*
> *not follow at all. They suggested either that the new physics had no*
> *wider implications, which seemed highly unlikely, or that these must*
> *remain incomprehensible to all but the experts. The intellectuals continued*
> *to speculate, of course, but the uneasy feeling grew that in the future*
> *great power would lie with those who had mastered the tensor calculus.*
> *This feeling became even stronger when it was learned in 1939 that*
> *Professor Einstein, who had fled to the United States to escape Hitler's*
> *persecution of the Jews, had informed President Roosevelt that it was*
> *now possible to construct an atomic bomb powerful enough to demolish*
> *an entire city in seconds.*
>
> *The bomb was constructed, and the city was demolished. Thus we now*
> *know a little more about the "wider human significance" of the new*
> *physics, but the whole question remains a baffling one. This is the problem*
> *with which the following essay by Werner Heisenberg deals. Heisenberg,*
> *director of the Kaiser Wilhelm Institute for Physics in Berlin (the post*
> *held by Einstein from 1913 to 1933), winner of the Nobel Prize in*
> *1932 for his work in quantum mechanics, is probably the world's most*
> *distinguished living physicist.*

## THE ROLE OF MODERN PHYSICS IN THE
## PRESENT DEVELOPMENT OF HUMAN THINKING

The philosophical implications of modern physics have been discussed in the foregoing chapters in order to show that this most modern part of science touches very

*Physics and Philosophy: The Revolution in Modern Science* (New York: Harper and Row Publishers, Inc., 1958), pp. 187–206.

old trends of thought at many points, that it approaches some of the very old problems from a new direction. It is probably true quite generally that in the history of human thinking the most fruitful developments frequently take place at those points where two different lines of thought meet. These lines may have their roots in quite different parts of human culture, in different times or different cultural environments or different religious traditions; hence if they actually meet, that is, if they are at least so much related to each other that a real interaction can take place, then one may hope that new and interesting developments will follow. Atomic physics as a part of modern science does actually penetrate in our time into very different cultural traditions. It is not only taught in Europe and the Western countries, where it belongs to the traditional activity in the natural sciences, but it is also studied in the Far East, in countries like Japan and China and India, with their quite different cultural background, and in Russia, where a new way of thinking has been established in our time; a new way related both to specific scientific developments of the Europe of the nineteenth century and to other entirely different traditions from Russia itself. It can certainly not be the purpose of the following discussion to make predictions about the probable result of the encounter between the ideas of modern physics and the older traditions. But it may be possible to define the points from which the interaction between the different ideas may begin.

In considering this process of expansion of modern physics it would certainly not be possible to separate it from the general expansion of natural science, of industry and engineering, of medicine, etc., that is, quite generally of modern civilization in all parts of the world. Modern physics is just one link in a long chain of events that started from the work of Bacon, Galileo and Kepler and from the practical application of natural science in the seventeenth and eighteenth centuries. The connection between natural science and technical science has from the beginning been that of mutual assistance: The progress in technical science, the improvement of the tools, the invention of new technical devices have provided the basis for more, and more accurate, empirical knowledge of nature; and the progress in the understanding of nature and finally the mathematical formulation of natural laws have opened the way to new applications of this knowledge in technical science. For instance, the invention of the telescope enabled the astronomers to measure the motion of the stars more accurately than before; thereby a considerable progress in astronomy and in mechanics was made possible. On the other hand, precise knowledge of the mechanical laws was of the greatest value for the improvement of mechanical tools, for the construction of engines, etc. The great expansion of this combination of natural and technical science started when one had succeeded in putting some of the forces of nature at the disposal of man. The energy stored up in coal, for instance, could then perform some of the work which formerly had to be done by man himself. The industries growing out of these new possibilities could first be considered as a natural continuation and expansion of the older trades; at many points the work of the machines still resembled the older handicraft and the work in the chemical factories could be considered as a continuation of the work in the dyehouses and the pharmacies of the older times. But later entirely new branches of industry developed which had no counterpart in the older trades; for instance, electrical engineering. The penetration of science into the more remote parts of nature enabled the engineers to use forces of nature which in former periods had scarcely been known; and the accurate knowledge of these forces in terms of a mathematical formulation of the laws governing them formed a solid basis for the construction of all kinds of machinery.

The enormous success of this combination of natural and technical science led to a strong preponderance of those nations or states or communities in which this kind of human activity flourished, and as a natural consequence this activity had to be taken up even by those nations which by tradition would not have been inclined toward natural and technical sciences. The modern means of communication and of traffic finally completed this process of expansion of technical civilization. Undoubtedly the process has fundamentally changed the conditions of life on our earth; and whether one approves of it or not, whether one calls it progress or danger, one must realize that it has gone far beyond any control through human forces. One may rather consider it as a biological process on the largest scale whereby the structures active in the human organism encroach on larger parts of matter and transform it into a state suited for the increasing human population.

Modern physics belongs to the most recent parts of this development, and its unfortunately most visible result, the invention of nuclear weapons, has shown the essence of this development in the sharpest possible light. On the one hand, it has demonstrated most clearly that the changes brought about by the combination of natural and technical sciences cannot be looked at only from the optimistic viewpoint; it has at least partly justified the views of those who had always warned against the dangers of such radical transmutation of our natural conditions of life. On the other hand, it has compelled even those nations or individuals who tried to keep apart from these dangers to pay the strongest attention to the new development, since obviously political power in the sense of military power rests upon the possession of atomic weapons. It can certainly not be the task of this volume to discuss extensively the political implications of nuclear physics. But at least a few words may be said about these problems because they always come first into the minds of people when atomic physics is mentioned.

It is obvious that the invention of the new weapons, especially of the thermonuclear weapons, has fundamentally changed the political structure of the world. Not only has the concept of independent nations or states undergone a decisive change, since any nation which is not in possession of such weapons must depend in some way on those very few nations that do produce these arms in large quantity; but also the attempt of warfare on a large scale by means of such weapons has become practically an absurd kind of suicide. Hence one frequently hears the optimistic view that therefore war has become obsolete, that it will not happen again. This view, unfortunately, is a much too optimistic oversimplification. On the contrary, the absurdity of warfare by means of thermonuclear weapons may, in a first approximation, act as an incentive for war on a small scale. Any nation or political group which is convinced of its historical or moral right to enforce some change of the present situation will feel that the use of conventional arms for this purpose will not involve any great risks; they will assume that the other side will certainly not have recourse to the nuclear weapons, since the other side being historically and morally wrong in this issue will not take the chance of war on a large scale. This situation would in turn induce the other nations to state that in case of small wars inflicted upon them by aggressors, they would actually have recourse to the nuclear weapons, and thus the danger obviously remains. It may quite well be that in about twenty or thirty years from now the world will have undergone so great changes that the danger of warfare on a large scale, of the application of all technical resources for the annihilation of the opponent, will have greatly diminished or disappeared. But the way to this new state will be full of the greatest dangers. We must as in all former times, realize that what looks historically or morally right to the one side may look wrong to the other side. The continuation of the status quo may not always be the correct solution; it may, on the contrary, be most important to find peaceful means of adjustments to new situations, and it may in many cases be extremely difficult to find any just decision at all. Therefore, it is probably not too pessimistic to say that the great war can be avoided only if all the different political groups are ready to renounce some of their apparently most obvious rights—in view of the fact that the question of right or wrong may look essentially different from the other side. This is certainly not a new point of view; it is in fact only an application of that human attitude which has been taught through many centuries by some of the great religions.

The invention of nuclear weapons has also raised entirely new problems for science and scientists. The political influence of science has become very much stronger than it was before World War II, and this fact has burdened the scientist, especially the atomic physicist, with a double responsibility. He can either take an active part in the administration of the country in connection with the importance of science for the community; then he will eventually have to face the responsibility for decisions of enormous weight which go far beyond the small circle of research and university work to which he was wont. Or he may voluntarily withdraw from any participation in political decisions; then he will still be responsible for wrong decisions which he could possibly have prevented had he not preferred the quiet life of the scientist. Obviously it is the duty of the scientists to inform their governments in detail about the unprecedented destruction that would follow from a war with thermonuclear weapons. Beyond that, scientists are frequently requested to participate in solemn resolutions in favor of world peace; but considering this latter demand I must confess that I have never been able to see any point in declarations of this kind. Such resolutions may seem a welcome proof of goodwill; but anyone who speaks in favor of peace without stating precisely the conditions of this peace must at once be suspected of speaking only about that kind of peace in which he and his group thrive best—which of course would be completely worthless. Any honest declaration for peace must be an enumeration of the sacrifices one is prepared to make for its preservation. But as a rule the scientists have no authority to make statements of this kind.

At the same time the scientist can do his best to promote international co-operation in his own field. The great importance that many governments attach to research in nuclear physics nowadays and the fact that the level of scientific work is still very different in different countries favors international co-operation in this work. Young scientists of many different countries may gather in research institutions in which a strong activity in the field of modern physics is going on and the common work on difficult scientific problems will foster mutual understanding. In one case, that of the Geneva organization, it has even been possible to reach an agreement between a number of different nations for building a common laboratory and for constructing by a combined effort the expensive experimental equipment for research in nuclear physics. This kind of co-operation will certainly help to establish a common attitude toward the problems of science—common even beyond the purely scientific problems —among the younger generation of scientists. Of course one does not know beforehand what will grow out of the seeds that have been sown in this way when the scientists return into their old environments and again take part in their own cultural traditions. But one can scarcely doubt that the exchange of ideas between young scientists of different countries and between the different generations in every country will help to approach without too much tension that new state of affairs in which a balance is reached between the older traditional forces and the inevitable necessities of modern life. It is especially one feature of science which makes it more than anything else suited for establishing the first strong connection between different cultural traditions. This is the fact that the ultimate decisions about the value of a special scientific work, about what is correct or wrong in the work, do not depend on any human authority. It may sometimes take many years before one knows the solution of a problem, before one can distinguish between truth and error; but finally the questions will be decided, and the decisions are made not by any group of scientists but by nature itself. Therefore, scientific ideas spread among those who are interested in science in an entirely different way from the propagation of political ideas.

While political ideas may gain a convincing influence among great masses of people just because they correspond or seem to correspond to the prevailing interests of the people, scientific ideas will spread only because they are true. There are objective and final criteria assuring the correctness of a scientific statement.

All that has here been said about international co-operation and exchange of ideas would of course be equally true for any part of modern science; it is by no means confined to atomic physics. In this respect modern physics is just one of the many branches of science, and even if its technical applications—the arms and the peaceful use of atomic energy—attach a special weight to this branch, there would be no reason for considering international co-operation in this field as far more important than in any other field. But we have now to discuss again those features of modern physics which are essentially different from the previous development of natural science, and we have for this purpose once more to go back to the European history of this development that was brought about by the combination of natural and technical sciences.

It has frequently been discussed among the historians whether the rise of natural science after the sixteenth century was in any way a natural consequence of earlier trends in human thinking. It may be argued that certain trends in Christian philosophy led to a very abstract concept of God, that they put God so far above the world that one began to consider the world without at the same time also seeing God in the world. The Cartesian partition may be called a final step in this development. Or one may point out that all the theological controversies of the sixteenth century produced a general discontent about problems that could not really be settled by reason and were exposed to the political struggles of the time; that this discontent favored interest in problems which were entirely separated from the theological disputes. Or one may simply refer to the enormous activity, the new spirit that had come into the European societies through the Renaissance. In any case during this period a new authority appeared which was completely independent of Christian religion or philosophy or of the Church, the authority of experience, of the empirical fact. One may trace this authority back into older philosophical trends, for instance, into the philosophy of Occam and Duns Scotus, but it became a vital force of human activity only from the sixteenth century onward. Galileo did not only *think* about the mechanical motions, the pendulum and the falling stone; he tried out by experiments, quantitatively, how these motions took place. This new activity was in its beginning certainly not meant as a deviation from the traditional Christian religion. On the contrary, one spoke of two kinds of revelation of God. The one was written in the Bible and the other was to be found in the book of nature. The Holy Scripture had been written by man and was therefore subject to error, while nature was the immediate expression of God's intentions.

However, the emphasis on experience was connected with a slow and gradual change in the aspect of reality. While in the Middle Ages what we nowadays call the symbolic meaning of a thing was in some way its primary reality, the aspect of reality changed toward what we can perceive with our senses. What we can see and touch became primarily real. And this new concept of reality could be connected with a new activity: we can experiment and see how things really are. It was easily seen that this new attitude meant the departure of the human mind into an immense field of new possibilities, and it can be well understood that the Church saw in the new movement the dangers rather than the hopes. The famous trial of Galileo in connection with his views on the Copernican system marked the beginning of a struggle that went on for more than a century. In this controversy the representatives of natural science could argue that experience offers an undisputable truth, that it cannot be left to any human authority to decide about what really happens in nature, and that this decision is made by nature or in this sense by God. The representatives of the traditional religion, on the other hand, could argue that by paying too much attention to the material world, to what we perceive with our senses, we lose the connection with the essential values of human life, with just that part of reality which is beyond the material world. These two arguments do not meet, and therefore the problem could not be settled by any kind of agreement or decision.

In the meantime natural science proceeded to get a clearer and wider picture of the material world. In physics this picture was to be described by means of those concepts which we nowadays call the concepts of classical physics. The world consisted of things in space and time, the things consist of matter, and matter can produce and can be acted upon by forces. The events follow from the interplay between matter and forces; every event is the result and the cause of other events. At the same time the human attitude toward nature changed from a contemplative one to the pragmatic one. One was not so much interested in nature as it is; one rather asked what one could do with it. Therefore, natural science turned into technical science; every advancement of knowledge was connected with the question as to what practical use could be derived from it. This was true not only in physics; in chemistry and biology the attitude was essentially the same, and the success of the new methods in medicine or in agriculture contributed essentially to the propagation of the new tendencies.

In this way, finally, the nineteenth century developed an extremely rigid frame for natural science which formed not only science but also the general outlook of great masses of people. This frame was supported by the fundamental concepts of classical physics, space, time, matter and causality; the concept of reality applied to the things or events that we could perceive by our senses or that could be observed by means of the refined tools that technical science had provided. Matter was the primary reality. The progress of science was pictured as a crusade of conquest into the material world. Utility was the watchword of the time.

On the other hand, this frame was so narrow and rigid that it was difficult to find a place in it for many concepts of our language that had always belonged to its very substance, for instance, the concepts of mind, of the human soul or of life. Mind could be introduced into the general picture only as a kind of mirror of the material world; and when one studied the properties of this mirror in the science of psychology, the scientists were always tempted—if I may carry the comparison further—to pay more attention to its mechanical than to its optical properties. Even there one tried to apply the concepts of classical physics, primarily that of causality. In the same way life was to be explained as a physical and chemical process, governed by natural laws, completely determined by causality. Darwin's concept of evolution provided ample evidence for this interpretation. It was especially difficult to find in this framework room for those parts of reality that had been the object of the traditional religion and seemed now more or less only imaginary. Therefore, in those European countries in which one was wont to follow the ideas up to their extreme consequences, an open hostility of science toward religion developed, and even in the other countries there was an increasing tendency toward indifference toward such questions; only the ethical values of the Christian religion were excepted from this trend, at least for the time being. Confidence in the scientific method and in rational thinking replaced all other safeguards of the human mind.

Coming back now to the contributions of modern physics, one may say that the most important change brought about by its results consists in the dissolution of this rigid frame of concepts of the nineteenth century. Of course many attempts had been made before to get away from this rigid frame which seemed obviously too narrow for an understanding of the essential parts of reality. But it had not been possible to see what could be wrong with the fundamental concepts like matter, space, time and causality that had been so extremely successful in the history of science. Only experimental research itself, carried out with all the refined equipment that technical science could offer, and its mathematical interpretation, provided the basis for a critical analysis—or, one may say, enforced the critical analysis—of these concepts, and finally resulted in the dissolution of the rigid frame.

This dissolution took place in two distinct stages. The first was the discovery, through the theory of relativity, that even such fundamental concepts as space and time could be changed and in fact must be changed on account of new experience. This change did not concern the somewhat vague concepts of space and time in natural language; but it did concern their precise formulation in the scientific language of Newtonian mechanics, which had erroneously been accepted as final. The second stage was the discussion of the concept of matter enforced by the experimental results concerning the atomic structure. The idea of the reality of matter had probably been the strongest part in that rigid frame of concepts of the nineteenth century, and this idea had at least to be modified in connection with the new experience. Again the concepts so far as they belonged to the natural language remained untouched. There was no difficulty in speaking about matter or about facts or about reality when one had to describe the atomic experiments and their results. But the scientific extrapolation of these concepts into the smallest parts of matter could not be done in the simple way suggested by classical physics, though it had erroneously determined the general outlook on the problem of matter.

These new results had first of all to be considered as a serious warning against the somewhat forced application of scientific concepts in domains where they did not belong. The application of the concepts of classical physics, e.g., in chemistry, had been a mistake. Therefore, one will nowadays be less inclined to assume that the concepts of physics, even those of quantum theory, can certainly be applied everywhere in biology or other sciences. We will, on the contrary, try to keep the doors open for the entrance of new concepts even in those parts of science where the older concepts have been very useful for the understanding of the phenomena. Especially at those points where the application of the older concepts seems somewhat forced or appears not quite adequate to the problem we will try to avoid any rash conclusions.

Furthermore, one of the most important features of the development and the analysis of modern physics is the experience that the concepts of natural language, vaguely defined as they are, seem to be more stable in the expansion of knowledge than the precise terms of scientific language, derived as an idealization from only limited groups of phenomena. This is in fact not surprising since the concepts of natural language are formed by the immediate connection with reality; they represent reality. It is true that they are not very well defined and may therefore also undergo changes in the course of the centuries, just as reality itself did, but they never lose the immediate connection with reality. On the other hand, the scientific concepts are idealizations; they are derived from experience obtained by refined experimental tools, and are precisely defined through axioms and definitions. Only through these precise definitions is it possible to connect the concepts with a mathematical scheme and to derive mathematically the infinite variety of possible phenomena in this field. But through this process of idealization and precise definition the immediate connection with reality is lost. The concepts still correspond very closely to reality in that part of nature which had been the object of the research. But the correspondence may be lost in other parts containing other groups of phenomena.

Keeping in mind the intrinsic stability of the concepts of natural language in the process of scientific development, one sees that—after the experience of modern physics—our attitude toward concepts like mind or the human soul or life or God will be different from that of the nineteenth century, because these concepts belong to the natural language and have therefore immediate connection with reality. It is true that we will also realize that these concepts are not well defined in the scientific sense and that their application may lead to various contradictions, for the time being we may have to take the concepts, unanalyzed as they are; but still we know that they touch reality. It may be useful in this connection to remember that even in the most precise part of science, in mathematics, we cannot avoid using concepts that involve contradictions. For instance, it is well known that the concept of infinity leads to contradictions that have been analyzed, but it would be practically impossible to construct the main parts of mathematics without this concept.

The general trend of human thinking in the nineteenth century had been toward an increasing confidence in the scientific method and in precise rational terms, and had led to a general skepticism with regard to those concepts of natural language which do not fit into the closed frame of scientific thought—for instance, those of religion. Modern physics has in many ways increased this skepticism; but it has at the same time turned it against the overestimation of precise scientific concepts, against a too-optimistic view on progress in general, and finally against skepticism itself. The skepticism against precise scientific concepts does not mean that there should be a definite limitation for the application of rational thinking. On the contrary, one may say that the human ability to understand may be in a certain sense unlimited. But the existing scientific concepts cover always only a very limited part of reality, and the other part that has not yet been understood is infinite. Whenever we proceed from the known into the unknown we may hope to understand, but we may have to learn at the same time a new meaning of the word "understanding." We know that any understanding must be based finally upon the natural language because it is only there that we can be certain to touch reality, and hence we must be skeptical about any skepticism with regard to this natural language and its essential concepts. Therefore, we may use these concepts as they have been used at all times. In this way modern physics has perhaps opened the door to a wider outlook on the relation between the human mind and reality.

This modern science, then, penetrates in our time into other parts of the world where the cultural tradition has been entirely different from the European civilization. There the impact of this new activity in natural and technical science must make itself felt even more strongly than in Europe, since changes in the conditions of life that have taken two or three centuries in Europe will take place there within a few decades. One should expect that in many places this new activity must appear as a decline of the older culture, as a ruthless and barbarian attitude, that upsets the sensitive balance on which all human happiness rests. Such consequences cannot be avoided; they must be taken as one aspect of our time. But even there the openness of modern physics may help to some extent to reconcile the older traditions with the new trends of thought. For instance, the great scientific contribution in theoretical physics that has come from Japan since the last war may be an indication for a certain relationship between philosophical ideas in the tradition of the Far East and the philosophical substance of quantum theory. It may be easier to adapt oneself to the quantum-theoretical concept of reality when one has not gone through the naïve materialistic way of thinking that still prevailed in Europe in the first decades of this century.

Of course such remarks should not be misunderstood as an underestimation of the damage that may be done or has been done to old cultural traditions by the impact of technical progress. But since this whole development has for a long time passed far beyond any control by human forces, we have to accept it as one of the most essential features of our time and must try to connect it as much as possible with the human values that have been the aim of the older cultural and religious traditions. It may be allowed at this point to quote a story from the Hasidic religion: There was an old rabbi, a priest famous for his wisdom, to whom all people came for advice. A man visited him in despair over all the changes that went on around him, deploring all the harm done by so-called technical progress. "Isn't all this technical nuisance completely worthless," he exclaimed, "if one considers the real values of life?" "This may be so," the rabbi replied, "but if one has the right attitude one can learn from everything." "No," the visitor rejoined, "from such foolish things as railway or telephone or telegraph one can learn nothing whatsoever." But the rabbi answered, "You are wrong. From the railway you can learn that you may by being one instant late miss everything. From the telegraph you can learn that every word counts. And from the telephone you can learn that what we say here can be heard there." The visitor understood what the rabbi meant and went away.

Finally, modern science penetrates into those large areas of our present world in which new doctrines were established only a few decades ago as foundations for new and powerful societies. There modern science is confronted both with the content of the doctrines, which go back to European philosophical ideas of the nineteenth century (Hegel and Marx), and with the phenomenon of uncompromising belief. Since modern physics must play a great role in these countries because of its practical applicability, it can scarcely be avoided that the narrowness of the doctrines is felt by those who have really understood modern physics and its philosophical meaning. Therefore, at this point an interaction between science and the general trend of thought may take place. Of course the influence of science should not be overrated; but it might be that the openness of modern science could make it easier even for larger groups of people to see that the doctrines are possibly not so important for the society as had been assumed before. In this way the influence of modern science may favor an attitude of tolerance and thereby may prove valuable.

On the other hand, the phenomenon of uncompromising belief carries much more weight than some special philosophical notions of the nineteenth century. We cannot close our eyes to the fact that the great majority of the people can scarcely have any well-founded judgment concerning the correctness of certain important general ideas or doctrines. Therefore, the word "belief" can for this majority not mean "perceiving the truth of something" but can only be understood as "taking this as the basis for life." One can easily understand that this second kind of belief is much firmer, is much more fixed than the first one, that it can persist even against immediate contradicting experience and can therefore not be shaken by added scientific knowledge. The history of the past two decades has shown by many examples that this second kind of belief can sometimes be upheld to a point where it seems completely absurd, and that it then ends only with the death of the believer. Science and history can teach us that this kind of belief may become a great danger for those who share it. But such knowledge is of no avail, since one cannot see how it could be avoided, and therefore such belief has always belonged to the great forces in human history. From the scientific tradition of the nineteenth century one would of course be inclined to hope that all belief should be based on a rational analysis of every argument, on careful deliberation; and that this other kind of belief, in which some real or apparent truth is simply taken as the basis for life, should not exist. It is true that cautious deliberation based on purely rational arguments can save us from many errors and dangers, since it allows readjustment to new situations, and this may be a necessary condition for life. But remembering our experience in modern physics it is easy to see that there must always be a fundamental complementarity between deliberation and decision. In the practical decisions of life it will scarcely ever be possible to go through all the arguments in favor of or against one possible decision, and one will therefore always have to act on insufficient evidence. The decision finally takes place by pushing away all the arguments—both those that have been understood and others that might come up through further deliberation—and by cutting of all further pondering. The decision may be the result of deliberation, but it is at the same time complementary to deliberation; it excludes deliberation. Even the most important decisions in life must always contain this inevitable element of irrationality. The decision itself is necessary, since there must be something to rely upon, some principle to guide our actions. Without such a firm stand our own actions would lose all force. Therefore, it cannot be avoided that some real or apparent truth form the basis of life; and this fact should be acknowledged with regard to those groups of people whose basis is different from our own.

Coming now to a conclusion from all that has been said about modern science, one may perhaps state that modern physics is just one, but a very characteristic, part of a general historical process that tends toward a unification and a widening of our present world. This process would in itself lead to a diminution of those cultural and political tensions that create the great danger of our time. But it is accompanied by another process which acts in the opposite direction. The fact that great masses of people become conscious of this process of unification leads to an instigation of all forces in the existing cultural communities that try to ensure for their traditional values the largest possible role in the final state of unification. Thereby the tensions increase and the two competing processes are so closely linked with each other that every intensification of the unifying process—for instance, by means of new technical progress—intensifies also the struggle for influence in the final state, and thereby adds to the instability of the transient state. Modern physics plays perhaps only a small role in this dangerous process of unification. But it helps at two very decisive points to guide the development into a calmer kind of evolution. First, it shows that the use of arms in the process would be disastrous and, second, through its openness for all kinds of concepts it raises the hope that in the final state of unification many different cultural traditions may live together and may combine different human endeavors into a new kind of balance between thought and deed, between activity and meditation.

# THE BROTHERS KARAMAZOV

*Fyodor Dostoyevsky*

*The reforms of Tsar Peter the Great (1672–1725) brought modern civilization to Russia, and by the nineteenth century St. Petersburg (now Leningrad) was a leading European cultural center. The Russian nobility traveled in western Europe and spoke French to each other; their contributions to the arts and sciences rivaled those of any other nation. But the two giants of Russian literature, Fyodor Dostoyevsky (1821–1881) and Leo Tolstoy (1828–1910), launched an attack against this civilization in favor of a mystical Christianity based on compassion for the suffering of the Russian peasantry.*

*Dostoyevsky, born into an impoverished noble family, nevertheless received an excellent "western" education, and in 1849, a year of revolutions throughout Europe, he was sentenced to four years at hard labor for participating in a revolutionary socialist circle. While in Siberia with prisoners from all walks of life, he experienced a religious conversion. Upon his return he started writing novels and stories in an agitated style which achieved an extraordinary emotional impact. His greatest novels,* Crime and Punishment *(1866),* The Idiot *(1869),* The Possessed *(1872), and* The Brothers Karamazov *(1880), portray the contradictions and confusions of modern man with an astonishing depth of psychological insight. Always western rationalism, scepticism, and materialism are pitted against the faith, suffering, and redemption he had rediscovered in Christianity and found embodied in the downtrodden of the earth.*

*The following passage from* The Brothers Karamazov, *climaxed by Ivan's tale of "The Grand Inquisitor," is one of the supreme moments in world literature. It represents a conversation between two members of the Karamazov family, a middle-class family torn—as are Russia and all mankind in Dostoyevsky's view—by tragic conflict. Ivan, the oldest brother, has returned home after years of studying western ideas; he is far more than a symbol of the westernized Russian intelligentsia, however, for all the passion and uncertainty of Dostoyevsky's own tortured soul are in him. He pours out his mind to Alyosha, the youngest brother, who has been preparing to spend his life in a monastery.*

117

### Rebellion

"I must make a confession to you," Ivan began. "I never could understand how one can love one's neighbours. In my view, it is one's neighbours that one can't possibly love, but only perhaps these who live far away. I read somewhere about 'John the Merciful' (some saint) who, when a hungry and frozen stranger came to him and begged him to warm him, lay down with him in his bed and, putting his arms round him, began breathing into his mouth, which was festering and fetid from some awful disease. I'm convinced that he did so from heartache, from heartache that originated in a lie, for the sake of love arising from a sense of duty, for the sake of a penance he had imposed upon himself. To love a man, it's necessary that he should be hidden, for as soon as he shows his face, love is gone."

"The elder Zossima has talked about it more than once," observed Alyosha. "He, too, declared that a man's face often prevented many people who were inexperienced in love from loving him. But then there's a great deal of love in mankind, almost Christ-like love, as I know myself, Ivan. . . ."

"Well, I'm afraid I don't know anything about it yet and I can't understand it, and an innumerable multitude of people are with me there. You see, the question is whether that is due to men's bad qualities or whether that is their nature. In my opinion, Christ's love for men is in a way a miracle that is impossible on earth. It is true he was a god. But we are no gods. Suppose, for instance, that I am capable of profound suffering, but no one else could ever know how much I suffer, because he is someone else and not I. Moreover, a man is rarely ready to admit that another man is suffering (as if it were some honour). Why doesn't he admit it, do you think? Because, I suppose, I have a bad smell or a stupid face, or because I once trod on his foot. Besides, there is suffering and suffering: there is humiliating suffering, which degrades me; a benefactor of mine, for instance, would not object to my being hungry, but he would not often tolerate some higher kind of suffering in me, for an idea, for instance. That he would only tolerate in exceptional cases, and even then he might look at me and suddenly realize that I haven't got the kind of face which, according to some fantastic notion of his, a man suffering for some idea ought to have. So he at once deprives me of all his benefactions, and not from an evil heart, either. Beggars, especially honourable beggars, should never show themselves in the streets, but ask for charity through the newspapers. Theoretically it is still possible to love one's neighbours, and sometimes even from a distance, but at close quarters almost never. If everything had been as on the stage, in the ballet, where, if beggars come in, they wear silken rags and tattered lace and beg for alms dancing gracefully, then it would still be possible to look at them with pleasure. But even then we might admire them but not love them. But enough of this. All I wanted is to make you see my point of view. I wanted to discuss the suffering of humanity in general, but perhaps we'd better confine ourselves to the sufferings of children. This will reduce the scope of my argument by a tenth, but I think we'd better confine our argument to the children. It's all the worse for me, of course.

F. Dostoyevsky, *The Brothers Karamazov,* trans. David Magarshack (Baltimore: Penguin Books, Inc., 1958), Vol. I, 276–308.

For, to begin with, one can love children even at close quarters and even with dirty and ugly faces (though I can't help feeling that children's faces are never ugly). Secondly, I won't talk about grown-ups because, besides being disgusting and undeserving of love, they have something to compensate them for it: they have eaten the apple and know good and evil and have become 'like gods.' They go on eating it still. But little children haven't eaten anything and so far are not guilty of anything. Do you love little children, Alyosha? I know you do and you will understand why I want to talk only about them now. If they, too, suffer terribly on earth, they do so, of course, for their fathers. They are punished for their fathers who have eaten the apple, but this is an argument from another world, an argument that is incomprehensible to the human heart here on earth. No innocent must suffer for another, and such innocents, too! You may be surprised at me, Alyosha, for I too love little children terribly. And note, please, that cruel men, passionate and carnal men, Karamazovs, are sometimes very fond of children. Children, while they are children, up to seven years, for instance, are very different from grown-up people: they seem to be quite different creatures with quite different natures. I knew a murderer in prison: in the course of his career he had murdered whole families in the houses he had broken into at night for the purpose of robbery, and while about it he had also murdered several children. But when he was in prison he showed a very peculiar affection for them. He used to stand by the window of his cell for hours watching the children playing in the prison yard. He trained one little boy to come up to his window and made great friends with him. You don't know why I'm telling you this, Alyosha? I'm afraid I have a headache and I'm feeling sad."

"You speak with a strange air," Alyosha observed uneasily, "as though you were not quite yourself."

"By the way, not so long ago a Bulgarian in Moscow told me," Ivan went on, as though not bothering to listen to his brother, "of the terrible atrocities committed all over Bulgaria by the Turks and Circassians who were afraid of a general uprising of the Slav population. They burn, kill, violate women and children, nail their prisoners' ears to fences and leave them like that till next morning when they hang them, and so on—it's impossible to imagine it all. And, indeed, people sometimes speak of man's 'bestial' cruelty, but this is very unfair and insulting to the beasts: a beast can never be so cruel as a man, so ingeniously, so artistically cruel. A tiger merely gnaws and tears to pieces, that's all he knows. It would never occur to him to nail men's ears to a fence and leave them like that overnight, even if he were able to do it. These Turks, incidentally, seemed to derive a voluptuous pleasure from torturing children, cutting a child out of its mother's womb with a dagger and tossing babies up in the air and catching them on a bayonet before the eyes of their mothers. It was doing it before the eyes of their mothers that made it so enjoyable. But one incident I found particularly interesting. Imagine a baby in the arms of a trembling mother, surrounded by Turks who had just entered her house. They are having great fun: they fondle the baby, they laugh to make it laugh and they are successful: the baby laughs. At that moment the Turk points a pistol four inches from the baby's face. The boy laughs happily, stretches out his little hands to grab the pistol, when suddenly the artist pulls the trigger in the baby's face and blows his brains out. . . . Artistic, isn't it? Incidentally, I'm told the Turks are very fond of sweets."

"Why are you telling me all this, Ivan?" asked Alyosha.

"I can't help thinking that if the devil doesn't exist and, therefore, man has created him, he has created him in his own image and likeness."

"Just as he did God, you mean."

"Oh, you're marvellous at 'cracking the wind of the poor phrase,' as Polonius says in *Hamlet*," laughed Ivan. "You've caught me there. All right. I'm glad. Your God is a fine one, if man created him in his own image and likeness. You asked me just now why I was telling you all this: you see, I'm a collector of certain interesting little facts and, you know, I'm jotting down and collecting from newspapers and books, from anywhere, in fact, certain jolly little anecdotes, and I've already a good collection of them. The Turks, of course, have gone into my collection, but they are, after all, foreigners. I've also got lovely stories from home. Even better than the Turkish ones. We like corporal punishment, you know. The birch and the lash mostly. It's a national custom. With us nailed ears are unthinkable, for we are Europeans, after all. But the birch and the lash are something that is our own and cannot be taken away from us. Abroad they don't seem to have corporal punishment at all now. Whether they have reformed their habits or whether they've passed special legislation prohibiting flogging—I don't know, but they've made up for it by something else, something as purely national as ours. Indeed, it's so national that it seems to be quite impossible in our country, though I believe it is taking root here too, especially since the spread of the religious movement among our aristocracy. I have a very charming brochure, translated from the French, about the execution quite recently, only five years ago, of a murderer in Geneva. The murderer, Richard, a young fellow of three and twenty, I believe, repented and was converted to the Christian faith before his execution. This Richard fellow was an illegitimate child who at the age of six was given by his parents *as a present* to some shepherds in the Swiss mountains. The shepherds brought him up to work for them. He grew up among them like a little wild animal. The shepherds taught him nothing. On the contrary, when he was seven they sent him to take the cattle out to graze in the cold and wet, hungry and in rags. And it goes without saying that they never thought about it or felt remorse, being convinced that they had every right to treat him like that, for Richard had been given to them just as a chattel and they didn't even think it necessary to feed him. Richard himself testified how in those years, like the prodigal son in the Gospel, he was so hungry that he wished he could eat the mash given to the pigs, which were fattened for sale. But he wasn't given even that and he was beaten when he stole from the pigs. And that was how he spent all his childhood and his youth, till he grew up and, having grown strong, he himself went to steal. The savage began to earn his living as a day labourer in Geneva, and what he earned he spent on drink. He lived like a brute and finished up by killing and robbing an old man. He was caught, tried, and sentenced to death. There are no sentimentalists there, you see. In prison he was immediately surrounded by pastors and members of different Christian sects, philanthropic ladies, and so on. They taught him to read and write in prison, expounded the Gospel to him, exhorted him, tried their best to persuade him, wheedled, coaxed, and pressed him till he himself at last solemnly confessed his crime. He was converted and wrote to the court himself that he was a monster and that at last it had been vouchsafed to him by God to see the light and obtain grace. Everyone in Geneva was excited about him—the whole of philanthropic and religious Geneva. Everyone who was well-bred and belonged to the higher circles of Geneva society rushed to the prison to see him. They embraced and kissed Richard: 'You are our brother! Grace has descended upon you!' Richard himself just wept with emotion: 'Yes, grace has descended upon me! Before in my childhood and youth I was glad of pigs' food, but now grace has descended upon me, too, and I'm dying in the Lord!' 'Yes, yes, Richard, die in the Lord. You've shed blood and you must die in the Lord. Though it was not your fault that you knew not the Lord when you coveted the pigs' food and when you were beaten for stealing it (what you did was very wrong, for it is forbidden to steal), you've shed blood and you must die.' And now the last day comes. Richard, weak and feeble, does nothing but cry and repeat every minute: 'This is the happiest day of my life. I'm going to the Lord!' 'Yes,' cry the pastors, the judges, and the philanthropic ladies, 'this is the happiest day of your life, for you are going to the Lord!' They all walked and drove in carriages behind the cart on which Richard was being taken to the scaffold. At last they arrived at the scaffold: 'Die, brother,' they cried to Richard, 'die in the Lord, for His grace has descended upon you!' And so, covered with the kisses of his brothers, they dragged brother Richard on to the scaffold, placed him on the guillotine, and chopped off his head in a most brotherly fashion because grace had descended upon him too. Yes, that's characteristic. That brochure has been translated into Russian by some aristocratic Russian philanthropists of the Lutheran persuasion and sent gratis to the newspapers and other editorial offices for the enlightenment of the Russian people. The incident with Richard is so interesting because it's national. Though we may consider it absurd to cut off the head of a brother of ours because he has become our brother and because grace has descended upon him, we have, I repeat, our own national customs which are not much better. The most direct and spontaneous historic pastime we have is the infliction of pain by beating. Nekrassov has a poem about a peasant who flogs a horse about its eyes, 'its gentle eyes.' Who hasn't seen that? That is a truly Russian characteristic. He describes how a feeble nag, which has been pulling too heavy a load, sticks in the mud with its cart and cannot move. The peasant beats it, beats it savagely and, in the end, without realizing why he is doing it and intoxicated by the very act of beating, goes on showering heavy blows upon it. 'Weak as you are, pull you must! I don't care if you die so long as you go on pulling!' The nag pulls hard but without avail, and he begins lashing the poor defenceless creature across its weeping, 'gentle eyes.' Beside itself with pain, it gives one tremendous pull, pulls out the cart, and off it goes, trembling all over and gasping for breath, moving sideways, with a curious sort of skipping motion, unnaturally and shamefully—it's horrible in Nekrassov. But it's only a horse and God has given us horses to be flogged. So the Tartars taught us and left us the whip as a present. But men, too, can be flogged. And there you have an educated and well-brought-up gentleman and his wife who birch their own little daughter, a child of seven—I have a full account of it. Daddy is glad that the twigs have knots, for, as he says, 'it will sting more' and so he begins 'stinging' his own daughter. I know for a fact that there are people who get so excited that they derive a sensual pleasure from every blow, literally a sensual pleasure, which grows progressively with every subsequent blow. They beat for a minute, five minutes, ten minutes. The more it goes on the more 'stinging' do the blows become. The child screams, at last it can scream no more, it is gasping for breath. 'Daddy, Daddy, dear Daddy!' The case, by some devilishly indecent chance, is finally brought to court. Counsel is engaged. The Russian people have long called an advocate—'a hired conscience.' Counsel shouts in his client's defence: 'It's such a simple thing, an ordinary domestic incident. A father has given a hiding to his daughter and, to our shame, it's been brought to court!' Convinced by him, the jurymen retire and bring in a verdict of not guilty. The public roars with delight that the torturer has been acquitted. Oh, what a pity I wasn't there! I'd have bawled out a proposal to found a scholarship in the name of the torturer! . . . Charming pictures. But I have still better ones about children. I've collected a great deal of facts about Russian children, Alyosha. A father and mother, 'most respectable people of high social position, of good education and breeding,' hated their little five-year-old daughter. You see, I repeat again most emphatically that this love of torturing children and only children is a peculiar characteristic of a great many people. All other individuals of the human species these torturers treat benevolently and mildly like educated and humane Europeans, but they are very fond of torturing children and, in a sense, this is their way of loving children. It's just the defencelessness of these little ones that tempts the torturers, the angelic trustfulness of the child, who has nowhere to go and no one to run to for protection—it is this that inflames the evil blood of the torturer. In every man, of course, a wild beast is hidden—the wild beast of irascibility, the wild beast of sensuous intoxication from the screams of the tortured victim. The wild beast let off the chain and allowed to roam free. The wild beast of diseases contracted in vice, gout, bad liver, and so on. This poor five-year-old girl was subjected to every possible torture by those educated parents. They beat her, birched her, kicked her, without themselves knowing why, till her body was covered with bruises; at last they reached the height of refinement: they shut her up all night, in the cold and frost, in the privy and because she didn't ask to get up at night (as though a child of five, sleeping its angelic, sound sleep, could be trained at her age to ask for such a thing), they smeared her face with excrement and made her eat it, and it was her mother, her mother who made her! And that mother could sleep at night, hearing the groans of the poor child locked up in that vile place! Do you realize what it means when a little creature like that, who's quite unable to understand what is happening to her, beats her little aching chest in that vile place, in the dark and cold, with her tiny fist and weeps searing, unresentful and gentle tears to 'dear, kind God' to protect her? Can you understand all this absurd and horrible business, my friend and brother, you meek and humble novice? Can you understand why all this absurd and horrible business is so necessary and has been brought to pass? They tell me that without it man could not even have existed on earth, for he would not have known good and evil. But why must we know that confounded good and evil when it costs so much? Why, the whole world of knowledge isn't worth that child's tears to her 'dear and kind God'! I'm not talking of the sufferings of grown-up people, for they have eaten the apple and to hell with them—let them all go to hell, but these little ones, these little ones! I'm sorry I'm torturing you, Alyosha. You're not yourself. I'll stop if you like."

"Never mind, I want to suffer too," murmured Alyosha.

"One more, only one more picture, and that, too, because it's so curious, so very characteristic, but mostly because I've only just read about it in some collection of Russian antiquities, in the *Archives* or *Antiquity*. I'll have to look it up, I'm afraid I've forgotten where I read it. It happened in the darkest days of serfdom, at the beginning of this century—and long live the liberator of the people! There was at the beginning of the century a General, a very rich landowner with the highest aristocratic connexions, but one of those (even then, it is true, rather an exception) who, after retiring from the army, are almost convinced that their service to the State has given them the power of life and death over their 'subjects.' There were such people in those days. Well, so the General went to live on his estate with its two thousand serfs, imagining himself to be God knows how big a fellow and treating his poorer neighbours as though they were his hangers-on and clowns. He had hundreds of hounds in his kennels and nearly a hundred whips—all mounted and wearing uniforms. One day, a serf-boy, a little boy of eight, threw a stone in play and hurt the paw of the General's favourite hound. 'Why is my favourite dog lame?' He was told that the boy had thrown a stone at it and hurt its paw. 'Oh, so it's you, is it?' said the General, looking him up and down. 'Take him!' They took him. They took him away from his mother, and he spent the night in the lock-up. Early next morning the General, in full dress, went out hunting. He mounted his horse, surrounded by his hangers-on, his whips, and his huntsmen, all mounted. His house-serfs were all mustered to teach them a lesson, and in front of them all stood the child's mother. The boy was brought out of the lock-up. It was a bleak, cold, misty autumn day, a perfect day for hunting. The General ordered the boy to be undressed. The little boy was stripped naked. He shivered, panic-stricken and not daring to utter a sound. 'Make him run!' ordered the General. 'Run, run!' the whips shouted at him. The boy ran. 'Sick him!' bawled the General, and set the whole pack of borzoi hounds on him. They hunted the child down before the eyes of his mother, and the hounds tore him to pieces! I believe the General was afterwards deprived of the right to administer his estates. Well, what was one to do with him? Shoot him? Shoot him for the satisfaction of our moral feelings? Tell me, Alyosha!"

"Shoot him!" Alyosha said softly, raising his eyes to his brother with a pale, twisted sort of smile.

"Bravo!" yelled Ivan with something like rapture. "If you say so, then—you're a fine hermit! So that's the sort of little demon dwelling in your heart, Alyosha Karamazov!"

"What I said was absurd, but—"

"Yes, but—that's the trouble, isn't it?" cried Ivan. "Let me tell you, novice, that absurdities are only too necessary on earth. The world is founded on absurdities and perhaps without them nothing would come to pass in it. We know a thing or two!"

"What do you know?"

"I understand nothing," Ivan went on as though in delirium, "and I don't want to understand anything now. I want to stick to facts. I made up my mind long ago not to understand. For if I should want to understand something, I'd instantly alter the facts and I've made up my mind to stick to the facts. . . ."

"Why are you putting me to the test?" exclaimed Alyosha, heartbrokenly. "Will you tell me at last?"

"Of course I will tell you. That's what I was leading up to. You're dear to me. I don't want to let you go and I won't give you up to your Zossima."

Ivan was silent for a minute and his face suddenly became very sad.

"Listen to me: I took only children to make my case clearer. I don't say anything about the other human tears with which the earth is saturated from its crust to its centre—I have narrowed my subject on purpose. I am a bug and I acknowledge in all humility that I can't understand why everything has been arranged as it is. I suppose men themselves are to blame: they were given paradise, they wanted freedom and they stole the fire from heaven, knowing perfectly well that they would become unhappy, so why should we pity them? Oh, all that my pitiful earthly Euclidean mind can grasp is that suffering exists, that no one is to blame, that effect follows cause, simply and directly, that everything flows and finds its level—but then this is only Euclidean nonsense. I know that and I refuse to live by it! What do I care that no one is to blame, that effect follows cause simply and directly and that I know it—I must have retribution or I shall destroy myself. And retribution not somewhere in the infinity of space and time, but here on earth, and so that I could see it myself. I was a believer, and I want to see for myself. And if I'm dead by that time, let them resurrect me, for if it all happens without me, it will be too unfair. Surely the reason for my suffering was not that I as well as my evil deeds and sufferings may serve as manure for some future harmony for someone else. I want to see with my own eyes the lion lie down with the lamb and the murdered man rise up and embrace his murderer. I want to be there when everyone suddenly finds out what it has all been for. All religions on earth are based on his desire, and I am a believer. But then there are the children, and what am I to do with them? That is the question I cannot answer. I repeat for the hundredth time—there are lots of questions, but I've only taken the children, for in their case it is clear beyond the shadow of a doubt what I have to say. Listen: if all have to suffer so as to buy eternal harmony by their suffering, what have the children to do with it— tell me, please? It is entirely incomprehensible why they, too, should have to suffer and why they should have to buy harmony by their sufferings. Why should they, too, be used as dung for someone's future harmony? I understand solidarity in sin among men, I understand solidarity in retribution, too, but, surely, there can be no solidarity in sin with children, and if it is really true that they share their fathers' responsibility for all their fathers' crimes, then that truth is not, of course, of this world and it's incomprehensible to me. Some humorous fellow may say that it makes no difference since a child is bound to grow up and sin, but, then, he didn't grow up: he was torn to pieces by dogs at the age of eight. Oh, Alyosha, I'm not blaspheming! I understand, of course, what a cataclysm of the universe it will be when everything in heaven and on earth blends in one hymn of praise and everything that lives and has lived cries aloud: 'Thou art just, O Lord, for thy ways are revealed!' Then, indeed, the mother will embrace the torturer who had her child torn to pieces by his dogs, and all three will cry aloud: 'Thou art just, O Lord!', and then, of course, the crown of knowledge will have been attained and everything will be explained. But there's the rub: for it is that I cannot accept. And while I'm on earth, I hasten to take my own measures. For, you see, Alyosha, it may really happen that if I live to that moment, or rise again to see it, I shall perhaps myself cry aloud with the rest, as I look at the mother embracing her child's torturer: 'Thou art just, O Lord!' But I do not want to cry aloud then. While there's still time, I make haste to arm myself against it, and that is why I renounce higher harmony altogether. It is not worth one little tear of that tortured little girl who beat herself on the breast and prayed to her 'dear, kind Lord' in the stinking privy with her unexpiated tears! It is not worth it, because her tears remained unexpiated. They must be expiated, for otherwise there can be no harmony. But how, how are you to expiate them? Is it possible? Not, surely, by their being avenged? But what do I want them avenged for? What do I want a hell for torturers for? What good can hell do if they have already been tortured to death? And what sort of harmony is it, if there is a hell? I want to forgive. I want to embrace. I don't want any more suffering. And if the sufferings of children go to make up the sum of sufferings which is necessary for the purchase of truth, then I say beforehand that the entire truth is not worth such a price. And, finally, I do not want a mother to embrace the torturer who had her child torn to pieces by his dogs! She has no right to forgive him! If she likes, she can forgive him for herself, she can forgive the torturer for the immeasurable suffering he has inflicted upon her as a mother; but she has no right to forgive him for the sufferings of her tortured child. She has no right to forgive the torturer for that, even if her child were to forgive him! And if that is so, if they have no right to forgive him, what becomes of the harmony? Is there in the whole world a being who could or would have the right to forgive? I don't want harmony. I don't want it, out of the love I bear to mankind. I want to remain with my suffering unavenged. I'd rather remain with my suffering unavenged and my indignation unappeased, *even if I were wrong*. Besides, too high a price has been placed on harmony. We cannot afford to pay so much for admission. And therefore I hasten to return my ticket of admission. And indeed, if I am an honest man, I'm bound to hand it back as soon as possible. This I am doing. It is not God that I do not accept, Alyosha. I merely most respectfully return him the ticket."

"This is rebellion," Alyosha said softly, dropping his eyes.

"Rebellion? I'm sorry to hear you say that," Ivan said with feeling. "One can't go on living in a state of rebellion, and I want to live. Tell me frankly, I appeal to you— answer me: imagine that it is you yourself who are erecting the edifice of human destiny with the aim of making men happy in the end, of giving them peace and contentment at last, but that to do that it is absolutely necessary, and indeed quite inevitable, to torture to death only one tiny creature, the little girl who beat her breast with her little fist, and to found the edifice on her unavenged tears—would you consent to be the architect on those conditions? Tell me and do not lie!"

"No, I wouldn't," Alyosha said softly.

"And can you admit the idea that the people for whom you are building it would agree to accept their happiness at the price of the unjustly shed blood of a little tortured child, and having accepted it, to remain for ever happy?"

"No, I can't admit it. Ivan," Alyosha said suddenly with flashing eyes, "you said just now, is there a being in the whole world who could or had the right to forgive?

But there is such a being, and he can forgive everything, everyone and everything and *for everything,* because he gave his innocent blood for all and for everything. You've forgotten him, but it is on him that the edifice is founded, and it is to him that they will cry aloud: 'Thou art just, O Lord, for thy ways are revealed!' "

"Oh, 'the only one without sin' and his blood! No, I have not forgotten him, and indeed I could not help being surprised at you all the time for not bringing him in, for in all your arguments you usually put him forward first of all. You know, Alyosha —don't laugh, but I made up a poem about a year ago. If you can spare me another ten minutes, I'll tell you about it."

"You wrote a poem?"

"Oh, no, I didn't write it," Ivan laughed. "And I've never composed two lines of poetry in my life. But I made up this poem and I remembered it. I made it up in a moment of inspiration. You will be my first reader, I mean, listener," Ivan grinned. "Shall I tell you or not?"

"I'd be glad to hear it," said Alyosha.

"My poem is called 'The Grand Inquisitor.' It's an absurd thing, but I'd like to tell you about it."

### The Grand Inquisitor

"I'm afraid here, too, it's impossible to begin without an introduction, that is, a literary introduction—oh, dear," Ivan laughed, "what a rotten author I'd make! You see, the action of my poem takes place in the sixteenth century and in those days, as you no doubt know from your lessons at school, it was the custom in poetical works to bring heavenly powers down to earth. Not to mention Dante, in France court clerks as well as monks in monasteries performed plays in which the Madonna, the angels, the saints, Christ, and even God himself were brought on the stage. In those days it was all done very artlessly. In Victor Hugo's *Notre Dame de Paris,* an edifying play, to which the people were admitted without charge, was performed at the Paris town hall in the reign of Louis XI to celebrate the birth of the French Dauphin. It was called *Le bon jugement de la très sainte et gracieuse Vierge Marie,* and she appeared in person and pronounced her *bon jugement.* We occasionally had almost identical performances of plays, based on Old Testament stories, in Moscow before the time of Peter the Great. But in addition to plays, there were in those days a great many stories and 'poems' in which, whenever required, holy angels and all the heavenly powers took part. In our monasteries monks were also occupied with translating, copying, and even composing such poems—and even under the Tartars. There is, for instance, one such monastery poem (translated from the Greek, of course): *The Holy Virgin's Journey Through Hell,* with descriptions as bold as those of Dante's. Our Lady visits hell and is shown round 'the torments' by the archangel Michael. She sees the sinners and their sufferings. There is there, incidentally, a highly diverting category of sinners in a burning lake: those who are thrown into this lake can never swim out of it, and these 'God forgets'—an expression of extraordinary depth and force. And so the Mother of God shocked and weeping, kneels before the throne of God and begs for a free pardon for all in hell, for all she has seen there, without distinction. Her conversation with God is extraordinarily interesting. She beseeches, she refuses to go away, and when God points to the stigmata on the hands and feet of her Son and asks her: 'How am I to forgive his torturers?'—she bids all the saints, all the martyrs, all the angels and archangels to kneel with her and pray for a free pardon for all without distinction. It ends by her obtaining from God a respite from torments every year from Good Friday to Trinity Sunday, and the sinners in hell at once give thanks to the Lord and cry out to him: 'Thou art just, O Lord, in that judgement!' Well, then, my little poem would also have been of that kind had it appeared at that time. In my poem he appears, though, it is true, he says nothing, but only appears and passes on. Fifteen centuries have passed since he gave the promise to come into his kingdom, fifteen centuries since his prophet wrote: 'Behold I come quickly.' 'Of that day and hour knoweth no man, not the angels of heaven, but my Father only,' as he said himself while still on earth. But mankind awaits him with the same faith and the same yearning. Oh, with greater faith even, for fifteen centuries have passed since the pledges given to man from heaven have ceased:

> Trust what thy heart doth tell thee,
> Trust no pledges from above.

"And only the faith in what your heart tells you remains! It is true there were many miracles in those days. There were saints who worked miraculous cures; according to their 'lives,' the Holy Mother of God herself came to visit some holy men. But the devil does not slumber, and many people were already beginning to doubt the truth of those miracles. Just then there appeared in the north of Germany a dreadful new heresy. A great star, 'burning as it were a lamp' (that is, the church), 'fell upon the fountains of waters and they became wormwood.' Those heresies began impiously to deny the existence of miracles. But those who remained faithful believed all the more ardently. The tears of mankind rose up to him as before, they waited for him, they loved him, they put their hope in him, they yearned to suffer and die for him as before. . . . And for countless ages mankind prayed with fiery faith, 'Oh Lord our God, appear unto us.' They called upon him for so many ages that he, in his infinite mercy, longed to come down to those who prayed to him. He had come down and had visited before that day some saints, martyrs, and holy hermits while they were still on earth, as is written in their 'lives.' In our own country, the poet Tyutchev, who believed sincerely in the truth of his words, proclaimed that:

> In slavish habit, the Heavenly King,
> By the burden of the Cross weighted down,
> Through my native land went wandering,
> Showering blessings upon village and town.

And I can assure you that it really was so. And now the time came when he wished to appear to the people, if only for a moment—to the tormented, suffering people, to the people sunk in filthy iniquity, but who loved him like innocent children. The action of my poem takes place in Spain, in Seville, during the most terrible time of the Inquisition, when fires were lighted every day throughout the land to the glory of God and

> In the splendid autos-da-fé
> Wicked heretics were burnt.

Oh, of course, this was not the second coming when, as he promised, he would appear at the end of time in all his heavenly glory, and which would be as sudden 'as the lightning cometh out of the east, and shineth even unto the west.' No, all he wanted was to visit his children only for a moment and just where the stakes of the heretics were crackling in the flames. In his infinite mercy he once more walked among men in the semblance of man as he had ' walked among men for thirty-three years fifteen centuries ago. He came down into the hot 'streets and lanes' of the southern city just at the moment when, a day before, nearly a hundred heretics had been burnt all at once by the cardinal, the Grand Inquisitor, *ad majorem gloriam Dei* in 'a magnificent auto da fé,' in the presence of the king, the court, the knights, the cardinals, and the fairest ladies of the Court and the whole population of Seville. He appeared quietly, inconspicuously, but everyone—and that is why it is so strange—recognized him. That might have been one of the finest passages in my poem—I mean, why they recognized him. The people are drawn to him by an irresistible force, they surround him, they throng about him, they follow him. He walks among them in silence with a gentle smile of infinite compassion. The sun of love burns in his heart, rays of Light, of Enlightenment, and of Power stream from his eyes and, pouring over the people, stir their hearts with responsive love. He stretches forth his hands to them, blesses them, and a healing virtue comes from contact with him, even with his garments. An old man, blind from childhood, cries out to him from the midst of the crowd, 'O Lord, heal me so that I may see thee,' and it is as though scales fell from his eyes, and the blind man sees him. The people weep and kiss the ground upon which he walks. Children scatter flowers before him, sing and cry out to him: 'Hosannah!' 'It is he, it is he himself,' they all repeat. 'It must be he, it can be no one but he.' He stops on the steps of the Cathedral of Seville at the moment when a child's little, open white coffin is brought in with weeping into the church: in it lies a girl of seven, the only daughter of a prominent citizen. The dead child is covered with flowers. 'He will raise up your child,' people shout from the crowd to the weeping mother. The canon, who has come out to meet the coffin, looks on perplexed and knits his brows. But presently a cry of the dead child's mother is heard. She throws herself at his feet. 'If it is thou,' she cries, holding out her hands to him, 'then raise my child from the dead!' The funeral cortège halts. The coffin is lowered on to the steps at his feet. He gazes with compassion and his lips once again utter softly the words, 'Talitha cumi'—'and the damsel arose.' The little girl rises in the coffin, sits up, and looks around her with surprise in her smiling, wide-open eyes. In her hands she holds the nosegay of white roses with which she lay in her coffin. There are cries, sobs, and confusion among the people, and it is at that very moment that the Cardinal himself, the Grand Inquisitor, passes by the cathedral in the square. He is an old man of nearly ninety, tall and erect, with a shrivelled face and sunken eyes, from which, though, a light like a fiery spark still gleams. Oh, he is not wearing his splendid cardinal robes in which he appeared before the people the day before, when the enemies of the Roman faith were being burnt—no, at that moment he is wearing only his old, coarse, monk's cassock. He is followed at a distance by his sombre assistants and his slaves and his 'sacred' guard. He stops in front of the crowd and watches from a distance. He sees everything. He sees the coffin set down at *his* feet, he sees the young girl raised from the dead, and his face darkens. He knits his grey, beetling brows and his eyes flash with an ominous fire. He stretches forth his finger and commands the guards to seize *him*. And so great is his power and so accustomed are the people to obey him, so humble and submissive are they to his will, that the crowd immediately makes way for the guards and, amid the death-like hush that descends upon the square, they lay hands upon *him* and lead him away. The crowd, like one man, at once bows down to the ground before the old Inquisitor, who blesses them in silence and passes on. The guards take their Prisoner to the dark, narrow, vaulted prison in the old building of the Sacred Court and lock him in there. The day passes and the night falls, the dark, hot and 'breathless' Seville night. The air is 'heavy with the scent of laurel and lemon.' Amid the profound darkness, the iron door of the prison is suddenly opened and the old Grand Inquisitor himself slowly enters the prison with a light in his hand. He is alone and the door at once closes behind him. He stops in the doorway and gazes for a long time, for more than a minute, into his face. At last he approaches him slowly, puts the lamp on the table and says to him:

" 'Is it you? You?'

"But receiving no answer, he adds quickly: 'Do not answer, be silent. And, indeed, what can you say? I know too well what you would say. Besides, you have no right to add anything to what you have said already in the days of old. Why, then, did you come to meddle with us? For you have come to meddle with us, and you know it. But do you know what is going to happen tomorrow? I know not who you are and I don't want to know: whether it is you or only someone who looks like him, I do not know, but tomorrow I shall condemn you and burn you at the stake as the vilest of heretics, and the same people who today kissed your feet, will at the first sign from me rush to rake up the coals at your stake tomorrow. Do you know that? Yes, perhaps you do know it,' he added after a moment of deep reflection without taking his eyes off his prisoner for an instant."

"I'm afraid I don't quite understand it, Ivan," said Alyosha, who had been listening in silence all the time, with a smile. "Is it just a wild fantasy, or has the old man made some mistake, some impossible *qui pro quo?*"

"You can assume it to be the latter," laughed Ivan, "if our modern realism has spoilt you so much that you can't bear anything fantastic. If you prefer a *qui pro quo,* then let it be so. It is true," he laughed again, "the old man was ninety and he might have long ago gone mad about his fixed idea. He might, too, have been struck by the Prisoner's appearance. It might, finally, have been simply delirium. A vision the ninety-year-old man had before his death, particularly as he had been greatly affected by the burning of a hundred heretics at the auto-da-fé the day before. What difference does it make to us whether it was a *qui pro quo* or a wild fantasy? The only thing that matters is that the old man should speak out, that at last he does speak out and says aloud what he has been thinking in silence for ninety years."

"And is the Prisoner also silent? Does he look at him without uttering a word?"

"Yes," Ivan laughed again, "that's how it should be in all such cases. The old man himself tells him that *he* has no right to add anything to what had already been said before. If you like, this is the most fundamental feature of Roman Catholicism, in my opinion at any rate: 'Everything,' he tells him, 'has been handed over by you to the Pope and, therefore, everything is now in the Pope's hands, and there's no need for you to come at all now—at any rate, do not interfere for the time being.' They not only speak, but also write in that sense. The Jesuits do at any rate. I've read it myself in the works of their theologians. 'Have you the right to reveal to us even one of the mysteries of the world you have come from?' my old man asks him and he replies for him himself. 'No, you have not. So that you may not add anything to what has been said before and so as not to deprive men of the freedom which you upheld so strongly when you were on earth. All that you might reveal anew would encroach on men's freedom of faith, for it would come as a miracle, and their freedom of faith was dearer to you than anything even in those days, fifteen hundred years ago. Was it not you who said so often in those days, "I shall make you free"? But now you have seen those "free" men,' the old man adds suddenly with a pensive smile. 'Yes, this business has cost us a great deal,' he goes on, looking sternly at him, 'but we've completed it at last in your name. For fifteen centuries we've been troubled by this freedom, but now it's over and done with for good. You don't believe that it is all over? You look meekly at me and do not deign even to be indignant with me? I want you to know that now—yes, today—these men are more than ever convinced that they are absolutely free, and yet they themselves have brought their freedom to us and humbly laid it at our feet. But it was we who did it. And was that what you wanted? Was that the kind of freedom you wanted?' "

"I'm afraid I don't understand again," Alyosha interrupted. "Is he being ironical, is he laughing?"

"Not in the least. You see, he glories in the fact that he and his followers have at last vanquished freedom and have done so in order to make men happy. 'For,' he tells him, 'it is only now (he is, of course, speaking of the Inquisition), that it has become possible for the first time to think of the happiness of men. Man is born a rebel, and can rebels be happy? You were warned,' he says to him. 'There has been no lack of warnings and signs, but you did not heed the warnings. You rejected the only way by which men might be made happy, but, fortunately, in departing, you handed on the work to us. You have promised and you have confirmed it by your own word. You have given us the right to bind and unbind, and of course you can't possibly think of depriving us of that right now. Why, then, have you come to interfere with us?' "

"And what's the meaning of 'there has been no lack of warnings and signs'?" asked Alyosha.

"That, you see, is the chief thing about which the old man has to speak out.

" 'The terrible and wise spirit, the spirit of self-destruction and non-existence,' the old man went on, 'the great spirit talked with you in the wilderness and we are told in the books that he apparently "tempted" you. Is that so? And could anything truer have been said than what he revealed to you in his three questions and what you rejected, and what in the books are called "temptations"? And yet if ever there has been on earth a real, prodigious miracle, it was on that day, on the day of the three temptations. Indeed, it was in the emergence of those three questions that the miracle lay. If it were possible to imagine, for the sake of argument, that those three questions of the terrible spirit had been lost without leaving a trace in the books and that we had to rediscover, restore, and invent them afresh and that to do so we had to gather together all the wise men of the earth—rulers, high priests, scholars, philosophers, poets—and set them the task of devising and inventing three questions which would not only correspond to the magnitude of the occasion, but, in addition, express in three words, in three short human sentences, the whole future history of the world and mankind, do you think that the entire wisdom of the earth, gathered together, could have invented anything equal in depth and force to the three questions which were actually put to you at the time by the wise and mighty spirit in the wilderness? From those questions alone, from the miracle of their appearance, one can see that what one is dealing with here is not the human, transient mind, but the absolute and everlasting one. For in those three questions the whole future history of mankind is, as it were, anticipated and combined in one whole and three images are presented in which all the insoluble historical contradictions of human nature all over the world will meet. At the time it could not be so clearly seen, for the future was still unknown, but now, after fifteen centuries have gone by, we can see that everything in those three questions was so perfectly divined and foretold and has been so completely proved to be true that nothing can be added or taken from them.

" 'Decide yourself who was right—you or he who questioned you then? Call to your mind the first question; its meaning, though not in these words, was this: "You want to go into the world and you are going empty-handed, with some promise of freedom, which men in their simplicity and their innate lawlessness cannot even comprehend, which they fear and dread—for nothing has ever been more unendurable to man and to human society than freedom! And do you see the stones in this parched and barren desert? Turn them into loaves, and mankind will run after you like a flock of sheep, grateful and obedient, though for ever trembling with fear that you might withdraw your hand and they would no longer have your loaves." But you did not want to deprive man of freedom and rejected the offer, for, you thought, what sort of freedom is it if obedience is bought with loaves of bread? You replied that man does not live by bread alone, but do you know that for the sake of that earthly bread the spirit of the earth will rise up against you and will join battle with you and conquer you, and all will follow him, crying "Who is like this beast? He has given us fire from heaven!" Do you know that ages will pass and mankind will proclaim in its wisdom and science that there is no crime and, therefore, no sin, but that there are only hungry people. "Feed them first and then demand virtue of them!"—that is what they will inscribe on their banner which they will raise against you and which will destroy your temple. A new building will rise where your temple stood, the dreadful Tower of Babel will rise up again, and though, like the first one, it will not be completed, yet you might have prevented the new tower and have shortened the sufferings of men by a thousand years—for it is to us that they will come at last, after breaking their hearts for a thousand years with their tower! Then they will look for us again under the ground, hidden in the catacombs (for we shall again be persecuted and tortured), and they will find us and cry out to us, "Feed us, for those who have promised us fire from heaven have not given it to us!" And then we shall finish building their tower, for he who feeds them will complete it, and we alone shall feed them in your name, and we shall lie to them that it is in your name. Oh, without us they will never, never feed themselves. No science will give them bread so long as they remain free. But in the end they will lay their freedom at our feet and say to us, "We don't mind being your slaves so long as you feed us!" They will, at last, realize themselves that there cannot be enough freedom and bread for everybody, for they will never, never be able to let everyone have his fair share! They will also be convinced that they can never be free because they are weak, vicious, worthless, and rebellious. You promised them bread from heaven, but, I repeat again, can it compare with earthly bread in the eyes of the weak, always vicious and always ignoble race of man? And if for the sake of the bread from heaven thousands and tens of thousands will follow you, what is to become of the millions and scores of thousands of millions of creatures who will not have the strength to give up the earthly bread for the bread of heaven? Or are only the scores of thousands of the great and strong dear to you, and are the remaining millions, numerous as the sand of the sea, who are weak but who love you, to serve only as the material for the great and the strong? No, to us the weak, too, are dear. They are vicious and rebellious, but in the end they will become obedient too. They will marvel at us and they will regard us as gods because, having become their masters, we consented to endure freedom and rule over them—so dreadful will freedom become to them in the end! But we shall tell them that we do your bidding and rule in your name. We shall deceive them again, for we shall not let you come near us again. That deception will be our suffering, for we shall be forced to lie. That was the meaning of the first question in the wilderness, and that was what you rejected in the name of freedom, which you put above everything else. And yet in that question lay hidden the great secret of this world. By accepting "the loaves," you would have satisfied man's universal and everlasting craving, both as an individual and as mankind as a whole, which can be summed up in the words "whom shall I worship?" Man, so long as he remains free, has no more constant and agonizing anxiety than to find as quickly as possible someone to worship. But man seeks to worship only what is incontestable, so incontestable, indeed, that all men at once agree to worship it all together. For the chief concern of those miserable creatures is not only to find something that I or someone else can worship, but to find something that all believe in and worship, and the absolutely essential thing is that they should do so *all together*. It is this need for *universal* worship that is the chief torment of every man individually and of mankind as a whole from the beginning of time. For the sake of that universal worship they have put each other to the sword. They have set up gods and called upon each other, "Give up your gods and come and worship ours, or else death to you and to your gods!" And so it will be to the end of the world, even when the gods have vanished from the earth: they will prostrate themselves before idols just the same. You knew, you couldn't help knowing this fundamental mystery of human nature, but you rejected the only absolute banner, which was offered to you, to make all men worship you alone incontestably—the banner of earthly bread, which you rejected in the name of freedom and the bread from heaven. And look what you have done further—and all again in the name of freedom! I tell you man has no more agonizing anxiety than to find someone to whom he can hand over with all speed the gift of freedom with which the unhappy creature is born. But only he can gain possession of men's freedom who is able to set their conscience at ease. With the bread you were given an incontestable banner: give him bread and man will worship you, for there is nothing more incontestable than bread; but if at the same time someone besides yourself should gain possession of his conscience—oh, then he will even throw away your bread and follow him who has ensnared his conscience. You were right about that. For the mystery of human life is not only in living, but in knowing why one lives. Without a clear idea of what to live for man will not consent to live and will rather destroy himself than remain on the earth, though he were surrounded by loaves of bread. That is so, but what became of it? Instead of gaining possession of men's freedom, you gave them greater freedom than ever! Or did you forget that a tranquil mind and even death is dearer to man than the free choice in the knowledge of good and evil? There is nothing more alluring to man than this freedom of conscience, but there is nothing more tormenting, either. And instead of firm foundations for appeasing man's conscience once and for all, you chose everything that was exceptional, enigmatic, and vague, you chose everything that was beyond the strength of men, acting, consequently, as though you did not love them at all—you who came to give your life for them! Instead of taking possession of men's freedom you multiplied it and burdened the spiritual kingdom of man with its sufferings for ever. You wanted man's free love so that he should follow you freely, fascinated and captivated by you. Instead of the strict ancient law, man had in future to decide for himself with a free heart what is good and what is evil, having only your image before him for guidance. But did it never occur to you that he would at last reject and call in question even your image and your truth, if he were weighed down by so fearful a burden as free-dom of choice? They will at last cry aloud that the truth is not in you, for it was impossible to leave them in greater confusion and suffering than you have done by leaving them with so many cares and insoluble problems. It was you yourself, there-fore, who laid the foundation for the destruction of your kingdom and you ought not to blame anyone else for it. And yet, is that all that was offered to you? There are three forces, the only three forces that are able to conquer and hold captive for ever the conscience of these weak rebels for their own happiness—these forces are: miracle, mystery, and authority. You rejected all three and yourself set the example for doing so. When the wise and terrible spirit set you on a pinnacle of the temple and said to you: "If thou be the Son of God, cast thyself down: for it is written, He shall give his angels charge concerning thee: and in their hands they shall bear thee up, lest at any time thou dash thy foot against a stone, and thou shalt prove then how great is thy faith in thy Father." But, having heard him, you rejected his proposal and did not give way and did not cast yourself down. Oh, of course, you acted proudly and mag-nificently, like God. But men, the weak, rebellious race of men, are they gods? Oh, you understood perfectly then that in taking one step, in making a move to cast your-self down, you would at once have tempted God and have lost all your faith in him, and you would have been dashed to pieces against the earth which you came to save, and the wise spirit that tempted you would have rejoiced. But, I repeat, are there many like you? And could you really assume for a moment that men, too, could be equal to such a temptation? Is the nature of man such that he can reject a miracle and at the most fearful moments of life, the moments of his most fearful, funda-mental, and agonizing spiritual problems, stick to the free decision of the heart? Oh, you knew that your great deed would be preserved in books, that it would go down to the end of time and the extreme ends of the earth, and you hoped that, following you, man would remain with God and ask for no miracle. But you did not know that as soon as man rejected miracle he would at once reject God as well, for what man seeks is not so much God as miracles. And since man is unable to carry on without a miracle, he will create new miracles for himself, miracles of his own, and will worship the miracle of the witch-doctor and the sorcery of the wise woman, rebel, heretic and infidel though he is a hundred times over. You did not come down from the cross when they shouted to you, mocking and deriding you: "If thou be the Son of God, come down from the cross." You did not come down because, again, you did not want to enslave man by a miracle and because you hungered for a faith based on free will and not on miracles. You hungered for freely given love and not for the servile raptures of the slave before the might that has terrified him once and for all. But here, too, your judgement of men was too high, for they are slaves, though rebels by nature. Look round and judge: fifteen centuries have passed, go and have a look at them: whom have you raised up to yourself? I swear, man has been created a weaker and baser creature than you thought him to be! Can he, can he do what you did? In respecting him so greatly, you acted as though you ceased to feel any compassion for him, for you asked too much of him—you who have loved him more than yourself! Had you respected him less, you would have asked less of him, and that would have been more like love, for his burden would have been lighter. He is weak and base. What does it matter if he does rebel against our authority everywhere now and is proud of his rebellion? It is the pride of a child and of a schoolboy. They are little children rioting in class and driving out their teacher. But an end will come to the transports of the children, too. They will pay dearly for it. They will tear down the temples and drench the earth with blood. But they will realize at last, the foolish children, that although they are rebels, they are impotent rebels who are unable to keep up with their rebellion. Dissolving into foolish tears, they will admit at last that he who created them rebels must undoubtedly have meant to laugh at them. They will say so in despair, and their utterance will be a blasphemy which will make them still more unhappy, for man's nature cannot endure blasphemy and in the end will always avenge it on itself. And so, unrest, confusion, and unhappiness—this is the present lot of men after all you suffered for their freedom! Your great prophet tells in a vision and in an allegory that he saw all those who took part in the first resurrection and that there were twelve thousand of them from each tribe. But if there were so many then, they, too, were not like men, but gods. They had borne your cross, they had endured scores of years of the hungry and barren wilderness, feeding on locusts and roots— and you can indeed point with pride to those children of freedom, freely given love, and free and magnificent sacrifice in your name. But remember that there were only a few thousand of them, and they, too, gods. But what of the rest? And why are the rest, the weak ones, to blame if they were not able to endure all that the mighty ones endured? Why is the weak soul to blame for being unable to receive gifts so terrible? Surely, you did not come only to the chosen and for the chosen? But if so, there is a mystery here and we cannot understand it. And if it is a mystery, then we, too, were entitled to preach a mystery and to teach them that it is neither the free verdict of their hearts nor love that matters, by the mystery which they must obey blindly, even against their conscience. So we have done. We have corrected your great work and have based it on *miracle, mystery, and authority.* And men rejoiced that they were once more led like sheep and that the terrible gift which had brought them so much suffering had at last been lifted from their hearts. Were we right in doing and teaching this? Tell me. Did we not love mankind when we admitted so humbly its impotence and lovingly lightened its burden and allowed men's weak nature even to sin, so long as it was with our permission? Why, then, have you come to meddle with us now? And why are you looking at me silently and so penetratingly with your gentle eyes? Get angry. I do not want your love because I do not love you myself. And what have I to hide from you? Or don't I know to whom I am speaking? All I have to tell you is already known to you. I can read it in your eyes. And would I conceal our secret from you? Perhaps it is just what you want to hear from my lips. Well, then, listen. We are not with you but with *him*: that is our secret! It's a long time—eight centuries—since we left you and went over to *him*. Exactly eight centuries ago we took from him what you rejected with scorn, the last gift he offered you, after having shown you all the kingdoms of the earth: we took from him Rome and the sword of Caesar and proclaimed ourselves the rulers of the earth, the sole rulers, though to this day we have not succeeded in bringing our work to total completion. But whose fault is it? Oh, this work is only beginning, but it has begun. We shall have to wait a long time for its completion and the earth will have yet much to suffer, but we shall reach our goal and be Caesars and it is then that we shall think about the universal happiness of man. And yet even in those days you could have taken up the sword of Caesar. Why did you reject that last gift? By accepting that third counsel of the mighty spirit, you would have accomplished all that man seeks on earth, that is to say, whom to worship, to whom to entrust his conscience and how at last to unite all in a common, harmonious, and incontestable ant-hill, for the need of universal unity is the third and last torment of men. Mankind as a whole has always striven to organize itself into a world state. There have been many great nations with great histories, but the more highly developed they were, the more unhappy they were, for they were more acutely conscious of the need for the world-wide union of men. The great conquerors, the Timurs and Ghenghis-Khans, swept like a whirlwind over the earth, striving to conquer the world, but, though unconsciously, they expressed the same great need of mankind for a universal and world-wide union. By accepting the world and Caesar's purple, you would have founded the world state and given universal peace. For who is to wield dominion over men if not those who have taken possession of their consciences and in whose hands is their bread? And so we have taken the sword of Caesar and, having taken it, we of course rejected you and followed *him*. Oh, many more centuries are yet to pass of the excesses of their free mind, of their science and cannibalism, for, having begun to build their Tower of Babel without us, they will end up with cannibalism. But then the beast will come crawling up to us and will lick our feet and will bespatter them with tears of blood from its eyes. And we shall sit upon the beast and raise the cup, and on it will be written: "Mystery!" And then, and only then, will the reign of peace and happiness come to men. You pride yourself upon your chosen ones, but you have only the chosen ones, while we will bring peace to all. But that is not all: how many of those chosen ones, of those mighty ones who could have become the chosen ones, have at last grown tired of waiting for you and have carried and will go on carrying the powers of their spirit and the ardours of their hearts to another field and will end by raising their *free* banner against you? But you raised that banner yourself. With us, however, all will be happy and will no longer rise in rebellion nor exterminate one another, as they do everywhere under your freedom. Oh, we will convince them that only then will they become free when they have resigned their freedom to us and have submitted to us. And what do you think? Shall we be right or shall we be lying? They will themselves be convinced that we are right, for they will remember the horrors of slavery and confusion to which your freedom brought them. Freedom, a free mind and science will lead them into such a jungle and bring them face to face with such marvels and insoluble mysteries that some of them, the recalcitrant and the fierce, will destroy themselves, others, recalcitrant but weak, will destroy one another, and the rest, weak and unhappy, will come crawling to our feet and cry aloud: "Yes, you were right, you alone possessed his mystery, and we come back to you—save us from ourselves!" In receiving loaves from us, they will, of course, see clearly that we are taking the loaves made by their own hands in order to distribute them among themselves, without any miracle. They will see that we have not made stones into loaves, but they will, in truth, be more pleased with receiving them from our hands than with the bread itself! For they will remember only too well that before, without us, the bread they made turned to stones in their hands, but that when they came back to us, the very stones turned to bread in their hands. They will appreciate only too well what it means to submit themselves to us for ever! And until men understand this, they will be unhappy. And who, pray, was more than anyone responsible for that lack of understanding? Who divided the flock and scattered it on unknown paths? But the flock will be gathered together again and will submit once more, and this time it will be for good. Then we shall give them quiet, humble happiness, the happiness of weak creatures, such as they were created. Oh, we shall at last persuade them not to be proud, for you raised them up and by virtue of that taught them to be proud; we shall prove to them that they are weak, that they are mere pitiable children, but that the happiness of a child is the sweetest of all. They will grow timid and begin looking up to us and cling to us in fear as chicks to the hen. They will marvel at us and be terrified of us and be proud that we are so mighty and so wise as to be able to tame such a turbulent flock of thousands of millions. They will be helpless and in constant fear of our wrath, their minds will grow timid, their eyes will always be shedding tears like women and children, but at the slightest sign from us they will be just as ready to pass to mirth and laughter, to bright-eyed gladness and happy childish song. Yes, we shall force them to work, but in their leisure hours we shall make their life like a children's game, with children's songs, in chorus, and with innocent dances. Oh, we shall permit them to sin, too, for they are weak and helpless, and they will love us like children for allowing them to sin. We shall tell them that every sin can be expiated, if committed with our permission; that we allow them to sin because we love them all and as for the punishment for their sins—oh well, we shall take it upon ourselves. And we shall take it upon ourselves, and they will adore us as benefactors who have taken their sins upon ourselves before God. And they will have no secrets from us. We shall allow or forbid them to live with their wives and mistresses, to have or not have children—everything according to the measure of their obedience—and they will submit themselves to us gladly and cheerfully. The most tormenting secrets of their conscience—everything, everything they will bring to us, and we shall give them our decision for it all, and they will be glad to believe in our decision, because it will relieve them of their great anxiety and of their present terrible torments of coming to a free decision themselves. And they will all be happy, all the millions of creatures, except the hundred thousand who rule over them. For we alone, we who guard the mystery, we alone shall be unhappy. There will be thousands of millions of happy infants and one hundred thousand sufferers who have taken upon themselves the curse of knowledge of good and evil. Peacefully they will die, peacefully will they pass away in your name, and beyond the grave they will find nothing but death. But we shall keep the secret and for their own happiness will entice them with the reward of heaven and eternity. For even if there were anything at all in the next world, it would not of course be for such as they. They declare and prophesy that you will come and be victorious again, that you will come with your chosen ones, with your proud and mighty ones, but we shall declare that they have only saved themselves, while we have saved all. It is said that the whore, who sits upon the beast and holds in her hands the *mystery,* will be put to shame, that the weak will rise up again, that they will rend her purple and strip naked her "vile" body. But then I will rise and point out to you the thousands of millions of happy babes who have known no sin. And we who, for their happiness, have taken their sins upon ourselves, we shall stand before you and say, "Judge us if you can and if you dare." Know that I am not afraid of you. Know that I, too, was in the wilderness, that I, too, fed upon locusts and roots, that I, too, blessed freedom, with which you have blessed men, and that I, too, was preparing to stand among your chosen ones, among the strong and mighty, thirsting "to make myself of the number." But I woke up and refused to serve madness. I went back and joined the hosts of those who have *corrected your work.* I went away from the proud and returned to the meek for the happiness of the meek. What I say to you will come to pass and our kingdom will be established. I repeat, tomorrow you will behold the obedient flock which at a mere sign from me will rush to heap up the hot coals against the stake at which I shall burn you because you have come to meddle with us. For if anyone has ever deserved our fire, it is you. Tomorrow I shall burn you. *Dixi!*' "

Ivan stopped. He had got worked up as he talked and he spoke with enthusiasm; but when he had finished, he suddenly smiled.

Alyosha, who had listened to him in silence, tried many times towards the end to interrupt him, restraining his great agitation with an effort. But now he suddenly burst into speech, as though carried away beyond control.

"But," he cried, reddening, "this is absurd! Your poem is in praise of Jesus and not in his disparagement as—as you wanted it to be. And who will believe you about freedom? Is that the way to understand it? Is that the way it is understood by the Greek Orthodox Church? It's Rome, and not the whole of Rome, either—it's not true. They are the worst among the Catholics—the Inquisitors, the Jesuits! . . . And, besides, there could never have been such a fantastic person as your Inquisitor. What are those sins of men they take upon themselves? Who are these keepers of the mystery who have taken some sort of curse upon themselves for the happiness of men? When have they been seen? We know the Jesuits, people speak ill of them— do you really think they are the people in your poem? They are certainly not the same at all. . . . They are simply the Romish army for the future establishment of a universal government on earth, with the Emperor—the Pontiff of Rome—at its head. That is their ideal, but without any mystery or lofty sadness about it. . . . It's the most ordinary lust for power, for filthy earthly gains, enslavement—something like a future regime of serfdom with them as the land-owners—that is all they are after. Perhaps they don't even believe in God. Your suffering Inquisitor is nothing but a fantasy. . . ."

"Wait, wait," Ivan laughed, "don't be so excited! You say it's a fantasy—very well, I don't deny it. Of course it's a fantasy. But, look here, you don't really think that the Catholic movement in the last few centuries is really nothing but a lust for power for the sake of some filthy gains. . . . It isn't by any chance Father Paissy's teachings, is it?"

"No, no, on the contrary, Father Paissy once said something of the same kind as you, but," Alyosha suddenly recollected himself, "of course, it's not the same thing at all. Not the same thing at all!"

"A very valuable piece of information all the same in spite of your 'not the same thing at all.' What I'd like to ask you is why your Jesuits and Inquisitors have united only for some vile material gains? Why shouldn't there be among them a sufferer tormented by great sorrow and loving humanity? You see, let us suppose that among all those who are only out for filthy material gains there's one, just one, who is like my old Inquisitor, who had himself fed on roots in the wilderness, a man possessed, who was eager to mortify his flesh so as to become free and perfect; and yet one who had loved humanity all his life and whose eyes were suddenly opened and who saw that it was no great moral felicity to attain complete control over his will and at the same time achieve the conviction that millions of other God's creatures had been created as a mockery, that they would never be able to cope with their freedom, that no giants would ever arise from the pitiful rebels to complete the tower, that the great idealist had not in mind such boobies when he dreamt of his harmony. Realizing that, he returned and joined—the clever fellows. That could have happened, couldn't it?"

"Whom did he join? What clever fellows?" cried Alyosha, almost passionately. "They are not so clever and they have no such mysteries and secrets. Except perhaps only godlessness, that's all their secret. Your inquisitor doesn't believe in God—that's all his secret!"

"Well, suppose it is so! At last you've guessed it! And, in fact, it really is so. That really is his whole secret. But is that not suffering, particularly for a man like him who had sacrificed his whole life for a great cause in the wilderness and has not cured himself of his love of humanity? In his last remaining years he comes to the clear conviction that it is only the advice of the great and terrible spirit that could bring some sort of supportable order into the life of the feeble rebels, 'the unfinished experimental creatures created as a mockery.' And so, convinced of that, he sees that one has to follow the instructions of the wise spirit, the terrible spirit of death and destruction. He therefore accepts lies and deceptions and leads men consciously to death and destruction. Keeps deceiving them all the way, so that they should not notice where they are being led, for he is anxious that those miserable, blind creatures should at least on the way think themselves happy. And, mind you, the deception is in the name of him in whose ideal the old man believed so passionately all his life! Is not that a calamity? And even if there were only one such man at the head of the whole army of men 'craving for power for the sake of filthy gains'—would not even one such man be sufficient to make a tragedy? Moreover, one man like that, standing at the head of the movement, is enough for the emergence of a real leading idea of the entire Roman Church with all its armies and Jesuits—the highest idea of this Church. I tell you frankly it's my firm belief that there was never any scarcity of such single individuals among those who stood at the head of the movement. Who knows, there may have been many such individuals among the Roman Pontiffs, too. Who knows, perhaps this accursed old man, who loves humanity so obstinately in his own particular way, still exists even now in the form of a whole multitude of such individual old men, and not by chance, either, but by agreement, as a secret society formed long ago to guard the mystery. To guard it from the weak and unhappy, so as to make them happy. I'm sure it exists and, indeed, it must be so. I can't help feeling that something of the same kind of mystery exists also among the freemasons at the basis of their organization. That is why the Catholics hate the freemasons so much, for they regard them as their competitors who are breaking up the unity of their idea, while there should be only one flock and one shepherd. However, I feel that in defending my theory I must appear to you as an author who resents your criticism. Let's drop it."

"You're probably a freemason yourself!' Alyosha cried, unable to restrain himself. "You don't believe in God," he added, but this time in great sorrow. He imagined, besides, that his brother was looking mockingly at him. "How does your poem end?" he asked suddenly, his eyes fixed on the ground. "Or was that the end?"

"I intended to end it as follows: when the Inquisitor finished speaking, he waited for some time for the Prisoner's reply. His silence distressed him. He saw that the Prisoner had been listening intently to him all the time, looking gently into his face and evidently not wishing to say anything in reply. The old man would have liked him to say something, however bitter and terrible. But he suddenly approached the old man and kissed him gently on his bloodless, aged lips. That was all his answer. The old man gave a start. There was an imperceptible movement at the corners of his mouth; he went to the door, opened it and said to him: 'Go, and come no more —don't come at all—never, never!' And he let him out into 'the dark streets and lanes of the city.' The Prisoner went away."

"And the old man?"

"The kiss glows in his heart, but the old man sticks to his idea.". . .

## ⤷ THE MYTH OF SISYPHUS

*Albert Camus*

> *Albert Camus insisted he was not an existentialist, and indeed his ideas are distinguishable from those of Jean-Paul Sartre (b. 1905), who accepts this much abused label. They both, however, are representatives of an approach to moral and philosophical problems which originated in the writings of Sören Kierkegaard (1813–1855) and Friedrich Nietzsche (1844–1900) and which swept Europe in the wake of the two world*

*wars of the twentieth century. Naturally, it is difficult to generalize about such a widespread phenomenon, but most existentialists stress the inadequacy of traditional philosophies and religions, at least as traditionally formulated, and also of modern science, whether experimental or dialectical, to serve as guides for human life under modern conditions. They believe that all these make too many assumptions, take too much for granted; and modern man has learned, from bitter experience, not to take anything for granted. The important thing is to be absolutely* honest, *with oneself and with others, especially when face to face with the question of the meaning of existence itself. In this sense, Camus'* The Myth of Sisyphus, *written in 1940 in the midst of France's greatest crisis, is definitely an existentialist book.*

*Born in Algeria in 1913, Camus spent a restless youth there as a clerk, a salesman, a journalist, a stockbroker's agent, and the director of an amateur theatrical company. In 1940 he came to Paris to seek a careeer as a writer; two years later he was active in the Resistance movement and turned the underground newspaper* Combat *into a force for social criticism and reconstruction which continued long after the war. It was his novels, plays, and essays, however, which won him the Nobel Prize for literature in 1957. In* The Stranger *(1942),* The Plague *(1947), and a philosophical essay called* The Rebel *(1951), he finds grounds for hope in the very depths of modern man's inquietude.*

*He maintains this stubborn optimism in* The Myth of Sisyphus *also, although the selection we have chosen does not make this clear. The selection consists of the opening sections of the essay in which he discusses the notion that human life is fundamentally absurd—that is, that there is no* ultimate *reason why things are as they are—and asks whether such thoughts should logically lead to suicide. It is typical of Camus, and of contemporary European thought generally, to insist on raising disquieting questions like this one. The selection also illustrates the quality of intellectual courage and lucidity, reminiscent of Descartes or Voltaire, which makes Camus a hero to many serious thinkers throughout the western world.*

## AN ABSURD REASONING

### Absurdity and Suicide

There is but one truly serious philosophical problem, and that is suicide. Judging whether life is or is not worth living amounts to answering the fundamental question

Albert Camus, *The Myth of Sisyphus, and Other Essays,* trans. Justin O'Brien (New York: Alfred A. Knopf, Inc., 1955), pp. 3–16.

of philosophy. All the rest—whether or not the world has three dimensions, whether the mind has nine or twelve categories—comes afterwards. These are games; one must first answer. And if it is true, as Nietzsche claims, that a philosopher, to deserve our respect, must preach by example, you can appreciate the importance of that reply, for it will precede the definitive act. These are facts the heart can feel; yet they call for careful study before they become clear to the intellect.

If I ask myself how to judge that this question is more urgent than that, I reply that one judges by the actions it entails. I have never seen anyone die for the onto-logical argument. Galileo, who held a scientific truth of great importance, abjured it with the greatest ease as soon as it endangered his life. In a certain sense, he did right. That truth was not worth the stake. Whether the earth or the sun revolves around the other is a matter of profound indifference. To tell the truth, it is a futile question. On the other hand, I see many people die because they judge that life is not worth living. I see others paradoxically getting killed for the ideas or illusions that give them a reason for living (what is called a reason for living is also an excellent reason for dying). I therefore conclude that the meaning of life is the most urgent of questions. How to answer it? On all essential problems (I mean thereby those that run the risk of leading to death or those that intensify the passion of living) there are probably here two methods of thought: the method of La Palisse and the method of Don Quixote. Solely the balance between evidence and lyricism can allow us to achieve simultaneously emotion and lucidity. In a subject at once so humble and so heavy with emotion, the learned and classical dialectic must yield, one can see, to a more modest attitude of mind deriving at one and the same time from common sense and understanding.

Suicide has never been dealt with except as a social phenomenon. On the con-trary, we are concerned here, at the outset, with the relationship between individual thought and suicide. An act like this is prepared within the silence of the heart, as is a great work of art. The man himself is ignorant of it. One evening he pulls the trigger or jumps. Of an apartment-building manager who had killed himself I was told that he had lost his daughter five years before, that he had changed greatly since, and that that experience had "undermined" him. A more exact word cannot be imagined. Beginning to think is beginning to be undermined. Society has but little connection with such beginnings. The worm is in man's heart. That is where it must be sought. One must follow and understand this fatal game that leads from lucidity in the face of existence to flight from light.

There are many causes for a suicide, and generally the most obvious ones were not the most powerful. Rarely is suicide committed (yet the hypothesis is not ex-cluded) through reflection. What sets off the crisis is almost always unverifiable. Newspapers often speak of "personal sorrows" or of "incurable illness." These explanations are plausible. But one would have to know whether a friend of the desperate man had not that very day addressed him indifferently. He is the guilty one. For that is enough to precipitate all the rancors and all the boredom still in suspension.

But if it is hard to fix the precise instant, the subtle step when the mind opted for death, it is easier to deduce from the act itself the consequences it implies. In a sense, and as in melodrama, killing yourself amounts to confessing. It is confessing that life is too much for you or that you do not understand it. Let's not go too far in such analogies, however, but rather return to everyday words. It is merely confessing that that "is not worth the trouble." Living, naturally, is never easy. You continue making the gestures commanded by existence for many reasons, the first of which is habit. Dying voluntarily implies that you have recognized, even instinctively, the ridiculous character of that habit, the absence of any profound reason for living, the insane character of that daily agitation, and the uselessness of suffering.

What, then, is that incalculable feeling that deprives the mind of the sleep necessary to life? A world that can be explained even with bad reasons is a familiar world. But, on the other hand, in a universe suddenly divested of illusions and lights, man feels an alien, a stranger. His exile is without remedy since he is deprived of the memory of a lost home or the hope of a promised land. This divorce between man and his life, the actor and his setting, is properly the feeling of absurdity. All healthy men having thought of their own suicide, it can be seen, without further explanation, that there is a direct connection between this feeling and the longing for death.

The subject of this essay is precisely this relationship between the absurd and suicide, the exact degree to which suicide is a solution to the absurd. The principle can be established that for a man who does not cheat, what he believes to be true must determine his action. Belief in the absurdity of existence must then dictate his conduct. It is legitimate to wonder, clearly and without false pathos, whether a conclusion of this importance requires forsaking as rapidly as possible an incomprehensible condition. I am speaking, of course, of men inclined to be in harmony with themselves.

Stated clearly, this problem may seem both simple and insoluble. But it is wrongly assumed that simple questions involve answers that are no less simple and that evidence implies evidence. *A priori* and reversing the terms of the problem, just as one does or does not kill oneself, it seems that there are but two philosophical solutions, either yes or no. This would be too easy. But allowance must be made for those who, without concluding, continue questioning. Here I am only slightly indulging in irony: this is the majority. I notice also that those who answer "no" act as if they thought "yes." As a matter of fact, if I accept the Nietzschean criterion, they think "yes" in one way or another. On the other hand, it often happens that those who commit suicide were assured of the meaning of life. These contradictions are constant. It may even be said that they have never been so keen as on this point where, on the contrary, logic seems so desirable. It is a commonplace to compare philosophical theories and the behavior of those who profess them. But it must be said that of the thinkers who refused a meaning to life none except Kirilov who belongs to literature, Peregrinos who is born of legend, and Jules Lequier who belongs to hypothesis, admitted his logic to the point of refusing that life. Schopenhauer is often cited, as a fit subject for laughter, because he praised suicide while seated at a well-set table. This is no subject for joking. That way of not taking the tragic seriously is not so grievous, but it helps to judge a man.

In the face of such contradictions and obscurities must we conclude that there is no relationship between the opinion one has about life and the act one commits to leave it? Let us not exaggerate in this direction. In a man's attachment to life there is something stronger than all the ills in the world. The body's judgment is as good as the mind's, and the body shrinks from annihilation. We get into the habit of living before acquiring the habit of thinking. In that race which daily hastens us toward death, the body maintains its irreparable lead. In short, the essence of that contradiction lies in what I shall call the act of eluding because it is both less and more than diversion in the Pascalian sense. Eluding is the invariable game. The typical act of eluding, the fatal evasion that constitutes the third theme of this essay, is hope. Hope of another life one must "deserve" or trickery of those who live not for life itself but for some great idea that will transcend it, refine it, give it a meaning, and betray it.

Thus everything contributes to spreading confusion. Hitherto, and it has not been wasted effort, people have played on words and pretended to believe that refusing to grant a meaning to life necessarily leads to declaring that it is not worth living. In truth, there is no necessary common measure between these two judgments. One merely has to refuse to be misled by the confusions, divorces, and inconsistencies previously pointed out. One must brush everything aside and go straight to the real problem. One kills oneself because life is not worth living, that is certainly a truth —yet an unfruitful one because it is a truism. But does that insult to existence, that flat denial in which it is plunged come from the fact that it has no meaning? Does its absurdity require one to escape it through hope or suicide—this is what must be clarified, hunted down, and elucidated while brushing aside all the rest. Does the Absurd dictate death? This problem must be given priority over others, outside all methods of thought and all exercises of the disinterested mind. Shades of meaning, contradictions, the psychology that an "objective" mind can always introduce into all problems have no place in this pursuit and this passion. It calls simply for an unjust—in other words, logical—thought. That is not easy. It is always easy to be logical. It is almost impossible to be logical to the bitter end. Men who die by their own hand consequently follow to its conclusion their emotional inclination. Reflection on suicide gives me an opportunity to raise the only problem to interest me: is there a logic to the point of death? I cannot know unless I pursue, without reckless passion, in the sole light of evidence, the reasoning of which I am here suggesting the source. This is what I call an absurd reasoning. Many have begun it. I do not yet know whether or not they kept to it.

When Karl Jaspers, [a German Christian existentialist philosopher, b. 1883] revealing the impossibility of constituting the world as a unity, exclaims: "This limitation leads me to myself, where I can no longer withdraw behind an objective point of view that I am merely representing, where neither I myself nor the existence of others can any longer become an object for me," he is evoking after many others those waterless deserts where thought reaches its confines. After many others, yes indeed, but how eager they were to get out of them! At that last crossroad where thought hesitates, many men have arrived and even some of the humblest. They then abdicated what was most precious to them, their life. Others, princes of the mind, abdicated likewise, but they initiated the suicide of their thought in its purest revolt. The real effort is to stay there, rather, in so far as that is possible, and to examine closely the odd vegetation of those distant regions. Tenacity and acumen are privileged spectators of this inhuman show in which absurdity, hope, and death carry on their dialogue. The mind can then analyze the figures of that elementary yet subtle dance before illustrating them and reliving them itself.

## Absurd Walls

Like great works, deep feelings always mean more than they are conscious of saying. The regularity of an impulse or a repulsion in a soul is encountered again in habits of doing or thinking, is reproduced in consequences of which the soul itself knows nothing. Great feelings take with them their own universe, splendid or abject. They light up with their passion an exclusive world in which they recognize their climate. There is a universe of jealousy, of ambition, of selfishness, or of generosity. A universe—in other words, a metaphysic and an attitude of mind. What is true of already specialized feelings will be even more so of emotions basically as inde- terminate, simultaneously as vague and as "definite," as remote and as "present" as those furnished us by beauty or aroused by absurdity.

At any streetcorner the feeling of absurdity can strike any man in the face. As it is, in its distressing nudity, in its light without effulgence, it is elusive. But that very difficulty deserves reflection. It is probably true that a man remains forever unknown to us and that there is in him something irreducible that escapes us. But *practically* I know men and recognize them by their behavior, by the totality of their deeds, by the consequences caused in life by their presence. Likewise, all those irra- tional feelings which offer no purchase to analysis. I can define them *practically*, appreciate them *practically*, by gathering together the sum of their consequences in the domain of the intelligence, by seizing and noting all their aspects, by outlining their universe. It is certain that apparently, though I have seen the same actor a hundred times, I shall not for that reason know him any better personally. Yet if I add up the heroes he has personified and if I say that I know him a little better at the hundredth character counted off, this will be felt to contain an element of truth. For this apparent paradox is also an apologue. There is a moral to it. It teaches that a man defines himself by his make-believe as well as by his sincere impulses. There is thus a lower key of feelings, inaccessible in the heart but partially disclosed by the acts they imply and the attitudes of mind they assume. It is clear that in this way I am defining a method. But it is also evident that that method is one of analysis and not of knowledge. For methods imply metaphysics; unconsciously they disclose conclusions that they often claim not to know yet. Similarly, the last pages of a book are already contained in the first pages. Such a link is inevitable. The method defined here acknowledges the feeling that all true knowledge is impossible. Solely appear- ances can be enumerated and the climate make itself felt.

Perhaps we shall be able to overtake that elusive feeling of absurdity in the differ- ent but closely related worlds of intelligence, of the art of living, or of art itself. The climate of absurdity is in the beginning. The end is the absurd universe and that attitude of mind which lights the world with its true colors to bring out the privileged and implacable visage which that attitude has discerned in it.

\* \* \*

All great deeds and all great thoughts have a ridiculous beginning. Great works are often born on a streetcorner or in a restaurant's revolving door. So it is with absurdity. The absurd world more than others derives its nobility from that abject birth. In certain situations, replying "nothing" when asked what one is thinking about may be pretense in a man. Those who are loved are well aware of this. But if that reply is sincere, if it symbolizes that odd state of soul in which the void becomes eloquent, in which the chain of daily gestures is broken, in which the heart vainly seeks the link that will connect it again, then it is as it were the first sign of absurdity.

It happens that the stage sets collapse. Rising, streetcar, four hours in the office or the factory, meal, streetcar, four hours of work, meal, sleep, and Monday Tuesday Wednesday Thursday Friday and Saturday according to the same rhythm—this path is easily followed most of the time. But one day the "why" arises and everything begins in that weariness tinged with amazement. "Begins"—this is important. Weariness comes at the end of the acts of a mechanical life, but at the same time it inaugurates the impulse of consciousness. It awakens consciousness and provokes what follows. What follows is the gradual return into the chain or it is the definitive awakening. At the end of the awakening comes, in time, the consequence: suicide or recovery. In itself weariness has something sickening about it. Here, I must conclude that it is good. For everything begins with consciousness and nothing is worth anything except through it. There is nothing original about these remarks. But they are obvious; that is enough for a while, during a sketchy reconnaissance in the origins of the absurd. Mere "anxiety," as Heidegger [German existentialist philosopher, b. 1889] says, is at the source of everything.

Likewise and during every day of an unillustrious life, time carries us. But a moment always comes when we have to carry it. We live on the future: "tomorrow," "later on," "when you have made your way," "you will understand when you are old enough." Such irrelevancies are wonderful, for, after all, it's a matter of dying. Yet a day comes when a man notices or says that he is thirty. Thus he asserts his youth. But simultaneously he situates himself in relation to time. He takes his place in it. He admits that he stands at a certain point on a curve that he acknowledges having to travel to its end. He belongs to time, and by the horror that seizes him, he recognizes his worst enemy. Tomorrow, he was longing for tomorrow, whereas everything in him ought to reject it. That revolt of the flesh is the absurd.

A step lower and strangeness creeps in: perceiving that the world is "dense," sensing to what a degree a stone is foreign and irreducible to us, with what intensity nature or a landscape can negate us. At the heart of all beauty lies something inhuman, and these hills, the softness of the sky, the outline of these trees at this very minute lose the illusory meaning with which we had clothed them, henceforth more remote than a lost paradise. The primitive hostility of the world rises up to face us across millennia. For a second we cease to understand it because for centuries we have understood in it solely the images and designs that we had attributed to it beforehand, because henceforth we lack the power to make use of that artifice. The world evades us because it becomes itself again. That stage scenery masked by habit becomes again what it is. It withdraws at a distance from us. Just as there are days when under the familiar face of a woman, we see as a stranger her we had loved months or years ago, perhaps we shall come even to desire what suddenly leaves us so alone. But the time has not yet come. Just one thing: that denseness and that strangeness of the world is the absurd.

Men, too, secrete the inhuman. At certain moments of lucidity, the mechanical aspect of their gestures, their meaningless pantomime makes silly everything that surrounds them. A man is talking on the telephone behind a glass partition; you cannot hear him, but you see his incomprehensible dumb show: you wonder why he is alive. This discomfort in the face of man's own inhumanity, this incalculable tumble before the image of what we are, this "nausea," as a writer of today [Jean-Paul Sartre, French existentialist philosopher and man of letters, b. 1905] calls it, is also the absurd. Likewise the stranger who at certain seconds comes to meet us in a mirror, the familiar and yet alarming brother we encounter in our own photographs is also the absurd.

I come at last to death and to the attitude we have toward it. On this point everything has been said and it is only proper to avoid pathos. Yet one will never be sufficiently surprised that everyone lives as if no one "knew." This is because in reality there is no experience of death. Properly speaking, nothing has been experienced but what has been lived and made conscious. Here, it is barely possible to speak of the experience of others' deaths. It is a substitute, an illusion, and it never quite convinces us. That melancholy convention cannot be persuasive. The horror comes in reality from the mathematical aspect of the event. If time frightens us, this is because it works out the problem and the solution comes afterward. All the pretty speeches about the soul will have their contrary convincingly proved, at least for a time. From this inert body on which a slap makes no mark the soul has disappeared. This elementary and definitive aspect of the adventure constitutes the absurd feeling. Under the fatal lighting of that destiny, its uselessness becomes evident. No code of ethics and no effort are justifiable *a priori* in the face of the cruel mathematics that command our condition.

Let me repeat: all this has been said over and over. I am limiting myself here to making a rapid classification and to pointing out these obvious themes. They run through all literatures and all philosophies. Everyday conversation feeds on them. There is no question of reinventing them. But it is essential to be sure of these facts in order to be able to question oneself subsequently on the primordial question. I am interested—let me repeat again—not so much in absurd discoveries as in their consequences. If one is assured of these facts, what is one to conclude, how far is one to go to elude nothing? Is one to die voluntarily or to hope in spite of everything? Beforehand, it is necessary to take the same rapid inventory on the plane of the intelligence.

*     *     *

The mind's first step is to distinguish what is true from what is false. However, as soon as thought reflects on itself, what it first discovers is a contradiction. Useless to strive to be convincing in this case. Over the centuries no one has furnished a clearer and more elegant demonstration of the business than Aristotle: "The often ridiculed consequence of these opinions is that they destroy themselves. For by asserting that all is true we assert the truth of the contrary assertion and consequently the falsity of our own thesis (for the contrary assertion does not admit that it can be true). And if one says that all is false, that assertion is itself false. If we declare that solely the assertion opposed to ours is false or else that solely ours is not false, we are nevertheless forced to admit an infinite number of true or false judgments. For the one who expresses a true assertion proclaims simultaneously that it is true, and so on *ad infinitum*."

This vicious circle is but the first of a series in which the mind that studies itself gets lost in a giddy whirling. The very simplicity of these paradoxes makes them irreducible. Whatever may be the plays on words and the acrobatics of logic, to understand is, above all, to unify. The mind's deepest desire, even in its most elaborate operations, parallels man's unconscious feeling in the face of his universe: it is an insistence upon familiarity, an appetite for clarity. Understanding the world for a man is reducing it to the human, stamping it with his seal. The cat's universe is not the universe of the anthill. The truism "All thought is anthropomorphic" has no other meaning. Likewise, the mind that aims to understand reality can consider itself satisfied only by reducing it to terms of thought. If man realized that the universe like him can love and suffer, he would be reconciled. If thought discovered in the shimmering mirrors of phenomena eternal relations capable of summing them up and summing themselves up in a single principle, then would be seen an intellectual joy of which the myth of the blessed would be but a ridiculous imitation. That nostalgia for unity, that appetite for the absolute illustrates the essential impulse of the human drama. But the fact of that nostalgia's existence does not imply that it is to be immediately satisfied. For if, bridging the gulf that separates desire from conquest, we assert with Parmenides the reality of the One (whatever it may be), we fall into the ridiculous contradiction of a mind that asserts total unity and proves by its very assertion its own difference and the diversity it claimed to resolve. This other vicious circle is enough to stifle our hopes.

These are again truisms. I shall again repeat that they are not interesting in themselves but in the consequences that can be deduced from them. I know another truism: it tells me that man is mortal. One can nevertheless count the minds that have deduced the extreme conclusions from it. It is essential to consider as a constant point of reference in this essay the regular hiatus between what we fancy we know and what we really know, practical assent and simulated ignorance which allows us to live with ideas which, if we truly put them to the test, ought to upset our whole life. Faced with this inextricable contradiction of the mind, we shall fully grasp the divorce separating us from our own creations. So long as the mind keeps silent in the motionless world of its hopes, everything is reflected and arranged in the unity of its nostalgia. But with its first move this world cracks and tumbles: an infinite number of shimmering fragments is offered to the understanding. We must despair of ever reconstructing the familiar, calm surface which would give us peace of heart. After so many centuries of inquiries, so many abdications among thinkers, we are well aware that this is true for all our knowledge. With the exception of professional rationalists, today people despair of true knowledge. If the only significant history of human thought were to be written, it would have to be the history of its successive regrets and its impotences.

Of whom and of what indeed can I say: "I know that!" This heart within me I can feel, and I judge that it exists. This world I can touch, and I likewise judge that it exists. There ends all my knowledge, and the rest is construction. For if I try to seize this self of which I feel sure, if I try to define and to summarize it, it is nothing but water slipping through my fingers. I can sketch one by one all the aspects it is able to assume, all those likewise that have been attributed to it, this upbringing, this origin, this ardor or these silences, this nobility or this vileness. But aspects cannot be added up. This very heart which is mine will forever remain indefinable to me. Between the certainty I have of my existence and the content I try to give to that assurance, the gap will never be filled. Forever I shall be a stranger to myself. In psychology as in logic, there are truths but no truth. Socrates' "Know thyself" has as much value as the "Be virtuous" of our confessionals. They reveal a nostalgia at the same time as an ignorance. They are sterile exercises on great subjects. They are legitimate only in precisely so far as they are approximate.

And here are trees and I know their gnarled surface, water and I feel its taste. These scents of grass and stars at night, certain evenings when the heart relaxes—how shall I negate this world whose power and strength I feel? Yet all the knowledge on earth will give me nothing to assure me that this world is mine. You describe it to me and you teach me to classify it. You enumerate its laws and in my thirst for knowledge I admit that they are true. You take apart its mechanism and my hope increases. At the final stage you teach me that this wondrous and multicolored universe can be reduced to the atom and that the atom itself can be reduced to the electron. All this is good and I wait for you to continue. But you tell me of an invisible planetary system in which electrons gravitate around a nucleus. You explain this world to me with an image. I realize then that you have been reduced to poetry: I shall never know. Have I the time to become indignant? You have already changed theories. So that science that was to teach me everything ends up in a hypothesis, that lucidity founders in metaphor, that uncertainty is resolved in a work of art. What need had I of so many efforts? The soft lines of these hills and the hand of evening on this troubled heart teach me much more. I have returned to my beginning. I realize that if through science I can seize phenomena and enumerate them, I cannot, for all that, apprehend the world. Were I to trace its entire relief with my finger, I should not know any more. And you give me the choice between a description that is sure but that teaches me nothing and hypotheses that claim to teach me but that are not sure. A stranger to myself and to the world, armed solely with a thought that negates itself as soon as it asserts, what is this condition in which I can have peace only by refusing to know and to live, in which the appetite for conquest bumps into walls that defy its assaults? To will is to stir up paradoxes. Everything is ordered in such a way as to bring into being that poisoned peace produced by thoughtlessness, lack of heart, or fatal renunciations.

Hence the intelligence, too, tells me in its way that this world is absurd. Its contrary, blind reason, may well claim that all is clear; I was waiting for proof and longing for it to be right. But despite so many pretentious centuries and over the heads of so many eloquent and persuasive men, I know that is false. On this plane, at least, there is no happiness if I cannot know. That universal reason, practical or ethical, that determinism, those categories that explain everything are enough to make a decent man laugh. They have nothing to do with the mind. They negate its profound truth, which is to be enchained. In this unintelligible and limited universe, man's fate henceforth assumes its meaning. A horde of irrationals has sprung up and surrounds him until his ultimate end. In his recovered and now studied lucidity, the feeling of the absurd becomes clear and definite. I said that the world is absurd, but I was too hasty. This world in itself is not reasonable, that is all that can be said. But what is absurd is the confrontation of this irrational and the wild longing for clarity whose call echoes in the human heart. The absurd depends as much on man as on the world. For the moment it is all that links them together. It binds them one to the other as only hatred can weld two creatures together. This is all I can discern clearly in this measureless universe where my adventure takes place. Let us pause here. If I hold to be true that absurdity that determines my relationship with life, if I become thoroughly imbued with that sentiment that seizes me in face of the world's scenes, with that lucidity imposed on me by the pursuit of a science, I must sacrifice everything to these certainties and I must see them squarely to be able to maintain them. Above all, I must adapt my behavior to them and pursue them in all their consequences. I am speaking here of decency. But I want to know beforehand if thought can live in those deserts.

## ᴥᴈ HONEST TO GOD

*John A. T. Robinson*

*In the nineteenth century the German universities became great centers of scholarly research, especially in the field of history. Following Hegel (see pages 4–17), the German scholars insisted on rigorous standards of methodology and on the necessity to understand social and cultural phenomena in their historical context. When this historical-critical approach was applied to the documents of Christianity, it led to important progressive or "liberal" implications. Early Christianity was seen as a product of its times, implying that the modern Christian must reinterpret his faith in terms of the values and problems of his own time. The holocaust of the twentieth century—world wars, totalitarian regimes, revolutions, class and racial hatred—has sent theologians back to the fundamental questions: Are we really making progress? Are we perhaps suffering the effects of a sinful attempt to go it alone without divine guidance? What does Christianity have to say to modern man with his triumphant science and technology and his traumatic social and spiritual problems?*

*Three of the most interesting and influential of recent theologians are Rudolf Bultmann (b. 1884), Paul Tillich (1886–1966), and Dietrich Bonhoeffer (1906–1945). All three were products of those same German universities. Bultmann, a New Testament scholar, produced a storm of controversy in 1941 with an essay on*

*"demythologizing" the Scriptures, meaning by "mythology" not only
the doctrines of the Virgin Birth and the Second Coming, but also the
Trinity, the Incarnation, the Resurrection, and Original Sin. Tillich,
who was dismissed from his professorship in Germany as early as 1933
for opposing the Nazis, continued his brilliant career for over thirty
years at several leading American universities. He incorporated insights
from psychoanalysis, existentialism, and the arts into his theology, which
was based on the idea that "God" is simply a word for the object of
each person's "ultimate concern." There could thus be no question
about the existence of God, Tillich thought, but only various theories
about his (or its) nature. Bonhoeffer was likewise persecuted by the
Nazis but returned to take part in an unsuccessful attempt to assassinate
Hitler in 1944. He was caught and hanged by the SS in 1945. In his*
Letters and Papers from Prison, *written during those two years, Bonhoeffer
welcomed modern secular civilization as man's coming of age; he called
upon Christians to put their faith not in organized religion, which he
thought outmoded and ineffectual, but in the spirit of the suffering Christ
of the Gospels.*

*Finally, in 1963, John A. T. Robinson (b. 1919), Suffragan Bishop of
Woolwich in England, added a new dimension to the whole question in
a little book entitled* Honest to God, *indicating that such radical notions
as these had penetrated even to the higher clergy of the traditionally
staid Church of England. The following selections from Bishop Robinson's
controversial book refer to Bultmann, Tillich, and Bonhoeffer and are
characteristic of progressive Christian theology today, at least among
Protestants. To some, these ideas will seem heretical and even atheistic;
to others, they will demonstrate the continuing vitality of Christianity
even in an age of science and materialism.*

## RELUCTANT REVOLUTION

The Bible speaks of a God "up there." No doubt its picture of a three-decker universe, of "the heaven above, the earth beneath and the waters under the earth," was once taken quite literally. No doubt also its more sophisticated writers, if pressed, would have been the first to regard this as symbolic language to represent and convey spiritual realities. Yet clearly they were not pressed. Or at any rate they were not oppressed by it. Even such an educated man of the world as St. Luke can express the

John A. T. Robinson, *Honest to God* (Philadelphia: The Westminster Press, 1956), pp. 11–18, 64–75.

conviction of Christ's ascension—the conviction that he is not merely alive but reigns in the might and right of God—in the crudest terms of being "lifted up" into heaven, there to sit down at the right hand of the Most High. He feels no need to offer any apology for this language, even though he of all New Testament writers was commending Christianity to what Schleiermacher called its "cultured despisers." This is the more remarkable because, in contrast, he leaves his readers in no doubt that what we might regard as the scarcely more primitive notions of God entertained by the Athenians, that the deity lives in temples made by man and needs to be served by human hands, were utterly superseded by Christianity.

Moreover, it is the two most mature theologians of the New Testament, St. John and the later Paul, who write most uninhibitedly of this "going up" and "coming down."

> No one has ascended into heaven but he who descended from heaven, the Son of man.
> Do you take offence at this? Then what if you were to see the Son of man ascending where he was before?
> In saying, "He ascended," what does it mean but that he had also descended into the lower parts of the earth? He who descended is he who also ascended far above all the heavens, that he might fill all things.

They are able to use this language without any sense of constraint because it had not become an embarrassment to them. Everybody accepted what it meant to speak of a God up there, even though the groundlings might understand it more grossly than the gnostics. For St. Paul, no doubt, to be "caught up to the third heaven" was as much a metaphor as it is to us (though for him a considerably more precise metaphor). But he could use it to the spiritually sophisticated at Corinth with no consciousness that he must "demythologize" if he were to make it acceptable.

For the New Testament writers the idea of a God "up there" created no embarrassment—because it had not yet become a difficulty. For us too it creates little embarrassment—because, for the most part, it has ceased to be a difficulty. We are scarcely even conscious that the majority of the words for what we value most are still in terms of height, though as Edwyn Bevan observed in his Gifford lectures, "The proposition: Moral and spiritual worth is greater or less in ratio to the distance outwards from the earth's surface, would certainly seem to be, if stated nakedly like that, an odd proposition." Yet it is one that we have long ago found it unnecessary to explain away. We may indeed continue to have to tell our children that heaven is not in fact over their heads nor God literally "above the bright blue sky." Moreover, whatever we may accept with the top of our minds, most of us still retain deep down the mental image of "an old man in the sky." Nevertheless, for most of us most of the time the traditional language of a three-storeyed universe is not a serious obstacle. It does not worry us intellectually, it is not an "offence" to faith, because we have long since made a remarkable transposition, of which we are hardly aware. In fact, we do not realize how crudely spatial much of the Biblical terminology is, for we have ceased to perceive it that way. It is as though when reading a musical score what we actually saw was not the notes printed but the notes of the key into which mentally we were transposing it. There are some notes, as it were, in the Biblical score which still strike us in the old way (the Ascension story, for instance) and which we have to make a conscious effort to transpose, but in general we assimilate the language without trouble.

*For in place of a God who is literally or physically "up there" we have accepted, as part of our mental furniture, a God who is spiritually or metaphysically "out there."* There are, of course, those for whom he is almost literally "out there." They may have accepted the Copernican revolution in science, but until recently at any rate they have still been able to think of God as in some way "beyond" outer space. In fact the number of people who instinctively seem to feel that it is no longer possible to believe in God in the space-age shows how crudely physical much of this thinking about a God "out there" has been. Until the last recesses of the cosmos had been explored or were capable of being explored (by radio-telescope if not by rocketry), it was still possible to locate God mentally in some *terra incognita.* But now it seems there is no room for him, not merely in the inn, but in the entire universe: for there are no vacant places left. In reality, of course, our new view of the universe has made not the slightest difference. Indeed, the limit set to "space" by the speed of light (so that beyond a certain point—not all that much further than our present range— everything recedes over the horizon of visibility) is even more severe. And there is nothing to stop us, if we wish to, locating God "beyond" it. And there he would be quite invulnerable—in a "gap" science could never fill. But in fact the coming of the space-age has destroyed this crude projection of God—and for that we should be grateful. For if God is "beyond," he is not *literally* beyond anything.

But the idea of a God spiritually or metaphysically "out there" dies very much harder. Indeed, most people would be seriously disturbed by the thought that it should need to die at all. For it *is* their God, and they have nothing to put in its place. And for the words "they" and "their" it would be more honest to substitute "we" and "our." For it is the God of our own upbringing and conversation, the God of our fathers and of our religion, who is under attack. Every one of us lives with some mental picture of a God "out there," a God who "exists" above and beyond the world he made, a God "to" whom we pray and to whom we "go" when we die. In traditional Christian theology, the doctrine of the Trinity witnesses to the self-subsistence of this divine Being outside us and apart from us. The doctrine of creation asserts that at a moment of time this God called "the world" into existence over against himself. The Biblical record describes how he proceeds to enter into contact with those whom he has made, how he establishes a "covenant" with them, how he "sends" to them his prophets, and how in the fullness of time he "visits" them in the person of his Son, who must one day "come again" to gather the faithful to himself.

This picture of a God "out there" coming to earth like some visitor from outer space underlies every popular presentation of the Christian drama of salvation, whether from the pulpit or the presses. Indeed, it is noticeable that those who have been most successful in communicating it in our day—Dorothy Sayers, C. S. Lewis, J. B. Phillips—have hesitated least in being boldly anthropomorphic in the use of this language. They have not, of course, taken it literally, any more than the New Testament writers take literally the God "up there," but they have not apparently felt it any embarrassment to the setting forth of the Gospel. This is sufficient testimony to the fact that there is a ready-made public for whom this whole frame of reference still presents no difficulties, and their very achievement should make us hesitate to pull it down or call it in question.

Indeed, the last thing I want to do is to appear to criticize from a superior position. I should like to think that it were possible to use this mythological language of the God "out there" and make the same utterly natural and unself-conscious transposition as I have suggested we already do with the language of the God "up there." Indeed, unless we become used to doing this and are able to take this theological notation, as it were, in our stride, we shall cut ourselves off from the classics of the Christian faith, just as we should be unable to read the Bible were we to stumble at *its* way of describing God. I believe, however, that we may have to pass through a century or more of reappraisal before this becomes possible and before this language ceases to be an offence to faith for a great many people. No one wants to live in such a period, and one could heartily wish it were not necessary. But the signs are that we are reaching the point at which the whole conception of a God "out there," which has served us so well since the collapse of the three-decker universe, is itself becoming more of a hindrance than a help.

In a previous age there came a moment when the three-decker likewise proved an embarrassment, even as a piece of mental furniture. But in this case there was a considerable interval between the time when it ceased to be taken literally as a model of the universe and the time when it ceased to perform a useful function as a metaphor. An illustration of this is to be seen in the doctrine of hell. In the old scheme, hell was "down there." By Shakespeare's time no one thought of it as literally under the earth, but still in *Hamlet* it is lively and credible enough as a metaphor. But a localized hell gradually lost more and more of its purchase over the imagination, and revivalist attempts to stoke its flames did not succeeed in restoring its power. The tragedy in this instance is that no effective translation into terms of the God "out there" was found for the Devil and his angels, the pit and the lake of fire. This element therefore tended to drop out of popular Christianity altogether—much to the detriment of the depth of the Gospel.

But the point I wish to make here is that the supersession of the old scheme was a gradual one. After it had been discredited scientifically, it continued to serve theologically as an acceptable frame of reference. The image of a God "up there" survived its validity as a literal description of reality by many centuries. But today I believe we may be confronted by a double crisis. The final psychological, if not logical, blow delivered by modern science and technology to the idea that there might *literally* be a God "out there" has *coincided* with an awareness that the *mental* picture of such a God may be more of a stumbling-block than an aid to belief in the Gospel. There is a double pressure to discard this entire construction, and with it any belief in God at all.

Moreover, it is not merely a question of the speed of adjustment required. The abandonment of a God "out there" represents a much more radical break than the transition to this concept from that of a God "up there." For this earlier transposition was largely a matter of verbal notation, of a change in spatial metaphor, important as this undoubtedly was in liberating Christianity from a flat-earth cosmology. But to be asked to give up any idea of a Being "out there" at all will appear to be an outright denial of God. For, to the ordinary way of thinking, to believe in God means to be convinced of the existence of such a supreme and separate Being. "Theists" are those who believe that such a Being exists, "atheists" those who deny that he does.

But suppose such a super-Being "out there" is really only a sophisticated version of the Old Man in the sky? Suppose belief in God does not, indeed cannot, mean being persuaded of the "existence" of some entity, even a supreme entity, which might or might not be there, like life on Mars? Suppose the atheists are right—but that this is no more the end or denial of Christianity than the discrediting of the God "up there," which must in its time have seemed the contradiction of all that the Bible said? Suppose that all such atheism does is to destroy an idol, and that we can and must get on without a God "out there" at all? Have we seriously faced the possibility that to abandon such an idol may in the future be the only way of making Christianity meaningful, except to the few remaining equivalents of flat-earthers (just as to have clung earlier to the God "up there" would have made it impossible in the modern world for any but primitive peoples to believe the Gospel)? Perhaps after all the Freudians are right, that such a God—the God of traditional popular theology—*is* a projection, and perhaps we are being called to live without that projection in any form. . . .

<br>

## THE MAN FOR OTHERS

The doctrine of the Incarnation and Divinity of Christ is on any count central to the entire Christian message and crucial therefore for any reinterpretation of it. It is also the point where resistance to reinterpretation is likely to be at its maximum and where orthodoxy has its heaviest investment in traditional categories. This is true both at the level of technical theology, where any restatement must run the gauntlet of the Chalcedonian Definition and the Athanasian Creed, and at the popular level, where one will quickly be accused of destroying the Christmas story. But if it is necessary in our thinking about God to move to a position "beyond naturalism and supranaturalism," this is no less important in our thinking about Christ. Otherwise we shall be shut up, as we have been hitherto, to an increasingly sterile choice between the two.

Traditional Christology has worked with a frankly supranaturalist scheme. Popular religion has expressed this mythologically, professional theology metaphysically. For this way of thinking, the Incarnation means that God the Son came down to earth, and was born, lived and died within this world as a man. From "out there" there graciously entered into the human scene one who was not "of it" and yet who lived genuinely and completely within it. As the God-man, he united in his person the supernatural and the natural: and the problem of Christology so stated is how Jesus can be fully God and fully man, and yet genuinely one person.

The orthodox "answer" to this problem, as formulated in the Definition of Chalcedon, is within its own terms unexceptionable—except that properly speaking it is not a solution but a statement of the problem. But as a correct statement, as "a signpost against all heresies," it had—and has—an irreplaceable value. "The Christological dogma saved the Church," says Tillich, "but with very inadequate conceptual tools." To use an analogy, if one had to present the doctrine of the person of Christ as a union of oil and water, then it made the best possible attempt to do so. Or rather it made the only possible attempt, which was to insist against all efforts to "confuse the substance" that there were two distinct natures and against all temptation to break the unity that there was but one indivisible person. It is not surprising, however, that in popular Christianity the oil and water separated, and that one or the other came to the top.

In fact, popular supranaturalistic Christology has always been dominantly docetic. That is to say, Christ only appeared to be a man or looked like a man: "underneath" he was God.

John Wren-Lewis gives a vivid description of an extreme form of this in the working-class religion in which he was brought up.

> I have heard it said again and again that the ordinary person sees Jesus as a good man and no more. Modernist clergy hold it up as a reason why doctrines like that of the Virgin Birth will not appeal widely, while Anglo-Catholic clergy urge that the ordinary man must be taught to recognize Jesus as *more* than a good man, but both agree in their estimate of where the ordinary man stands, and I am sure they are quite wrong, even today. Certainly up to the Second World War, the commonest vision of Jesus was not as a human being *at all*. He was a God in human form, full of supernatural knowledge and miraculous power, very much like the Olympian gods were supposed to be when they visited the earth in disguise.

But even if such a view would be indignantly repudiated by orthodox Churchmen, and however much they would insist that Jesus was "perfect man" as well as "perfect God," still the traditional supranaturalistic way of describing the Incarnation almost inevitably suggests that Jesus was really God almighty walking about on earth, dressed up as a man. Jesus was not a man born and bred—he was God for a limited period taking part in a charade. He looked like a man, he talked like a man, he felt like a man, but underneath he was God dressed up—like Father Christmas. However guardedly it may be stated, the traditional view leaves the impression that God took a space-trip and arrived on this planet in the form of a man. Jesus was not really one of us; but through the miracle of the Virgin Birth he contrived to be born so as to appear one of us. Really he came from outside.

I am aware that this is a parody, and probably an offensive one, but I think it is perilously near the truth of what most people—and I would include myself—have been brought up to believe at Christmas time. Indeed, the very word "incarnation" (which, of course, is not a Biblical term) almost inevitably suggests it. It conjures up the idea of a divine substance being plunged in flesh and coated with it like chocolate or silver plating. And if this is a crude picture, substitute for it that of the Christmas collect, which speaks of the Son of God "taking our nature upon him," or that of Wesley's Christmas hymn, with its "veiled in flesh the Godhead see."

But my point is not to ask how far particular expressions, or the general trend of thought they present, verge on the limits of orthodoxy but to put the question whether the entire supranaturalistic frame of reference does not make anything but a Christological *tour de force* impossible. For as long as God and man are thought of as two "beings," each with distinct natures, one from "the other side" and one from "this side," then it is impossible to create out of them more than a God-man, a divine visitant from "out there" who chooses in every respect to live like the natives. The supranaturalist view of the Incarnation can never really rid itself of the idea of the prince who appears in the guise of a beggar. However genuinely destitute the beggar may be, he *is* a prince; and that in the end is what matters.

But suppose the whole notion of "a God" who "visits" the earth in the person of "his Son" is as mythical as the prince in the fairy story? Suppose there is no realm "out there" from which the "Man from heaven" arrives? Suppose the Christmas myth (the invasion of "this side" by "the other side")—as opposed to the Christmas history (the birth of the man Jesus of Nazareth)—has to go? Are we prepared for that? Or are we to cling here to this last vestige of the mythological or metaphysical world-view as the only garb in which to clothe story with power to touch the imagination? Cannot perhaps the supranaturalist scheme survive at least as part of the "magic" of Christmas?

Yes, indeed, it can survive—as myth. For myth has its perfectly legitimate, and indeed profoundly important, place. The myth is there to indicate the significance of the events, the divine depth of the history. And we shall be grievously impoverished if our ears cannot tune to the angels' song or our eyes are blind to the wise men's star. But we must be able to read the nativity story without assuming that its truth depends on there being a literal interruption of the natural by the supernatural, that Jesus can only be Emmanuel—God with us—if, as it were, he came through from another world. For, as supranaturalism becomes less and less credible, to tie the action of God to such a way of thinking is to banish it for increasing numbers into the preserve of the pagan myths and thereby to sever it from any real connection with history. As Christmas becomes a pretty story, naturalism—the attempt to explain Christ, like everything else, on humanistic presuppositions—is left in possession of the field as the only alternative with any claim to the allegiance of intelligent men.

Naturalism has on the whole been remarkably favourable to Christianity in the realm of Christology. Once the "dogma" of his deity has been put out of the way, the humanist picture of Jesus is noticeably sympathetic, especially when compared with the sharpness of its "antitheism." Indeed, the non-Christian secularist view of Jesus shades imperceptibly into the estimate of his person in Liberal Christianity. To do it justice, let us then take the naturalistic interpretation of Christ at its highest and most positive.

This has even been ready to use the epithet "divine" of Jesus—in the sense that he was the most God-like man that ever lived, that what he said and did was so beautiful and so true that he must have been a revelation, indeed, the supreme revelation, of God. According to this view, the divine is simply the human raised to the power of "*x*." As Kierkegaard put it in a devastating parody more than a hundred years ago, "If the thing is well said, the man is a genius—and if it is unusually well said, then God said it." And by this Jesus is put "on the same level as all those who have no authority, on the same level as geniuses, poets and the thinkers." He is one of them, albeit the highest of them.

Unfortunately this is clearly not what the New Testament is saying of Jesus. Nor does the naturalist interpretation of Christ side with Athanasius on what he recognized to be the crucial divide. To say that Jesus had a unique experience of God, that he displayed all the qualities of God, that he was like God or that God was like him—this can never add up to saying that he was "of one substance" with the father. And on that line Athanasius was correct in seeing that the battle must be fought, however much one may legitimately deplore the categories in which that test of orthodoxy had to be framed.

Yet the Liberals were entirely justified in the courage with which they were prepared to abandon the supranaturalistic scaffolding by which hitherto the whole structure had been supported. That house had to collapse, and they had the faith to see that Christianity need not collapse with it. Moreover, however inadequate the Liberal theology may now appear to us, it undoubtedly helped many to hold on to their faith at a time when otherwise they might have thrown it up completely. As the supranaturalistic scheme of things became incredible, a naturalistic theology was all that stood between an entire generation and abandoning the spirit and power of Jesus altogether. And the spirit and power was able in many cases to prove itself greater than the theology. Yet equally the theology has not sufficed to commend the spirit and power. Modern humanistic naturalism has found less and less need to speak of Jesus as in any sense "divine." The belief that we are at this point and in this person in touch with *God* has increasingly been left to the religious minority that can still accept the old mythology as physically or metaphysically true. This is a dangerous situation for the Christian faith, and in no way helps to answer Bonhoeffer's searching question: "How can Christ become the Lord even of those with no religion?"

But before we ask, with Bonhoeffer, "What *is* Christ, for us today?," we should stop and pose the prior question of what it is we have to reinterpret, of what in fact the New Testament is saying. For I believe that the supranaturalist, like the naturalist, estimate of Christ, whatever its intention, tends to be a distortion of the Biblical truth. I do not say it necessarily is, since the mythological-metaphysical framework can obviously provide the setting, as it has in the past, for an entirely orthodox Christology. But in practice popular preaching and teaching presents a supranaturalistic view of Christ which cannot be substantiated from the New Testament. It says simply that Jesus *was* God, in such a way that the terms "Christ" and "God" are interchangeable. But nowhere in Biblical usage is this so. The New Testament says that Jesus was the Word of God, it says that God was in Christ, it says that Jesus is the Son of God; but it does not say that Jesus was God, simply like that.

What it does say is defined as succinctly and accurately as it can be in the opening verse of St. John's Gospel. But we have to be equally careful about the translation. The Greek runs: *kai theos en ho logos.* The so-called Authorized Version has: "And the Word was God." This would indeed suggest the view that "Jesus" and "God" were identical and interchangeable. But in Greek this would most naturally be represented by "God" with the article, not *theos* but *ho theos.* But, equally, St. John is not saying that Jesus is a "divine" man, in the sense with which the ancient world was familiar or in the sense in which the Liberals spoke of him. That would be *theios.* The Greek expression steers carefully between the two. It is impossible to represent it in a single English word, but the New English Bible, I believe, gets the sense pretty exactly with its rendering, "And what God was, the Word was." In other words, if one looked at Jesus, one saw God—for "he who has seen me, has seen the Father." He was the complete expression, the Word, of God. Through him, as through no one else, God spoke and God acted: when one met him one was met—and saved and judged—by God. And it was to this conviction that the Apostles bore their witness. In this man, in his life, death and resurrection they had experienced God at work; and in the language of their day they confessed, like the centurion at the Cross, "Truly this man was the Son of God." Here was more than just a man: here was a window into God at work. For "God was in Christ reconciling the world to himself."

The essential difference comes out in the matter of Jesus' claims. We are often asked to accept Christ as divine because he claimed to be so—and the familiar argument is pressed: "A man who goes around claiming to be God must either be God—or else he is a madman or a charlatan (*aut deus aut malus homo*)." And, of course, it is not easy to read the Gospel story and to dismiss Jesus as either mad or bad. Therefore, the conclusion runs, he must be God.

But I am not happy about this argument. None of the disciples in the Gospels acknowledged Jesus because he claimed to be God, and the Apostles never went out saying, "This man claimed to be God, therefore you must believe in him." In fact, Jesus himself said in so many words, "If I claim anything for myself, do not believe me." It is, indeed, an open question whether Jesus ever claimed to be the Son of God, let alone God. He may have acknowledged it from the lips of others—but on his own he preferred "the Son of Man." In Mark 14.61 f., he is reported to reply to the question at his trial, "Are you the Christ, the Son of the Blessed?," with the simple words, "I am." But in the parallel passage in Matthew he gives an equivocal answer: "The words are yours" (as he does in all the Gospels when questioned by Pilate)—and what conceivable interest would Matthew have in watering down Jesus' claim? We cannot be sure what titles Jesus claimed, and we should be wise, like the Apostles, not to rest our faith on them. Their message was rather that "God has made him both Lord and Christ, this Jesus whom you crucified." That is to say, through the Resurrection God vindicated and set his seal upon this man as the one through whom he spoke and acted in final and decisive fashion. He vested himself utterly and completely in the man Christ Jesus; in him all his fullness dwelt. What God was, the Word was.

There is a paradox running through all the Gospels that Jesus makes no claims for himself in his own right and at the same time makes the most tremendous claims about what God is doing through him and uniquely through him. Men's response to him *is* men's response to God: men's rejection of him *is* men's rejection of God. And the fourth Gospel merely highlights this paradox (it does not, as is usually said, present quite a different picture of the claims of Jesus) when it combines the saying that "the Son can do nothing of his own accord, but only what he sees the Father doing" with the uncompromising assertion, "No one comes to the Father, but by me." Jesus never claims to be God, personally: yet he always claims to bring God, completely.

This paradox is the point from which our reinterpretation of Christology must start. As the summary of his ministry in the fourth Gospel, Jesus cries out and says, "He who believes in me, believes not in me but in him who sent me. And he who sees me sees him who sent me." Jesus, that is to say, reveals God by being utterly transparent to him, precisely as he is nothing "in himself." And Tillich makes this the criterion of the whole Christian claim that Jesus is the final revelation of God:

> The question of the final revelation is the question of a medium of revelation which overcomes its own finite conditions by sacrificing them, and itself with them. He who is the bearer of the final revelation must surrender his finitude—not only his life but also his finite power and knowledge and perfection. In doing so, he affirms that he is the bearer of final revelation (the "Son of God" in classical terms). He became completely transparent to the mystery he reveals. But, in order to be able to surrender himself completely, he must possess himself completely. And only he can possess—and therefore surrender—himself completely who is united with the ground of his being and meaning without separation and disruption. In the picture of Jesus as the Christ we have the picture of a man who possesses these qualities, a man who, therefore, can be called the medium of final revelation.

And thus it comes about that it is only on the Cross that Jesus can be the bearer of the final revelation and the embodiment of God's decisive act: it is "Christ crucified" who is "the power of God and the wisdom of God." For it is in this ultimate surrender of self, in love "to the uttermost," that Jesus is so completely united to the Ground of his being that he can say, "I and the Father are one. . . . The Father is in me and I am in the Father."

It is in Jesus, and Jesus alone, that there is nothing of self to be seen, but solely the ultimate, unconditional love of God. It is as he emptied himself utterly of himself that he became the carrier of "the name which is above every name," the revealer of the Father's glory—for that name and that glory is simply Love. The "kenotic" theory of Christology, based on this conception of self-emptying, is, I am persuaded, the only one that offers much hope of relating at all satisfactorily the divine and the human in Christ. Yet the fatal weakness of this theory as it is stated in supranaturalist terms is that it represents Christ as stripping himself precisely of those attributes of transcendence which make him the revelation of God. The underlying assumption is that it is his omnipotence, his omniscience, and all that makes him "superhuman," that must be shed in order for him to become truly man. On the contrary, it is as he empties himself not of his Godhead but of himself, of any desire to focus attention on himself, of any craving to be "on an equality with God," that he reveals God. For it is in making himself nothing, in his utter self-surrender to others in love, that he discloses and lays bare the Ground of man's being as Love.

# Part Two

# The Advent of a Mass Society, 1850–1914

## ✍§ DEMOCRACY IN AMERICA

*Alexis Clérel de Tocqueville*

*At a time when the term "sociology" had not yet been coined and long
before political science was recognized as a respectable academic discipline,
Alexis Clérel de Tocqueville (1805–1859) excelled in combining both
of these approaches in a brilliant and profound study of American society
and politics. A member of a French aristocratic family whose lineage
could be traced to the time of the Norman conquest, Tocqueville early
in life became preoccupied with the problems of the increasingly
egalitarian society he felt to be inevitable. When the revolution of 1830
made questionable his career as a judge, Tocqueville embarked for the
United States, ostensibly to study the American prison system but actually
to study the country where equality—or democracy, as he often termed
it—had progressed further than anywhere else.*

*Several years after his trip to the United States, Tocqueville published in
succession the two volumes of his* Democracy in America, *which were
immediately hailed as a masterpiece not only in France but also in England
and the United States. Tocqueville's subsequent political career—for years
he sat in the French parliament (see Vol. III, page 487) and for a brief
time was foreign minister—was largely based on his reputation as a
political analyst, a reputation that has endured remarkably well.*

*Even though for the most part* Democracy in America *focuses on the
peculiar egalitarian conditions of the United States and the institutions
growing out of them, in the selection that follows, drawn from the
conclusion of the second volume, Tocqueville gives vent to his misgivings
about the prospects of the Western world in general. While he had
expressed such misgivings even before his American trip, his stay in the
United States did little to dispel them; for him the central and tragic
issue of the times remained the problem of preserving liberty in the
midst of a growing equality, or, as he negatively put it, "what sort of
despotism democratic nations have to fear."*

I had remarked during my stay in the United States, that a democratic state of society,
similar to that of the Americans, might offer singular facilities for the establishment
of despotism; and I perceived, upon my return to Europe, how much use had already

Alexis Clérel de Tocqueville, *Democracy in America,* trans. Henry Reeve (New York:
Colonial Press, 1899), Vol. II, 330–344.

been made by most of our rulers, of the notions, the sentiments, and the wants engendered by this same social condition, for the purpose of extending the circle of their power. This led me to think that the nations of Christendom would perhaps eventually undergo some sort of oppression like that which hung over several of the nations of the ancient world. A more accurate examination of the subject, and five years of further meditations, have not diminished my apprehensions, but they have changed the object of them. No sovereign ever lived in former ages so absolute or so powerful as to undertake to administer by his own agency, and without the assistance of intermediate powers, all the parts of a great empire: none ever attempted to subject all his subjects indiscriminately to strict uniformity of regulation, and personally to tutor and direct every member of the community. The notion of such an undertaking never occurred to the human mind; and if any man had conceived it, the want of information, the imperfection of the administrative system, and above all, the natural obstacles caused by the inequality of conditions, would speedily have checked the execution of so vast a design. When the Roman emperors were at the height of their power, the different nations of the empire still preserved manners and customs of great diversity; although they were subject to the same monarch, most of the provinces were separately administered; they abounded in powerful and active municipalities; and although the whole government of the empire was centered in the hands of the emperor alone, and he always remained, upon occasions, the supreme arbiter in all matters, yet the details of social life and private occupations lay for the most part beyond his control. The emperors possessed, it is true, an immense and unchecked power, which allowed them to gratify all their whimsical tastes, and to employ for that purpose the whole strength of the State. They frequently abused that power arbitrarily to deprive their subjects of property or of life: their tyranny was extremely onerous to the few, but it did not reach the greater number; it was fixed to some few main objects, and neglected the rest; it was violent, but its range was limited.

But it would seem that if despotism were to be established amongst the democratic nations of our days, it might assume a different character; it would be more extensive and more mild; it would degrade men without tormenting them. I do not question, that in an age of instruction and equality like our own, sovereigns might more easily succeed in collecting all political power into their own hands, and might interfere more habitually and decidedly within the circle of private interests, than any sovereign of antiquity could ever do. But this same principle of equality which facilitates despotism, tempers its rigor. We have seen how the manners of society become more humane and gentle in proportion as men become more equal and alike. When no member of the community has much power or much wealth, tyranny is, as it were, without opportunities and a field of action. As all fortunes are scanty, the passions of men are naturally circumscribed—their imagination limited, their pleasures simple. This universal moderation moderates the sovereign himself, and checks within certain limits the inordinate extent of his desires.

Independently of these reasons drawn from the nature of the state of society itself, I might add many others arising from causes beyond my subject; but I shall keep within the limits I have laid down to myself. Democratic governments may become violent and even cruel at certain periods of extreme effervescence or of great danger: but these crises will be rare and brief. When I consider the petty passions of our contemporaries, the mildness of their manners, the extent of their education, the purity of their religion, the gentleness of their morality, their regular and industrious habits, and the restraint which they almost all observe in their vices no less than in their virtues, I have no fear that they will meet with tyrants in their rulers, but rather guardians. I think then that the species of oppression by which democratic nations are menaced is unlike anything which ever before existed in the world: our contemporaries will find no prototype of it in their memories. I am trying myself to choose an expression which will accurately convey the whole of the idea I have formed of it, but in vain; the old words "despotism" and "tyranny" are inappropriate: the thing itself is new; and since I cannot name it, I must attempt to define it.

I seek to trace the novel features under which despotism may appear in the world. The first thing that strikes the observation is an innumerable multitude of men all equal and alike, incessantly endeavoring to procure the petty and paltry pleasures with which they glut their lives. Each of them, living apart, is as a stranger to the fate of all the rest—his children and his private friends constitute to him the whole of mankind; as for the rest of his fellow-citizens, he is close to them, but he sees them not —he touches them, but he feels them not; he exists but in himself and for himself alone; and if his kindred still remain to him, he may be said at any rate to have lost his country. Above this race of men stands an immense and tutelary power, which takes upon itself alone to secure their gratifications, and to watch over their fate. That power is absolute, minute, regular, provident, and mild. It would be like the authority of a parent, if, like that authority, its object was to prepare men for manhood; but it seeks on the contrary to keep them in perpetual childhood: it is well content that the people should rejoice, provided they think of nothing but rejoicing. For their happiness such a government willingly labors, but it chooses to be the sole agent and the only arbiter of that happiness: it provides for their security, foresees and supplies their necessities, facilitates their pleasures, manages their principal concerns, directs their industry, regulates the descent of property, and subdivides their inheritances—what remains, but to spare them all the care of thinking and all the trouble of living? Thus it every day renders the exercise of the free agency of man less useful and less frequent; it circumscribes the will within a narrower range, and gradually robs a man of all the uses of himself. The principle of equality has prepared men for these things: it has predisposed men to endure them, and oftentimes to look on them as benefits.

After having thus successively taken each member of the community in its powerful grasp, and fashioned them at will, the supreme power then extends its arm over the whole community. It covers the surface of society with a net-work of small complicated rules, minute and uniform, through which the most original minds and the most energetic characters cannot penetrate, to rise above the crowd. The will of man is not shattered, but softened, bent, and guided: men are seldom forced by it to act, but they are constantly restrained from acting: such a power does not destroy, but it prevents existence; it does not tyrannize, but it compresses, enervates, extinguishes, and stupefies a people, till each nation is reduced to be nothing better than a flock of timid and industrious animals, of which the government is the shepherd.

I have always thought that servitude of the regular, quiet, and gentle kind which I have just described, might be combined more easily than is commonly believed with some of the outward forms of freedom; and that it might even establish itself under the wing of the sovereignty of the people. Our contemporaries are constantly excited by two conflicting passions; they want to be led, and they wish to remain free: as they cannot destroy either one or the other of these contrary propensities, they strive to satisfy them both at once. They devise a sole, tutelary, and all-powerful form of government, but elected by the people. They combine the principle of centralization and that of popular sovereignty; this gives them a respite; they console themselves for being in tutelage by the reflection that they have chosen their own guardians. Every man allows himself to be put in leading-strings, because he sees that it is not a person or a class of persons, but the people at large that holds the end of his chain. By this system the people shake off their state of dependence just long enough to select their master, and then relapse into it again. A great many persons at the present day are quite contented with this sort of compromise between administrative despotism and the sovereignty of the people; and they think they have done enough for the protection of individual freedom when they have surrendered it to the power of the nation at large. This does not satisfy me: the nature of him I am to obey signifies less to me than the fact of extorted obedience.

I do not however deny that a constitution of this kind appears to me to be infinitely preferable to one, which, after having concentrated all the powers of government, should vest them in the hands of an irresponsible person or body of persons. Of all the forms which democratic despotism could assume, the latter would assuredly be the worst. When the sovereign is elective, or narrowly watched by a legislature which is really elective and independent, the oppression which he exercises over individuals is sometimes greater, but it is always less degrading; because every man, when he is oppressed and disarmed, may still imagine, that whilst he yields obedience it is to himself he yields it, and that it is to one of his own inclinations that all the rest give way. In like manner I can understand that when the sovereign represents the nation, and is dependent upon the people, the rights and the power of which every citizen is deprived, not only serve the head of the State, but the State itself; and that private persons derive some return from the sacrifice of their independence which they have made to the public. To create a representation of the people in every centralized country is, therefore, to diminish the evil which extreme centralization may produce, but not to get rid of it. I admit that by this means room is left for the intervention of individuals in the more important affairs; but it is not the less suppressed in the smaller and more private ones. It must not be forgotten that it is especially dangerous to enslave men in the minor details of life. For my own part, I should be inclined to think freedom less necessary in great things than in little ones, if it were possible to be secure of the one without possessing the other. Subjection in minor affairs breaks out every day, and is felt by the whole community indiscriminately. It does not drive men to resistance, but it crosses them at every turn, till they are led to surrender the exercise of their will. Thus their spirit is gradually broken and their character enervated; whereas that obedience, which is exacted on a few important but rare occasions, only exhibits servitude at certain intervals, and throws the burden of it upon a small number of men. It is in vain to summon a people, which has been rendered so dependent on the central power, to choose from time to time the representatives of that power; this rare and brief exercise of their free choice, however important it may be, will not prevent them from gradually losing the faculties of thinking, feeling, and acting for themselves, and thus gradually falling below the level of humanity. I add that they will soon become incapable of exercising the great and only privilege which remains to them. The democratic nations which have introduced freedom into their political constitution, at the very time when they were augmenting the despotism of their administrative constitution, have been led into strange paradoxes. To manage those minor affairs in which good sense is all that is wanted—the people are held to be unequal to the task, but when the government of the country is at stake, the people are invested with immense powers; they are alternately made the playthings of their ruler, and his masters—more than kings, and less than men. After having exhausted all the different modes of election, without finding one to suit their purpose, they are still amazed, and still bent on seeking further; as if the evil they remark did not originate in the constitution of the country far more than in that of the electoral body. It is, indeed, difficult to conceive how men who have entirely given up the habit of self-government should succeed in making a proper choice of those by whom they are to be governed; and no one will ever believe that a liberal, wise, and energetic government can spring from the suffrages of a subservient people. A constitution, which should be republican in its head and ultra-monarchical in all its other parts, has ever appeared to me to be a short-lived monster. The vices of rulers and the ineptitude of the people would speedily bring about its ruin; and the nation, weary of its representatives and of itself, would create freer institutions, or soon return to stretch itself at the feet of a single master.

I believe that it is easier to establish an absolute and despotic government amongst a people in which the conditions of society are equal, than amongst any other; and I think that if such a government were once established amongst such a people, it would not only oppress men, but would eventually strip each of them of several of the highest qualities of humanity. Despotism therefore appears to me peculiarly to be dreaded in democratic ages. I should have loved freedom, I believe, at all times, but in the time in which we live I am ready to worship it. On the other hand, I am persuaded that all who shall attempt, in the ages upon which we are entering, to base freedom upon aristocratic privilege, will fail—that all who shall attempt to draw and to retain authority within a single class, will fail. At the present day no ruler is skilful or strong enough to found a despotism, by re-establishing permanent distinctions of rank amongst his subjects: no legislator is wise or powerful enough to preserve free institutions, if he does not take equality for his first principle and his watchword. All those of our contemporaries who would establish or secure the independence and the dignity of their fellow-men, must show themselves the friends of equality; and the only worthy means of showing themselves as such, is to be so: upon this depends the success of their holy enterprise. Thus the question is not how to reconstruct aristocratic society, but how to make liberty proceed out of that democratic state of society in which God has placed us.

These two truths appear to me simple, clear, and fertile in consequences; and they naturally lead me to consider what kind of free government can be established amongst a people in which social conditions are equal.

It results from the very constitution of democratic nations and from their necessities, that the power of government amongst them must be more uniform, more centralized, more extensive, more searching, and more efficient than in other countries. Society at large is naturally stronger and more active, individuals more subordinate and weak; the former does more, the latter less; and this is inevitably the case. It is not therefore to be expected that the range of private independence will ever be as extensive in democratic as in aristocratic countries—nor is this to be desired; for, amongst aristocratic nations, the mass is often sacrificed to the individual, and the prosperity of the greater number to the greatness of the few. It is both necessary and desirable that the government of a democratic people should be active and powerful: and our object should not be to render it weak or indolent, but solely to prevent it from abusing its aptitude and its strength.

The circumstance which most contributed to secure the independence of private persons in aristocratic ages, was, that the supreme power did not affect to take upon itself alone the government and administration of the community; those functions were necessarily partially left to the members of the aristocracy; so that as the supreme power was always divided, it never weighed with its whole weight and in the same manner on each individual. Not only did the government not perform everything by its immediate agency; but as most of the agents who discharged its duties derived their power not from the State, but from the circumstance of their birth, they were not perpetually under its control. The government could not make or unmake them in an instant, at pleasure, nor bend them in strict uniformity to its slightest caprice—this was an additional guarantee of private independence. I readily admit that recourse cannot be had to the same means at the present time: but I discover certain democratic expedients which may be substituted for them. Instead of vesting in the government alone all the administrative powers of which corporations and nobles have been deprived, a portion of them may be entrusted to secondary public bodies, temporarily composed of private citizens: thus the liberty of private persons will be more secure, and their equality will not be diminished.

The Americans, who care less for words than the French, still designate by the name of "county" the largest of their administrative districts: but the duties of the count or lord-lieutenant are in part performed by a provincial assembly. At a period of equality like our own it would be unjust and unreasonable to institute hereditary officers; but there is nothing to prevent us from substituting elective public officers to a certain extent. Election is a democratic expedient which insures the independence of the public officer in relation to the government, as much and even more than hereditary rank can insure it amongst aristocratic nations. Aristocratic countries abound in wealthy and influential persons who are competent to provide for themselves, and who cannot be easily or secretly oppressed: such persons restrain a government within general habits of moderation and reserve. I am very well aware that democratic countries contain no such persons naturally; but something analogous to them may be created by artificial means. I firmly believe that an aristocracy cannot again be founded in the world; but I think that private citizens, by combining together, may constitute bodies of great wealth, influence, and strength, corresponding to the persons of an aristocracy. By this means many of the greatest political advantages of aristocracy would be obtained without its injustice or its dangers. An association for political, commercial, or manufacturing purposes, or even for those of science and literature, is a powerful and enlightened member of the community, which cannot be disposed of at pleasure, or oppressed without remonstrance; and which, by defending its own rights against the encroachments of the government, saves the common liberties of the country.

In periods of aristocracy every man is always bound so closely to many of his fellow-citizens, that he cannot be assailed without their coming to his assistance. In ages of equality every man naturally stands alone; he has no hereditary friends whose co-operation he may demand—no class upon whose sympathy he may rely: he is easily got rid of, and he is trampled on with impunity. At the present time, an oppressed member of the community has therefore only one method of self-defence—he may appeal to the whole nation; and if the whole nation is deaf to his complaint, he may appeal to mankind: the only means he has of making this appeal is by the press. Thus the liberty of the press is infinitely more valuable amongst democratic nations than amongst all others; it is the only cure for the evils which equality may produce. Equality sets men apart and weakens them; but the press places a powerful weapon within every man's reach, which the weakest and loneliest of them all may use. Equality deprives a man of the support of his connections; but the press enables him to summon all his fellow-countrymen and all his fellow-men to his assistance. Printing has accelerated the progress of equality, and it is also one of its best correctives.

I think that men living in aristocracies may, strictly speaking, do without the liberty of the press: but such is not the case with those who live in democratic countries. To protect their personal independence I trust not to great political assemblies, to parliamentary privilege, or to the assertion of popular sovereignty. All these things may, to a certain extent, be reconciled with personal servitude—but that servitude cannot be complete if the press is free: the press is the chiefest democratic instrument of freedom.

Something analogous may be said of the judicial power. It is a part of the essence of judicial power to attend to private interests, and to fix itself with predilection on minute objects submitted to its observation; another essential quality of judicial power is never to volunteer its assistance to the oppressed, but always to be at the disposal of the humblest of those who solicit it; their complaint, however feeble they may themselves be, will force itself upon the ear of justice and claim redress, for this is inherent in the very constitution of the courts of justice. A power of this kind is therefore peculiarly adapted to the wants of freedom, at a time when the eye and finger of the government are constantly intruding into the minutest details of human actions, and when private persons are at once too weak to protect themselves, and too much isolated for them to reckon upon the assistance of their fellows. The strength of the courts of law has ever been the greatest security which can be offered to personal independence; but this is more especially the case in democratic ages: private rights and interests are in constant danger, if the judicial power does not grow more extensive and more strong to keep pace with the growing equality of conditions.

Equality awakens in men several propensities extremely dangerous to freedom, to which the attention of the legislator ought constantly to be directed. I shall only remind the reader of the most important amongst them. Men living in democratic ages do not readily comprehend the utility of forms: they feel an instinctive contempt for them—I have elsewhere shown for what reasons. Forms excite their contempt and often their hatred; as they commonly aspire to none but easy and present gratifications, they rush onwards to the object of their desires, and the slightest delay exasperates them. This same temper, carried with them into political life, renders them hostile to forms, which perpetually retard or arrest them in some of their projects. Yet this objection which the men of democracies make to forms is the very thing which renders forms so useful to freedom; for their chief merit is to serve as a barrier between the strong and the weak, the ruler and the people, to retard the one, and give the other time to look about him. Forms become more necessary in proportion as the government becomes more active and more powerful, whilst private persons are becoming more indolent and more feeble. Thus democratic nations naturally stand more in need of forms than other nations, and they naturally respect them less. This deserves most serious attention. Nothing is more pitiful than the arrogant disdain of most of our contemporaries for questions of form; for the smallest questions of form have acquired in our time an importance which they never had before: many of the greatest interests of mankind depend upon them. I think that if the statesmen of aristocratic ages could sometimes contemn forms with impunity, and frequently rise above them, the statesmen to whom the government of nations is now confined ought to treat the very least among them with respect, and not neglect them without imperious necessity. In aristocracies the observance of forms was superstitious; amongst us they ought to be kept with a deliberate and enlightened deference.

Another tendency, which is extremely natural to democratic nations and extremely dangerous, is that which leads them to despise and undervalue the rights of private persons. The attachment which men feel to a right, and the respect which they display for it, is generally proportioned to its importance, or to the length of time during which they have enjoyed it. The rights of private persons amongst democratic nations are commonly of small importance, of recent growth, and extremely precarious—the consequence is that they are often sacrificed without regret, and almost always violated without remorse. But it happens that at the same period and amongst the same nations in which men conceive a natural contempt for the rights of private persons, the rights of society at large are naturally extended and consolidated; in other words, men become less attached to private rights at the very time at which it would be most necessary to retain and to defend what little remains of them. It is therefore most especially in the present democratic ages, that the true friends of the liberty and the greatness of man ought constantly to be on the alert to prevent the power of government from lightly sacrificing the private rights of individuals to the general execution of its designs. At such times no citizen is so obscure that it is not very dangerous to allow him to be oppressed—no private rights are so unimportant that they can be surrendered with impunity to the caprices of a government. The reason is plain:—if the private right of an individual is violated at a time when the human mind is fully impressed with the importance and the sanctity of such rights, the injury done is confined to the individual whose right is infringed; but to violate such a right, at the present day, is deeply to corrupt the manners of the nation and to put the whole community in jeopardy, because the very notion of this kind of right constantly tends amongst us to be impaired and lost.

There are certain habits, certain notions, and certain vices which are peculiar to a state of revolution, and which a protracted revolution cannot fail to engender and to propagate, whatever be, in other respects, its character, its purpose, and the scene on which it takes place. When any nation has, within a short space of time, repeatedly varied its rulers, its opinions, and its laws, the men of whom it is composed eventually contract a taste for change, and grow accustomed to see all changes effected by sudden violence. Thus they naturally conceive a contempt for forms which daily prove ineffectual; and they do not support without impatience the dominion of rules which they have so often seen infringed. As the ordinary notions of equity and morality no longer suffice to explain and justify all the innovations daily begotten by a revolution, the principle of public utility is called in, the doctrine of political necessity is conjured up, and men accustom themselves to sacrifice private interests without scruple, and to trample on the rights of individuals in order more speedily to accomplish any public purpose.

These habits and notions, which I shall call revolutionary, because all revolutions produce them, occur in aristocracies just as much as amongst democratic nations; but amongst the former they are often less powerful and always less lasting, because there they meet with habits, notions, defects, and impediments, which counteract them: they consequently disappear as soon as the revolution is terminated, and the nation reverts to its former political courses. This is not always the case in democratic countries, in which it is ever to be feared that revolutionary tendencies, becoming more gentle and more regular, without entirely disappearing from society, will be gradually transformed into habits of subjection to the administrative authority of the government. I know of no countries in which revolutions are more dangerous than in democratic countries; because, independently of the accidental and transient evils which must always attend them, they may always create some evils which are permanent and unending. I believe that there are such things as justifiable resistance and legitimate rebellion: I do not therefore assert, as an absolute proposition, that the men of democratic ages ought never to make revolutions; but I think that they have especial reason to hesitate before they embark in them, and that it is far better to endure many grievances in their present condition than to have recourse to so perilous a remedy.

I shall conclude by one general idea, which comprises not only all the particular ideas which have been expressed in the present chapter, but also most of those which it is the object of this book to treat of. In the ages of aristocracy which preceded our own, there were private persons of great power, and a social authority of extreme weakness. The outline of society itself was not easily discernible, and constantly confounded with the different powers by which the community was ruled. The principal efforts of the men of those times were required to strengthen, aggrandize, and secure the supreme power; and on the other hand, to circumscribe individual independence within narrower limits, and to subject private interests to the interests of the public. Other perils and other cares await the men of our age. Amongst the greater part of modern nations, the government, whatever may be its origin, its constitution, or its name, has become almost omnipotent, and private persons are falling, more and more, into the lowest stage of weakness and dependence. In olden society everything was different; unity and uniformity were nowhere to be met with. In modern society everything threatens to become so much alike, that the peculiar characteristics of each individual will soon be entirely lost in the general aspect of the world. Our forefathers were ever prone to make an improper use of the notion, that private rights ought to be respected; and we are naturally prone on the other hand to exaggerate the idea that the interest of a private individual ought always to bend to the interest of the many. The political world is metamorphosed: new remedies must henceforth be sought for new disorders. To lay down extensive, but distinct and settled limits, to the action of the government; to confer certain rights on private persons, and to secure to them the undisputed enjoyment of those rights; to enable individual man to maintain whatever independence, strength, and original power he still possesses; to raise him by the side of society at large, and uphold him in that position—these appear to me the main objects of legislators in the ages upon which we are now entering. It would seem as if the rulers of our time sought only to use men in order to make things great; I wish that they would try a little more to make great men; that they would set less value on the work, and more upon the workman; that they would never forget that a nation cannot long remain strong when every man belonging to it is individually weak, and that no form or combination of social polity has yet been devised, to make an energetic people out of a community of pusillanimous and enfeebled citizens.

I trace amongst our contemporaries two contrary notions which are equally injurious. One set of men can perceive nothing in the principle of equality but the anarchical tendencies which it engenders: they dread their own free agency—they fear themselves. Other thinkers, less numerous but more enlightened, take a different view: besides that track which starts from the principle of equality to terminate in anarchy, they have at last discovered the road which seems to lead men to inevitable servitude. They shape their souls beforehand to this necessary condition; and, despairing of remaining free, they already do obeisance in their hearts to the master who is soon to appear. The former abandon freedom, because they think it dangerous; the latter, because they hold it to be impossible. If I had entertained the latter conviction, I should not have written this book, but I should have confined myself to deploring in secret the destiny of mankind. I have sought to point out the dangers to which the principle of equality exposes the independence of man, because I firmly believe that these dangers are the most formidable, as well as the least foreseen, of all those which futurity holds in store: but I do not think that they are insurmountable. The men who live in the democratic ages upon which we are entering have naturally a taste for independence: they are naturally impatient of regulation, and they are wearied by the permanence even of the condition they themselves prefer. They are fond of power; but they are prone to despise and hate those who wield it, and they easily elude its grasp by their own mobility and insignificance. These propensities will always manifest themselves, because they originate in the groundwork of society, which will undergo no change: for a long time they will prevent the establishment of any despotism, and they will furnish fresh weapons to each succeeding generation which shall struggle in favor of the liberty of mankind. Let us then look forward to the future with that salutary fear which makes men keep watch and ward for freedom, not with that faint and idle terror which depresses and enervates the heart.

# ✂ ON LIBERTY

### John Stuart Mill

*While most European intellectuals were being successfully wooed by the soul-searching, semimystical intangibles of romanticism, John Stuart Mill (1806–1873) adhered to common-sense empirical analysis for his conclusions. Mill's philosopher father, James Mill, a rigid advocate of Bentham's utilitarianism, gave him a rigorous daily dosage of mathematics, Greek, and logic. Mill dutifully followed his father's standard until the latter's death in 1836 freed him of filial responsibility. Mill then felt able to criticize the tenets of utilitarianism (though remaining in the movement) and to embark on a bold and broad philosophical career embracing economics, psychology, logic, mathematics, and politics. A drab but undemanding clerkship in the East India Company provided an income, leaving him time to organize political associations and produce a steady stream of pungent periodical essays, as well as larger and more significant works. Only once did he step down from the role of constructive critic: he ran for Parliament and in the House of Commons (1865–1868) gained a reputation for being too high-minded and abstruse for the practical compromise necessary in politics.*

*Mill's* On Liberty *(1859), like his* Considerations on Representative Government *(1861), liberated democracy from a centuries-old dependence on philosophical abstraction by illustrating how liberty could be applied to specific situations, both political and social. He espoused total freedom of thought and action, assuming that in the market place of human affairs false ideas would be discarded and true ideas tested and approved. Mill knew the limits of the democratic process and advised the creation of a permanent corps of well-trained civil servants both to add intelligent administrative continuity and to provide well-informed advice to current heads of state. Yet he remained faithful to the democratic principle that local and central control should always be in the hands of the people in constant rotation among the largest possible number, in order to prevent the emergence of professional officeholders.*

## CHAPTER I. INTRODUCTORY

The subject of this Essay is not the so-called Liberty of the Will, so unfortunately opposed to the misnamed doctrine of Philosophical Necessity; but Civil, or Social

John Stuart Mill, *On Liberty* (Boston: Ticknor and Fields, 1863), pp. 7–15, 22–29, 33–36, 40–42, 44–47, 68–69, 88–93, 107–109, 112–114, 117–119, 144–146, 154–155, 156, 158–160, 219–223.

Liberty: the nature and limits of the power which can be legitimately exercised by society over the individual. A question seldom stated, and hardly ever discussed, in general terms, but which profoundly influences the practical controversies of the age by its latent presence, and is likely soon to make itself recognized as the vital question to the future. It is so far from being new, that, in a certain sense, it has divided mankind, almost from the remotest ages; but in the stage of progress into which the more civilized portions of the species have now entered, it presents itself under new conditions, and requires a different and more fundamental treatment.

The struggle between Liberty and Authority is the most conspicuous feature in the portions of history with which we are earliest familiar, particularly in that of Greece, Rome, and England. But in old times this contest was between subjects, or some classes of subjects, and the government. By liberty, was meant protection against the tyranny of the political rulers. The rulers were conceived (except in some of the popular governments of Greece) as in a necessarily antagonistic position to the people whom they ruled. They consisted of a governing One, or a governing tribe or caste, who derived their authority from inheritance or conquest; who, at all events, did not hold it at the pleasure of the governed, and whose supremacy men did not venture, perhaps did not desire, to contest, whatever precautions might be taken against its oppressive exercise. Their power was regarded as necessary, but also as highly dangerous; as a weapon which they would attempt to use against their subjects, no less than against external enemies. To prevent the weaker members of the community from being preyed upon by innumerable vultures, it was needful that there should be an animal of prey stronger than the rest, commissioned to keep them down. But as the king of the vultures would be no less bent upon preying on the flock than any of the minor harpies, it was indispensable to be in a perpetual attitude of defence against his beak and claws. The aim, therefore, of patriots, was to set limits to the power which the ruler should be suffered to exercise over the community; and this limitation was what they meant by liberty. It was attempted in two ways. First, by obtaining a recognition of certain immunities, called political liberties or rights, which it was to be regarded as a breach of duty in the ruler to infringe, and which, if he did infringe, specific resistance, or general rebellion, was held to be justifiable. A second, and generally a later expedient, was the establishment of constitutional checks; by which the consent of the community, or of a body of some sort supposed to represent its interests, was made a necessary condition to some of the more important acts of the governing power. To the first of these modes of limitation, the ruling power, in most European countries, was compelled, more or less, to submit. It was not so with the second; and to attain this, or when already in some degree possessed, to attain it more completely, became everywhere the principal object of the lovers of liberty. And so long as mankind were content to combat one enemy by another, and to be ruled by a master, on condition of being guaranteed more or less efficaciously against his tyranny, they did not carry their aspirations beyond this point.

A time, however, came, in the progress of human affairs, when men ceased to think it a necessity of nature that their governors should be an independent power, opposed in interest to themselves. It appeared to them much better that the various magistrates of the State should be their tenants or delegates, revocable at their pleasure. In that way alone, it seemed, could they have complete security that the powers of government

would never be abused to their disadvantage. By degrees, this new demand for elective and temporary rulers became the prominent object of the exertions of the popular
party, wherever any such party existed; and superseded, to a considerable extent, the
previous efforts to limit the power of rulers. As the struggle proceeded for making
the ruling power emanate from the periodical choice of the ruled, some persons began
to think that too much importance had been attached to the limitation of the power
itself. *That* (it might seem) was a resource against rulers whose interests were
habitually opposed to those of the people. What was now wanted was, that the rulers
should be identified with the people; that their interest and will should be the interest
and will of the nation. The nation did not need to be protected against its own will.
There was no fear of its tyrannizing over itself. Let the rulers be effectually responsible to it, promptly removable by it, and it could afford to trust them with power of
which it could itself dictate the use to be made. Their power was but the nation's own
power, concentrated, and in a form convenient for exercise. This mode of thought,
or rather perhaps of feeling, was common among the last generation of European
liberalism, in the Continental section of which, it still apparently predominates. Those
who admit any limit to what a government may do, except in the case of such governments as they think ought not to exist, stand out as brilliant exceptions among the
political thinkers of the Continent. A similar tone of sentiment might by this time
have been prevalent in our own country, if the circumstances which for a time encouraged it had continued unaltered.

But, in political and philosophical theories, as well as in persons, success discloses
faults and infirmities which failure might have concealed from observation. The
notion, that the people have no need to limit their power over themselves, might seem
axiomatic, when popular government was a thing only dreamed about, or read of as
having existed at some distant period of the past. Neither was that notion necessarily
disturbed by such temporary aberrations as those of the French Revolution, the worst
of which were the work of an usurping few, and which, in any case, belonged, not
to the permanent working of popular institutions, but to a sudden and convulsive
outbreak against monarchical and aristocratic despotism. In time, however, a democratic republic came to occupy a large portion of the earth's surface, and made itself
felt as one of the most powerful members of the community of nations; and elective
and responsible government became subject to the observations and criticisms which
wait upon a great existing fact. It was now perceived that such phrases as "self-
government," and "the power of the people over themselves," do not express the true
state of the case. The "people" who exercise the power, are not always the same
people with those over whom it is exercised; and the "self-government" spoken of,
is not the government of each by himself, but of each by all the rest. The will of the
people, moreover, practically means, the will of the most numerous or the most active
*part* of the people; the majority, or those who succeed in making themselves accepted
as the majority: the people, consequently, *may* desire to oppress a part of their number; and precautions are as much needed against this, as against any other abuse
of power. The limitation, therefore, of the power of government over individuals,
loses none of its importance when the holders of power are regularly accountable to
the community, that is, to the strongest party therein. This view of things, recommending itself equally to the intelligence of thinkers and to the inclination of those im-

portant classes in European society to whose real or supposed interests democracy is adverse, has had no difficulty in establishing itself; and in political speculations "the tyranny of the majority" is now generally included among the evils against which society requires to be on its guard.

Like other tyrannies, the tyranny of the majority was at first, and is still vulgarly, held in dread, chiefly as operating through the acts of the public authorities. But reflecting persons perceived that when society is itself the tyrant—society collectively, over the separate individuals who compose it—its means of tyrannizing are not restricted to the acts which it may do by the hands of its political functionaries. Society can and does execute its own mandates: and if it issues wrong mandates instead of right, or any mandates at all in things with which it ought not to meddle, it practises a social tyranny more formidable than many kinds of political oppression, since, though not usually upheld by such extreme penalties, it leaves fewer means of escape, penetrating much more deeply into the details of life, and enslaving the soul itself. Protection, therefore, against the tyranny of the magistrate is not enough; there needs protection also against the tyranny of the prevailing opinion and feeling; against the tendency of society to impose, by other means than civil penalties, its own ideas and practices as rules of conduct on those who dissent from them; to fetter the development, and, if possible, prevent the formation, of any individuality not in harmony with its ways, and compel all characters to fashion themselves upon the model of its own. There is a limit to the legitimate interference of collective opinion with individual independence; and to find that limit, and maintain it against encroachment, is as indispensable to a good condition of human affairs, as protection against political despotism.

But though this proposition is not likely to be contested in general terms, the practical question, where to place the limit—how to make the fitting adjustment between individual independence and social control—is a subject on which nearly everything remains to be done. All that makes existence valuable to any one, depends on the enforcement of restraints upon the actions of other people. Some rules of conduct, therefore, must be imposed, by law in the first place, and by opinion on many things which are not fit subjects for the operation of law. What these rules should be, is the principal question in human affairs; but if we except a few of the most obvious cases, it is one of those which least progress has been made in resolving. No two ages, and scarcely any two countries, have decided it alike; and the decision of one age or country is a wonder to another. Yet the people of any given age and country no more suspect any difficulty in it, than if it were a subject on which mankind had always been agreed. The rules which obtain among themselves appear to them self-evident and self-justifying. This all but universal illusion is one of the examples of the magical influence of custom, which is not only, as the proverb says, a second nature, but is continually mistaken for the first. . . .

The object of this Essay is to assert one very simple principle, as entitled to govern absolutely the dealings of society with the individual in the way of compulsion and control, whether the means used be physical force in the form of legal penalties, or the moral coercion of public opinion. That principle is, that the sole end for which mankind are warranted, individually or collectively, in interfering with the liberty of action of any of their number, is self-protection. That the only purpose for which power can be rightfully exercised over any member of a civilized community, against his will, is to prevent harm to others. His own good, either physical or moral, is not a sufficient warrant. He cannot rightfully be compelled to do or forbear because it will be better for him to do so, because it will make him happier, because, in the opinions of others, to do so would  be wise, or even right. These are good reasons for remonstrating with him, or reasoning with him, or persuading him, or entreating him, but not for compelling him, or visiting him with any evil, in case he do otherwise. To justify that, the conduct from which it is desired to deter him must be calculated to produce evil to some one else. The only part of the conduct of any one, for which he is amenable to society, is that which concerns others. In the part which merely concerns himself, his independence is, of right, absolute. Over himself, over his own body and mind, the individual is sovereign.

It is, perhaps, hardly necessary to say that this doctrine is meant to apply only to human beings in the maturity of their faculties. We are not speaking of children, or of young persons below the age which the law may fix as that of manhood or womanhood. Those who are still in a state to require being taken care of by others, must be protected against their own actions as well as against external injury. For the same reason, we may leave out of consideration those backward states of society in which the race itself may be considered as in its nonage. The early difficulties in the way of spontaneous progress are so great, that there is seldom any choice of means for overcoming them; and a ruler full of the spirit of improvement is warranted in the use of any expedients that will attain an end, perhaps otherwise unattainable. Despotism is a legitimate mode of government in dealing with barbarians, provided the end be their improvement, and the means justified by actually effecting that end. Liberty, as a principle, has no application to any state of things anterior to the time when mankind have become capable of being improved by free and equal discussion. Until then, there is nothing for them but implicit obedience to an Akbar or a Charlemagne, if they are so fortunate as to find one. But as soon as mankind have attained the capacity of being guided to their own improvement by conviction or persuasion (a period long since reached in all nations with whom we need here concern ourselves), compulsion, either in the direct form or in that of pains and penalties for non-compliance, is no longer admissible as a means to their own good, and justifiable only for the security of others.

It is proper to state that I forego any advantage which could be derived to my argument from the idea of abstract right, as a thing independent of utility. I regard utility as the ultimate appeal on all ethical questions; but it must be utility in the largest sense, grounded on the permanent interests of man as a progressive being. Those interests, I contend, authorize the subjection of individual spontaneity to external control, only in respect to those actions of each, which concern the interest of other people. If any one does an act hurtful to others, there is a *primâ facie* case for punishing him, by law, or, where legal penalties are not safely applicable, by general disapprobation. There are also many positive acts for the benefit of others, which he may rightfully be compelled to perform; such as, to give evidence in a court of justice; to bear his fair share in the common defence, or in any other joint work necessary to the interest of the society of which he enjoys the protection; and to perform certain acts of individual beneficence, such as saving a fellow creature's life, or interposing to protect the defenceless against ill-usage, things which whenever it is obviously a man's duty to do, he may rightfully be made responsible to society for not doing. A person may cause evil to others not only by his actions but by his inaction, and in either case he is justly accountable to them for the injury. The latter case, it is true, requires a much more cautious exercise of compulsion than the former. To make any one answerable for doing evil to others, is the rule; to make him answerable for not preventing evil, is, comparatively speaking, the exception. Yet there are many cases clear enough and grave enough to justify that exception. In all things which regard the external relations of the individual, he is *de jure* amenable to those whose interests are concerned, and if need be, to society as their protector. There are often good reasons for not holding him to the responsibility; but these reasons must arise from the special expediencies of the case: either because it is a kind of case in which he is on the whole likely to act better, when left to his own discretion, than when controlled in any way in which society have it in their power to control him; or because the attempt to exercise control would produce other evils, greater than those which it would prevent. When such reasons as these preclude the enforcement of responsibility, the conscience of the agent himself should step into the vacant judgment-seat, and protect those interests of others which have no external protection; judging himself all the more rigidly, because the case does not admit of his being made accountable to the judgment of his fellow-creatures.

But there is a sphere of action in which society, as distinguished from the individual, has, if any, only an indirect interest; comprehending all that portion of a person's life and conduct which affects only himself, or, if it also affects others, only with their free, voluntary, and undeceived consent and participation. When I say only himself, I mean directly, and in the first instance: for whatever affects himself, may affect others *through* himself; and the objection which may be grounded on this contingency, will receive consideration in the sequel. This, then, is the appropriate region of human liberty. It comprises, first, the inward domain of consciousness; demanding liberty of conscience, in the most comprehensive sense; liberty of thought and feeling; absolute freedom of opinion and sentiment on all subjects, practical or speculative, scientific, moral, or theological. The liberty of expressing and publishing opinions may seem to fall under a different principle, since it belongs to that part of the conduct of an individual which concerns other people; but, being almost of as much importance as the liberty of thought itself, and resting in great part on the same reasons, is practically inseparable from it. Secondly, the principle requires liberty of tastes and pursuits; of framing the plan of our life to suit our own character; of doing as we like, subject to such consequences as may follow; without impediment from our fellow-creatures, so long as what we do does not harm them, even though they should think our conduct foolish, perverse, or wrong. Thirdly, from this liberty of each individual, follows the liberty, within the same limits, of combination among individuals; freedom to unite, for any purpose not involving harm to others: the persons combining being supposed to be of full age, and not forced or deceived.

No society in which these liberties are not, on the whole, respected, is free, whatever may be its form of government; and none is completely free in which they do not exist absolute and unqualified. The only freedom which deserves the name, is that of pursuing our own good in our own way, so long as we do not attempt to deprive others of theirs, or impede their efforts to obtain it. Each is the proper guardian of his own health, whether bodily, or mental and spiritual. Mankind are greater gainers by suffering each other to live as seems good to themselves, than by compelling each to live as seems good to the rest.

## CHAPTER II. OF THE LIBERTY OF THOUGHT AND DISCUSSION

The time, it is to be hoped, is gone by, when any defence would be necessary of the "liberty of the press" as one of the securities against corrupt or tyrannical government. No argument, we may suppose, can now be needed, against permitting a legislature or an executive, not identified in interest with the people, to prescribe opinions to them, and determine what doctrines or what arguments they shall be allowed to hear. This aspect of the question, besides, has been so often and so triumphantly enforced by preceding writers, that it needs not be specially insisted on in this place. Though the law of England, on the subject of the press, is as servile to this day as it was in the time of the Tudors, there is little danger of its being actually put in force against political discussion, except during some temporary panic, when fear of insurrection drives ministers and judges from their propriety; and, speaking generally, it is not, in constitutional countries, to be apprehended, that the government, whether completely responsible to the people or not, will often attempt to control the expression of opinion, except when in doing so it makes itself the organ of the general intolerance of the public. Let us suppose, therefore, that the government is entirely at one with the people, and never thinks of exerting any power of coercion unless in agreement with what it conceives to be their voice. But I deny the right of the people to exercise such coercion, either by themselves or by their government. The power itself is illegitimate. The best government has no more title to it than the worst. It is as noxious, or more noxious, when exerted in accordance with public opinion, than when in opposition to it. If all mankind minus one, were of one opinion, and only one person were of the contrary opinion, mankind would be no more justified in silencing that one person, than he, if he had the power, would be justified in silencing mankind. Were an opinion a personal possession of no value except to the owner; if to be obstructed in the enjoyment of it were simply a private injury, it would make some difference whether the injury was inflicted only on a few persons or on many. But the peculiar evil of silencing the expression of an opinion is, that it is robbing the human race; posterity as well as the existing generation; those who dissent from the opinion, still more than those who hold it. If the opinion is right, they are deprived of the opportunity of exchanging error for truth: if wrong, they lose, what is almost as great a benefit, the clearer perception and livelier impression of truth, produced by its collision with error.

It is necessary to consider separately these two hypotheses, each of which has a distinct branch of the argument corresponding to it. We can never be sure that the opinion we are endeavoring to stifle is a false opinion; and if we were sure, stifling it would be an evil still.

First: the opinion which it is attempted to suppress by authority may possibly be true. Those who desire to suppress it, of course deny its truth; but they are not infallible. They have no authority to decide the question for all mankind, and exclude every other person from the means of judging. To refuse a hearing to an opinion, because they are sure that it is false, is to assume that *their* certainty is the same thing as *absolute* certainty. All silencing of discussion is an assumption of infallibility. Its condemnation may be allowed to rest on this common argument, not the worse for being common. . . .

When we consider either the history of opinion, or the ordinary conduct of human life, to what is it to be ascribed that the one and the other are no worse than they are? Not certainly to the inherent force of the human understanding; for, on any matter not self-evident, there are ninety-nine persons totally incapable of judging of it, for one who is capable; and the capacity of the hundredth person is only comparative; for the majority of the eminent men of every past generation held many opinions now known to be erroneous, and did or approved numerous things which no one will now justify. Why is it, then, that there is on the whole a preponderance among mankind of rational opinions and rational conduct? If there really is this preponderance—which there must be, unless human affairs are, and have always been, in an almost desperate state—it is owing to a quality of the human mind, the source of everything respectable in man either as an intellectual or as a moral being, namely, that his errors are corrigible. He is capable of rectifying his mistakes, by discussion and experience. Not by experience alone. There must be discussion, to show how experience is to be interpreted. Wrong opinions and practices gradually yield to fact and argument: but facts and arguments, to produce any effect on the mind, must be brought before it. Very few facts are able to tell their own story, without comments to bring out their meaning. The whole strength and value, then, of human judgment, depending on the one property, that it can be set right when it is wrong, reliance can be placed on it only when the means of setting it right are kept constantly at hand. In the case of any person whose judgment is really deserving of confidence, how has it become so? Because he has kept his mind open to criticism of his opinions and conduct. Because it has been his practice to listen to all that could be said against him; to profit by as much of it as was just, and expound to himself, and upon occasion to others, the fallacy of what was fallacious. Because he has felt, that the only way in which a human being can make some approach to knowing the whole of a subject, is by hearing what can be said about it by persons of every variety of opinion, and studying all modes in which it can be looked at by every character of mind. No wise man ever acquired his wisdom in any mode but this; nor is it in the nature of human intellect to become wise in any other manner. . . .

In the present age—which has been described as "destitute of faith, but terrified at scepticism,"—in which people feel sure, not so much that their opinions are true, as that they should not know what to do without them—the claims of an opinion to be protected from public attack are rested not so much on its truth, as on its importance to society. There are, it is alleged, certain beliefs, so useful, not to say indispensable to well-being, that it is as much the duty of governments to uphold those beliefs, as to protect any other of the interests of society. In a case of such necessity, and so directly in the line of their duty, something less than infallibility may, it is maintained, warrant, and even bind, governments, to act on their own opinion, confirmed by the general opinion of mankind. It is also often argued, and still oftener thought, that none but bad men would desire to weaken these salutary beliefs; and there can be nothing wrong, it is thought, in restraining bad men, and prohibiting what only such men would wish to practise. This mode of thinking makes the justification of restraints on discussion not a question of the truth of doctrines, but of their usefulness; and flatters itself by that means to escape the responsibility of ,claiming to be an infallible judge of opinions. But those who thus satisfy themselves, do not perceive that the assumption of infallibility is merely shifted from one point to another. The usefulness of an opinion is itself matter of opinion: as disputable, as open to discussion, and requiring discussion as much, as the opinion itself. There is the same need of an infallible judge of opinions to decide an opinion to be noxious, as to decide it to be false, unless the opinion condemned has full opportunity of defending itself. And it will not do to say that the heretic may be allowed to maintain the utility or harmlessness of his opinion, though forbidden to maintain its truth. The truth of an opinion is part of its utility. If we would know whether or not it is desirable that a proposition should be believed, is it possible to exclude the consideration of whether or not it is true? In the opinion, not of bad men, but of the best men, no belief which is contrary to truth can be really useful: and can you prevent such men from urging that plea, when they are charged with culpability for denying some doctrine which they are told is useful, but which they believe to be false? Those who are on the side of received opinions, never fail to take all possible advantage of this plea; you do not find *them* handling the question of utility as if it could be completely abstracted from that of truth: on the contrary, it is, above all, because their doctrine is "the truth," that the knowledge or the belief of it is held to be so indispensable. There can be no fair discussion of the question of usefulness, when an argument so vital may be employed on one side, but not on the other. And in point of fact, when law or public feeling do not permit the truth of an opinion to be disputed, they are just as little tolerant of a denial of its usefulness. The utmost they allow is an extenuation of its absolute necessity, or of the positive guilt of rejecting it. . . .

Let us now pass to the second division of the argument, and dismissing the supposition that any of the received opinions may be false, let us assume them to be true, and examine into the worth of the manner in which they are likely to be held, when their truth is not freely and openly canvassed. However unwillingly a person who has a strong opinion may admit the possibility that his opinion may be false, he ought to be moved by the consideration that however true it may be, if it is not fully, frequently, and fearlessly discussed, it will be held as a dead dogma, not a living truth.

There is a class of persons (happily not quite so numerous as formerly) who think it enough if a person assents undoubtingly to what they think true, though he has no knowledge whatever of the grounds of the opinion, and could not make a tenable defence of it against the most superficial objections. Such persons, if they can once get their creed taught from authority, naturally think that no good, and some harm, comes of its being allowed to be questioned. Where their influence prevails, they make it nearly impossible for the received opinion to be rejected wisely and considerately, though it may still be rejected rashly and ignorantly; for to shut out discussion entirely is seldom possible, and when it once gets in, beliefs not grounded on conviction are apt to give way before the slightest semblance of an argument. Waiving, however, this possibility—assuming that the true opinion abides in the mind, but abides as a prejudice, a belief independent of, and proof against, argument—this is not the way in which truth ought to be held by a rational being. This is not knowing the truth. Truth, thus held, is but one superstition the more, accidentally clinging to the words which enunciate a truth. . . .

It still remains to speak of one of the principal causes which make diversity of opinion advantageous, and will continue to do so until mankind shall have entered a stage of intellectual advancement which at present seems at an incalculable distance. We have hitherto considered only two possibilities: that the received opinion may be false, and some other opinion, consequently, true; or that, the received opinion being true, a conflict with the opposite error is essential to a clear apprehension and deep feeling of its truth. But there is a commoner case than either of these; when the conflicting doctrines, instead of being one true and the other false, share the truth between them; and the nonconforming opinion is needed to supply the remainder of the truth, of which the received doctrine embodies only a part. Popular opinions, on subjects not palpable to sense, are often true, but seldom or never the whole truth. They are a part of the truth; sometimes a greater, sometimes a smaller part, but exaggerated, distorted, and disjoined from the truths by which they ought to be accompanied and limited. Heretical opinions, on the other hand, are generally some of these suppressed and neglected truths, bursting the bonds which kept them down, and either seeking reconciliation with the truth contained in the common opinion, or fronting it as enemies, and setting themselves up, with similar exclusiveness, as the whole truth. The latter case is hitherto the most frequent; as, in the human mind, one-sidedness has always been the rule, and many-sidedness the exception. Hence, even in revolutions of opinion, one part of the truth usually sets while another rises. Even progress, which ought to superadd, for the most part only substitutes one partial and incomplete truth for another; improvement consisting chiefly in this, that the new fragment of truth is more wanted, more adapted to the needs of the time, than that which it displaces. Such being the partial character of prevailing opinions, even when resting on a true foundation; every opinion which embodies somewhat of the portion of truth which the common opinion omits, ought to be considered precious, with whatever amount of error and confusion that truth may be blended. No sober judge of human affairs will feel bound to be indignant because those who force on our notice truths which we should otherwise have overlooked, overlook some of those which we see. Rather, he will think that so long as popular truth is one-sided, it is more desirable than otherwise that unpopular truth should have one-sided asserters too; such being usually the most energetic, and the most likely to compel reluctant attention to the fragment of wisdom which they proclaim as if it were the whole.

Thus, in the eighteenth century, when nearly all the instructed, and all those of the uninstructed who were led by them, were lost in admiration of what is called civilization, and of the marvels of modern science, literature, and philosophy, and while greatly overrating the amount of unlikeness between the men of modern and those of ancient times, indulged the belief that the whole of the difference was in their own favor; with what a salutary shock did the paradoxes of Rousseau explode like bombshells in the midst, dislocating the compact mass of one-sided opinion, and forcing its elements to recombine in a better form and with additional ingredients. Not that the current opinions were on the whole farther from the truth than Rousseau's were;

on the contrary, they were nearer to it; they contained more of positive truth, and very much less of error. Nevertheless there lay in Rousseau's doctrine, and has floated down the stream of opinion along with it, a considerable amount of exactly those truths which the popular opinion wanted; and these are the deposit which was left behind when the flood subsided. The superior worth of simplicity of life, the enervating and demoralizing effect of the trammels and hypocrisies of artificial society, are ideas which have never been entirely absent from cultivated minds since Rousseau wrote; and they will in time produce their due effect, though at present needing to be asserted as much as ever, and to be asserted by deeds, for words, on this subject, have nearly exhausted their power.

In politics, again, it is almost a commonplace, that a party of order or stability, and a party of progress or reform, are both necessary elements of a healthy state of political life; until the one or the other shall have so enlarged its mental grasp as to be a party equally of order and of progress, knowing and distinguishing what is fit to be preserved from what ought to be swept away. Each of these modes of thinking derives its utility from the deficiencies of the other; but it is in a great measure the opposition of the other that keeps each within the limits of reason and sanity. Unless opinions favorable to democracy and to aristocracy, to property and to equality, to coöperation and to competition, to luxury and to abstinence, to sociality and individuality, to liberty and discipline, and all the other standing antagonisms of practical life, are expressed with equal freedom, and enforced and defended with equal talent and energy, there is no chance of both elements obtaining their due; one scale is sure to go up, and the other down. Truth, in the great practical concerns of life, is so much a question of the reconciling and combining of opposites, that very few have minds sufficiently capacious and impartial to make the adjustment with an approach to correctness, and it has to be made by the rough process of a struggle between combatants fighting under hostile banners. . . .

## CHAPTER III. OF INDIVIDUALITY, AS ONE OF THE ELEMENTS OF WELL-BEING

Such being the reasons which make it imperative that human beings should be free to form opinions, and to express their opinions without reserve; and such the baneful consequences to the intellectual, and through that to the moral nature of man, unless this liberty is either conceded, or asserted in spite of prohibition; let us next examine whether the same reasons do not require that men should be free to act upon their opinions—to carry these out in their lives, without hindrance, either physical or moral, from their fellow-men, so long as it is at their own risk and peril. This last proviso is of course indispensable. No one pretends that actions should be as free as opinions. On the contrary, even opinions lose their immunity, when the circumstances in which they are expressed are such as to constitute their expression a positive instigation to some mischievous act. An opinion that corn-dealers are starvers of the poor, or that private property is robbery, ought to be unmolested when simply circulated through the press, but may justly incur punishment when delivered orally to an excited mob assembled before the house of a corn-dealer, or when handed about among the same mob in the form of a placard. Acts, of whatever kind, which, without justifiable cause, do harm to others, may be, and in the more important cases absolutely require to be, controlled by the unfavorable sentiments, and, when needful, by the active interference of mankind. The liberty of the individual must be thus far limited; he must not make himself a nuisance to other people. But if he refrains from molesting others in what concerns them, and merely acts according to his own inclination and judgment in things which concern himself, the same reasons which show that opinion should be free, prove also that he should be allowed, without molestation, to carry his opinions into practice at his own cost. That mankind are not infallible; that their truths, for the most part, are only half-truths; that unity of opinion, unless resulting from the fullest and freest comparison of opposite opinions, is not desirable, and diversity not an evil, but a good, until mankind are much more capable than at present of recognizing all sides of the truth, are principles applicable to men's modes of action, not less than to their opinions. As it is useful that while mankind are imperfect there should be different opinions, so is it that there should be different experiments of living; that free scope should be given to varieties of character, short of injury to others; and that the worth of different modes of life should be proved practically, when any one thinks fit to try them. It is desirable, in short, that in things which do not primarily concern others, individuality should assert itself. Where, not the person's own character, but the traditions or customs of other people are the rule of conduct, there is wanting one of the principal ingredients of human happiness, and quite the chief ingredient of individual and social progress. . . .

The traditions and customs of other people are, to a certain extent, evidence of what their experience has taught *them;* presumptive evidence, and as such, have a claim to his deference: but, in the first place, their experience may be too narrow; or they may not have interpreted it rightly. Secondly, their interpretation of experience may be correct, but unsuitable to him. Customs are made for customary circumstances, and customary characters: and his circumstances or his character may be uncustomary. Thirdly, though the customs be both good as customs, and suitable to him, yet to conform to custom, merely *as* custom, does not educate or develop in him any of the qualities which are the distinctive endowment of a human being. The human faculties of perception, judgment, discriminative feeling, mental activity, and even moral preference, are exercised only in making a choice. He who does anything because it is the custom, makes no choice. He gains no practice either in discerning or in desiring what is best. The mental and moral, like the muscular powers, are improved only by being used. The faculties are called into no exercise by doing a thing merely because others do it, no more than by believing a thing only because others believe it. If the grounds of an opinion are not conclusive to the person's own reason, his reason cannot be strengthened, but is likely to be weakened by his adopting it: and if the inducements to an act are not such as are consentaneous to his own feelings and character (where affection, or the rights of others, are not concerned), it is so much done towards rendering his feelings and character inert and torpid, instead of active and energetic.

He who lets the world, or his own portion of it, choose his plan of life for him, has no need of any other faculty than the ape-like one of imitation. He who chooses his plan for himself, employs all his faculties. He must use observation to see, reasoning and judgment to foresee, activity to gather materials for decision, discrimination to decide, and when he has decided, firmness and self-control to hold to his deliberate decision. And these qualities he requires and exercises exactly in proportion as the part of his conduct which he determines according to his own judgment and feelings is a large one. It is possible that he might be guided in some good path, and kept out of harm's way, without any of these things. But what will be his comparative worth as a human being? It really is of importance, not only what men do, but also what manner of men they are that do it. Among the works of man, which human life is rightly employed in perfecting and beautifying, the first in importance surely is man himself. Supposing it were possible to get houses built, corn grown, battles fought, causes tried, and even churches erected and prayers said, by machinery—by automatons in human form—it would be a considerable loss to exchange for these automatons even the men and women who at present inhabit the more civilized parts of the world, and who assuredly are but starved specimens of what nature can and will produce. Human nature is not a machine to be built after a model, and set to do exactly the work prescribed for it, but a tree, which requires to grow and develop itself on all sides, according to the tendency of the inward forces which make it a living thing. . . .

In some early states of society, these forces might be, and were, too much ahead of the power which society then possessed of disciplining and controlling them. There has been a time when the element of spontaneity and individuality was in excess, and the social principle had a hard struggle with it. The difficulty then was, to induce men of strong bodies or minds to pay obedience to any rules which required them to control their impulses. To overcome this difficulty, law and discipline, like the Popes struggling against the Emperors, asserted a power over the whole man, claiming to control all his life in order to control his character—which society had not found any other sufficient means of binding. But society has now fairly got the better of individuality; and the danger which threatens human nature is not the excess, but the deficiency, of personal impulses and preferences. Things are vastly changed, since the passions of those who were strong by station or by personal endowment were in a state of habitual rebellion against laws and ordinances, and required to be rigorously chained up to enable the persons within their reach to enjoy any particle of security. In our times, from the highest class of society down to the lowest, every one lives as under the eye of a hostile and dreaded censorship. Not only in what concerns others, but in what concerns only themselves, the individual, or the family, do not ask themselves—what do I prefer? or, what would suit my character and disposition? or, what would allow the best and highest in me to have fair play, and enable it to grow and thrive? They ask themselves, what is suitable to my position? what is usually done by persons of my station and pecuniary circumstances? or (worse still) what is usually done by persons of a station and circumstances superior to mine? I do not mean that they choose what is customary, in preference to what suits their own inclination. It does not occur to them to have any inclination, except for what is customary. Thus the mind itself is bowed to the yoke: even in what people do for pleasure, conformity is the first thing thought of; they like in crowds; they exercise choice only among things commonly done: peculiarity of taste, eccentricity of conduct, are shunned equally with crimes: until by dint of not following their own nature, they have no nature to follow: their human capacities are withered and starved: they become incapable of any strong wishes or native pleasures, and are generally without either opinions or feelings of home growth, or properly their own. Now is this, or is it not, the desirable condition of human nature? . . .

CHAPTER IV. OF THE LIMITS TO THE AUTHORITY OF SOCIETY
OVER THE INDIVIDUAL

What, then, is the rightful limit to the sovereignty of the individual over himself? Where does the authority of society begin? How much of human life should be assigned to individuality, and how much to society?

Each will receive its proper share, if each has that which more particularly concerns it. To individuality should belong the part of life in which it is chiefly the individual that is interested; to society, the part which chiefly interests society.

Though society is not founded on a contract, and though no good purpose is answered by inventing a contract in order to deduce social obligations from it, every one who receives the protection of society owes a return for the benefit, and the fact of living in society renders it indispensable that each should be bound to observe a certain line of conduct towards the rest. This conduct consists, first, in not injuring the interests of one another; or rather certain interests, which, either by express legal provision or by tacit understanding, ought to be considered as rights; and secondly, in each person's bearing his share (to be fixed on some equitable principle) of the labors and sacrifices incurred for defending the society or its members from injury and molestation. These conditions society is justified in enforcing, at all costs to those who endeavor to withhold fulfilment. Nor is this all that society may do. The acts of an individual may be hurtful to others, or wanting in due consideration for their welfare, without going the length of violating any of their constituted rights. The offender may then be justly punished by opinion, though not by law. As soon as any part of a person's conduct affects prejudicially the interests of others, society has jurisdiction over it, and the question whether the general welfare will or will not be promoted by interfering with it, becomes open to discussion. But there is no room for entertaining any such question when a person's conduct affects the interests of no persons besides himself, or needs not affect them unless they like (all the persons concerned being of full age, and the ordinary amount of understanding). In all such cases there should be perfect freedom, legal and social, to do the action and stand the consequences. . . .

The distinction here pointed out between the part of a person's life which concerns only himself, and that which concerns others, many persons will refuse to admit. How (it may be asked) can any part of the conduct of a member of society be a matter of indifference to the other members? No person is an entirely isolated being; it is impossible for a person to do anything seriously or permanently hurtful to himself, without mischief reaching at least to his near connections, and often far beyond them. If he injures his property, he does harm to those who directly or indirectly derived support from it, and usually diminishes, by a greater or less amount, the general resources of the community. If he deteriorates his bodily or mental faculties,

he not only brings evil upon all who depended on him for any portion of their happiness, but disqualifies himself for rendering the services which he owes to his
fellow-creatures generally; perhaps becomes a burden on their affection or benevolence; and if such conduct were very frequent, hardly any offence that is committed
would detract more from the general sum of good. Finally, if by his vices or follies
a person does no direct harm to others, he is nevertheless (it may be said) injurious
by his example; and ought to be compelled to control himself, for the sake of those
whom the sight or knowledge of his conduct might corrupt or mislead. . . .

I fully admit that the mischief which a person does to himself, may seriously affect,
both through their sympathies and their interests, those nearly connected with him,
and in a minor degree, society at large. When, by conduct of this sort, a person is
led to violate a distinct and assignable obligation to any other person or persons, the
case is taken out of the self-regarding class, and becomes amenable to moral disapprobation in the proper sense of the term. . . .

But with regard to the merely contingent, or, as it may be called, constructive
injury which a person causes to society, by conduct which neither violates any specific
duty to the public, nor occasions perceptible hurt to any assignable individual except
himself; the inconvenience is one which society can afford to bear, for the sake of the
greater good of human freedom. If grown persons are to be punished for not taking
proper care of themselves, I would rather it were for their own sake, than under pretence of preventing them from impairing their capacity of rendering to society benefits
which society does not pretend it has a right to exact. But I cannot consent to argue
the point as if society had no means of bringing its weaker members up to its ordinary standard of rational conduct, except waiting till they do something irrational,
and then punishing them, legally or morally, for it. Society has had absolute power
over them during all the early portion of their existence: it has had the whole period
of childhood and nonage in which to try whether it could make them capable of
rational conduct in life. The existing generation is master both of the training and
the entire circumstances of the generation to come; it cannot indeed make them
perfectly wise and good, because it is itself so lamentably deficient in goodness and
wisdom; and its best efforts are not always, in individual cases, its most successful
ones; but it is perfectly well able to make the rising generation, as a whole, as good
as, and a little better than, itself. If society lets any considerable number of its members grow up mere children, incapable of being acted on by rational consideration of
distant motives, society has itself to blame for the consequences. Armed not only with
all the powers of education, but with the ascendency which the authority of a received
opinion always exercises over the minds who are least fitted to judge for themselves;
and aided by the *natural* penalties which cannot be prevented from falling on those
who incur the distaste or the contempt of those who know them; let not society pretend that it needs, besides all this, the power to issue commands and enforce obedience
in the personal concerns of individuals, in which, on all principles of justice and
policy, the decision ought to rest with those who are to abide the consequences. . . .

To determine the point at which evils, so formidable to human freedom and advancement, begin, or rather at which they begin to predominate over the benefits
attending the collective application of the force of society, under its recognized chiefs,
for the removal of the obstacles which stand in the way of its well-being; to secure

as much of the advantages of centralized power and intelligence, as can be had without turning into governmental channels too great a proportion of the general activity, is one of the most difficult and complicated questions in the art of government. It is, in a great measure, a question of detail, in which many and various considerations must be kept in view, and no absolute rule can be laid down. But I believe that the practical principle in which safety resides, the ideal to be kept in view, the standard by which to test all arrangements intended for overcoming the difficulty, may be conveyed in these words: the greatest dissemination of power consistent with efficiency; but the greatest possible centralization of information, and diffusion of it from the centre. Thus, in municipal administration, there would be, as in the New England States, a very minute division among separate officers, chosen by the localities, of all business which is not better left to the persons directly interested; but besides this, there would be, in each department of local affairs, a central superintendence, forming a branch of the general government. The organ of this superintendence would concentrate, as in a focus, the variety of information and experience derived from the conduct of that branch of public business in all the localities, from everything analogous which is done in foreign countries, and from the general principles of political science. This central organ should have a right to know all that is done, and its special duty should be that of making the knowledge acquired in one place available for others. Emancipated from the petty prejudices and narrow views of a locality by its elevated position and comprehensive sphere of observation, its advice would naturally carry much authority; but its actual power, as a permanent institution, should, I conceive, be limited to compelling the local officers to obey the laws laid down for their guidance. In all things not provided for by general rules, those officers should be left to their own judgment, under responsibility to their constituents. For the violation of rules, they should be responsible to law, and the rules themselves should be laid down by the legislature; the central administrative authority only watching over their execution, and if they were not properly carried into effect, appealing, according to the nature of the case, to the tribunal to enforce the law, or to the constituencies to dismiss the functionaries who had not executed it according to its spirit. Such, in its general conception, is the central superintendence which the Poor Law Board is intended to exercise over the administrators of the Poor Rate throughout the country. Whatever powers the Board exercises beyond this limit, were right and necessary in that peculiar case, for the cure of rooted habits of mal-administration in matters deeply affecting not the localities merely, but the whole community; since no locality has a moral right to make itself by mismanagement a nest of pauperism, necessarily overflowing into other localities, and impairing the moral and physical condition of the whole laboring community. The powers of administrative coercion and subordinate legislation possessed by the Poor Law Board (but which, owing to the state of opinion on the subject, are very scantily exercised by them), though perfectly justifiable in a case of a first-rate national interest, would be wholly out of place in the superintendence of interests purely local. But a central organ of information and instruction for all the localities, would be equally valuable in all departments of administration. A government cannot have too much of the kind of activity which does not impede, but aids and stimulates, individual exertion and development. The mischief begins when, instead of calling forth the activity and powers of individuals and bodies, it substitutes its own activity for theirs; when, instead of informing, advising, and, upon occasion, denouncing, it makes them work in fetters, or bids them stand aside and does their work instead of them. The worth of a State, in the long run, is the worth of the individuals composing it; and a State which postpones the interests of *their* mental expansion and elevation, to a little more of administrative skill, or that semblance of it which practice gives, in the details of business; a State which dwarfs its men, in order that they may be more docile instruments in its hands even for beneficial purposes, will find that with small men no great thing can really be accomplished; and that the perfection of machinery to which it has sacrificed everything, will in the end avail it nothing, for want of the vital power which, in order that the machine might work more smoothly, it has preferred to banish.

## ~§ THE MAN VERSUS THE STATE

*Herbert Spencer*

*By the mid-nineteenth century the Liberal party in England was completely in the hands of the followers of Adam Smith, and so successful was its economic warfare against the old system of mercantilism that in 1851 its leaders could boast that England had totally established free trade: no protective tariffs for grain, no regulations on selling or buying abroad, no restrictions on deployment of capital. The enormous riches accumulated by inventors and entrepreneurs working from the ground floor up provided fertile ground for the legend of the self-made man rising from rags to riches, from slum to mansion—the legend portrayed, for example, in the popular works of the industrial biographer Samuel Smiles. This new aristocracy felt it had rightly displaced the old, for its successes hinged not on family inheritance but on prudence and ability. From 1850, with the publication of* Social Statics, *Herbert Spencer was the man whose books increasingly graced the businessman's study and from whom the businessman derived philosophical justification for his desire for unrestricted competition and his convictions about the aristocracy of wealth.*

*Herbert Spencer (1820–1903) was raised in the bleak environment of religious sectarianism which took a highly moral view of the universe. He taught himself rudimentary mechanics, becoming one of the first engineers on the railroad operating between London and Birmingham. An intelligent student of the laissez-faire doctrine, he quickly rose to editorship of the* London Economist, *a mouthpiece for industrial capitalism, thenceforth supporting himself with the income from his writings supplemented by occasional large donations from British*

*and American tycoons. During the 1850s, influenced by early works
on evolution, he compounded a single law of universal progress
characterized by his favorite phrase, "from the homogeneous to the
heterogeneous." By this he meant that all things—not only animals,
but societies, governments, and ethical systems—had begun from single
or simple-structured cells and had struggled through successive stages of
environmental adaptation to become highly complex structures able to
cope with wide ranges of problems. Darwin's* Origin of Species *(1859)
was hailed by Spencer as final proof for his own theory of social natural
selection. Spencer showed how survival of the fittest had operated in
scores of social settings, arriving at the conclusion that higher cultures
are manifestations of successful evolution and that even moral growth
is the result of purging degenerate forms: if man is left to his own
devices, he will inevitably evolve into a creature of ultimate nobility,
virtue, and perfection.*

*Needless to say, Spencer took the dimmest view of social legislation
which protected the poor or the working class from the operation of
natural law. In order to improve the strain, nature must annihilate the
weak: this was the theme enunciated in scores of Spencer's works—*
Synthetic Philosophy: Its Law and Cause, Principles of Psychology,
Principles of Sociology, Principles of Ethics. *Most of his analysis was
faulty and purely analogical as a result of his borrowing biological laws
to prove his views about society; nevertheless, Spencer was immensely
popular with late nineteenth-century scholars, politicians, statesmen, and
businessmen, who have become known as "Social Darwinists."*

## THE COMING SLAVERY

The kinship of pity to love is shown among other ways in this, that it idealizes its object. Sympathy with one in suffering suppresses, for the time being, remembrance of his transgressions. The feeling which vents itself in "poor fellow!" on seeing one in agony, excludes the thought of "bad fellow," which might at another time arise. Naturally, then, if the wretched are unknown or but vaguely known, all the demerits they may have are ignored; and thus it happens that when, as just now, the miseries of the poor are depicted, they are thought of as the miseries of the deserving poor, instead of being thought of, as in large measure they should be, as the miseries of the undeserving poor. Those whose hardships are set forth in pamphlets and proclaimed in sermons and speeches which echo throughout society, are assumed to be all worthy

Herbert Spencer, *The Man versus the State* (New York: D. Appleton & Company, Inc., 1885), pp. 18–20, 23–24, 26–28, 30–35, 39–43.

souls, grievously wronged; and none of them are thought of as bearing the penalties of their own misdeeds.

On hailing a cab in a London street, it is surprising how frequently the door is officiously opened by one who expects to get something for his trouble. The surprise lessens after counting the many loungers about tavern-doors, or after observing the quickness with which a street-performance, or procession, draws from neighbouring slums and stable-yards a group of idlers. Seeing how numerous they are in every small area, it becomes manifest that tens of thousands of such swarm through London. "They have no work," you say. Say rather that they either refuse work or quickly turn themselves out of it. They are simply good-for-nothings, who in one way or other live on the good-for-somethings—vagrants and sots, criminals and those on the way to crime, youths who are burdens on hard-worked parents, men who appropriate the wages of their wives, fellows who share the gains of prostitutes; and then, less visible and less numerous, there is a corresponding class of women.

Is it natural that happiness should be the lot of such? or is it natural that they should bring unhappiness on themselves and those connected with them? Is it not manifest that there must exist in our midst an immense amount of misery which is a normal result of misconduct, and ought not to be dissociated from it? There is a notion, always more or less prevalent and just now vociferously expressed, that all social suffering is removable, and that it is the duty of somebody or other to remove it. Both these beliefs are false. To separate pain from ill-doing is to fight against the constitution of things, and will be followed by far more pain. Saving men from the natural penalties of dissolute living, eventually necessitates the infliction of artificial penalties in solitary cells, on tread-wheels, and by the lash. I suppose a dictum, on which the current creed and the creed of science are at one, may be considered to have as high an authority as can be found. Well, the command "if any would not work neither should he eat," is simply a Christian enunciation of that universal law of Nature under which life has reached its present height—the law that a creature not energetic enough to maintain itself must die: the sole difference being that the law which in the one case is to be artificially enforced, is, in the other case, a natural necessity. And yet this particular tenet of their religion which science so manifestly justifies, is the one which Christians seem least inclined to accept. The current assumption is that there should be no suffering, and that society is to blame for that which exists.

"But surely we are not without responsibilities, even when the suffering is that of the unworthy?"

If the meaning of the word "we" be so expanded as to include with ourselves our ancestors, and especially our ancestral legislators, I agree. I admit that those who made, and modified, and administered, the old Poor Law, were responsible for producing an appalling amount of demoralization, which it will take more than one generation to remove. I admit, too, the partial responsibility of recent and present law-makers for regulations which have brought into being a permanent body of tramps, who ramble from union to union; and also their responsibility for maintaining a constant supply of felons by sending back convicts into society under such conditions that they are almost compelled again to commit crimes. Moreover, I admit that the philanthropic are not without their share of responsibility; since, that they may aid the offspring of the unworthy, they disadvantage the offspring of the worthy through burdening their parents by increased local rates. Nay, I even admit that these swarms of good-for-nothings, fostered and multiplied by public and private agencies, have, by sundry mischievous meddlings, been made to suffer more than they would otherwise have suffered. Are these the responsibilities meant? I suspect not. . . .

It is said that when railways were first opened in Spain, peasants standing on the tracks were not unfrequently run over; and that the blame fell on the engine-drivers for not stopping: rural experiences having yielded no conception of the momentum of a large mass moving at a high velocity.

The incident is recalled to me on contemplating the ideas of the so-called "practical" politician, into whose mind there enters no thought of such a thing as political momentum, still less of a political momentum, which, instead of diminishing or remaining constant, increases. The theory on which he daily proceeds is that the change caused by his measure will stop where he intends it to stop. He contemplates intently the things his act will achieve, but thinks little of the remoter issues of the movement his act sets up, and still less its collateral issues. When, in war-time, "food for powder" was to be provided by encouraging population—when Mr. Pitt said, "Let us make relief in cases where there are a number of children a matter of right and honour, instead of a ground for opprobrium and contempt;" it was not expected that the poor-rates would be quadrupled in fifty years, that women with many bastards would be preferred as wives to modest women, because of their incomes from the parish, and that hosts of ratepayers would be pulled down into the ranks of pauperism. Legislators who in 1833 voted £20,000 a year to aid in building school-houses, never supposed that the step they then took would lead to forced contributions, local and general, now amounting to £6,000,000; they did not intend to establish the principle that A should be made responsible for educating B's offspring; they did not dream of a compulsion which would deprive poor widows of the help of their elder children; and still less did they dream that their successors, by requiring impoverished parents to apply to Boards of Guardians to pay the fees which School Boards would not remit, would initiate a habit of applying to Boards of Guardians and so cause pauperization. Neither did those who in 1834 passed an Act regulating the labour of women and children in certain factories, imagine that the system they were beginning would end in the restriction and inspection of labour in all kinds of producing establishments where more than fifty people are employed; nor did they conceive that the inspection provided would grow to the extent of requiring that before a "young person" is employed in a factory, authority must be given by a certifying surgeon, who, by personal examination (to which no limit is placed) has satisfied himself that there is no incapacitating disease or bodily infirmity: his verdict determining whether the "young person" shall earn wages or not. . . .

The blank form of a question daily asked is—"We have already done this; why should we not do that?" And the regard for precedent suggested by it, is ever pushing on regulative legislation. Having had brought within their sphere of operation more and more numerous businesses, the Acts restricting hours of employment and dictating the treatment of workers are now to be made applicable to shops. From inspecting lodging-houses to limit the numbers of occupants and enforce sanitary conditions, we have passed to inspecting all houses below a certain rent in which there are members of more than one family, and are now passing to a kindred inspection of all small houses. The buying and working of telegraphs by the State is made a reason for urging that the State should buy and work the railways. Supplying children with food for their minds by public agency is being followed in some cases by supplying food for their bodies; and after the practice has been made gradually more general, we may anticipate that the supply, now proposed to be made gratis in the one case, will eventually be proposed to be made gratis in the other: the argument that good bodies as well as good minds are needful to make good citizens, being logically urged as a reason for the extension. And then, avowedly proceeding on the precedents furnished by the church, the school, and the reading-room, all publicly provided, it is contended that "pleasure, in the sense it is now generally admitted, needs legislating for and organizing at least as much as work."

Not precedent only prompts this spread, but also the necessity which arises for supplementing ineffective measures, and for dealing with the artificial evils continually caused. Failure does not destroy faith in the agencies employed, but merely suggests more stringent use of such agencies or wider ramifications of them. Laws to check intemperance, beginning in early times and coming down to our own times, when further restraints on the sale of intoxicating liquors occupy nights every session, not having done what was expected, there come demands for more thorough-going laws, locally preventing the sale altogether; and here, as in America, these will doubtless be followed by demands that prevention shall be made universal. All the many appliances for "stamping out" epidemic diseases not having succeeded in preventing outbreaks of small-pox, fevers, and the like, a further remedy is applied for in the shape of police-power to search houses for diseased persons, and authority for medical officers to examine any one they think fit, to see whether he or she is suffering from an infectious or contagious malady. Habits of improvidence having for generations been cultivated by the Poor-Law, and the improvident enabled to multiply, the evils produced by compulsory charity are now proposed to be met by compulsory insurance.

The extension of this policy, causing extension of corresponding ideas, fosters everywhere the tacit assumption that Government should step in whenever anything is not going right. "Surely you would not have this misery continue!" exclaims some one, if you hint a demurrer to much that is now being said and done. Observe what is implied by this exclamation. It takes for granted, first, that all suffering ought to be prevented, which is not true: much suffering is curative, and prevention of it is prevention of a remedy. In the second place, it takes for granted that every evil can be removed: the truth being that with the existing defects of human nature, many evils can only be thrust out of one place or form into another place or form—often being increased by the change. The exclamation also implies the unhesitating belief, here especially concerning us, that evils of all kinds should be dealt with by the State. There does not occur the inquiry whether there are at work other agencies capable of dealing with evils, and whether the evils in question may not be among those which are best dealt with by these other agencies. And obviously, the more numerous governmental interventions become, the more confirmed does this habit of thought grow, and the more loud and perpetual the demands for intervention. . . .

These various influences working from above downwards meet with an increasing response of expectations and solicitations proceeding from below upwards. The hard-worked and over-burdened who form the great majority, and still more the incapables perpetually helped who are ever led to look for more help, are ready supporters of schemes which promise them this or the other benefit by State agency, and ready believers of those who tell them that such benefits can be given, and ought to be given. They listen with eager faith to all builders of political air-castles, from Oxford graduates down to Irish irreconcilables; and every additional tax-supported appliance for their welfare raises hopes of further ones. Indeed the more numerous public instrumentalities become, the more is there generated in citizens the notion that everything is to be done for them, and nothing by them. Each generation is made less familiar with the attainment of desired ends by individual actions or private combinations, and more familiar with the attainment of them by governmental agencies; until, eventually, governmental agencies come to be thought of as the only available agencies. This result was well shown in the recent Trades-Unions Congress at Paris. The English delegates, reporting to their constituents, said that between themselves and their foreign colleagues "the point of difference was the extent to which the State should be asked to protect labour:" reference being thus made to the fact, conspicuous in the reports of the proceedings, that the French delegates always invoked governmental power as the only means of satisfying their wishes.

The diffusion of education has worked, and will work still more, in the same direction. "We must educate our masters," is the well-known saying of a Liberal who opposed the last extension of the franchise. Yes, if the education were worthy to be so called, and were relevant to the political enlightenment needed, much might be hoped from it. But knowing rules of syntax, being able to add up correctly, having geographical information, and a memory stocked with the dates of kings' accessions and generals' victories, no more implies fitness to form political conclusions than acquirement of skill in drawing implies expertness in telegraphing, or than ability to play cricket implies proficiency on the violin. "Surely," rejoins some one, "facility in reading opens the way to political knowledge." Doubtless; but will the way be followed? Table-talk proves that nine out of ten people read what amuses them or interests them rather than what instructs them; and that the last thing they read is something which tells them disagreeable truths or dispels groundless hopes. That popular education results in an extensive reading of publications which foster pleasant illusions rather than of those which insist on hard realities, is beyond question. Says "A Mechanic," writing in the *Pall Mall Gazette* of December 3, 1883:—

> "Improved education instils the desire for culture—culture instils the desire for many things as yet quite beyond working men's reach. . . . In the furious competition to which the present age is given up they are utterly impossible to the poorer classes; hence they are discontented with things as they are, and the more educated the more discontented. Hence, too, Mr. Ruskin and Mr. Morris are regarded as true prophets by many of us."

And that the connexion of cause and effect here alleged is a real one, we may see clearly enough in the present state of Germany.

Being possessed of electoral power, as are now the mass of those who are thus led to nurture sanguine anticipations of benefits to be obtained by social reorganization, it results that whoever seeks their votes must at least refrain from exposing their mistaken beliefs; even if he does not yield to the temptation to express agreement with them. Every candidate for Parliament is prompted to propose or support some new piece of *ad captandum* legislation. Nay, even the chiefs of parties—these anxious to retain office and those to wrest it from them—severally aim to get adherents by out-bidding one another. Each seeks popularity by promising more than his opponent has promised, as we have lately seen. And then, as divisions in Parliament show us, the traditional loyalty to leaders overrides questions concerning the intrinsic propriety of proposed measures. Representatives are unconscientious enough to vote for Bills which they believe to be wrong in principle, because party-needs and regard for the next election demand it. And thus a vicious policy is strengthened even by those who see its viciousness.

Meanwhile there goes on out-of-doors an active propaganda to which all these influences are ancillary. Communistic theories, partially indorsed by one Act of Parliament after another, and tacitly if not avowedly favoured by numerous public men seeking supporters, are being advocated more and more vociferously under one or other form by popular leaders, and urged on by organized societies. There is the movement for land-nationalization which, aiming at a system of land-tenure equitable in the abstract, is, as all the world knows, pressed by Mr. George and his friends with avowed disregard for the just claims of existing owners, and as the basis of a scheme going more than half-way to State-socialism. And then there is the thorough-going Democratic Federation of Mr. Hyndman and his adherents. We are told by them that "the handful of marauders who now hold possession [of the land] have and can have no right save brute force against the tens of millions whom they wrong." They exclaim against "the shareholders who have been allowed to lay hands upon (!) our great railway communications." They condemn "above all, the active capitalist class, the loan-mongers, the farmers, the mine exploiters, the contractors, the middle-men, the factory-lords—these, the modern slave drivers" who exact "more and yet more surplus value out of the wage-slaves whom they employ." And they think it "high time" that trade should be "removed from the control of individual greed."

It remains to point out that the tendencies thus variously displayed, are being strengthened by press-advocacy, daily more pronounced. Journalists, always chary of saying that which is distasteful to their readers, are some of them going with the stream and adding to its force. Legislative meddlings which they would once have condemned they now pass in silence, if they do not advocate them; and they speak of *laissez-faire* as an exploded doctrine. "People are no longer frightened at the thought of socialism," is the statement which meets us one day. On another day, a town which does not adopt the Free Libraries Act is sneered at as being alarmed by a measure so moderately communistic. And then, along with editorial assertions that this economic evolution is coming and must be accepted, there is prominence given to the contributions of its advocates. Meanwhile those who regard the recent course of legislation as disastrous, and see that its future course is likely to be still more disastrous, are being reduced to silence by the belief that it is useless to reason with people in a state of political intoxication.

See, then, the many concurrent causes which threaten continually to accelerate the transformation now going on. There is that spread of regulation caused by following precedents, which become the more authoritative the further the policy is carried.

There is that increasing need for administrative compulsions and restraints, which results from the unforeseen evils and shortcomings of preceding compulsions and restraints. Moreover, every additional State-interference strengthens the tacit assumption that it is the duty of the State to deal with all evils and secure all benefits. Increasing power of a growing administrative organization is accompanied by decreasing power of the rest of the society to resist its further growth and control. The multiplication of careers opened by a developing bureaucracy, tempts members of the classes regulated by it to favour its extension, as adding to the chances of safe and respectable places for their relatives. The people at large, led to look on benefits received through public agencies as gratis benefits, have their hopes continually excited by the prospects of more. A spreading education, furthering the diffusion of pleasing errors rather than of stern truths, renders such hopes both stronger and more general. Worse still, such hopes are ministered to by candidates for public choice, to augment their chances of success; and leading statesmen, in pursuit of party ends, bid for popular favour by countenancing them. Getting repeated justifications from new laws harmonizing with their doctrines, political enthusiasts and unwise philanthropists push their agitations with growing confidence and success. Journalism, ever responsive to popular opinion, daily strengthens it by giving it voice; while counter-opinion, more and more discouraged, finds little utterance.

Thus influences of various kinds conspire to increase corporate action and decrease individual action. And the change is being on all sides aided by schemers, each of whom thinks only of his pet project and not at all of the general re-organization which his, joined with others such, are working out. It is said that the French Revolution devoured its own children. Here an analogous catastrophe seems not unlikely. The numerous socialistic changes made by Act of Parliament, joined with the numerous others presently to be made, will by-and-by be all merged in State-Socialism—swallowed in the vast wave which they have little by little raised.

"But why is this change described as 'the coming slavery'?" is a question which many will still ask. The reply is simple. All socialism involves slavery.

What is essential to the idea of a slave? We primarily think of him as one who is owned by another. To be more than nominal, however, the ownership must be shown by control of the slave's actions—a control which is habitually for the benefit of the controller. That which fundamentally distinguishes the slave is that he labours under coercion to satisfy another's desires. The relation admits of sundry gradations. Remembering that originally the slave is a prisoner whose life is at the mercy of his captor, it suffices here to note that there is a harsh form of slavery in which, treated as an animal, he has to expend his entire effort for his owner's advantage. Under a system less harsh, though occupied chiefly in working for his owner, he is allowed a short time in which to work for himself, and some ground on which to grow extra food. A further amelioration gives him power to sell the produce of his plot and keep the proceeds. Then we come to the still more moderated form which commonly arises where, having been a free man working on his own land, conquest turns him into what we distinguish as a serf; and he has to give to his owner each year a fixed amount of labour or produce, or both: retaining the rest himself. Finally, in some cases, as in Russia until recently, he is allowed to leave his owner's estate and work or trade for himself elsewhere, under the condition that he shall pay an annual sum.

What is it which, in these cases, leads us to qualify our conception of the slavery as more or less severe? Evidently the greater or smaller extent to which effort is compulsorily expended for the benefit of another instead of for self-benefit. If all the slave's labour is for his owner the slavery is heavy, and if but little it is light. Take now a further step. Suppose an owner dies, and his estate with its slaves comes into the hands of trustees; or suppose the estate and everything on it to be bought by a company; is the condition of the slave any the better if the amount of his compulsory labour remains the same? Suppose that for a company we substitute the community; does it make any difference to the slave if the time he has to work for others is as great, and the time left for himself is as small, as before? The essential question is— How much is he compelled to labour for other benefit than his own, and how much can he labour for his own benefit? The degree of his slavery varies according to the ratio between that which he is forced to yield up and that which he is allowed to retain; and it matters not whether his master is a single person or a society. If, without option, he has to labour for the society, and receives from the general stock such portion as the society awards him, he becomes a slave to the society. Socialistic arrangements necessitate an enslavement of this kind; and towards such an enslavement many recent measures, and still more the measures advocated, are carrying us. . . .

Evidently then, the changes made, the changes in progress, and the changes urged, will carry us not only towards State-ownership of land and dwellings and means of communication, all to be administered and worked by State-agents, but towards State-usurpation of all industries: the private forms of which, disadvantaged more and more in competition with the State, which can arrange everything for its own convenience, will more and more die away; just as many voluntary schools have, in presence of Board-schools. And so will be brought about the desired ideal of the socialists.

And now when there has been compassed this desired ideal, which "practical" politicians are helping socialists to reach, and which is so tempting on that bright side which socialists contemplate, what must be the accompanying shady side which they do not contemplate? It is a matter of common remark, often made when a marriage is impending, that those possessed by strong hopes habitually dwell on the promised pleasures and think nothing of the accompanying pains. A further exemplification of this truth is supplied by these political enthusiasts and fanatical revolutionists. Impressed with the miseries existing under our present social arrangements, and not regarding these miseries as caused by the ill-working of a human nature but partially adapted to the social state, they imagine them to be forthwith curable by this or that rearrangement. Yet, even did their plans succeed it could only be by substituting one kind of evil for another. A little deliberate thought would show that under their proposed arrangements, their liberties must be surrendered in proportion as their material welfares were cared for.

For no form of co-operation, small or great, can be carried on without regulation, and an implied submission to the regulating agencies. Even one of their own organizations for effecting social changes yields them proof. It is compelled to have its councils, its local and general officers, its authoritative leaders, who must be obeyed under penalty of confusion and failure. And the experience of those who are loudest in their advocacy of a new social order under the paternal control of a Government, shows that even in private voluntarily-formed societies, the power of the regulative organization becomes great, if not irresistible: often, indeed, causing grumbling and restiveness among those controlled. Trades Unions which carry on a kind of industrial war in defence of workers' interests *versus* employers' interests, find that subordination almost military in its strictness is needful to secure efficient action; for divided councils prove fatal to success. And even in bodies of cooperators, formed for carrying on manufacturing or distributing businesses, and not needing that obedience to leaders which is required where the aims are offensive or defensive, it is still found that the administrative agency gains such supremacy that there arise complaints about "the tyranny of organization." Judge then what must happen when, instead of relatively small combinations, to which men may belong or not as they please, we have a national combination in which each citizen finds himself incorporated, and from which he cannot separate himself without leaving the country. Judge what must under such conditions become the despotism of a graduated and centralized officialism, holding in its hands the resources of the community, and having behind it whatever amount of force it finds requisite to carry out its decrees and maintain what it calls order. Well may Prince Bismarck display leanings towards State-socialism.

And then after recognizing, as they must if they think out their scheme, the power possessed by the regulative agency in the new social system so temptingly pictured, let its advocates ask themselves to what end this power must be used. Not dwelling exclusively, as they habitually do, on the material well-being and the mental gratifications to be provided for them by a beneficent administration, let them dwell a little on the price to be paid. The officials cannot create the needful supplies: they can but distribute among individuals that which the individuals have joined to produce. If the public agency is required to provide for them, it must reciprocally require them to furnish the means. There cannot be, as under our existing system, agreement between employer and employed—this the scheme excludes. There must in place of it be command by local authorities over workers, and acceptance by the workers of that which the authorities assign to them. And this, indeed, is the arrangement distinctly, but as it would seem inadvertently, pointed to by the members of the Democratic Federation. For they propose that production should be carried on by "agricultural and industrial *armies* under State-control:" apparently not remembering that armies pre-suppose grades of officers, by whom obedience would have to be insisted upon; since otherwise neither order nor efficient work could be ensured. So that each would stand toward the governing agency in the relation of slave to master.

"But the governing agency would be a master which he and others made and kept constantly in check; and one which therefore would not control him or others more than was needful for the benefit of each and all."

To which reply the first rejoinder is that, even if so, each member of the community as an individual would be a slave to the community as a whole. Such a relation has habitually existed in militant communities, even under quasi-popular forms of government. In ancient Greece the accepted principle was that the citizen belonged neither to himself nor to his family, but belonged to his city—the city being with the Greek equivalent to the community. And this doctrine, proper to a state of constant warfare, is a doctrine which socialism unawares re-introduces into a state intended to be purely industrial. The services of each will belong to the aggregate of all; and for these services, such returns will be given as the authorities think proper. So that even if the administration is of the beneficent kind intended to be secured, slavery, however mild, must be the outcome of the arrangement.

A second rejoinder is that the administration will presently become not of the intended kind, and that the slavery will not be mild. The socialist speculation is vitiated by an assumption like that which vitiates the speculations of the "practical" politician. It is assumed that officialism will work as it is intended to work, which it never does. The machinery of Communism, like existing social machinery, has to be framed out of existing human nature; and the defects of existing human nature will generate in the one the same evils as in the other. The love of power, the selfishness, the injustice, the untruthfulness, which often in comparatively short times bring private organisations to disaster, will inevitably, where their effects accumulate from generation to generation, work evils far greater and less remediable; since, vast and complex and possessed of all the resources, the administrative organization once developed and consolidated, must become irresistible. And if there needs proof that the periodic exercise of electoral power would fail to prevent this, it suffices to instance the French Government, which, purely popular in origin, and subject at short intervals to popular judgment, nevertheless tramples on the freedom of citizens to an extent which the English delegates to the late Trades Unions Congress say "is a disgrace to, an anomaly in, a Republican nation."

The final result would be a revival of despotism. A disciplined army of civil officials, like an army of military officials, gives supreme power to its head—a power which has often led to usurpation, as in mediæval Europe and still more in Japan—nay, has thus so led among our neighbours, within our own times. The recent confessions of M. de Maupas have shown how readily a constitutional head, elected and trusted by the whole people, may, with the aid of a few unscrupulous confederates, paralyze the representative body and make himself autocrat. That those who rose to power in a socialistic organization would not scruple to carry out their aims at all costs, we have good reason for concluding. When we find that shareholders who, sometimes gaining but often losing, have made that railway-system by which national prosperity has been so greatly increased, are spoken of by the council of the Democratic Federation as having "laid hands" on the means of communication, we may infer that those who directed a socialistic administration might interpret with extreme perversity the claims of individuals and classes under their control. And when, further, we find members of this same council urging that the State should take possession of the railways, "with or without compensation," we may suspect that the heads of the ideal society desired, would be but little deterred by considerations of equity from pursuing whatever policy they thought needful: a policy which would always be one identified with their own supremacy. It would need but a war with an adjacent society, or some internal discontent demanding forcible suppression, to at once transform a socialistic administration into a grinding tyranny like that of ancient Peru; under which the mass of the people, controlled by grades of officials, and leading lives that were inspected out-of-doors and in-doors, laboured for the support of the organisation which regulated them, and were left with but a bare subsistence for themselves. And then would be completely revived, under a different form, that *régime* of status—that system of compulsory co-operation, the decaying tradition of which is represented by the old Toryism, and towards which the new Toryism is carrying us back.

"But we shall be on our guard against all that—we shall take precautions to ward off such disasters," will doubtless say the enthusiasts. Be they "practical" politicians with their new regulative measures, or communists with their schemes for re-organizing labour, their reply is ever the same:—"It is true that plans of kindred nature have, from unforeseen causes or adverse accidents, or the misdeeds of those concerned, been brought to failure; but this time we shall profit by past experiences and succeed." There seems no getting people to accept the truth, which nevertheless is conspicuous enough, that the welfare of a society and the justice of its arrangements are at bottom dependent on the characters of its members; and that improvement in neither can take place without that improvement in character which results from carrying on peaceful industry under the restraints imposed by an orderly social life.

The belief, not only of the socialists but also of those so-called Liberals who are diligently preparing the way for them, is that by due skill and ill-working humanity may be framed into well-working institutions. It is a delusion. The defective natures of citizens will show themselves in the bad acting of whatever social structure they are arranged into. There is no political alchemy by which you can get golden conduct out of leaden instincts.

## ✑ THE AUSTRIAN REICHSRAT: DEBATE ON CHURCH AND STATE

> During the nineteenth century western and central Europe witnessed the extension of a process begun by the "enlightened despots" and the revolutionaries of the eighteenth century: the building of a rationally organized secular state with transcendent claims to the loyalty of its subjects or citizens. This trend prevailed whether the substance of power remained in royal hands, as in Prussia or Austria, or whether a country was a true constitutional monarchy, like Piedmont after 1849 and Italy after 1861, a liberal federal state, like Switzerland after 1848, or a unitary democratic republic, like France after 1871.
>
> Everywhere this extension of effective state power entailed the subordination of institutions that had traditionally enjoyed considerable autonomy, notably the Catholic Church. The state's determination to mold the allegiance of its citizenry was bound to come into conflict with the age-old claims of the church to control education or to exercise jurisdiction over its own clergy. Quite aside from the jurisdictional issue, the social and political orientation of Catholicism could not easily be

*reconciled with the requirements of the modern state. Throughout the period, save for a constitutional fling from 1846 to 1848, the papacy resolutely rejected the articles of faith of the nineteenth century—such as nationalism, religious toleration, individual liberty—that even conservative states like Prussia and Austria had come to honor. The official position of the head of the Catholic Church was spelled out in the Syllabus of Errors (1864), a long list of modern "errors" condemned by the Pope that included most of the political and ideological innovations introduced since the eighteenth century. The church's uncompromising stance was further underlined when the Vatican Council of 1870 agreed on the dogma of papal infallibility, which was widely interpreted as a declaration of war on the modern secular state.*

*Although church-state conflict had erupted decades earlier in countries such as Switzerland and Italy, in Prussia and Austria it was the proclamation of papal infallibility that precipitated the struggle. In Prussia the so-called Kulturkampf reached extraordinary intensity, but Austria's reaction was considerably more moderate: the liberal government, interpreting the proclamation of papal infallibility as an abrogation of the Concordat (the treaty governing the church-state relationship), sought unilaterally to redefine the jurisdiction of the church within the state. The following debates of March 5 and 9, 1874, centered on comprehensive government proposals before the liberal-dominated lower house of the Austrian parliament, outlining the church's role in the Austrian state.*

**Dr. Schaffer** I have mentioned the Prussian May Laws [laws passed in 1873 subjecting the Roman Catholic clergy to state authority in the course of the so-called Kulturkampf, the conflict of church and state in Germany, 1871 to 1883]. Neither the explanation accompanying the government proposal—which, by the way, deserves praise for its excellent presentation—nor the report of the honorable committee contains the slightest mention of this legislation. It nevertheless seems natural that at this moment, when we are in the process of reordering the relationship of the state to the Catholic Church, we should pay attention to parallel legislation in a neighboring country, particularly where this legislation is both epoch-making and of such recent date. (Calls of "Very true!" on the right.)

If we may do so very briefly, I would like above all to recall that in its main outlines our legislation was antecedent to that of Prussia. Even though our religious proposals reached the discussion stage almost a year after those in Prussia, our

Austria, Reichsrat, *Protokoll des Haus der Abgeordneten,* Session I, Vol. I, 839–840, 859–868. 943–945, 956–958, 960–961. (Translated by Peter Amann.)

program had already been formulated before any part of the Prussian [legislation] became known.

In fact, the two pieces of legislation came into existence under markedly different circumstances. In our case, the legislation was taken under advisement as a natural, consistent, unavoidable legislative duty stemming from the abrogation of the Concordat [the agreement governing church-state relationships in the Habsburg domains had been concluded with the Vatican in 1855 and was rescinded by the Austrian government following the proclamation of papal infallibility in 1870]. The laws were worked out without any extraordinary incidents, while taking existing circumstances into consideration. The Prussian legislation, on the other hand, was produced by the pressure of events. In part it was formulated as a weapon of defense against threatening dangers in the midst of bitter struggles.

Thus from the outset, the two legislative approaches have borne a certain imprint, which, even though it does not permit a judgment of their relative merits, should nonetheless . . . be considered if we are to make a realistic comparison. . . .

The ways and means by which the Prussian laws were enacted . . . lend them, in my opinion at least, an undeniable appearance of persecution, particularly in those aspects by which these laws differ from ours; hence I cannot agree with those who would deem such striking and exaggerated provisions to be especially urgent and desirable.

The peculiar circumstances surrounding the religious legislation in Prussia have resulted in an embittered struggle all along the line, adding up to a state of war with no end in sight. Indeed, in order to safeguard its authority, the state has been forced to resort to ever stronger measures. The latest additions to the Prussian code constitute the most extreme means of defense at the state's disposal.

The situation as it has developed in Prussia seems to present yet another drawback in providing a totally unnecessary martyrdom for a provocative hierarchy which the latter will everywhere and always exploit to its benefit. Refractory priests and bishops are needlessly stamped as being oppressed and persecuted, thus enhancing their following among the uneducated masses and lending themselves the appearance of being victims of [arbitrary] state power, something that ought to be avoided. I hope, given the ways and means by which we are putting the laws into effect, that nothing similar will happen here. I would see a distinct threat in the opposite, i.e., the Prussian method, entailing as it would an even more embittered struggle than in Prussia. As we would scarcely have the resources to overcome such opposition, the loss of our recently gained achievements might well end such a conflict. . . .

*Weiss von Starkenfels* . . . When the power of the state rested in the hands of a single individual and the absolute ruler assumed the role of the state, he was addressed [from all sides]: "Surrender your dignity, descend from your throne and sacrifice part of that majesty really embodied in you!" ("Good!") For myself, I was never able to grasp how I could have done so, had the fate of peoples and nations lain in my hands, had I been able to make happy nations as well as the humblest hut, had I been master of peace or war according to my will. I do not grasp how I could have resigned my lofty position if I respected the right and authority of the Church and when, in short, within and through the Church I was rendering unto God what is God's in order thereby to instruct my subjects to render unto Caesar what is Caesar's.

Ever since the end of absolutism, in order to enlist their support, the masses have been hoodwinked into believing that the sovereignty of the state was being diminished and encroached upon. The sovereignty of the state indeed! And in order to make this more comprehensible, people have suddenly taken offense at the saying, "We must obey God rather than men," a dictum that has been distorted into a threat to the state, disregarding the fact that these words were first pronounced and put into practice almost two thousand years ago. Pluck this phrase out of the Bible if you find it offensive!

In this connection I recall something which recently happened in the committee of which I have the honor of being a member. This occurrence did not arouse mock anger but really made people step back in indignation. The committee reporter, having the constitution of the Jesuit order before him, was citing the place where it says (at least according to his translation and reading) that in the name of Christ the superior has the right to order a member to commit any deadly or venial sin and that the member in question must obey. All of [the committee members] were indignant. Yet if this be the case, permit us to be equally indignant when we are required to do something against God's command that we deem to be a sin. Do not expect us to do this, to obey man rather than God! This is not going to be done. In this matter the Catholic world is but one in spirit and sentiment, holding but a single doctrine: the Church is not vainly called Catholic, that is, universal.

In England, clear-cut statements have recently been made condemning the despotism prevailing here as being of the most contemptible sort, in that it claims to anticipate the wishes of the people, in that it takes refuge behind the will and interest of the people. Such contemptible despotism, it was asserted, has been witnessed from Nero to Cromwell (this was said in England) and from Cromwell to Bismarck. . . . Yes, despotism has always been the same and always will be the same. Yet all its efforts are [nonetheless] in vain. You cannot root out the Catholic Church. Do you think that the letter of the law holds up in the face of the firm and determined faith of Catholics? To you who simulated such indignation when you heard the assertion [in the course of the debate] that "We Tyroleans will not heed the law"? I tell you this: not Catholics alone, but all men who are endowed with a sense of feeling for what is moral and right share, above all, the awareness that any law that is meant to be enforced and to last must have justice as its essential requirement. You may preserve all the forms, from taking a vote to obtaining the consent of the crown, yet the dictum remains valid: every law that lacks the requirement of justice is only a mock law that is really an act of violence ("Bravo!" on the right.) and man rises up against every act of violence, . . . but especially when it is committed in this sphere.

You may perhaps achieve one thing. Enact your law; extend your persecution from other lands to our lands. All you will achieve will be to shake the rotten fruits from the tree. Yet as to the tree itself—which you did not plant, for which someone on high provided the roots—you will never be able to uproot this tree. (Lively applause on the right.)

*Fux* Honored Chamber! . . . The business with which we are concerned today is epoch-making in importance. What is involved is not merely a piece of legislation but a phase in the international conflict over culture that is stirring all of civilized mankind. I may well say without exaggeration that for years to come our decisions with regard to this proposal will exercise a decisive influence on the parliamentary and political situation of our imperial state, on the fulfillment of its cultural mission, on the spiritual welfare of its population.

A happy solution of this affair is equally important to the good sense of the state, to liberalism, and to patriotism. This is why each one of us feels the heavy responsibility that hinges on his vote. This is also the reason why everyone will admit that such an issue cannot be dealt with on the basis of transient expedience, but must be met by fidelity to principles. More than ever must we abide by the ideal that whatsoever does not flow from the well of conviction is evil. Above all, I regret that we Germans, with but scattered support from the Slavic and Romanic side, should stand alone in this burning struggle. I do not level a reproach at anyone, I merely note a fact. I regret that the representatives of the Polish nation, whether for reasons of sentiment or in consideration of certain national Polish dreams and ideals, should have withheld their cooperation, thus gambling with the sympathies which the educated world has always shown toward the plight of this noble nation. (Applause on the left.) I regret no less that the descendants of those who five and a half centuries ago were the pathbreakers and pioneers of the Reformation should today disown the noblest man produced by their nation, a man whose great soul expired at the burning stake at Constance. [The reference is to the Czechs and the burning of John Hus by the Council of Constance in 1415.] (Lively applause on the left. Isolated shouts of disapproval on the far right. Hilarity on the left.)

And why do they hold firm to this unnatural alliance, save perhaps to wield the national hammer? As though we would ever consent to be their anvil! As though, within the framework of the fundamental constitution of the state, they could not take their place around the table of freedom! (Applause on the left.)

I feel deeply inspired by these mightily changing times when a matter such as this should come up for free discussion in an Austrian legislature. The times when dark religious compulsion celebrated its orgies have receded into a misty distance. The terrible idea that "You must believe what I believe because I believe it," which once fired thousands and millions to sheer insanity, smothering even the natural inclination toward love of one's neighbor and of mankind (Calls of "Unfortunately true."), this too has passed. We have also happily left behind the stage of merely tolerating other religions.

Today our point of departure is the fundamental law of the state, the ideas which, in spirit if not in letter, are deposited in this treasure-trove, the ideas of the secular character of the state, the separation of the state from the church. . . . We must test the legislative proposal before us according to this standard and these basic principles. We must wish and strive that it pass this test. (Calls of "True!") We must not simply and blindly rely on historical precedent lest it be used as a claim or pretext for retreating. We must keep in mind the greatest of all historical facts, constituting a definitive break with earlier viewpoints, namely, the concept of the constitutional state which has indeed given birth to these ideas. We must be faithful to our convictions and firmly adhere to these ideas; otherwise we could not truly exclaim, "We are not going to Canossa," without self-deception. [The reference is to Emperor Henry IV's supposed capitulation to Pope Gregory VII in 1077.] We have just returned from Canossa [i.e., the Concordat of 1855 between Austria and the Vatican, considered unduly favorable to the Church, had just been abrogated], and we must not stop half way. We must be on our guard for fear of being maneuvered and pushed back to Canossa. (Great applause on the left.) . . .

It was the Church that always sought to widen the control over her own affairs, to the point of reaching for omnipotence. . . . The Church has always had a universalist tendency. The Church has always striven to intervene in all possible areas, including all areas of public and private law. Essentially the Church still claims what Boniface VIII claimed in one of his bulls: "Every human being is subject to the papacy"—whether it be the Pope deposing kings, giving away countries and peoples, confiscating by means of the interdict the right of generations to eternal salvation, or whether it be in our own days the Syllabus [of Errors of 1864] proclaiming the supremacy of the Church, or Pius IX elevating himself to infallible lawgiver and judge in matters of faith and morals and seeking to annul any legislation opposed to his interest. (Applause on the left.) . . .

We have yet another illustration of this. When the provinces of Alsace and Lorraine were transferred to Germany by the Treaty of Frankfurt [which concluded the Franco-Prussian War in 1871], the issue arose as to whether the French Concordat could be considered annulled as far as these provinces were concerned. The solution to this riddle was confided to a Jesuit, the recently deceased Cardinal Tarquini. He announced that the Pope could unilaterally annul without addressing himself to the secular rulers concerned. In concluding concordats, [Tarquini asserted] the Pope merely grants concessions to any one state, depending upon temporary circumstances. Though the Pope could demand far more, he acquiesces in less for the time being, without, however, surrendering his full powers which he holds in reserve. (Hilarity on the left.)

Princes and peoples are really simply subjects of the Pope, and the latter remains free to cancel concordats whenever he feels so inclined. You see, therefore, to what extent concordats should be viewed as treaties! You see what is left for the state in the face of the Church's drive for omnipotence! [This becomes a problem] not for the [old] state under the Church's sway, but for the modern state and society that can finally say, "This is the limit of your jurisdiction, dear Pope. No further, for the rest is mine." ("Bravo!" on the left.)

Such is the origin and fundamental orientation of this legislation.

This striving for omnipotence was originally confined to the spiritual realm, as the Church was not, after all, a kingdom of this world. Indeed, every church is free to broaden the realm of faith as it sees fit. Who will deny that Christianity has conquered individual rights for man, that the idea of immortality has elevated man to infinity, that man has been comforted by the words, "Come unto me, ye who are heavy-laden." To be truthful, Christianity was indeed imbued with a genuine democratic spirit. ("Bravo!" on the left.)

Primitive Christianity even overstepped the bounds of socialism in practicing community of goods. (Calls of "Very true!") Yet when we contemplate the alterations undergone since then in the Church's spirit and constitution, may we not rightfully say, "If the lofty founder of the religion were to reappear among his own, would he even recognize his instrument?" (Applause on the left.)

I do not want to develop in detail how the Pope, initially enjoying no more than a primacy based on reputation and jurisdiction, how this servant of God's servants gradually rose to worldly rule; how he sought to become the suzerain of all kings and all peoples; how he strove not merely to play Osiris but be Pharaoh as well; . . . how the Church, after overcoming a severe crisis, bore the storms of the Reformation with the help of that Armada [i.e., Spain] that forced the sacrifice of intellect upon the Pope; how the Church even lived through the revolution of 1789 without, however, overcoming it—something it was unable to do because the germs of the ideas of equality, liberty, and fraternity were to be found in Christianity itself; how later on this Church itself took a hand in the politics of the restoration and reaction after 1848 and, going over to the offensive, became once again the Church Militant.

It was the Church that staged this attack. It was the Church that issued the declaration of war in the form of the Syllabus [of Errors] of 1864—that assault on the ideas of modern society. It was the Church that proclaimed the dogma of papal infallibility, despite the remonstrances of judicious bishops. This system as a whole proclaims the supremacy of the Church over the state and over the state's legislation. The papacy demands unconditional subjection from every state in matters of law, for the Church always retains the final say as to whether or not legislation is in harmony with canon law.

[The papacy] demands the suppression of all other religions! (Calls of disapproval on the right; "Yes, yes, that is so!" on the left. Applause on the left.) . . .

Gentlemen! This system simply demands a state church, which we must oppose. This system is today overflowing with a combativeness, an aggressiveness which demands a response of solidarity on the part of liberals in all lands. We are not the irreconcilables; the other side is. ("Bravo!" on the left.) The eightieth statement of the Syllabus reads explicitly: "The Pope cannot be reconciled to or make his peace with modern civilization." . . .

What follows from all this? What follows is that the modern state and modern society have, through the fault of the [papal] Curia, been placed on a permanent war footing. . . .

I tell you this much: today liberalism will no longer crawl humbly to the cross, it will no longer kiss the hem of some cardinal's robe. (Applause on the left.) Today, [liberalism] aware of its own vigor and force, is altogether conscious of being something, of being capable, if need be, to match the challenge. While you may believe, hope, and have confidence in your ideals, you will not shake our faith, our hopes, our confidence in the future. We too hold firmly to our ideals. (Applause on the left.)

To tell the truth, if it is a matter of gauging the [opposing] forces [accurately], we are not at all the underdogs. While the authority for our ideas is also founded on a spiritual and intangible basis, your own broad basis [of support, namely] the ignorance of the masses, is daily eroding.

We are sharpening and tempering our weapons, popular education and enlightenment, which are the most reliable and, in my opinion, the only means of expelling the Jesuits and consolidating liberty. (Lively shouts of "Bravo" on the left.) And as we are today in possession of the legislative power, of many legislatures and governmental authorities, we are indeed to be reckoned with.

If you seek to reach a *modus vivendi* with us, give up your rigid viewpoint exemplified by the Syllabus and the Encyclical. . . .

In conclusion I will say only one more thing. The struggle being waged here is not new. It is a struggle fought from century to century, the struggle between Guelfs [the medieval supporters of papal supremacy] and Ghibellines [the medieval supporters of imperial supremacy]. And let it be known in high places that we are the Ghibellines, that we are those who seek to render to the emperor what is the emperor's. (Lively applause on the left.)

Today the stakes of victory are higher than in those times. The question is no longer that of the state's emancipation within the Church, no longer whether the emperor is to invest the bishop with staff and ring or merely with staff. Nor is the most important thing whether civil marriage will be introduced and the birth and death register turned over to the mayor. These are not even questions of liberalism from which liberalism benefits—as events in Belgium, France, and the Rhineland have shown. These are merely by-products of the principle of separating the state from the church.

One thing we must keep in sight: the principle of untrammeled theocratic authority within modern society must be broken. . . . We must see to it that our dear Austria assumes her rightful place in this struggle waged by a Europe striving for rationality and freedom.

It is from this point of view that I consider this whole law. It may well be—to quote Lord Chatham on the reform movement in England—that it perhaps entails some ambition, some rebellion, some violence; yet we console ourselves with the thought that we have lent our support to the cause of freedom, not to that of tyranny. (Lively and prolonged applause and clapping on the left.) . . .

*Baron von Giovanelli* . . . Usually it is a parliamentary custom for the speaker at the conclusion of a general debate to present a summary of the course of the proceedings, of the arguments raised by one side and opposed on the other. This is impossible for me, because, first of all, I would have to be too lengthy and diffuse; and also because I find certain confusion in the variety of points of view expressed. The gentlemen on that [left] side of the House have raised what seem to me to be conflicting viewpoints. The thought of one group is inconsistent with that of another group.

One group explains: We too are Catholics but not Ultramontanes—as though there could be Catholicism not founded in Rome. The others say: We respect religion, but one must distinguish between religion and the Church—as though there could be a religion without a church.

There are still others who say: We respect the Church, but the Church consists of the people, not of priests and bishops. We are opposed to the hierarchy.

Finally, we have heard remarks which challenge God and the divine attributes.

The speaker I found most telling was the one who said: "The Jesuits are the fly in the ointment." I think so too, and if it isn't the Jesuits, it is at least the followers of Jesus.

As far as I am concerned, I pride myself on taking my stand from a Catholic vantage point. I am a Catholic, and with God's help I shall not disown my convictions during my lifetime. I can therefore present only Catholic opinions to you. In the great and important question with which we are dealing, I perceive two powers, Church and state, and the issue concerns their relationship.

According to the Catholic viewpoint, what is the Church? The Church is an institution of salvation appointed by God, teaching true salvation to all men in order to lead them to their eternal destinies. The Church teaches and rules men to guide them toward these goals. The Church says of itself that, thanks to its divine appointment, it enjoys a threefold power, in terms of which its essential nature must be understood. One is the Church's apostolic mission, which its founder formulated in the words, "Go ye unto all nations preaching the Gospel." A second is the power of the sacraments, according to which the priest makes the offering and disposes of the instruments of grace and salvation. A third is the power of judgment, according to which the Church governs and guides toward salvation those who are confided to her care. The chief members of this jurisdiction are appointed by God: the Pope, the bishops, and the priests. The Church claims to be for all times and all peoples. There is only one Church, which everywhere propagates the same doctrine, offers the same sacraments, disposes of the same grace, exercises the same jurisdiction. This universal and perpetual character of the Church in itself indicates that she cannot be subordinated to secular powers in spiritual matters. The Church cannot arbitrarily alter its laws and its doctrine. These constitute the backdrop for divine revelation, and God is unchanging. It is not simply a matter of doctrine nor simply a dogmatic dictum; it is the very essence of the Church that she was endowed by her divine founder with power independent of the state. The Church has the mission of prevailing for all eternity. How could it be subjected to temporal power in its essential institutions, in its appointment of bishops and priests, in the exercise of its official authority? . . .

Gentlemen! The Church's concept of the state is in sharp opposition to the modern view. The Church teaches that all power, spiritual and secular, comes from above, and that the fundamental reason why subjects obey the authorities, be they good or evil, is because the authorities' power derives from God. If power did not emanate from above, no man would be obliged to obey, the individual will would then indeed be autonomous. Because all power is from God, therefore all power is subject to God. Hence the maxim, "We must obey God rather than man."

The state has the duty to direct and order civil affairs. Within its sphere of action it is independent, and the Church neither should nor indeed does infringe upon it. The Church demands as much of the state; yet in the Christian state law is not derived from the state's own will nor from that of its ruler, whether this ruler be a single person or an assembly. In a Christian state law is derived from God. According to the Christian viewpoint, law must be the external reflection of justice, and legislation is the expression of what human understanding considers to be the outward manifestation of the demands of justice. (Calls on the right: "Very good!")

Such is law according to the Christian viewpoint—the [very] opposite of arbitrary power.

In the secular state, on the other hand, gentlemen, the difference between concepts of right, might, and arbitrary power disappears.

In the secular state, the state ascribes power to itself and does not recognize any norm higher than itself, since it is itself the source of law. In the secular state, whatever the majority wants at any given moment is law, and it remains law as long as and because the majority wills it to be so. There is no authoritative standard above the arbitrary will of the majority. The sovereign authority of the state, refusing to bow to any law outside itself, to a divine law, seeks to regulate everything of and by itself. This struggle, this opposition between human arbitrary power and divine law is nothing new; it is as old as the struggle between good and evil, the struggle and rebellion of human pride against divine law. (Hilarity on the left. "Bravo! (bravo!" on the right.)

It is strange, gentlemen, that the invention of the secular state is claimed as an achievement of modern science. Oh no! There have always been men who would have nothing to do with God and his commandments, who, to the best of their ability, regarded their own arbitrary power and their own passions as the final arbiter of their actions and thoughts. . . .

Religious enthusiasm, whether true or false, has always been in back of the greatest achievements of world history. There has never been a state without reverence for God, a state of atheists. Wherever there is disbelief, there is death and despair; atheism is the philosophy of suicide. (Agreement on the right.)

The ghastly increase in the [rate of suicide] furnishes a frightful corroboration [to my argument]. (Calls of "Very true!" on the right.)

The science of godlessness about which you are bragging is the science of despair. This science teaches that man came out of slime, that his spiritual life is merely the motion of matter, that man returns to slime—for after death there is no hereafter. Yes, gentlemen, this science leads to annihilation by depriving man of his inner peace, by depriving him of the hope of a future. Faith is the greatest good of man: it teaches subjection to God's will; it also teaches subjection to a cruel tyrant; it teaches subjection to every oppression for the sake of God's will. Confidence in God, self-denial, humility, chastity, renunciation of the world, hope, love of God and one's fellow—all these are the blossoms of faith. Faith provides everything that ennobles life and elevates the spirit. Your wisdom (turning to the left) slays the spirit, annihilates the sense of community; it leads to dissolution and despair.

Admittedly there are matters which, though of a spiritual nature, do have repercussions in civil life. In such instances an agreement is necessary, or at least desirable. Yet such agreement can only be reached on the basis of a Christian view of the world; and when such a presupposition is lacking, the Church cannot enter into an accord. . . .

**Dr. Weeber**   Keeping in mind and looking back on the debate we have witnessed in the last few days, we must confess in the first place that it went far beyond the framework of the legislative proposal under consideration.

While this legislative proposal was uniquely and solely designed to order and regulate the religious affairs with regard to the external legal position of the Catholic Church, the debate extended to the whole broad range of church affairs, immersed itself in historical accounts of centuries long past, and even roamed over the area of faith and religion. . . .

It is my task, which I fulfill from the profoundest depth of my conviction, to speak for the legislative proposal brought forward by the government and complemented on some points by the committee. The legislative proposal grew out of the conviction that, given present circumstances, the state is forced by utter necessity, by its duty of self-preservation, to draw a line between the rights of the Church and those of the state. The Ultramontane tendency of one part of the Church has encouraged and promoted encroachments upon the state's sphere, jeopardizing the future of the state and endangering its mission.

No weightier and more irrefutable evidence in support of this claim can be mustered than the words spoken by the gentlemen from the Tyrol and Upper Austria [as fervent Catholics, they had threatened civil disobedience if the law were put into effect], who thus set a frightful example. (Calls of "True! Bravo!" and hilarity on the left and in the center.)

I do not wish to linger over these incidents that must be highly disagreeable to every good Austrian. In going back to the main lines of the debate, in summing up and trying to systematize the factual, concrete arguments that were brought up against the legislative proposal, I permit myself in the first place to speak to a representative on the left side of this lofty chamber. He pointed to the law as defective and incomplete in not fully carrying out the principle upon which it is based. In theory I fully agree with him. I would very much like to adopt his point of view and carry out the principle in all its consequences—but on one condition: that as soon as the law is put into effect, the actual conditions of the whole realm should be instantly transformed in such a manner that conditions would correspond to the law. (Calls of "Very good!" in the center.)

This, however, is not possible. Therefore the law must be adapted to circumstances; it must use the existing circumstances as a starting point in order to lead and press forward in the direction corresponding to the principle, to the purpose of the whole thing.

It cannot be denied, however, that the level of education is not equally high in all countries, nor in all the classes and sections of the population. While the lawmaking authorities have indeed the duty to take forward strides, it should not be forgotten that these authorities should not advance so rapidly that a great part of the people be unable to keep pace.

Therein, gentlemen, lies the explanation as to why this law may well seem defective on theoretical grounds. It is my conviction, however, that from the standpoint of practical needs, the law is apt. ("Bravo!" on the left.) . . .

When objections against the law were raised from this (right) side of the lofty chamber, to the effect that it breeds skepticism; when it was said that this was a struggle of faith against disbelief and that the law contains attacks upon religion and religious conviction, I can only confine myself to a simple denial until such time as the gentlemen on the right see fit to show me the paragraphs containing infringements upon religion and an attack upon the Catholic faith. Having read over the individual sections of the law, I did not find any such encroachments, nor did I find a contradiction between the law and religious prescriptions. Were I to go through the law once again, I would still not find them. Or is paragraph 1, perhaps, which determines the qualifications for holding church offices and benefices incompatible with the [Catholic] faith? This seems scarcely possible!

Is paragraph 2, requiring Austrian citizenship and a clean moral and civic record for the holding of a church office, contrary to religion? I believe this will never be claimed from a religious point of view. Or are perhaps those paragraphs opposed to faith and religion that concede the right of presentation [to a church office] to a territorial ruler or private patron?

Well, how could the Catholic Church and its head recognize these same rights for hundreds of years which are [here] being spelled out once again? Or is it perhaps paragraph 8 containing the decision that a priest, found guilty of criminal or other punishable offenses, be declared ineligible to exercise his office? Surely this cannot be considered offensive to religion; yet this paragraph has a very peculiar history which is brought out in the government's brief on the proposal.

In this brief we have read that within a few years 112 churchmen have been condemned for criminal or other punishable offenses, without the Church deeming it necessary to remove them from office. The fact that punishable offenses occur within the priesthood is not meant as a reproach. Such things happen in every walk of life, and no walk of life can be deemed immune. Yet that in 112 cases there should not have been a single instance in which the rulers of the Church saw fit to safeguard the right of the state by removing from the exercise of spiritual functions persons condemned for criminal acts against the state, for [the crime of] *lèse-majesté* [i.e., insulting the emperor], for offenses against public security and the like—this fact and this history of paragraph 8 is indeed significant in indicating that the state must look out for itself, being unable to count upon support from the Church.

I could cite paragraph after paragraph to prove that they do not impinge on faith or religion. I must therefore unconditionally reject the accusation that the law offends against religion. I shall deem this accusation to be false, just as long as the representatives from the right side of this chamber shall not have produced one paragraph, one article, even one word directed against the Catholic faith. . . .

## ⁓§ SPEECH ON WOMEN'S SUFFRAGE

*John Stuart Mill*

> *The movement to gain equality for women had its roots in the very ideology of the Enlightenment, in its aspiration to free the individual from the trammels of custom and society and to provide for his full and harmonious development as a human being. Several of the philosophes, among whom Condorcet (see Vol. III, pages 258–259) is the most notable,*

*advocated, among many other reforms, an end to discrimination based on sex. As early as the 1790s, the cry was to be taken up by several feminists who put this reform first on their agenda.*

*It took several generations to bridge the gap between feminism as an abstract doctrine and women's suffrage as a potent political movement. Even though votes for women had figured briefly in the demands of the English Chartists in 1838, the issue was not really publicly raised in Parliament until 1867. At this time, during the debate on extending suffrage by reducing property qualifications for voting, John Stuart Mill (see page 73) shocked the staid House of Commons by bringing up the question of women's suffrage. Specifically, he proposed a seemingly innocuous but actually startling amendment to the Reform Bill of 1867 to change the word "man" to "person." The speech that follows was delivered in support of that amendment. Mill's championship was no passing fancy; his bitter book* The Subjection of Women (1869) *was to become the bible of European femininism during the remainder of the nineteenth century.*

*Although Mill's efforts to extend the franchise were not immediately successful, the British Parliament proved more responsive in removing some of the legal disabilities of women in a series of laws passed during the 1870s and 1880s. It took the militant agitation of the decade preceding World War I to gain the municipal franchise for women; complete political participation by women was not achieved in Great Britain until 1928. By this time parallel movements for women's suffrage had succeeded in many Western countries, though few would argue that the effective and full equality of women in the social, economic, and political spheres had been fully achieved.*

**Mr. J. Stuart Mill**   I rise, Sir, to propose an extension of the suffrage which can excite no party or class feeling in this House; which can give no umbrage to the keenest asserter of the claims either of property or of numbers; an extension which has not the smallest tendency to disturb what we have heard so much about lately, the balance of political power, which cannot afflict the most timid alarmist with revolutionary terrors, or offend the most jealous democrat as an infringement of popular rights, or a privilege granted to one class of society at the expense of another. There is nothing to distract our attention from the simple question, whether there is any adequate justification for continuing to exclude an entire half of the community, not only from admission, but from the capability of being ever admitted within the pale

Great Britain, 3 *Hansard's Parliamentary Debates*, CLXXXVII (1867), 817–829, 838–840, 843.

of the Constitution, though they may fulfil all the conditions legally and constitution-
ally sufficient in every case but theirs. Sir, within the limits of our Constitution this
is a solitary case. There is no other example of an exclusion which is absolute. If the
law denied a vote to all but the possessors of £5,000 a year, the poorest man in the
nation might—and now and then would—acquire the suffrage; but neither birth,
nor fortune, nor merit, nor exertion, nor intellect, nor even that great disposer of
human affairs, accident, can ever enable any woman to have her voice counted in
those national affairs which touch her and hers as nearly as any other person in the
nation.

Nor, Sir, before going any further, allow me to say that a *primâ facie* case is already made out. It is not just to make distinctions, in rights and privileges, without
a positive reason. I do not mean that the electoral franchise, or any other public
function, is an abstract right, and that to withhold it from any one, on sufficient
grounds of expediency, is a personal wrong; it is a complete misunderstanding of
the principle I maintain, to confound this with it; my argument is entirely one of
expediency. But there are different orders of expediency; all expediencies are not
exactly on the same level; there is an important branch of expediency called justice;
and justice, though it does not necessarily require that we should confer political
functions on every one, does require that we should not, capriciously and without
cause, withhold from one what we give to another. As was most truly said by my right
hon. Friend the Member for South Lancashire, in the most misunderstood and mis-
represented speech I ever remember; to lay a ground for refusing the suffrage to any
one, it is necessary to allege either personal unfitness or public danger. Now, can
either of these be alleged in the present case? Can it be pretended that women who
manage an estate or conduct a business—who pay rates and taxes, often to a large
amount, and frequently from their own earnings—many of whom are responsible
heads of families, and some of whom, in the capacity of schoolmistresses, teach much
more than a great number of the male electors have ever learnt—are not capable of
a function of which every male householder is capable? Or is it feared that if they
were admitted to the suffrage they would revolutionize the State—would deprive us
of any of our valued institutions, or that we should have worse laws, or be in any
way whatever worse governed through the effect of their suffrages? No one, Sir, believes anything of the kind. And it is not only the general principles of justice that
are infringed, or at least set aside, by the exclusion of women, merely as women,
from any share in the representation; that exclusion is also repugnant to the particular principles of the British Constitution. It violates one of the oldest of our
constitutional maxims—a doctrine dear to Reformers, and theoretically acknowledged
by most Conservatives—that taxation and representation should be co-extensive. Do
not women pay taxes? Does not every woman who is *sui juris* contribute exactly as
much to the revenue as a man who has the same electoral qualification? If a stake
in the country means anything, the owner of freehold or leasehold property has the
same stake, whether it is owned by a man or a woman. There is evidence in our
constitutional records that women have voted, in counties and in some boroughs, at
former, though certainly distant, periods of our history.

The House, however, will doubtless expect that I should not rest my case solely
on the general principles either of justice or of the Constitution, but should produce

what are called practical arguments. Now, there is one practical argument of great weight, which, I frankly confess, is entirely wanting in the case of women; they do not hold great meetings in the Parks, or demonstrations at Islington. How far this omission may be considered to invalidate their claim, I will not undertake to decide; but other practical arguments, practical in the most restricted meaning of the term, are not wanting; and I am prepared to state them, if I may be permitted first to ask, what are the practical objections? The difficulty which most people feel on this subject is not a practical objection; there is nothing practical about it, it is a mere feeling —a feeling of strangeness; the proposal is so new; at least they think so, though this is a mistake; it is a very old proposal. Well, Sir, strangeness is a thing which wears off; some things were strange enough to many of us three months ago which are not at all so now; and many are strange now, which will not be strange to the same persons a few years hence, or even, perhaps, a few months. And as for novelty, we live in a world of novelties; the despotism of custom is on the wane; we are not now satisfied with knowing what a thing is, we ask whether it ought to be; and in this House at least, I am bound to believe that an appeal lies from custom to a higher tribunal, in which reason is judge. Now, the reasons which custom is in the habit of giving for itself on this subject are usually very brief. That, indeed, is one of my difficulties; it is not easy to refute an interjection; interjections, however, are the only arguments among those we usually hear on this subject, which it seems to me at all difficult to refute. The others mostly present themselves in such aphorisms as these:—Politics are not women's business, and would distract them from their proper duties; women do not desire the suffrage, but would rather be without it; women are sufficiently represented by the representation of their male relatives and connections; women have power enough already.

I shall probably be thought to have done enough in the way of answering, if I answer all this; and it may, perhaps, instigate any hon. Gentleman who takes the trouble of replying to me, to produce something more recondite. Politics, it is said, are not a woman's business. Well, Sir, I rather think that politics are not a man's business either; unless he is one of the few who are selected and paid to devote their time to the public service, or is a Member of this or of the other House. The vast majority of male electors have each his own business which absorbs nearly the whole of his time; but I have not heard that the few hours occupied, once in a few years, in attending at a polling-booth, even if we throw in the time spent in reading newspapers and political treatises, ever causes them to neglect their shops or their counting-houses. I have never understood that those who have votes are worse merchants, or worse lawyers, or worse physicians, or even worse clergymen than other people. One would almost suppose that the British Constitution denied a vote to every one who could not give the greater part of his time to politics; if this were the case we should have a very limited constituency. But allow me to ask, what is the meaning of political freedom? Is it anything but the control of those who do make their business of politics, by those who do not? Is it not the very essence of constitutional liberty, that men come from their looms and their forges to decide, and decide well, whether they are properly governed, and whom they will be governed by? And the nations which prize this privilege the most, and exercise it most fully, are invariably those who excel the most in the common concerns of life.

The ordinary occupations of most women are, and are likely to remain, principally domestic; but the notion that these occupations are incompatible with the keenest interest in national affairs, and in all the great interests of humanity, is as utterly futile as the apprehension, once sincerely entertained, that artizans would desert their workshops and their factories if they were taught to read. I know there is an obscure feeling—a feeling which is ashamed to express itself openly—as if women had no right to care about anything, except how they may be the most useful and devoted servants of some man. But as I am convinced that there is not a single Member of this House, whose conscience accuses him of so mean a feeling, I may say without offence, that this claim to confiscate the whole existence of one half of the species for the supposed convenience of the other, appears to me, independently of its injustice, particularly silly. For who that has had ordinary experience of human affairs, and ordinary capacity of profiting by that experience, fancies that those do their own work best who understand nothing else? A man has lived to little purpose who has not learnt that without general mental cultivation, no particular work that requires understanding is ever done in the best manner. It requires brains to use practical experience; and brains, even without practical experience, go further than any amount of practical experience without brains.

But perhaps it is thought that the ordinary occupations of women are more antagonistic than those of men are to the comprehension of public affairs. It is thought, perhaps, that those who are principally charged with the moral education of the future generations of men, cannot be fit to form an opinion about the moral and educational interests of a people; and that those whose chief daily business is the judicious laying-out of money, so as to produce the greatest results with the smallest means, cannot possibly give any lessons to right hon. Gentlemen on the other side of the House on this, who contrive to produce such singularly small results with such vast means. I feel a degree of confidence, Sir, on this subject, which I could not feel, if the political change, in itself not great or formidable, which I advocate, were not grounded, as beneficent and salutary political changes almost always are, upon a previous social change. The notion of a hard and fast line of separation between women's occupations and men's—of forbidding women to take interest in the things which interest men—belongs to a gone-by state of society which is receding further and further into the past. We talk of political revolutions, but we do not sufficiently attend to the fact that there has taken place around us a silent domestic revolution; women and men are, for the first time in history, really each other's companions. Our traditions respecting the proper relations between them have descended from a time when their lives were apart—when they were separate in their thoughts, because they were separate equally in their amusements and in their serious occupations. In former days a man passed his life among men; all his friendships, all his real intimacies, were with men; with men alone did he consult on any serious business; the wife was either a plaything, or an upper servant. All this, among the educated classes, is now changed.  The man no longer gives his spare hours to violent outdoor exercises and boisterous conviviality with male associates; the two sexes now pass their lives together; the women of a man's family are his habitual society; the wife is his chief associate, his most confidential friend, and often his most trusted adviser. Now, does a man wish to have for his nearest companion so closely linked with him, and whose wishes and preferences have so strong a claim on him, one whose thoughts are alien to those which occupy his own mind—one who can neither be a help, a comfort, nor a support, to his noblest feelings and purposes? Is this close and almost exclusive companionship compatible with women's being warned off all large subjects—being taught that they ought not to care for what it is men's duty to care for, and that to have any serious interests outside the household is stepping beyond their province? Is it good for a man to live in complete communion of thoughts and feelings with one who is studiously kept inferior to himself, whose earthy interests are forcibly confined within four walls, and who cultivates, as a grace of character, ignorance and indifference about the most inspiring subjects, those among which his highest duties are cast? Does any one suppose that this can happen without detriment to the man's own character?

Sir, the time is now come when, unless women are raised to the level of men, men will be pulled down to theirs. The women of a man's family are either a stimulus and a support to his highest aspirations, or a drag upon them. You may keep them ignorant of politics, but you cannot prevent them from concerning themselves with the least respectable part of politics—its personalities; if they do not understand and cannot enter into the man's feelings of public duty, they do care about his personal interest, and that is the scale into which their weight will certainly be thrown. They will be an influence always at hand, co-operating with the man's selfish promptings, lying in wait for his moments of moral irresolution, and doubling the strength of every temptation. Even if they maintain a modest forbearance, the mere absence of their sympathy will hang a dead-weight on his moral energies, making him unwilling to make sacrifices which they will feel, and to forego social advantages and successes in which they would share, for objects which they cannot appreciate. Supposing him fortunate enough to escape any actual sacrifice of conscience, the indirect effect on the higher parts of his own character is still deplorable. Under an idle notion that the beauties of character of the two sexes are mutually incompatible, men are afraid of manly women; but those who have considered the nature and power of social influences well know, that unless there are manly women, there will not much longer be manly men. When men and women are really companions, if women are frivolous, men will be frivolous; if women care for nothing but personal interest and idle vanities, men in general will care for little else; the two sexes must now rise or sink together.

It may be said that women may take interest in great public questions without having votes; they may, certainly; but how many of them will? Education and society have exhausted their power in inculcating on women that their proper rule of conduct is what society expects from them; and the denial of the vote is a proclamation intelligible to every one, that whatever else society may expect, it does not expect that they should concern themselves with public interests. Why, the whole of a girl's thoughts and feelings are toned down by it from her schooldays; she does not take the interest even in national history which her brothers do, because it is to be no business of hers when she grows up. If there are women—and now happily there are many—who do interest themselves in these subjects, and do study them, it is because the force within is strong enough to bear up against the worst kind of discouragment, that which acts not by interposing obstacles, which may be struggled against, but by deadening the spirit which faces and conquers obstacles.

We are told, Sir, that women do not wish for the suffrage. If the fact were so, it would only prove that all women are still under this deadening influence; that the opiate still benumbs their mind and conscience. But great numbers of women do desire the suffrage, and have asked for it by petitions to this House. How do we know how many more thousands there may be who have not asked for what they do not hope to get; or for fear of what may be thought of them by men, or by other women; or from the feeling, so sedulously cultivated in them by their education— aversion to make themselves conspicuous? Men must have a rare power of self-delu- sion, if they suppose that leading questions put to the ladies of their family or of their acquaintance will elicit their real sentiments, or will be answered with complete sincerity by one woman in 10,000. No one is so well schooled as most women are in making a virtue of necessity; it costs little to disclaim caring for what is not offered; and frankness in the expression of sentiments which may be unpleasing and may be thought uncomplimentary to their nearest connections, is not one of the virtues which a woman's education tends to cultivate, and is, moreover, a virtue at- tended with sufficient risk, to induce prudent women usually to reserve its exercise for cases in which there is a nearer and a more personal interest at stake. However this may be, those who do not care for the suffrage will not use it; either they will not register, or if they do, they will vote as their male relatives advise—by which, as the advantage will probably be about equally shared among all classes, no harm will be done. Those, be they few or many, who do value the privilege, will exercise it, and will receive that stimulus to their faculties, and that widening and liberalizing influ- ence over their feelings and sympathies, which the suffrage seldom fails to produce on those who are admitted to it. Meanwhile an unworthy stigma would be removed from the whole sex. The law would cease to decleare them incapable of serious things; would cease to proclaim that their opinions and wishes are unworthy of regard, on things which concern them equally with men, and on many things which concern them much more than men. They would no longer be classed with children, idiots, and lunatics, as incapable of taking care of either themselves or others, and needing that everything should be done for them, without asking their consent. If only one woman in 20,000 used the suffrage, to be declared capable of it would be a boon to all women. Even that theoretical enfranchisement would remove a weight from the expansion of their faculties, the real mischief of which is much greater than the apparent.

Then it is said, that women do not need direct power, having so much indirect, through their influence over their male relatives and connections. I should like to carry this argument a little further. Rich people have a great deal of indirect in- fluence. Is this a reason for refusing them votes? Does any one propose a rating qualification the wrong way, or bring in a Reform Bill to disfranchise all who live in a £500 house, or pay £100 a year indirect taxes? Unless this rule for distributing the franchise is to be reserved for the exclusive benefit of women, it would follow that persons of more than a certain fortune should be allowed to bribe, but should not be allowed to vote. Sir, it is true that women have great power. It is part of my case that they have great power; but they have it under the worst possible conditions because it is indirect, and therefore irresponsible. I want to make this great power a responsible power. I want to make the woman feel her conscience interested in its honest exercise. I want her to feel that it is not given to her as a mere means of personal ascendency. I want to make her influence work by a manly interchange of opinion, and not by cajolery. I want to awaken in her the political point of honour. Many a woman already influences greatly the political conduct of the men connected with her, and sometimes, by force of will, actually governs it; but she is never supposed to have anything to do with it; the man whom she influences, and perhaps misleads, is alone responsible; her power is like the back-stairs influence of a favourite. Sir, I demand that all who exercise power should have the burden laid on them of knowing something about the things they have power over. With the acknowledged right to a voice, would come a sense of the corresponding duty. Women are not usually inferior in tenderness of conscience to men. Make the woman a moral agent in these matters; show that you expect from her a political conscience; and when she has learnt to understand the transcendent importance of these things, she will know why it is wrong to sacrifice political convictions to personal interest or vanity; she will understand that political integrity is not a foolish personal crotchet, which a man is bound, for the sake of his family, to give up, but a solemn duty; and the men whom she can influence will be better men in all public matters, and not, as they often are now, worse men by the whole amount of her influence.

But at least, it will be said, women do not suffer any practical inconvenience, as women, by not having a vote. The interests of all women are safe in the hands of their fathers, husbands, and brothers, who have the same interest with them, and not only know, far better than they do, what is good for them, but care much more for them then they care for themselves. Sir, this is exactly what is said of all unrepresented classes. The operatives, for instance; are they not virtually represented by the representation of their employers? Are not the interest of the employers and that of the employed, when properly understood, the same? To insinuate the contrary, is it not the horrible crime of setting class against class? Is not the farmer equally interested with the labourer in the prosperity of agriculture—the cotton manufacturer equally with his workmen in the high price of calicoes? Are they not both interested alike in taking off taxes? And, generally, have not employers and employed a common interest against all outsiders, just as husband and wife have against all outside the family? And what is more, are not all employers good, kind, benevolent men, who love their workpeople, and always desire to do what is most for their good? All these assertions are as true, and as much to the purpose, as the corresponding assertions respecting men and women. Sir, we do not live in Arcadia, but, as we were lately reminded, *in fæce Romuli:* and in that region workmen need other protection than that of their employers, and women other protection than that of their men. I should like to have a Return laid before this House of the number of women who are annually beaten to death, kicked to death, or trampled to death by their male protectors; and, in an opposite column, the amount of the sentences passed in those cases in which the dastardly criminals did not get off altogether. I should also like to have, in a third column, the amount of property, the unlawful taking of which was, at the same sessions or assizes, by the same judge, thought worthy of the same amount of punishment. We should then have an arithmetical estimate of the value set by a male legislature and male tribunals on the murder of a woman, often by torture continued through years, which, if there is any shame in us, would make us hang our heads.

Sir, before it is affirmed that women do not suffer in their interests, as women, by the denial of a vote, it should be considered whether women have no grievances; whether the laws, and those practices which laws can reach, are in every way as favourable to women as to men. Now, how stands the fact? In the matter of education, for instance. We continually hear that the most important part of national education is that of mothers, because they educate the future men. Is this importance really attached to it? Are there many fathers who care as much, or are willing to expend as much, for the education of their daughters as of their sons? Where are the Universities, where the high schools, or the schools of any high description, for them? If it be said that girls are better educated at home, where are the training-schools for governesses? What has become of the endowments which the bounty of our ancestors destined for the education, not of one sex only but of both indiscriminately? I am told by one of the highest authorities on the subject, that in the majority of the endowments the provision made is not for boys, but for education generally; in one great endowment, Christ's Hospital, it is expressly for both; that institution now maintains and educates 1,100 boys, and exactly twenty-six girls. And when they attain womanhood, how does it fare with that great and increasing portion of the sex, who, sprung from the educated classes, have not inherited a provision, and not having obtained one by marriage, or disdaining to marry merely for a provision, depend on their exertions for subsistence? Hardly any decent educated occupation, save one, is open to them. They are either governesses or nothing. . . . No sooner do women show themselves capable of competing with men in any career, than that career, if it be lucrative or honourable, is closed to them. A short time ago women might be associates of the Royal Academy; but they were so distinguishing themselves, they were assuming so honourable a place in their art, that this privilege also has been withdrawn.

This is the sort of care taken of women's interests by the men who so faithfully represent them. This is the way we treat unmarried women. And how is it with the married? They, it may be said, are not interested in this Motion; and they are not directly interested; but it interests, even directly, many who have been married, as well as others who will be. Now, by the common law of England, all that a wife has, belongs absolutely to the husband; he may tear it all from her, squander every penny of it in debauchery, leave her to support by her labour herself and her children, and if by heroic exertion and self-sacrifice she is able to put by something for their future wants, unless she is judicially separated from him he can pounce down upon her savings, and leave her penniless. And such cases are of quite common occurrence.

Sir, if we were besotted enough to think these things right, there would be more excuse for us; but we know better. The richer classes take care to exempt their own daughters from the consequences of this abominable state of the law. By the contrivance of marriage settlements, they are able in each case to make a private law for themselves, and they invariably do so. Why do we not provide that justice for the daughters of the poor, which we take care to provide for our own daughters? Why is not that which is done in every case that we personally care for, made the law of the land, so that a poor man's child, whose parents could not afford the expense of a settlement, may retain a right to any little property that may devolve on her, and may have a voice in the disposal of her own earnings, which, in the case of many husbands, are the best and only reliable part of the incomings of the family?

I am sometimes asked what practical grievances I propose to remedy by giving women a vote. I propose, for one thing, to remedy this. I give these instances to prove that women are not the petted children of society which many people seem to think they are—that they have not the overabundance, the superfluity of power that is ascribed to them, and are not sufficiently represented by the representation of the men who have not had the heart to do for them this simple and obvious piece of justice. Sir, grievances of less magnitude than the law of the property of married women, when suffered by parties less inured to passive submission, have provoked revolutions. We ought not to take advantage of the security we feel against any such consequence in the present case, to withhold from a limited number of women that moderate amount of participation in the enactment and improvement of our laws, which this Motion solicits for them, and which would enable the general feelings of women to be heard in this House through a few male representatives. We ought not to deny to them, what we are conceding to everybody else—a right to be consulted; the ordinary chance of placing in the great Council of the nation a few organs of their sentiments—of having, what every petty trade or profession has, a few members who feel specially called on to attend to their interests, and to point out how those interests are affected by the law, or by any proposed changes in it. No more is asked by this Motion; and when the time comes, as it certainly will come, when this will be granted, I feel the firmest conviction that you will never repent of the concession.

*Mr. Laing* thanked the hon. Member for Westminster for the pleasant interlude he had interposed to the grave and somewhat sombre discussions on the subject of Reform, in which the Committee had hitherto been engaged. The hon. Member for Westminster had referred in very feeling terms to the wickets which he had spoken of as having been shut by the male against the fair sex; and he wished to ask him whether among those wickets he included those which closed the entrance to that House? Because the logical inference from the argument of the hon. Member was that if women ought to be allowed to elect representatives they ought to be eligible to seats in the House of Commons. Indeed, he had said as much, for he had pointed to the office of Chancellor of the Exchequer as one which could not be better filled than by a person whose life was spent in obtaining the greatest results from the smallest possible pecuniary means. But there were a great many practical considerations to be taken into account before the hon. Gentleman's views could be carried out to that extent. The Committee would recollect that there had been a discussion a few nights before as to the number of cubic feet which should be required to constitute a dwelling-house in the case of the compound-householder, and space must undoubtedly form a very material element in any scheme which might be devised for giving women a place in the deliberations of the Legislature. The question of rating, too, would have a very important bearing in determining whether the suffrage should be conferred upon them, for, if he was not mistaken, it entered very largely into the intercourse of a certain Mr. and Mrs. Caudle, who were some years ago so humorously described in the pages of a well-known periodical. But, to speak seriously on the subject, it would, he thought, be well in dealing with it to reflect for a moment how small a part mere logic played in political and social life. The instinct, he felt assured, of nine men out of ten—nay, of nine women out of ten—was opposed to the proposal which had been laid before the Committee by the hon. Member for Westminster with so much force and acumen, and although they might not be able to give a single argument for their opinion he would back their instinct against the logic of the hon. Member. The most narrow of all possible views to take of the question was, he contended, to look upon women as being a sort of half-developed men, whose rights were to be made dependent on such things as rating and voting and the like, and who was held to be kept in a position of humiliation if she was not assimilated in every respect to the male half of creation. The real standard of the true career for human beings, whether male or female, to pursue in search of happiness was that ideal pattern of perfection which was in the mind of the Creator when He called both man and woman into existence. Taking that standard of ideal perfection in the case of woman, he would ask whether it had any relation whatsoever to their having a voice in the election of Members of Parliament? Between the two sexes it was abundantly evident that Nature had drawn clear lines of distinction. There were certain things which women could do better than men, and others which they could not do so well. In all that required rough, rude, practical force, stability of character, and intellect, man was superior: whereas in all those relations of life that demanded mildness, softness of character, and amiability, women far excelled. He would appeal in support of the view which he took from the political economists to those who were higher authorities in such matters—the poets. How did that poet who was admitted on all hands to have held most truly the mirror up to nature represent ideal women? Who could fancy the Julias, Ophelias, and Desdemonas, who were surrounded with so great a charm in his pages, as interesting themselves in and voting at municipal or Parliamentary elections? Which was the most likely to figure in the character of a ratepayer and elector—the gentle Cordelia or the hateful and unattractive Goneril or Regan? He did not wish to pursue the question further, but at the bottom of it lay, he firmly believed, the distinction which he had endeavoured to point out. With regard to the law of property as it affected married women he would admit that in those cases in which that law bore hardly on the female sex it was a matter well worthy of consideration how it should be revised and placed upon a footing more in accordance with the civilization of the age. The contests of political life, and the rude and rough work which men had so often to go through, were not, however, he thought, suited to the nature of woman, and, unless he was greatly mistaken, the majority of women themselves were of that opinion. The question, he would add, was not one of a purely speculative character. There was one country in which women took a leading part in the concerns of active life, in which they were regarded as constituting the safety and ornament of the Throne, and monopolized the rewards of the Court—even those which were the most seductive of all—the rewards of military virtue and honour. That Court was the Court of Dahomey. Now, he must confess he had no wish to see the institutions of Dahomey imported into our own happy land; in other words, he hoped the day was far distant when our women should become masculine and our men effeminate. The maxim *propria quæ maribus* had remained fixed in his mind ever since in early youth it had been installed into it under the influence of the birch, and he could not help thinking that it was more fitting that men should retain what was proper to men, and the women retain all the privileges that could becomingly be conceded to women.

Question put, "That the word 'man' stand part of the Clause."
The Committee *divided:*—Ayes 196; Noes 73: Majority 123.

## THE SCHOOL AND SOCIETY

*John Dewey*

*In any society, the ideas and skills instilled in the young and the methods used to instill them reveal what their elders consider a necessary preparation for life. Modern democratic society is no exception: going to school today, especially in America, is a very different experience from what it was only a century ago. The names of many educators are associated with this change, beginning with Rousseau and Pestalozzi in the eighteenth century. But no one has perceived the nature and significance of the recent trends in education as clearly or with as much depth of historical and philosophical perspective as John Dewey (1859–1952). And no other movement has so dominated the modern pedagogical scene, even in Europe, as has progressive education.*

*John Dewey did not invent progressive education. It was only one aspect of the Progressive movement, a wave of social reform which had its roots in the Western and Middle Western United States in the 1890s and which demanded greater democracy in politics and in American life generally. Its political leaders were Robert M. La Follette, George W. Norris, and Theodore Roosevelt, but Dewey was its chief intellectual spokesman. His philosophy, which he called "instrumentalism" or "pragmatism," stressed the biological and social functions of intelligence and the kinship between the scientific method and the democratic process as techniques of collective problem solving. He criticized traditional education for being authoritarian and for treating ideas in isolation from the context in which they originated and in which they were being placed: the developing mind of the child. In 1896 he and his wife founded at the University of Chicago a Laboratory School designed to base education on the findings of the new sciences of psychology and sociology and, above all, to make it relevant to the needs both of the child and of society. At the same time, Dewey was explaining his ideas to graduate students and other professors as head of the University's new department of philosophy, psychology, and pedagogy. In 1904 he moved to Columbia University and helped its Teachers College to dominate American education for half a century. During his long life—he died at the age of ninety-three—he also found time to write dozens of influential books and hundreds of important articles. The fullest statement of his educational philosophy is in* Democracy and Education *(1916); but the following selection from* The School and Society *(1899), in which he describes his Laboratory School, catches the enthusiasm of the movement at an early stage and brings out its relations to modern democracy and industrialism.*

## CHAPTER I. THE SCHOOL AND SOCIAL PROGRESS

We are apt to look at the school from an individualistic standpoint, as something between teacher and pupil, or between teacher and parent. That which interests us most is naturally the progress made by the individual child of our acquaintance, his normal physical development, his advance in ability to read, write, and figure, his growth in the knowledge of geography and history, improvement in manners, habits of promptness, order, and industry—it is from such standards as these that we judge the work of the school. And rightly so. Yet the range of the outlook needs to be enlarged. What the best and wisest parent wants for his own child, that must the community want for all of its children. Any other ideal for our schools is narrow and unlovely; acted upon, it destroys our democracy. All that society has accomplished for itself it puts, through the agency of the school, at the disposition of its future members. All its better thoughts of itself it hopes to realize through the new possibilities thus opened to its future self. Here individualism and socialism are at one. Only by being true to the full growth of all the individuals who make it up, can society by any chance be true to itself. And in the self-direction thus given nothing counts as much as the school, for, as Horace Mann said, "Where anything is growing, one former is worth a thousand re-formers."

Whenever we have in mind the discussion of a new movement in education, it is especially necessary to take the broader, or social view. Otherwise, changes in the school institution and tradition will be looked at as the arbitrary inventions of particular teachers, at the worst transitory fads, and at the best merely improvements in certain details—and this is the plane upon which it is too customary to consider school changes. It is as rational to conceive of the locomotive or the telegraph as personal devices. The modification going on in the method and curriculum of education is as much a product of the changed social situation, and as much an effort to meet the needs of the new society that is forming, as are the changes in modes of industry and commerce.

John Dewey, *The School and Society* (Chicago: The University of Chicago Press, 1899), Chap. I: "The School and Social Progress," pp. 15–40.

It is to this, then, that I especially ask your attention: the effort to conceive what roughly may be termed the "New Education" in the light of larger changes in society. Can we connect this "New Education" with the general march of events? If we can, it will lose its isolated character, and will cease to be an affair which proceeds only from the over-ingenious minds of pedagogues dealing with particular pupils. It will be seen as part and parcel of the whole social evolution, and, in its more general features at least, as inevitable. Let us then ask after the main aspects of the social movement; and afterwards turn to the school to find what signs it shows of effort to put itself in line. And since it is quite impossible to cover the whole ground, I shall for the most part confine myself to one typical thing in the modern school movement—that which passes under the name of manual training, hoping if the meaning of that appears under changed social conditions, we shall be ready to concede the point regarding other educational innovations as well.

I make no apology for not dilating at length upon the social changes in question. Those I shall mention are writ so large that he who runs may read. The change that comes first to mind, the one that overshadows and even controls all others, is the industrial one—the application of science resulting in the great inventions that have utilized the forces of nature on a vast and inexpensive scale: the growth of a world-wide market as the object of production, of vast manufacturing centers to supply this market, of cheap and rapid means of communication and distribution between all its parts. Even as to its feebler beginnings, this change is not much more than a century old; in many of its most important aspects it belongs within the short span of those now living. One can hardly believe there has been a revolution in all history so rapid, so extensive, so complete. Through it the face of the earth is making over, even as to its physical forms; political boundaries are wiped out and moved about, as if they were indeed only lines on a paper map; population is hurriedly gathered into cities from the ends of the earth; habits of living are altered with startling abruptness and thoroughness; the search for the truths of nature is infinitely stimulated and facilitated and their application to life made not only practicable, but commercially necessary. Even our moral and religious ideas and interests, the most conservative because the deepest-lying things in our nature, are profoundly affected. That this revolution should not affect education in other than formal and superficial fashion is inconceivable.

Back of the factory system lies the household and neighborhood system. Those of us who are here today need go back only one, two, or at most three generations, to find a time when the household was practically the center in which were carried on, or about which were clustered, all the typical forms of industrial occupation. The clothing worn was for the most part not only made in the house, but the members of the household were generally familiar with the shearing of the sheep, the carding and spinning of the wool, and the plying of the loom. Instead of pressing a button and flooding the house with electric light, the whole process of getting illumination stood revealed in its toilsome length, from the killing of the animal and the trying of fat, to the making of wicks and dipping of candles. The supply of flour, of lumber, of foods, of building materials, of household furniture, even of metal ware, of nails, hinges, hammers, etc., was in the immediate neighborhood, in shops which were constantly open to inspection and often centers of neighborhood congregation. The entire industrial process stood revealed, from the production on the farm of the raw materials, till the finished article was actually put to use. Not only this, but practically every member of the household had his own share in the work. The children, as they gained in strength and capacity, were gradually initiated into the mysteries of the several processes. It was a matter of immediate and personal concern, even up to the point of actual participation.

We cannot overlook the factors of discipline and of character-building involved in all this training in habits of order and of industry, and the idea of responsibility, of obligation to do something, to produce something, in the world. There was always something which really needed to be done, and a real necessity that each member of the household should do his own part faithfully and in coöperation with others. Personalities which became effective in action were bred and tested in the medium of action. Again, we cannot overlook the importance for educational purposes of the close and intimate acquaintance got with nature at first hand, with real things and materials, with the actual processes of their manipulation, and the knowledge of their social necessities and uses. In all this there was continual training of observation, of ingenuity, constructive imagination, of logical thought, and of the sense of reality acquired through first-hand contact with actualities. The educative forces of the domestic spinning and weaving, of the saw-mill, the grist-mill, the cooper shop, and the blacksmith forge, were continuously operative.

No number of object-lessons, got up *as* object-lessons for the sake of giving information, can afford even the shadow of a substitute for acquaintance with the plants and animals of the farm and garden, acquired through actual living among them and caring for them. No training of sense-organs in school, introduced for the sake of training, can begin to compete with the alertness and fullness of sense-life that comes through daily intimacy and interest in familiar occupations. Verbal memory can be trained in committing tasks, a certain discipline of the reasoning powers can be acquired through lessons in science and mathematics; but, after all, this is somewhat remote and shadowy compared with the training of attention and of judgment that is acquired in having to do things with a real motive behind and a real outcome ahead. At present, concentration of industry and division of labor have practically eliminated household and neighborhood occupations—at least for educational purposes. But it is useless to bemoan the departure of the good old days of children's modesty, reverence, and implicit obedience, if we expect merely by bemoaning and by exhortation to bring them back. It is radical conditions which have changed, and only an equally radical change in education suffices. We must recognize our compensations—the increase in toleration, in breadth of social judgment, the larger acquaintance with human nature, the sharpened alertness in reading signs of character and interpreting social situations, greater accuracy of adaptation to differing personalities, contact with greater commercial activities. These considerations mean much to the city-bred child of today. Yet there is a real problem: how shall we retain these advantages, and yet introduce into the school something representing the other side of life—occupations which exact personal responsibilities and which train the child with relation to the physical realities of life?

When we turn to the school, we find that one of the most striking tendencies at present is toward the introduction of so-called manual training, shop-work, and the household arts—sewing and cooking.

This has not been done "on purpose," with a full consciousness that the school must now supply that factor of training formerly taken care of in the home, but rather by instinct, by experimenting and finding that such work takes a vital hold of pupils and gives them something which was not to be got in any other way. Consciousness of its real import is still so weak that the work is often done in a half-hearted, confused, and unrelated way. The reasons assigned to justify it are painfully inadequate or sometimes even positively wrong.

If we were to cross-examine even those who are most favorably disposed to the introduction of this work into our school system, we should, I imagine, generally find the main reasons to be that such work engages the full spontaneous interest and attention of the children. It keeps them alert and active, instead of passive and perceptive; it makes them more useful, more capable, and hence more inclined to be helpful at home; it prepares them to some extent for the practical duties of later life —the girls to be more efficient house managers, if not actually cooks and sempstresses; the boys (were our educational system only adequately rounded out into trade schools) for their future vocations. I do not underestimate these reasons. Of those indicated by the changed attitude of the children I shall indeed have something to say in my next talk, when speaking directly of the relationship of the school to the child, not to society. But the point of view is, upon the whole, unnecessarily narrow. We must conceive of work in wood and metal, of weaving, sewing, and cooking, as methods, not as distinct studies of life on its active and social sides. We must conceive of them in their social significance, as types of the processes by which society keeps itself going, as agencies for bringing home to the child some of the primal necessities of community life, and as the ways in which these have been met by the growing insight and ingenuity of man; in short, as instrumentalities through which the school itself shall be made a genuine form of active community life, instead of a place set apart in which to learn lessons.

A society is a number of people held together because they are working along common lines, in a common spirit, and with reference to common aims. The common needs and aims demand a growing interchange of thought and growing unity of sympathetic feeling. The radical reason that the present school cannot organize itself as a natural social unit is because just this element of common and productive activity is absent. Upon the playground, in game and sport, social organization takes place spontaneously and inevitably. There is something to do, some activity to be carried on, requiring natural divisions of labor, selection of leaders and followers, mutual coöperation and emulation. In the schoolroom the motive and the cement of social organization are alike wanting. Upon the ethical side, the tragic weakness of the present school is that it endeavors to prepare future members of the social order in a medium in which the conditions of the social spirit are eminently wanting.

The difference that appears when occupations are made the articulating centers of school life is not easy to describe in words; it is a difference in motive, of spirit and atmosphere. As one enters a busy workshop in which a group of children are actively engaged in the preparation of food, the psychological difference, the change from more or less passive and inert recipiency and restraint to one of buoyant outgoing energy, is so obvious as fairly to strike one in the face. Indeed, to those whose image of the school is rigidly set the change is sure to give a shock. But the change in the social attitude is equally marked. The mere absorption of facts and truths is so exclusively individual an affair that it tends very naturally to pass into selfishness. There is no obvious social motive for the acquirement of mere learning, there is no clear social gain in success thereat. Indeed, almost the only measure for success is a competitive one, in the bad sense of that term—a comparison of results in the recitation or in the examination to see which child has succeeded in getting ahead of others in storing up, in accumulating the maximum of information. So thoroughly is this the prevalent atmosphere that for one child to help another in his task has become a school crime. Where the school work consists in simply learning lessons, mutual assistance, instead of being the most natural form of coöperation and association, becomes a clandestine effort to relieve one's neighbor of his proper duties. Where active work is going on all this is changed. Helping others, instead of being a form of charity which impoverishes the recipient, is simply an aid in setting free the powers and furthering the impulse of the one helped. A spirit of free communication, of interchange of ideas, suggestions, results, both successes and failures of previous experiences, becomes the dominating note of the recitation. So far as emulation enters in, it is in the comparison of individuals, not with regard to the quantity of information personally absorbed, but with reference to the quality of work done—the genuine community standard of value. In an informal but all the more pervasive way, the school life organizes itself on a social basis.

Within this organization is found the priniciple of school discipline or order. Of course, order is simply a thing which is relative to an end. If you have the end in view of forty or fifty children learning certain set lessons, to be recited to a teacher, your discipline must be devoted to securing that result. But if the end in view is the development of a spirit of social coöperation and community life, discipline must grow out of and be relative to this. There is little order of the first sort where things are in process of construction; there is a certain disorder in any busy workshop; there is not silence; persons are not engaged in maintaining certain fixed physical postures; their arms are not folded; they are not holding their books thus and so. They are doing a variety of things, and there is the confusion, the bustle, that results from activity. But out of occupation, out of doing things that are to produce results, and out of doing these in a social and coöperative way, there is born a discipline of its own kind and type. Our whole conception of school discipline changes when we get this point of view. In critical moments we all realize that the only discipline that stands by us, the only training that becomes intuition, is that got through life itself. That we learn from experience, and from books or the sayings of others *only* in their vital relation to experience, are not mere phrases. But the school has been so set apart, so isolated from the ordinary conditions and motives of life, that the place where children are sent for discipline is the one place in the world where it is most difficult to get experience—the mother of all discipline worth the name. It is only where a narrow and fixed image of traditional school discipline dominates, that one is in any danger of overlooking that deeper and infinitely wider discipline that comes from having a part to do in constructive work, in contributing to a result which, social in spirit, is none the less obvious and tangible in form—and hence in a form with reference to which responsibility may be exacted and accurate judgment passed.

The great thing to keep in mind, then, regarding the introduction into the school of various forms of active occupation, is that through them the entire spirit of the school is renewed. It has a chance to affiliate itself with life, to become the child's habitat, where he learns through directed living, instead of being only a place to learn lessons having an abstract and remote reference to some possible living to be done in the future. It gets a chance to be a miniature community, an embryonic society. This is the fundamental fact, and from this arise continuous and orderly sources of instruction. Under the industrial *régime* described, the child, after all, shared in the work, not for the sake of the sharing, but for the sake of the product. The educational results secured were real, yet incidental and dependent. But in the school the typical occupations followed are freed from all economic stress. The aim is not the economic value of the products, but the development of social power and insight. It is this liberation from narrow utilities and openness to the possibilities of the human spirit that makes these practical activities in the school allies of art and centers of science and history.

The unity of all the sciences is found in geography. The significance of geography is that it presents the earth as the enduring home of the occupations of man. The world without its relationship to human activity is less than a world. Human industry and achievement, apart from their roots in the earth, are not even a sentiment, hardly a name. The earth is the final source of all man's food. It is his continual shelter and protection, the raw material of all his activities, and the home to whose humanizing and idealizing all his achievement returns. It is the great field, the great mine, the great source of the energies of heat, light, and electricity; the great scene of ocean, stream, mountain, and plain, of which all our agriculture and mining and lumbering, all our manufacturing and distributing agencies, are but the partial elements and factors. It is through occupations determined by this environment that mankind has made its historical and political progress. It is through these occupations that the intellectual and emotional interpretation of nature has been finally fixed. It is through what we do in and with the world that we read its meaning and measure its value.

In educational terms this means that these occupations in the school shall not be mere practical devices or modes of routine employment, the gaining of better technical skill as cooks, sempstresses, or carpenters, but active centers of scientific insight into natural materials and processes, points of departure whence children shall be led out into a realization of the historic development of man. The actual significance of this can be told better through one illustration taken from actual school work than by general discourse.

There is nothing which strikes the average intelligent visitor as stranger than to see boys as well as girls of ten, twelve, and thirteen years of age engaged in sewing and weaving. If we look at this from the standpoint of preparation of the boys for sewing on buttons and making patches, we get a narrow and utilitarian conception— a basis that hardly justifies giving prominence to this sort of work in the school. But if we look at it from another side, we find that this work gives the point of departure from which the child can begin to follow the progress of mankind in history, getting an insight also into the materials he is using and the mechanical principles involved.

In connection with these occupations, the historic development of man is recapitulated. For example, the children are first given the raw material—the flax, the cotton plant, the wool as it comes from the back of the sheep (if we could take them to the place where the sheep are sheared, so much the better). Then a study is made of these materials from the standpoint of their adaptation to the uses to which they may be put. For instance, a comparison of the cotton fiber with wool fiber is made. I did not know until the children told me, that the reason for the late development of the cotton industry as compared with the woolen is, that the cotton fiber is so very difficult to free by hand from the seeds. The children in one group worked thirty minutes freeing cotton fibers from the boll and seeds, and succeeded in getting out less than one ounce. They could easily believe that one person could only gin one pound a day by hand, and could understand why their ancestors wore woolen instead of cotton clothing. Among other things discovered as affecting their relative utilities was the shortness of the cotton fiber as compared with that of wool, the former being one-tenth of an inch in length, while that of the latter is an inch in length; also that the fibers of cotton are smooth and do not cling together, while the wool has a certain roughness which makes the fibers stick, thus assisting the spinning. The children worked this out for themselves with the actual material, aided by questions and suggestions from the teacher.

They then followed the processes necessary for working the fibers up into cloth. They re-invented the first frame for carding the wool—a couple of boards with sharp pins in them for scratching it out. They re-devised the simplest process for spinning the wool—a pierced stone or some other weight through which the wool is passed, and which as it is twirled draws out the fiber, next the top, which was spun on the floor, while the children kept the wool in their hands until it was gradually drawn out and wound upon it. Then the children are introduced to the invention next in historic order, working it out experimentally, thus seeing its necessity, and tracing its effects, not only upon that particular industry, but upon modes of social life—in this way passing in review the entire process up to the present complete loom, and all that goes with the application of science in the use of our present available powers. I need not speak of the science involved in this—the study of the fibers, of geographical features, the conditions under which raw materials are grown, the great centers of manufacture and distribution, the physics involved in the machinery of production; nor, again, of the historical side—the influence which these inventions have had upon humanity. You can concentrate the history of all mankind into the evolution of the flax, cotton, and wool fibers into clothing. I do not mean that this is the only, or the best, center. But it is true that certain very real and important avenues to the consideration of the history of the race are thus opened—that the mind is introduced to much more fundamental and controlling influences than usually appear in the political and chronological records that pass for history.

Now, what is true of this one instance of fibers used in fabrics (and, of course, I have only spoken of one or two elementary phases of that) is true in its measure of every material used in every occupation, and of the processes employed. The occupation supplies the child with a genuine motive; it gives him experience at first hand; it brings him into contact with realities. It does all this, but in addition it is liberalized throughout by translation into its historic values and scientific equivalencies. It ceases

with the growth of the child's mind in power and knowledge to be a pleasant occupation merely, and becomes more and more a medium, an instrument, an organ—
and is thereby transformed.

This, in turn, has its bearing upon the teaching of science. Under present conditions, all activity, to be successful, has to be directed somewhere and somehow by
the scientific expert—it is a case of applied science. This connection should determine
its place in education. It is not only that the occupations, the so-called manual or
industrial work in the school, give the opportunity for the introduction of science
which illuminates them, which makes them material, freighted with meaning, instead
of being mere devices of hand and eye; but that the scientific insight thus gained
becomes an indispensable instrument of free and active participation in modern social
life. Plato somewhere speaks of the slave as one who in his actions does not express
his own ideas, but those of some other man. It is our social problem now, even more
urgent than at the time of Plato, that method, purpose, understanding, shall be found
in the one who does the work, that his activity shall have meaning to him.

When occupations in the school are conceived in this broad and generous way,
I can only stand lost in wonder at the objections so often heard, that such occupations are out of place in the school because they are materialistic, utilitarian, or even
menial in their tendency. It sometimes seems to me that those who make these objections must live in quite another world. The world in which most of us live is
a world in which everyone has a calling and occupation, something to do. Some
are managers and others are subordinates. But the great thing for one as for the
other is that each shall have had the education which shall enable him to see within
his daily work all there is of large and human significance. How many of the employed are today mere appendages to the machines which they operate! This may be
due in part to the machine itself, or to the *régime* which lays so much stress upon
the products of the machine; but it is certainly due in large part to the fact that
the worker has had no opportunity to develop his imagination and his sympathetic
insight into the social and scientific values found in his work. At present, the impulses
which lie at the basis of the industrial system are either practically neglected or
positively distorted during the school period. Until the instincts of construction and
production are systematically laid hold of in the years of childhood and youth,
until they are trained in social directions, enriched by historical interpretation, controlled and illuminated by scientific methods, we certainly are in no position even
to locate the source of our economic evils, much less to deal with them effectively.

If we go back a few centuries, we find a practical monopoly of learning. The term
*possession* of learning was, indeed, a happy one. Learning was a class matter. This
was a necessary result of social conditions. There were not in existence any means
by which the multitude could possibly have access to intellectual resources. These
were stored up and hidden away in manuscripts. Of these there were at best only
a few, and it required long and toilsome preparation to be able to do anything
with them. A high-priesthood of learning, which guarded the treasury of truth and
which doled it out to the masses under severe restrictions, was the inevitable expression of these conditions. But, as a direct result of the industrial revolution of which
we have been speaking, this has been changed. Printing was invented; it was made
commercial. Books, magazines, papers were multiplied and cheapened. As a result

of the locomotive and telegraph, frequent, rapid, and cheap intercommunication by mails and electricity was called into being. Travel has been rendered easy; freedom of movement, with its accompanying exchange of ideas, indefinitely facilitated. The result has been an intellectual revolution. Learning has been put into circulation. While there still is, and probably always will be, a particular class having the special business of inquiry in hand, a distinctively learned class is henceforth out of the question. It is an anachronism. Knowledge is no longer an immobile solid; it has been liquefied. It is actively moving in all the currents of society itself.

It is easy to see that this revolution, as regards the materials of knowledge, carries with it a marked change in the attitude of the individual. Stimuli of an intellectual sort pour in upon us in all kinds of ways. The merely intellectual life, the life of scholarship and of learning, thus gets a very altered value. Academic and scholastic, instead of being titles of honor, are becoming terms of reproach.

But all this means a necessary change in the attitude of the school, one of which we are as yet far from realizing the full force. Our school methods, and to a very considerable extent our curriculum, are inherited from the period when learning and command of certain symbols, affording as they did the only access to learning, were all-important. The ideals of this period are still largely in control, even where the outward methods and studies have been changed. We sometimes hear the introduction of manual training, art and science into the elementary, and even the secondary schools, deprecated on the ground that they tend toward the production of specialists—that they detract from our present scheme of generous, liberal culture. The point of this objection would be ludicrous if it were not often so effective as to make it tragic. It is our present education which is highly specialized, one-sided and narrow. It is an education dominated almost entirely by the mediæval conception of learning. It is something which appeals for the most part simply to the intellectual aspect of our natures, our desire to learn, to accumulate information, and to get control of the symbols of learning; not to our impulses and tendencies to make, to do, to create, to produce, whether in the form of utility or of art. The very fact that manual training, art and science are objected to as technical, as tending toward mere specialism, is of itself as good testimony as could be offered to the specialized aim which controls current education. Unless education had been virtually identified with the exclusively intellectual pursuits, with learning as such, all these materials and methods would be welcome, would be greeted with the utmost hospitality.

While the training for the profession of learning is regarded as the type of culture as a liberal education, that of a mechanic, a musician, a lawyer, a doctor, a farmer, a merchant, or a railroad manager is regarded as purely technical and professional. The result is that which we see about us everywhere—the division into "cultured" people and workers, the separation of theory and practice. Hardly one per cent. of the entire school population ever attains to what we call higher education; only five per cent. to the grade of our high school; while much more than half leave on or before the completion of the fifth year of the elementary grade. The simple facts of the case are that in the great majority of human beings the distinctively intellectual interest is not dominant. They have the so-called practical impulse and disposition. In many of those in whom by nature intellectual interest is strong, social conditions prevent its adequate realization. Consequently by far the larger number of pupils leave school as soon as they have acquired the rudiments of learning, as soon as they have enough of the symbols of reading, writing, and calculating to be of practical use to them in getting a living. While our educational leaders are talking of culture, the development of personality, etc., as the end and aim of education, the great majority of those who pass under the tuition of the school regard it only as a narrowly practical tool with which to get bread and butter enough to eke out a restricted life. If we were to conceive our educational end and aim in a less exclusive way, if we were to introduce into educational processes the activities which do appeal to those whose dominant interest is to do and to make, we should find that the hold of the school upon its members would be more vital, more prolonged.

But why should I make this labored presentation? The obvious fact is that our social life has undergone a thorough and radical change. If our education is to have any meaning for life, it must pass through an equally complete transformation. This transformation is not something to appear suddenly, to be executed in a day by conscious purpose. It is already in progress. Those modifications of our school system which appear often (even to those most actively concerned with them, to say nothing of their spectators) as mere changes of detail, mere improvements within the school mechanism, are in reality signs and evidences of this change. The introduction of active occupations, of nature study, of elementary science, of art, of history; the relegation of the merely symbolic and formal to a secondary position; the change in the moral school atmosphere, in the relation of pupils and teachers—of discipline; the introduction of more active, expressive, and self-directing factors—all these are not mere accidents, they are necessities of the larger social evolution. It remains but to organize all these factors, to appreciate them in their fullness of meaning, and to put the ideas and ideals involved in complete, uncompromising possession of our school system. To do this means to make each one of our schools an embryonic community life, active with types of occupations that reflect the life of the larger society, and permeated throughout with the spirit of art, history, and science. When the school introduces and trains each child of society into membership within such a little community, saturating him with the spirit of service, and providing him with the instruments of effective self-direction, we shall have the deepest and best guarantee of a larger society which is worthy, lovely, and harmonious.


## ✐ THE INDUSTRIAL COMMISSION: REPORT ON TRUSTS AND COMBINATIONS

*During the last two decades of the nineteenth century, the organization of capitalist production in the more advanced countries of the West changed radically and irreversibly. Vast markets, opened up by intricate and efficient transportation networks, were paralleled by the increasing scale of organization, investment, and technological complexity of business enterprise. By the turn of the century, in leading industrial countries*

*like England, Germany, and the United States, immense corporate
enterprises commanding a large share of the national market were
displacing the small, individually owned firms around which the classical
economists had built their theories and nineteenth-century liberals had
created their myths of economic freedom and equal opportunity.*

*Although in Europe there was little opposition to this trend toward
consolidation, in the United States it encountered strong, although in the
final analysis ineffective, opposition. In any case, the bitterly debated
Sherman Antitrust Act of 1890, undercut by judicial interpretation and
undermined by lax enforcement, failed in its announced purpose of
stemming the tide toward monopoly. The Industrial Commission, created
by act of Congress in 1898 and sitting until 1902, was the best that
antimonopoly forces of the period were able to achieve. Designed as a
nonpartisan commission to gather information on the problems of labor,
agriculture, and capital, the commission devoted much of its effort to
hearing testimony on industrial combinations. Aside from publishing
nineteen massive volumes of testimony and analysis, the Industrial
Commission does not seem to have any tangible achievement to its credit.*

*The selection which follows is taken from the "Review of the Evidence,"
introducing the first published volume of the commission's reports, which
was devoted to the problems of trusts and industrial combinations.*

Among the causes which have led to the formation of industrial combinations, most
of the witnesses were of the opinion that competition, so vigorous that profits of
nearly all competing establishments were destroyed, is to be given first place. . . .
Many of the witnesses say that their organization was formed to make economies,
to lessen competition and to get higher profits—another way of saying that competition is the cause without conceding that the separate plants were forced to combine.
One or two witnesses simply mention the higher profits wanted or some like ambition,
as when Chairman Gates asserts that the American Steel and Wire Company was
formed because its organizers "wished to be the wire manufacturers of the world."
    The methods by which the combinations hope to effect savings so as to keep new
competitors from coming into the field will be mentioned under the advantages of
combination, but it may be noted that they usually assert that they expect the increased
profits to come from savings and lessened cost of production, and not from higher
prices.
    While the form of organization of the industrial combinations is not of so great
importance, perhaps, as their effects upon prices and wages and society at large, it is

Industrial Commission, *Preliminary Report on Trusts and Industrial Combinations* (Washington, D.C.: U.S. Government Printing Office, 1900), Vol. I, 9–22, 24–26, 29–32.

nevertheless of consequence to see what legal form has been taken by those that from the point of view of their managers are most successful, especially if an effort is to be made to legislate regarding them.

The form of organization that has given them their name "trusts" was the one started by the Standard Oil Trust in 1882, afterwards followed by the Whisky combination—the Distillers and Cattle Feeders' Trust—and by the Sugar Trust—the American Sugar Refineries Company. The plan of that organization was as follows: The stockholders of the different corporations entering the combination assigned their stock in trust to a board of trustees without the power of revocation. That board of trustees then held the voting power of the stocks of the different companies and was thus enabled, through the election of directors, to control them absolutely. In place of the stock thus received the trustees issued trust certificates upon which the former holders of the stock drew their dividends, these being paid upon the certificates regardless of what disposition was made of the plants of the different corporations. Owing largely to hostile legislation and to the bitter feeling against the trusts above named, these trusts, after some adverse decisions of the courts, went out of existence, reorganizing as single corporations in most cases, and none at the present time remain.

A somewhat similar form of organization, however—the voting trust—is found at times. In this form of trust the holders of at least a majority of stock of a single corporation put their stock into the hands of trustees for the purpose of voting it, retaining for themselves all the privileges of drawing dividends and making transfers. Such a voting trust has been formed, it is claimed, in the case of the Pure Oil Company—an organization of the independent oil interests—for the sake of protecting a majority of the stock against purchase by the Standard Oil Company. The Standard had bought large blocks of stock before in another independent company with the probable purpose of securing control. It will be observed that the purpose of such a trust is not to unite various corporations under one management, but to secure in perpetuity an agreed-upon policy without danger of interference through sales of individual shareholders. Some profess to find danger in this form of voting trust, while others think it decidedly beneficial. It is, however, true that this form of trust may put the direction of a company into the hands of a comparatively few members, the trustees, who are in this way able to manage the affairs of the company and to secure it a permanent policy (whatever later wishes of stockholders may be) such as could not be secured under the ordinary corporate management with so great certainty. At any rate, as a form of corporate combination for the sake of securing monopolistic control, the voting trust does not seem to be now in vogue.

The form of organization that seems most common at the present time is that of the single large corporation, which owns outright the different plants. A combination of this kind is formed by the purchase of all of the plants of the different corporations or individuals who enter into it, the corporations then dissolving as separate corporations. Often payments for the plants are made largely in stock of the new corporation, so that many of the former owners maintain their interest in the business. The affairs are then managed entirely by the stockholders of the one corporation through their board of directors, elected in the ordinary way. It is usual for these larger corporations to choose a very liberal form of charter.

A third form of organization, which is in many particulars quite like the original trust form, is that which has been taken by the Federal Steel Company, by the Distilling Company of America, and others. In this form the central company, instead of purchasing the plants of the different corporations which it is proposed to unite, simply buys a majority of the stock, or possibly the entire stock of each one of the corporations. The separate corporations keep in separate corporate existence, but a majority of the stock being held by the one larger corporation, its officers, of course, elect the boards of directors of all of the separate corporations, and in this way hold ultimately complete control. It is usually true that the separate corporations manage their own affairs practically independently, although they are furnished information regarding the workings of the other establishments in the combination through the central officers, and are doubtless largely directed in their policy in this way. . . .

## General Statements Regarding the Evil

During the past few years the total capitalization of the new industrial combinations has reached an enormous sum, well into the billions, and in many cases at least the nominal capitalization of the corporations far exceeds the cash value of their property. The impressions among different people regarding the effect of this over-capitalization vary. Some of the witnesses who have appeared before the Commission are of the opinion that the question of the capitalization of any corporation is of slight consequence. They think that if the amount of stock issued is only three or four times in par value more than the cash value of the plants themselves, no especial harm is done. If the plant shows that its earning capacity is sufficient to pay dividends on the large capitalization, the stock will hold its value fairly well, and the capitalization is justified. If the earning capacity of the establishment is not sufficient to pay dividends, this condition will show itself in the value of the stocks. While some individuals who are careless about their methods of doing business may be injured by the purchase of stock through misrepresentation, that is not a matter that concerns materially the general public. People who deal in stocks are likely at times to lose. The State, it is said, can not act as guardian for foolish individuals. It is not believed by these witnesses that overcapitalization has any effect upon prices which is injurious to the public.

Other witnesses believe that this overcapitalization is a serious injury to the public. Not merely do the misrepresentations of the promoters of these corporations, and perhaps also of the underwriters of their stocks, mislead prospective buyers of stock, but it is thought also that the attempt to pay dividends on the inflated capitalization seriously affects the prices of the products to consumers and the wages of employees. These witnesses are inclined to believe that possibly the chief evil of the great industrial combinations comes at the time of their organization, when private bankers and others acting as financial agents or underwriters, together with promoters, make huge profits from floating the new corporations, which will afterwards find themselves unable to pay dividends to stockholders and which must within a comparatively short time go through a process of reorganization to the great loss of those who have invested their money in good faith. Some of the witnesses are inclined to think that this overcapitalization has been so prevalent within the past two or three years that the result must inevitably be a financial crisis which will prove injurious to the public at large, aside from those who have foolishly, perhaps, invested their money in these stocks.

The position seems well taken that the methods of promotion and financiering are often decidedly against public interest and ought to be checked. The overcapitalization, too, is probably felt somewhat in increased prices at times.

### The Facts from the Testimony

Regarding most of the combinations concerning which testimony has been taken the facts appear quite clear.

None of the witnesses believe that the Standard Oil Company is on the whole overcapitalized, as compared with the present value of the plants. Its opponents believe that its profits are enormous on the capitalization. The witnesses representing the Standard Oil Company itself, while admitting very large profits and presenting no very definite facts regarding the capitalization, still give the same impression from their testimony.

The American Sugar Refining Company seems to be, beyond question, capitalized at a sum twice as large at least as the cost of reconstruction of the plants themselves. The capitalization was shown to be several times the original capitalization of its constituent members, the testimony taken before the Lexow Committee on this point being confirmed in terms, although the capitalization of some of these constituent members had little relation to their actual value. . . . The dividends by the American Sugar Refining Company for some years past, 7 per cent on the preferred stock and 12 per cent on the common, together with the sum set aside for surplus, would seem to show that, while the capitalization may be far above the cost of the plants, it is not above the earning capacity of the establishments at the range of prices which has prevailed for the past few years. This raises the question whether the power of the combination has not enabled it to keep prices up so that its earnings could pay dividends on an excessive capitalization, and whether the high capitalization has not been an added temptation to hold prices high. . . .

Perhaps the clearest testimony on this subject of capitalization came from the witnesses connected with some of the iron and steel companies. The witnesses regarding the tin-plate combination were in substantial agreement in stating that the owners of most of the plants gave an option on their plants at what they considered was the fair cash value, although, owing to the good times and to the fact that, in many cases, the industries were quite prosperous, the prices were high. They were then given, by the promoter, the option of taking this valuation of their property in cash, or of taking instead the same amount in preferred stock with a like amount of common stock added as bonus. The witnesses who appeared before the Commission had chosen to take stock instead of cash, believing that the business could carry that capitalization, and the price of stock on the market shows that the common and preferred together have so far ranged above the cash valuation.

One of the witnesses, at least, conceded that the total amount of stock thus paid for the plants, since the cash option was taken in prosperous times and included not merely the value of the plant but also the good will of the running business, probably amounted in some instances to three or four or even five times the cash cost of the plants at that time. Owing, however, to the greatly increased value of material and the increased wages of labor, some of the witnesses were of the opinion that the preferred stock alone of the tin-plate company would probably not equal the cost of reproduction of its plants at the present time. . . .

The International Silver Company, according to the testimony of its president, has from 45 to 50 per cent of its capitalization represented by plants, machinery, merchandise, etc., and the rest by brands or "good will."

Mr. Gates, president of the American Steel and Wire Company, estimates that of their $80,000,000 of capital stock, some $10,000,000 to $15,000,000 are considered good will, the rest plants and material. It is to be noted, however, that the valuation of the plants given by Mr. Gates is based on the great increase in cost of all iron material for the last year, and not on the value at the time the organization was capitalized. Forty million dollars would come more nearly the cash value at the time, 1897–98, when Mr. Morgan's estimate was made of $28,000,000 for some 70 per cent of the value of all the plants.

The National Shear Company was clearly capitalized at far beyond its cash value. Mr. Wiss was of the opinion that the stock issued was five times more than the cash value of the plants; and the fact that the stock was practically unsalable would seem to justify his conclusion, even though there were difficulties in connection with the management of the establishments which would tend to lower the value of the stock.

As was intimated above, one of the chief causes of this overcapitalization comes from the high profits that are secured by the promoters and by the underwriters of the stock when the combinations are made. Mention has just been made of the ten millions of common stock paid to the promoter of the American Tin Plate Company, and of the five millions paid in each case to the promoter of the National Steel Company and of the American Steel Hoop Company.

According to the testimony of Mr. Clarke, when the Standard Distilling and Distributing Company was organized, for each $100,000 of cash advanced to buy the plants the underwriters received $100,000 in preferred stock and $150,000 in common stock, while the promoter likewise received $150,000 in common stock.

According to the agreement made with the organizers of the Distilling Company of America, they were to turn over all the stock of the constituent companies at a ratio agreed upon, and were then to furnish $1,500,000 cash as working capital and two distilleries which, it was testified, cost $2,000,000. After full exchange in stock at the agreed ratios was made, there would be left in their hands, with which to secure the $3,500,000 cash needed, $10,710,000 of preferred stock and $13,360,000 of common. At the average market price of the stocks during the month after the company was organized, July, 1897, 56½ and 21, respectively, these stocks would have been worth $8,856,750, although, of course, they would not have realized this if thrown on the market. Promoters' profits seemed thus very large. By December, however, the stock had so fallen that it was worth less than $4,000,000; so that the ultimate gains were possibly not so large as they at first appeared. . . .

According to the testimony of Mr. Gary the Federal Steel Company was capitalized at almost precisely the actual value of the plants, estimated by a board of appraisers, together with the actual cash put in. Considerable has been allowed for increased values of lands, and, of course, the exact basis of the appraisement did not appear. He testified also that J. P. Morgan & Co., the bankers who effected the exchange of the stocks of the constituent companies for that of the Federal Steel Company, received some $200,000 for their services. He admitted, however, that before this arrangement was made by J. P. Morgan & Co. for the syndicate that was organizing the Federal Steel Company, J. P. Morgan & Co. already controlled a majority of the stock of all the constituent companies. The price paid by them for this stock did not appear, so that their real profits are not clearly in evidence.

On the whole, from the testimony given before the Commission, the inference seems a fair one that the capitalization of these combinations is usually a sum considerably above the value of the plants together with patents, but exclusive of brands and good will, of the companies that enter into the combination. In cases that are considered fairly conservative, the amount of stock issued, including both preferred and common stock, is from two to three times more than this value, while in not a few instances—for example, the one cited by Mr. Dill where value of possibly $500,000 was capitalized for $8,000,000—the capital stock seems to bear little relation to actual value of plants and patents.

### Raw Material

The statement is frequently made that owing to the fact that a large combination becomes a principal buyer of raw material it has great influence in decreasing its price. Thus it is said that, as the chief purchaser of raw sugar, the American Sugar Refining Company is able to get a certain advantage. Mr. Havemeyer concedes that the fact that he is a very large buyer gives him some advantage in selecting his markets. All seem to be agreed, however, that this advantage probably does not on the average amount to more than one-sixteenth of a cent per pound.

In the case of the American Tin Plate Company it was said that owing to the fact it was a very large buyer of steel it could at times get contracts at better rates than smaller buyers, although apparently it could not get any better rates than several other large buyers of steel doing different classes of business. Especially, however, does the fact that the directors of the American Tin Plate Company are in large part the same as the directors of the National Steel Company, that the business conditions of each are known to the other, and that their interests are closely allied, enable the Tin Plate Company at times to secure rather better rates from the National Steel Company than would be given by that company to an outsider. Similar statements are made regarding the American Steel Hoop Company, which is similarly associated with the National Steel Company.

Nearly all of the opponents of the Standard Oil Company who appeared before the commission testified that owing to the fact that the Standard had control of the main pipe lines and was the chief refiner of petroleum it could practically fix the price of crude oil, and had done so for many years, often to the detriment or even financial ruin of the producer. By virtue of its control over the pipe lines the Standard Oil Company, when in competition with smaller pipe lines in certain localities, had frequently put premiums upon the oil produced there, thus paying more than the regular market rate for it. Sometimes through this practice the competing pipe lines found themselves deprived of oil, were financially ruined, and were at length bought up by the Standard Oil Company, which then recouped itself by removing the premium, and perhaps making a general reduction in the price of crude oil. The opponents of the Standard Oil Company seem to be of the opinion that this payment of premiums has been almost altogether for the sake of forcing the competitors out of the business. The Standard Oil witnesses, on the other hand, asserted that the premiums were often, perhaps usually, and at present only, made because of the better quality of the oil from these special localities; but they also conceded that at times the Standard has paid premiums for the sake of forcing a competitor out of the business, and that under similar circumstances it would do it again.

It is charged also that where the Standard Oil Company has had exclusive control of the pipe lines in certain territory it has frequently held the price of crude oil so low that it could at length buy up the wells or the oil lands from the producers and owners, after which the price of crude oil would be raised again to a fair price. There can be little doubt that when a company is the owner of the only pipe line in any district, this gives it great control over the price of oil, and in consequence over the welfare of the producers themselves. . . .

It is asserted by the Standard Oil Company itself that its prices for crude petroleum, as of late years announced through the Seep Purchasing Agency, are fixed on the world demand and supply, and that in the main these prices have been fair to the producers. It is probably true in general that the extent of the output has been the main factor in determining prices, though the fact of very many individual cases of arbitrary shifting of prices to a degree ruinous, in certain localities, to the competitors and to the producers, may also be considered established.

## Prices of Product

Several of the combinations, as appears from the testimony of their officers, control a large proportion of the entire output of the country. The American Sugar Refining Company was selling at the time of the testimony about 90 per cent of the output. The American Tin Plate Company was probably also, at the time when its representatives appeared, controlling something more than 90 per cent. The whisky combination has controlled at times as high as 95 per cent of the production of spirits, and has probably during most of the time for the past 12 years controlled more than 80 per cent of the output. Most of the iron and steel companies claim, on the other hand, that they make no attempt to control so large a percentage of the output, and that they make no approach to monopolistic power, but secure their advantages by bringing together different branches of the industry which insures them a steady supply of raw material or, on the other hand, a sure customer for part of the product. Thus the Federal Steel Company controls possibly some 30 per cent of the output of its main products, and carries the processes from the mines to the finished product. The National Steel Company controls about 18 per cent, and it also operates mines, fleets, and mills. In the case of the American Steel and Wire Company, however, the combination at the time of the testimony was selling from 75 to 80 per cent of the total output of steel rods, the same percentage of smooth wire, and 65 to 90 per cent of wire nails. Moreover, the American Steel and Wire Company has practically a monopoly of barbed-wire and woven-wire fencing through the patents which it holds, and not merely by virtue of its large capital. With the exception of the monopoly secured through these patents Mr. Gates, chairman of the company, thinks it does not control competition.

The proportion of refined petroleum produced by the Standard Oil Company has varied materially at different times, but during the past few years has, as stated by its own officers, increased gradually from 81.4 per cent in 1894 to 83.7 per cent in 1898. Opponents of the combination are inclined to put the figures as high as 90 or 95 per cent. The control of the crude petroleum field by the combination is much less, but is, nevertheless, considerable. It is not claimed, however, that the Standard fixes the price of crude petroleum by virtue of the fact that it is the greatest producer, but rather by the fact that it owns the pipe lines and is the chief buyer.

A manufacturer who controls so large a proportion of the product as do some of these combinations can, beyond question, to a considerable degree control the price. Throwing into the market a large amount of goods at one time tends to lower the price. Likewise, one who controls plants enough to supply the entire normal demand of the country can, evidently, by closing some of these plants, readily raise the price.

The custom has regularly been for some years for the Standard Oil Company to announce from day to day the price which it would pay for crude petroleum and the price at which it would sell refined petroleum. This price is generally accepted as the market price, and competitors follow.

Likewise, the American Sugar Refining Company first posts the prices for the day, and is then followed by its competitors, who post theirs. Generally they take the prices fixed by the American Sugar Refining Company; but at times, if they have a little surplus stock on hand, or if it is difficult for them to secure a customer, they will cut the price perhaps one-sixteenth of a cent per pound. One or two of the chief competitors seem to be forced to put their prices quite frequently at one-sixteenth of a cent below that of the American Sugar Refining Company. In spite of its control over the output it is said by Mr. Post that the American Sugar Refining Company has not, in his judgment, unduly restricted the output. It is probable, he thinks, that had that company not been formed the competitive system would have ruined many established refineries, so that as many would have been closed as is now the case and the output would have been fully as small, probably even less. Practically all of the witnesses, both members of the combination and their opponents, concede that while there is a certain arbitrariness in fixing the prices it has been exercised in most cases only within comparatively narrow limits, and then mainly to meet competition or stifle it.

While prices may be kept at rates sufficient, by virtue of the economies of combination, to pay reasonable, even considerable, profits, though still largely excluding competition, any attempt, it is claimed by many witnesses, to secure extortionate prices defeats itself by provoking competition. Thus the whisky combination, in the days of the Distillers and Cattle Feeders' Trust and the Distilling and Cattle Feeding Company, in certain instances put up the prices to an excessively high point. The result was that numerous competitive distilleries were built, so that either the trust was forced to buy them out at high figures or else the competitors secured enough control of the market so that the prices were comparatively soon forced down. . . .

The fact, however, that in the main the great combinations fix the prices and their competitors follow would seem to show a certain element of monopoly. When they make a cut in the price the others must follow, and their action is substantially an arbitrary one. They, on the other hand, having so large a control of the market, need not follow the cut of a competitor in a comparatively small market, although, of course, they can not permit the competitor to widen his market materially, provided they wish to hold the control. So, on the other hand, this monopolistic element is shown by the fact that the increased price fixed at any time by a combination must be taken, at least temporarily, by most consumers, since the combination is, substantially, at the moment the chief source of supply, its competitors being utterly unable to meet the needs of the market. This is true in spite of the fact that if the prices are made unreasonably high, competitors would, in the long run, deprive the combination of its trade. . . .

From the standpoint of the competitors of the combinations, the greatest evil perhaps is not the fixing of prices too high, although assertions against the monopolies are not infrequently made on this ground, but rather that they cut prices to an unreasonable extent in certain localities, and even to individuals at certain times for the sake of driving out their rivals. This practice has been most frequently charged against the Standard Oil Company. Doubtless, too, in order to get into new fields, the competitors will at times cut the price, and to hold its market the Standard follows, or makes still lower prices; or again, to prevent a competitor from entering a market which he seems to be threatening, a first cut is made by the Standard. Witnesses disagree as to the side which usually makes the first cut, and doubtless all depends upon the circumstances of the special case in question. The same policy has also been followed by the American Sugar Refining Company, at any rate in its earlier days, and of late since it has been competing against the new refineries of Arbuckle Brothers and Doscher.

The opponents of the Standard Oil Company do not hesitate to charge it with employing competitive methods which they consider dishonorable. They assert that persons are engaged to follow wagons of competitors to learn who their customers are, and that then they make lower offers to those customers; and it is still further asserted that at times the employees in the offices of rivals are bribed to disclose the business to the Standard Oil Company.

The Standard Oil Company denies authorizing or approving any such methods of learning its competitors' business, although it is acknowledged that it takes practically every honorable means of finding out what its competitors are doing in order that it may properly meet the competitors on their own field. The methods of competition charged, it is said, may rarely be followed by an overzealous employee, but such action would be discountenanced in every case by the company. . . .

Most of the witnesses who so far have been heard before the Industrial Commission on the subject of trusts have been directly connected with the industries concerned as manufacturers. Practically all of them testify in favor of the tariff upon the industry represented, whether they be members of the combination or its opponents.

The tariff, of course, has practically no influence in connection with the Standard Oil Company, except indirectly in its manufacture of tin cans and other collateral industries.

Mr. Havemeyer, president of the American Sugar Refining Company, asserts with much vigor that he believes the customs tariff law to be the mother of all trusts—except the Sugar Trust. When the protection is very high, instead of fighting one another he thinks the manufacturers get together to take all the profit possible. If this is not their attitude at first, vigorous competition among themselves, brought about by the great number tempted into the industry by the tariff itself, is likely to force them to see what they are losing, and combination follows. He is strongly inclined to the belief that the tariff on all industries should be kept as low as 10 per cent, thinking that to afford sufficient protection against foreign countries, while at the same time it is low enough so that trusts would not be encouraged, as he believes they are now, by the "inordinate protection" granted. He has particularly in mind, apparently, the steel and iron industries, although he also concedes that had it not been for the high protective tariff existing at the time the original Sugar Trust was formed he would probably not have taken the risk of putting his refineries into the trust.

As regards the present tariff on sugar, Mr. Havemeyer thinks that the differential in favor of refined sugar, one-eighth of one cent per pound, is too low, and is of the opinion that it should be as high as one-fourth of a cent. . . .

Judge Gary, President of the Federal Steel Company, while admitting that protection may sometimes perhaps permit monopolistic prices, does not think the plan of reducing it by Executive order practicable. That would injure firms and individuals outside the combination. It would be justifiable only in case the combination were distinctly illegal, and in that event the present laws are sufficient to suppress the monopoly. He believes that some tariff is still needed for the proper protection of the various steel industries, and does not believe that at the present time there is any monopoly in them. . . .

One of the chief causes, in the opinion of some of the witnesses, of industrial combinations, and at any rate one of the greatest evils in connection with them, is the discriminations which it is claimed they have received in the freight rates given by the railroads. In other investigations carried on by the Industrial Commission, especially that on transportation, it has been quite generally conceded by railroad men and shippers that even up to the present time discriminating rates are made in favor of large shippers.

So far as this especial investigation is concerned, discriminations have been emphatically denied by the manufacturers of sugar, both Mr. Havemeyer, of the American Sugar Refining Company, and one of his opponents. Apparently all of these refineries receive the advantage of free storage of sugar in the railroad warehouses at the distributing points, but there seems to be no discrimination in this regard. Sugar freights out of New York are divided among the different railroads in a certain proportion which has been agreed upon.

In the case of iron, steel, and tin-plate shipments, while discriminations were not acknowledged, there was hesitation on the part of the officers of two of the companies, at any rate, in denying directly that favors were received. Outsiders knew of no discriminations.

On the other hand, charges of the most emphatic and unequivocal nature were made by the opponents of the Standard Oil Company with reference to freight discriminations received by it.

It was charged by most of the leading opponents of the Standard Oil Company that the chief reason for the rapid growth of the Standard, and its apparent great success in underselling rivals and winning markets, was the special advantages that it had received from the railroads. It was claimed that the company not merely received discriminating rates on its own shipments, but that it was frequently paid rebates on the shipments of its competitors. It was conceded by representatives of the Standard Oil Company that before the passage of the interstate-commerce act special freight rates and rebates were frequently received. . . .

Much greater differences of opinion exist with reference to the condition of affairs since the passage of the interstate-commerce act. It has been charged as a matter of general belief on the part of almost all of the opponents of the Standard Oil Company that these discriminations in various forms have been continually received, even up to date. On the other hand, these charges have been denied in toto and most emphatically by every representative of the Standard Oil Company with reference to all cases excepting one, which they claim was a mistake, the amount of freight due being promptly paid on discovery of the error. The Standard Oil Company not merely challenged the opponents to bring forth proof of any case, but produced many letters from leading officials of railroads to show that the company had in no case received any favors or asked for them. . . .

The opponents of the Standard Oil Company claim further that, owing to agreements which exist between the railroads and the pipe lines in which the Standard Oil Company has controlling interest, the Standard Oil Company is benefited. By such agreements freight rates are kept fully as high as pipe-line charges, and the latter, it is claimed by opponents of the Standard, are several times greater than the actual cost of transportation in pipe lines. The Standard thus gains an advantage on its own oil transported through pipe lines. . . .

There can be no question from the testimony, but that the Standard Oil Company in certain sections of the country, particularly in New England, receives decided advantages from the location of its refineries in or near those sections. The more distant location of independent refiners places them at a disadvantage, while in certain cases at least the railroads refuse to give the shippers into that territory through rates on petroleum, such as are granted on almost every other kind of freight, but compel shippers of petroleum to pay the arbitrary local rates.

For example, shippers of goods from Titusville, Pa., to points in Vermont, Rhode Island, Connecticut, and other New England States, on most articles pay Boston rates; on petroleum the rate is arbitrary, a local rate being added to the through rate. In consequence refiners of petroleum in Titusville and Bradford, Pa., and other places, find it impossible to ship oil to such points as they think they could easily reach, provided Boston rates obtained. The Standard Oil Company, on the other hand, by shipping its oil into this territory from its refineries on the seaboard, either directly by rail or by tank steamers and rail, pays lower rates and in this way is enabled to control the oil market in that whole territory.

A somewhat similar condition of affairs seems to exist as regards the freight rates on Standard Oil shipments from its large refinery at Whiting, near Chicago, to southern and western points, as compared with rates from Cleveland and other points somewhat farther east. It is not claimed by anyone that the railroads in making these rates are doing anything illegal, or that the Standard Oil Company is receiving any illegal advantage. It pays exactly the same rates as its competitors pay when they make shipments in the same way; its only advantage comes from the fact that, considering the way the tariffs are made up, its refineries are more favorably situated. When one considers the way in which the railroads make up their freight schedules, naturally the opponents of the Standard Oil Company think they are arranged with special reference to the Standard Oil Company's interests. The Standard Oil Company certainly gains from this custom of the railroad companies, in refusing to give through rates. . . .

Several of the witnesses who have appeared before the Commission say that one effect of the combinations is to lessen the cost of production by lessening the number of laborers needed in certain departments.

The witness who was most insistent upon this view, Mr. Dowe, president of the Commercial Travelers' National League, estimated that large numbers of commercial travelers were out of work, owing to the new methods of business adopted by the combinations, and that many more had had their wages decidedly lessened. The lack of competition brought about by the combinations had made it, in his judgment, possible to employ a less skilled class of commercial travelers than was required under the former competitive system, as well as greatly to diminish the number. He believes common workmen are also displaced by combination.

Other witnesses, heads of industrial combinations, agreed with Mr. Dowe in part. Mr. Bradley, one of the directors of the Distilling Company of America, thought there was a decided lessening in the number of salesmen; his combination will be able to dispense with about 300 altogether. Others, like Mr. Clarke, were of the opinion that few employees had been discharged as a consequence of the combination; and that in all probability had the combination not been formed an equal number, or perhaps more, would have been discharged on account of the failures that certainly would have resulted from the competitive system. In the whisky business, however, both Mr. Clarke and Mr. Rice testified that common labor is, relatively speaking, an unimportant factor.

Mr. Gates, of the American Steel and Wire Company, testified that it had dispensed with the services of all but 15 or 20 out of 200 or 300 traveling men, as well as with those of about 50 per cent of its  high-priced men—superintendents, officers, etc.

While Mr. Lee was inclined to believe that the closing of refineries by the Standard Oil Company has worked, on the whole, against the interest of the workingman, he nevertheless agreed with practically all the other witnesses who gave evidence on this point that the Standard Oil Company pays good wages and gives steady employment to its men. Mr. Archbold, of the Standard Oil Company, said that he was a believer in combinations of labor, as he was in combinations of capital, and thought that the interests of the two were not opposed.

In the sugar combination not many men, though possibly a few, have been thrown out by the absorption of competing refineries, and those remaining have received, on the whole, probably better wages than before.

The officers of several of the large combinations, particularly those in the iron and steel industries, testified that there had been no lessening, but rather, owing to the great demand for the product, with the consequent enlarged output, a decided increase of the number of laborers employed in the ordinary branches of the business. On the other hand, the services of presidents, superintendents, and other high officials of the individual plants had been dispensed with when the combination was formed. . . .

On the other hand, these men state that in the steel manufacture and its allied industries there has been a very decided increase, both in the number of men employed and in the rates of wages, since the formation of these corporations. For example, the Tin Plate Company has advanced the wages of its employees from 15 or 20 per cent upward, some few of the men receiving advances as high as 50 per cent. Mr. Reid furnished details of wages for some years tending to confirm his statements. In the National Steel Company wages have advanced from 15 to 20 per cent, while the American Steel and Wire Company has advanced wages, on the average, perhaps 40 per cent, and is employing from 30 to 40 per cent more labor.

In the Federal Steel Company also there has been an average increase of some 11 per cent, common labor being advanced about 16 per cent, while high officers and clerks at headquarters have had their pay lessened more than 6 per cent. President Gary furnished a table showing advances in wages in the different classes of employment, as well as the increased number employed. The American Steel Hoop Company had also advanced wages from 15 to 25 per cent. It should be remembered, in connection with all of these steel companies, that there has been a very decided improvement in business during the last year or two, and prices as well as wages have therefore gone up enormously. Part of the increase in certain cases is in fact to be explained by the operation of the sliding-scale system, although the base prices of the scales have also been advanced.

Mr. Griffiths, while recognizing that there has been an advance of wages by the American Tin Plate Company, testified that the feeling among the laborers was not at all in favor of the combination. While the workingmen knew that there had been some increase in their wages, they felt that on the whole they were more within the power of their employers than before. Some of the plants were closed down, for a time at least, early in the winter 1899–1900, and the men believed that the formation of the combination would help the employers in an attempt to lower wages in 1900. He based these statements largely on a letter from one of the workingmen employed by the American Tin Plate Company. . . .

The opinion was general that when plants were closed in any industry there might and probably would be at least a temporary displacement of labor, though in many cases men would be simply transferred to other establishments.

In the case of the International Silver Company, the workingmen have also received an advance in wages since the combination of from 5 to 10 per cent; there are no unions among the men employed in its establishments and the employees are dealt with individually. Many of the laborers are fairly well off, being permanent residents of the place where the works are established and owning their own homes.

Nearly all of the combinations whose representatives appeared before the Commission manifest no hostility to labor organizations, but are on the whole inclined to favor them. As has been said, the Standard Oil Company believes in trade unions. The National Steel Company, the American Steel Hoop Company, the American Tin Plate Company, and the Federal Steel Company all employ union labor largely, although not exclusively. They deal regularly with the Amalgamated Association of

Iron, Steel, and Tin Workers, and pay as a rule to the nonunion men wages that are substantially based upon the Amalgamated scale.

Chairman Gates, of the American Steel and Wire Company, asserted that his company did not recognize union labor as such, although it employs large numbers of men belonging to the Amalgamated Association. The various employers meet with committees of the men to agree upon rates of wages, but do not deal with the unions as such. In all of their establishments they expect to pay good rates; those which prevail in the locality for those grades of labor.

Some of the witnesses were of opinion that in case of a conflict between employers and employees the large organization would have a decided advantage by virtue of its great wealth, perhaps chiefly from the fact that having a number of establishments in different sections of the country it would be possible to close two or three without materially affecting the prosperity of the organization.

The great combination might also, if it controlled practically all of the establishments in the country, carry out an effectual boycott against individual employees who had opposed its policy.

In some of the testimony that has been given before the Industrial Commission in other lines of investigation, leaders of labor organizations have testified that they do not fear the industrial combinations on the ground that has been mentioned, but that they believe that the unions are able to hold their own as effectually against the combinations as they could against the individual employers. They are further of the opinion that if the combinations are able, by virtue of their savings, to increase the profits of the industry, the laborers can perhaps, by pressure, maintain or increase their wages quite as readily as before the combinations were made. On this subject more testimony is expected.

The testimony is practically universal that the combinations have had little or no trouble in the way of strikes, although Mr. Griffiths testifies as regards the tin-plate workers that they have been dissatisfied, and that there has been some tendency at least toward strikes.

The opponents of the large industrial combinations believe that one of the most injurious effects to the country from such organizations is that people are deprived thereby of the opportunities for independent management of business enterprises, and that in consequence the mental and moral fiber of the community is weakened. Even witnesses who assert that combinations in certain lines of industry are on the whole advantageous and desirable speak with not a little feeling on this evil effect of them.

Witnesses on the other side, however, believe that under the combinations there is every opportunity for individual initiative and independent activity that could be found outside the combinations, while the benefits in the way of greater financial profits, greater stability of business conditions, and potential lowering of prices would, at any rate in the long run, more than compensate for any possible disadvantage that might arise. Attention is called to the fact that when the combinations are effected, men well advanced in years, who would perhaps find it difficult to withdraw from business under other circumstances, seize the opportunity to withdraw from active management of affairs, while younger men of greater energy, who are glad to take up the burden, are put in their stead. The fact that the combination is managed by a board of directors mostly made up of men themselves actively engaged in the business, while the superintendents in charge of the separate plants, often their former owners, have large discretionary powers and responsibility, seems to these witnesses to show that there is no lack of incentive to individual activity or possibility of weakened individual judgment.

The power which such combinations exert over persons whom they supply with goods or who are in any way dependent upon them brings out in a somewhat startling light this social effect. As laborers have, it is said, often been coerced by employers upon whom they were dependent, so some persons feared to give evidence or to let it be publicly known that they objected to the methods of business of some of the trusts, lest they be driven out of business by them.

## ✑§ THE THEORY OF BUSINESS ENTERPRISE

*Thorstein Veblen*

*Thorstein Veblen (1857–1929), economist and sociologist, evinced many characteristics of previous creative thinkers, including some of the same social deficiencies. Like Socrates, he was in the habit of asking those embarrassing questions about society which pluck away the façade of pompous respectability; like Swift, alienating those who could help his career, he presented his findings in pungently objective prose and with complete and disarming honesty; like Rousseau, he was personally and morally obnoxious to polite society. He was requested to leave by the University of Chicago, Stanford University, and the University of Missouri (settling finally at the New School for Social Research in New York) because of scandalous behavior, scruffy dress, an inability to lecture above a mumble, and an incapacity to find in his students' work anything worthy of more than a C grade. He died in obscurity in California, leaving behind the most cogent analyses of American society since Tocqueville.*

*Veblen brought to the study of American economics a wide knowledge of the new schools of European social study, which had gone beyond mere tabulations of purchases and sales or cycles and population figures to explore class tastes and the values of producer and consumer. He was a devotee of the new study of anthropology, especially in the areas of taboos and social status symbols and their relationship to economic consumption. His first book,* The Theory of the Leisure Class *(1899), began the tradition which has since produced writers like Vance Packard, C. Wright Mills, and William H. Whyte, Jr., and is famous for introducing the concept of "conspicuous consumption," denoting the*

*process whereby social leaders flaunt their status by surrounding themselves
with exotic and useless items. Today, as the acquisition of status symbols
is facilitated by larger incomes and easy access to superfluous goods, the
term has far wider relevance; but in Veblen's day "conspicuous
consumption" had special applicability to people like the Goulds and
the Rockefellers, whose opulence gave the designation "the Gilded Age"
to the 1890s.*

*The following selection, from* The Theory of Business Enterprise *(1904),
is typical of Veblen's style of exposition. Using his words like scalpels
to dissect an aspect of business life, he lays bare the intrinsic irrationality
of business practices which, to everyone else, seemed logical. The reader
should not be put off by his monumental prose or his choice of vocabulary;
as a matter of fact, this was a source of deep humor for Veblen, an
eccentricity he cultivated to poke fun at the long-winded scholar.*

. . . The modern industrial system is a concatenation of processes which has much
of the character of a single, comprehensive, balanced mechanical process. A disturbance of the balance at any point means a differential advantage (or disadvantage) to
one or more of the owners of the sub-processes between which the disturbance falls;
and it may also frequently mean gain or loss to many remoter members in the
concatenation of processes, for the balance throughout the sequence is a delicate one,
and the transmission of a disturbance often goes far. It may even take on a cumulative
character, and may thereby seriously cripple or accelerate branches of industry that
are out of direct touch with those members of the concatenation upon which the
initial disturbance falls. Such is the case, for instance, in an industrial crisis, when
an apparently slight initial disturbance may become the occasion of a widespread
derangement. And such, on the other hand, is also the case when some favorable
condition abruptly supervenes in a given industry; as, *e.g.*, when a sudden demand
for war stores starts a wave of prosperity by force of a large and lucrative demand
for the products of certain industries, and these in turn draw on their neighbors in
the sequence, and so transmit a wave of business activity.

The keeping of the industrial balance, therefore, and adjusting the several industrial processes to one another's work and needs, is a matter of grave and far-
reaching consequence in any modern community, as has already been shown. Now,
the means by which this balance is kept is business transactions, and the men in
whose keeping it lies are the business men. The channel by which disturbances are
transmitted from member to member of the comprehensive industrial system is the
business relations between the several members of the system; and, under the modern
conditions of ownership, disturbances, favorable or unfavorable, in the field of

Thorstein Veblen, *The Theory of Business Enterprise* (New York: New American Library
of World Literature, Inc., 1958), pp. 18–29.

industry are transmitted by nothing but these business relations. Hard times or prosperity spread through the system by means of business relations, and are in their primary expression phenomena of the business situation simply. It is only secondarily that the disturbances in question show themselves as alterations in the character or magnitude of the mechanical processes involved. Industry is carried on for the sake of business, and not conversely; and the progress and 'activity of industry are conditioned by the outlook of the market, which means the presumptive chance of business profits.

All this is a matter of course which it may seem simply tedious to recite. But its consequences for the theory of business make it necessary to keep the nature of this connection between business and industry in mind. The adjustments of industry take place through the mediation of pecuniary transactions, and these transactions take place at the hands of the business men and are carried on by them for business ends, not for industrial ends in the narrower meaning of the phrase.

The economic welfare of the community at large is best served by a facile and uninterrupted interplay of the various processes which make up the industrial system at large; but the pecuniary interests of the business men in whose hands lies the discretion in the matter are not necessarily best served by an unbroken maintenance of the industrial balance. Especially is this true as regards those greater business men whose interests are very extensive. The pecuniary operations of these latter are of large scope, and their fortunes commonly are not permanently bound up with the smooth working of a given sub-process in the industrial system. Their fortunes are rather related to the larger conjunctures of the industrial system as a whole, the interstitial adjustments, or to conjunctures affecting large ramifications of the system. Nor is it at all uniformly to their interest to enhance the smooth working of the industrial system at large in so far as they are related to it. Gain may come to them from a given disturbance of the system whether the disturbance makes for heightened facility or for widespread hardship, very much as a speculator in grain futures may be either a bull or a bear. To the business man who aims at a differential gain arising out of interstitial adjustments or disturbances of the industrial system, it is not a material question whether his operations have an immediate furthering or hindering effect upon the system at large. The end is pecuniary gain, the means is disturbance of the industrial system,—except so far as the gain is sought by the old-fashioned method of permanent investment in some one industrial or commercial plant, a case which is for the present left on one side as not bearing on the point immediately in hand. The point immediately in question is the part which the business man plays in what are here called the interstitial adjustments of the industrial system; and so far as touches his transactions in this field it is, by and large, a matter of indifference to him whether his traffic affects the system advantageously or disastrously. His gains (or losses) are related to the magnitude of the disturbances that take place, rather than to their bearing upon the welfare of the community.

The outcome of this management of industrial affairs through pecuniary transactions, therefore, has been to dissociate the interests of those men who exercise the discretion from the interests of the community. This is true in a peculiar degree and increasingly since the fuller development of the machine industry has brought about a close-knit and wide-reaching articulation of industrial processes, and has at the same time given rise to a class of pecuniary experts whose business is the strategic management of the interstitial relations of the system. Broadly, this class of business men, in so far as they have no ulterior strategic ends to serve, have an interest in making the disturbances of the system large and frequent, since it is in the conjunctures of change that their gain emerges. Qualifications of this proposition may be needed, and it will be necessary to return to this point presently.

It is, as a business proposition, a matter of indifference to the man of large affairs whether the disturbances which his transactions set up in the industrial system help or hinder the system at large, except in so far as he has ulterior strategic ends to serve. But most of the modern captains of industry have such ulterior ends, and of the greater ones among them this is peculiarly true. Indeed, it is this work of far-reaching business strategy that gives them full title to the designation, "Captains of Industry." This large business strategy is the most admirable trait of the great business men who with force and insight swing the fortunes of civilized mankind. And due qualification is accordingly to be entered in the broad statement made above. The captain's strategy is commonly directed to gaining control of some large portion of the industrial system. When such control has been achieved, it may be to his interest to make and maintain business conditions which shall facilitate the smooth and efficient working of what has come under his control, in case he continues to hold a large interest in it as an investor; for, other things equal, the gains from what has come under his hands permanently in the way of industrial plant are greater the higher and more uninterrupted its industrial efficiency.

An appreciable portion of the larger transactions in railway and "industrial" properties, *e.g.*, are carried out with a view to the permanent ownership of the properties by the business men into whose hands they pass. But also in a large proportion of these transactions the business men's endeavors are directed to a temporary control of the properties in order to close out at an advance or to gain some indirect advantage; that is to say, the transactions have a strategic purpose. The business man aims to gain control of a given block of industrial equipment—as, *e.g.*, given railway lines or iron mills that are strategically important—as a basis for further transactions out of which gain is expected. In such a case his efforts are directed, not to maintaining the permanent efficiency of the industrial equipment, but to influencing the tone of the market for the time being, the apprehensions of other large operators, or the transient faith of investors. His interest in the particular block of industrial equipment is, then, altogether transient, and while it lasts it is of a factitious character.

The exigencies of this business of interstitial disturbance decide that in the common run of cases the proximate aim of the business man is to upset or block the industrial process at some one or more points. His strategy is commonly directed against other business interests and his ends are commonly accomplished by the help of some form of pecuniary coercion. This is not uniformly true, but it seems to be true in appreciably more than half of the transactions in question. In general, transactions which aim to bring a coalition of industrial plants or processes under the control of a given business man are directed to making it difficult for the plants or processes in question to be carried on in severalty by their previous owners or managers. It is commonly a struggle between rival business men, and more often than not the outcome of the struggle depends on which side can inflict or endure the greater pecuniary damage. And pecuniary damage in such a case not uncommonly involves a set-back to the industrial plants concerned and a derangement, more or less extensive, of the industrial system at large.

The work of the greater modern business men, in so far as they have to do with the ordering of the scheme of industrial life, is of this strategic character. The dispositions which they make are business transactions, "deals," as they are called in the business jargon borrowed from gaming slang. These do not always involve coercion of the opposing interests; it is not always necessary to "put a man in a hole" before he is willing to "come in on" a "deal." It may often be that the several parties whose business interests touch one another will each see his interest in reaching an amicable and speedy arrangement; but the interval that elapses between the time when a given "deal" is seen to be advantageous to one of the parties concerned and the time when the terms are finally arranged is commonly occupied with business maneuvers on both or all sides, intended to "bring the others to terms." In so playing for position and endeavoring to secure the largest advantage possible, the manager of such a campaign of reorganization not infrequently aims to "freeze out" a rival or to put a rival's industrial enterprise under suspicion of insolvency and "unsound methods," at the same time that he "puts up a bluff" and manages his own concern with a view to a transient effect on the opinions of the business community. Where these endeavors occur, directed to a transient derangement of a rival's business or to a transient, perhaps specious, exhibition of industrial capacity and earning power on the part of one's own concern, they are commonly detrimental to the industrial system at large; they act temporarily to lower the aggregate serviceability of the comprehensive industrial process within which their effects run, and to make the livelihood and the peace of mind of those involved in these industries more precarious than they would be in the absence of such disturbances. If one is to believe any appreciable proportion of what passes current as information on this head, in print and by word of mouth, business men whose work is not simply routine constantly give some attention to maneuvering of this kind and to the discovery of new opportunities for putting their competitors at a disadvantage. This seems to apply in a peculiar degree, if not chiefly, to those classes of business men whose operations have to do with railways and the class of securities called "industrials." Taking the industrial process as a whole, it is safe to say that at no time is it free from derangements of this character in any of the main branches of modern industry. This chronic state of perturbation is incident to the management of industry by business methods and is unavoidable under existing conditions. So soon as the machine industry had developed to large proportions, it became unavoidable, in the nature of the case, that the business men in whose hands lies the conduct of affairs should play at cross-purposes and endeavor to derange industry. But chronic perturbation is so much a matter of course and prevails with so rare interruptions, that, being the normal state of affairs, it does not attract particular notice.

In current discussion of business, indeed ever since the relation of business men to the industrial system has seriously engaged the attention of economists, the point to which attention has chiefly been directed is the business man's work as an organizer of comprehensive industrial processes. During the later decades of the nineteenth century, particularly, has much interest centered, as there has been much provocation for its doing, on the formation of large industrial consolidations; and the evident good effects of this work in the way of heightened serviceability and economies of production are pointed to as the chief and characteristic end of this work of reorganization. So obvious are these good results and so well and widely has the matter been expounded, theoretically, that it is not only permissible, but it is a point of conscience, to shorten this tale by passing over these good effects as a matter of common notoriety. But there are other features of the case, less obtrusive and less attractive to the theoreticians, which need more detailed attention than they have commonly received.

The circumstances which condition the work of consolidation in industry and which decide whether a given move in the direction of a closer and wider organization of industrial processes will be practicable and will result in economies of production,—these circumstances are of a mechanical nature. They are facts of the comprehensive machine process. The conditions favorable to industrial consolidation on these grounds are not created by the business men. They are matters of "the state of the industrial arts," and are the outcome of the work of those men who are engaged in the industrial employments rather than of those who are occupied with business affairs. The inventors, engineers, experts, or whatever name be applied to the comprehensive class that does the intellectual work involved in the modern machine industry, must prepare the way for the man of pecuniary affairs by making possible and putting in evidence the economies and other advantages that will follow from a prospective consolidation.

But it is not enough that the business man should see a chance to effect economies of production and to heighten the efficiency of industry by a new combination. Conditions favorable to consolidation on these grounds must be visible to him before he can make the decisive business arrangements; but these conditions, taken by themselves, do not move him. The motives of the business man are pecuniary motives, inducements in the way of pecuniary gain to him or to the business enterprise with which he is identified. The end of his endeavors is, not simply to effect an industrially advantageous consolidation, but to effect it under such circumstances of ownership as will give him control of large business forces or bring him the largest possible gain. The ulterior end sought is an increase of ownership, not industrial serviceability. His aim is to contrive a consolidation in which he will be at an advantage, and to effect it on the terms most favorable to his own interest.

But it is not commonly evident at the outset what are the most favorable terms that he can get in his dealings with other business men whose interests are touched by the proposed consolidation, or who are ambitious to effect some similar consolidation of the same or of competing industrial elements for their own profit. It rarely happens that the interests of the business men whom the prospective consolidation touches all converge to a coalition on the same basis and under the same management. The consequence is negotiation and delay. It commonly also happens that some of the business men affected see their advantage in staving off the coalition until a time more propitious to their own interest, or until those who have the work of consolidation in hand can be brought to compound with them for the withdrawal of whatever obstruction they are able to offer. Such a coalition involves a loss of independent standing, or even a loss of occupation, to many of the business men interested in the deal. If a prospective industrial consolidation is of such scope as to require the concurrence or consent of many business interests, among which no one is very decidedly preponderant in pecuniary strength or in strategic position, a long time will be consumed in the negotiations and strategy necessary to define the terms on which the several business interests will consent to come in and the degree of solidarity and central control to which they will submit.

It is notorious, beyond the need of specific citation, that the great business coalitions and industrial combinations which have characterized the situation of the last few years have commonly been the outcome of a long-drawn struggle, in which the industrial ends, as contrasted with business ends, have not been seriously considered, and in which great shrewdness and tenacity have commonly been shown in the staving off of a settlement for years in the hope of more advantageous terms. The like is true as regards further coalitions, further consolidations of industrial processes ·which have not been effected, but which are known to be feasible and desirable so far as regards the mechanical circumstances of the case. The difficulties in the way are difficulties of ownership, of business interest, not of mechanical feasibility.

These negotiations and much of the strategy that leads up to a business consolidation are of the nature of derangements of industry, after the manner spoken of above. So that business interests and maneuvers commonly delay consolidations, combinations, correlations of the several plants and processes, for some appreciable time after such measures have become patently advisable on industrial grounds. In the meantime the negotiators are working at cross-purposes and endeavoring to put their rivals in as disadvantageous a light as may be, with the result that there is chronic derangement, duplication, and misdirected growth of the industrial equipment while the strategy is going forward, and expensive maladjustment to be overcome when the negotiations are brought to a close.

Serviceability, industrial advisability, is not the decisive point. The decisive point is business expediency and business pressure. In the normal course of business touching this matter of industrial consolidation, therefore, the captain of industry works against, as well as for, a new and more efficient organization. He inhibits as well as furthers the higher organization of industry. Broadly, it may be said that industrial consolidations and the working arrangements made for the more economical utilization of resources and mechanical contrivances are allowed to go into effect only after they are long overdue.

In current economic theory the business man is spoken of under the name of "entrepreneur" or "undertaker," and his function is held to be the coördinating of industrial processes with a view to economies of production and heightened serviceability. The soundness of this view need not be questioned. It has a great sentimental value and is useful in many ways. There is also a modicum of truth in it as an account of facts. In common with other men, the business man is moved by ideals of serviceability and an aspiration to make the way of life easier for his fellows. Like other men, he has something of the instinct of workmanship. No doubt such aspirations move the great business man less urgently than many others, who are, on that account, less successful in business affairs. Motives of this kind detract from business efficiency, and an undue yielding to them on the part of business men is to be deprecated as an infirmity. Still, throughout men's dealings with one another and with the interests of the community there runs a sense of equity, fair dealing, and workmanlike integrity; and in an uncertain degree this bent discountenances gain that is got at an undue cost to others, or without rendering some colorable equivalent. Business men are also, in a measure, guided by the ambition to effect a creditable improvement in the industrial processes which their business traffic touches. These sentimental factors in business exercise something of a constraint, varying greatly from one person to another, but not measurable in its aggregate results. The careers of most of the illustrious business men show the presence of some salutary constraint of this kind. Not infrequently an excessive sensitiveness of this kind leads to a withdrawal from business, or from certain forms of business which may appeal to a vivid fancy as peculiarly dishonest or peculiarly detrimental to the community. Such grounds of action, and perhaps others equally genial and equally unbusinesslike, would probably be discovered by a detailed scrutiny of any large business deal. Probably in many cases the business strategist, infected with this human infirmity, reaches an agreement with his rivals and his neighbors in the industrial system without exacting the last concession that a ruthless business strategy might entitle him to. The result is, probably, a speedier conclusion and a smoother working of the large coalitions than would follow from the unmitigated sway of business principles.

But the sentiment which in this way acts in constraint of business traffic proceeds on such grounds of equity and fair dealing as are afforded by current business ethics; it acts within the range of business principles, not in contravention of them; it acts as a conventional restraint upon pecuniary advantage, not in abrogation of it. This code of business ethics consists, after all, of mitigations of the maxim, *Caveat emptor.* It touches primarily the dealings of man with man, and only less directly and less searchingly inculcates temperance and circumspection as regards the ulterior interests of the community at large. Where this moral need of a balance between the services rendered the community and the gain derived from a given business transaction asserts itself at all, the balance is commonly sought to be maintained in some sort of pecuniary terms; but pecuniary terms afford only a very inadequate measure of serviceability to the community.

Great and many are the items of service to be set down to the business man's account in connection with the organization of the industrial system, but when all is said, it is still to be kept in mind that his work in the correlation of industrial processes is chiefly of a permissive kind. His furtherance of industry is at the second remove, and is chiefly of a negative character. In his capacity as business man he does not go creatively into the work of perfecting mechanical processes and turning the means at hand to new or larger uses. That is the work of the men who have in hand the devising and oversight of mechanical processes. The men in industry must first create the mechanical possibility of such new and more efficient methods and correlations, before the business man sees the chance, makes the necessary business arrangements, and gives general directions that the contemplated industrial advance shall go into effect. The period between the time of earliest practicability and the effectual completion of a given consolidation in industry marks the interval by which the business man retards the advance of industry. Against this are to be offset the cases, comparatively slight and infrequent, where the business men in control push the advance of industry into new fields and prompt the men concerned with the mechanics of the case to experiment and exploration in new fields of mechanical process.

When the recital is made, therefore, of how the large consolidations take place at the initiative of the business men who are in control, it should be added that the fact of their being in control precludes industrial correlations from taking place except by their advice and consent. The industrial system is organized on business principles and for pecuniary ends. The business man is at the center, he holds the discretion and he exercises it freely, and his choice falls out now on one side, now on the other. The retardation as well as the advance is to be set down to his account.

As regards the economies in cost of production effected by these consolidations, there is a further characteristic feature to be noted, a feature of some significance for any theory of modern business. In great measure the saving effected is a saving of the costs of business management and of the competitive costs of marketing products and services, rather than a saving in the prime costs of production. The heightened facility and efficiency of the new and larger business combinations primarily affect the expenses of office work and sales, and it is in great part only indirectly that this curtailment and consolidation of business management has an effect upon the methods and aims of industry proper. It touches the pecuniary processes immediately, and the mechanical processes indirectly and in an uncertain degree. It is of the nature of a partial neutralization of the wastes due to the presence of pecuniary motives and business management,—for the business management involves waste wherever a greater number of men or transactions are involved than are necessary to the effective direction of the mechanical processes employed. The amount of "business" that has to be transacted per unit of product is much greater where the various related industrial processes are managed in severalty than where several of them are brought under one business management. A pecuniary discretion has to be exercised at every point of contact or transition, where the process or its product touches or passes the boundary between different spheres of ownership. Business transactions have to do with ownership and changes of ownership. The greater the parcelment in point of ownership, the greater the amount of business work that has to be done in connection with a given output of goods or services, and the slower, less facile, and less accurate, on the whole, is the work. This applies both to the work of bargain and contract, wherein pecuniary initiative and discretion are chiefly exercised, and to the routine work of accounting, and of gathering and applying information and misinformation.

The standardization of industrial processes, products, services, and consumers, spoken of in an earlier chapter, very materially facilitates the business man's work in reorganizing business enterprises on a larger scale; particularly does this standardization serve his ends by permitting a uniform routine in accounting, invoices, contracts, etc., and so admitting a large central accounting system, with homogeneous ramifications, such as will give a competent conspectus of the pecuniary situation of the enterprise at any given time.

The great, at the present stage of development perhaps the greatest, opportunity for saving by consolidation, in the common run of cases, is afforded by the ubiquitous and in a sense excessive presence of business enterprise in the economic system. It is in doing away with unnecessary business transactions and industrially futile maneuvering on the part of independent firms that the promoter of combinations finds his most telling opportunity. So that it is scarcely an over-statement to say that probably the largest, assuredly the securest and most unquestionable, service rendered by the great modern captains of industry is this curtailment of the business to be done,—this sweeping retirement of business men as a class from the service and the definitive cancelment of opportunities for private enterprise.

So long as related industrial units are under different business managements, they are, by the nature of the case, at cross-purposes, and business consolidation remedies this untoward feature of the industrial system by eliminating the pecuniary element from the interstices of the system as far as may be. The interstitial adjustments of the industrial system at large are in this way withdrawn from the discretion of rival business men, and the work of pecuniary management previously involved is in large part dispensed with, with the result that there is a saving of work and an avoidance of that systematic mutual hindrance that characterizes the competitive management of industry. To the community at large the work of pecuniary management, it appears, is less serviceable the more there is of it. The heroic rôle of the captain of industry is that of a deliverer from an excess of business management. It is a casting out of business men by the chief of business men.

The theory of business enterprise sketched above applies to such business as is occupied with the interstitial adjustments of the system of industries. This work of keeping and of disturbing the interstitial adjustments does not look immediately to the output of goods as its source of gain, but to the alterations of values involved in disturbances of the balance, and to the achievement of a more favorable business situation for some of the enterprises engaged. This work lies in the middle, between commercial enterprise proper, on the one hand, and industrial enterprise in the stricter sense, on the other hand. It is directed to the acquisition of gain through taking advantage of those conjunctures of business that arise out of the concatenation of processes in the industrial system.

## ENGLISH PROGRESS TOWARDS SOCIAL DEMOCRACY

*Sidney Webb*

*The group later known as the Fabian Socialists held their first meeting in the Westminster Palace Hotel in 1881. At the time, Victorian respectability eyed socialism as "merely a French or German eccentricity, due to militarism or protectionism" and was positive that "it could never rear its head in 'free' England." But the members of the Society— a cross section of literary wits, such as George Bernard Shaw and H. G.*

*Wells, drama critics, academics, labor leaders, and clergymen—agitated
over the cloying complacency which infected the ruling circles and were
convinced that England would profit by a socialist program of its own.
They demonstrated first for Irish independence and then for land reform;
but by 1883 the group became aware that it was wasting its energies on
occasional causes when the whole of society needed change. Throughout
the autumn frequent gatherings were held at members' homes; as one
member later recounted in 1908, "It would be too long a tale to tell
of the endless discussions which took place, of the dull men and the
brilliant men, the cranks and the thinkers, the men with long hair and
the women with short hair, who debated and argued, and went for one
another, and then debated and argued again."*

*The member whom we have quoted, William Clarke, also explained the
Fabian Society's name:*

> Few readers have not heard of the Roman general, Quinctus Fabius
> Maximus. . . . That illustrious man is the patron saint of the
> society, through which, being dead, he yet speaketh. . . . The Fabian
> Society proposes . . . to conquer by delay; to carry its programmes,
> not by a hasty rush, but through the slower but, as it thinks, surer
> methods of patient discussion, exposition, and political action. . . .
> For a convenient motto the society has taken the following sentence:
> 'For the right moment you must wait, as Fabius did, most patiently,
> when warring against Hannibal, though many censured his delays;
> but when the time comes you must strike hard, as Fabius did, or
> your waiting will be in vain and fruitless.' This double policy, then,
> of waiting and striking, is the general idea of the society.

*The main aim was, and still is, the promulgation of socialism, though
the Fabians still concentrate on political education rather than on the
recruitment of politicians to their cause. Their connection with the British
Labour Party to this day is as a semiofficial platform committee, although
the Society also acts as a training ground for future Labour leaders.
There is still the emphasis on peaceful means of persuasion; consequently
the Society has drawn the fire of Communist groups who regard its
passivity as tantamount to betrayal of the working class, a delusive intrigue
and conspiracy with the capitalists.*

*The following selection by Sidney Webb (1859–1947), economic
historian and one of the Society's founders, is a sample of the tracts which
have poured from the Society since 1888. The announcement on the title
page, "Price, One Penny," indicates the effort to keep the cost within the
means of the workingman.*

There are three stages through which every new notion in England has to pass: It is impossible: It is against the Bible: We knew it before. Socialism is rapidly reaching the third of these stages. "We are all Socialists now," said one of Her Majesty's late Ministers; and, in sober truth, there is no anti-Socialist political party. That which has long formed part of the unconscious basis of our practice is now formulated as a definite theory, and the tide of Democratic Collectivism is rolling in upon us. All the authorities, whatever their own views, can but note its rapid progress. If we look back along the line of history, we see the irresistible sweep of the growing tendency: if we turn to contemporary industrial development, it is there: if we fly to biological science, we do not escape the lesson: on all sides the sociologic evolution compels our adherence. There is no resting place for stationary Toryism in the scientific universe. The whole history of the human race cries out against the old-fashioned Individualism.

Economic Science, at any rate, will now have none of it. When the Editor of the new issue of the Encyclopædia Britannica lately required from some eminent Economist an article on Political Economy, fully representing the present position of that science, it was to an avowed Socialist that he addressed himself, and the article took the form of an elaborate survey of the inevitable convergence of all the economic tendencies towards Socialism. Professor Alfred Marshall's new work will be as repugnant to Mr. Herbert Spencer and the Liberty and Property Defence League as John Stuart Mill's conversion was to his respectable friends. Have we not seen Professor Sidgwick, that most careful of men, contributing an article to the *Contemporary Review*, to prove that the main principles of Socialism are a plain deduction from accepted economic doctrines, and in no way opposed to them?

Indeed, those who remember John Stuart Mill's emphatic adhesion to Socialism, both the name and the thing, in his "Autobiography," cannot be surprised at this tendency of economists. The only wonder is, that interested defenders of economic monopoly are still able to persuade the British public that Political Economy is against Socialism, and are able to make even Bishops believe that its laws "forbid" anything save the present state of things.

It is, however, time to give a plain definition of Socialism, to prevent any mistake as to meanings. Nothing is more common than the statement, "I can't understand what Socialism is." But this is sheer intellectual laziness. The word is to be found in our modern dictionaries. The Encyclopædia Britannica contains exhaustive articles upon its every aspect. There are enough Socialist lectures in London every week, good, bad, and indifferent, to drive the meaning into every willing ear.

The abstract word "Socialism" denotes a particular principle of social organisation. We may define this principle either from the constitutional or the economic standpoint. We may either put it as "the control by the community of the means of production for public advantage, instead of for private profit," or "the absorption of rent and interest by the community collectively." Its opposite is the abandonment of our means of production to the control of competing private individuals, stimulated by the prospect of securing the rent and interest gratuitously.

Sidney Webb, *English Progress towards Social Democracy,* Fabian Tract No. 15 (London, 1890), complete.

But this definition does not satisfy some people. They want a complete description of a Socialist State, an elaborately worked out, detailed plan, like Sir Thomas More's "Utopia" or Gulliver's Travels. Such fancy sketches have, indeed, at times been thrown off by Socialists as by all other thinkers; but with the growing realisation of social evolution, men gradually cease to expect the fabrication of a perfect and final social state; and the dreams of Fourier and Cabet, like those of Godwin and Comte, become outworn and impossible to us. There will never come a moment when we can say, "*Now* let us rest, for Socialism is established:" any more than we say, "*Now* Radicalism is established." The true principles of social organisation must already have secured partial adoption, as a condition of the continuance of every existing social organism; and the progress of Socialism is but their more complete recognition and their conscious adoption as the lines upon which social improvement advances.

Looking back over the record of human progress, we see one main economic characteristic underlying every form of society. As soon as production is sufficiently advanced to furnish more than maintenance, there arises, wherever two or three are gathered together, a fierce struggle for the surplus product. This struggle varies in outward form according to the time and circumstances, but remains essentially the same in economic character. The individuals or classes who possess social power, have at all times, consciously or unconsciously, made use of that power in such a way as to leave to the great majority of their fellows practically nothing beyond the means of subsistence according to the current local standard. The additional product, determined by the relative differences in productive efficiency of the different sites, soils, capitals, and forms of skill above the margin of cultivation, has gone to those exercising control over these valuable but scarce productive factors. This struggle to secure the surplus or "economic rent" is the key to the confused history of European progress, and an underlying, unconscious motive of all revolutions. The student of history finds that the great world moves, like the poet's snake, on its belly.

The social power which has caused this unequal division of the worker's product has taken various forms. Beginning, probably, in open personal violence in the merely predatory stage of society, it has passed in one field, through tribal war, to political supremacy, embodied, for instance, in a "Jingo" foreign policy, and at home in vindictive class legislation. A survival in England at the present time is the severity of the punishment for trifling offences against property compared with that for personal assaults; and its effect is curiously seen when the legal respect for person and that for property are, to some extent, opposed to each other, as in the case of wife-beating.

The social power does not, however, always take the forms of physical strength or political supremacy. From the Indian medicine man and the sun-priests of Peru down to the Collector of Peter's Pence and the Treasurer of the Salvation Army, theological influences have ever been used to divert a portion of the rent to spiritual uses, often nourishing (like the meats offered to idols) whole classes of non-producers, many of whom have been of no real spiritual advantage to the community.

But by far the most important means of appropriating the surplus product has been in the organisation of labour. The industrial leader, who can oblige his fellows to organise their toil under his direction, is able thereby to cause an enormous increase in their productivity. The advantages of co-operative or associated labour were discovered long before they were described by Adam Smith or Fourier; and human history is the record of their ever-increasing adoption. Civilisation itself is nothing but an ever-widening co-operation.

But who is to get the benefit of the increased productivity? In all times this question has been decided by the political condition of the labourer. The universally first form of industrial organisation is chattel slavery. At a certain stage in social development there seems to have been possible no other kind of industrial co-operation. The renunciation of personal independence is, as Darwin observed of the Fuegian, the initial step towards civilisation.

As a slave, the worker obtained at first nothing but bare maintenance at the lowest economic rate. Cato even advises the Roman noble that the bailiff or foreman need not have so large a ration as the other slaves, his work, though more skilled, being less exhausting. On the other hand, the surplus value was not yet differentiated into its component economic parts, and went in an undivided stream of profit all to the master.

Advancing civilisation, itself rendered possible only by chattel slavery, gradually made this form of servitude incompatible with intellectual and moral development, and inadequate to industrial needs. The slave became the feudal serf or the tribal dependent. As a chattel he had ceded all but his maintenance to his master: as a serf he rendered to his lord three or four days' unpaid labour per week, maintaining himself on the product of the rest.

The further development of the social organism proved no more favourable to feudalism than to chattel slavery; and the modern "free labourer" came into existence. But the economic servitude of the worker did not drop off with his feudal fetters. With the chains of innate status, there disappeared also its economic privileges; and the "free labourer" found himself, especially in England, in a community where the old common rights over the soil were being gradually but effectually extinguished. He became a landless stranger in his own country.

The development of competitive production for sale, and the industrial revolution of the past century, have made subsistence dependent, not merely upon access to the land, but upon the use, in addition, of increasingly large masses of capital, at first in agriculture, then in foreign trade, then in manufacture, and now, finally, also in distributive industries. The mere worker became steadily less and less industrially independent as his legal freedom increased. From an independent producing unit, he passed into a mere item in a vast industrial army, over the organisation of which he had no control. He was free, but free only to work at the market wage or to starve. Other resource he had none; and even now the freedom to work at all is denied to many at a time for varying periods, and we have the constantly recurring phenomenon of the unemployed. When it suits any person having the use of land and capital to employ the worker, he does so only on condition that two important deductions, rent and interest, can be made from the product for the gratuitous benefit of those possessing the legal ownership of land and capital. The reward of labour being thus reduced on an average by at least one third, the remaining eightpence out of the shilling is then shared between the various classes who *have* co-operated in the production, that is, the inventor, the managing employer, and the mere wage-worker—but in the competitive struggle it is shared in such a way that at least fourpence goes to a favoured set of educated workers numbering one-fifth of the whole, leaving four-fifths to divide less than fourpence out of the shilling between them. We have the direct consequence in the social condition around us. A fortunate few, owing to their legal power over the instruments of wealth production, are able to command the services of thousands of industrial slaves whose faces they have never seen, without rendering any return whatever to them or to society. A larger body of persons contribute some labour, but are able, from their education or their cultivated ability, to choose occupations for which the competition wage is still high, owing to the relatively small number of possible competitors. These two classes together number only one-fifth of the whole. On the other side is the great mass of the people, the weekly wage-earners, four out of every five of the nation, toiling perpetually for less than a third of the aggregate product of labour, at an annual wage averaging at most £35 per adult, hurried into unnecessarily early graves by the severity of their lives, and dying, as regards, at least, one-third of them, destitute or actually in receipt of poor-law relief.

When we have bound the labourer fast to his wheel; when we have practically excluded the average man from every real chance of improving his condition; when we have virtually denied to him the means of sharing in the higher feelings and the larger sympathies of the cultured race; when we have shortened his life in our service, stunted his growth in our factories, racked him with unnecessary disease by our exactions, tortured his soul with that worst of all pains, the constant fear of poverty, condemned his wife and children to sicken and die before his eyes, in spite of his own perpetual round of toil—then we are aggrieved that he often loses hope, gambles for the windfall that is denied to his industry, attempts to drown his cares in drink, and, driven by his misery irresistibly down the steep hill of vice, passes into that evil circle where vice begets poverty, and poverty intensifies vice, until Society unrelentingly stamps him out as vermin. Thereupon we lay the flattering unction to our souls that it was his own fault, that he had his chance; and we preach to his fellows thrift and temperance, prudence and virtue, but always industry, that industry of others which keeps the industrial machine in motion, so that we can still enjoy the opportunity of taxing it. Nay, so that we may not lose his labour, we keep him when we can from absolute starvation; and when the world has taken his all, we offer him the pauper's dole. Nothing gives a more striking picture of his condition than the official statistics of our pauperism. We have clogged our relief with irksome and humiliating conditions, so that the poor often die lingering deaths rather than submit to them. Yet there is a class in receipt of this bitter bread during any one year, numbering between three and four millions, one in ten of the whole population, one in eight of the wage-earning class. In some rural districts *every* aged labourer is a pauper. Of all persons over 70 years of age, 40 per cent. are permanent paupers. When the Queen in June, 1888, passed in review the whole population of London, she may, perhaps, have reflected that for one in every five of that whole crowd, a pauper's death was waiting. One fifth of the population of the richest city in the world die in the workhouse or the hospital (not including recipients of outdoor relief), and the proportion for the wage-earning class alone must, of course, be much greater.

This is the net result of our social arrangements after a generation of gradual *improvement*, greater, we are told, than England ever before knew. The distress is only normal. The condition of the people exhibits a marked advance in prosperity. It may be that this is true: nay, owing to the silent progress of Socialism, it probably is true; yet the problem for *us* is no lighter. Are things *now* such as we can dare to be responsible for? Let a sober, non-Socialist authority of weight answer. Mr. Frederic Harrison, writing just five years ago, said:—"To me at least, it would be enough to condemn modern society as hardly an advance on slavery or serfdom, if the permanent condition of industry were to be that which we now behold, that 90 per cent. of the actual producers of wealth have no home that they can call their own beyond the end of a week; have no bit of soil or so much as a room that belongs to them; have nothing of value of any kind except as much old furniture as will go in a cart; have the precarious chance of weekly wages which barely suffice to keep them in health; are housed for the most part in places that no man thinks fit for his horse: are separated by so narrow a margin of destitution that a month of bad trade, sickness or unexpected loss, brings them face to face with hunger and pauperism. . . . This is the normal state of the average workmen in town or country." (Report of Industrial Remuneration Conference, 1886, p. 429.)

Such then is our position to-day. Those who believe it possible that the festering evils of social ulceration can be cured without any fundamental change in property relations, rely mainly on three leading remedies, Trade Unions, Co-operation, and a general recrudescence of a Christ-like unselfishness. What does the dry light of science say to these homœopathic "pills against the earthquake"?

The belief in universal Trade Unionism as a means of greatly and permanently raising wages all round must be at once dismissed as involving a logical fallacy. Certainly, the workers in some trades have managed to improve their economic position by strict Trade Unions. We are never allowed to forget the splendid incomes earned by these aristocrats of labour, a mere tenth of the whole labour class. But those who merely counsel the rest to go and do likewise forget that the only permanently effective Trade Union victories are won by limitation of the numbers in the particular trade, and the excluded candidates necessarily go to depress the condition of the outsiders. The Trade Unionist can usually only raise himself on the bodies of his less fortunate comrades. If all were equally strong, all would be equally powerless—a point clearly proved by Prof. Cairnes, and obvious to all Trade Unionists themselves.

Co-operation is a more seductive means of escape: and most social reformers cannot, even now, refrain from keeping alive lingering hopes that some solution may here be found. But a whole generation of experiment has done little more than show the futility of expecting real help from this quarter. Less than one four-hundredth part of the industry of the country is yet carried on by Co-operation. The whole range of industrial development in the larger industries seems against it; and no ground for hope in Co-operation as a complete answer to the social problem can be gained from economic science. It fails to deal even with the real elements of the case. It may claim to obviate competition; but, as Mill himself quotes, "the deepest root of the evils and iniquities which fill the industrial world is *not* competition, but the subjection of labour to capital, and the enormous share which the possessors of the instruments of production are able to take from the produce." Co-operation can make no real defence against the continuance of the exaction of this "enormous share"—rent and interest—the continued individual enjoyment of which it, indeed, actually presupposes. It affords a valuable moral training, a profitable savings bank for investments, and a temporary means of interesting the worker in the industrial affairs of his country. But ordinary joint stock investment is now rapidly outgrowing it, and is already a hundred and sixty times as great as Co-operation. Now even the most enthusiastic believer in the virtues of association will hardly expect salvation merely from a *régime* of Joint Stock Companies; and this, and not Co-operation, is clearly the line in which our industrial development is rapidly travelling, so far as all large enterprises are concerned. The final goal of many industries is, moreover, obviously not the Co-operative Society, but the municipality. Nearly twice as much capital is already invested by town councils in a single industry (gas supply) as the whole twelve millions of the accumulations of the 1,500 co-operative societies. A larger extension of "municipal industry" is made every year than the progress, great as it is, of the Co-operative industry. Already where there is most Co-operation, there is also most municipalisation. Nevertheless, it may be some time before the more enthusiastic co-operators realise the industrial tendency, or even become aware that modern economic science turns regretfully against them; yet such eminent authorities as Cliffe Leslie, Professor Walker, Mr. Leonard Courtney, and Dr. J. K. Ingram, concur in dismissing the idea of universal Co-operation as chimerical. Nor is Co-operation really a rival of Socialism. The real import of the Co-operative movement is not profit-sharing, but the collective control of the consumer over industry; not the division of so-called "profits" among a larger number, but their elimination as far as is safely possible. Similarly, the purpose of Socialism is not the division of wealth among the poor but the assertion of the right of the community to the complete control over the means of production by which the community lives. Both movements had their rise in the inspiring propaganda of Robert Owen, which, seeming at the time to fail, had really so splendidly succeeded. Owen's advocacy of factory legislation, national education, and other measures, now rightly described as Socialistic in principle, led the way to the tremendous development of unconsciously Socialist legislation which has since taken place. His constant insistence on the corporate duty of the community to its individual members was really the fore-runner of the successful "municipal Socialism" which our great cities have since taken up. In all these matters "consumers" co-operate as citizens. But Owen lacked the teachings of Democracy, and when his followers learnt this lesson, they turned from his kind paternalism to the "collective freedom" asserted by the Chartist movement. It was largely from the Chartist followers of Owen that the modern Co-operative movement has derived its most enduring inspiration. Many of the founders of the most successful stores had been Chartist agitators. With its completely democratic organization, its assertion of the principle of public control over industry, and its repudiation of even benevolent dictation, modern Co-operation shows its affinity, not only to Chartism, but also to modern Socialism of the English type. The two movements have not only the same ends, but also the same principle—

the main idea of each being the control of industry neither by individuals nor for individuals, but by the public for the public. Both express the economic and industrial obverse of political democracy. Both recognise that political freedom can be but a mockery to the poorer worker so long as he has no control over the industry by which alone he can live. The two movements differ rather in their spheres than in their methods. No reasonable Socialist thinks it possible for the State immediately to take over the grocers' shops. The "democratisation" of retail trade, and of some other branches of industry, can, it has been triumphantly proved, be effected by the store and the "Wholesale," where neither the national government nor the local authority could yet venture to step in. On the other hand, co-operators easily recognize that there are industries for which the appropriate unit of administration is not the store, but the town council. The co-operators of Lancashire and Yorkshire have made greater strides in municipal Socialism than they have even in Co-operation. Municipal Socialism is, indeed, already twenty-five times as great as Co-operation, but its sphere lies outside that of the co-operative society, and every co-operator is bound by his principles to be also a good citizen, taking as keen an interest in the election of his town council as in that of his store committee. Nor is the National Government without its sphere in this progressive "democratisation" of industry. Co-operators need not refuse to admit that, for some services, the most convenient unit of administration is neither the store nor the town council, but the central executive. Our post office, and soon our railways, our Factory Acts and our taxation of unearned incomes, must all be national, not local. The greatest possible extension of the co-operative movement would therefore still leave an enormous sphere for both national and municipal collectivism.

There remains the ideal of the rapid spread of a Christ-like unselfishness. Of this hope let us speak with all the respect which so ancient a dream deserves. If it were realised it would, indeed, involve an upset of present property arrangements, compared with which Socialism is a mere trifle; yet science must perforce declare that the expectation of any but the slowest real improvement in general moral habit is absolutely without warrant. Forms of egoism may change, and moral habits vary; but, constituted as we are, it seems inevitable for healthy personal development that an at best instructed and unconscious egoism should preponderate in the individual. It is the business of the community not to lead into temptation this healthy natural feeling, but so to develop social institutions that individual egoism is necessarily directed to promote only the well-being of all. The older writers, led by Rousseau, in the reaction against aristocratic government, saw this necessary adjustment in absolute freedom. But that crude vision has long been demolished. "It is, indeed, certain," sums up Dr. Ingram, "that industrial society will not permanently remain without a systematic organisation. The mere conflict of private interests will never produce a well-ordered commonwealth of labour."

Is there then no hope? Is there no chance of the worker ever being released from the incubus of what Mill called, "the great social evil of a non-labouring class," whose monopolies cause the taxation of the industrious for the support of indolence, if not of plunder?

Mill tells us how, as he investigated more closely the history and structure of Society, he came to find a sure and certain hope in the Progress of Socialism, which he foresaw and energetically aided. We who call ourselves Socialists to-day in England, largely through Mill's teaching and example, find a confirmation of this hope in social history and economics, and see already in the distance the glad vision of a brighter day, when, practically, the whole product of labour will be the worker's and the worker's alone, and at last social arrangements will be deliberately based upon the Apostolic rule ignored by so many Christians, that if a man do not work, neither shall he eat.

But it must clearly be recognised that no mere charitable palliation of existing individualism can achieve this end. Against this complacent delusion of the philanthropist, Political Economy emphatically protests. So long as the instruments of production are in unrestrained private ownership, so long must the tribute of the workers to the drones continue: so long will the toilers' reward inevitably be reduced by their exactions. No tinkering with the Land Laws can abolish or even diminish Economic Rent. The whole series of Irish Land Acts, for instance, have not reduced its amount by a single penny, however much they have altered its distribution. The *whole* equivalent of every source of fertility or advantage of all land over and above the very worst land in use, is necessarily abstracted from the mere worker. So long as Lady Matheson can "own" the island of Lewis, and "do what she likes with her own," it is the very emphatic teaching of Political Economy that the earth may be the Lord's, but the fulness thereof must, inevitably, be the landlord's.

There is an interesting episode in English history in which James the First, disputing with the City Corporation, then the protector of popular liberties, threatened, as a punishment upon London, to remove the Court to Oxford. "Provided only your Majesty leave us the Thames," cleverly replied the Lord Mayor. But economic dominion is more subtle than king-craft: our landlords have stolen from us even the Thames. No Londoner who is not in some way a landlord obtains one farthing of economic benefit from the existence of London's ocean highway: the whole equivalent of its industrial advantage goes to swell our compulsory tribute of 37 millions sterling —London's annual rental.

And it is precisely the same with industrial capital. The worker in the factory gets, as a worker, absolutely no advantage from the machinery which causes the product of his labour to be multiplied a hundredfold. He gets no more of that product as wages for himself, in a state of free and unrestrained competition, than his colleague labouring at the very margin of cultivation with the very minimum of capital. The artisan producing shoes by the hundred in the modern machine works of Southwark or Northampton gets no higher wages than the surviving hand cobbler in the bye street. The whole advantage of industrial capital, like the whole advantage of superior land, necessarily goes to him who legally owns it. The mere worker can have none of them. "The remuneration of labour, as such," wrote Professor Cairnes in 1874, "skilled or unskilled, can never rise much above its present level."

Nor is it the increase of population which effects this result. During the present century, indeed, in spite of an unparalleled increase in numbers, the wealth annually produced in England *per head* has nearly doubled. If population became stationary tomorrow, other things being equal, the present rent and interest would not be affected: our numbers determine indeed how far the margin of cultivation will spread (and this is of vital import) ; but, increase or no increase, the unrestrained private ownership of land and capital necessarily involves the complete exclusion of the mere worker, as such, from all the advantages of the fertile soil on which he is born, and of the buildings, railways, and machinery he finds around him.

So much the orthodox economists tell us clearly enough. Where then is the Socialist hope?

In the political power of the workers. The industrial evolution has left them landless strangers in their own country; but the political evolution is about to make them its rulers. If unrestrained private ownership of the means of production necessarily keeps the many workers permanently poor without any fault on their part, in order to make a few idlers rich without any merit on theirs (and this is the teaching of economic science), unrestrained private ownership will inevitably go. In this country many successive inroads have already been made in it; and these constitute the Progress of Socialism.

Three hundred years ago, for fear of the horde of "sturdy beggars," which even hanging had failed to extirpate, the wise Cecil was led to institute the general system of poor relief, a deduction from rent and interest for the benefit of those who were excluded from directly sharing in them. But the industrial evolution had not yet made this condition universal; and little further progress was made in Socialism until the beginning of our century. Then, indeed, the acme of individualism was reached. No sentimental regulations hindered the free employment of land and capital to the highest possible personal advantage, however many lives of men, women, and children were used up in the process. Capitalists still speak of that bright time with exultation. "It was not five per cent. or ten per cent.," says one, "but thousands per cent. that made the fortune of Lancashire." But opinion turned against *Laisser faire* fifty years ago. Mainly by the heroic efforts of a young nobleman, who lately passed away from us as Lord Shaftesbury, a really effective Factory Act was won; and the insatiate greed of the manufacturers was restrained by political power, in the teeth of their most determined opposition. Since then the progress has been rapid. Slice after slice has, in the public interest, been cut off the profits of land and capital, and therefore off their value, by Mines Regulation Acts, Truck Acts, Factory Acts, Adulteration Acts, Land Acts. Slice after slice has been cut off the already diminished incomes of the classes enjoying rent and interest, by the gradual shifting of taxation from the whole nation as consumers of taxed commodities to the holders of incomes above £150, the average family income of the Kingdom. Step by step political power and political organisation have been used for industrial ends, until a Minister of the Crown is the largest employer of labour in the country, and at least 200,000 men, not counting the army and navy, are directly in the service of the community, without the intervention of the profit of any middleman. All the public needs supplied by the labour of these public servants were at one time left to private enterprise, and were a source of legitimate individual investment of capital. Step by step the community has absorbed them, wholly or partially; and the area of private exploitation has been lessened. Parallel with this progressive nationalisation or municipalisation of industry, a steady elimination of the purely personal element in business management has gone on. The older economists doubted whether anything but banking could be carried on by joint-stock enterprise: now every conceivable industry, down to baking and milk-selling, is successfully managed by the salaried officers of large corporations of idle shareholders. More than one-third of the whole business of England, measured by the capital employed, is now done by joint-stock companies, whose shareholders could be expropriated by the community with little more dislocation of industry than is caused by the daily purchase of shares on the Stock Exchange.

Besides its direct supersession of private enterprise, the State now registers, inspects, and controls nearly all the industrial functions which it has not yet absorbed. The inspection is often detailed and rigidly enforced. The State in most of the larger industrial operations prescribes the age of the worker, the hours of work, the amount of air, light, cubic space, heat, lavatory accommodation, holidays, and meal-times; where, when, and how wages shall be paid; how machinery, staircases, lift-holes, mines, and quarries are to be fenced and guarded; how and when the plant shall be cleaned, repaired, and worked. Even the kind of package in which some articles shall be sold is duly prescribed, so that the individual capitalist shall take no advantage of his position. On every side he is being registered, inspected, controlled; eventually he will be superseded by the community, and he is compelled in the meantime to cede for public purposes an ever-increasing share of his rent and interest.

This is the rapid progress of "Collectivism" which is so noticeable in our generation. England is already the most Socialist of all European communities, though the young Emperor of Germany is now compelled by the uneasy ground swell of German politics to emulate us very closely. English Collectivism will, however, inevitably be Democratic—a real "Social Democracy" instead of the mere Political Democracy with which Liberals coquet. As the oldest industrial country, we are likely to keep the lead, in spite of those old-fashioned politicians who innocently continue to regard Socialism as a dangerous and absolutely untried innovation. Are there not still, in obscure nooks, disbelievers and despisers of all science? The schoolmaster never penetrates into *all* the corners in the same generation.

But some will be inclined to say, "This is not what we thought Socialism meant? We imagined that Socialists wanted to bring about a sanguinary conflict in the streets, and then the next day to compel all delicately nurtured people to work in the factories at a fixed rate of wages."

It is not only in the nursery that bogey-making continues to be a very general though quite unnecessary source of anxiety. Socialists do but foretell the probable direction of English social evolution; and it needs nothing but a general recognition of that development and a clear determination not to allow the selfish interests of any class to hinder or hamper it, for Socialism to secure universal assent. All other changes will easily flow from this acquiescent state of mind, and they need not be foreshadowed in words.

"But will not Socialism abolish private property?" It will certainly seriously change ideas concerning that which the community will lend its force to protect in the personal enjoyment of any individual.

It is already clear that no really democratic government, whether consciously Socialist or not, will lend its soldiers or its police to enforce the "rights" of such an owner as Lord Clanricarde. Even Matthew Arnold declared the position of the mere landlord to be an "anachronism." "Landlordism" in Ireland is admittedly doomed, and opinion in England is rapidly ripening in favour of collective control over the soil. The gradual limitation of the sphere of private property which has been steadily taking place will doubtless continue; and just as courts of justice, private mints, slaves, public office, pocket boroughs, votes, army commissions, post offices, telegraph lines, and now even continental telegraph cables landing on English shores, have ceased to be permissible personal possessions, so will the few remaining private gasworks, waterworks, docks, tramways, and schools be quickly absorbed, and an end be also made to private railways and town ground-rents. Ultimately, and as soon as may be possible, we look to see this absorption cover all land, and at least all the larger forms of industrial capital. In these, as Herbert Spencer pointed out forty years ago as regards land, private ownership will eventually no more be possible than it is now in a post office or a court of justice, both of which were once valuable sources of individual profit. Beyond the vista of this extension of collectivism, it is at present unnecessary to look; but we may at any rate be sure that social evolution will no more stop there than at any previous stage.

This is the Progress of Socialism. To an ever growing number of students of history and science, its speedy acceleration appears at once our evident destiny and our only hope. Political Economy, at least, whatever the economist may think of Socialism, now recognises no other alternative. So long as land and industrial capital remain in unrestrained private ownership, so long must "the subjection of labour to capital, and the enormous share which the possessors of the instruments of industry are able to take from the produce" inevitably continue, and even increase. The aggregate product may continue to grow; but "the remuneration of labour as such, skilled or unskilled, can never rise much above its present level."

The *only* effectual means of raising the material condition of the great mass of the people, is for them to resume, through their own public organisations, that control over their own industry which industrial evolution has taken from them, and to enter collectively into the enjoyment of the fertile lands and rich mines from which they are now so relentlessly excluded. This is the teaching of economic science; and, however little individual economists may relish the application, the workers are rapidly coming to appreciate it.

In this direction, too, is the mighty sweep and tendency of social evolution. Without our knowledge, even against our will, we in England have already been carried far by the irresistible wave. What Canute will dare to set a limit to its advance? One option we have, and one only. It is ours, if we will, to recognise a rising force, to give it reasonable expression, nay, within limits, even to direct its course. This is why we are Socialists, and why you must become so. For if the conscious intelligence of the natural leaders of the community lag behind the coming thought; if it ignore the vast social forces now rapidly organising for common action; if it leave poverty and repression and injustice to go on breeding their inevitable births of angry brutality and fierce revenge: then, indeed, social evolution may necessarily be once more accomplished by social cataclysm. From this catastrophe, our gradual adoption of Social Democracy is the path of escape.

# ✍ THE CONDITION OF LABOR

*Leo XIII*

*Throughout much of the nineteenth century the papacy, maintaining
its opposition to ideological and political innovation, remained aloof
from the problems of a rapidly changing, industrializing society. During
the last years of the pontificate of Pius IX (1846–1878), conflict between
the rigidly traditional papacy and the secular-minded national states had
reached a critical stage (see pages 200–211); by the time Pius died,
the Catholic Church was in a state of declared or undeclared war
with most of the important European states.*

*Pius's successor, Leo XIII (1878–1903), began a cautious adaptation
of the papacy to an age of mass politics and to an urban, industrial society.
On one hand, this involved a new departure in diplomacy to liquidate
outstanding church-state conflicts without sacrificing fundamental
ecclesiastical interests; on the other hand, it required a refocusing of
traditional Catholic social doctrine. The papal encyclical (that is, an open
papal letter on a subject of general concern to the Catholic Church,
authoritatively defining the Church's position without being absolutely
binding on all Catholics) of 1891 on* The Condition of Labor *was such
an application of traditional principles to new conditions. From the first
two words of its Latin text, Leo's encyclical is often known as* Rerum
Novarum.

*Neither in form nor in content can* The Condition of Labor *be considered
a pioneering effort in the realm of Catholic social doctrine. Similar ideas
had been put forward earlier by churchmen like Bishop Ketteler in
Germany and laymen like Albert de Mun in France, who had sought
to make Catholic teachings relevant among belching smokestacks,
mushrooming slums, and a dehumanized proletariat. Indeed, in a number
of countries—Belgium, Germany, and Austria are the most prominent—
Catholic-inspired mass parties were then competing with Marxist Socialists
for the allegiance of the working class. In this sense both the Church's
traditional concern with social justice and the expediency of party politics
dictated an official Catholic stand on the problems of capital and labor.
What makes* The Condition of Labor *both significant and novel is that
for the first time this reorientation of Catholic social thought was officially
recognized and sanctioned by the Pope.*

269

It is not surprising that the spirit of revolutionary change, which has so long been predominant in the nations of the world, should have passed beyond politics and made its influence felt in the cognate field of practical economy. The elements of a conflict are unmistakable: the growth of industry, and the surprising discoveries of science; the changed relations of masters and workmen; the enormous fortunes of individuals, and the poverty of the masses; the increased self-reliance and the closer mutual combination of the working population; and, finally, a general moral deterioration. The momentous seriousness of the present state of things just now fills every mind with painful apprehension; wise men discuss it; practical men propose schemes; popular meetings, legislatures, and sovereign princes, all are occupied with it—and there is nothing which has a deeper hold on public attention.

Therefore, venerable brethren, as on former occasions, when it seemed opportune to refute false teaching, we have addressed you in the interests of the Church and of the common weal, and have issued letters on "Political Power," on "Human Liberty," on the "Christian Constitution of the State," and on similar subjects, so now we have thought it useful to speak on the "Condition of Labor." It is a matter on which we have touched once or twice already. But in this letter the responsibility of the Apostolic office urges us to treat the question expressly and at length in order that there may be no mistake as to the principles which truth and justice dictate for its settlement. The discussion is not easy, nor is it free from danger. It is not easy to define the relative rights and the mutual duties of the wealthy and of the poor, of capital and of labor. And the danger lies in this, that crafty agitators constantly make use of these disputes to pervert men's judgments and to stir up the people to sedition.

But all agree, and there can be no question whatever, that some remedy must be found, and quickly found, for the misery and wretchedness which press so heavily at this moment on the large majority of the very poor. The ancient workmen's guilds were destroyed in the last century, and no other organization took their place. Public institutions and the laws have repudiated the ancient religion. Hence by degrees it has come to pass that workingmen have been given over, isolated and defenceless, to the callousness of employers and the greed of unrestrained competition. The evil has been increased by rapacious usury, which, although more than once condemned by the Church, is nevertheless, under a different form but with the same guilt, still practised by avaricious and grasping men. And to this must be added the custom of working by contract, and the concentration of so many branches of trade in the hands of a few individuals, so that a small number of very rich men have been able to lay upon the masses of the poor a yoke little better than slavery itself.

To remedy these evils the *Socialists*, working on the poor man's envy of the rich, endeavor to destroy private property, and maintain that individual possessions should become the common property of all, to be administered by the State or by municipal bodies. They hold that, by thus transferring property from private persons to the

*The Condition of Labor. The Encyclical Letter of His Holiness Pope Leo XIII* (Mount Loretto, Staten Island, N.Y.: Press of the Mission of the Immaculate Virgin, 1891), pp. 3–5, 7–15, 17–28, 30.

community, the present evil state of things will be set to rights, because each citizen will then have its equal share of whatever there is to enjoy. But their proposals are so clearly futile for all practical purposes that if they were carried out the working-man himself would be among the first to suffer. Moreover they are emphatically unjust, because they would rob the lawful possessor, bring the State into a sphere that is not its own, and cause complete confusion in the community.

It is surely undeniable that, when a man engages in remunerative labor, the very reason and motive of his work is to obtain property, and to hold it as his own private possession. If one man hires out to another his strength or his industry, he does this for the purpose of receiving in return what is necessary for food and living; he thereby expressly proposes to acquire a full and real right, not only to the remuneration, but also to the disposal of that remuneration as he pleases. Thus, if he lives sparingly, saves money, and invests his savings, for greater security, in land, the land in such a case is only his wages in another form; and, consequently, a workingman's little estate thus purchased should be as completely at his own disposal as the wages he received for his labor. But it is precisely in this power of disposal that ownership consists, whether the property be land or movable goods. The *Socialists*, therefore, in endeavoring to transfer the possessions of individuals to the community, strike at the interests of every wage-earner, for they deprive him of the liberty of disposing of his wages, and thus of all hope and possibility of increasing his stock and of bettering his condition in life. . . .

With reason, therefore, the common opinion of mankind, little affected by the few dissentients who have maintained the opposite view, has found in the study of nature, and in the law of nature herself, the foundations of the division of property, and has consecrated by the practice of all ages the principle of private ownership, as being preëminently in conformity with human nature, and as conducing in the most unmistakable manner to the peace and tranquility of human life. The same principle is confirmed and enforced by the civil laws—laws which, as long as they are just, derive their binding force from the law of nature. The authority of the divine law adds its sanction, forbidding us in the gravest terms even to covet that which is another's: *Thou shalt not covet thy neighbor's wife; nor his house, nor his field, nor his man servant, nor his maid servant, nor his ox, nor his ass, nor anything which is his.*

The rights here spoken of, belonging to each individual man, are seen in a much stronger light if they are considered in relation to man's social and domestic obligations. . . .

That right of property, . . . which has been proved to belong naturally to individual persons, must also belong to a man in his capacity of head of a family; nay, such a person must possess this right so much the more clearly in proportion as his posi-tion multiplies his duties. For it is a most sacred law of nature that a father must provide food and all necessaries for those whom he has begotten; and, similarly, nature dictates that a man's children, who carry on, as it were, and continue his own personality, should be provided by him with all that is needful to enable them honorably to keep themselves from want and misery in the uncertainties of this mortal life. Now in no other way can a father effect this except by the ownership of profitable property, which he can transmit to his children by inheritance. A family, no less than a State, is, as we have said, a true society, governed by a power within itself, that is to say, by the father. Wherefore, provided the limits be not transgressed which are prescribed by the very purposes for which it exist, the family has at least equal rights with the State in the choice and pursuit of those things which are needful to its preservation and its just liberty.

We say, at least equal rights; for since the domestic household is anterior both in idea and in fact to the gathering of men into a commonwealth, the former must necessarily have rights and duties which are prior to those of the latter, and which rest more immediately on nature. If the citizens of a State—that is to say, the families —on entering into association and fellowship, experienced at the hands of the State hindrance instead of help, and found their rights attacked instead of being protected, such association were rather to be repudiated than sought after.

The idea, then, that the civil government should, at its own discretion, penetrate and pervade the family and the household, is a great and pernicious mistake. True, if a family finds itself in great difficulty, utterly friendless, and without prospect of help, it is right that extreme necessity be met by public aid; for each family is part of the commonwealth. In like manner, if within the walls of the household there occur grave disturbance of mutual rights, the public power must interfere to force each party to give the other what is due; for this is not to rob citizens of their rights, but justly and properly to safeguard and strengthen them. But the rulers of the State must go no further; nature bids them stop here. Paternal authority can neither be abolished by the State nor absorbed, for it has the same source as human life itself. "The child belongs to the father," and is, as it were, the continuation of the father's personality; and, to speak with strictness, the child takes its place in civil society not in its own right, but in its quality as a member of the family in which it is begotten. And it is for the very reason that "the child belongs to the father" that, as St. Thomas of Aquin says, "before it attains the use of free will, it is in the power and care of its parents." The *Socialists*, therefore, in setting aside the parent and introducing the providence of the State, act *against natural justice*, and threaten the very existence of family life.

And such interference is not only unjust, but is quite certain to harass and disturb all classes of citizens and to subject them to odious and intolerable slavery. It would open the door to envy, to evil speaking, and to quarrelling; the sources of wealth would themselves run dry, for no one would have any interest in exerting his talents or his industry; and that ideal equality of which so much is said would in reality be the levelling down of all to the same condition of misery and dishonor.

Thus it is clear that the main tenet of *Socialism,* the community of goods, must be utterly rejected; for it would injure those whom it is intended to benefit, it would be contrary to the natural rights of mankind, and it would introduce confusion and disorder into the commonwealth. Our first and most fundamental principle, therefore, when we undertake to alleviate the condition of the masses, must be the inviolability of private property. This laid down, we go on to show where we must find the remedy that we seek. . . .

Let it be laid down, in the first place, that humanity must remain as it is. It is impossible to reduce human society to a level. The *Socialists* may do their utmost, but all striving against nature is vain. There naturally exist among mankind innumerable differences of the most important kind; people differ in capability, in diligence, in health, and in strength; and unequal fortune is a necessary result of inequality in condition. Such inequality is far from being disadvantageous either to individuals or to the community; social and public life can only go on by the help of various kinds of capacity and the playing of many parts: and each man, as a rule, chooses the part which peculiarly suits his case. As regards bodily labor, even had man never fallen from *the state of innocence,* he would not have been wholly unoccupied; but that which would then have been his free choice and his delight, became afterward compulsory, and the painful expiation of his sin. *Cursed be the earth in thy work; in thy labor thou shalt eat of it all the days of thy life.* In like manner, the other pains and hardships of life will have no end or cessation on this earth; for the consequences of sin are bitter and hard to bear, and they must be with man as long as life lasts. To suffer and to endure, therefore, is the lot of humanity; let men try as they may, no strength and no artifice will ever succeed in banishing from human life the ills and troubles which beset it. If any there are who pretend differently—who hold out to a hard-pressed people freedom from pain and trouble, undisturbed repose, and constant enjoyment—they cheat the people and impose upon them, and their lying promises will only make the evil worse than before. There is nothing more useful than to look at the world as it really is—and at the same time to look elsewhere for a remedy to its troubles.

The great mistake that is made in the matter now under consideration, is to possess one-self of the idea that class is naturally hostile to class: that rich and poor are intended by nature to live at war with one another. So irrational and so false is this view, that the exact contrary is the truth. Just as the symmetry of the human body is the result of the disposition of the members of the body, so in a State it is ordained by nature that these two classes should exist in harmony and agreement, and should, as it were, fit into one another, so as to maintain the equilibrium of the body politic. Each requires the other; capital cannot do without labor, nor labor without capital. Mutual agreement results in pleasantness and good order: perpetual conflict necessarily produces confusion and outrage. Now, in preventing such strife as this, and in making it impossible, the efficacy of Christianity is marvellous and manifold. First of all, there is nothing more powerful than religion (of which the Church is the interpreter and guardian) in drawing rich and poor together, by reminding each class of its duties to the other, and especially of the duties of justice. Thus religion teaches the laboring man and the workman to carry out honestly and well all equitable agreements freely made; never to injure capital, or to outrage the person of an employer; never to employ violence in representing his own cause, or to engage in riot or disorder; and to have nothing to do with men of evil principles, who work upon the people with artful promises, and raise foolish hopes which usually end in disaster and in repentance when too late. Religion teaches the rich man and the employer that their work-people are not their slaves; that they must respect in every man his dignity as a man and as a Christian; that labor is nothing to be ashamed of, if we listen to right reason and to christian philosophy, but is an honorable employment, enabling a man to sustain his life in an upright and creditable way; and that it is shameful and inhuman to treat men like chattels to make money by, or to look upon them merely as so much muscle or physical power.

Thus, again, religion teaches that, as among the workman's concerns are religion herself and things spiritual and mental, the employer is bound to see that he has time for the duties of piety; that he be not exposed to corrupting influences and dangerous occasions, and that he be not led away to neglect his home and family, or to squander his wages. Then, again, the employer must never tax his work-people beyond their strength, nor employ them in work unsuited to their sex or age. His great and principal obligation is to give to every one that which is just. Doubtless before we can decide whether wages are adequate, many things have to be considered, but rich men and masters should remember this—that to exercise pressure for the sake of gain, upon the indigent and the destitute, and to make one's profit out of the need of another, is condemned by all laws, human and divine. To defraud any one of wages that are his due is a crime which cries to the avenging anger of Heaven. *Behold, the hire of the laborers which by fraud hath been kept back by you, crieth; and the cry of them hath entered into the ears of the Lord of Sabaoth.* Finally, the rich must religiously refrain from cutting down the workman's earnings, either by force, by fraud, or by usurious dealing; and with the more reason because the poor man is weak and unprotected, and because his slender means should be sacred in proportion to their scantiness.

Were these precepts carefully obeyed and followed, would not strife die out and cease?

But the Church, with Jesus Christ for its Master and Guide, aims higher still. It lays down precepts yet more perfect, and tries to bind class to class in friendliness and good understanding. The things of this earth cannot be understood or valued rightly without taking into consideration the life to come, the life that will last forever. Exclude the idea of futurity, and the very notion of what is good and right would perish; nay, the whole system of the universe would become a dark and unfathomable mystery. The great truth which we learn from nature herself is also the grand Christian dogma on which religion rests as on its base—that when we have done with this present life, then we shall really begin to live. God has not created us for the perishable and transitory things of earth, but for things heavenly and everlasting. He has given us this world, as a place of exile, and not as our true country. Money, and the other things which men call good and desirable—we may have them in abundance, or we may want them altogether—as far as eternal happiness is concerned, it is no matter; the only thing that is important is to use them aright. . . .

The chiefest and most excellent rule for the right use of money is one which the heathen philosophers indicated, but which the Church has traced out clearly, and has not only made known to men's minds, but has impressed upon their lives. It rests on the principle that it is one thing to have a right to the possession of money, and another to have a right to use money as one pleases. Private ownership, as we have seen, is the natural right of man; and to exercise that right, especially as members of society, is not only lawful, but absolutely necessary. *It is lawful,* says St. Thomas of Aquin, *for a man to hold private property: and it is also necessary for the carrying on of human life.* But if the question be asked, How must one's possessions be used? the Church replies without hesitation in the words of the same holy doctor: *Man should not consider his outward possessions as his own, but as common to all, so as to share them without difficulty when others are in need. Whence the Apostle saith, Command the rich of this world . . . to give with ease, to communicate.* True, no one is commanded to distribute to others that which is required for his own necessities and those of his household; nor even to give away what is reasonably required to keep up becomingly his condition in life; *for no one ought to live unbecomingly.* But when necessity has been supplied, and one's position fairly considered, it is a duty to give to the indigent out of that which is over. *That which remaineth, give alms.* It is a duty, not of justice (except in extreme cases), but of Christian charity—a duty which is not enforced by human law. . . .

But, if Christian precepts prevail, the two classes will not only be united in the bonds of friendship, but also in those of brotherly love. For they will understand and feel that all men are the children of the common Father, that is, of God; that all have the same last end, which is God Himself, who alone can make either men or angels absolutely and perfectly happy; that all and each are redeemed by Jesus Christ and raised to the dignity of children of God, and are thus united in brotherly ties, both with each other and with Jesus Christ, *the first born among many brethren;* that the blessings of nature and the gifts of grace belong in common to the whole human race, and that to all, except to those who are unworthy, is promised the inheritance of the Kingdom of Heaven. *If sons, heirs also; heirs indeed of God, and co-heirs of Christ.*

Such is the scheme of duties and of rights which is put forth to the world by the Gospel. Would it not seem that strife must quickly cease were society penetrated with ideas like these?

But the Church, not content with pointing out the remedy, also applies it. For the Church does its utmost to teach and train men, and to educate them; and by means of its Bishops and clergy it diffuses its salutary teachings far and wide. It strives to influence the mind and heart so that all may willingly yield themselves to be formed and guided by the commandments of God. It is precisely in this fundamental and principal matter, on which everything depends, that the Church has a power peculiar to itself. The agencies which it employs are given it for the very purpose of reaching the hearts of men, by Jesus Christ Himself, and derive their efficiency from God. . . .

It cannot, however, be doubted that, to attain the purpose of which we treat, not only the Church, but all human means must conspire. All who are concerned in the matter must be of one mind and must act together. It is in this, as in the Providence which governs the world; results do not happen save where all the causes coöperate.

Let us, now, therefore, inquire what part the State should play in the work of remedy and relief.

By the State we here understand, not the particular form of government which prevails in this or that nation, but the State as rightly understood; that is to say, any Government conformable in its institutions to right, reason, and natural law, and to those dictates of the Divine wisdom which we have expounded in the Encyclical on the Christian Constitution of the State. The first duty, therefore, of the rulers of the State should be to make sure that the laws and institutions, the general character and administration of the commonwealth, shall be such as to produce of themselves public well being and private prosperity. This is the proper office of wise statesmanship and the work of the heads of the State. Now a State chiefly prospers and flourishes by morality, by well-regulated family life, by respect for religion and justice, by the moderation and equal distribution of public burdens, by the progress of the arts and of trade, by the abundant yield of the land—by everything which makes the citizens better and happier. Here, then, it is in the power of a ruler to benefit every order of the State, and among the rest to promote in the highest degree the interests of the poor; and this, by virtue of his office, and without being exposed to any suspicion of undue interference—for it is the province of the commonwealth to consult for the common good. And the more that is done for the working population by the general laws of the country, the less need will there be to seek for particular means to relieve them.

There is another and a deeper consideration which must not be lost sight of. To the State the interests of all are equal, whether high or low. The poor are members of the national community equally with the rich; they are real component parts, living parts, which make up, through the family, the living body; and it need hardly be said that they are by far the majority. It would be irrational to neglect one portion of the citizens and to favor another; and therefore the public administration must duly and solicitously provide for the welfare and the comfort of the working people, or else that law of justice will be violated which ordains that each shall have his due. . . .

But although all citizens, without exception, can and ought to contribute to that common good in which individuals share so profitably to themselves, yet it is not to be supposed that all can contribute in the same way and to the same extent. No matter what changes may be made in forms of government, there will always be differences and inequalities of condition in the State; Society cannot exist or be conceived without them. Some there must be who dedicate themselves to the work of the commonwealth, who make the laws, who administer justice, whose advice and authority govern the nation in times of peace and defend it in war. Such men clearly occupy the foremost place in the State, and should be held in the foremost estimation, for their work touches most nearly and effectively the general interests of the community. Those who labor at a trade or calling do not promote the general welfare in such a fashion as this; but they do in the most important way benefit the nation, though less directly. We have insisted that, since it is the end of society to make men better, the chief good that society can be possessed of is virtue. Nevertheless, in all well-constituted States it is a by no means unimportant matter to provide those bodily and external commodities, *the use of which is necessary to virtuous action.* And in the provision of material well being, the labor of the poor—the exercise of their skill and the employment of their strength in the culture of the land and the workshops of trade—is most efficacious and altogether indispensable. Indeed, their coöperation in this respect is so important that it may be truly said that it is only by the labor of the workingman that States grow rich. Justice, therefore, demands that the interests of the poorer population be carefully watched over by the administration, so that they who contribute so largely to the advantage of the community may themselves share in the benefits they create—that being housed, clothed, and enabled to support life, they may find their existence less hard and more endurable. It follows that whatever shall appear to be conducive to the well being of those who work should receive favorable consideration. Let it not be feared that solicitude of this kind will injure any interest; on the contrary, it will be to the advantage of all; for it cannot but be good for the commonwealth to secure from misery those on whom it so largely depends. . . .

Whenever the general interest or any particular class suffers or is threatened with evils which can in no other way be met, the public authority must step in to meet them. Now among the interests of the public as of private individuals, are these: that peace and good order should be maintained; that family life should be carried on in accordance with God's laws and those of nature; that religion should be reverenced and obeyed; that a high standard of morality should prevail in public and private life; that the sanctity of justice should be respected, and that no one should injure another with impunity; that the members of the commonwealth should grow up to man's estate strong and robust, and capable, if need be, of guarding and defending their country. If by a strike, or other combination of workmen, there should be imminent danger of disturbance to the public peace; or if circumstances were such that among the laboring population the ties of family were relaxed; if religion were found to suffer through the workmen not having time and opportunity to practise it; if in workshops and factories there were danger to morals through the mixing of the sexes or from any occasion of evil; or if employers laid burdens upon the workmen which were unjust, or degraded them with conditions that were repugnant to their dignity as human beings; finally, if health were endangered by excessive labor, or by work unsuited to sex or age—in these cases there can be no question that, within certain limits, it would be right to call in the help and authority of the law. The limits must be determined by the nature of the occasion which calls for the law's interference—the principle being this, that the law must not undertake more, or go further, than is required for the remedy of the evil or the removal of the danger. . . .

Here, however, it will be advisable to advert expressly to one or two of the more important details. It must be borne in mind that the chief thing to be secured is the safeguarding, by legal enactment and policy, of private property. Most of all is it essential in these times of covetous greed, to keep the multitude within the line of duty; for if all may justly strive to better their condition, yet neither justice nor the common good allows any one to seize that which belongs to another, or, under the pretext of futile and ridiculous equality, to lay hands on other people's fortunes. It is most true that by far the larger part of the people who work prefer to improve themselves by honest labor rather than by doing wrong to others. But there are not a few who are imbued with bad principles and are anxious for revolutionary change, and whose purpose it is to stir up tumult and bring about a policy of violence. The authority of the State should intervene to put restraint upon these disturbers, to save the workmen from their seditious arts, and to protect lawful owners from spoliation.

When work people have recourse to a strike, it is frequently because the hours of labor are too long, or the work too hard, or because they consider their wages insufficient. The grave inconvenience of this not uncommon occurrence should be obviated by public remedial measure; for such paralysis of labor not only affects the masters and their work people, but is extremely injurious to trade, and to the general interests of the public; moreover, on such occasions violence and disorder are generally not far off, and thus it frequently happens that the public peace is threatened. The laws should be beforehand, and prevent these troubles from arising; they should lend their influence and authority to the removal in good time of the causes which lead to conflicts between masters and those whom they employ.

But if the owners of property must be made secure, the workman, too, has property and possessions in which he must be protected: and, first of all, there are his spiritual and mental interests. Life on earth, however good and desirable in itself, is not the final purpose for which man is created; it is only the way and the means to that attainment of truth, and that practice of goodness, in which the full life of the soul consists. . . .

From this follows the obligation of the cessation of work and labor on Sundays and certain festivals. This rest from labor is not to be understood as mere idleness; much less must it be an occasion of spending money and of vicious excess, as many would desire it to be; but it should be rest from labor consecrated by religion. Repose united with religious observance disposes man to forget for a while the business of this daily life, and to turn his thoughts to heavenly things and to the worship which he so strictly owes to the Eternal Deity. . . .

If we turn now to things exterior and corporeal, the first concern of all is to save the poor workers from the cruelty of grasping speculators, who use human beings as mere instruments for making money. It is neither justice nor humanity so to grind men down with excessive labor as to stupefy their minds and wear out their bodies. Man's powers, like his general nature, are limited, and beyond these limits he cannot go. His strength is developed and increased by use and exercise, but only on condition of due intermission and proper rest. Daily labor, therefore, must be so regulated that it may not be protracted during longer hours than strength admits. How many and how long the intervals of rest should be will depend on the nature of the work, on circumstances of time and place, and on the health and strength of the workman. Those who labor in mines and quarries, and in work within the bowels of the earth, should have shorter hours in proportion as their labor is more severe and more trying to health. Then again, the season of the year must be taken into account; for not unfrequently a kind of labor is easy at one time which at another is intolerable or very difficult. Finally, work which is suitable for a strong man cannot reasonably be required from a woman or a child. And, in regard to children, great care should be taken not to place them in workshops and factories until their bodies and minds are sufficiently mature. For just as rough weather destroys the buds of spring, so too early an experience of life's hard work blights the young promise of a child's powers, and makes any real education impossible. Women, again, are not suited to certain trades; for a woman is by nature fitted for home work, and it is that which is best adapted at once to preserve her modesty and to promote the good bringing up of children and the well-being of the family. As a general principle it may be laid down that a workman ought to have leisure and rest in proportion to the wear and tear of his strength; for the waste of strength must be repaired by the cessation of work. . . .

We now approach a subject of very great importance, and one on which, if extremes are to be avoided, right ideas are absolutely necessary. Wages, we are told, are fixed by free consent; and therefore the employer, when he pays what was agreed upon, has done his part, and is not called upon for anything further. The only way, it is said, in which injustice could happen would be if the master refused to pay the whole of the wages, or the workman would not complete the work undertaken; when this happens the State should intervene, to see that each obtains his own,— but not under any other circumstances. . . .

Let it be granted . . . that as a rule workman and employer should make free agreements, and in particular should freely agree as to wages. Nevertheless, there is a dictate of nature more imperious and more ancient than any bargain between man and man, that the remuneration must be enough to support the wage earner in reasonable and frugal comfort. If through necessity or fear of a worse evil the workman accepts harder conditions because an employer or a contractor will give him no better, he is the victim of force and injustice. . . .

If a workman's wages be sufficient to enable him to maintain himself, his wife, and his children in reasonable comfort, he will not find it difficult, if he is a sensible man, to study economy; and he will not fail, by cutting down expenses, to put by a little property; nature and reason would urge him to do this. We have seen that this great labor question cannot be solved except by assuming as a principle that private ownership must be held sacred and inviolable. The law, therefore, should favor ownership, and its policy should be to induce as many of the people as possible to become owners. . . .

In the last place, employers and workmen may themselves effect much in the matter of which we treat, by means of those institutions and organizations which afford opportune assistance to those in need, and which draw the two orders more closely together. Among these may be enumerated: Societies for mutual help: various foundations established by private persons for providing for the workman, and for his widow or his orphans, in sudden calamity, in sickness, and in the event of death; and what are called "patronages" or institutions for the care of boys and girls, for young people, and also for those of more mature age.

The most important of all are workmen's associations, for these virtually include all the rest. History attests what excellent results were effected by the artificers' guilds of a former day. They were the means not only of many advantages to the workmen, but in no small degree of the advancement of art, as numerous monuments remain to prove. Such associations should be adapted to the requirements of the age in which we live—an age of greater instruction, of different customs, and of more numerous requirements in daily life. It is gratifying to know that there are actually in existence not a few societies of this nature, consisting either of workmen alone or of workmen and employers together; but it were greatly to be desired that they should multiply and become more effective. We have spoken of them more than once; but it will be well to explain here how much they are needed, to show that they exist by their own right, and to enter into their organization and their work. . . .

There are times, no doubt, when it is right that the law should interfere to prevent association; as when men join together for purposes which are evidently bad, unjust, or dangerous to the State. In such cases the public authority may justly forbid the formation of associations, and may dissolve them when they already exist. But every precaution should be taken not to violate the rights of individuals and not to make unreasonable regulations under the pretence of public benefit. For laws only bind when they are in accordance with right reason, and, therefore with the eternal law of God. . . .

Associations of every kind, and especially those of workingmen, are now far more common than formerly. In regard to many of these there is no need at present to inquire whence they spring, what are their objects, or what means they use. But there is a good deal of evidence which goes to prove that many of these societies are in the hands of invisible leaders, and are managed on principles far from compatible with Christianity and the public well-being; and that they do their best to get into their hands the whole field of labor, and to force workmen either to join them or to starve. Under these circumstances, Christian workmen must do one of two things: either join associations in which their religion will be exposed to peril, or form associations among themselves—unite their forces and courageously shake off the yoke of an unjust and intolerable oppression. No one who does not wish to expose man's chief good to extreme danger will hesitate to say that the second alternative must by all means be adopted.

Those Catholics are worthy of all praise—and there are not a few—who, understanding what the times require, have, by various enterprises and experiments, endeavored to better the condition of the working people without any sacrifice of principle. They have taken up the cause of the workingman, and have striven to make both families and individuals better off; to infuse the spirit of justice into the mutual relations of employer and employed; to keep before the eyes of both classes the precepts of duty and the laws of the Gospel—that Gospel which, by inculcating self-restraint, keeps men within the bounds of moderation, and tends to establish harmony among the divergent interests and various classes which compose the State. It is with such ends in view that we see men of eminence meeting together for discussion, for the promotion of united action, and for practical work. Others, again, strive to unite working people of various kinds into associations, help them with their advice and their means, and enable them to obtain honest and profitable work. The Bishops, on their part, bestow their ready good will and support; and with their approval and guidance many members of the clergy, both secular and regular, labor assiduously on behalf of the spiritual and mental interests of the members of associations. . . .

At this moment the condition of the working population is the question of the hour; and nothing can be of higher interest to all classes of the State than that it should be rightly and reasonably decided. But it will be easy for Christian workingmen to decide it aright if they form associations, choose wise guides, and follow the same path which with so much advantage to themselves and the commonwealth was trod by their fathers before them. Prejudice, it is true, is mighty, and so is the love of money, but if the sense of what is just and right be not destroyed by depravity of heart, their fellow-citizens are sure to be won over to a kindly feeling toward men whom they see to be so industrious and so modest, who so unmistakably prefer honesty to lucre, and the sacredness of duty to all other considerations.

And another great advantage would result from the state of things we are describing; there would be so much more hope and possibility of recalling to a sense of their duty those workingmen who have either given up their faith altogether, or whose lives are at variance with its precepts. These men in most cases, feel that they have been fooled by empty promises and deceived by false appearances. They cannot but perceive that their grasping employers too often treat them with the greatest inhumanity and hardly care for them beyond the profit their labor brings, and if they belong to an association, it is probably one in which there exists, in place of charity and love, that intestine strife which always accompanies unresigned and irreligious poverty. Broken in spirit and worn down in body, how many of them would gladly free themselves from this galling slavery? But human respect, or the dread of starvation, makes them afraid to take the step. To such as these, Catholic associations are of incalculable service, helping them out of their difficulties, inviting them to companionship, and receiving the repentant to a shelter in which they may securely trust. . . .

# Social Justice through the Organization of Labor

*During the last quarter of the nineteenth century, as the pace of industrialization quickened, factory, mine, and railroad workers succeeded in setting up bargaining and protective associations capable of surviving depressions and employers' hostility. By 1900 some sort of national labor movement had emerged in advanced countries such as England, Germany, the United States, Belgium, and France. The tactical problems of labor unions in dealing with individual employers were similar from country to country, but there were great differences in strategy and ultimate aims. In France, for instance, syndicalism sought to overturn the existing capitalist society by means of the revolutionary general strike; in the United States the dominant American Federation of Labor worked essentially to gain a larger share of the national product for skilled labor without challenging the prevailing economic system. Yet this does not mean that the modest demands of American or British unions met with less resistance from employers than the revolutionary objectives of French or German labor.*

*The selections which follow illustrate the clash of viewpoints between labor and employer in the United States during the mid-1890s, a time of economic depression and social dislocation. Samuel Gompers (1850–1924), speaking for the workers, was president and architect of the American Federation of Labor, which concentrated on collective bargaining for short-term economic gains by organized craftsmen. His opponent, P. J. Grosscup, a judge of the Federal court at Chicago, was widely regarded as an unofficial spokesman for employers, though far more vehement antiunion views than his could be found at the time. The occasion for this controversy was the national railway strike of 1894, which, blossoming from a local strike against the sleeping-car manufacturer Pullman, was decisively broken by the judicial and military intervention of the Federal government.*

## THE RAILWAY STRIKE

*Samuel Gompers*

On Decoration Day, May 30th, 1894, Judge Grosscup of the United States Courts in his oration commemorative of the day, took occasion to say that "The growth of labor organizations must be checked by law," yet when the sounds of his voice have scarcely died away we have in the midst of us the greatest and most extensive labor struggle that has ever taken place among the wage-workers of America, and possibly of the world.

Thousands of miles of railroads in all directions are at a stand still, and nearly a hundred thousand workmen in voluntary idleness to secure what they regard as justice to their fellow workmen. It has been questioned whether the boycott or strike was wise, or whether it was justifiable. With the first question there may be some difference of opinion. It may sincerely be doubted whether it was wise for an organization such as the American Railway Union, within a year of its formation to attempt to inaugurate a movement which in its inception, of necessity, assumed gigantic proportions.

The policy or wisdom of entering into so great a movement without consultation with, or against the advice of the older railroad and bona fide labor organizations of the country, is open to serious question. Nor will I attempt from the usual standpoint of trade disputes to justify the strike. Sufficient for me are the facts which provoked it, and to which I shall allude later; but that the railroad men deliberately entered a contest which entailed many sacrifices and dangers in an attempt to redress grievances not of their own, but of other workmen, workmen, who by an insidious system of hypocrisy and deceit had become so thoroughly enervated and enslaved and impoverished, without organization or previous understanding, in sheer desperation threw down their work and unmasking before the world's wondrous gaze the second of the twin of modern Pecksniffs, George M. Pullman, is indeed to their credit. The first of these twins, Andrew Carnegie, was for years regarded as the ideal of the "Captains of Industry," the paragon of virtue and business probity, the *Ne Plus Ultra* of political devotion to our "Triumphant Democracy," and the most adored of men when he reduced his workmen at Homestead, to a condition of poverty and

Samuel Gompers, "The Railway Strike," *American Federationist,* I (1894), 121–124.

misery. To-day he stands before the world convicted of defrauding the government he pretended to worship, the people whom he led to believe he loved and trusted.

A little more than twenty years ago George M. Pullman conceived the idea of starting in connection with his car shops a town. One that should bear his name and hand down to posterity a monument of his enterprise and philanthropy. He builded houses for his employees to live in, stores to make their purchases and churches to do their praying. The workers were told their interests and Pullman's were one and the same, that what would bring him a greater prosperity, would redound to their advantage. They were warned that to belong to a trade union would be inimical to their *joint* enterprise, hence workmen who would purpose forming a union among them would be discharged, regarded as a common enemy and driven out of the town. They were to depend entirely upon Pullman's generosity and foresight in all things. To paraphrase a stanza of a well known poem they were much like the men at Balaklava.

> Pullman to the front of them,
>> Pullman to the rear of them;
> Bulldozed and plundered.
>> Theirs not to ask the reason why?
> Theirs but to work and die
>> Too long had they slumbered.

The result was that the workers at Pullman were huddled together in the (exteriorly) neat houses, for which they were required to pay higher rents than are paid for similar accommodations in Chicago. They were reduced in wages as often as the seasons would recur and opportunities either arose or were made. This was carried on until last February, when a reduction in wages was offered varying from 25 to 33⅓ and in a few instances 50 per cent.

Here are a few figures which may be taken as a fair criterion of the extent of the reduction in wages offered.

| | Price per piece, 1893 | Price offered, 1894 |
|---|---|---|
| Making trolley roofs | $ 2 25 | $ 1 40 |
| Framework car seat | 1 25 | 79 |
| Cutting carpets | 3 00 | 1 50 |
| Making mattresses double | 25 | 15 |
| Cutting Brussels carpet | 2 50 | 1 10 |
| Blacksmith work, platform | 4 00 | 2 65 |
| Truck setting | 45 | 16 |
| Sleeping car bodies | 180 00 | 115 50 |

Driven to desperation by this latest attempt of Pullman to force the men, women and children further down in the social scale a meeting was held. Who called it no one knows, how it came about not a vestige of evidence is at hand. It was held and a committee appointed to wait upon Mr. Pullman or a representative of the company to show that it was absolutely impossible to live on the wages offered; that a middle ground should be sought; that if wages were to be reduced the rents should also come down.

Instead of the request of the men being considered by Pullman, the committee was summarily dismissed and discharged almost instantly. Is it surprising that these men in their rude awakening to the true character of this modern philanthropist who had led them to depend entirely upon him, deceived them into the belief that self reliance and organization for their common protection was their greatest enemy, now that they asked for a respectful hearing and consideration of their grievances, found themselves injured and insulted and their spokesmen discharged and blacklisted and themselves without an organization to protect or defend them, without the means of properly laying their grievances before organized labor of the country, they struck work declaring that they might as well remain idle and starve as to work and slowly meet that fate.

Organized labor of Chicago becoming aware of the unusual commotion at Pullman did not hold the spurned attempt to organize the workers of that town against them. It was readily appreciated that these men were wholly misled by the false promises and covert threats of Pullman's "Pantata." Relief committees were at once formed and it is firmly declared that the average workman of that philanthropist-ridden town have fared better since they have engaged in the contest and fraternized with their fellow workmen than they have for the past two years while working.

It was during this time, when relief committees from the Pullman strikers were making their visits to organizations, that the convention of the American Railway Union was holding its first convention in Chicago and a committee called for its financial and moral assistance. A committee from the convention was appointed to wait upon the company with the request that the matter in dispute might be submitted to arbitration. The committee was told there was nothing to arbitrate and that the company refused to discuss the matter at all. Insulted, humiliated by the manner their disinterested efforts at restoring amicable relations between Pullman and his former servile employees were received, the committee made its report. The convention in a moment reflected the feelings of the committee and though at first sullen, silent and indignant they resolved amidst the wildest enthusiasm that unless the Pullman Company either adjusted the matter in controversy with their employees or submitted it to an arbitration the members of the American Railway Union would not handle Pullman cars and would ask all workmen to act likewise. No heed was given to the request, resolution or threat (call it what you will) and the great boycott (strike) was on.

I can scarcely bring myself to the belief that the convention imagined that the movement would be as extended as it developed into, nor that it would last as long as it has. Be that as it may, we certainly find ourselves in the midst of one of the greatest labor struggles.

Now comes the question repeated. Was the strike wise or justifiable? The answer to which must always depend upon the character and position of the party giving it. As to the wisdom time can only tell. Since "Nothing succeeds so well as success" in all efforts of life I presume this element will finally set its quietus upon this consideration of the subject. But as to its justification, what of that? From the standpoint of the employer, no! From the standpoint of a labor organization having an agreement with an employer which would violate its provisions, no! From the standpoint of the A. R. U., having no agreement with either of the railroad companies involved and expressing the inarticulate protest of the masses against the wrongs inflicted upon any of their brothers and their yearning for justice to all mankind, yes! a thousand times yes!

It is something not yet fully understood how fully organized labor stands as the sturdy pioneer of all the hopes of the masses for justice and humane conditions, of their aspirations for a nobler manhood resultant from an equality of opportunities. It is in consequence of these facts that organized labor feels itself frequently called upon to espouse the cause of those who have neglected their own interests and who have even antagonized any effort to bring them within the fold of organization. Labor men feel and know that the wealth producers would certainly avail themselves of their only means of defending and advancing their position in life were it not that they in many instances had their prejudices aroused and ignorance of actual conditions preyed upon by the instruments of their oppression in the hands of the corporate and employing class.

But the men are on strike, the police armed to the teeth are on guard to protect life and property, the militia are called out ostensibly for the same purpose and the regular army of the United States are marshaled into the fields by order of the President to enforce injunctions, restraining "everybody" from even writing a letter, issued by the Judge who only a few days ago expressed the firm conviction that the growth of labor organizations must be checked by law.

Is it not somewhat strange that under the provisions of the Interstate Commerce Law, a law passed by Congress in compliance with the demand of the people of our country to protect them against the greed and outrageous discriminations of the railroads it can be distorted to such a degree as to appal its authors and promoters and should be perverted from its true purpose and made to do service as an instrument to oppress the parties to whom it was never intended to apply, workingmen engaged in a contest to redress grievances?

One may look almost in vain for the restraint the law has put upon the avarice and injustice practiced by the railroad corporations, but the reform elements in our country seem to have unconsciously created their own Frankenstein, the breath of life being injected into it by plutocracy in the shape of ill gotten gains.

There was no desire nor even a tendency on the part of organized labor to have its movement go beyond the limits of the law, but I submit that there is a standpoint from which this great problem should be considered other than a sycophantic judge's injunction, a policeman's club or the point of a bayonet. The fact of the matter is that industrial conditions have changed to a wonderful extent within the past thirty years, that wealth has been accumulated as never before, that new forces are at play in the production and transportation of wealth, and that the civil law of our States and country has simply not kept pace in becoming accommodated to the altered conditions.

Do what you will, declaim as you may industrial and commercial development cannot be confined within the limits of laws enacted to fit past decades, the theories of which are sought to be applied to modern conditions.

Civilization of the past and present is based upon labor, and yet the laborer has no standing nor protection in the economy of our life. It may well be asked that if the State ignores dealing out some degree of justice and guaranteeing protection to labor, what interest the labor has in the State? As a matter of fact the organizations of labor are endeavoring to secure that protection and guarantee to the workingmen which the State has failed to take cognizance of. Without organization the workmen would simply be reduced to a much worse condition than the slaves in antebellum days, and all attempts to strain the law, construing the exercise of natural rights to be criminal, will only react upon the heads of the legal prestidigitators.

If in monarchical England with its old and effete traditions and crusty customs the Parliament can afford to liberalize its laws and legalize the action of workingmen engaged in the maintenance of their organizations and their effort to obtain better conditions, certainly the Republic of these United States should not only keep pace with that spirit, but advance beyond it and not bring the entire military and civil forces to aid the strong and help crush out the weak.

Labor cannot and will not if it could, utilize the Havemeyer process of securing legislation; it relies upon the justice of its cause, the nobility of its purposes, the humanizing influences of its efforts.

Pullman it is said is willing to spend millions of dollars if necessary to bring his former employees "to their senses." This man who compels the public to pay the wages in the shape of tips to his employees on the Pullman cars, who forces his workmen down to the very lowest dregs of human misery, is willing to spend millions of dollars to bring his workmen to the sense of their utter dependence upon him.

This is evidently his purpose. It is the purpose of many another corporation king. He and a few others may possibly win in the present contest, but the people of America when once aroused to a sense of the wrong inflicted upon them will not be slow in so shaping our laws and industrial conditions as will surprise their most supercilious critics.

We insist upon the right to organize, the right to think, to act, to protect ourselves, our homes and our liberties and work out our emancipation. We are confident we shall secure them, and that the world will stand surprised that they were accomplished through the means of an enlightened public opinion and by peaceful means. For

> "We love no triumphs sprung from force—
> They stain their brightest cause;
> 'Tis not in blood that liberty
> Inscribes her civic laws.
> She writes them on the people's heart,
> In language clear and plain:
> True thoughts have moved the world before
> And so they shall again."

# In re CHARGE TO GRAND JURY
## (District Court, N. D. Illinois. July 10, 1894.)

*P. J. Grosscup*

A grand jury, having been called to consider the offenses alleged to have been committed during the strike of the American Railway Union against the railroads hauling Pullman cars, was instructed by the court as follows:

GROSSCUP, District Judge. Gentlemen of the Grand Jury: You have been summoned here to inquire whether any of the laws of the United States within this judicial district have been violated. You have come in an atmosphere and amid occurrences that may well cause reasonable men to question whether the government and laws of the United States are yet supreme. Thanks to resolute manhood, and to that enlightened intelligence which perceives the necessity of a vindication of law before any other adjustments are possible, the government of the United States is still supreme.

You doubtless feel, as I do, that the opportunities of life, under present conditions, are not entirely equal, and that changes are needed to forestall some of the dangerous tendencies of current industrial tendencies. But neither the torch of the incendiary, nor the weapon of the insurrectionist, nor the inflamed tongue of him who incites to fire and sword is the instrument to bring about reforms. To the mind of the American people; to the calm, dispassionate sympathetic judgment of a race that is not afraid to face deep changes and responsibilities, there has, as yet, been no appeal. Men who appear as the champions of great changes must first submit them to discussion, discussion that reaches, not simply the parties interested, but the outer circles of society, and must be patient as well as persevering until the public intelligence has been reached, and a public judgment made up. An appeal to force before that hour is a crime, not only against government of existing laws, but against the cause itself; for what man of any intelligence supposes that any settlement will abide which is induced under the light of the torch or the shadow of an overpowering threat?

With the questions behind present occurrences, therefore, we have, as ministers of the law and citizens of the republic, nothing now to do. The law as it is must first be vindicated before we turn aside to inquire how law or practice, as it ought be, can be effectually brought about. Government by law is imperiled, and that issue is paramount.

The government of the United States has enacted laws designed, first, to protect itself and its authority as a government, and, secondly, its control over those agencies to which, under the constitution and laws, it extends governmental regulation. For the former purpose,—namely, to protect itself and its authority as a government,—it has enacted that every person who incites, sets on foot, assists, or engages in, any rebellion or insurrection against the authority of the United States or the laws thereof, or gives aid or comfort thereto, "and any two or more persons in any state or territory who conspire to overthrow, put down, or destroy by force the government

*U.S. vs. Debs.* Judge Grosscup's charge to the Grand Jury, *Federal Reporter*, LXII (1894), 828–833.

of the United States, or to levy war against them, or to oppose by force the authority thereof; or by force to prevent, hinder or delay the execution of any law of the United States contrary to the authority thereof," shall be visited with certain penalties therein named.

Insurrection is a rising against civil or political authority,—the open and active opposition of a number of persons to the execution of law in a city or state. Now, the laws of the United States forbid, under penalty, any person from obstructing or retarding the passage of the mail, and make it the duty of the officers to arrest such offenders, and bring them before the court. If, therefore, it shall appear to you that any person or persons have willfully obstructed or retarded the mails, and that their attempted arrest for such offense has been opposed by such a number of persons as would constitute a general uprising in that particular locality, and as threatens for the time being the civil and political authority, then the fact of an insurrection, within the meaning of the law, has been established; and he who by speech, writing, or other inducement assists in setting it on foot, or carrying it along, or gives it aid or comfort, is guilty of a violation of law. It is not necessary that there should be bloodshed; it is not necessary that its dimensions should be so portentous as to insure probable success, to constitute an insurrection. It is necessary, however, that the rising should be in opposition to the execution of the laws of the United States, and should be so formidable as for the time being to defy the authority of the United States. When men gather to resist the civil or political power of the United States, or to oppose the execution of its laws, and are in such force that the civil authorities are inadequate to put them down, and a considerable military force is needed to accomplish that result, they become insurgents; and every person who knowingly incites, aids, or abets them, no matter what his motives may be, is likewise an insurgent. The penalty for the offense is severe, and, as I have said, is designed to protect the government and its authority against direct attack. There are other provisions of law designed to protect those particular agencies which come within governmental control. To these I will now call your attention.

The mails are in the special keeping of the government and laws of the United States. To insure their unhindered transmission, it is made an offense to knowingly and willfully obstruct or retard the passage of the mail, or any carriage, horse, driver, or carrier carrying the same. It is also provided that "if two or more persons conspire together to commit any offense against the United States and one or more of such parties do any act to effect the object of the conspiracy," all the parties thereto shall be subject to a penalty. Any person knowingly and willfully doing any act which contributes, or is calculated to contribute, to obstructing or hindering the mails, or who knowingly and willfully takes a part in such acts, no matter how trivial, if intentional, is guilty of violating the first of these provisions; and any person who conspires with one or more persons, one of whom subsequently commits the offense, is likewise guilty of an offense against the United States. What constitutes conspiracy to hinder or obstruct the mails will be touched upon in connection with the subject to which I now call your attention.

The constitution places the regulation of commerce between the several states, and between the states and foreign nations, within the keeping of the United States government. Anything which is designed to be transported for commercial purposes from one state to another, and is actually in transit, and any passenger who is actually engaged in any such interstate commercial transaction, and any car or carriage actually transporting or engaged in transporting such passenger or thing, are the agencies and subject-matter of interstate commerce, and any conspiracy in restraint of such trade or commerce is an offense against the United States. To restrain is to prohibit, limit, confine, or abridge a thing. The restraint may be permanent or temporary. It may be intended to prohibit, limit, or abridge for all time, or for a day only. The law draws no distinction in this respect. Commerce of this character is intended to be free, except subject to regulation by law, at all times, and for all periods. Temporary restraint is therefore as intolerable as permanent, and practical restraint by actual physical interference, as criminal as that which flows from the arrangements of business and organization. Any physical interference, therefore, which has the effect of restraining any passenger, car, or thing constituting an element of interstate commerce, forms the foundation for this offense. But to complete this offense, as also that of conspiracy to obstruct the mails, there must exist, in addition to the overt act and purpose, the element of criminal conspiracy.

What is criminal conspiracy? If it shall appear to you that any two or more persons corruptly or wrongfully agreed with each other that the trains carrying the mails and interstate commerce should be forcibly arrested, obstructed, and restrained, such would clearly constitute a conspiracy. If it shall appear to you that two or more persons corruptly or wrongfully agreed with each other that the employés of the several railroads carrying the mails and interstate commerce should quit, and that successors should, by threats, intimidation, or violence, be prevented from taking their places, such would constitute a conspiracy.

I recognize, however, the right of labor to organize. Each man in America is a freeman, and, so long as he does not interfere with the rights of others, has the right to do with that which is his what he pleases. In the highest sense, a man's arm is his own, and, aside from contract relations, no one but he can direct when it shall be raised to work, or shall be dropped to rest. The individual option to work or to quit is the imperishable right of a freeman. But the raising and dropping of the arm is the result of a will that resides in the brain, and, much as we may desire that such wills should remain entirely independent, there is no mandate of law which prevents their association with others, and response to a higher will. The individual may feel himself, alone, unequal to cope with the conditions that confront him, or unable to comprehend the myriad of considerations that ought to control his conduct. He is entitled to the highest wage that the strategy of work or cessation from work may bring, and the limitations upon his intelligence and opportunities may be such that he does not choose to stand upon his own perception of strategic or other conditions. His right to choose a leader, one who observes, thinks, and wills for him,—a brain skilled to observe his interest,—is no greater pretension than that which is recognized in every other department of industry. So far, and within reasonable limits, associations of this character are not only not unlawful, but are, in my judgment, beneficial, when they do not restrain individual liberty, and are under enlightened and conscientious leadership.

But they are subject to the same laws as other associations. The leaders to whom are given the vast power of judging and acting for the members are simply, in that respect, their trustees. Their conduct must be judged, like that of other trustees, by the extent of their lawful authority, and the good faith with which they have executed it. No man, in his individual right, can lawfully demand and insist upon conduct by others which will lead to an injury to a third person's lawful rights. The railroads carrying the mails and interstate commerce have a right to the service of each of their employés until each lawfully chooses to quit; and any concerted action upon the part of others to demand or insist, under any effective penalty or threat, upon their quitting, to the injury of the mail service or the prompt transportation of interstate commerce, is a conspiracy, unless such demand or insistence is in pursuance of a lawful authority conferred upon them by the employés themselves, and is made in good faith in the execution of such authority. The demand and insistence under effective penalty or threat, and injury to the transportation of the mails or interstate commerce being proven, the burden falls upon those making the demand or insistence to show lawful authority and good faith in its execution.

Let me illustrate: Twelve carpenters are engaged in building a house. Aside from contract regulations, they each can quit at pleasure. A thirteenth and fourteenth man, strangers to them, by concerted threats of holding them up to public odium or private malice, induce them to quit, and leave the house unfinished. The latter in no sense represent the former or their wishes, but are simply interlopers for mischief, and are guilty of conspiracy against the employers of the carpenters. But if, upon a trial for such, it results that, instead of being strangers, they are the trustees, agents, or leaders of the twelve, with full power to determine for them whether their wage is such that they ought to continue or quit, and that they have in good faith determined that question, they are not then, so far as the law goes, conspirators. But if it should further appear that the supposed authority was used, not in the interests of the twelve, but to further a personal ambition or malice of the two, it would no longer justify their conduct. Doing a thing under cloak of authority is not doing it with authority. The injury of the two to the employer, in such an instance, would only be aggravated by their treachery to the associated twelve, and both the employer and employés should, with equal insistence, ask for the visitation of the law.

If it appears to you, therefore,—applying the illustration to the occurrences that will be brought to your attention,—that any two or more persons, by concert, insisted or demanded, under effective penalties and threats, upon men quitting the employment of the railways, to the obstruction of the mails or interstate commerce, you may inquire whether they did these acts as strangers to these men, or whether they did them under the pretension of trustees or leaders of an association to which these men belong. And, if the latter appears, you may inquire whether their acts and conduct in that respect were in faithful and conscientious execution of their supposed authority, or were simply a use of that authority as a guise to advance personal ambition or satisfy private malice. There is honest leadership among these, our laboring fellow citizens, and there is doubtless dishonest leadership. You should not brand any act of leadership as done dishonestly or in bad faith unless it clearly so appears. But if it does so appear,—if any person is shown to have betrayed the trust of these toiling men, and their acts fall within the definition of crime, as I have given it to you,—it is alike the interest, the pleasure, and the duty of every citizen to bring them to swift and heavy punishment.

I wish again, in conclusion, to impress upon you the fact that the present emergency is to vindicate law. If no one has violated the law, under the rules I have laid down, it needs no vindication; but, if there has been such violation, there should be quick, prompt, and adequate indictment. I confess that the problems which are made the occasion or pretext for our present disturbances have not received the consideration they deserve. It is our duty, as citizens, to take them up, and, by candid and courageous discussion, ascertain what wrongs exist, and what remedies can be applied. But neither the existence of such problems, nor the neglect of the public hitherto to adequately consider them, justify the violation of law, or the bringing on of general lawlessness. Let us first restore peace, and punish the offenders of the law, and then the atmosphere will be clear to think over the claims of those who have real grievances. First vindicate the law. Until that is done, no other questions are in order.

## ◄§ A LETTER FROM JUDGE GROSSCUP AND ITS ANSWER

*Samuel Gompers*

New York, August 14, 1894.
*Hon. P. J. Grosscup, Judge of the United States Court, Chicago, Ill.:*

DEAR SIR:—I have the honor to acknowledge the receipt of your favor of the 31st ult., the contents of which I have carefully noted. Possibly I should have written you earlier, but more important matters demanded my immediate consideration. I hope, however, that you have suffered no inconvenience or pain of injustice done you by reason of this delay. . . .

You say that as you stated in your charge to the Grand Jury, you believe in labor organizations within such lawful and reasonable limits as will make them a service to the laboring man, and not a menace to the lawful institutions of the country.

I have had the pleasure of reading your charge to the Grand Jury, and have only partially been able to discover how far you believe in labor organizations. You would certainly have no objection officially or personally to workingmen organizing, and in their meetings discuss perhaps "the origin of man," benignly smiling upon each other, and declaring that all existing things are right, going to their wretched homes to find some freedom in sleep from gnawing hunger. You would have them extol the virtues of monopolists and wreckers of the people's welfare. You would not have them consider seriously the fact that more than two millions of their fellows are unemployed, and though willing and able, cannot find the opportunity to work, in order that they may sustain themselves, their wives and their children. You would not have them consider seriously the fact that Pullman who has grown so rich from the toil of his workmen, that he can riot in luxury, while he heartlessly turns these very workmen out of their tenements into the streets and leaves them to the tender mercies of corporate greed. Nor would you have them ponder upon the hundreds of other Pullmans of different names.

"A Letter from Judge Grosscup and Its Answer," *American Federationist,* I (1894), 149–152.

You know, or ought to know, that the introduction of machinery is turning into idleness thousands, faster than new industries are founded, and yet, machinery certainly should not be either destroyed or hampered in its full development. The laborer is a man, he is made warm by the same sun and made cold—yes, colder—by the same winter as you are. He has a heart and brain, and feels and knows the human and paternal instinct for those depending upon him as keenly as do you.

What shall the workers do? Sit idly by and see the vast resources of nature and the human mind be utilized and monopolized for the benefit of the comparative few? No. The laborers must learn to think and act, and soon, too, that only by the power of organization, and common concert of action, can either their manhood be maintained, their rights to life (work to sustain it) be recognized, and liberty and rights secured.

Since you say that you favor labor organizations within certain limits, will you kindly give to thousands of your anxious fellow citizens what you believe the workers could and should do in their organizations to solve this great problem? Not what they should not do. You have told us that.

I am not one of those who regards the entire past as a failure. I recognize the progress made and the improved conditions of which nearly the entire civilized world are the beneficiaries. I ask you to explain, however, that if the wealth of the whole world is, as you say, "Pre-eminently and beneficially the nation's wealth," how is it that thousands of able-bodied, willing, earnest men and women are suffering the pangs of hunger? We may boast of our wealth and civilization, but to the hungry man and woman and child our progress is a hollow mockery, our civilization a sham, and our "national wealth" a chimera.

You recognize that the industrial forces set in motion by steam and electricity have materially changed the structure of our civilization. You also admit that a system has grown up where the accumulations of the individual have passed from his control into that of representative combinations and trusts, and that the tendency in this direction is on the increase. How, then, can you consistently criticize the workingmen for recognizing that as individuals they can have no influence in deciding what the wages, hours of toil and conditions of employment shall be?

You evidently have observed the growth of corporate wealth and influence. You recognize that wealth, in order to become more highly productive, is concentrated into fewer hands, and controlled by representatives and directors, and yet you sing the old siren song that the workingman should depend entirely upon his own "individual effort."

The school of *laissez faire*, of which you seem to be a pronounced advocate, has produced great men in advocating the theory of each for himself, and his Satanic Majesty taking the hindermost, but the most pronounced advocates of your school of thought in economics have, when practically put to the test, been compelled to admit that combination and organization of the toiling masses are essential both to prevent the deterioration and to secure an improvement in the condition of the wage earners.

If, as you say, the success of commercial society depends upon the full play of competition, why do not you and your confreres turn your attention and direct the shafts of your attacks against the trusts and corporations, business wreckers and manipulators in the food products—the necessities of the people. Why garland your thoughts in beautiful phrases when speaking of these modern vampires, and steep your pen in gall when writing of the laborers' efforts to secure some of the advantages accruing from the concentrated thought and genius of the ages?

You charge that before a boy can learn a trade he must receive a permit from the union and assume obligations which the union imposes. I am sure you have read the current history of industry but superficially, or you would certainly have discovered that with the introduction of modern methods of production, the apprenticeship system has almost been entirely eliminated. Professors, the learned men concerned in the welfare of our people, insist upon a maintenance of a technical knowledge of crafts and trades. They are endeavoring to substitute manual training schools in order that the youth of our country may be supplied with a knowledge of the trades and crafts of which modern methods of production have deprived them.

For the sake of your argument, let me admit that what you may say in connection with this matter is true. I ask you whether it is not true that before a boy can properly learn your trade, is it not necessary for him to enter a term of apprenticeship? Of course, you have a more euphonius name for it, student life, I believe. Would judges permit any one to practice law in their courts where justice is dispensed (with) unless he could produce his working card? Pardon, I mean his diploma.

One becomes enraptured in reading the beauty of your description of modern progress. Could you have had in mind the miners of Spring Valley or Pennsylvania, or the clothing workers of the sweat shops of New York or Chicago when you grandiloquently dilate, "Who is not rich to-day when compared with his ancestors of a century ago? The steamboat and the railroad bring to his breakfast table the coffees of Java and Brazil, the fruits from Florida and California, and the steaks from the plains. The loom arrays him in garments and the factories furnish him with a dwelling that the richest contemporaries of his grandfather would have envied. With health and industry he is a prince."

Probably you have not read within the past year of babes dying of starvation at their mothers' breasts. More than likely the thousands of men lying upon the bare stones night after night in the City Hall of Chicago last winter escaped your notice. You may not have heard of the cry for bread that was sounded through this land of plenty by thousands of honest men and women. But should these and many other painful incidents have passed you by unnoticed, I am fearful that you may learn of them with keener thoughts with the coming sleets and blasts of winter.

You say that "labor cannot afford to attack capital." Let me remind you that labor has no quarrel with capital, as such. It is merely the possessors of capital who refuse to accord to labor the recognition, the right, the justice which is the laborers' due, with whom we contend.

See what is implied by your contemptuous reference to the laborer when you ask, "Will the conqueror destroy his trophy?" Who ever heard of a conqueror marching unitedly with his *trophy*, as you would have them? But if by your comparison you mean that the conqueror is the corporation, the trust, the capitalist class, and ask then whether they would destroy their *trophy*, I would have you ask the widows and orphans of the thousands of men killed annually through the avarice of railroad corporations refusing to avail themselves of modern appliances in coupling and other improvements on their railroads.

Inquire from the thousands of women and children whose husbands or fathers were suffocated or crushed in the mines through the rapacious greed of stockholders clamoring for more dividends. Investigate the sweating dens of the large cities. Go to the mills, factories, through the country. Visit the modern tenement houses or hovels in which thousands of workers are compelled to eke out an existence. Ask these whether the conqueror (monopoly) cares whether his trophy (the laborers) is destroyed or preserved. Ascertain from employers whether the laborer is not regarded the same as a machine, thrown out as soon as all the work possible has been squeezed out of him.

Are you aware that all the legislation ever secured for the ventilation or safety of mines, factory or workshop is the result of the efforts of organized labor? Do you know that the trade unions were the shield for the seven-year-old children from being the conqueror's trophy until they become somewhat older? And that the reformatory laws now on the statute books, protecting or defending the trophies of both sexes, young and old, from the fond care of the conquerors, were wrested from Congresses, legislatures and parliaments despite the Pullmans, the Jeffries, the Ricks, the Tafts, the Williams, the Woods, or the Grosscups.

By what right, sir, do you assume that the labor organizations do not conduct their affairs within lawful limits, or that they are a menace to the lawful institutions of the country? Is it because some thoughtless or over-zealous member at a time of great excitement and smarting under a wrong may violate under a law or commit an improper act? Would you apply the same rule to the churches, the other moral agencies and organizations that you do to the organizations of labor? If you did, the greatest moral force of life to-day, the trade unions, would certainly stand out the clearest, brightest and purest. Because a certain class (for which you and a number of your colleagues on the bench seem to be the special pleaders) have a monopoly in their lines of trade, I submit that this is no good reason for their claim to have a monopoly on true patriotism or respect for the lawful institutions of the country.

But speaking of law reminds me of the higher law of the land. The constitution prescribes that all rights not specifically granted to the general government are reserved to the States. There is another provision prohibiting the President from sending armed forces into any State except for the purpose of maintaining "a republican form of government," and then only upon the requisition of the Legislature of the State or of the Governor, when the Legislature is not in session. Yet when, during the recent railroad strike, the President sent the troops into Illinois, it was not in compliance with the request of the Legislature of that State, nor of the Governor, but in spite of his protest. Yes, even when the Governor remonstrated he was practically told by the President to stop arguing the law upon the question. Pardon the simplicity of my inquiry, but does not the law require that its limits shall be observed by a president, a judge, equally as by a labor organization?

If I remember aright you based the injunctions recently issued by you upon the provisions of the Interstate Commerce Law, a law enacted by Congress upon the demand of the farmers and shippers of our country, to protect them against the unjust and outrageous discriminations imposed by the railroads. Where in the law can you find one word to justify your course applying to workingmen organized and engaged in a strike?

Read the discussions in Congress when that law was under consideration. You will not find a remote reference to the application of the laws as you construe it. In fact, I am informed upon excellent authority that when the law was before the Senate in the form of a bill Senator Morgan, of Alabama, proposed an amendment which if adopted would have had the effect of empowering judges to issue an order of the nature you have, in the recent railroad strike, but it was not adopted, it was defeated. How then in the face of this you can issue your omnibus restraining order passes the comprehension of ordinary men.

In his last report to Congress, the Postmaster-General recommended the passage of a law by Congress declaring that any train in which there should be but one pouch of mail matter should be considered a mail train, thus recognizing that there was no law by which other than regular "mail trains" come under the operation of the postal laws. Hence it is not a grave stretch of the imagination to regard this latest court-made law as an invention to break the strike.

I am not versed in the law, but somewhere I read that Blackstone says that a law which is not based on justice is not law, and presumably judges who distort law so that injustice is done are not the ablest or purest devotees of the "blind goddess." I do not quote this for the purpose of converting your mind to some degree of impartiality for labor, but merely to show what a sycophantic knave Blackstone was.

Year by year man's liberties are trampled under foot at the bidding of corporations and trusts, rights are invaded and law perverted. In all ages wherever a tyrant has shown himself he has always found some willing judge to clothe that tyranny in the robes of legality, and modern capitalism has proven no exception to the rule.

You may not know that the labor movement as represented by the trades unions, stands for right, for justice, for liberty. You may not imagine that the issuance of an injunction depriving men of a legal as well as a natural right to protect themselves, their wives and little ones, must fail of its purpose. Repression or oppression never yet succeeded in crushing the truth or redressing a wrong.

In conclusion let me assure you that labor will organize, and more compactly than ever and upon practical lines, and despite relentless antagonism, achieve for humanity a nobler manhood, a more beautiful womanhood and a happier childhood.

Very respectfully yours,

SAMUEL GOMPERS, President,
American Federation of Labor.

Although in many cases nineteenth-century European colonization in Africa and Asia was promoted by strategic considerations and rivalries among the great powers, the Congo Free State was unique from its beginning in being an almost purely economic enterprise. Unlike other colonies in the possession of one of the European states, the Congo became the personal preserve of Leopold II, King of the Belgians, constitutional monarch in Europe, absolute ruler in Africa.

The Congo Free State had come into existence through the promotion of Leopold II, who, in his private capacity, formed a company for the exploration and economic exploitation of the Congo basin. In 1884–1885, an international conference meeting in Berlin recognized Leopold's claims, though stipulating that the new state should be open to the commerce of all nations and should also benefit the native population, conditions which were soon to be violated. Aside from land retained by the natives, the Congo gradually came to be divided into three types of European control: the domaine privé (private domain) which in 1905 included about one-fourth of the area and which was exploited directly by the Congo Free State in order, so it was claimed, to raise funds for needed public improvements and the cost of administration; the domaine de la couronne (crown lands), lands owned and exploited by agents of Leopold for his private benefit; and lands leased to concessionary companies exploiting the natural resources of the area.

In 1889, Leopold II had guaranteed that the Congo Free State should ultimately revert to Belgium, which had had no control over her King's African possessions. Twelve years later, a move to annex the area failed in the Belgian parliament where it was defeated by supporters of the King. By that time, widespread abuses in the treatment of the natives had come to light, particularly through the reports of a British consul. This led to agitation, in England, America, and ultimately Belgium, against Leopold's personal rule. Under pressure from public opinion in Belgium, Leopold appointed a commission of inquiry that returned from Africa in 1905 with a report criticizing some of the harsher measures of oppression of the natives. The document which follows consists of selections from a five-day debate of the commission of inquiry's report before the Belgian Lower House of Parliament in February, 1906. The debate ended with the passage of a motion supporting Leopold's position, though in 1908 the Congo Free State *was annexed by Belgium after ample compensation had been provided for Leopold. In the years that followed, some of the most flagrant abuses for which the Congo had become notorious were gradually eliminated.*

## FIRST DAY'S DEBATE (FEBRUARY 20)

### M. Vandervelde's Opening Speech

**M. Vandervelde (Leader of the Belgian Labour Party)**    Gentlemen, the question which I have the honour of bringing before the House is not a party question. It is distinct also from the opinion which each of us may hold as to the advantages or the disadvantages of colonial enterprises in general. I should like, in making this interpellation, to be able to forget my republican convictions, as I should also like you to set aside your monarchical convictions. The whole subject resolves itself into this—whether the system adopted in the Congo does not involve nefarious consequences, as well for the natives, who are its victims, as for Belgium, its alleged gainer. . . .

It has been repeatedly said that the Congo is a Belgian enterprise, and, under these circumstances, it is perfectly natural that Belgium should be interested in what takes place there. If, on the other hand, those who contradict me still wish to refer to my republican convictions I will answer to-day that those who protest against the Administration of the Congo State belong to all parties. Some of them are Liberals, some are Royalists like Felicien Cattier, others are Catholics and loyalists, like those missionaries who have felt at length the imperious need of freeing their consciences. . . .

And if I am told that, in making these charges against the Congo Administration, I am associating myself with a campaign carried out in the interests of England, I reply there is no English campaign. There is a campaign carried on in all countries, by Englishmen like the venerable Fox Bourne, like E. D. Morel, like the Bishops of Durham, Liverpool, and Rochester, like statesmen who are now included in the new Liberal Cabinet; by Americans like Mark Twain and Professor Reinsch; by Italians like Deputy Santini; finally, by Frenchmen like Paul Violet, the learned Catholic jurist, Francis de Préssensé, Pierre Mille, or Anatole France, who said a few days ago only, with regard to the abuses which have taken place in the French portion of the Congo Basin:

"It is necessary for us Frenchmen to denounce first of all the crimes committed in our name; our honour is involved, without reckoning that, speaking of what concerns us, what is our affair, we have a little more hope of not speaking in vain."

U.S. Senate, *Verbatim Report of the Five Days' Congo Debate in the Belgian House of Representatives, February 20, 27, 28, March 1, 2, 1906* (Washington, D.C.: U.S. Government Printing Office, 1906), pp. 3–12, 14–15, 28, 41–43, 50–51, 54, 64–68, 70–75, 98–102, 105–106, 108–109, 112–113, 117–121, 123, 171–172.

I will not, therefore, trouble myself longer with the charge of furthering foreign ambitions. There remains, then, a last argument which has been invoked against us, viz., that what we affirm is either exaggerated or calumnious. . . .

Well, to-day, in order to repeat the language we used before, and in order to justify us at the same time from the reproach of having brought before this House exaggerations or calumnies, I have the right of invoking a final opinion, the opinion of the three men of conscience, heart and character, who formed part of the Commission of Inquiry which the British Government compelled the Congo State to send out. When this Commission was appointed, we certainly could not entertain much hope in regard to it. Its mandate had been limited in such a way that the accomplishment of its mission was impossible. It had to act "conformably with the instructions of the Secretary of State." Thereupon a renewed intervention of the British Government took place, with the result that the Commissioners' mandate was enlarged, and it is thanks to that circumstance that we possess to-day documents which my colleague, M. Neujean, was abundantly justified in asking should be distributed, and which every member of the House ought to read. . . .

I now come to the Report itself, and I notice that it may be said to be divided into two parts; one part contains praise for what has been done in the Congo in the last twenty-five years; the other is a formidable indictment of the abuses of which the natives have been the victims. To deal with the first part. In a large measure I agree with the praise given. I admire, as do the Commissioners of Inquiry, the immense effort of persevering energy which was necessary to construct the Lower Congo Railway, to create in this enormous territory a vast system of postal and telegraphic communication, to provide the young colony with a powerful economic machinery. But the real grandeur of the results obtained must make us all the more severe in considering the conditions under which the native population is placed. It has been said many times that the Congo State was formed, above all, with an object of civilisation and humanity. Reference has been made, and with truth, to what has been done to stop the sale of liquor, and, what is more essential, to suppress the slave trade. Nevertheless, we find that, after twenty years, after the cessation of internal wars amongst the tribes, after the Arabs have been driven from the territory, when security reigns throughout the Colony, the population is less numerous than it was before. An attempt has been made to explain this fact. It has been said that the depopulation has been due to epidemics, to smallpox, to sleeping sickness. And certainly, in some measure, this is true; but how can we explain the small resisting power of the natives against these epidemics? It is due to the system forced upon them, and to the inhuman treatment inflicted upon them. Similarly, in our industrial cities, thousands of workmen die from consumption; but why do they suffer more than do the moneyed classes? Because they are poorly fed and ill-treated (applause from the extreme left). . . .

To support the statement that the depopulation of the Congo is largely due to the system of extortion, of which the natives are the victims, I have the right to invoke the report of the Commission, which shows the frightful gulf which separates a system of rational colonisation, and a system of colonisation such as exists in the Congo. A system of rational colonisation, of ideal colonisation, which up to the present has only been realised in a very incomplete manner, would be to recognize native land tenure, and to recognize to the natives the right of exchanging the products of their free labour on fair terms.

Now, the Congo system is exactly the antithesis of the system of ideal colonisation which I have described, and I exaggerate in no way in saying that this Congo system is founded upon the confiscation of the land of the natives, upon forced labour, and a system of compulsion which brings about the most frightful abuses.

I say first, upon the confiscation of the land of the natives. This is not a new charge. It was replied to formerly by saying, "The Congo State has respected the property of the natives. It has left them the right of proprietorship over their fields and their huts. It has limited itself to taking that which it was entitled to—the vacant lands —the lands which were occupied by no one." Gentlemen, there is in this statement a flagrant error, not to use a stronger expression. What the natives have been robbed of are not the lands which they have not occupied, but communal property which belonged to their village communities, and which was indispensable to the development of the latter, What has been done towards the Congo native is precisely what might be done to-morrow if, in *La Campine* or in the Ardennes, the ownership of the inhabitants in their houses and in their fields which they cultivate was left to them, but if their communal rights, their heaths and the woods over which they preserve their rights of usage, were confiscated.

In the Congo the individual ownership of the natives has been respected, but communal ownership has been suppressed, and this, moreover, is admitted by the Commission of Inquiry.

"As the greater portion of the land in the Congo is not cultivated, this interpretation of the words 'vacant lands' concedes to the State an absolute and exclusive ownership over virtually the whole of the land, with this consequence, that it can itself dispose solely of all the products of the land, prosecute as a poacher anyone who takes from that land the least of its fruits, or as a receiver of stolen goods anyone who receives such fruit, forbid anyone to establish himself on the greater part of the territory. The activity of the natives is thus limited to very restricted areas, and their economic condition is immobilised. Thus applied, such legislation would prevent any development of native life. In this manner, not only has the native been often forbidden to shift his village, but he has often been forbidden to visit even temporarily a neighbouring village without special permit."

Well, gentlemen, by what name can we call this system? We were taught at school that, under the old régime, men were not free, that serfs were attached to glebe land. If this Congo system, which forbids natives from leaving their village and going to a neighbouring village, even for a few days, is not serfdom, what is it? (Interruption.)

*M. Anseele*   It is the system which we apply to the cattle on our frontiers! . . .

*M. Vandervelde*   To sum up, therefore, the Congo natives have been despoiled of their land, and the Commission admits that in many places it is impossible for them to trade, because all the fruits of the land belong to the State.

But this is not all. After having taken their land, forced labour has been imposed upon them. I know that this system of forced labour is disguised under the words "taxation in kind," and we heard lately the Minister of Foreign Affairs and the Chancellor of the Exchequer declare:—

"Does not taxation, and even the *corvée*, exist in Belgium?"
"Moreover, the taxation in kind established by the Congo State only involves a light imposition. The natives are only asked to provide forty hours labour per month."

Now, when the Minister for Foreign Affairs spoke in this manner, in July, 1903, the laws of the Congo had not, in point of fact, specified any time for the duration of the forced labour imposed upon the natives. The law of forty hours was then only projected, and it was quite arbitrarily that the population was taxed. In certain districts worked by the *Domaine Privé*, the natives were compelled to bring in from four to eight pounds of rubber per month; in the A.B.I.R. district, twelve pounds of rubber per month; in the Mongalla district eighteen pounds of rubber per month.

It was a decision of the Boma Appeal Court which compelled the State to establish a more regular system, which is the law—or, to be more accurate, for we are dealing with an absolutism, the *ukase*—of 18th November, 1903. By virtue of this decree, the native can be subjected to forced labour, which must not exceed forty hours per month, but the Commission of Inquiry, which approves of this, which finds that this imposition is not too heavy, which considers that this forced labour is legitimate, declares at the same time that, throughout the country, the law of forty hours has been outrageously violated.

When the Report of the Commission of Inquiry has been distributed to you, I would ask you to give special attention, if you have not already done so, to what the Commissioners have to say upon the different forms of forced labour imposed upon the natives. There are four kinds, the tax in ground nuts, the tax in porterage, the tax in foodstuffs, and, finally and specially, the tax in rubber.

As regards the porterage tax, it is not necessary for me to recall to you the fearful and murderous consequences which it had at the time when the Cataract Railway was being constructed, and before this railway was completed. Thousands of human lives were sacrificed on the road between Matadi and Stanley Pool; but, whatever may be the regrets with which we are inspired by this decimation of the native population, we must at any rate recognise that it has had the result of making the Congo exploitable, and in freeing the natives to-day of porterage (*corvée*) in that particular region. But, if it has disappeared in that region, it has been maintained in others. A porterage service is organised on the one hand towards Lakes Kivu and Tanganyika, and on the other hand towards the Lado Enclave, where, during the last few years, an enormous amount of war material has been accumulated. Now, the Commission admits, from the reports of a large number of missionaries, that this system of porterage "leads to the partial destruction of the population which is called upon to submit to it."

Then comes the forced tax in food-stuffs. The natives are compelled to furnish various articles for the victualling of the stations, and notably native bread (kwanga). The Commission finds that these impositions are in themselves relatively light; to plant manioca, prepare it, cook it, and carry it are agricultural or household duties to which the women of the country have long been accustomed. But the Commission adds that, in certain regions, where there are military stations, such, for instance, as Coquilhatville and Leopoldville, this system of forced labour in food-stuffs involves the most disastrous consequences to the people. You will at once understand why I take Leopoldville as an example. There are some 3,000 soldiers of the Force Publique there, who must be fed by the natives in the neighbourhood. Now, to procure manioc bread in sufficient quantities to feed the Leopoldville soldiers, villages are called upon to produce it, some of which are situated forty-five miles away! The result is, that the natives who are called upon to furnish the State with material which represents the value of one franc and a half, are compelled every twelve days to travel ninety miles to fulfil their obligations! Assume that to-morrow the people of Huy, Waremme, Dinant, Bruges and Antwerp were compelled every twelve days to bring 1.50 francs to the Chancellor of the Exchequer, and you will understand in what condition these unhappy natives live, who have no railways to carry them to the place where the tax has to be paid, and back again. But the forced tax in food-stuffs and porterage, and the tax in ground nuts, are, when all is said and done, only accessories to this vast "financial machine," which is called the Congo State. That which is essential, that which gives to the State its revenues, to the Concessionaires of the A.B.I.R. and the Mongalla, and to the *Domaine de la Couronne*, profits which continue on an increasing scale—is the rubber tax. Here I will not limit myself to a *résumé*, and, since you have not all received a copy of the Report of the Commission, I shall take the liberty of reading to you what it has to say on the suffering involved for the natives in the course of the frantic exploitation of the rubber forests:—

> "In the majority of cases, the native must go one or two days' march every fortnight, until he arrives at that part of the forest where the rubber vines can be met with in a certain degree of abundance. There the collector passes a number of days in a miserable existence. He has to build himself an improvised shelter, which cannot, obviously, replace his hut. He has not the food to which he is accustomed. He is deprived of his wife, exposed to the inclemencies of the weather and the attacks of wild beasts. When once he has collected the rubber, he must bring it to the State station, or to that of the Company, and only then can he return to his village, where he can sojourn for barely more than two or three days, because the next demand is upon him. The result of this, therefore, is that, whatever may be his activity in the rubber forests, the native, on account of the numerous displacement which he is compelled to undergo, sees the majority of his time absorbed in the collection of indiarubber. It is hardly necessary to add that this state of affairs is a flagrant violation of the forty hours law."

Well, I ask those who used to reply to me that taxation in kind on the Congo was a light imposition, what they have to say in answer to this official admission of the Commission of Inquiry. Remember that these unfortunate natives are compelled every fortnight to spend eight or twelve days in the forest, exposed to the attacks of wild beasts, compelled often to work in swampy ground, waist deep in water, subjected to the supervision of soldiers of the Force Publique, many of whom are heartless wretches, who, in the words of the Commission, "kill without pity all those who resist," and you will understand how absurd it was to profess that this system is analogous to the obligations of the *Communes* in Belgium to keep the roads clear, and to the taxation which our own citizens are called upon to bear. Here again, gentlemen, I refer you to the Report of the Commission. You will see what are the means employed to exercise this coercion; the *chicotte*, the hippopotamus whip, which leaves bloody weals on the bodies of those upon whom it is used; servile labours imposed upon the chiefs; the seizing of hostages, which was recommended in 1897, in an official circular by Baron Wahis, the present Governor of the Congo State, and finally, what is more terrible than all, the black soldiers of the Force Publique, whose intervention is indispensable to the working of the system. Here is what the Commission has to say on the subject of these black soldiers:—

> "According to the witnesses, these auxiliaries, especially those who are stationed in the villages, abuse the authority placed in them, making themselves into despots, claiming the women, and food, not only for themselves, but for the band of parasites and scallywags which the love of rapine associates with them, and with whom they surround themselves as by a veritable bodyguard; they kill, without pity, all those who attempt to resist their exigencies and whims."

. . . Gentlemen, I ask you all, because, as I said when I began my speech, this is not a party question, but a question of humanity, is there in this House, is there in Belgium, a single man who dares to defend the system of hostages, sentries, punitive expeditions, and who can say that it is right, that it is just, that it is necessary, when one burns a village, when one massacres its inhabitants, to kill the innocent as well as the guilty, leaving God to recognise his own? (Applause on the extreme left.) . . .

I have, therefore, the right to say that these abominations have been committed in the Congo, have been tolerated and encouraged by the Congo State, and I add that that State is responsible for these crimes, because it has profited by them. The beneficiaries of this system, whose only equivalent is to be found in the history of the old Spanish Colonies, is, in the first place, the State itself; in the second place, the Concessionnaire Companies of the State, in which the State holds half the shares; and, finally, the *Domaine de la Couronne*.

First of all the State itself, and awhile ago, when I recognised the great things accomplished in the Congo in the last twenty years, I could not bring myself to forget that the revenue necessary to accomplish them has been obtained from the exploitation of the *Domaine Privé*, which has caused so much suffering, and engendered so much misery. But, apart from the profits realised by the Colony to satisfy the needs of the Colony, there are other profits, which have been acquired by individuals; others, again, which have been employed for objects which have nothing whatever in common with the development of the Congo. As regards, first of all, the profits of individuals, it is well, gentlemen, that it should be known what are the profits drawn by certain parties from the régime which I have just described.

I will take two Concessionnaire Societies, the most typical, those which have the most sinister reputation: the Société Anversoise du Commerce au Congo, and the A.B.I.R. In the one, as in the other, the Congo State holds half the shares. The first-named Company, from 1898 to 1903, has paid an average annual dividend of

425 francs to its shareholders on every 500-franc share. That is the Society presided over by our ex-colleague, M. De Browne de Tiège, whom I regret not to see any longer in his seat. (Laughter on the extreme left.)

*M. A. Daens*   Most unfortunate!

*M. Vandervelde*   I might have asked him, had he been here, if he were still prepared to maintain, as he did two years ago, that the charges brought against him were calumnious. Since then, indeed, the State has, under the pressure of public opinion, suspended for fifteen years the exercise of the concession of this Company.

Let us now deal with the A.B.I.R. We find that this Company was created in 1892, with a capital of 1,000,000 francs, of which only 232,000 francs were paid up. What has become of these shares, of so small a value? In 1898 each share brought in 1,100 francs in dividends, and was worth 14,600 francs. In 1899 each share brought in 1,225 francs in dividends, and was worth 17,950 francs. In 1900 each share brought in 2,100 francs and was worth 25,250 francs. In 1901 each share brought in 900 francs, and was worth 14,550 francs. In 1902 each share brought in 850 francs, and was worth 13,400 francs. In 1903 each share brought in 1,200 francs, and was worth 15,800 francs.

If you now wish to know what are the proceedings employed in order to secure such profits, you have only to turn to the Report of the Commission of Inquiry:—

> "It was hardly denied that in the various Posts of the A.B.I.R. which were visited, the imprisonment of women hostages, the subjugation of the chiefs to servile labour, the humiliations forced upon them, the *chicotte* given to defaulters, and the brutalities of the soldiers employed in getting the prisoners, was the rule habitually followed."

*M. Caeluwaert*   It is scandalous!

*M. Vandervelde*   Add to this, punitive expeditions, burning of villages, the massacre of natives, hands cut off by the sentinels, either from dead bodies, or from people yet alive, and you know the sources of the riches of the shareholders and administrators of the A.B.I.R.!

*M. A. Daens*   It is revolting!

*M. Vandervelde*   No doubt these gentlemen would be personally incapable of inflicting such tortures, but they knew what was taking place; they were not ignorant of the proceedings adopted to fill their coffers, and they find that the money they have thus obtained has no scent, not even the scent of blood. (Applause on the extreme left.)

. . . When we spoke in the past you might not have believed us; you might have suspected our intentions. You had the right to ignore what was not revealed in official documents; but to-day you know, you ought to know, you can no longer ignore, you can no longer remain deaf to the complaints and the protests which arise from all sides—and I address myself to you, members of the Clerical Party. I ask you to forget the links which bind you to the Government, and to cling, above all, to that which your conscience dictates to you. In presence of facts denounced by all ministers of Christianity, Protestant and Catholic, you have no right to remain impassive, and to wash your hands of the blood which has been shed, because if you were to do so, if you were to refuse justice to the natives, if you were to withhold from them the bread of life which they ask, the words of one of the Fathers of your Church might be applied to you:

> "Thy brother asked for help and protection; thou remainest deaf to his appeal; thou hast not gone to his assistance, therefore thou hast killed him."

(Loud applause on the Socialist benches. The orator is congratulated by his political friends.)

## SECOND DAY'S DEBATE (FEBRUARY 27)

### *Speech by M. Verhaegen*

**M. Verhaegen** Gentlemen, M. Vandervelde, in interpellating the Minister for Foreign Affairs "on the duties incumbent on Belgium as signatory Power to the Act of Berlin, 1885," based himself, on the one hand, on Article 6 of Chapter 1 of the saïd Act of Berlin; and, on the other, on the Report of the Congo Commission of Inquiry. I shall indicate presently the extent to which I think myself justified in associating myself with the protests which the honourable member has brought against the acts and the abuses pointed out by the Commission of Inquiry, respecting the Administration of the Congo State, acts and proceedings which have undoubtedly shaken public opinion in Belgium to its depths. Before dealing with this part of my speech, I desire, however, placing myself also from the point of view of Article 6 of the Act of Berlin, to examine the duties which are incumbent upon Belgium towards the Belgian missionaries who go to the Congo. Article 6 of the Act of Berlin is precise:—

> "All the Powers shall protect and favour, without distinction of nationality or creed, all religious, scientific, or charitable Institutions and enterprises, Christian missionaries, scientists, explorers, their escorts, their goods, their belongings, shall be the object of special protection."

I do not overlook the fact that the Act of Berlin does not authorize the signatory Powers to intervene in the affairs of the Congo State. This rule must give way when the essential interests of their subjects are affected. The Foreign Minister recognised, by quoting the principles of international law, and by invoking in this connection the authority of the Duke of Wellington at the Congress of Verona. "The Government of His Majesty," said the noble Duke, "is of the opinion that to censure the internal affairs of an independent State, unless the essential interests of the subjects of His Majesty are affected, is incompatible with the principles according to which the British Government has invariably acted on all questions relating to the internal affairs of other countries."

Now, such is precisely the case which faces us in relation to the Belgian missionaries on the Congo. Amongst the essential interests of those citizens, professional honour, which is their sole property on this earth, figures in the front rank. I shall attempt to convince the House that Belgium cannot remain indifferent to the essential interests of her citizens. Catholic missionaries, nearly all Belgians, hastened to comply with the appeal of the Congo State, which answered at the same time to the suggestions of their own hearts, and proceeded to Central Africa. They settled in the spots assigned to them without any thought of the dangers of the climate. Young and old rivalled one another in ardour, hard for themselves, tender for the unhappy natives, a splendid band, before whom I bow with respect, recruited from all social classes, and amongst whom I note the son of our sympathetic colleague, M. Van Naeman; the missionaries have laboured incessantly on the Congo; much money has been spent by them, through the charity of Belgian Catholics. They have sacrificed their health; many have died, or have only returned to die.

What did they go out there for? To collect ivory, rubber, or gold? Better than that. To receive substantial salaries? To receive honours, or a name on the scroll of history? Better still. They have received, and they receive every day, the blessings of the natives. They bring the word and the love of God to the land of Africa. They are expanding Christian civilisation in the Congo—that is to say, the civilisation which has made Europe. Thanks to the missionaries, thanks to the King, who opened the road for them, and who appealed to them, deserving, therefore, the gratitude of all civilised humanity, millions of negroes, plunged in an abyss of degradation, have seen the light which the Saviour brought into the world. They have heard, and they have had practised towards them, the law which dominates, and which at the same time summarises, all divine teaching, "Love one another." Thanks to the missionaries, native customs in the regions which they evangelise have become purer. The secular humiliation in which woman is placed has been altered for a higher ideal, family life has taken hold in the Congo. Monogamy has become respected. The native begins to understand that from the law of work a higher social standard emanates. Christianity will put an end to the material and moral degradation of populations plunged for many centuries in the backwash of barbarism. I do not wish to uselessly prolong my speech, but the House will allow me to point out a single example of the zeal and success attained by the Belgian missionaries. The small town of Baudouinville, founded near Lake Tanganyika by the White Fathers, numbers to-day 300 families, formed of young negroes and negresses, whom the White Fathers and the nuns have brought up and inured to labour. Monogamy is the absolute rule, and produces its beneficent results. Whilst, under a polygamous régime, black women have usually only one child, the three hundred young couples have alone increased the population of Baudouinville to 1,700 souls, and it seems that the process continues (laughter on the extreme left).

To these 1,700 souls have been added 300 other natives from regions not worked by the missionaries; the 2,000 inhabitants of Baudouinville cultivate, without any coercion, a thousand *hectares* of land, and enjoy a material prosperity, which is increasing, and which will develop if the State grants them other land. Gentlemen, is not this a magnificent result? And should we not desire that many cities like Baudouinville should exist on the Congo? Will it not be due to such enterprises that civilisation will penetrate rapidly, in a durable fashion, in the land of the black man? A few figures will permit the House to realise the work accomplished by the Belgian missionaries.

Catholic missions in the Congo include at this moment 119 Priests, 51 Fathers, 88 Nuns, or a total of 258 Missionaries, divided among the White Fathers, the

Premontrès, the Trappists, the Missionaries of Scheut, the Jesuits, the Redemptorists, the Fathers *du Coeur de Jesus*, apart from the congregations of women. These missionaries control 23,000 Christians whom they have baptised; they instruct 54,000 Catechumens, and give instruction to more than 9,000 children. They have 48 principal schools, 460 secondary schools, farms, chapels, agricultural colonies, apart from their hospitals and their schools. They receive from Belgian Catholics proof of the interest which the latter have in the Congo Missions, and spend each year more than £24,000; 120 missionaries have died on the field.

What figures cannot show, is the admiration which is inspired in the native by the apostolic life of these religious men, the veneration and the confidence with which the latter are surrounded, the prodigious influence exercised upon the natives by the absolute unselfishness of which the missionaries give an example. Such, gentlemen, is the secret of their power. They are expanding the field of civilisation, without coercion, solely by their moral ascendancy, and one can say that they alone really civilise the native, because too often certain servants of the State, and certain agents of the Companies propagate around them nothing but terror and hatred. . . .

It is to-day made clear that if the civilisation of the Congo natives does not progress; if in many places it seems compromised for a long time; if the Protestant missionaries easily find causes for complaints, which permit them to decry the Government of the Congo State, and enable them to boast of the superior humanity and generosity of England; if, in certain regions, the population is going down, instead of increasing; if morality around the official stations is worse than before the arrival of the white man; the present administration of the Congo State has serious things to answer for. I shall be told, perhaps, that I exaggerate. I should look upon exaggeration as a crime. Profound admirer of the civilising thought which inspired the King, admiring his energy and his perseverance, I would say more, admiring his genius—I gave public testimony to my sympathies in the Congo work by signing, a few years ago, the Bill proposed by the Hon. M. Beernaert, relating to the immediate annexation of the Congo by Belgium. But I am compelled, as all honest men must be compelled, to bow before the evidence of facts:—

> "The Congo State," thus it is the Report expresses itself in conclusion, "owes it to itself to introduce as soon as possible the reforms which we have suggested. . . . Notably the interpretation of a large and liberal application of the land laws, the effective application of the law limiting the labour tax to forty hours per month, the suppression of the sentry system, the suppression of the permits for the *capitas* to carry arms, the withdrawal of the right of coercion conferred upon the commercial companies, supervision over military expeditions, and the freedom of the Judiciary from administrative tutelage."

It is not I, gentlemen, who have traced this programme, which constitutes the counterpart of a formidable act of accusation. It is sufficient, moreover, to remember the extracts of the Report read to the House last week by M. Vandervelde, in order to be convinced that the Sovereign of the Congo State is, perhaps, not served at this moment as he ought to be. It is not the laws which he has passed which are subject to criticism (they form a remarkable legislative whole) ; it is their application which has become bad, tyrannical, anti-Christian. . . .

Gentlemen, when one has gone to the root of things, one acquires the conviction that the Congo State is not served at this moment by a sufficiency of competent men, men with high and humanitarian views, with civilising tendencies, such as were the servants of the State when the King founded it. I am well aware that neither Belgium nor the other signatory Powers of the Act of Berlin has the right to interfere in the internal administration of the Congo State, and I do not dream of inviting the Government to do so, but I am entitled to note what the Minister for Foreign Affairs said himself (and in the same terms as he used), that "the Congo, watered with our blood, must remain a Belgian work." But I might be allowed to add, "must remain a work worthy of Belgians." I am also entitled, basing myself upon the close solidarity which exists, in practice, between Belgium and the Congo, to express publicly the wish that a more generous, a higher and more Christian, a more worthy inspiration of Belgium and its King, and, to sum up, a more humane inspiration, should henceforth be applied to the Congo administration. It has been sought to reply to the reproaches addressed to the Congo State, by pointing out that other Powers, and, in particular, France and England, treat the natives of their Colonies even worse. This, gentlemen, is a detestable argument. Even if this were so, the Congo State owes it to itself, if it wishes to maintain the sympathies of Belgians, and that is a very important matter for it, not to imitate the bad examples of others, and to act paternally towards beings who, if they are black and barbarians, are none the less men like us, and our brethren. I fear much (I see it with sorrow) that Belgian public opinion, which has become so favourable to the great work of the King, will end by turning away from it, if the Congo State does not make up its mind to treat the natives as they are treated with so much success by the missionaries, and if it does not seek to raise them morally as well as materially. Finally, this is what I ask, and this is the measure in which I associate myself with the proposals of M. Vandervelde.

. . . I do not share the suspicions of M. Vandervelde towards the Commission for Reforms. I am convinced that these resolutions will be characterized by generosity, by a real Belgian spirit, and by a strong reforming zeal. I hope that the Congo state will profit by the salutary humiliation which has been inflicted upon its administration by the Commission of Inquiry, and will deem its own honour involved in putting a stop to all the abuses which have been pointed out. If, officially, we are not called upon to trouble ourselves about, nor to answer for the treatment inflicted upon the natives of the Congo, our honour, and the good name of Belgium, is interested in a country governed by our King, and administered to a great extent by Belgians, and that it must be worthy of the esteem and the confidence of civilised humanity (applause on various benches).

## Speech by M. Woeste

**M. Woeste** Gentlemen, the debate which is before the House was opened by a prejudiced speech. (Protests on the extreme left.) No doubt, here and there within it were to be noted a few platonic compliments towards the Congo enterprise, but criticism was not the less long, constant, or bitter on that account. Everything was blamed, everything was condemned; the past, the present, were not pardoned by M. Vandervelde; and as for the future, he stigmatised it in advance by saying that the Congo State was incapable of reforming itself. So implacable an indictment does not respond, in my opinion, to the average opinion of the public, and it will not be favourably received by the country. I do not deny that a sort of gale is at present blowing upon the Congo State. This gale has come from England, and has crossed the channel. England had accustomed us to expect more sympathy and good feeling. I would point out, however, that there are many English statesmen who render homage to the grandeur, to the importance, to the brilliancy of the Congo enterprise.

. . . But, however this may be, the attacks of which I speak have crossed the channel; they have found in Belgium a feeding ground in that school of disparagement whose adepts are numerous in our country, and whose mission it is to criticise everything which emanates from Belgium. Let one place before many Belgians an enterprise, an institution, an establishment created by their compatriots, and they will not seek to find in it any advantage; they will merely look for defects in detail. Is there a shadow in a picture—they will only see that shadow; they will make the entire picture of that shadow. As far as I am concerned, gentlemen, I do not associate myself with this injustice. I was one of the first to help, with my vote and with my voice, the Congo enterprise; and I remain attached to that enterprise, whose grandeur I cannot, without injustice, fail to recognise. The Commission of Inquiry itself admitted that it had felt, in travelling in the Congo, a sense of wonderment. Is it not true that, twenty-five years ago, the Congo was delivered over to murders, to pillage, to cannibalism, to the slave trade, to hateful superstitions? Is it not true that it was a closed continent, and that to-day it is open, thanks to the initiative of the King of the Belgians? Is it not true that the Congo State, constituted in the heart of Africa, boasts of a regular system of administration? Is it not true, too, that all moral civilisation and religious interests are therein protected? Is it not true that numerous ways of communication have been opened, allowing relations between the natives, and relations between the natives and foreigners? Is it not true that commercial relations have been established between the Congo State and the greater part of the European States, and Belgium, and that our compatriots feel the salutary effects of this? Could Belgium, under these conditions, decline to consider the Congo as becoming one day her colony? I have just heard, in the Resolution presented by the Left, that opinion is reserved in this respect. No doubt the Belgian Chamber is not called upon at this moment to give a vote on the subject, but, to allow it to be thought that Belgium might one day renounce the Congo, would be an ingratitude towards the Sovereign which created it! It would be for Belgium a real moral decadence, because she would be renouncing to contribute to the work of civilisation in Africa. It would also be an immense deception for our compatriots who have considered, and who still consider, the Congo a field of activity open to their efforts and their labours. So, gentlemen, the accusers of the Congo do not place themselves precisely upon that ground; what they say is, that out in the Congo there is a system to be indicted, that there are numerous abuses, that these abuses must be stigmatised, that they must disappear. Gentlemen, those who speak thus seem to me to commit, in certain respects, a double error. But assuredly, I am not amongst those who desire that abuses which have been pointed out should not disappear, but how great is the error of those who think that in a day, or even in a few years, a barbarous country can be transformed into a civilised one. Civilisation has had a struggle there. It has had a struggle elsewhere, against inveterate habits, against profoundly low customs, against influences of education and environment, and it is only by long continuity of effort that the natives can be raised from this degraded state. Remember, gentlemen, the origin of all European States. Remember the origin of the French monarchy. What illimitable disorders, what crimes were committed for several centuries, which only disappeared under the persistent influence of Christianity. History teaches us that it is only in the long run that public conscience can be improved, and customs humanised.

. . . Alongside this primary error there is a secondary one, and that is the idea that a barbarous country can be governed on the lines of a civilised country. No doubt we must approximate to these lines as much as possible, but account must be taken of the mental condition of those whose civilisation is aimed at. Proceedings which might have full success in our country, would be doomed there to complete sterility. Where you have an advanced state of civilisation, force must be set aside as much as possible. In barbarous countries, among infant peoples, coercion is often necessary; authority must be felt, in order to be respected. It is due to the influence of the two errors which I am pointing out that so many inaccurate judgments have been pronounced, and are still pronounced, on the Congo State. The Congo State is looked upon, and I understand the desire up to a certain point, as another Belgium. I hope, gentlemen, it may be so one day; but, before this day comes, we must admit the necessity in which the governing element finds itself of often employing means other than those which are current in our civilised Europe. The Belgian Government is asked what it means to do to prevent the state of affairs which has been pointed out, as if the Belgian Government were the government of the Congo State! When one goes to the root of matters, it will be recognised that the personality aimed at here is the Sovereign of the Congo State himself.

**M. A. Daens** That is obvious.

**M. Woeste** It is obvious, I am told! I thank the interrupter for this admission.

. . . Who amongst us would have had sufficient initiative and organising capacity to create the Congo State? Who amongst us would have had sufficient initiative and organising capacity to drag Europe, in a certain measure, behind him? Who amongst us would have had sufficient initiative and organising capacity to create in twenty-five years this State, in giving to it an administration, judicial machinery, a regular police, and having already succeeded, in a large measure in humanising the savage customs which prevailed therein? If such be the case, how can it be suggested that he who created and organised the Congo, should be incapable of assisting in its development? While associating myself with all my heart with the desire put forward by M. Beernaert, by virtue of which the House is asked to examine the proposed Bill on the government of Colonial possessions, I must point out that a country like the Congo cannot be governed like a country with a Parliamentary system. A representative system is fitted for advanced civilisations, but not for civilisations in a primitive state. Emile Augier placed in the mouth of Richelieu these words: "Despotism alone brings order out of chaos." I do not maintain that despotism should use any kind of means to do so, but I maintain that it is from personal power that energetic initiative, rapidly executed, can be expected, which obtains in a few years magnificent results such as those obtained in the Congo.

*M. Lorand*    Despotisms like those of Russia, Turkey and the Congo.

*M. Woeste*    Gentlemen, I hold in my hand a remarkable code of laws and regulations, which have been promulgated for the Congo for the last twenty-five years. If the Congo had been under a Parliamentary régime, if the Belgian House had been expected to deliberate with regard to it, I state as a fact that not a twentieth part of these laws would have been drafted; not a twentieth part of these regulations would have issued:

*M. Vandervelde*    Such as the forty hours law, for instance!

*M. Woeste*    This is what must be recognised. This is what common sense and history teach us; but we are told there are many abuses there. M. Vandervelde told us: "I pointed out these abuses in the past; I was not believed; now facts confirm my statements." The honourable member is mistaken. It was never denied that abuses existed in the Congo, but to this admission was added that it was almost impossible that there should not be any. These abuses arise from the immensity of the territory, from the small number of Belgians who administrate it, from ingrained habits which object to the innovations introduced by the Belgians. And also—why should I not say so?—from the fact that, especially at first, the officials have not always been picked. When the King initiated the Congo enterprise, there were a number of people who considered his action as utopian. Belgians whose position at home is a stable and sure one were little tempted to emigrate into unknown regions, and to risk their lives and their future therein. It was necessary to accept the services of all willing men who came forward. But it is not the less true that as the enterprise grew, and as it will grow, the personnel will steadily improve, and that this personnel will consider its honour is involved in causing the abuses which have been pointed out to disappear. The only reproach which might be brought against the Congo State, if it be founded, would be that, when abuses have been pointed out to it, it has not wished to suppress them. Now, gentlemen, if we consult the laws of the Congo, and the regulations which have been issued, and to which I alluded a moment ago, it will be seen that the constant effort of those who direct the Congo State has been to place the Congo under a regular and normal régime, and when, latterly, *lacunoe* have been shown in its legislation, when necessary reforms were pointed to, and abuses requiring suppression, the Congo State itself constituted a Commission of Inquiry, and when the latter made its report, it was again the Congo State, which, without delay, appointed another Commission to prepare the necessary legislation required to bring about reforms. . . .

But still, we are told, there are abuses. There are reprehensible things taking place in the Congo. Assuredly, and I admitted so much a moment ago, but what exaggeration there is also. Thus, M. Vandervelde did not hesitate to say that the slave trade was still rife in the Congo. But what is the slave trade? It consists in the fact that men, being owners of other men, sell the latter. Now, to justify the charge which the honourable member directed against the Congo State, what does he advance? He quoted the fact that recruiting was carried out in the Congo on the basis of bonuses granted to the recruiters. Is that, gentlemen, the slave trade? I appeal to your common sense, and to your consciences. No one will reply in the affirmative. These recruiting operations constitute a legitimate act in themselves, and the labour which the recruiters undertake deserves recompense. Certainly, the sojourn of Arabs in the Congo has left some traces. Mohammedans from Zanzibar, and Arabised natives, have formed here and there small communities where disguised slavery and gross immorality is practised. We know that. The Congo State has sought, to the extent which was humanely possible, to remedy this state of affairs. The past is for us a guarantee of the future. What it has already done it will continue to do, but the injustice consists in saying that, in a country eighty times as large as Belgium, and in twenty-five years, all ills can be extirpated, as it were, instantaneously. Abuses have been spoken of. I return to the criticisms directed against the Congo State. The land régime is complained of. In this connection, what is the paramount factor? It is shown by the Commission of Inquiry itself in the following terms: "The greater portion of the land in the Congo is not cultivated." Not being cultivated, and the natives not being able to produce titles to these lands (Outcry on the Socialist benches.), they belong to the State in strict law, and in conformity with general principles. (Laughter on the same benches.) But, along with the question of law, there is the question of practice, and it was precisely to regulate the latter question that the Commission of Reforms has been constituted. The fact is that the natives went and came. They gathered the produce of the forests, not, as has been insinuated, in order to collect rubber, because rubber was not collected by them.

*M. Vandervelde*   That is inaccurate.

*M. Woeste*   In any case, they did collect some produce, and I understand that, under these conditions, the Congo State, in constituting the Commission for Reforms, desired especially to draw its attention to this point, in order to give greater satisfaction to the natives than that which they possess through the strict and rigorous application of the principles to which I referred a moment ago. . . . It is always thus that things occur in countries which are still barbarous like the Congo. A principle is laid down, it is sought to be applied, and cannot be applied at once in a complete manner; that is a matter of time. Those who refuse to recognise that time has here to play a great part, forget the lessons of history; and if they will not admit those lessons, they must be left to the one-sided views which influence them. Another complaint has been made against the Congo State. It has been said that the profits which accrue from the exploitation of the Congo had gone to Belgium, continue to go to Belgium—had served, and continue to serve, Belgian enterprises. Gentlemen, in the note which was sent in 1901 to the Central Committee of this House, which note was concerned in settling definitely the situation of the Congo State towards Belgium, we may read the following passage:—

> "The Congo State declares once more that it has no private objects or interests, and that it pursues its mission with the view to the sole advantage of Belgium. Its past bears witness to, and confirms the sincerity of this declaration. Its action, its constant effort to increase the economic prosperity of Belgium, its persevering efforts to this effect, the results which it has obtained, protest against certain suspicions which exist at the present time, and which hardly seem to be inspired by the public interest."

That was a great and noble thought, which should be everywhere appreciated in our country. The Congo has been created and organised in the interests of the country which one day will be its mother country. Is it not right that Belgium should profit in a fair measure from the benefits which she is giving to the Congo? How can one fail to recognise, for instance, that the revenues which have served to construct the Colonial Palace at Tervueren, allow of our countrymen appreciating the advantages which result from closer relationship with the Congo? How can it be contended that these revenues, thus applied, are not useful to the two States, and to the two peoples? I am, moreover, convinced that the Congo State will understand increasingly that, without wishing to withdraw absolutely from Belgium the revenues obtained from the Congo, it is necessary to devote a large portion of its resources, perhaps the greater portion, to improving the morality, the civilisation, and the development of the Congo from every point of view.

*M. Vandervelde*   That will be the beginning of wisdom.

*M. Woeste*   I am told it will be the beginning of wisdom. I do not admit the accuracy of the interruption, because I have said already that the Congo was created and organised, thanks to the efforts and the labours of the King and of Belgium, and that it is legitimate that the profits of these efforts and this labour should not be wholly withheld from Belgium. But we are entering a new phase, and this new phase should be characterized, in my opinion, by a fair division. The revenues of the Congo should be used, before anything else, for the moral and intellectual improvement of the natives, in the organising of their country; the balance, being used for Belgium, will cause Belgium to devote herself more and more to the needs of the future Colony.

. . . Gentlemen, I have attempted to be as brief as possible. I think, however, that I have placed matters from the true point of view, from the point of view which they should be looked at. Following the Minister for Foreign Affairs, I have not denied, and I do not deny, that reforms are useful in the Congo State, that they may be even necessary. Neither have I denied, and neither do I deny, that regrettable events have occurred therein, although it is difficult to conceive how it could have been otherwise. But, taking the enterprise as a whole, it must be admitted that it deserves praise and encouragement, not blame and criticism, and this is why, far from censuring the Congo State, I desire, in conclusion, only to address towards it words of cordial sympathy. I desire also that the Congo State shall, in order to fulfil its mission, protect more and more all the moral, intellectual and religious affairs which are developing themselves so freely out there. Latterly the missionaries have been violently attacked. They were not sufficiently heard; their establishments were not sufficiently inspected! But facts speak louder than attacks and insinuations; the missionaries clear the ground; they found schools; they propagate the Bible (which is always good tidings) ; they improve the natives by familiarising them with a regular and normal life; they influence them towards the law of work; they impose upon them a moral discipline; and, in a word, they remove them from savage life. These services, which their predecessors have rendered to all European States, and to America, are services which cannot be exaggerated. They testify higher than the critics and censorians who do not know them, who have not studied their work, who allow themselves to be influenced by I do not know what blamable hatred. One day they will be thanked for what they have done in the Congo, as history thanks the priests and the nuns who have contributed to the civilisation of European and American States. The work of the Congo will remain, I am convinced, in all impartial eyes, a grand and fine enterprise. Such also will be the judgment of posterity. Whatever may be done, whatever may be said, it will be to the honour of King Leopold II, as it will be to the honour also of all those in Belgium who, only considering the moral and material interests of the native population. . . .

*M. Vandervelde*    The shareholders of the A.B.I.R., for instance. (Laughter on the extreme left.)

*M. Woeste*    . . . have devoted themselves to those interests, following the King, and have refused to allow themselves to be shaken by critics, the least of whose faults is a total lack of generosity and justice. I am tempted to say, in closing, to the Congo State, "Courage, courage. (Laughter and outcry on the extreme left.) No human enterprise is sheltered from charges and calumnies; reform what it may be necessary to reform in your affairs, reform. . . .

*M. Vandervelde*    Very good, very good!

*M. Woeste*    . . . but allow the flood of calumnies and charges to pass without allowing yourself to be arrested in your progressive march. These charges will fall heavily on those who bring them." (Applause on the right.)


THIRD DAY'S DEBATE (FEBRUARY 28)

## Speech by M. Lorand

*M. Lorand*    . . . Here is the passage in the Report of the Commission of Inquiry. You will see if I am exaggerating. It is concerned with punitive expeditions against villages which have not delivered a sufficiency of rubber, and whose inhabitants have fled to the bush. First of all, the women are tied up. This is another Congolese expression, which I point out to you. "Tied up"; the *capitas* tie up the women. These are curious methods and, as for the women, sometimes it is forgotten to untie them, and they are allowed to die of hunger, as happened in the case of the 58 women of Banghi, in the Upper Congo, and as happened in the Mongalla case —a very great number of women. As we said in a previous interpellation, the natives whose wives have been tied up flee. They are pursued by a black patrol, "often not commanded by a white man, according to the regulations," and then says the Commission:—

> "The black soldier, left to himself, falls back upon the sanguinary instincts which the severest discipline has difficulty in suppressing. It is in the course of such patrols that the greater number of murders, of which the soldiers of the State are accused, have occurred."

And now here is how the Report of the Commission of Inquiry characterises a punitive expedition:—

> "The order confided to the Commandant of the detachment was then drawn up in the following general way: 'N - - - - - is instructed to punish such and such a village.' "

In the Congo the communal property of the native is not respected, but collective punishments are applied (laughter on the extreme left). I continue my perusal of the Report:—

> "The Commission is aware of many expeditions of this type; the consequences have often been very destructive, and we must not be astonished if, in the course of the delicate operations, whose object it is to take hostages, and intimidate the natives, a perpetual control cannot always be exercised to prevent the sanguinary instincts of the natives"—of the natives in the service of the Congo State, note this well—"from giving themselves free scope. When the order to punish comes from a superior authority, it is very difficult that the expedition should not degenerate into massacres, accompanied by pillage and incendiarism."

The text of the Report itself finds that it is very difficult that the manner in which taxes are recovered should not lead to pillage and incendiarism.

> "Military action," continues the Report, "thus understood, always exceeds the object in view, punishment being in flagrant disproportion to the sin committed. The innocent and the guilty are confounded in the same punishment."

Did we exaggerate? But the commission thinks it advisable to invoke extenuating circumstances for these Belgian officers, who, under the pretext of civilisation, are thus employed in spreading massacre, pillage, and incendiarism in the Congo territories. I will read you this passage also, as it is right to do so, but I will then ask you if other responsibilities are not terribly involved:—

> "The responsibility for these abuses," says the Commission, "must not fall entirely upon the Commanders of military expeditions. Note must be taken in examining these facts of the deplorable confusion which exists still in the Upper Congo, between a state of war and a state of peace, between administration and repression, between those who may be considered as enemies, and those who ought to be considered as citizens of the State, and treated according to its laws. The Commission was struck with the general tone of the reports relating to the operations referred to. Often, while stating that the expedition was solely brought about by arrears in taxation, and without even making any sort of mention of attack or resistance on the part of the natives, which would alone justify the use of arms, the authors of these reports speak of 'villages surprised,' 'energetic pursuit,' 'numerous enemies killed and wounded,' 'plunder,' 'prisoners of war,' 'terms of peace.' Obviously, these officers thought they were at war, acted as though they were at war, and that, indeed, is what their superiors intended."

It is there that the responsibility lies!

> "In handing these reports to the supreme authority, what, in a general way, are the annotations inscribed on them by the District Commissioners? Among advice, or criticism, or technical military observations, blame or praise with regard to the incidents of the campaign, very rarely do they consider whether the use of arms was justified. Under such circumstances, we should be inclined to

excuse subalterns who have not thoroughly understood the pacific character of their mission."

If extenuating circumstances can be pleaded for the subalterns, how infinitely graver becomes the responsibility for their superiors!

"This position of affairs cannot be prolonged in the interest of the people, and in the interests of the officials of the State. The natives must not be exposed to being treated as enemies outside the law, and, on the other hand, measures must be taken so that officers who are conducting what may be accurately termed warlike operations, should not be liable to be hauled before the courts to explain these operations, as though it were a matter of an offence against the common law."

There are Courts of Justice on the Congo, although the organisation of justice is deplorable, and but too often interfered with by the administrative authority. The Report of the Commission admits this, and if, Sir (addressing the Premier), you had really desired to put an end to these abuses, it would merely have been necessary to ascertain the contents of the verdicts rendered by the Boma Tribunals, in which those who are prosecuted for violence towards the natives constantly give as an excuse, or as extenuating circumstances, the orders which they received from their superiors. This alone ought to have been sufficient to make you take action, and these verdicts alone exclude all idea of good faith, and every plea of ignorance on the part of the Congo Government.

Instructions to officials are, indeed of two kinds, as was said the other day in the French House. Instructions No. 1 are drawn up for European consumption, full of beautiful humanitarian phrases, and suggestions of kindness and gentleness. Then there are orders No. 2, which are not meant for publication, but which tell officials plainly what notice they need take, in practice, of the humanitarian instructions drafted to humbug European opinion. . . .

*M. Vandervelde* Notably the circular of M. Wahis, as regards hostages.

*M. Lorand* Precisely, and the circulars of the A.B.I.R., reproduced recently in the *Cahiers de la Quinzaine*, on which were inscribed the number of women taken from their homes, whom a sentry might detain, and the way in which coercion and the taking of hostages should be exercised, and the manner in which feeding hostages should be inscribed in the books, "in order that the monthly statement should give the administrators an exact idea of the general operations of the Society." (Sensation.) All these circulars exist. Those of the A.B.I.R. were recently published by M. Pierre Mille, in the *Cahiers de la Quinzaine*, and personally I have received confirmation of them recently in a report which I hold. But amongst the documents which have come into my possession are others which are worth communicating to the House, because they give a good idea of the daily proceedings of the Congo authorities. Here, for instance, are two memorandums, written in pencil by officials of the Congo State:—

"Ndumby is authorised to go to Lakondue, to fetch a woman and a girl belonging to him, and who have taken refuge there." Lusbo, 10th April, 1901. The Lieutenant (signed "Chenot"). (Outcry.)

"Klomoni is instructed to go to Lakondue to fetch two women, Galula and Makassi Moiqui, who belong to the interpreter Sebastian." The Commissioner (signed Pimpurniaux). (Renewed outcry.)

Here is another document, which is still more edifying. I shall be told, perhaps, that it is concerned with the preservation of the forests, and of measures to be taken to prevent their destruction! As you know, it is forbidden to cut the rubber vines. This practice must be prevented, and we are now about to see the method adopted to do so. Here is the photograph of a document, of which the original is in the hands of a person whom I know, and in whom we can have every confidence.

*M. Vandervelde*   Who wrote the document?

*M. Lorand*   It is signed by an official of the State, a District Commissioner, whom I know personally; who, moreover, is very well known, whose handwriting is known to me, and to colleagues to whom I have shown this document, and who, like myself, are perfectly convinced of its authenticity. It reads as follows:

"M. le Chef de Poste,
   "Decidedly these people of Inoryo are a bad lot. They have just been and cut some rubber vines at Huli. We must fight them until their absolute submission has been obtained, or their complete extinction. Warn for the last time the people of Inoryo, and put into execution as soon as possible your project of accompanying them to the forest or else go to the village with a good trique. When you arrive at the first hut, speak as follows to the owner thereof: 'Here is a basket; you are to fill it with rubber. Go to the forest at once, and if in a week you have not returned with 10 lbs. of rubber, I shall set fire to your hut and you will burn.' The trique may be used to drive into the forest those who refuse to leave the village. By burning one hut after another I think you will not be compelled to proceed to last extremities before being obeyed. Inform the natives that if they cut another single vine, I will exterminate them to the last man."

(Sensation—outcry on extreme left.) . . .

Gentlemen, this is the system which has been prevalent hitherto, which will continue to be applied, because no remedy will be brought until the State is compelled. Then, in comparison with the overwhelming testimony furnished by the Commission of Inquiry, the reform proposals are so vague and insufficient, would take so long to carry out; such care is taken of the financial situation of the Congo State, that one feels that, if the State does anything, it will do very little; and if the Congo State appointed a Commission of Reforms immediately after the return of the Commission of Inquiry, we must ask ourselves if this was not done in order to still further delay the moment when it will have to bring about reforms. Purposes of delay are but too often served by a Commission, and, as M. Vandervelde said, this Commission of Reforms has been constituted in such a manner that we have no kind of confidence in its results. We see amongst the members appointed some of the high officials of the Congo State, who could not have been ignorant of the facts which have taken place, and for which they are responsible. We see, I think, among them also, one of the signatories of the instructions which I have just read. We see among them the administrators of certain Concessionnaire Societies, and notably an administrator of the A.B.I.R. To cut a long story short, apart from two or three Belgian magistrates, who have no special competence in colonial affairs, the Commission does not contain a single person able to represent the protest of outraged humanity, and of the rights of man, which have been stamped upon. . . .

Well, to-day, gentlemen, the cup is full; it is overflowing. You refused to hear the indignant protests of the public in other civilised countries, and of independent individuals in Belgium; now you can no longer escape the movement of reprobation which is becoming universal. You can certainly no longer escape from it by saying that the charges brought against the Congo State are British calumnies, seeing that all the charges levelled at the Congo State have been admitted by the Commission of Inquiry as being the result of the Congo State's own system of outrageous exploitation of the people, enslaved to produce rubber, fought and massacred when they did not produce it. What sanction are you going to give to these overwhelming disclosures? I understand and I respect the feelings of those who recoil before the idea of denouncing to foreign Powers, signatories to the Act of Berlin, actions which constitute a flagrant violation of that Act, and which may provoke a new International Conference. But what I do not understand is that the Belgian Government, which is in daily touch with the Congo State, should not say to it, "Enough! You have pursued up to the present a system of whose consequences you have probably been ignorant, but which has led to a mass of abuses which you had not foreseen. To-day, these abuses are admitted; they are the result of the system adopted by you to draw the largest possible profits from the Colony. They are of a kind which call for vengeance, and which cannot be tolerated. They must disappear immediately, and radically, and Belgium will not remain a single day responsible with you for a state of affairs recognised by the Commission of Inquiry. You shall have no more officers, no more magistrates, no more officials of the Belgian State, if you do not immediately make up your mind to alter radically an admitted situation!" . . .

## Speech by the Premier

**M. de Smet de Naeyer (Premier, Chancellor of the Exchequer, and Minister of Public Works)**  Gentlemen, the Hon. M. Lorand is living in a fool's paradise if he thinks that anybody is going to believe in the impartiality of which he boasted in the opening part of his speech. The honourable member told us that he had no animosity against the King, or against his African work. Now, if in Belgium, from the very first moment, there has been found a systematic adversary of the African enterprise, from the very first that adversary has been M. Lorand.

**M. Flechet**  That proves that he saw clearly.

**M. de Smet de Naeyer**  The Belgians had hardly set foot in Africa before the honourable member denounced the enterprise of our countrymen as being of evil omen to the mother country.

**M. Lorand**  I was not mistaken.

**M. de Smet de Naeyer**  You are an anti-coloniser, an anti-colonial by principle, and, in consequence, I ask the House to receive your opinions with suspicion.

**M. Lorand**  My mistake has been to predict for twenty years everything which has happened. (Applause on the extreme left—protests on the right.)

*M. de Smet de Naeyer*    For my part, I intend to render homage at once to the colonial work accomplished in the Congo. First as regards the actual and immediate interest of our country. It cannot be denied that, without the Congo, we should be ten years behindhand in our economic expansion. Did not M. Lorand, as a new Cassandra, predict not so long ago that the construction of the Congo Railway was an enterprise bound to fail, and to be the tomb of black workmen? The honourable member even proposed, at a given moment, to abandon the enterprise. He was prepared to sacrifice the millions already subscribed to it by Belgium. Well, we know what the Congo railway has become! And M. Lorand, with such errors to his debit, returns once more to-day to throw opprobrium on the Congo enterprise.

*M. Pepin*    You are seeking a diversion. What you are saying has no significance.

*M. de Smet de Naeyer*    I have the right to examine, as the House has the right to ask, if we are in the presence of a critic sincerely desirous of enlightening himself, or of an adversary full of partiality.

*M. Lorand*    You can decide as you please.

*M. de Smet de Naeyer*    Let us then discuss the point. I ask to be heard. Why did the Hon. M. Lorand not speak to us of the abuses which have taken place in French and German Africa? (Interruption.) Must all colonisation be condemned because abuses are committed in the colonies? Must Belgium be judged from the contents of her prisons?

*M. Terwagne*    Belgium will be judged from her Government, and that is enough!

*M. de Smet de Naeyer*    I do not fear the verdict. To listen to M. Lorand, it would really seem as though the Commission of Inquiry had painted the desolating picture which he has drawn for us, as regards the moral condition of that African colony. It would almost seem as though the honourable member has failed to read the Report through.

*M. Lorand*    I have done nothing else but read the Report.

*M. de Smet de Naeyer*    You displayed everything which related to abuses, which all deplore as much as you do. You systematically left in the shade, and in silence, passages where the Commissioners proclaimed emphatically the beauty and the grandeur of the Congo enterprise.

. . . On what side is real patriotism? On the side of all those who, having founded, and pursued with unceasing perseverance, that admirable Congo enterprise, condemn individual abuses as much as M. Lorand can condemn them; or of those who only wish to see these abuses, to generalise them, in order the better to criticise the enterprise itself? (Applause on the right.)

*M. Bertrand*    It is the system which is condemned.

*M. de Smet de Naeyer*    I am in a position to inform the Chamber of an inquiry which has recently confirmed the testimony I have just read. Governor-General Wahis has recently closed a tour of inspection which was carried out in the Congo State. He has found that the condition of the natives is satisfactory, and two Protestant missionaries have testified before him—I mention this since some people appear to attach so much importance to their testimony—and stated that, in their region, which extends from the mouth of the Mongalla to Stanleyville, there is no complaint to formulate. On the other hand, the Hon. M. Verhaegen, who paid yesterday to our valiant and devoted Catholic missionaries so well-deserved a homage, quoted the declaration of Monsignor Roelens, whose jurisdiction extends to Tanganyika, and who says that he has only witnessed a single abuse in fourteen years, and that this abuse was remedied the moment it was denounced. The reprehensible acts and actions noticed here and there are, therefore, far from characterising a system.

*M. Vandervelde*   The abuses are the consequence of the system.

*M. de Smet de Naeyer*   They are not inherent to the system.

*M. Vandervelde*   Why, it is palpable.

*M. Lorand*   Absolutely so.

*M. de Smet de Naeyer*   One may always argue that abuses applied are the consequences of such and such a system. Nothing is easier, when one wishes to attack a system itself, and the principles upon which it is founded. In the present case, the general conclusions of the inquiry do not bear that out, but, obviously, what remains to be determined is whether the organisation of the system should be modified—I do not say to the extent of wholly suppressing abuses in a day, which would bring about a *millennium* on the Congo, but in order to reduce more and more these individual abuses. It is to this end that the Congo State is working ceaselessly, without it being necessary for us to intervene to press it to do so.

*M. Vandervelde*   At last, then, you admit that the abuses are the outcome of the system?

*M. de Smet de Naeyer*   I admit nothing of the kind, and I am certain that the House has understood me. Gentlemen, the question of porterage has been touched on, and that is one of the greatest difficulties which faces us in Africa. The porterage requirements were specially noteworthy in the Cataracts region, and, to the great benefit of the natives, a railway has been constructed there, which has suppressed this primitive method of transport. . . . What I was about to remark was that the evils of the porterage system had been very much reduced since the Nile route has been utilised for the supplies consigned to the Lado Enclave. Now the British steamship companies on the Nile are refusing to undertake the transport of this material, and the natives will have to begin once more their hard task of head carriage.

. . . In all this affair, gentlemen, there is a certain person who is fulminated against, who is as an accused party, who is condemned in advance, and who has not been heard (Approval on the right.) ; this someone is the Congo State, or rather all those who touch the Congo. The accused parties and the condemned parties, of whom I speak, constitute the Government of the Congo State, the *Domaine de la Couronne,* the Sovereign King, the *Force Publique,* the Administration, the Magistracy, the Commercial Companies. Faults of organisation, vices in application, abuses, and excesses have been pointed out. The Government of the Congo State instituted a Commission of Inquiry, in order to verify the facts, and to make ultimate suggestions for improvement. The Commission handed in its Report on the 13th October, 1905, and the Congo Government sent a copy of it to the Governor-General, published it, and appointed a Commission, "instructed to consider its conclusions, to formulate proposals which they thought necessary, and to seek for practical means of realising them," and it is at this moment, under cover of an interpellation addressed to the Belgian Government, that attacks of all kinds, and the gravest accusations against the Congo enterprise as a whole, are brought before this House! In favour of the gale which, as M. Woeste well said, blows at this moment upon the Congo State, members can be found who come here and make a chorus with those who are endeavouring to hound on public opinion against an enterprise, a study of which on the spot, in its fundamental organisation, and in its present state of advancement, dragged from the Commission of Inquiry a cry of admiration! (Applause on the right.) You have heard, gentlemen, that passage, so sincerely eulogious, from the Report of the Commission of Inquiry, which I quoted at the beginning of my speech. Never, so far as I know, have any of the friends of the Congo State, who are naturally suspicious, in the eyes of M. Vandervelde and M. Lorand, gone so far in praising the work of Belgians in Africa. (Applause on the right.)

. . . The truth is that we have led the country into a channel of prosperity which it had never known in the past, and the African enterprise has helped it enormously. Gentlemen, the House will not expect me to follow, point by point, the Report of the Commission of Inquiry, and the speeches of my critics. In order to meet the specific and general statements they have made, I will limit myself to a few points which should especially be noted. Much has been said of the so-called appropriation of the land and of rubber collection. Now, it is well that one should understand, because the opponents of the Congo have been very careful not to say so, that an identical régime is practised in all other colonies.

**M. Lorand**  In his book, M. Cattier compared the systems prevailing in different colonies, and proved that the one which is in force in the Congo exists nowhere else.

**M. de Smet de Naeyer**  I am about to show you that he is wrong. Passages of the Report of the Commission of Inquiry have been read out relating to the abuses connected with rubber collection. These abuses are certainly to be deplored, and they must be remedied. That is what the Congo State wishes, and one of the objects of the Report of the Commission of Inquiry will be to study the means of preventing their repetition. But there are other facts that are studiously concealed. The Commission of Inquiry recognised that the abuses are only individual faults, that they are not inherent to the system established, and stated explicitly:

1   That the State had the right to appropriate vacant land.
2   That the State had the right, and that it was necessary for it to itself exploit the forests and the lands of its domain.
3   The legitimacy and the necessity of establishing a labour tax.
4   The legitimacy and the necessity of applying coercion.

The Commission bases all its remarks on this initial admission:—

"All production of trade in the Congo is only possible at the present time, and will only be possible for a long time to come, through native labour."

and the report justifies coercion by the natural indolence of the native.

**M. Masson**  Is it by coercion that you intend to lead the natives to work?

**M. de Smet de Naeyer**  In the earlier stages a certain amount of coercion cannot be avoided. (Interruption—uproar.)

**M. Janson**  It is with such arguments that slavery is justified.

**M. de Smet de Naeyer**  You forget that one of the first acts of the Congo State was to suppress slavery.

**M. Janson**  It was thus that the South American planters justified slavery.

*M. Lorand*    The condition of the natives of the Congo is worse than the condition of the South American slaves ever was.

*M. de Smet de Naeyer*    It is ridiculous. Why, in the Congo it is only a matter of four or five days' labour per month.

*M. Lorand*    It is not four or five days per month which are demanded of the negro; it is all the month, with the exception of four or five days. The Commission of Inquiry admits that in the most formal manner.

*M. de Smet de Naeyer*    Not at all; the Commission admits the principle of the law, which is called the forty hours law.

*M. Lorand*    The Report acknowledges, on the contrary, that the native has only three or four days left to him in the month, and is ever weighed down under the knowledge of new privations and new dangers, which he has to incur in returning to the forest.

*M. de Smet de Naeyer*    The Commission points out the faults of organisation, and indicates reforms which appear to it to be useful. The Congo State will not fail, through the Commission of Reforms, to understand the evil, and apply the remedy. In any case, you will admit with me that labour which consists in making an incision in the rubber vines is not in itself very arduous. (Interruption—uproar.) Moreover, gentlemen, forced labour is only a transitory step; the native will learn to work voluntarily, to satisfy the needs which have been created in him. You should know that all the Congo tribes are not equally indolent. Those who have been in contact for centuries with Portuguese merchants are accustomed to work. In certain colonies the negroes have been incited to work by filling them with alcohol. Is that what you want?

*M. Mansart*    The *chicotte* is still worse.

*M. de Smet de Naeyer*    You forget to realise the state of affairs which existed in the Congo before the constitution of the State. Let the reports of the explorers of the Congo basin—Livingstone, Stanley, Cameron, and all the Belgians who have illustrated geographical science—be read, and you will see in the midst of what crime and atrocities the native populations were living. Their activity was confined to intertribal warfare, and the slave trade. The abolition of the slave trade did not suppress slavery in the interior of Africa, nor these intertribal wars, which have become with these people a habit and a need. If the State did not make its direct and continuous influence felt over these peoples, the majority of them would return quickly to their primitive state of savagery. Where the action of the State is not absolutely effective, abominable abuses take place, which shows what is still today the mental condition of the native when left to his own instincts.

. . . The only means to restore order and security in this country is to subject the natives to discipline. The labour tax brought about this result, and thus conferred a benefit. All the Companies established in the Congo, with the exception of the Kasai Company, which is in an especially favoured region, declared that they could not make the natives do anything, without coercion, and they begged the authorities of the State to intervene to compel the natives to work, or to give them means of exercising direct coercion upon them. I refer to the Companies established in the Upper Congo, where the collection of rubber has been abandoned to individuals, through the decree of the 8th November, 1903. The natives are free to bring, or not to bring, the produce of the forests to the Commercial Companies. All these Companies claimed the intervention of the State, by saying that neither promise nor offer of even exaggerated salaries can make the natives work. The people have very few means, and they prefer to live in a miserable state rather than to work for paid labour. Yet they reside in the forest, in regions where the collection of rubber only requires a minimum of effort. It will be seen, therefore, that the labour tax is as necessary to the civilisation and to the education of the negro as to the development of trade on the Congo. That is the opinion which is very clearly expressed by Mons. Augouard, French Bishop of Brazzaville.

. . . M. Vandervelde protested with indignation because the natives are prevented from travelling outside their villages without authority from the District Commissioner. The honourable member saw in this measure an act of oppression, and he thinks, no doubt, that there is nothing like it in any other country which is being colonised. This is a double error, as the Commission of Inquiry remarked quite rightly, in regard to other matters in the passage of this Report, which I quoted a short while ago. One must be careful not to look upon such regulations with European ideas. To raise the moral and material level of the native, the colonising State is imbued with the principle that the natives cannot be left isolated in their natural surroundings. The tribe is the moral status of the native, the condition of his political and social development. Separated from his tribe, the native becomes a vagabond. It is, therefore, with the object of protecting him that the State seeks to maintain natural and traditional communities. . . .

No criminal or oppressive act, no abuse of force or authority, will find defenders on the part of the Congo State, here or elsewhere. The Congo Government has given a complete proof of its intentions, and of its resolves, by instituting a Commission of Inquiry, followed by a Commission of Reforms. . . .


FOURTH DAY'S DEBATE (MARCH 1)

*Speech by De Heer P. Daens*

**De Heer P. Daens**  You ought to sit here as great friends and great defenders of truth; whereas the truth about the Congo is persistently killed. The mouths of all the officials in the Congo are shut; silence is imposed upon the missionaries, and if they attempt to speak they are accused of being revolutionaries and democrats. By this means your capitalists have drawn millions and millions from the Congo. Nevertheless, notwithstanding everything, truth is piercing the clouds, and to-day you are compelled to admit that there are systematic abuses in the Congo. These are proved, not only by official documents, but by all the speeches pronounced here yesterday. We listened to M. de Smet de Naeyer. He wandered among his notes, and his words were produced with difficulty. He vainly tried to escape from the striking light of facts! He is blinded by his aristocratic ideas to such an extent that he dares to say that those who speak against the Congo are anti-patriotic and enemies of civilisation. A magnificent civilisation, in very truth! M. Verhaegen spoke eloquently in congratulating the missionaries; but he forgot to say how they suffered in seeing their work crushed by the infamous conduct of European civilisers. We also heard the great hero, M. Woeste. He is fully informed of everything that takes place in the Congo; but he does not desire that the abuses should cease. M. Woeste knows of the evils which exist on the

Congo, but he will not have any reforms. He did not end his speech by saying, "Institute an inquiry. Seek out abuses, and put an end to them." No, he ended by saying, "Continue, and do not listen to calumny!" Yesterday, again, in the course of the eloquent speech of M. Lorand, when M. Terwangne gave a fine homage to truth, we heard M. Woeste, like a schoolmaster, read a lesson to his young pupil. You seem to be of opinion, M. Woeste, that this immense colony can be oppressed in an inhuman fashion, in order to extract millions from it. And what do you make of religion? Did not Christ give to His Apostles other means of civilising and conquering the world? Are you ignorant of the fact that St. Amans and St. Lievien adopted quite different means to convert our country? Have you never read the bitter complaints of Christopher Columbus, at the sight of the exploitation and the horrors committed by the Spaniards? . . . Francis Xavier said that in the islands of the Indian Archipelago, where Spanish traders had passed, not a solitary human being was left. The European civilisers, by their thirst for gold and sensual pleasure, had plunged the natives into such a condition of degradation that the work of the missionaries remained sterile. Do you not fear, gentlemen, that the same state of affairs will take place in the Congo? And will not these unfortunate natives, tired of being oppressed and ground down, rise some day to throw off the yoke which oppresses them so cruelly, and kills them? I think it is a disgrace for the Conservative Party to refuse to cause these abuses to cease; abuses pointed out on all sides, and to allow the Liberal and Socialist Parties to make themselves the vehicle of complaints. The masses of the people, which did not regard favourably this enterprise at the beginning, saw clearly and gauged the situation. You say that markets are required for Belgian industry and commerce. But these markets exist in the interior of our country. Open your eyes, and see the great number of families who are lacking in necessary food, and to whose interests you should devote in the first place your riches, to take them out of their misery, and put an end to their existence and privations. Not only is this talk of markets a flare of trumpets, but religion itself has dwindled more during the last twenty-four years of Conservative Government, than during the fifty preceding years. Open your eyes, and you will see in Brussels around your magnificent monuments, besides starving families, and yet you come to speak to us of openings for Belgian gold. And all the promises which rich men make here on such occasions are, as always, vain promises. But the day will come when the light of truth will be thrown upon the Congo, and you will be plunged in shadow. For truth is comparable to steam, which, when compressed, acquires a stronger power. Beware of the explosion, for it will destroy you!

*Part Three*

# *Impressions of an Age*

# The Bourgeois Age

*We are inclined to think of a historical era as something that may be
objectively ascertained and evaluated if only we gather enough facts
and add them up with sufficient care. Such a scientific approach might
seem particularly rewarding in appraising an age about which we have
the wealth of information and documentation that we possess for the
period in European history that ended abruptly in 1914.*

*That the problem is actually not quite so simple is demonstrated by the
two contrasting assessments of the prewar era that follow. Each is the
work of an outstanding representative of the generation that reached
maturity around the turn of the century. Charles Péguy (1873–1914)
was a French man of letters of shining, if prickly, integrity. A Socialist
who despised the Socialist party, a republican who rallied to the Republic
while loathing republicans, a Catholic repelled by the hierarchy and
the faithful alike, a nationalist with a low opinion of his conationals,
Péguy was a highly individual figure who influenced a whole generation
of French intellectuals. The selection which follows is from "Money," a
semiautobiographical essay published in 1913. The second selection is
a chapter from* The Economic Consequences of the Peace, *a book that
appeared in 1920. Its author, John Maynard Keynes (1883–1946), who
many years later was to emerge as the most influential economist of the
twentieth century, had been a minor member of the British delegation
to the Versailles Peace Conference in 1919. His widely read indictment
of the settlement imposed on Germany—Keynes maintained that it would
prevent European economic recovery and stabilization—was influential
in shaping English and American attitudes toward the peace treaties.
Keynes's analysis of prewar European society included here was meant
to contrast with the dislocated European economy which he predicted
would result from the reparations claims on Germany stipulated by the
Versailles Treaty.*

## ⋖§ MONEY

### Charles Péguy

. . . Having arrived at an age where I am ready to write my *Confessions,* and hoping
to find time, amid so many unfinished plans and projects, to set down a world I used
to know, I shall attempt to give some small idea of that whole admirable life of 1880,
that whole world of worker and peasant which we can sum up in one word: the people.

Charles Péguy, "L'Argent," *Oeuvres en Prose, 1909–1914* (Paris: Bibliothèque de la Pléiade,
1957), pp. 1046–1056. Translated by Dolores M. Burdick.

To be exact, it was still the world of Old France, with its people intact. It was a world in which the fine old meanings of the word "people" still applied, for this word drew its origins from the old regime. When you say "the people" nowadays, you are referring to a fiction, and one of the lowest forms at that; you are creating a vote-getting and political kind of literature.

The people no longer exists. Everyone is bourgeois, since everybody reads his daily paper. What little remained of the old aristocracy has become a crass bourgeoisie. The old nobility has degenerated into a middle class based on money, alongside the former middle classes from whom they are now indistinguishable. As for the workers, they have only one idea nowadays, namely, to become bourgeois themselves. That is what they mean by going socialist. The peasants alone have remained true to themselves, have clung profoundly to the role and tradition of the peasantry.

We were brought up in another kind of world. One can say that a child reared in a town like Orléans between 1873 and 1880 has literally been in contact with Old France, that he actually participated in Old France and knew its people. One can even say that this was his sole and total participation, for Old France was still whole and intact. That era collapsed all of a piece, at one fell stroke, in a breakup that took only a few years.

In a word, we were the children of Old France. We knew its people, we touched them, we were of the people at a time when it still existed. The lowliest laborer of those days was a man of Old France, while today the most intolerable of M. Maurras' disciples [Charles Maurras (1868–1945), longtime leader of conservative and monarchist French thought] has not a drop of Old France in his blood.

Let us try to illustrate this more clearly. A very intelligent woman who was gracefully moving toward seventy-odd used to say: "The world changed less during my first sixty years than it has during the last ten." One must go beyond her statement, and add that the world changed less since the days of Jesus Christ than it has in the past three decades. First there was the ancient (and Biblical) world. Then came the Christian era. Now we are in the modern age. A farm in Beauce, right after the [Franco-Prussian] war was infinitely closer to a Gallo-Roman farm—in manners, customs, dignity, even in its very make-up and structure—than to a farm of the present day.

We knew a time when any good woman of the people seemed to speak words that rose from the roots of the race itself, from the very depths of its being and spirit. And when a worker sat back and lit his cigarette, you knew that what he was about to say was not something he had just read in the morning papers. The freethinkers of those times were more Christian than our most pious churchgoers of today. An average parish of those times was infinitely closer to a parish of the fifteenth, or the fourth, or the fifth, or the eighth century than to a parish of today. . . .

When we say "the people" today, we are using a figure of speech, and a poor and empty one at that, for there is no referent, no substance to the image. It is merely a political turn of phrase. But when Michelet [Jules Michelet (1798–1874), liberal French historian and man of letters, often connected with the Romantic movement] and others of his ilk spoke of the people, they referred to a living reality, an entity they had truly *known*.

We of my generation knew this same people at the height of its powers, at the peak of its authenticity. And there were no omens; it seemed certain that nothing would ever change. Ten years later, nothing was left. The people, in what seemed one great burst of exertion, had, almost in a single moment of time, joined ranks to annihilate itself, to suppress and erase the people from the flow of history. . . .

Believe it or not, we were nurtured by a people full of gaiety. In those days, a workshop was one place on earth where men were happy. Today a workshop is a place where men blame each other, hold grudges, come to grips, and do battle, occasionally unto death.

In my day, everyone used to sing. (Except for me, but I was unworthy of those times.) In most places where men worked together, they sang. Today they grumble. In those days they earned nothing, so to speak. The salaries were low beyond belief. And yet everyone somehow managed to eat. In the lowliest of households there was a sort of well-being that you find nowhere today. People managed to bring up their young, and in goodly numbers too. There was none of that fearful economic strangulation which now tightens its grip on us from year to year. People earned nothing, spent nothing, and everybody seemed to get along.

There was, I repeat, none of this economic stranglehold we feel today—scientific, cold, rectangular, regular, clean, neat, seamless, implacable, well-behaved, common, constant, convenient—a strangling against which we can say nothing, and in which he who gets strangled is obviously in the wrong.

We will never know the full extent of the decency and fairness of the people; that brand of finesse and depth of soul will never be found again. Nor such concern with decency of speech. Those people would have blushed at the sound of our highest modern "tone," which is of course the bourgeois tone. And nowadays everyone is bourgeois.

It is hard to believe, I suppose, but we actually knew workers who *wanted* to work. That was all one thought of doing. We knew workers who got up in the morning— and at what an hour!—with a song in their hearts at the mere idea of going to work. At eleven o'clock they would sing as they went off to their midday soup. . . . Working was their sole joy, the profound root and source of their being. Their *reason* for being. There was an incredible *honor* in work, the finest honor of all, the most Christian, the only honor perhaps which could hold water. That is why, for example, I say that a freethinker of those days was more Christian than a modern zealot, because a modern zealot is bound to be a bourgeois. Today everyone is bourgeois.

We knew an honor of work identical with that form of honor which guided hands and hearts in the Middle Ages. That honor had been preserved intact. We saw *care*, the equal desire for perfection of the whole and of the infinitesimal part. We knew that reverence for a piece of work well done, a piety that pressed the worker to extremes of self-discipline. During my childhood I saw chairs repaired with exactly the same spirit, heart, and hand as cathedrals had been built in earlier times.

What remains of all this today? How have we managed to make out of the most industrious people on earth, perhaps the only people who adored labor for its own and honor's sake—how have we managed, I repeat, to make of them a people who channel all their energies into getting away with as little work as possible on the job? This transformation will doubtless go down in history as the greatest and perhaps the sole victory of intellectual bourgeois demagoguery. But we cannot deny that this victory has had a resounding impact on the people.

There was the Christian revolution. Then there was the modern one. They are the two that count. An artisan of my youth was like any artisan of any Christian period, and no doubt like any ancient artisan as well. An artisan of today is no longer an artisan at all.

In that fine honor of work converged all the noblest of sentiments—a dignity, a real pride. "Never have to ask anything of anyone"—that was the watchword. There you have the kind of ideas upon which we were nurtured. For to ask for work was not considered asking at all. It was the most natural, normal request in the world, hardly even a request; it was a simple taking of one's proper place in the workshop. It was the simple finding of your niche in a working community where your niche already awaited you. A worker of those days simply didn't know what it meant to beg. Only the bourgeoisie knows how, and the bourgeoisie taught begging to the people when it made them into bourgeois. Today, in the very insolence, brutality, and incoherence which they bring to their demands, it is easy to sense a kind of underlying shame at being forced to "ask," at being brought by the events of economic history down to the level of begging. Oh, they are asking somebody for something all right, these days! They are asking *everyone* for something! To demand one's rights is still a form of "asking." Only a servant asks.

Our workers did not serve. They worked. Their honor was an absolute, as is any form of honor. The humblest crosspiece of the lowliest chair must be fashioned with precision; this was understood and accepted as an unquestioned first premise. Perfect and well made, and *not* just because you were being paid for it. Well made—not for the boss, not for the esthete, not even for the customer. It had to be well made *itself*, in itself and for itself alone. A whole tradition welling up from the depths of the race, a whole history, an absolute value, an *honor*—all insisted on that crosspiece being perfect. Any part of the chair that was not visible was as carefully fashioned as the parts you could see. Was this not the very principle of the cathedrals? . . .

Just to ruffle the priests, they used to say that "working is praying." They didn't realize how well they spoke. For their work was, in effect, a prayer. And the shop a chapel. Work was the carrying out of a lovely ritual. What would have been the disgust, nay, the incredulity of those men if someone had told them that a few years hence, the workers would make official proposals to do as little work as possible, and that these latter-day workers would consider this a great victory! Such an idea, supposing they could even imagine it, would have come as a body blow, a direct attack upon themselves, an insult to their being; it would have amounted to questioning their ability to produce, insinuating that they would not give as fully of themselves as they were able. One might as well suppose of a soldier that he would choose not to be victorious. . . .

Earning nothing, living on nothing, people were happy. Please spare me your immediate recourse to sociological statistics. It happens to be a fact, one of the rare facts of which we were certain, which we could embrace and bear witness to, one of those few truths which is actually incontestable.

Add to this the fact that the modern worker doesn't really enjoy his new-won leisure in the shop. He would much rather be working. It is not for nothing that he springs from that industrious race. He hears its call: the hand that itches to be occupied, the arm that wearies of doing nothing. . . . Like their fathers before them, the workers hear the muffled call of work waiting to be done, and at bottom they are disgusted with themselves for letting the tools lie idle. But wait a moment! Some very fine gentlemen—scientists, bourgeois—have explained to them that that's what socialism is, that's what the revolution is about.

For we cannot repeat it too often: the whole problem was started by the bourgeoisie. The whole error, the whole crime. It is the capitalist bourgeoisie that infected the people with, to be precise, a spirit both bourgeois and capitalistic.

Note that I specify the capitalist bourgeoisie, the high bourgeoisie. The petty bourgeoisie, in contrast, has become the most hard pressed of all social classes, the only one really working these days, and thus the only one which has preserved the working-class virtues. For its reward, it is the only class which really lives in abject poverty. The petty bourgeoisie alone has stood firm, by some miracle; and if there should some day be a return to the old ways, it will be thanks to the petty bourgeoisie's having maintained its status quo. Thus it is not the workers who have preserved the virtues of their class, but rather the petty bourgeoisie.

The capitalist bourgeoisie, on the other hand, contaminated everything. It has infected both itself and the people, but the latter doubly: first, by merely existing and being itself; and secondly, by the way it has inoculated bits of itself into the people.

It has thus infected the people both as antagonist and as mentor. It has infected the people by itself and in itself. If the bourgeoisie had remained not so much what it already was, but rather what it *should* have been, what *might* have been—namely, the economic arbiter of salable value—then the working class would have asked nothing better than to remain what it had always been, namely, the economic *source* of salable value.

We must never fail to remind ourselves that it was the bourgeoisie itself that first began to undermine the system. Only because the bourgeoisie began to treat a man's labor as something to be bought and sold did the worker in turn begin to consider his own labor as a commodity with a price. Only because the bourgeoisie began to speculate and bargain in regard to a man's labor did the worker, through imitation—one might almost say collusion—begin to play the same game. It is only because the bourgeoisie began to exercise an endless blackmail upon man's labor that we now live under this regime of perpetual speculation and blackmail we call strikes. The notion of a fair price has disappeared, a notion our bourgeois intellectuals may ridicule all they like, but which used to provide nonetheless a sound basis for a whole way of life.

For—and here you have that second and no less insidious infection—while the bourgeoisie was introducing and using this sabotage to its own advantage, it was at the same time unwittingly introducing into working-class circles licensed theoreticians of sabotage. While it was setting an example and serving as a model, it was also giving lessons on the side. The *political* socialist party is entirely made up of bourgeois intellectuals. They are the ones who invented sabotage along with the double desertion —that of work and of the tool. Not to mention military desertion, which is a particular case of the greater desertion, just as military glory is a particular case of the greater glory. They are the ones who made the people believe that was what socialism and the revolution were all about. The *syndicalist* [labor-union oriented] socialist parties managed to go on thinking—more or less sincerely—that they were a reaction against the political parties, or against a unified party; but through a common historical phenomenon, through a new application and verification of a very old law of opposites, this reaction against politics happens to be political itself, and this party turns out to be a new political party, another political party, a rival political party!

The syndicalist parties are themselves infected, and as badly as the rest—infected with elements political, intellectual, and bourgeois, just like the others. They managed to go on believing—more or less sincerely—that they had gotten rid of the old political socialist personnel. But they have not rid themselves of the old political socialist spirit, which was eminently bourgeois in origin, hardly a spirit that came from the people. At first glance it might seem that there are more real workers in the syndicalist socialist parties than in the political socialist groups, which latter are composed of nothing but bourgeois. And it is true, I suppose, if you want to prove it by counting, that superficial method of the sociological census. But it only *appears* to be true. In reality, they [the syndicalist socialist parties] are infiltrated with elements purely intellectual and bourgeois. And most important, the very great number of workers you find there are not really workers at all, since they do not spring directly from the authentic people. They are really workers of a second zone, a second wave—they are "bourgeoisified" workers decked out, if I may use the image, in their bourgeois Sunday best. . . . [They are] presumptuous workers, more stupid, if that is possible, than their models the bourgeois or their teachers the intellectuals; miserable creatures not only rotten with pride, but enslaved by this same conceit; awkward, muddled in metaphysics they cannot begin to comprehend—presumptuous workers, cut off from their people and their race—in a word, poor empty souls pretending to shrewdness and profundity.


### ✒§ THE ECONOMIC CONSEQUENCES OF THE PEACE

*John Maynard Keynes*


#### EUROPE BEFORE THE WAR

Before 1870 different parts of the small continent of Europe had specialized in their own products; but, taken as a whole, it was substantially self-subsistent. And its population was adjusted to this state of affairs.

After 1870 there was developed on a large scale an unprecedented situation, and the economic condition of Europe became during the next fifty years unstable and peculiar. The pressure of population on food, which had already been balanced by the accessibility of supplies from America, became for the first time in recorded history definitely reversed. As numbers increased, food was actually easier to secure. Larger proportional returns from an increasing scale of production became true of agriculture as well as industry. With the growth of the European population there were more emigrants on the one hand to till the soil of the new countries, and, on the other, more

John Maynard Keynes, *The Economic Consequences of the Peace* (New York: Harcourt, Brace and Howe, 1920), pp. 9–22.

workmen were available in Europe to prepare the industrial products and capital goods which were to maintain the emigrant populations in their new homes, and to build the railways and ships which were to make accessible to Europe food and raw products from distant sources. Up to about 1900 a unit of labor applied to industry yielded year by year a purchasing power over an increasing quantity of food. It is possible that about the year 1900 this process began to be reversed, and a diminishing yield of Nature to man's effort was beginning to reassert itself. But the tendency of cereals to rise in real cost was balanced by other improvements; and—one of many novelties —the resources of tropical Africa then for the first time came into large employ, and a great traffic in oil-seeds began to bring to the table of Europe in a new and cheaper form one of the essential foodstuffs of mankind. In this economic Eldorado, in this economic Utopia, as the earlier economists would have deemed it, most of us were brought up.

That happy age lost sight of a view of the world which filled with deep-seated melancholy the founders of our Political Economy. Before the eighteenth century man-kind entertained no false hopes. To lay the illusions which grew popular at that age's latter end, Malthus disclosed a Devil. For half a century all serious economical writings held that Devil in clear prospect. For the next half century he was chained up and out of sight. Now perhaps we have loosed him again.

What an extraordinary episode in the economic progress of man that age was which came to an end in August, 1914! The greater part of the population, it is true, worked hard and lived at a low standard of comfort, yet were, to all appearances, reasonably contented with this lot. But escape was possible, for any man of capacity or character at all exceeding the average, into the middle and upper classes, for whom life offered, at a low cost and with the least trouble, conveniences, comforts, and amenities beyond the compass of the richest and most powerful monarchs of other ages. The inhabitant of London could order by telephone, sipping his morning tea in bed, the various prod-ucts of the whole earth, in such quantity as he might see fit, and reasonably expect their early delivery upon his doorstep; he could at the same moment and by the same means adventure his wealth in the natural resources and new enterprises of any quarter of the world, and share, without exertion or even trouble, in their prospective fruits and advantages; or he could decide to couple the security of his fortunes with the good faith of the townspeople of any substantial municipality in any continent that fancy or information might recommend. He could secure forthwith, if he wished it, cheap and comfortable means of transit to any country or climate without passport or other formality, could despatch his servant to the neighboring office of a bank for such supply of the precious metals as might seem convenient, and could then proceed abroad to foreign quarters, without knowledge of their religion, language, or customs, bearing coined wealth upon his person, and would consider himself greatly aggrieved and much surprised at the least interference. But, most important of all, he regarded this state of affairs as normal, certain, and permanent, except in the direction of further improvement, and any deviation from it as aberrant, scandalous, and avoidable. The projects and politics of militarism and imperialism, of racial and cultural rivalries, of monopolies, restrictions, and exclusion, which were to play the serpent to this paradise, were little more than the amusements of his daily newspaper, and appeared to exercise almost no influence at all on the ordinary course of social and economic life, the internationalization of which was nearly complete in practice.

It will assist us to appreciate the character and consequences of the Peace which we have imposed on our enemies, if I elucidate a little further some of the chief unstable elements, already present when war broke out, in the economic life of Europe.

## I. Population

In 1870 Germany had a population of about 40,000,000. By 1892 this figure had risen to 50,000,000, and by June 30, 1914, to about 68,000,000. In the years immediately preceding the war the annual increase was about 850,000, of whom an insignificant proportion emigrated. This great increase was only rendered possible by a far-reaching transformation of the economic structure of the country. From being agricultural and mainly self-supporting, Germany transformed herself into a vast and complicated industrial machine, dependent for its working on the equipoise of many factors outside Germany as well as within. Only by operating this machine, continuously and at full blast, could she find occupation at home for her increasing population and the means of purchasing their subsistence from abroad. The German machine was like a top which to maintain its equilibrium must spin ever faster and faster.

In the Austro-Hungarian Empire, which grew from about 40,000,000 in 1890 to at least 50,000,000 at the outbreak of war, the same tendency was present in a less degree, the annual excess of births over deaths being about half a million, out of which, however, there was an annual emigration of some quarter of a million persons.

To understand the present situation, we must apprehend with vividness what an extraordinary center of population the development of the Germanic system had enabled Central Europe to become. Before the war the population of Germany and Austria-Hungary together not only substantially exceeded that of the United States, but was about equal to that of the whole of North America. In these numbers, situated within a compact territory, lay the military strength of the Central Powers. But these same numbers—for even the war has not appreciably diminished them—if deprived of the means of life, remain a hardly less danger to European order.

European Russia increased her population in a degree even greater than Germany—from less than 100,000,000 in 1890 to about 150,000,000 at the outbreak of war; and in the year immediately preceding 1914 the excess of births over deaths in Russia as a whole was at the prodigious rate of two millions per annum. This inordinate growth in the population of Russia, which has not been widely noticed in England, has been nevertheless one of the most significant facts of recent years.

The great events of history are often due to secular changes in the growth of population and other fundamental economic causes, which, escaping by their gradual character the notice of contemporary observers, are attributed to the follies of statesmen or the fanaticism of atheists. Thus the extraordinary occurrences of the past two years in Russia, that vast upheaval of Society, which has overturned what seemed most stable —religion, the basis of property, the ownership of land, as well as forms of government and the hierarchy of classes—may owe more to the deep influences of expanding numbers than to Lenin or to Nicholas; and the disruptive powers of excessive national fecundity may have played a greater part in bursting the bonds of convention than either the power of ideas or the errors of autocracy.

## II. *Organization*

The delicate organization by which these peoples lived depended partly on factors internal to the system.

The interference of frontiers and of tariffs was reduced to a minimum, and not far short of three hundred millions of people lived within the three Empires of Russia, Germany, and Austria-Hungary. The various currencies, which were all maintained on a stable basis in relation to gold and to one another, facilitated the easy flow of capital and of trade to an extent the full value of which we only realize now, when we are deprived of its advantages. Over this great area there was an almost absolute security of property and of person.

These factors of order, security, and uniformity, which Europe had never before enjoyed over so wide and populous a territory or for so long a period, prepared the way for the organization of that vast mechanism of transport, coal distribution, and foreign trade which made possible an industrial order of life in the dense urban centers of new population. This is too well known to require detailed substantiation with figures. But it may be illustrated by the figures for coal, which has been the key to the industrial growth of Central Europe hardly less than of England; the output of German coal grew from 30,000,000 tons in 1871 to 70,000,000 tons in 1890, 110,000,000 tons in 1900, and 190,000,000 tons in 1913.

Round Germany as a central support the rest of the European economic system grouped itself, and on the prosperity and enterprise of Germany the prosperity of the rest of the Continent mainly depended. The increasing pace of Germany gave her neighbors an outlet for their products, in exchange for which the enterprise of the German merchant supplied them with their chief requirements at a low price.

The statistics of the economic interdependence of Germany and her neighbors are overwhelming. Germany was the best customer of Russia, Norway, Holland, Belgium, Switzerland, Italy, and Austria-Hungary; she was the second best customer of Great Britain, Sweden, and Denmark; and the third best customer of France. She was the largest source of supply to Russia, Norway, Sweden, Denmark, Holland, Switzerland, Italy, Austria-Hungary, Roumania, and Bulgaria; and the second largest source of supply to Great Britain, Belgium, and France.

In our own case we sent more exports to Germany than to any other country in the world except India, and we bought more from her than from any other country in the world except the United States.

There was no European country except those west of Germany which did not do more than a quarter of their total trade with her; and in the case of Russia, Austria-Hungary, and Holland the proportion was far greater.

Germany not only furnished these countries with trade, but, in the case of some of them, supplied a great part of the capital needed for their own development. Of Germany's pre-war foreign investments, amounting in all to about $6,250,000,000, not far short of $2,500,000,000 was invested in Russia, Austria-Hungary, Bulgaria, Roumania, and Turkey. And by the system of "peaceful penetration" she gave these countries not only capital, but, what they needed hardly less, organization. The whole of Europe east of the Rhine thus fell into the German industrial orbit, and its economic life was adjusted accordingly.

But these internal factors would not have been sufficient to enable the population to support itself without the co-operation of external factors also and of certain general dispositions common to the whole of Europe. Many of the circumstances already treated were true of Europe as a whole, and were not peculiar to the Central Empires. But all of what follows was common to the whole European system.

## III. The Psychology of Society

Europe was so organized socially and economically as to secure the maximum accumulation of capital. While there was some continuous improvement in the daily conditions of life of the mass of the population, Society was so framed as to throw a great part of the increased income into the control of the class least likely to consume it. The new rich of the nineteenth century were not brought up to large expenditures, and preferred the power which investment gave them to the pleasures of immediate consumption. In fact, it was precisely the *inequality* of the distribution of wealth which made possible those vast accumulations of fixed wealth and of capital improvements which distinguished that age from all others. Herein lay, in fact, the main justification of the Capitalist System. If the rich had spent their new wealth on their own enjoyments, the world would long ago have found such a régime intolerable. But like bees they saved and accumulated, not less to the advantage of the whole community because they themselves held narrower ends in prospect.

The immense accumulations of fixed capital which, to the great benefit of mankind, were built up during the half century before the war, could never have come about in a Society where wealth was divided equitably. The railways of the world, which that age built as a monument to posterity, were, not less than the Pyramids of Egypt, the work of labor which was not free to consume in immediate enjoyment the full equivalent of its efforts.

Thus this remarkable system depended for its growth on a double bluff or deception. On the one hand the laboring classes accepted from ignorance or powerlessness, or were compelled, persuaded, or cajoled by custom, convention, authority, and the well-established order of Society into accepting, a situation in which they could call their own very little of the cake that they and Nature and the capitalists were co-operating to produce. And on the other hand the capitalist classes were allowed to call the best part of the cake theirs and were theoretically free to consume it, on the tacit underlying condition that they consumed very little of it in practice. The duty of "saving" became nine-tenths of virtue and the growth of the cake the object of true religion. There grew round the non-consumption of the cake all those instincts of puritanism which in other ages has withdrawn itself from the world and has neglected the arts of production as well as those of enjoyment. And so the cake increased; but to what end was not clearly contemplated. Individuals would be exhorted not so much to abstain as to defer, and to cultivate the pleasures of security and anticipation. Saving was for old age or for your children; but this was only in theory,—the virtue of the cake was that it was never to be consumed, neither by you nor by your children after you.

In writing thus I do not necessarily disparage the practices of that generation. In the unconscious recesses of its being Society knew what it was about. The cake was really very small in proportion to the appetites of consumption, and no one, if it were shared all round, would be much the better off by the cutting of it. Society was working not for the small pleasures of today but for the future security and improvement of the race,—in fact for "progress." If only the cake were not cut but was allowed to grow in the geometrical proportion predicted by Malthus of population, but not less true of compound interest, perhaps a day might come when there would at last be enough to go round, and when posterity could enter into the enjoyment of *our* labors. In that day overwork, overcrowding, and underfeeding would have come to an end, and men, secure of the comforts and necessities of the body, could proceed to the nobler exercises of their faculties. One geometrical ratio might cancel another, and the nineteenth century was able to forget the fertility of the species in a contemplation of the dizzy virtues of compound interest.

There were two pitfalls in this prospect: lest, population still outstripping accumulation, our self-denials promote not happiness but numbers; and lest the cake be after all consumed, prematurely, in war, the consumer of all such hopes.

But these thoughts lead too far from my present purpose. I seek only to point out that the principle of accumulation based on inequality was a vital part of the pre-war order of Society and of progress as we then understood it, and to emphasize that this principle depended on unstable psychological conditions, which it may be impossible to recreate. It was not natural for a population, of whom so few enjoyed the comforts of life, to accumulate so hugely. The war has disclosed the possibility of consumption to all and the vanity of abstinence to many. Thus the bluff is discovered; the laboring classes may be no longer willing to forego so largely, and the capitalist classes, no longer confident of the future, may seek to enjoy more fully their liberties of consumption so long as they last, and thus precipitate the hour of their confiscation.

*≈§ Part Four*

# *Mass Society in Crisis: Since 1914*

# ⇜§ WHAT IS BACK OF THE WAR

*Albert J. Beveridge*

*The outbreak of World War I unleashed not only the horrors of modern
total war and modern totalitarianism, but also a host of technological
and social revolutions which have made the nineteenth century in many
ways as distant from our own age as are the Middle Ages.*

*Debate as to the origin of the conflict probably will never end, though
by now most of the materials for understanding at least the superficial
aspects of the story are available to the historian. Endless pages have
been spent on the question of responsibility—an issue necessarily
involving more than an objective recitation of the facts. On the whole,
historians have tended to reject the wartime sentiment that either side
bears sole guilt. Aside from determining blame, many have turned their
attention to separating the various levels on which the background of
the war can be discussed: the immediate diplomatic activity in the
summer of 1914, between the date of the assassination of the heir
to the Austro-Hungarian throne and the onset of hostilities; the
medium-range international tensions of the decade or two before 1914,
during which the rivalries between Germany and England and between
Russia and Austria-Hungary intensified to the point of violence,
crystallizing into the two massive alliances which faced each other that
summer; and the underlying implications of the entire modern state
system and of advanced capitalism.*

*The following selection seeks to introduce the subject in a concrete
manner. Albert J. Beveridge was an American newspaperman who visited
Europe in the first year of the war to determine what was "back of the
war," as the title of his book states. His conversations with people of
many countries and social positions give an impression of what alert
Europeans thought they were fighting for. The reading consists of two of
these conversations: the first with the German shipping magnate Albert
Ballin, a very influential force in the circles surrounding the German
Emperor William II, and the second with the French munitions
manufacturer Eugene Schneider. Through these conversations we
encounter not only the political and economic reasons (or rationalizations)
for the war, but also a good deal of the subrational national hostility,
reflecting the poisoned atmosphere of what one writer has called the
"international anarchy." It is interesting to detect the differences in the
way Germany and France approached the war. It is no less interesting,
however, to observe the similarities of their positions and arguments.*

*They were all Europeans, and the fact that the Frenchman's name is of*
*German derivation and the German's of French symbolizes that the war*
*was really more of a civil war within European civilization than a struggle*
*between two different ways of life.*

## The Master Builder of Germany's Sea-going Commerce

Consider now the views of one of Germany's greatest business men. General Director Albert Ballin is the genius who built up the Hamburg-American Line from a small concern, hopelessly bankrupt, to the largest steamship company in the world. In Germany he is considered one of the greatest, if not the very first, constructive business mind in Europe. There are Germans who say that, as a commercial organizer, he is unequalled by any living man in any country.

General Director Ballin is the direct antithesis of Professor von Harnack; he devotes his large ability to purely practical business and he is an Hebrew—yet his patriotism is as intense and self-sacrificing as is that of the purely Teutonic thinker and divine.

General Director Ballin is now giving all his energy to the organization of Germany's food production and distribution.

"I never worked so hard in my life, not even when I was a young man," said Director Ballin; "and I never worked so gladly."

"I am trying to get at the bottom of this war," I remarked. "We Americans want to know the real cause of it, and who began it."

"Well," answered General Director Ballin, "if you put aside the incidents and get down to the first cause, you will find that it was commercial rivalry, and at bottom England began it. She could have prevented it. Russia never would have gone on if she had not been sure about England; even at the last, England could have ended the whole thing without war. But she did not want to do it, and she did not do it. We hold her responsible; and she is responsible."

"I can not understand," I observed, "why England should have wanted such a war as this."

"She was not farsighted," answered Director Ballin, "and she miscalculated. England was sure that with her aid, Russia and France would overwhelm Germany very quickly. England thought that the combination of allies which she had arranged would bring us to our knees very soon, and that then she could dictate the terms of peace. But she had no idea of the strength of the German people."

"But what was her reason?" I pressed.

"She wished to break down her greatest commercial rival. We work harder, longer and more scientifically than the English. A long monopoly of the world's markets made them too rich. Compared with the Germans, they are idle—all of us Germans,

Albert J. Beveridge, *What Is Back of the War* (Indianapolis: The Bobbs-Merrill Company, Inc., 1915), pp. 176–184, 296–305.

rich and poor alike, work every day and at long hours every day. The result was that we were dividing the world's markets with England, and, indeed, taking her markets from her. That is the real cause of England's action."

"But how could she help that by beating you in war?" I asked.

"In many ways; breaking up our commercial connections over the world would be one way," said Herr Ballin.

"But that would mean a long war," I observed. "A quick victory over Germany would not break up your foreign trade, seriously. You could recover it very quickly. Nothing but a long war, a war for years could root out your commercial connections in other countries, so that you would have to begin all over again, and start where you started forty years ago. Do you think that it will be a long war?"

"I hardly think Russia and France will care to go to such lengths. Still, it may be a long war—a very long war," responded Herr Ballin.

"Frankly, how long can Germany keep up the war?" I ventured to inquire.

"We can keep it up for years, and we shall if necessary," said Herr Ballin. "We know that it is a question of existence with us. I suppose you have heard that statement before; but it is true."

"Have you the requisite resources?" I asked.

"Why, yes," quickly replied Herr Ballin, with emphasis. "Have you not seen that already? Financially we are in wonderful condition. Take the question of food. Have you seen any lack of it?"

"Why, then, your new food law?" I inquired.

"That is the best proof of all," answered Herr Ballin. "We have more than enough for this year without any law. But we are looking out for next year and the year after that and the year after that."

"But America thinks you do not have enough copper."

"We have large quantities of copper," declared Director Ballin. "We have not even touched our extra copper. Just take one item. If worst came to worst, the wires on our electric street-car lines alone would give us 120,000 tons of copper, which is more than enough for one year. We could easily replace them with iron wires. But that would only be an emergency which is not yet in sight. Then we could take the copper roofs of houses. And with both of these used up, we still would have left from other sources many times the quantity of copper yielded by both these sources.

"But without touching even our electric street-car wires, we have enough copper to last for a very long time. And if we had to use all the copper of every kind, for the purposes of war, which is now in use in Germany, in other forms, we could carry the war on almost indefinitely."

"And oil? We in America think you are short of oil. Is not Galicia your chief natural supply of oil in such a war as this, and was it not for that reason that Russia made the drive on Galicia?" I inquired.

"It may have been; I do not know. But the oil question does not trouble us," Herr Ballin asserted. "We are making a substitute for benzine; wood alcohol is another excellent substitute; and there are still others. Besides we have plenty of oil and are getting more."

"Is is not rather wasteful to use your oil on taxicabs and automobiles? I notice the usual number of taxicabs in Berlin, Hamburg and every other city. Is not that a great waste of oil?"

"Oh," said Herr Ballin, "those taxicabs are run by alcohol. That is a good example of why we are not troubled about oil."

"But getting back to how England can hurt you commercially by war; while she might break up your commerce by a long-drawn-out conflict, she could not do that by a quick victory which you said she thought she would have," I remarked.

"Oh, yes," answered Herr Ballin, "if she could make terms of peace she could do anything she liked. She could limit the size of our ships. She could put a war indemnity on us so heavy as to break us. Worst of all, she could require the dismemberment of our Imperial government—that is, our central government."

"I have heard that before," I observed. "I have been told that Germany's industrial and economic development—her management of railway rates, trusts, tariffs and all the elements of Germany's economic progress, has been possible only by reason of your central government; and that it could not have been accomplished in the divided condition that existed before the central Imperial government was established, and would be ended if the central government were overthrown and the old condition restored."

"That is exactly true," answered Herr Ballin; "and that is exactly what England would have required had she won. At least I think so."

"Is that what is meant, then, by the talk about loving the German people, the Germany of Goethe and Schiller, but hating this Imperial government with its militarism?"

"Why, of course it is!"

"Most of the talk I have heard, whether at the front in France, or in a village in the heart of Germany, alwayst goes back to what you said—the necessity of Germany's getting her goods to market, and England's wanting to prevent her from doing so; at least business men and working men, whom I find very well informed indeed, reason it out that way. The Hamburg-American line is the center of Germany's shipping activities—how far is it willing to go; how far are you willing to go?" I asked.

"To the very end; to the last ship," exclaimed the great shipping magnate. "As for myself, I am willing and prepared to come out of this a poor man, if necessary. I should be happy to do so if that would help Germany to win, as she will."

"Americans do not understand how you can win. After weeks in Germany it is hard for me to grasp this seemingly unanimous faith of the German people in victory. Do you really think, yourself, that Germany will win? You may speak to me in frankness and confidence. I give you my word that I will not repeat your answer if you do not wish me to," said I.

"Yes, I believe we shall win," replied Herr Ballin. "I know we will win. I do not think it, I *know* it. And you may repeat it as much as you like. I have not the least doubt on that point."

"In the United States there are those who fear that Germany intends to violate our Monroe Doctrine by occupying parts of South America."

"That, of course, is sheer nonsense. We want to trade in South America as we are doing now; and every place else. But nothing more."

"But it is said that your idea is to get possessions all over the world."

"The facts are the best answer to that," said Herr Ballin. "Since 1870 France has built up a great colonial empire-—Algiers, Tunis, for example. What have we got? A part of east Africa and southwest Africa, and the Kiouw Chow experiment. That is all."

"But Belgium; will you keep Belgium?"

"I don't know," said Herr Ballin; "but personally I hope so. But the main thing we do want is such a peace as will leave us alone to work and trade without interference."

"Speaking of Belgium, your violation of her neutrality was one cause of America's unfavorable public opinion toward Germany. Do the business men of Germany approve the attack on Belgium?" I inquired.

"Belgium had a treaty with Germany as well as with France and England; yet she made a secret agreement with France and England in violation of her treaty with Germany," asserted the General Director. "She destroyed her own neutrality. We have proved this to the world now, and nobody has denied it. We have still more proof. One single circumstance ought to satisfy anybody—I mean the large stores of English war material which we found in Maubeuge. That is only one example of many that the agreement was being carried through. But besides these examples we have the documentary proof; and as I say, it is not denied. Answering your question directly, German business men heartily approve our advance through Belgium under the circumstances.

"This suggests to me the food question again," continued Herr Ballin. "We are fighting this war in the enemy's country—in France on one side and in Russian Poland on the other side. So the country we occupy, especially in the west, is furnishing a good deal of the food consumed by our armies. This is not an important item, for we have enough food within Germany itself. And yet, it is important, too, when you think that we already have nearly 700,000 prisoners in Germany, whom we must feed, and are feeding very well indeed."[1]

"Does the fact that you are fighting the war in France and Russian Poland have anything to do with your belief, your confidence that Germany will win?" I asked.

"Yes, of course, They never can drive us back to the German frontier and carry the war into Germany. That ought to be plain to anybody. But that is not the chief reason for our certainty of winning. The spirit of the people; their absolute unity; the feeling of all of us that it is life or death with us; the willingness of every German, high and low, rich and poor, man and woman, to go to the end, even to poverty and death itself; the superiority of our men in the field, both officers and men—things like these are what make us know that we shall win in the end."

"But, will the women of Germany consent to allow the war to go to such lengths?" I asked.

"The women of Germany are as strong for the war as any man in the country," declared Herr Ballin. "I can give you dozens of examples, within my own personal knowledge. Here is one, which came to my attention only yesterday. A friend of mine, a lady of wealth, who already has four sons at the front; her fifth son is in America and has not been able to get back. The mother is grieving because this fifth son has not been able to get to the front also, to fight for Germany. You can write a book of

[1] *This conversation occurred January 28, 1915.*

examples of this spirit among the German women. They are our strongest support. I suggest that you talk to German women yourself. You will find there the best proof of the spirit that animates Germany in this war."

*     *     *

### France's Master Manufacturer

To only a few men in France is accorded industrial supremacy. One of these everybody in France agrees is Eugene Schneider, owner and active manager of the world-famed Le Creusot works, and whose artillery has attracted the attention of all nations. There are those in France who say that Monsieur Schneider is the leading business man of the Republic. He is still a young man, only forty-six years old. Earnestness and sincerity are the qualities which first strike the observer when meeting this unusual man.

But it is not in his constructive business genius and its remarkable results that Monsieur Schneider takes most pride. On the contrary, it is the social betterment of his forty thousand employees which to him, and, indeed, to his whole family, are the chief source of gratification.

In familiar talk at a family luncheon the conversation turned, of course, to France's desperate crisis. Madame Schneider's comments are typical of those of many French women of the highest classes.

"We are all one family," said Madame Schneider. "Since four generations the contact was always absolutely close. The elderly people say with pride and devotion: 'I worked under the orders of your grandfather and father,' and should anything happen to one of our children we feel the whole population would go through the same anxiety as ourselves. Everybody in the place is ready to help and protect them, if needed, as we are ready to help and protect any of theirs!"

"You see," said Monsieur Schneider, "it is the spirit back of any enterprise that makes it successful, and not merely the mechanics of business plan and detail."

"And," remarked Madame Schneider, "just that is the most remarkable thing in regenerated France. It began a few years before the war. The young generation talked of the serious, the elevated. We noticed it in our sons, and everybody else's children we found to be just the same. The solid, the noble, a mixture of energy and kindness are in vogue; the frivolous is no longer fashionable."

"Yes," said Monsieur Schneider, "this spirit of our people is the soul of the conflict, so far as France is concerned. It surprised everybody, even ourselves; most of all, it surprised the Germans. They thought us decadent; they found us and we found ourselves, recrudescent. Indeed, they did find us weak, in the sense that we were not prepared. But now we are strong; from the first day we grew stronger. At first we were weakest; now we are strongest."

"What, Monsieur Schneider, is the opinion of the French business world as to the real cause of this war?" I asked.

"The carrying into action of the German tendency to take what they want, or think they need, whether it belongs to them or not," answered the famous French gun manufacturer. "It is part of the German mental make-up to take, take, take. We have been threatened with this for more than forty years. There was always over us the shadow of aggression."

"Do you mean that French business opinion thought Germany intended to take anything from France, in a physical sense, such as territory or colonies?" I inquired.

"Yes, we are convinced that this was Germany's purpose," he replied. "The northern and eastern parts of our country are very, very rich. Our best ore and coal mines are there; our best agricultural district is there; our finest textile establishments, such as lace factories, are there; our greatest, or at least very important, steel and iron works are there. And this territory adjoins Germany or Belgium. The Germans said: 'We like that country—why not take it?' There is the adjacent district, with its ports of Calais, Le Havre, Dunkirk and Cherbourg. The Germans said: 'These ports are good for us to have, too. From them we look across the Channel to England. With them we could at least divide the Channel with England. They would be an immense advantage in our program of sea power; in any event, it is good for us to have them. Let us take them then.' "

"But," I remarked, "would not Germany see that this might be another Alsace and Lorraine—a source of trouble and of possible revolution within her own dominion? If so, would the Germans want to take this French territory as a matter of cold deliberate plan? Would she not have another hostile population on her hands?"

"She would not reason so from her experience in Alsace and Lorraine," Monsieur Schneider responded. "Many of the inhabitants of those provinces left rather than to endure German rule. Others stayed for as long as twenty years, and then left. The places of all these were taken by Germans. So Germany could well reason that the Champaigne, Picardy and other districts would also become Germanized. I do not think that the difficulty of an unfriendly population would have deterred her."

"But may not Germany have learned a lesson from her own experience with Alsace and Lorraine, just as the British did from their treatment of us and our revolution, which their treatment caused?"

"Perhaps she might," answered Monsieur Schneider. "Perhaps she has learned that kindness, rather than force, is the wise treatment of a subject people. But all of that is immaterial in view of her actual purpose to take and our purpose to resist being taken. We do not intend that France shall become Germanized."

"But," I remarked, in surprise, "do French business men really think that the Germans intend to Germanize France?"

"Why, they were doing it already. Perhaps it would have been wiser for them if they had gone on with their program of peaceful Germanization."

"What do you mean by peaceful Germanization?"

"Why," said Monsieur Schneider, "all over France German business men were coming in and taking our commerce. German laborers were displacing French working men. And with all this went Germany's desire to be the first Power of Europe, and later on, of the world."

"But what we Americans can not see is how Germany's asserting that she was the first Power would hurt France, or any other nation, practically. Would not French business men go on doing their business, French working men continue at their labor and France exist?"

"Well," answered Monsieur Schneider, "that might be if they only intended to assert that they were the first Power. But then they would at once use their power to take our place (and, perhaps, later on, your own place) in the commerce of the world. Then, of course, we might still exist, but under German power, and only to do as we should be told to do by Germany and the Germans, and never to do what we might want to do ourselves."

"Do you mean that, even without war? Just by the fact that Germany claimed to be and was acknowledged to be the first Power of Europe?" I asked.

"Yes, indeed," said Monsieur Schneider, "more concrete and immediate. If Germany wins, a great part of France is gone. That is plain from what already has happened. Germany to-day occupies some of the richest territory of France—the mining district, where also is located our best textile and metal industries—is still in German hands now. It is clear to us that if Germany wins France is reduced to nothing. That would mean the reduction of millions of French men and women to a worse position than that of the Alsatians before the war; the loss of some of the most venerated places and monuments in France, the battlefields of Valny and Montmirail, the cathedral of Rheims, the cottage of Joan of Arc, etc. So it is war for existence on our part."

"In America the feminist movement is very strong, and the question is on the lips of our people: How long will the women of France let this war go on?"

"I can answer that," said Madame Schneider. "Our sons are young, hardly more than boys. When the war began they enrolled at once, and, dear as they are to us, I immediately consented. France is our common mother, and no mother in France would keep her sons away from that absolute duty; to protect and save France. You should read, as I have, the letters of French mothers to their sons, and the letters of these sons to their mothers."

"May it be, then," I asked, "that this is a people's war?"

"It seems to be," answered Monsieur Schneider.

"If that is so, it may last for a long time."

"It may, indeed," replied Monsieur Schneider, "though I do not know. But long or short, we shall fight to the end."

"Yes," said Madame Schneider, "we want to finish while we are about it. We do not want our children to go through what we are going through now."

I said, "The Schneider guns are playing an important part in the war and are considered by French military men as superior to the Krupp guns. The world is interested in your establishment. How did it make headway?"

"Our works made most of the French guns from the time of Louis XVI, 1782, to the end of Napoleon's reign, 1815," Monsieur Schneider explained. "Then after the final peace a law passed that no private enterprise should make guns for foreign countries. This law was enforced until after the Franco-Prussian War (one of the many reasons for France's failure in that 1870 war was the inferiority of our artillery). After the Franco-Prussian War this law was repealed. During this long period gun manufacture was a government monopoly; we then manufactured machinery, engines, metallic bridges, all kinds of iron and steel work, ships, and also a large amount of parts of guns, which were designed and mounted in government's concerns. I then said to my father: 'Artillery is the future weapon of war. So let us make guns again, not only, or even chiefly, as a good business plan, but also and principally for our country's defense.' Meanwhile, of course, the Krupps had built their great establishment, which was encouraged by the German government, whereas we were not encouraged by our own government."

"How were you not encouraged by your government, and how were you then able to make guns at all? For whom did you make guns?" I inquired.

"We always made parts of guns for the French navy and army—but we were only allowed to make parts of guns," answered Monsieur Schneider. "These parts were mounted by and in government concerns."

"How then, did you get any foothold at all?" I asked.

"Only by making better guns, and asking other governments to test our guns with any others," responded Monsieur Schneider. "It was a hard pull. I would go to a country and say: 'We have better guns.' That country's government would say: 'Why, then, does not your own government let you make its guns entirely; the Germans do that? The Kaiser says the Krupp guns are best. Your government does not say yours are best.' And all I could answer was: 'Try them. Test them. Compare them.' So, little by little, we made headway. If our artillery should prove better, it is only because I never have been satisfied that anything we did was the best that we could do; but kept on trying to do better. Now the Schneider guns have been adopted by most governments in the world, as well as by the French government; and, of course, you know, for example, in the Balkan war, the Servians, Greeks and Bulgarians proved they were the best."

"What do you expect, Monsieur Schneider, will be the result of the war?"

"Our victory," answered Monsieur Schneider. "That is settled now."

"But," I suggested, "what will you do with your victory if you get it?"

"We shall make it impossible for France to be disturbed again—at least for one or two generations," responded Monsieur Schneider.

"And how will you do that if, as you seem to think possible, this is a war of peoples? There must now be shaping in the public mind some outline, however vague, of what you will do if you win. Especially should this be true of business men whose habit of mind is to think in concrete terms," I suggested.

"That is in the future. Events shape policies, not policies events," Monsieur Schneider answered.

"If you mean to destroy the military power of Germany, would you do it by dismembering the Imperial government," I asked.

"I do not know, I can not say," answered Monsieur Schneider. "That would be difficult. It is hard to tell people what they must do, and then make them do it."

"Do French business men contemplate disarmament of all nations?" I asked; "would this mean a limitation of navies as well as armies? If so, on what principle? For example, must England have only the same size navy as France? Would England agree to that?" I inquired.

"That is a hard problem. It is for the future," said Monsieur Schneider.

"Suppose disarmament did come, how would that affect your industry?"

"Scarcely at all," said Monsieur Schneider. "We should at once turn all our energies to the manufacture of engines, locomotives and other things made of metal. Indeed, that is our chief business, anyhow."

"But," said I, "what would become of the Krupps?"

"Just the same," answered Monsieur Schneider. "They, too, manufacture as many things for peace as for war."

"As a result of this war, do you anticipate that both you and the Krupps will cease making guns, armor plate, battleships, submarines?" I asked.

(For the Schneider works, like the Krupp works, manufacture armor plate, build ships, construct submarines; and the Schneiders have factories at Le Havre, Bordeaux and other places, just as the Krupps have factories at Kiel, Stettin, etc.)

"I do not," positively answered Monsieur Schneider. "That would mean universal peace. But universal peace would mean that every nation, people and country would agree never to fight again, and that some power could force them to keep that compact. Such a prospect is not in the immediate future, to say the least," said Monsieur Schneider. "I say this disinterestedly, for we make more work for purposes of peace than we do guns and armor plate and ships for purposes of war. It is a matter of self-respecting safety. After all, a nation is like a man. What do I do myself? I fence and ride every.day. I do this in order to keep my body and mind in perfect condition to do my work principally, but also there always is the thought of being my own man and being prepared to assert that fact. I mean to harm nobody; but if a highwayman holds me up on the street I hope I should be able to give a good account of myself. The man who is weak, flaccid and powerless is anybody's prey. True, nobody may harm him, but anybody could harm him. It is just so with nations."

# *Wilsonianism and Realpolitik*

*The cynical policy of unscrupulous expediency frequently called* Realpolitik *is often pointed to as one of the major roots of modern war. World War I seemed to many the most egregious example of all time; what seemed to be needed was an international environment in which strictly ethical principles dominated all policy decisions in international conduct. So ran the public statements, for example, of Woodrow Wilson, President of the United States. Considering the enormous following Wilson received as a result of these utterances, the concept of ethical diplomacy may be called "Wilsonianism." Wilson continued into the postwar settlement of 1919 his wartime crusade against the "method of the Congress of Vienna" (i.e., emphasis on power politics and peace negotiations on the basis of power relationships), and his stance has become the normal one for most European and American statesmen ever since, at least in their public messages. Hostility to power politics has by no means been unanimous, however; to many observers,* Realpolitik *is a normal and necessary constituent of international politics, and the Wilsonian position is either naïveté, folly, or a mask for an even more unscrupulous policy of deceit and hunger for power.*

*The following selections, although belonging to a moment in February, 1918, raise the controversy over* Realpolitik *in a number of ways that show its continued relevance. The first selection is a speech in which Wilson reiterates the terms of his policy of a just peace (elsewhere embodied in the famous Fourteen Points for postwar reconstruction) and comments on the replies of the Austrian and German governments to his peace offers. The second selection consists of summaries of various German press reactions to the speech. It was to be another nine months before the German army was brought to the point of collapse and an armistice signed. Since the Germans assumed the peace would embody the Wilsonian concept and since the 1919 peace treaties in fact bore little resemblance to it, there seemed some justification in postwar Germany for the cynical view that not only had* Realpolitik *triumphed once more, but international relations would always be based on power.*

## ADDRESS OF THE PRESIDENT OF THE UNITED STATES DELIVERED AT A JOINT SESSION OF THE TWO HOUSES OF CONGRESS, FEBRUARY 11, 1918

*Woodrow Wilson*

GENTLEMEN OF THE CONGRESS: On the 8th of January I had the honor of addressing you on the objects of the war as our people conceive them. The Prime Minister of Great Britain had spoken in similar terms on the 5th of January. To these addresses the German Chancellor [Count v. Hertling] replied on the 24th and Count Czernin, for Austria, on the same day. It is gratifying to have our desire so promptly realized that all exchanges of view on this great matter should be made in the hearing of all the world.

Count Czernin's reply, which is directed chiefly to my own address of the 8th of January, is uttered in a very friendly tone. He finds in my statement a sufficiently encouraging approach to the views of his own Government to justify him in believing that it furnishes a basis for a more detailed discussion of purposes by the two Governments. He is represented to have intimated that the views he was expressing had been communicated to me beforehand and that I was aware of them at the time he was uttering them; but in this I am sure he was misunderstood. I had received no intimation of what he intended to say. There was, of course, no reason why he should communicate privately with me. I am quite content to be one of his public audience.

Count von Hertling's reply is, I must say, very vague and very confusing. It is full of equivocal phrases and leads it is not clear where. But it is certainly in a very dif-

*Papers Relating to the Foreign Relations of the United States:* Supplement 1 (The World War) (Washington, D.C.: U.S. Government Printing Office, 1933), I, 108–113.

ferent tone from that of Count Czernin, and apparently of an opposite purpose. It confirms, I am sorry to say, rather than removes, the unfortunate impression made by what we had learned of the conferences at Brest-Litovsk.* His discussion and acceptance of our general principles lead him to no practical conclusions. He refuses to apply them to the substantive items which must constitute the body of any final settlement. He is jealous of international action and of international counsel. He accepts, he says, the principle of public diplomacy, but he appears to insist that it be confined, at any rate in this case, to generalities and that the several particular questions of territory and sovereignty, the several questions upon whose settlement must depend the acceptance of peace by the twenty-three states now engaged in the war, must be discussed and settled, not in general council, but severally by the nations most immediately concerned by interest or neighborhood. He agrees that the seas should be free, but looks askance at any limitation to that freedom by international action in the interest of the common order. He would without reserve be glad to see economic barriers removed between nation and nation, for that could in no way impede the ambitions of the military party with whom he seems constrained to keep on terms. Neither does he raise objection to a limitation of armaments. That matter will be settled of itself, he thinks, by the economic conditions which must follow the war. But the German colonies, he demands, must be returned without debate. He will discuss with no one but the representatives of Russia what disposition shall be made of the peoples and the lands of the Baltic provinces; with no one but the Government of France the "conditions" under which French territory shall be evacuated; and only with Austria what shall be done with Poland. In the determination of all questions affecting the Balkan states he defers, as I understand him, to Austria and Turkey; and with regard to the agreements to be entered into concerning the non-Turkish peoples of the present Ottoman Empire, to the Turkish authorities themselves. After a settlement all around, effected in this fashion, by individual barter and concession, he would have no objection, if I correctly interpret his statement, to a league of nations which would undertake to hold the new balance of power steady against external disturbance.

It must be evident to everyone who understands what this war has wrought in the opinion and temper of the world that no general peace, no peace worth the infinite sacrifices of these years of tragical suffering, can possibly be arrived at in any such fashion. The method the German Chancellor proposes is the method of the Congress of Vienna. We cannot and will not return to that. What is at stake now is the peace of the world. What we are striving for is a new international order based upon broad and universal principles of right and justice,—no mere peace of shreds and patches. Is it possible that Count von Hertling does not see that, does not grasp it, is in fact living in his thought in a world dead and gone? Has he utterly forgotten the Reichstag resolutions of the 19th of July,† or does he deliberately ignore them? They spoke of the conditions of a general peace, not of national aggrandizement or of arrangements between state and state. The peace of the world depends upon the just settlement of each of the several problems to which I adverted in my

* [Between Germany and the Russian Bolshevik leaders, attempting to create a peace treaty which would take Russia out of the war. (*Ed.*)]

† [The German parliament had passed a resolution advocating an end to the war based on a peace without territorial aggrandizement. (*Ed.*)]

recent address to the Congress. I, of course, do not mean that the peace of the world depends upon the acceptance of any particular set of suggestions as to the way in which those problems are to be dealt with. I mean only that those problems each and all affect the whole world; that unless they are dealt with in a spirit of unselfish and unbiased justice, with a view to the wishes, the natural connections, the racial aspirations, the security, and the peace of mind of the peoples involved, no permanent peace will have been attained. They cannot be discussed separately or in corners. None of them constitutes a private or separate interest from which the opinion of the world may be shut out. Whatever affects the peace affects mankind, and nothing settled by military force, if settled wrong, is settled at all. It will presently have to be reopened.

Is Count von Hertling not aware that he is speaking in the court of mankind, that all the awakened nations of the world now sit in judgment on what every public man, of whatever nation, may say on the issues of a conflict which has spread to every region of the world? The Reichstag resolutions of July themselves frankly accepted the decisions of that court. There shall be no annexations, no contributions, no punitive damages. Peoples are not to be handed about from one sovereignty to another by an international conference or an understanding between rivals and antagonists. National aspirations must be respected; peoples may now be dominated and governed only by their own consent. "Self-determination" is not a mere phrase. It is an imperative principle of action, which statesmen will henceforth ignore at their peril. We cannot have general peace for the asking, or by the mere arrangements of a peace conference. It cannot be pieced together out of individual understandings between powerful states. All the parties to this war must join in the settlement of every issue anywhere involved in it; because what we are seeking is a peace that we can all unite to guarantee and maintain and every item of it must be submitted to the common judgment whether it be right and fair, an act of justice, rather than a bargain between sovereigns.

The United States has no desire to interfere in European affairs or to act as arbiter in European territorial disputes. She would disdain to take advantage of any internal weakness or disorder to impose her own will upon another people. She is quite ready to be shown that the settlements she has suggested are not the best or the most enduring. They are only her own provisional sketch of principles and of the way in which they should be applied. But she entered this war because she was made a partner, whether she would or not, in the sufferings and indignities inflicted by the military masters of Germany, against the peace and security of mankind; and the conditions of peace will touch her as nearly as they will touch any other nation to which is entrusted a leading part in the maintenance of civilization. She cannot see her way to peace until the causes of this war are removed, its renewal rendered as nearly as may be impossible.

This war had its roots in the disregard of the rights of small nations and of nationalities which lacked the union and the force to make good their claim to determine their own allegiances and their own forms of political life. Covenants must now be entered into which will render such things impossible for the future; and those covenants must be backed by the united force of all the nations that love justice and are willing to maintain it at any cost. If territorial settlements and the political relations of great populations which have not the organized power to resist are to be determined by the contracts of the powerful governments which consider themselves most directly affected, as Count von Hertling proposes, why may not economic questions also? It has come about in the altered world in which we now find ourselves that justice and the rights of peoples affect the whole field of international dealing as much as access to raw materials and fair and equal conditions of trade. Count von Hertling wants the essential bases of commercial and industrial life to be safeguarded by common agreement and guarantee, but he cannot expect that to be conceded him if the other matters to be determined by the articles of peace are not handled in the same way as items in the final accounting. He cannot ask the benefit of common agreement in the one field without according it in the other. I take it for granted that he sees that separate and selfish compacts with regard to trade and the  essential materials of manufacture would afford no foundation for peace. Neither, he may rest assured, will separate and selfish compacts with regard to provinces and peoples.

Count Czernin seems to see the fundamental elements of peace with clear eyes and does not seek to obscure them. He sees that an independent Poland, made up of all the indisputably Polish peoples who lie contiguous to one another, is a matter of European concern and must of course be conceded; that Belgium must be evacuated and restored, no matter what sacrifices and concessions that may involve; and that national aspirations must be satisfied, even within his own Empire, in the common interest of Europe and mankind. If he is silent about questions which touch the interest and purpose of his allies more nearly than they touch those of Austria only, it must of course be because he feels constrained, I suppose, to defer to Germany and Turkey in the circumstances. Seeing and conceding, as he does, the essential principles involved and the necessity of candidly applying them, he naturally feels that Austria can respond to the purpose of peace as expressed by the United States with less embarrassment than could Germany. He would probably have gone much farther had it not been for the embarrassments of Austria's alliances and of her dependence upon Germany.

After all, the test of whether it is possible for either government to go any further in this comparison of views is simple and obvious. The principles to be applied are these:

First, that each part of the final settlement must be based upon the essential justice of that particular case and upon such adjustments as are most likely to bring a peace that will be permanent;

Second, that peoples and provinces are not to be bartered about from sovereignty to sovereignty as if they were mere chattels and pawns in a game, even the great game, now forever discredited, of the balance of power; but that

Third, every territorial settlement involved in this war must be made in the interest and for the benefit of the populations concerned, and not as a part of any mere adjustment or compromise of claims amongst rival states; and

Fourth, that all well defined national aspirations shall be accorded the utmost satisfaction that can be accorded them without introducing new or perpetuating old elements of discord and antagonism that would be likely in time to break the peace of Europe and consequently of the world.

A general peace erected upon such foundations can be discussed. Until such a peace can be secured we have no choice but to go on. So far as we can judge, these principles that we regard as fundamental are already everywhere accepted as imperative except among the spokesmen of the military and annexationist party in Germany. If they have anywhere else been rejected, the objectors have not been sufficiently numerous or influential to make their voices audible. The tragical circumstance is that this one party in Germany is apparently willing and able to send millions of men to their death to prevent what all the world now sees to be just.

I would not be a true spokesman of the people of the United States if I did not say once more that we entered this war upon no small occasion, and that we can never turn back from a course chosen upon principle. Our resources are in part mobilized now, and we shall not pause until they are mobilized in their entirety. Our armies are rapidly going to the fighting front, and will go more and more rapidly. Our whole strength will be put into this war of emancipation,—emancipation from the threat and attempted mastery of selfish groups of autocratic rulers,—whatever the difficulties and present partial delays. We are indomitable in our power of independent action and can in no circumstances consent to live in a world governed by intrigue and force. We believe that our own desire for a new international order under which reason and justice and the common interests of mankind shall prevail is the desire of enlightened men everywhere. Without that new order the world will be without peace and human life will lack tolerable conditions of existence and development. Having set our hand to the task of achieving it, we shall not turn back.

I hope that it is not necessary for me to add that no word of what I have said is intended as a threat. That is not the temper of our people. I have spoken thus only that the whole world may know the true spirit of America,—that men everywhere may know that our passion for justice and for self-government is no mere passion of words but a passion which, once set in action, must be satisfied. The power of the United States is a menace to no nation or people. It will never be used in aggression or for the aggrandizement of any selfish interest of our own. It springs out of freedom and is for the service of freedom.

## ❧ GERMAN PRESS COMMENT

*The Minister in the Netherlands (Garrett) to the Secretary of State*

THE HAGUE, *February 14, 1918*

*Tageblatt,* 13th: Wilson makes distinction between speeches of Hertling and Czernin. Difference did not pass unnoticed by German press at time, some papers favoring Hertling's language, others Czernin's. Hertling's speech did not entirely satisfy anybody. Wilson compliments Czernin's but does not take up suggestion which made his

*Papers Relating to the Foreign Relations of the United States:* Supplement I (The World War) (Washington, D.C.: U.S. Government Printing Office, 1933), I, 116–121.

speech particularly noteworthy, namely, exchange of opinion between two countries. Perhaps Wilson replied indirectly by saying that peace problems concerned all mankind, but all Wilson's fine words cannot make us forget decision of Versailles conference to continue war with utmost vigor until Allies' terms are accepted. Although United States was not represented at conference by delegate, Wilson must know there is no consequence [*consonance?*] between his message and Versailles declaration. President mentions Reichstag peace resolution which he thinks Hertling disregarded, but it must be remembered that resolution was not answered at time by any similar manifesto by Entente. It is true resolution lost much of its effect by Pan-German agitation* against it, but that very agitation was encouraged by Entente's continuance of "might policy," Clemenceau's elevation to power in France,† and repudiation Lansdowne's letter in England.‡ Wilson's speech is such in words and thoughts with which we can declare agreement forthwith; but very perspicacity with which [he] determines the difference between Berlin and Vienna utterances, Hertling's speech and Reichstag peace resolution, must reveal the differences between his words and Versailles declaration. He considers German Military and Annexationist Party sole obstacle to peace, but forgets that Clemenceau, the English times [*sic*] politicians and even Italian super-annexationists are still very influential. This new message shows Wilson's inclination to continue peace discussion and four principles which he [lays] down afford opportunity for serious reply as did his former fourteen points, but all this can have no practical value until whole policy of Entente decides in favor of general peace.

*Vorwärts*,§ 13th: Message brings us back to fundamental question, peace by force or peace by accommodation. American troops may appear in Europe but fact remains we cannot force America to peace nor can she force us. We are reminded of the words that Wilson said when still at peace with Germany, words that found readier echo in Germany than anything else he said: "If one side cannot overcome the other an understanding must be found." Question is whether new message can contribute to this understanding. In form it is undoubtedly highly peaceable and moderate, but leaves open the possibility that war must be pursued with all energy. Like so many speeches it is peace instrument and war means at same time. As war means it endeavours separate Germany and Austria and accentuate conflicts in Germany. It is fact that there are differences between German and Austrian policy and differences in Germany, that unity of military front is not equalled by unity of political front. There is unity in idea of defense alone. Hertling's speech was much criticized in Germany also, but it is not thinkable that Czernin's offer of Austro-American mediation will be made against wishes of German Government. On contrary it must be assumed Germany agreed. Undeniably there is close connection between German Government which Wilson treats so curtly and Austrian Government of which he speaks in such friendly manner. Germany cannot be completely alien to Austria's

* [I.e. extreme chauvinist activity. (*Ed.*)]

† [Clemenceau was thought of in Germany as violently anti-German. (*Ed.*)]

‡ [Advocating peace. (*Ed.*)]

§ [Official organ of the Social-Democratic Party. (*Ed.*)]

peace endeavors any more than Austria can be mere German satrap. Preliminary negotiations between Austria and America may initiate general peace. They might remove sharp conflict of views between Hertling and Wilson regarding method of negotiation. We cannot repeat too often that nothing stands in way of general conferences since whole German people is ready to reject with all means at its disposal claims of enemy imperialism to German possessions, and gratification of annexationist wishes is not will of German people, and cannot justify prolongation of war. German people stand united in defense against foreign annexationism, resisting in its overwhelming majority annexationism at home and waits impatiently for Government which will lead it to general peace. Wilson's four principles can be generally accepted in their general wording, but attempt to carry them out will immediately disclose antagonism of imperialism combating imperialism. Each side accepts general principles, but with ulterior [motives], and it is the hidden thoughts which must be given up before peace can be arranged. It remains to be seen whether Pan-Germans are obstacles to just peace as Wilson maintains or whether Pan-English, Pan-French or perhaps Pan-Poles, whom Wilson is favoring in remarkable manner, stand in way. The main point remains that both sides must recognize that an understanding is absolutely necessary to peace for this reason. Appropriate action must be taken by Germany to ascertain whether Wilson's statement that nothing stands in way of immediate peace discussion is mere diplomatic move or in reality the work for mankind. The German reply can only be that we too are immediately ready for peace discussions.

*Vossische*, 13th: Noteworthy that Wilson almost entirely approves Czernin's speech while he treats Hertling's speech with little approbation. It is plain from Wilson rejection of separate negotiations insisted on by Hertling that America wants presiding seat in international tribunal in order to realize America's real war aims which include prevention German-Russian-Japanese alliance which would defeat Anglo-Saxon world supremacy plans. Gerard endeavored to induce Bethmann Hollweg* to annex in east, likewise aimed at permanent hostility between Russia and Germany who are natural allies. Wilson's insinuation that Czernin favors uniting all territory inhabited by Poles in new Poland is part of deep plan to perpetuate animosity in the east, and can only tend to encourage advocates of wrong Polish policy. Wilson's friendliness is far more dangerous than Lloyd George's fulminations and Germany must recognize reality of that in order to avert it.

*Lokal-Anzeiger*, 13th: Wilson's plain intention is to drive wedge between Austria and Germany. His principles of peace might be discussed if he had not declared the tribunal of mankind solely competent to apply them, for such tribunal would simply mean that Anglo-Saxons and their serfs would vote down Centrals at conference table.

*Magdeburgische Zeitung*, 13th: Analysis of speech shows nothing but heap of elastic phrases and hopeless attempt to postpone for time discussion of reasonable peace terms by sowing discord in central Europe; Czernin's bashful offer of negotiations is complete failure.

*Berliner Neueste Nachrichten*, 13th: It is not devoid of interest to observe how wily America tries to catch Hertling by his inheritance from Bethmann Hollweg, the

* [The preceding Chancellor of Germany, removed in July 1917. (*Ed.*)]

Reichstag resolution. We should recognize from this again how much damage that resolution has done us; it not only fills enemy with new courage, but gives them opportunity to trap any government that does not openly repudiate it.

*Tageszeitung:* Wilson attempts to incite Austria against Germany and German Reichstag Majority against supreme military command, this again illustrates what valuable weapon was furnished Wilson in Reichstag peace resolution.

*Tägliche Rundschau:* Wilson cannot conceal his main object of establishing Anglo-American supremacy under name of society of nations. The unfortunate Reichstag peace resolution which Wilson delights in repeating is really only thing he likes in Germany, gives him courage to make his maximum demands. We must stand by the facts of our victories and our invincible military situation.

*Frankfurter Zeitung:* Message seems [less] favorable to peace than last speech; its warlike tones are only intended to make clear the powers of invincible America and weight of her Wilson's voice. Wilson's four principles are so abstract that nobody can say anything against them. We agree with him that general peace could be arranged on such basis, but we do not agree that spokesmen of Military and Annexationist Parties in Germany are sole obstacle. Versailles declaration and Lloyd George's latest speech plainly show that Entente has not courage to decide for peace of accommodation and understanding.

GARRETT

## The Chargé in Switzerland (Wilson) to the Secretary of State

BERNE, *February 16, 1918*

*Münchner Neueste Nachrichten,* 13th: President's speech shows clear desire continue public discussion between Washington and Central Powers. Tone even milder than January speech which showed great progress over former speeches. Message justified recent articles in this paper written by Germans knowing American situation who painted other picture of Wilson than many of our shallow daily newspapers and comic papers; not as bribed agent Wall Street and champion of trust imperialism grasping rapaciously for world supremacy, but as pacifist of extreme puritanic fanaticism determined use every effort to win victory his ideals of right and justice. In this doctrinairism lies perhaps Wilson's moral greatness and suggestive strength for Americans. German statesmen will do well to realize that if Germany comes to no *modus vivendi* with the Wilson mentality it will find in America its most tenacious and richest opponent with inexhaustible resources. Important to observe how greatly Wilson differs in tone and substance from declarations other Entente statesmen. Easily understood today why America not politically represented Versailles, because Wilson's present policy not Clemenceau's and Lloyd George's. Wilson mistaken in assuming existing difference between Military Party and German people but his mistake conceivable when considering recent unprincipled machinations of certain German party which hysterically cried for military *coup d'état.* Hoped that Reichstag in close cooperation with Government will immediately convince Wilson of error. Should not be difficult for Hertling, Czernin, by defining more closely former declarations, to come to agreement in principle with Wilson, but latter should also see justice of applying this beautiful principle to Allies. Altogether Wilson shows himself as only opponent with whom discussion possible. Therefore, duty of German statesmen to procure greatest possible benefits from this discussion. If agreement with America succeeds before its war machine assumes irresistible momentum the whole Entente will be unhinged.

*Münchener Post*, 13th: Wilson's reply to Hertling, Czernin, shows strong desire for general peace even more emphatic this regard than January message which this paper warmly supported. Must be admitted President entirely right in many points of his [polemic] against Hertling. Latter spoke but formulated no positive program. President places himself on basis Reichstag July resolution and thus general peace reconciliation becomes possible. Paper expects Chancellor to now build binding bridge to America. Professor Bonn recently properly declared that possibility for general peace depends on Germany's attitude toward American peace principles. Decision will not be difficult for German Government if it still holds to spirit July resolution and it must then subscribe to Wilson's developed general principles for general and just peace.

WILSON

## ⤳§ REFLECTIONS ON VIOLENCE

*Georges Sorel*

> *By the end of the nineteenth century, the western European and American Socialists had become, for the most part, respectable and respected party politicians. Although it was often conceded that violence and terror might still be justifiable weapons for the achievement of social justice in a country like Russia which was still under autocratic despotism, parliamentarism and reformism were clearly the norm in the West. It came as somewhat of a shock, therefore, when outspokenly revolutionary and terroristic trends began to appear. Anarchism, whose bomb-throwing image overshadowed its anticoercive libertarianism, and revolutionary Marxism, which advocated conspiracy and a return to direct action instead of merely waiting for capitalism to fall apart, were joined by a movement usually called "syndicalism," from the French word for trade union. Especially strong in France, Spain, and Italy, syndicalism was represented even in the United States by the International Workers of the World (IWW, commonly called "Wobblies"). Shunning parliamentary activity, the syndicalists advocated the general strike as a political weapon and, as an ultimate goal, a society operated politically and economically by local trade-union elements. Its opposition to the coercive state put it in contact with anarchism (and later with English guild socialism); its activism and close-knit party organization influenced both Lenin's bolshevism and, more directly, Mussolini's fascism.*

*One of the founders of syndicalism in France was Georges Sorel*
*(1847–1922), a writer who has had a far greater influence on*
*twentieth-century social movements and social science than his somewhat*
*meager fame would indicate. Sorel's* Reflections on Violence *(1906) is*
*a remarkable book, an unusual mixture of syndicalist propaganda,*
*political philosophy, and social psychology. An outgrowth of his discussion*
*of the role of the strike in syndicalism was his conception of the "myth"*
*in social movements in particular and in society in general, an idea which*
*has been of inestimable value both to totalitarian theoreticians and social*
*scientists interested in the subrational forces which make for social*
*cohesion. The following selections are from Chapter IV, "The Proletarian*
*Strike," and from "Letter to Daniel Halévy," which Sorel later used as*
*a preface to the* Reflections.

Every time that we attempt to obtain an exact conception of the ideas behind proletarian violence we are forced to go back to the notion of the general strike; and this
same conception may render many other services, and throw an unexpected light on
all the obscure parts of Socialism. In the last pages of the first chapter I compared
the general strike to the Napoleonic battle which definitely crushes an adversary;
this comparison will help us to understand the part played by the general strike in
the world of ideas.

Military writers of to-day, when discussing the new methods of war necessitated
by the employment of troops infinitely more numerous than those of Napoleon,
equipped with arms much more deadly than those of his time, do not for all that
imagine that wars will be decided in any other way than that of the Napoleonic battle.
The new tactics proposed must fit into the drama Napoleon had conceived; the
detailed development of the combat will doubtless be quite different from what it
used to be, but the end must always be the catastrophic defeat of the enemy. The
methods of military instruction are intended to prepare the soldier for this great and
terrible action, in which everybody must be ready to take part at the first signal.
From the highest to the lowest, the members of a really solid army have always in
mind this catastrophic issue of international conflicts.

The revolutionary Syndicates argue about Socialist action exactly in the same
manner as military writers argue about war; they restrict the whole of Socialism to
the general strike; they look upon every combination as one that should culminate
in this catastrophe; they see in each strike a reduced facsimile, an essay, a preparation
for the great final upheaval.

The *new school,* which calls itself Marxist, Syndicalist, and revolutionary, declared
in favour of the idea of the general strike as soon as it became clearly conscious of
the true sense of its own doctrine, of the consequences of its activity, and of its own

Georges Sorel, *Reflections on Violence,* trans. T. Hulme (New York: The Free Press of
Glencoe, 1950), pp. 119–128, 46–53.

originality. It was thus led to leave the old official, Utopian, and political tabernacles, which hold the general strike in horror, and to launch itself into the true current of the proletarian revolutionary movement; for a long time past the proletariat had made adherence to the principle of the general strike the *test* by means of which the Socialism of the workers was distinguished from that of the amateur revolutionaries.

Parliamentary Socialists can only obtain great influence if they can manage, by the use of a very confused language, to impose themselves on very diverse groups; for example, they must have working-men constituents simple enough to allow themselves to be duped by high-sounding phrases about future collectivism; they are compelled to represent themselves as profound philosophers to stupid middle-class people who wish to appear to be well informed about social questions; it is very necessary also for them to be able to exploit rich people who think that they are earning the grati- tude of humanity by taking shares in the enterprises of Socialist politicians. This influence is founded on balderdash, and our bigwigs endeavour—sometimes only too successfully—to spread confusion among the ideas of their readers; they detest the general strike because all propaganda carried on from that point of view is too socialistic to please philanthropists.

In the mouths of these self-styled representatives of the proletariat all socialistic formulas lose their real sense. The class war still remains the great principle, but it must be subordinated to national solidarity. Internationalism is an article of faith about which the most moderate declare themselves ready to take the most solemn oaths; but patriotism also imposes sacred duties. The emancipation of the workers must be the work of the workers themselves—their newspapers repeat this every day,—but real emancipation consists in voting for a professional politician, in securing for him the means of obtaining a comfortable situation in the world, in subjecting oneself to a leader. In the end the State must disappear—and they are very careful not to dispute what Engels has written on this subject—but this disappearance will take place only in a future so far distant that you must prepare yourself for it by using the State meanwhile as a means of providing the politicians with titbits; and the best means of bringing about the disappearance of the State consists in strength- ening meanwhile the Governmental machine. This method of reasoning resembles that of Gribouille, who threw himself into the water in order to escape getting wet in the rain.

Whole pages could be filled with the bare outlines of the contradictory, comical, and quack arguments which form the substance of the harangues of our great men; nothing embarrasses them, and they know how to combine, in pompous, impetuous, and nebulous speeches, the most absolute irreconcilability with the most supple oppor- tunism. A learned exponent of Socialism has said that the art of reconciling opposites by means of nonsense is the most obvious result which he had got from the study of the works of Marx. I confess my extreme incompetence in these difficult matters; moreover, I make no claim whatever to be counted among the people upon whom politicians confer the title of learned; yet I cannot easily bring myself to admit that this is the sum and substance of the Marxian philosophy. . . .

Against this noisy, garrulous, and lying Socialism, which is exploited by ambitious people of every description, which amuses a few buffoons, and which is admired by decadents—revolutionary Syndicalism takes its stand, and endeavours, on the contrary, to leave nothing in a state of indecision; its ideas are honestly expressed, without trickery and without mental reservations; no attempt is made to dilute doctrines by a stream of confused commentaries. Syndicalism endeavours to employ methods of expression which throw a full light on things, which put them exactly in the place assigned to them by their nature, and which bring out the whole value of the forces in play. Oppositions, instead of being glozed over, must be thrown into sharp relief if we desire to obtain a clear idea of the Syndicalist movement; the groups which are struggling one against the other must be shown as separate and as compact as possible; in short, the movements of the revolted masses must be represented in such a way that the soul of the revolutionaries may receive a deep and lasting impression.

These results could not be produced in any very certain manner by the use of ordinary language; use must be made of a body of images which, *by intuition alone,* and before any considered analyses are made, is capable of evoking as an undivided whole the mass of sentiments which corresponds to the different manifestations of the war undertaken by Socialism against modern society. The Syndicalists solve this problem perfectly, by concentrating the whole of Socialism in the drama of the general strike; there is thus no longer any place for the reconciliation of contraries in the equivocations of the professors; everything is clearly mapped out, so that only one interpretation of Socialism is possible. This method has all the advantages which "integral" knowledge has over analysis, according to the doctrine of Bergson; and perhaps it would not be possible to cite another example which would so perfectly demonstrate the value of the famous professor's doctrines.

The possibility of the actual realisation of the general strike has been much discussed; it has been stated that the Socialist war could not be decided in one single battle. To the people who think themselves cautious, practical, and scientific the difficulty of setting great masses of the proletariat in motion at the same moment seems prodigious; they have analysed the difficulties of detail which such an enormous struggle would present. It is the opinion of the Socialist-sociologists, as also of the politicians, that the general strike is a popular dream, characteristic of the beginnings of a working-class movement; we have had quoted against us the authority of Sidney Webb, who has decreed that the general strike is an illusion of youth, of which the English workers—whom the monopolists of sociology have so often presented to us as the depositaries of the true conception of the working-class movement—soon rid themselves.

That the general strike is not popular in contemporary England, is a poor argument to bring against the historical significance of the idea, for the English are distinguished by an extraordinary lack of understanding of the class war; their ideas have remained very much dominated by medieval influences: the guild, privileged, or at least protected by laws, still seems to them the ideal of working-class organisation; it is for England that the term *working-class aristocracy,* as a name for the trades unionists, was invented, and, as a matter of fact, trades unionism does pursue the acquisition of legal privileges. We might therefore say that the aversion felt by England for the general strike should be looked upon as strong presumptive evidence in favour of the latter by all those who look upon the class war as the essence of Socialism. . . .

Neither do I attach any importance to the objections made to the general strike based on considerations of a practical order. The attempt to construct hypotheses about the nature of the struggles of the future and the means of suppressing capitalism, on the model furnished by history, is a return to the old methods of the Utopists. There is no process by which the future can be predicted scientifically, nor even one which enables us to discuss whether one hypothesis about it is better than another; it has been proved by too many memorable examples that the greatest men have committed prodigious errors in thus desiring to make predictions about even the least distant future.

And yet without leaving the present, without reasoning about this future, which seems for ever condemned to escape our reason, we should be unable to act at all. Experience shows that the *framing of a future, in some indeterminate time,* may, when it is done in a certain way, be very effective, and have very few inconveniences; this happens when the anticipations of the future take the form of those myths, which enclose with them all the strongest inclinations of a people, of a party or of a class, inclinations which recur to the mind with the insistence of instincts in all the circumstances of life; and which give an aspect of complete reality to the hopes of immediate action by which, more easily than by any other method, men can reform their desires, passions, and mental activity. We know, moreover, that these social myths in no way prevent a man profiting by the observations which he makes in the course of his life, and form no obstacle to the pursuit of his normal occupations.

The truth of this may be shown by numerous examples.

The first Christians expected the return of Christ and the total ruin of the pagan world, with the inauguration of the kingdom of the saints, at the end of the first generation. The catastrophe did not come to pass, but Christian thought profited so greatly from the apocalyptic myth that certain contemporary scholars maintain that the whole preaching of Christ referred solely to this one point. The hopes which Luther and Calvin had formed of the religious exaltation of Europe were by no means realised; these fathers of the Reformation very soon seemed men of a past era; for present-day Protestants they belong rather to the Middle Ages than to modern times, and the problems which troubled them most occupy very little place in contemporary Protestantism. Must we for that reason deny the immense result which came from their dreams of Christian renovation? It must be admitted that the real developments of the Revolution did not in any way resemble the enchanting pictures which created the enthusiasm of its first adepts; but without those pictures would the Revolution have been victorious? Many Utopias were mixed up with the Revolutionary myth, because it had been formed by a society passionately fond of imaginative literature, full of confidence in the "science," and very little acquainted with the economic history of the past. These Utopias came to nothing; but it may be asked whether the Revolution was not a much more profound transformation than those dreamed of by the people who in the eighteenth century had invented social Utopias. In our own times Mazzini pursued what the wiseacres of his time called a mad chimera; but it can no longer be denied that, without Mazzini, Italy would never have become a great power, and that he did more for Italian unity than Cavour and all the politicians of his school.

A knowledge of what the myths contain in the way of details which will actually form part of the history of the future is then of small importance; they are not astrological almanacs; it is even possible that nothing which they contain will ever come to pass,—as was the case with the catastrophe expected by the first Christians. In our own daily life, are we not familiar with the fact that what actually happens is very different from our preconceived notion of it? And that does not prevent us from continuing to make resolutions. Psychologists say that there is heterogeneity between the ends in view and the ends actually realised: the slightest experience of life reveals this law to us, which Spencer transferred into nature, to extract therefrom his theory of the multiplication of effects.

The myth must be judged as a means of acting on the present; any attempt to discuss how far it can be taken literally as future history is devoid of sense. *It is the myth in its entirety which is alone important*: its parts are only of interest in so far as they bring out the main idea. No useful purpose is served, therefore, in arguing about the incidents which may occur in the course of a social war, and about the decisive conflicts which may give victory to the proletariat; even supposing the revolutionaries to have been wholly and entirely deluded in setting up this imaginary picture of the general strike, this picture may yet have been, in the course of the preparation for the Revolution, a great element of strength, if it has embraced all the aspirations of Socialism, and if it has given to the whole body of Revolutionary thought a precision and a rigidity which no other method of thought could have given.

To estimate, then, the significance of the idea of the general strike, all the methods of discussion which are current among politicians, sociologists, or people with pretensions to political science, must be abandoned. Everything which its opponents endeavour to establish may be conceded to them, without reducing in any way the value of the theory which they think they have refuted. The question whether the general strike is a partial reality, or only a product of popular imagination, is of little importance. All that it is necessary to know is, whether the general strike contains everything that the Socialist doctrine expects of the revolutionary proletariat.

To solve this question we are no longer compelled to argue learnedly about the future; we are not obliged to indulge in lofty reflections about philosophy, history, or economics; we are not on the plane of theories, and we can remain on the level of observable facts. We have to question men who take a very active part in the real revolutionary movement amidst the proletariat, men who do not aspire to climb into the middle class and whose mind is not dominated by corporative prejudices. These men may be deceived about an infinite number of political, economical, or moral questions; but their testimony is decisive, sovereign, and irrefutable when it is a question of knowing what are the ideas which most powerfully move them and their comrades, which most appeal to them as being identical with their socialistic conceptions, and thanks to which their reason, their hopes, and their way of looking at particular facts seem to make but one indivisible unity.

Thanks to these men, we know that the general strike is indeed what I have said: the *myth* in which Socialism is wholly comprised, i.e. a body of images capable of evoking instinctively all the sentiments which correspond to the different manifestations of the war undertaken by Socialism against modern society. Strikes have engendered in the proletariat the noblest, deepest, and most moving sentiments that they possess; the general strike groups them all in a co-ordinated picture, and, by bringing them together, gives to each one of them its maximum of intensity; appealing to their painful memories of particular conflicts, it colours with an intense life all the details of the composition presented to consciousness. We thus obtain that intuition of Socialism which language cannot give us with perfect clearness—and we obtain it as a whole, perceived instantaneously. . . .

[*From "Letter to Daniel Halévy"*]    The mind of man is so constituted that it cannot remain content with the mere observation of facts, but always attempts to penetrate into the inner reason of things. I therefore ask myself whether it might not be desirable to study this theory of myths more thoroughly, utilising the enlightenment we owe to the Bergsonian philosophy. The attempt I am about to submit to you is doubtless very imperfect, but I think that it has been planned in accordance with the only method which can possibly throw light on the problem. In the first place, we should notice that the discussions of the moralists hardly ever come into contact with what is truly fundamental in our individuality. As a rule, they simply try to appraise our already completed acts with the help of the moral valuations formulated in advance by society, for the different types of action commonest in contemporary life. They say that in this way they are determining motives; but these motives are of the same nature as those which jurists take account of in criminal justice; they are merely social valuations of facts known to everybody. Many philosophers, especially the ancients, have believed that all values could be deduced from utility, and if any social valuation does exist, it is surely this latter,—theologians estimate transgressions by the place they occupy on the road which, according to average human experience, leads to mortal sin; they are thus able to ascertain the degree of viciousness of any given sin,—while the moderns usually teach that we act after having established a particular maxim (which is, as it were, an abstraction or generalisation of our projected conduct), and justify this maxim by deducing it (more or less sophistically) from general principles which are, to a certain extent, analogous to the Declaration of the Rights of Man; and, as a matter of fact, this theory was probably inspired by the admiration excited by the Bill of Rights placed at the head of each American constitution.

We are all so extremely concerned in knowing what the world thinks of us that, sooner or later, considerations analogous to those the moralists speak of do pass through our mind; as a result of this the moralists have been able to imagine that they have really made an appeal to experience for the purpose of finding out what exists at the bottom of the creative conscience, when, as a matter of fact, all they have done is to consider already accomplished acts from the point of view of its social effects.

Bergson asks us, on the contrary, to consider the inner depths of the mind and what happens there during a creative moment. "There are," he says, "two different selves, one of which is, as it were, the external projection of the other, its spatial and, so to speak, social representation. We reach the former by deep introspection, which leads us to grasp our inner states as living things, constantly *becoming*, as states not amenable to measure. . . . But the moments at which we thus grasp ourselves are rare, and that is just why we are rarely free. The greater part of our time we live outside ourselves, hardly perceiving anything of ourselves but our own ghost, a colourless shadow. . . . Hence we live for the external world rather than for ourselves; we speak rather than think; we are acted rather than act ourselves. To act freely is to recover possession of oneself, and to get back into pure duration."

In order to acquire a real understanding of this psychology we must "carry ourselves back in thought to those moments of our life, when we made some serious decision, moments unique of their kind, which will never be repeated—any more than the past phases in the history of a nation will ever come back again." It is very evident that we enjoy this liberty pre-eminently when we are making an effort to create a new individuality in ourselves, thus endeavouring to break the bonds of habit which enclose us. It might at first be supposed that it would be sufficient to say that, at such moments, we are dominated by an overwhelming emotion; but everybody now recognises that movement is the essence of emotional life, and it is, then, in terms of movement that we must speak of creative consciousness.

It seems to me that this psychology of the deeper life must be represented in the following way. We must abandon the idea that the soul can be compared to something moving, which, obeying a more or less mechanical law, is impelled in the direction of certain given motive forces. To say that we are acting, implies that we are creating an imaginary world placed ahead of the present world and composed of movements which depend entirely on us. In this way our freedom becomes perfectly intelligible. Starting from a study of these artificial constructions which embrace everything that interests us, several philosophers, inspired by Bergsonian doctrines, have been led to formulate a rather startling theory. Edouard Le Roy, for example, says: "Our real body is the entire universe in as far as it is experienced by us. And what common sense more strictly calls our body is only the region of least unconsciousness and greatest liberty in this greater body, the part which we most directly control and by means of which we are able to act on the rest." But we must not, as this subtle philosopher constantly does, confuse a passing state of our willing activity with the stable affirmations of science.

These artificial worlds generally disappear from our minds without leaving any trace in our memory; but when the masses are deeply moved it then becomes possible to trace the outlines of the kind of representation which constitutes a social myth.

This belief in "glory" which Renan praised so much quickly fades away into rhapsodies when it is not supported by myths; these myths have varied greatly in different epochs: the citizen of the Greek republics, the Roman legionary, the soldier of the wars of Liberty, and the artist of the Renaissance did not picture their conception of glory by the help of the same set of images. Renan complained that "the faith in glory" is compromised by the *limited historical outlook* more or less prevalent at the present day. "Very few," he said, "act with a view to immortal fame. . . . Everyone wants to enjoy his own glory; they eat it in the green blade, and do not gather the sheaves after death." In my opinion, this limited historical outlook is, on the contrary, not a cause but a consequence; it results from the weakening of the heroic myths which had such great popularity at the beginning of the nineteenth century; the belief in "glory" perished and a limited historic outlook became predominant at the time when these myths vanished.

As long as there are no myths accepted by the masses, one may go on talking of revolts indefinitely, without ever provoking any revolutionary movement; this is what gives such importance to the general strike and renders it so odious to socialists who are afraid of a revolution; they do all they can to shake the confidence felt by the workers in the preparations they are making for the revolution; and in order to succeed in this they cast ridicule on the idea of the general strike—the only idea that could have any value as a motive force. One of the chief means employed by them is to represent it as a Utopia; this is easy enough, because there are very few myths which are perfectly free from any Utopian element.

The revolutionary myths which exist at the present time are almost free from any such mixture; by means of them it is possible to understand the activity, the feelings and the ideas of the masses preparing themselves to enter on a decisive struggle; the myths are not descriptions of things, but expressions of a determination to act. A Utopia is, on the contrary, an intellectual product; it is the work of theorists who, after observing and discussing the known facts, seek to establish a model to which they can compare existing society in order to estimate the amount of good and evil it contains. It is a combination of imaginary institutions having sufficient analogies to real institutions for the jurist to be able to reason about them; it is a construction which can be taken to pieces, and certain parts of it have been shaped in such a way that they can (with a few alterations by way of adjustment) be fitted into approaching legislation. Whilst contemporary myths lead men to prepare themselves for a combat which will destroy the existing state of things, the effect of Utopias has always been to direct men's minds towards reforms which can be brought about by patching up the existing system; it is not surprising, then, that so many makers of Utopias were able to develop into able statesmen when they had acquired a greater experience of political life. A myth cannot be refuted, since it is, at bottom, identical with the convictions of a group, being the expression of these convictions in the language of movement; and it is, in consequence, unanalysable into parts which could be placed on the plane of historical descriptions. A Utopia, on the contrary, can be discussed like any other social constitution; the spontaneous movements it presupposes can be compared with the movements actually observed in the course of history, and we can in this way evaluate its verisimilitude; it is possible to refute Utopias by showing that the economic system on which they have been made to rest is incompatible with the necessary conditions of modern production.

Liberal political economy is one of the best examples of a Utopia that could be given. A state of society was imagined which could contain only the types produced by commerce, and which would exist under the law of the fullest competition; it is recognised to-day that this kind of ideal society would be as difficult to realise as that of Plato; but several great statesmen of modern times have owed their fame to the efforts they made to introduce something of this ideal of commercial liberty into industrial legislation.

We have here a Utopia free from any mixture of myth; the history of French democracy, however, presents a very remarkable combination of Utopias and myths. The theories that inspired the authors of our first constitutions are regarded to-day as extremely chimerical; indeed, people are often loth to concede them the value which they have been so long recognised to possess—that of an ideal on which legislators, magistrates, and administrators should constantly fix their eyes, in order to secure for men a little more justice. With these Utopias were mixed up the myths which represented the struggle against the ancient regime; so long as the myths survived, all the refutations of liberal Utopias could produce no result; the myth safeguarded the Utopia with which it was mixed.

For a long time Socialism was scarcely anything but a Utopia; the Marxists were right in claiming for their master the honour of bringing about a change in this state of things; Socialism has now become the preparation of the masses employed in great industries for the suppression of the State and property; and it is no longer necessary, therefore, to discuss how men must organise themselves in order to enjoy future happiness; everything is reduced to the *revolutionary apprenticeship* of the proletariat. Unfortunately Marx was not acquainted with facts which have now become familiar to us; we know better than he did what strikes are, because we have been able to observe economic conflicts of considerable extent and duration; the myth of the "general strike" has become popular, and is now firmly established in the minds of the workers; we possess ideas about violence that it would have been difficult for him to have formed; we can then complete his doctrine, instead of making commentaries on his text, as his unfortunate disciples have done for so long.

In this way Utopias tend to disappear completely from Socialism; Socialism has no longer any need to concern itself with the organisation of industry since capitalism does that. I think, moreover, that I have shown that the general strike corresponds to a kind of feeling which is so closely related to those which are necessary to promote production in any very progressive state of industry, that a revolutionary apprenticeship may at the same time be considered as an apprenticeship which will enable the workmen to occupy a high rank among the best workmen of his own trade.

People who are living in this world of "myths," are secure from all refutation; this has led many to assert that Socialism is a kind of religion. For a long time people have been struck by the fact that religious convictions are unaffected by criticism, and from that they have concluded that everything which claims to be beyond science must be a religion. It has been observed also that Christianity tends at the present day to be less a system of dogmas than a Christian life, *i.e.* a moral reform penetrating to the roots of one's being; consequently, a new analogy has been discovered between religion and the revolutionary Socialism which aims at the apprenticeship, preparation, and even reconstruction of the individual,—a gigantic task. But Bergson has taught us that it is not only religion which occupies the profounder region of our mental life; revolutionary myths have their place there equally with religion. The arguments which Yves Guyot urges against Socialism on the ground that it is a religion, seem to me, then, to be founded on an imperfect acquaintance with the new psychology.

Renan was very surprised to discover that Socialists are beyond discouragement.

"After each abortive experiment they recommence their work: the solution is not yet found, but it will be. The idea that no solution exists never occurs to them, and in this lies their strength." The explanation given by Renan is superficial; it regards Socialism as a Utopia, that is, as a thing which can be compared to observed realities; if this were true, it would be scarcely possible to understand how confidence can survive so many failures. But by the side of the Utopias there have always been myths capable of urging on the workers to revolt. For a long time these myths were founded on the legends of the Revolution, and they preserved all their value as long as these legends remained unshaken. To-day the confidence of the Socialists is greater than ever since the myth of the general strike dominates all the truly working-class movement. No failure proves anything against Socialism since the latter has become a work of preparation (for revolution); if they are checked, it merely proves that the apprenticeship has been insufficient; they must set to work again with more courage, persistence, and confidence than before; their experience of labour has taught workmen that it is by means of patient apprenticeship that a man may become a true comrade, and it is also the way of becoming a true revolutionary. . . .

# ✑§ POLITICAL PARTIES

*Robert Michels*

*The political ideals growing out of the eighteenth-century revolutions have frequently been derided in the name of custom or attacked for their overly optimistic assumptions about human nature. By contrast, it was the empirical study and personal experience of twentieth-century mass movements that led Robert Michels (1876–1936) to question the soundness of the democratic political tradition. Michels, a social scientist of German-Italian middle-class parentage, early in life became involved in the pre-World War I German Socialist party and the trade-union movement, institutions that advertised their complete adherence to democratic procedures and aims. It was Michels' disillusionment with the substance of party democracy that led him to formulate his "iron law of oligarchy," discussed in the selection which follows, though he was also influenced by conservative theorists, such as the Italian sociologist Gaetano Mosca, who stressed the role of elites in society. Michels' study of the oligarchical tendencies in modern democratic parties appeared as early as 1911, long before avowedly totalitarian movements had become important in European politics. By the 1920s, in a move reflecting his own ideological evolution, Michels accepted a university appointment in Fascist Italy, where he spent the remaining years of his life.*

## DEMOCRACY AND THE IRON LAW OF OLIGARCHY

Whilst the majority of the socialist schools believe that in a future more or less remote it will be possible to attain to a genuinely democratic order, and whilst the greater number of those who adhere to aristocratic political views consider that democracy, however dangerous to society, is at least realizable, we find in the scientific world a conservative tendency voiced by those who deny resolutely and once for all that there is any such possibility. As was shown in an earlier chapter, this tendency is particularly strong in Italy, where it is led by a man of weight, Gaetano Mosca, who declares that no highly developed social order is possible without a "political class," that is to say, a politically dominant class, the class of a minority. Those who do not believe in the god of democracy are never weary of affirming that this god is the creation of a childlike mythopœic faculty, and they contend that all phrases representing the idea of the rule of the masses, such terms as state, civic rights, popular representation, nation, are descriptive merely of a legal principle, and do not correspond to any actually existing facts. They contend that the eternal struggles between aristocracy and democracy of which we read in history have never been anything more than struggles between an old minority, defending its actual predominance, and a new and ambitious minority, intent upon the conquest of power, desiring either to fuse with the former or to dethrone and replace it. On this theory, these class struggles consist merely of struggles between successively dominant minorities. The social classes which under our eyes engage in gigantic battles upon the scene of history, battles whose ultimate causes are to be found in economic antagonism, may thus be compared to two groups of dancers executing a *chassé croisé* in a quadrille.

The democracy has an inherent preference for the authoritarian solution of important questions. It thirsts simultaneously for splendour and for power. When the English burghers had conquered their liberties, they made it their highest ambition to possess an aristocracy. Gladstone declared that the love of the English people for their liberties was equalled only by their love for the nobility. Similarly it may be said that it is a matter of pride with the socialists to show themselves capable of maintaining a discipline which, although it is to a certain extent voluntary, none the less signifies the submission of the majority to the orders issued by the minority, or at least to the rules issued by the minority in obedience to the majority's instructions. Vilfredo Pareto has even recommended socialism as a means favourable for the creation of a new working-class *élite*, and he regards the courage with which the socialist leaders face attack and persecution as a sign of their vigour, and as the first condition requisite to the formation of a new "political class." Pareto's *théorie de la circulation des élites* must, however, be accepted with considerable reserve, for in most cases there is not a simple replacement of one group of *élites* by another, but a continuous process of intermixture, the old elements incessantly attracting, absorbing, and assimilating the new.

This phenomenon was perhaps recognized at an earlier date, in so far as the

Robert Michels, *Political Parties: A Sociological Study of the Oligarchical Tendencies in Modern Democracy,* trans. E. and C. Paul (New York: The Free Press of Glencoe, 1958), pp. 393–407, 417–425.

*circulation des élites* was effected within the limits of a single great social class and took place on the political plane. In states where a purely representative government prevails, the constitutional opposition aims simply at such a circulation. In England, for instance, the opposition possesses the same simple and resistent structure as the party which holds the reins of government; its programme is clearly formulated, directed to purely practical and proximate ends; it is thoroughly disciplined, and is led by one lacking theoretical profundity but endowed with strategic talent; all its energies are devoted to overthrowing the government, to taking the reins of power into its own hands, while in other respects leaving matters exactly as they were; it aims, in a word, at the substitution of one clique of the dominant classes for another. Sooner or later the competition between the various cliques of the dominant classes ends in a reconciliation, which is effected with the instinctive aim of retaining dominion over the masses by sharing it among themselves. The opinion is very generally held that as a result of the French Revolution, or that in any case in the Third Republic, the old order had socially speaking been completely suppressed in France. This view is utterly erroneous. In the present year of grace we find that the French nobility is represented in the cavalry regiments and in the republican diplomatic service to an extent altogether disproportionate to its numerical strength; and although in the French Chamber there does not exist, as in Germany, a declared conservative party of the nobility, we find that of 584 deputies no less than 61 belong to the old aristocracy (*noblesse d'épée* and *noblesse de robe*).

As we have said, the theory that a directive social group is absolutely essential is by no means a new one. . . . It is a less familiar fact, but one no less interesting, that the leading intellectual progenitors of the theory of Mosca and Pareto are to be found among the members of the school against which these writers more especially direct their attacks, namely among socialist thinkers, and especially among the earlier French socialists. In their work we discover the germs of the doctrine which at a later date was elaborated by Mosca and Pareto into a sociological system.

The school of Saint-Simon, while holding that the concept of class would some day cease to be characterized by any economic attribute, did not look for a future without class distinctions. The Saint-Simonians dreamed of the creation of a new hierarchy which was to be founded, not upon the privileges of birth, but upon acquired privileges. This class was to consist of "les plus aimants, les plus intelligents, et les plus forts, personnification vivante du triple progrès de la société," and "capables de la diriger dans une plus vaste carrière." At the head of their socialist state the Saint-Simonians desired to place those whom they termed "hommes généraux," who would be able to prescribe for each individual his quantum of social labour, the individual's special aptitudes being taken into account in this connection; here it is obvious that dependence must be placed upon the discretion of these supermen. One of the most ardent followers of Saint-Simon, an enthusiastic advocate of the "nouvelle dynastie," when forced to defend himself against the accusation that his doctrine paved the way for despotism, did not hesitate to declare that the majority of human beings ought to obey the orders of the most capable; they should do this, he contended, not only for the love of God, but also on grounds of personal egoism, and finally because man, even if he could live in isolation, would always need some external support. The necessity for issuing orders on one side and the necessity for complying with them on the other are furnished with metaphysical justification. Such authority would only be "une transformation politique de l'amour qui unit tous les hommes en Dieu. Et pouvez-vous lui préférer cette triste indépendance qui aujourd'hui isole les sentiments, les opinions, les efforts, et qui, sous un nom pompeux, n'est rien autre chose que l'égoisme accompagnée de tous les maux qu'il enfante?" The Saint-Simonian system is authoritarian and hierarchical through and through. The disciples of Saint-Simon were so little shocked by the Cæsarism of Napoleon III that most of them joyfully accepted it, imagining that they would find in it the principles of economic socialization.

The school of Fourier went further still. With a wealth of detail bordering on pedantry and exhibiting more than one grotesque feature, Fourier thought out a vast and complex system. To-day we can hardly restrain a smile when we study the tables he drew up describing his "spherical hierarchy," consisting of a thousand grades and embracing all possible forms of dominion from "anarchie" to "omniarchie," each of them having its special "hautes dignités," and its appropriate "hautes fonctions." Sorel has well shown that the socialism of the days prior to Louis Blanc was intimately connected with the Napoleonic era, so that the Saint-Simonian and Fourierist utopias could not live and prosper elsewhere than in the soil of the idea of authority to which the great Corsican had furnished a new splendour. According to Berth, Fourier's whole system presupposes for its working the invisible but real and indispensable ubiquity of Fourier himself, for he alone, the Napoleon, as it were, of socialism, would be capable of activating and harmonizing the diverse passions of humanity.

Socialists of the subsequent epoch, and above all revolutionary socialists, while not denying the possibility, in the remote future, of a democratic government by majority, absolutely denied that such a government could exist in the concrete present. Bakunin opposed any participation of the working class in elections. He was convinced that in a society where the people, the mass of the wage-earners, is under the economic dominion of a minority consisting of possessors, the freest of electoral systems could be nothing more than an illusion. "Qui dit pouvoir, dit domination, et toute domination présume l'existence d'une masse dominée." Democracy is even regarded as the worst of all the bourgeois regimes. The republic, which is presented to us as the most elevated form of bourgeois democracy, was said by Proudhon to possess to an extreme degree that fanatical and petty authoritative spirit (zèle gouvernemental) which believes that it can dare everything with impunity, being always ready to justify its despotic acts under the convenient pretext that they are done for the good of the republic and in the general interest. Even the political revolution signifies merely "un déplacement de l'autorité" [a displacement of authority].

The only scientific doctrine which can boast of ability to make an effective reply to all the theories, old or new, affirming the immanent necessity for the perennial existence of the "political class" is the Marxist doctrine. In this doctrine the state is identified with the ruling class—an identification from which Bakunin, Marx's pupil, drew the extreme consequences. The state is merely the executive committee of the ruling class; or, to quote the expression of a recent neo-Marxist, the state is merely a "trade-union formed to defend the interest of the powers-that-be." It is obvious that this theory greatly resembles the conservative theory of Gaetano Mosca. Mosca, in fact, from a study of the same diagnostic signs, deduces a similar prognosis, but abstains from lamentations and recriminations on account of a phenomenon which, in the light of his general political views, he regards not merely as inevitable, but as actually advantageous to society. Aristide Briand, in the days when he was an active member of the socialist party, and before he had become prime minister of the "class-state," pushed the Marxist notion of the state to its utmost limits by recommending the workers to abandon isolated and local economic struggles, to refrain from dissipating their energies in partial strikes, and to deliver a united assault upon the state in the form of the general strike, for, he said, you can reach the bourgeoisie with your weapons in no other way than by attacking the state.

The Marxist theory of the state, when conjoined with a faith in the revolutionary energy of the working class and in the democratic effects of the socialization of the means of production, leads logically to the idea of a new social order which to the school of Mosca appears utopian. According to the Marxists the capitalist mode of production transforms the great majority of the population into proletarians, and thus digs its own grave. As soon as it has attained maturity, the proletariat will seize political power, and will immediately transform private property into state property. "In this way it will eliminate itself, for it will thus put an end to all social differences, and consequently to all class antagonisms. In other words, the proletariat will annul the state, *qua* state. Capitalist society, divided into classes, has need of the state as an organization of the ruling class, whose purpose it is to maintain the capitalist system of production in its own interest and in order to effect the continued exploitation of the proletariat. Thus to put an end to the state is synonymous with putting an end to the existence of the dominant class." But the new collectivist society, the society without classes, which is to be established upon the ruins of the ancient state, will also need elective elements. It may be said that by the adoption of the preventive rules formulated by Rousseau in the *Contrat Social*, and subsequently reproduced by the French revolutionists in the *Déclaration des Droits de l'Homme* [Declaration of the Rights of Man], above all by the strict application of the principle that all offices are to be held on a revocable tenure, the activity of these representatives may be confined within rigid limits. It is none the less true that social wealth cannot be satisfactorily administered in any other manner than by the creation of an extensive bureaucracy. In this way we are led by an inevitable logic to the flat denial of the possibility of a state without classes. The administration of an immeasurably large capital, above all when this capital is collective property, confers upon the administrator influence at least equal to that possessed by the private owner of capital. Consequently the critics in advance of the Marxist social order ask whether the instinct which to-day leads the members of the possessing classes to transmit to their children the wealth which they (the parents) have amassed, will not exist also in the administrators of the public wealth of the socialist state, and whether these administrators will not utilize their immense influence in order to secure for their children the succession to the offices which they themselves hold.

The constitution of a new dominant minority would, in addition, be especially facilitated by the manner in which, according to the Marxist conception of the revolution, the social transformation is to be effected. Marx held that the period between the destruction of capitalist society and the establishment of communist society would be bridged by a period of revolutionary transition in the economic field, to which would correspond a period of political transition, "when the state could not be anything other than the revolutionary dictatorship of the proletariat." To put the matter less euphemistically, there will then exist a dictatorship in the hands of those leaders who have been sufficiently astute and sufficiently powerful to grasp the sceptre of dominion in the name of socialism, and to wrest it from the hands of the expiring bourgeois society. . . .

There is little difference, as far as practical results are concerned, between individual dictatorship and the dictatorship of a group of oligarchs. Now it is manifest that the concept *dictatorship* is the direct antithesis of the concept *democracy*. The attempt to make dictatorship serve the ends of democracy is tantamount to the endeavour to utilize war as the most efficient means for the defence of peace, or to employ alcohol in the struggle against alcoholism. It is extremely probable that a social group which had secured control of the instruments of collective power would do all that was possible to retain that control. Theophrastus noted long ago that the strongest desire of men who have attained to leadership in a popularly governed state is not so much the acquirement of personal wealth as the gradual establishment of their own sovereignty at the expense of popular sovereignty. The danger is imminent lest the social revolution should replace the visible and tangible dominant classes which now exist and act openly, by a clandestine demagogic oligarchy, pursuing its ends under the cloak of equality.

The Marxist economic doctrine and the Marxist philosophy of history cannot fail to exercise a great attraction upon thinkers. But the defects of Marxism are patent directly we enter the practical domains of administration and public law, without speaking of errors in the psychological field and even in more elementary spheres. Wherever socialist theory has endeavoured to furnish guarantees for personal liberty, it has in the end either lapsed into the cloudland of individualist anarchism, or else has made proposals which (doubtless in opposition to the excellent intentions of their authors) could not fail to enslave the individual to the mass. Here is an example: to ensure that the literature of socialist society shall be elevated and moral, and to exclude *a priori* all licentious books, August Bebel proposed the nomination of a committee of experts to decide what might and what might not be printed. To obviate all danger of injustice and to secure freedom of thought and expression, Bebel added that every author must have the right of appeal to the collectivity. It is hardly necessary to point out the impracticability of this proposal, which is in effect that the books, however large, regarding which an appeal is made, must be printed by the million and distributed to the public in order that the public may decide whether they are or are not fit for publication!

The problem of socialism is not merely a problem in economics. In other words, socialism does not seek merely to determine to what extent it is possible to realize a distribution of wealth which shall be at once just and economically productive. Socialism is also an administrative problem, a problem of democracy, and this not in the technical and administrative sphere alone, but also in the sphere of psychology. In the individualist problem is found the most difficult of all that complex of questions which socialism seeks to answer. Rudolf Goldschied, who aims at a renascence of the socialist movement by the strengthening of the more energetic elements in that movement, rightly draws attention to a danger which socialism incurs, however brilliantly it may handle the problems of economic organization. If socialism, he says, fails to study the problem of individual rights, individual knowledge, and individual will, it will suffer shipwreck from a defective understanding of the significance of the problem of freedom for the higher evolution of our species—will suffer shipwreck no less disastrous than that of earlier conceptions of world reform which, blinded by the general splendour of their vision, have ignored the individual light-sources which combine to produce that splendour.

The youthful German labour party had hardly succeeded in detaching itself, at the cost of severe struggles, from the bourgeois democracy, when one of its sincerest friends drew attention to certain urgent dangers. In an open letter to the Leipzig committee of the Allgemeine Deutsche Arbeiterverein, Rodbertus wrote: "You are separating yourselves from a political party because, as you rightly believe, this political party does not adequately represent your social interests. But you are doing this in order to found a new political party. Who will furnish you with guarantees against the danger that in this new party the adversaries of your class (*die antisozialen Elemente*) may some day gain the upper hand?" In this observation Rodbertus touches the very essence of the political party. An analysis of the elements which enter into the composition of a party will show the perfect justice of his criticism. A party is neither a social unity nor an economic unity. It is based upon its programme. In theory this programme may be the expression of the interests of a particular class. In practice, however, anyone may join a party, whether his interests coincide or not with the principles enunciated in the party programme. The socialist party, for example, is the ideological representative of the proletariat. This, however, does not make it a class organism. From the social point of view it is a mixture of classes, being composed of elements fulfilling diverse functions in the economic process. But since the programme has a class origin, an ostensible social unity is thereby conferred upon the party. All socialists as such, whatever their economic position in private life, admit in theory the absolute pre-eminence of one great class, the proletariat. Those non-proletarians affiliated to the party, and those who are but partial proletarians, "adopt the outlook of the working class, and recognize this class as predominant." It is tacitly presupposed that those members of a party who do not belong to the class which that party represents will renounce their personal interests whenever these conflict with the interests of the proletarian class. On principle, the heterogeneous elements will subordinate themselves to the "idea" of a class to which they themselves do not belong. So much for theory. In practice, the acceptance of the programme does not suffice to abolish the conflict of interests between capital and labour. Among the members belonging to higher social strata who have made their adhesion to the political organization of the working class, there will be some who will, when the occasion demands it, know how to sacrifice themselves, who will be able to unclass themselves. The majority of such persons, however, notwithstanding their outward community of ideas with the proletariat, will continue to pursue economic interests opposed to those of the proletariat. There is, in fact, a conflict of interests, and the decision in this conflict will be determined by the relationship which the respective interests bear towards the principal necessities of life. Consequently it is by no means impossible that an economic conflict may arise between the bourgeois members and the proletarian members of the party, and that as this conflict extends it will culminate in political dissensions. Economic antagonism stifles the ideological superstructure. The programme then becomes a dead letter, and beneath the banner of "socialism" and within the bosom of the party, a veritable class struggle goes on. We learn from actual experience that in their conduct towards persons in their employ the bourgeois socialists do not always subordinate personal interests to those of their adoptive class. When the party includes among its members the owners of factories and workshops, it may be noticed that these, notwithstanding personal goodwill and notwithstanding the pressure which is exercised on them by the party, have the same economic conflict with their employees as have those employers whose convictions harmonize with their economic status, and who think not as socialists but as bourgeois.

But there exists yet another danger. The leadership of the socialist party may fall into the hands of persons whose practical tendencies are in opposition with the programme of the working class, so that the labour movement will be utilized for the service of interests diametrically opposed to those of the proletariat. This danger is especially great in countries where the working-class party cannot dispense with the aid and guidance of capitalists who are not economically dependent upon the party; it is least conspicuous where the party has no need of such elements, or can at any rate avoid admitting them to leadership.

When the leaders, whether derived from the bourgeoisie or from the working class, are attached to the party organism as employees, their economic interest coincides as a rule with the interest of the party. This, however, serves to eliminate only one aspect of the danger. Another aspect, graver because more general, depends upon the opposition which inevitably arises between the leaders and the rank and file as the party grows in strength.

The party, regarded as an entity, as a piece of mechanism, is not necessarily identifiable with the totality of its members, and still less so with the class to which these belong. The party is created as a means to secure an end. Having, however, become an end in itself, endowed with aims and interests of its own, it undergoes detachment, from the teleological point of view, from the class which it represents. In a party, it is far from obvious that the interests of the masses which have combined to form the party will coincide with the interests of the bureaucracy in which the party becomes personified. The interests of the body of employees are always conservative, and in a given political situation these interests may dictate a defensive and even a reactionary policy when the interests of the working class demand a bold and aggressive policy; in other cases, although these are very rare, the rôles may be reversed. By a universally applicable social law, every organ of the collectivity, brought into existence through the need for the division of labour, creates for itself, as soon as it becomes consolidated, interests peculiar to itself. The existence of these special interests involves a necessary conflict with the interests of the collectivity. Nay, more, social strata fulfilling peculiar functions tend to become isolated, to produce organs fitted for the defence of their own peculiar interests. In the long run they tend to undergo transformation into distinct classes.

The sociological phenomena whose general characteristics have been discussed in this chapter and in preceding ones offer numerous vulnerable points to the scientific opponents of democracy. These phenomena would seem to prove beyond dispute that society cannot exist without a "dominant" or "political" class, and that the ruling class, whilst its elements are subject to a frequent partial renewal, nevertheless constitutes the only factor of sufficiently durable efficacy in the history of human development. According to this view, the government, or, if the phrase be preferred, the state, cannot be anything other than the organization of a minority. It is the aim of this minority to impose upon the rest of society a "legal order," which is the outcome of the exigencies of dominion and of the exploitation of the mass of helots effected by the ruling minority, and can never be truly representative of the majority. The majority is thus permanently incapable of self-government. Even when the discontent of the masses culminates in a successful attempt to deprive the bourgeoisie of power, this is after all, so Mosca contends, effected only in appearance; always and necessarily there springs from the masses a new organized minority which raises itself to the rank of a governing class. Thus the majority of human beings, in a condition of eternal tutelage, are predestined by tragic necessity to submit to the dominion of a small minority, and must be content to constitute the pedestal of an oligarchy.

The principle that one dominant class inevitably succeeds to another, and the law deduced from that principle that oligarchy is, as it were, a preordained form of the common life of great social aggregates, far from conflicting with or replacing the materialist conception of history, completes that conception and reinforces it. There is no essential contradiction between the doctrine that history is the record of a continued series of class struggles and the doctrine that class struggles invariably culminate in the creation of new oligarchies which undergo fusion with the old. The existence of a political class does not conflict with the essential content of Marxism, considered not as an economic dogma but as a philosophy of history; for in each particular instance the dominance of a political class arises as the resultant of the relationships between the different social forces competing for supremacy, these forces being of course considered dynamically and not quantitatively. . . .

Moreover, by not a few party leaders the war was looked upon as a useful means of propaganda for the attraction of new recruits. This applies above all to the socialist party, eager to overthrow the barriers which separate from the party many sympathizers among the manual, operative, and shopkeeping classes, who are loth to join a party professing internationalist views. In a great public meeting held at Stuttgart on February 22, 1915, Heymann, a deputy to the diet of Würtemberg and one of the best-known leaders of the socialist party in that state, triumphantly declared: "Many have ardently desired to join our party. But there was an obstacle. Well, that obstacle no longer exists!" Unquestionably principles are often a stumbling-block to a party whose main desire is to increase its membership; and to disregard inconvenient principles may bring electoral advantage, if at the cost of honour. The leaders are the first to favour such a tendency, for the more widely extended the foundations of their party, the greater grows their own individual power. In fact, the individual power of the leaders undergoes an immeasurable increase at a time when the majority of the members of all parties are under arms, and for this reason may be considered as politically non-existent because they are unable to exercise any influence upon the executive of the party to which they belong. On the Continent, even those members who have not been summoned to the colours no longer possess any power of controlling their leaders, owing to the suppression of the freedom of the press and of the rights of public meeting and of combination. Wherever martial law prevails, the leader is omnipotent.

*    *    *

Leadership is a necessary phenomenon in every form of social life. Consequently it is not the task of science to inquire whether this phenomenon is good or evil, or predominantly one or the other. But there is great scientific value in the demonstration that every system of leadership is incompatible with the most essential postulates of democracy. We are now aware that the law of the historic necessity of oligarchy is primarily based upon a series of facts of experience. Like all other scientific laws, sociological laws are derived from empirical observation. In order, however, to deprive our axiom of its purely descriptive character, and to confer upon it that status of analytical explanation which can alone transform a formula into a law, it does not suffice to contemplate from a unitary outlook those phenomena which may be empirically established; we must also study the determining causes of these phenomena. Such has been our task.

Now, if we leave out of consideration the tendency of the leaders to organize themselves and to consolidate their interests, and if we leave also out of consideration the gratitude of the led towards the leaders, and the general immobility and passivity of the masses, we are led to conclude that the principal cause of oligarchy in the democratic parties is to be found in the technical indispensability of leadership.

The process which has begun in consequence of the differentiation of functions in the party is completed by a complex of qualities which the leaders acquire through their detachment from the mass. At the outset, leaders arise SPONTANEOUSLY; their functions are ACCESSORY and GRATUITOUS. Soon, however, they become PROFESSIONAL leaders, and in this second stage of development they are STABLE and IRREMOVABLE.

It follows that the explanation of the oligarchical phenomenon which thus results is partly PSYCHOLOGICAL; oligarchy derives, that is to say, from the psychical transformations which the leading personalities in the parties undergo in the course of their lives. But also, and still more, oligarchy depends upon what we may term the PSYCHOLOGY OF ORGANIZATION ITSELF, that is to say, upon the tactical and technical necessities which result from the consolidation of every disciplined political aggregate. Reduced to its most concise expression, the fundamental sociological law of political parties (the term "political" being here used in its most comprehensive significance) may be formulated in the following terms: "It is organization which gives birth to the dominion of the elected over the electors, of the mandataries over the mandators, of the delegates over the delegators. Who says organization, says oligarchy."

Every party organization represents an oligarchical power grounded upon a democratic basis. We find everywhere electors and elected. Also we find everywhere that the power of the elected leaders over the electing masses is almost unlimited. The oligarchical structure of the building suffocates the basic democratic principle. That which IS oppresses THAT WHICH OUGHT TO BE. For the masses, this essential difference between the reality and the ideal remains a mystery. Socialists often cherish a sincere belief that a new *élite* of politicians will keep faith better than did the old. The notion of the representation of popular interests, a notion to which the great majority of democrats, and in especial the working-class masses of the German-speaking lands, cleave with so much tenacity and confidence, is an illusion engendered by a false illumination, is an effect of mirage. In one of the most delightful pages of his analysis of modern Don Quixotism, Alphonse Daudet shows us how the "brav' commandant" Bravida, who has never quitted Tarascon, gradually comes to persuade himself, influenced by the burning southern sun, that he has been to Shanghai and has had all kinds of heroic adventures. Similarly the modern proletariat, enduringly influenced by glib-tongued persons intellectually superior to the mass, ends by believing that by flocking to the poll and entrusting its social and economic cause to a delegate, its direct participation in power will be assured.

The formation of oligarchies within the various forms of democracy is the outcome of organic necessity, and consequently affects every organization, be it socialist or even anarchist. Haller long ago noted that in every form of social life relationships of dominion and of dependence are created by Nature herself. The supremacy of the leaders in the democratic and revolutionary parties has to be taken into account in every historic situation present and to come, even though only a few and exceptional minds will be fully conscious of its existence. The mass will never rule except *in abstracto*. Consequently the question we have to discuss is not whether ideal democracy is realizable, but rather to what point and in what degree democracy is desirable, possible, and realizable at a given moment. In the problem as thus stated we recognize the fundamental problem of politics as a science. Whoever fails to perceive this must, as Sombart says, either be so blind and fanatical as not to see that the democratic current daily makes undeniable advance, or else must be so inexperienced and devoid of critical faculty as to be unable to understand that all order and all civilization must exhibit aristocratic features. The great error of socialists, an error committed in consequence of their lack of adequate psychological knowledge, is to be found in their combination of pessimism regarding the present, with rosy optimism and immeasurable confidence regarding the future. A realistic view of the mental condition of the masses shows beyond question that even if we admit the possibility of moral improvement in mankind, the human materials with whose use politicians and philosophers cannot dispense in their plans of social reconstruction are not of a character to justify excessive optimism. Within the limits of time for which human provision is possible, optimism will remain the exclusive privilege of utopian thinkers.

The socialist parties, like the trade unions, are living forms of social life. As such they react with the utmost energy against any attempt to analyse their structure or their nature, as if it were a method of vivisection. When science attains to results which conflict with their apriorist ideology, they revolt with all their power. Yet their defence is extremely feeble. Those among the representatives of such organizations whose scientific earnestness and personal good faith make it impossible for them to deny outright the existence of oligarchical tendencies in every form of democracy, endeavour to explain these tendencies as the outcome of a kind of atavism in the mentality of the masses, characteristic of the youth of the movement. The masses, they assure us, are still infected by the oligarchic virus simply because they have been oppressed during long centuries of slavery, and have never yet enjoyed an autonomous existence. The socialist regime, however, will soon restore them to health, and will furnish them with all the capacity necessary for self-government. Nothing could be

more anti-scientific than the supposition that as soon as socialists have gained possession of governmental power it will suffice for the masses to exercise a little control
over their leaders to secure that the interests of these leaders shall coincide perfectly
with the interests of the led. This idea may be compared with the view of Jules
Guesde, no less anti-scientific than anti-Marxist (though Guesde proclaims himself a
Marxist), that whereas Christianity has made God into a man, socialism will make
man into a god.

The objective immaturity of the mass is not a mere transitory phenomenon which
will disappear with the progress of democratization *au lendemain du socialisme* [in
the wake of socialism]. On the contrary, it derives from the very nature of the mass
as mass, for this, even when organized, suffers from an incurable incompetence for
the solution of the diverse problems which present themselves for solution—because
the mass *per se* is amorphous, and therefore needs division of labour, specialization,
and guidance. "L'espèce humaine veut être gouvernée; elle le sera. J'ai honte de mon
espèce," wrote Proudhon from his prison in 1850.* Man as individual is by nature
predestined to guided, and to be guided all the more in proportion as the functions
of life undergo division and subdivision. To an enormously greater degree is guidance
necessary for the social group.

From this chain of reasoning and from these scientific convictions it would be erroneous to conclude that we should renounce all endeavours to ascertain the limits
which may be imposed upon the powers exercised over the individual by oligarchies
(state, dominant class, party, etc.). It would be an error to abandon the desperate
enterprise of endeavouring to discover a social order which will render possible the
complete realization of the idea of popular sovereignty. In the present work, as the
writer said at the outset, it has not been his aim to indicate new paths. But it seemed
necessary to lay considerable stress upon the pessimist aspect of democracy which is
forced on us by historical study. We had to inquire whether, and within what limits,
democracy must remain purely ideal, possessing no other value than that of a moral
criterion which renders it possible to appreciate the varying degrees of that oligarchy
which is immanent in every social regime. In other words, we have had to inquire if,
and in what degree, democracy is an ideal which we can never hope to realize in
practice. A further aim of this work was the demolition of some of the facile and
superficial democratic illusions which trouble science and lead the masses astray.
Finally, the author desired to throw light upon certain sociological tendencies which
oppose the reign of democracy, and to a still greater extent oppose the reign of
socialism.

The writer does not wish to deny that every revolutionary working-class movement,
and every movement sincerely inspired by the democratic spirit, may have a certain
value as contributing to the enfeeblement of oligarchic tendencies. The peasant in the
fable, when on his death-bed, tells his sons that a treasure is buried in the field. After
the old man's death the sons dig everywhere in order to discover the treasure. They
do not find it. But their indefatigable labour improves the soil and secures for them
a comparative well-being. The treasure in the fable may well symbolize democracy.
Democracy is a treasure which no one will ever discover by deliberate search. But in

* ["Mankind seeks to be governed and so it will be. I am ashamed of my species." (*Ed.*)]

continuing our search, in labouring indefatigably to discover the indiscoverable, we shall perform a work which will have fertile results in the democratic sense. We have seen, indeed, that within the bosom of the democratic working-class party are born the very tendencies to counteract which that party came into existence. Thanks to the diversity and to the unequal worth of the elements of the party, these tendencies often give rise to manifestations which border on tyranny. We have seen that the replacement of the traditional legitimism of the powers-that-be by the brutal plebiscitary rule of Bonapartist parvenus does not furnish these tendencies with any moral or æsthetic superiority. Historical evolution mocks all the prophylactic measures that have been adopted for the prevention of oligarchy. If laws are passed to control the dominion of the leaders, it is the laws which gradually weaken, and not the leaders. Sometimes, however, the democratic principle carries with it, if not a cure, at least a palliative, for the disease of oligarchy. When Victor Considérant formulated his "democratico-pacificist" socialism, he declared that socialism signified, not the rule of society by the lower classes of the population, but the government and organization of society in the interest of all, through the intermediation of a group of citizens; and he added that the numerical importance of this group must increase *pari passu* with social development. This last observation draws attention to a point of capital importance. It is, in fact, a general characteristic of democracy, and hence also of the labour movement, to stimulate and to strengthen in the individual the intellectual aptitudes for criticism and control. We have seen how the progressive bureaucratization of the democratic organism tends to neutralize the beneficial effects of such criticism and such control. None the less it is true that the labour movement, in virtue of the theoretical postulates it proclaims, is apt to bring into existence (in opposition to the will of the leaders) a certain number of free spirits who, moved by principle, by instinct, or by both, desire to revise the base upon which authority is established. Urged on by conviction or by temperament, they are never weary of asking an eternal "Why?" about every human institution. Now this predisposition towards free inquiry, in which we cannot fail to recognize one of the most precious factors of civilization, will gradually increase in proportion as the economic status of the masses undergoes improvement and becomes more stable, and in proportion as they are admitted more effectively to the advantages of civilization. A wider education involves an increasing capacity for exercising control. Can we not observe every day that among the well-to-do the authority of the leaders over the led, extensive though it be, is never so unrestricted as in the case of the leaders of the poor? Taken in the mass, the poor are powerless and disarmed vis-à-vis their leaders. Their intellectual and cultural inferiority makes it impossible for them to see whither the leader is going, or to estimate in advance the significance of his actions. It is, consequently, the great task of social education to raise the intellectual level of the masses, so that they may be enabled, within the limits of what is possible, to counteract the oligarchical tendencies of the working-class movement.

In view of the perennial incompetence of the masses, we have to recognize the existence of two regulative principles:—

1    The *ideological* tendency of democracy towards criticism and control;

2   The *effective* counter-tendency of democracy towards the creation of parties ever more complex and ever more differentiated—parties, that is to say, which are increasingly based upon the competence of the few.

To the idealist, the analysis of the forms of contemporary democracy cannot fail to be a source of bitter deceptions and profound discouragement. Those alone, perhaps, are in a position to pass a fair judgment upon democracy who, without lapsing into dilettantist sentimentalism, recognize that all scientific and human ideals have relative values. If we wish to estimate the value of democracy, we must do so in comparison with its converse, pure aristocracy. The defects inherent in democracy are obvious. It is none the less true that as a form of social life we must choose democracy as the least of evils. The ideal government would doubtless be that of an aristocracy of persons at once morally good and technically efficient. But where shall we discover such an aristocracy? We may find it sometimes, though vary rarely, as the outcome of deliberate selection; but we shall never find it where the hereditary principle remains in operation. Thus monarchy in its pristine purity must be considered as imperfection incarnate, as the most incurable of ills; from the moral point of view it is inferior even to the most revolting of demagogic dictatorships, for the corrupt organism of the latter at least contains a healthy principle upon whose working we may continue to base hopes of social resanation. It may be said, therefore, that the more humanity comes to recognize the advantages which democracy, however imperfect, presents over aristocracy, even at its best, the less likely is it that a recognition of the defects of democracy will provoke a return to aristocracy. Apart from certain formal differences and from the qualities which can be acquired only by good education and inheritance (qualities in which aristocracy will always have the advantage over democracy—qualities which democracy either neglects altogether, or, attempting to imitate them, falsifies them to the point of caricature), the defects of democracy will be found to inhere in its inability to get rid of its aristocratic scoriæ. On the other hand, nothing but a serene and frank examination of the oligarchical dangers of democracy will enable us to minimize these dangers, even though they can never be entirely avoided.

The democratic currents of history resemble successive waves. They break ever on the same shoal. They are ever renewed. This enduring spectacle is simultaneously encouraging and depressing. When democracies have gained a certain stage of development, they undergo a gradual transformation, adopting the aristocratic spirit, and in many cases also the aristocratic forms, against which at the outset they struggled so fiercely. Now new accusers arise to denounce the traitors; after an era of glorious combats and of inglorious power, they end by fusing with the old dominant class; whereupon once more they are in their turn attacked by fresh opponents who appeal to the name of democracy. It is probable that this cruel game will continue without end.

# ✑ WHAT IS TO BE DONE?

*Nicolai Lenin*

*Vladimir Ilich Ulianov (1870–1924), better known to the world by his underground alias, Nicolai Lenin, is second only to Marx as a socialist theoretician and perhaps to none as an interpreter of Marx's own writings. Lenin was also one of the few intellectuals to make an unqualified success in politics. He proved to be a great revolutionary organizer during the fifteen years preceding the Russian revolution of 1917 when communism was threatened with either collapse or absorption. His flexible and wide-ranging administration at the helm of Russian affairs from 1917 to his death tempered the movement, giving it the resolute momentum we know today as an international force.*

*Early twentieth-century Russia was an absolute despotism scarcely moving toward democracy or even minimal liberalism in an age when the rest of European civilization had long since implemented the basic eighteenth-century Enlightenment demands. It was an overwhelmingly agrarian country, barely freed from serfdom, where a generation of rather rapid industrialization had hardly brought into view the potentialities of the industrial age. Lenin's bolshevism was Marxism adjusted to the peculiar circumstances of Russia: a country where an enormous peasant mass overshadowed a tiny proletariat. Russia would have seemed the last place one would expect a great Marxist revolution. Lenin's brilliant appraisal of the Russian situation in a series of polemical pamphlets, in which he attacked rival socialists, played a major role in creating the climate for revolution and in turning it toward its Bolshevist conclusion.*

*In 1898 a group of Russian Marxists founded the Social Democratic party, a heterogeneous collection of parliamentary "legalists," of "economists" whose primary aim was an improvement in the material well-being of the workers, and of revolutionaries such as Lenin and his followers who were demanding a professional and conspiratorial movement. At a party congress in 1903, Lenin's faction temporarily won dominance, and hence the right to call themselves Bolsheviks (i.e., the majority). The previous year, Lenin had published the pamphlet* What Is to Be Done? *which had attacked the more moderate positions and had been effective in rallying the membership to his views. The following selections are from this work, written long before the Bolshevik conquest of power in 1917; for a statement of Lenin's views on democracy after 1917, see* Theses and Report on Bourgeois Democracy and the Dictatorship of the Proletariat *(pages 398–404).*

## ORGANISATION OF WORKERS AND ORGANISATION OF REVOLUTIONARIES

It is only natural that a Social-Democrat, who conceives the political struggle as being identical with the "economic struggle against the employers and the government," should conceive of an "organisation of revolutionaries" as being more or less identical with an "organisation of workers." And this, in fact, is what actually happens; so that when we talk about organisation, we literally talk in different tongues. I recall a conversation I once had with a fairly consistent Economist, with whom I had not been previously acquainted. We were discussing the pamphlet *Who Will Make the Political Revolution?* and we were very soon agreed that the principal defect in that brochure was that it ignored the question of organisation. We were beginning to think that we were in complete agreement with each other—but as the conversation proceeded, it became clear that we were talking of different things. My interlocutor accused the author of the brochure just mentioned of ignoring strike funds, mutual aid societies, etc.; whereas I had in mind an organisation of revolutionaries as an essential factor in "making" the political revolution. After that became clear, I hardly remember a single question of importance upon which I was in agreement with that Economist!

What was the source of our disagreement? The fact that on questions of organisation and politics the Economists are forever lapsing from Social-Democracy into trade unionism. The political struggle carried on by the Social-Democrats is far more extensive and complex than the economic struggle the workers carry on against the employers and the government. Similarly (and indeed for that reason), the organisation of a revolutionary Social-Democratic Party must inevitably *differ* from the organisations of the workers designed for the latter struggle. A workers' organisation must in the first place be a trade organisation; secondly, it must be as wide as possible; and thirdly, it must be as public as conditions will allow (here, and further on, of course, I have only autocratic Russia in mind). On the other hand, the organisations of revolutionaries must consist first and foremost of people whose profession is that of a revolutionary (that is why I speak of organisations of *revolutionaries*, meaning revolutionary Social-Democrats). In view of this common feature of the members of such an organisation, *all distinctions as between workers and intellectuals*, and certainly distinctions of trade and profession, must be obliterated. Such an organisation must of necessity be not too extensive and as secret as possible. Let us examine this threefold distinction.

In countries where political liberty exists the distinction between a trade union and a political organisation is clear, as is the distinction between trade unions and Social-Democracy. The relation of the latter to the former will naturally vary in each country according to historical, legal and other conditions—it may be more or less close or more or less complex (in our opinion it should be as close and simple as possible); but trade union organisations are certainly not in the least identical with the Social-Democratic Party organisations in free countries. In Russia, however, the yoke of autocracy appears at first glance to obliterate all distinctions between a Social-Democratic organisation and trade unions, because *all* workers' associations and *all* circles are prohibited, and because the principal manifestation and weapon of the workers' economic struggle—the strike—is regarded as a criminal offence (and sometimes even

V. I. Lenin, *Selected Works* (London: Lawrence and Wishart, Ltd., 1936), II, 126–134, 138–154.

as a political offence!). Conditions in our country, therefore, strongly "impel" the workers who are conducting the economic struggle to concern themselves with political questions. They also "impel" the Social-Democrats to confuse trade unionism with Social-Democracy (and our Krichevskys, Martynovs and their like, while speaking enthusiastically of the first kind of "impelling," fail to observe the "impelling" of the second kind). Indeed, picture to yourselves the people who are immersed ninety-nine per cent in "the economic struggle against the employers and the government." Some of them have never, *during the whole course of their activity* (four to six months), thought of the need for a more complex organisation of revolutionaries; others, perhaps, come across the fairly widely distributed Bernsteinian literature, from which they become convinced of the profound importance of the forward march of "the drab everyday struggle." Still others are carried away, perhaps, by the seductive idea of showing the world a new example of "close and organic contact with the proletarian struggle"—contact between the trade union and Social-Democratic movements. Such people would perhaps argue that the later a country enters into the arena of capitalism and, consequently, of the labour movement, the more the Socialists in that country may take part in, and support, the trade union movement, and the less reason is there for non-Social-Democratic trade unions. So far, the argument is absolutely correct; unfortunately, however, some go beyond that and hint at the complete fusion of Social-Democracy with trade unionism. We shall soon see, from the example of the rules of the St. Petersburg League of Struggle, what a harmful effect these dreams have upon our plans of organisation.

The workers' organisations for carrying on the economic struggle should be trade union organisations; every Social-Democratic worker should, as far as possible, support and actively work inside these organisations. That is true. But it is not in the least in our interest to demand that only Social-Democrats be eligible for membership in the trade unions, for this would only restrict our influence over the masses. Let every worker who understands the need for organisation in order to carry on the struggle against the employers and the government join the trade unions. The very objects of the trade unions would be unattainable unless they were extremely *wide* organisations. The wider these organisations are, the wider our influence over them will be, and this influence will be exercised not only through the "spontaneous" development of the economic struggle, but also by the direct and conscious effect the Socialist members of the union have on their comrades. But a wide organisation cannot apply the methods of strict secrecy (since the latter demands far greater training than is required for the economic struggle). How is the contradiction between the need for a large membership and the need for strictly secret methods to be reconciled? How are we to make the trade unions as public as possible? Generally speaking, there are perhaps only two ways to this end: either the trade unions become legalised (which in some countries precedes the legalisation of the socialist and political unions), or the organisation is kept a secret one, but so "free" and amorphous, *lose* as the Germans say, that the need for secret methods becomes almost negligible as far as the bulk of the members is concerned.

The legalisation of the non-socialist and non-political labour unions in Russia has already begun, and there is no doubt that every advance our rapidly growing Social-Democratic working class movement makes will increase and encourage the attempts at legalisation. These attempts proceed for the most part from supporters of the existing order, but they will proceed also from the workers themselves and from the liberal intellectuals. The banner of legality has already been unfurled by the Vassilyevs and the Zubatovs. Support has been promised by the Ozerovs and the Wormses, and followers of the new tendency are to be found among the workers. Henceforth, we must reckon with this tendency. How are we to reckon with it? There can be no two opinions about this among Social-Democrats. We must constantly expose any part played in this movement by the Zubatovs and the Vassilyevs, the gendarmes and the priests, and explain to the workers what their real intentions are. We must also expose the conciliatory, "harmonious" undertones that will be heard in the speeches delivered by liberal politicians at the legal meetings of the workers, irrespective of whether they proceed from an earnest conviction of the desirability of peaceful class collaboration, whether they proceed from a desire to curry favour with the employers, or are simply the result of clumsiness. We must also warn the workers against the traps often set by the police, who at such open meetings and permitted societies spy out the "hotheads" and who, through the medium of the legal organisations, endeavour to plant their *agents provocateurs* in the illegal organisations.

But while doing all this, we must not forget that *in the long run* the legalisation of the working class movement will be to our advantage, and not to that of the Zubatovs. On the contrary, our campaign of exposure will help to separate the tares from the wheat. What the tares are, we have already indicated. By the wheat, we mean attracting the attention of still larger and more backward sections of the workers to social and political questions, and freeing ourselves, the revolutionaries, from functions which are essentially legal (the distribution of legal books, mutual aid, etc.), the development of which will inevitably provide us with an increasing quantity of material for agitation. In this sense, we may say, and we should say, to the Zubatovs and the Ozerovs: keep at it, gentlemen, do your best! When you place a trap in the path of the workers (either by way of direct provocation, or by the "honest" corruption of the workers with the aid of "Struve-ism"), we shall see to it that you are exposed. But whenever you take a real step forward, even if it is timid and vacillating, we shall say: please continue! And the only step that can be a real step forward is a real, if small, extension of the workers' field of action. Every such extension will be to our advantage and will help to hasten the advent of legal societies, not of the kind in which *agents provocateurs* hunt for Socialists, but of the kind in which Socialists will hunt for adherents. In a word, our task is to fight down the tares. It is not our business to grow wheat in flower-pots. By pulling up the tares, we clear the soil for the wheat. And while the old-fashioned folk are tending their flower-pot crops, we must prepare reapers, not only to cut down the tares of today, but also to reap the wheat of tomorrow.

Legalisation, therefore, will *not solve* the problem of creating a trade union organisation that will be as public and as extensive as possible (but we would be extremely glad if the Zubatovs and the Ozerovs provided even a partial opportunity for such a solution—to which end we must fight them as strenuously as possible!). There only remains the path of secret trade union organisation; and *we must* offer all possible assistance to the workers, who (as we definitely know) have already adopted this path. Trade union organisations may not only be of tremendous value in developing and consolidating the economic struggle, but may also become a very important auxiliary to political agitation and revolutionary organisation. In order to achieve this purpose, and in order to guide the nascent trade union movement in the direction the Social-Democrats desire, we must first fully understand the foolishness of the plan of organisation with which the St. Petersburg Economists have been occupying themselves for nearly five years. That plan is described in the "Rules for a Workers' Benefit Fund" of July 1897 (*Listok Rabotnika*, No. 9-10, p. 46, in *Rabochaya Mysl*, No. 1), and also in the "Rules for a Trade Union Workers' Organisation," of October 1900. (Special leaflet printed in St. Petersburg and quoted in *Iskra*, No 1.) The fundamental error contained in both these sets of rules is that they give a detailed formulation of a wide workers' organisation and confuse the latter with the organisation of revolutionaries. Let us take the last-mentioned set of rules, since it is drawn up in greater detail. The body of it consists of *fifty-two* paragraphs. Twenty-three paragraphs deal with structure, the method of conducting business and the competence of the "workers' circles," which are to be organised in every factory ("not more than ten persons") and which elect "central (factory) groups." "The central group," says paragraph 2, "observes all that goes on in its factory or workshop and keeps a record of events." "The central group presents to the contributors a monthly report on the state of the funds" (par. 17), etc. Ten paragraphs are devoted to the "district organisation," and nineteen to the highly complex interconnection between the Committee of the Workers' Organisation and the Committee of the St. Petersburg League of Struggle (delegates from each district and from the "executive groups"—"groups of propagandists, groups for maintaining contact with the provinces and with the organisation abroad, and for managing stores, publications and funds").

Social-Democracy = "executive groups" in relation to the economic struggle of the workers! It would be difficult to find a more striking illustration than this of how the Economists' ideas deviate from Social-Democracy to trade unionism, and how foreign to them is the idea that a Social-Democrat must concern himself first and foremost with an organisation of revolutionaries, capable of guiding the *whole* proletarian struggle for emancipation. To talk of "the political emancipation of the working class" and the struggle against "tsarist despotism," and at the same time to draft rules like these, indicates a complete failure to understand what the real political tasks of Social-Democracy are. Not one of the fifty or so paragraphs reveals the slightest glimmer of understanding that it is necessary to conduct the widest possible political agitation among the masses, an agitation that deals with every phase of Russian absolutism and with every aspect of the various social classes in Russia. Rules like these are of no use even for the achievement of trade union aims, let alone political aims, for that requires organisation *according to trade*, and yet the rules do not contain a single reference to this.

But most characteristic of all, perhaps, is the amazing top-heaviness of the whole "system," which attempts to bind every factory with the "committee" by a permanent string of uniform and ludicrously petty rules and a three-stage system of election. Hemmed in by the narrow outlook of Economism, the mind is lost in details which positively reek of red tape and bureaucracy. In practice, of course, three-fourths of the clauses are never applied; on the other hand, however, a "conspiratorial" organisation of this kind, with its central group in each factory, makes it very easy for the gendarmes to carry out raids on a large scale. Our Polish comrades have already passed through a similar phase in their own movement, when everybody was extremely enthusiastic about the extensive organisation of workers' funds; but these ideas were very quickly abandoned when it was found that such organisations only provided rich harvests for the gendarmes. If we are out for wide workers' organisations, and not for wide arrests, if it is not our purpose to provide satisfaction to the gendarmes, these organisations must remain absolutely loose. But will they be able to function? Well, let us see what the functions are: ". . . to observe all that goes on in the factory and keep a record of events." (Par. 2 of the Rules.) Do we need a special group for this? Could not the purpose be better served by correspondence conducted in the illegal papers and without setting up special groups? ". . . to lead the struggles of the workers for the improvement of their workshop conditions." (Par. 3 of the Rules.) This, too, requires no special group. Any agitator with any intelligence at all can gather what demands the workers want to advance in the course of ordinary conversation and transmit them to a narrow—not a wide—organisation of revolutionaries to be embodied in a leaflet. ". . . to organise a fund . . . to which contributions of two kopeks per ruble should be made" (par. 9) . . . to present monthly reports to the contributors on the state of the funds (par. 17) . . . to expel members who fail to pay their contributions (par. 10), and so forth. Why, this is a very paradise for the police; for nothing would be easier than for them to penetrate into the ponderous secrecy of a "central factory fund," confiscate the money and arrest the best members. Would it not be simpler to issue one-kopek or two-kopek coupons bearing the official stamp of a well-known (very exclusive and very secret) organisation, or to make collections without coupons of any kind and to print reports in a certain agreed code in the illegal paper? The object would thereby be attained, but it would be a hundred times more difficult for the gendarmes to pick up clues.

I could go on analysing the rules, but I think that what has been said will suffice. A small, compact core, consisting of reliable, experienced and hardened workers, with responsible agents in the principal districts and connected by all the rules of strict secrecy with the organisations of revolutionaries, can, with the wide support of the masses and without an elaborate organisation, perform *all* the functions of a trade union organisation, and perform them, moreover, in the manner Social-Democrats desire. Only in this way can we secure the *consolidation* and development of a *Social-Democratic* trade union movement, in spite of the gendarmes.

It may be objected that an organisation which is so loose that it is not even definitely formed, and which even has no enrolled and registered members, cannot be called an organisation at all. That may very well be. I am not out for names. But this "organisation without members" can do everything that is required, and will, from the very outset, guarantee the closest contact between our future trade unions and socialism. Only an incorrigible utopian would want a *wide* organisation of workers, with elections, reports, universal suffrage, etc., under the autocracy.

The moral to be drawn from this is a simple one. If we begin with the solid foundation of a strong organisation of revolutionaries, we can guarantee the stability of the movement as a whole and carry out the aims of both Social-Democracy and of trade unionism. If, however, we begin with a wide workers' organisation, supposed to be most "accessible" to the masses, when as a matter of fact it will be most accessible to the gendarmes and will make the revolutionaries most accessible to the police, we shall achieve the aims neither of Social-Democracy nor of trade unionism; we shall not escape from our primitiveness, and because we constantly remain scattered and broken up, we shall make only the trade unions of the Zubatov and Ozerov type most accessible to the masses. . . .

"A dozen wise men can be more easily caught than a hundred fools!" This wonderful truth (which the hundred fools will applaud) appears obvious only because in the very midst of the argument you have skipped from one question to another. You began by talking, and continued to talk, of catching a "committee," of catching an "organisation," and now you skip to the question of getting hold of the "roots" of the movement in the "depths." The fact is, of course, that our movement cannot be caught precisely because it has hundreds and hundreds of thousands of roots deep down among the masses; but that is not the point we are discussing. As far as "deep roots" are concerned, we cannot be "caught" even now, in spite of all our primitiveness; but we all complain, and cannot but complain, that the *organisations* are caught, with the result that it is impossible to maintain continuity in the movement. If you agree to discuss the question of catching the *organisations* and to stick to that question, then I assert that it is far more difficult to catch a dozen wise men than it is to catch a hundred fools. And this position I shall defend no matter how much you instigate the crowd against me for my "anti-democratic" views, etc. As I have already said, by "wise men," in connection with organisation, I mean *professional revolutionaries*, irrespective of whether they are trained from among students or workingmen. I assert: 1) that no movement can be durable without a stable organisation of leaders to maintain continuity; 2) that the more widely the masses are spontaneously drawn into the struggle and form the basis of the movement and participate in it, the more necessary is it to have such an organisation, and the more stable must it be (for it is much easier for demagogues to side-track the more backward sections of the masses); 3) that the organisation must consist chiefly of persons engaged in revolutionary activities as a profession; 4) that in a country with an autocratic government, the more we *restrict* the membership of this organisation to persons who are engaged in revolutionary activities as a profession and who have been professionally trained in the art of combating the political police, the more difficult will it be to catch the organisation; and 5) the *wider* will be the circle of men and women of the working class or of other classes of society able to join the movement and perform active work in it.

I invite our Economists, terrorists and "Economists-terrorists" to confute these propositions. At the moment, I shall deal only with the last two points. The question as to whether it is easier to catch "a dozen wise men" or "a hundred fools" reduces itself to the question we have considered above, namely, whether it is possible to have a mass *organisation* when the maintenance of strict secrecy is essential. We can never give a mass organisation that degree of secrecy which is essential for the persistent and continuous struggle against the government. But to concentrate all secret functions in the hands of as small a number of professional revolutionaries as possible does not mean that the latter will "do the thinking for all" and that the crowd will not take an active part in the *movement*. On the contrary, the crowd will advance from its ranks increasing numbers of professional revolutionaries, for it will know that it is not enough for a few students and workingmen, waging economic war, to gather together and form a "committee," but that it takes years to train professional revolutionaries; the crowd will "think" not of primitive ways but of training professional revolutionaries. The centralisation of the secret functions of the *organisation* does not mean the centralisation of all the functions of the *movement*. The active participation of the broad masses in the dissemination of illegal literature will not diminish because a dozen professional revolutionaries centralise the secret part of the work; on the contrary, it will *increase tenfold*. Only in this way will the reading of illegal literature, the contribution to illegal literature and to some extent even the distribution of illegal literature *almost cease to be secret work*, for the police will soon come to realise the folly and futility of setting the whole judicial and administrative machine into motion to intercept every copy of a publication that is being broadcast in thousands. This applies not only to the press, but to every function of the movement, even to demonstrations. The active and widespread participation of the masses will not suffer; on the contrary, it will benefit by the fact that a "dozen" experienced revolutionaries, no less professionally trained than the police, will centralise all the secret side of the work—prepare leaflets, work out approximate plans and appoint bodies of leaders for each urban district, for each factory district and for each educational institution, etc. (I know that exception will be taken to my "undemocratic" views, but I shall reply to this altogether unintelligent objection later on.) The centralisation of the more secret functions in an organisation of revolutionaries will not diminish, but rather increase the extent and the quality of the activity of a large number of other organisations intended for wide membership and which, therefore, can be as loose and as public as possible, for example, trade unions, workers' circles for self-education and the reading of illegal literature, and socialist and also democratic circles for *all other sections of the population*, etc., etc. We must have *as large a number as possible* of such organisations having the widest possible variety of functions, but it is absurd and dangerous to *confuse these with organisations of revolutionaries*, to erase the line of demarcation between them, to dim still more the masses' already incredibly hazy appreciation of the fact that in order to "serve" the mass movement we must have people who will devote themselves exclusively to Social-Democratic activities, and that such people must *train* themselves patiently and steadfastly to be professional revolutionaries.

Aye, this appreciation has become incredibly dim. The most grievous sin we have committed in regard to organisation is that *by our primitiveness we have lowered the prestige of revolutionaries in Russia*. A man who is weak and vacillating on theoretical questions, who has a narrow outlook, who makes excuses for his own slackness on the ground that the masses are awakening spontaneously, who resembles a trade union secretary more than a people's tribune, who is unable to conceive of a broad and bold plan, who is incapable of inspiring even his opponents with respect for himself, and who is inexperienced and clumsy in his own professional art—the art of combating the political police—such a man is not a revolutionary but a wretched amateur!

Let no active worker take offence at these frank remarks, for as far as insufficient training is concerned, I apply them first and foremost to myself. I used to work in a circle that set itself great and all-embracing tasks; and every member of that circle suffered to the point of torture from the realisation that we were proving ourselves to be amateurs at a moment in history when we might have been able to say, paraphrasing a well-known epigram: "Give us an organisation of revolutionaries, and we shall overturn the whole of Russia!" And the more I recall the burning sense of shame I then experienced, the more bitter are my feelings towards those pseudo-Social-Democrats whose teachings bring disgrace on the calling of a revolutionary, who fail to understand that our task is not to degrade the revolutionaries to the level of an amateur, but to *exalt* the amateur to the level of a revolutionary.

### THE SCOPE OF ORGANISATIONAL WORK

. . . The critical, transitional state of our movement in this connection may be formulated as follows: *there are no people—yet there are enormous numbers of people.* There are enormous numbers of people, because the working class and the most diverse strata of society, year after year, advance from their ranks an increasing number of discontented people who desire to protest, who are ready to render all the assistance they can in the fight against absolutism, the intolerableness of which is not yet recognised by all, but is nevertheless more and more acutely sensed by increasing masses of the people. At the same time we have no people, because we have no leaders, no political leaders, we have no talented organisers capable of organising extensive and at the same time uniform and harmonious work that would give employment to all forces, even the most inconsiderable. "The growth and development of revolutionary organisations" not only lag behind the growth of the labour movement, . . . but also behind the general democratic movement among all strata of the people. . . . The scope of revolutionary work is too narrow compared with the breadth of the spontaneous basis of the movement. It is too hemmed in by the wretched "economic struggle against the employers and the government" theory. And yet, at the present time, not only Social-Democratic political agitators, but also Social-Democratic organisers must "go among all classes of the population."

There is hardly a single practical worker who would have any doubt about the ability of Social-Democrats to distribute the thousand and one minute functions of their organisational work among the various representatives of the most varied classes. Lack of specialisation is one of our most serious technical defects. . . . The smaller each separate "operation" in our common cause will be, the more people we shall find capable of carrying out such operations (people, who, in the majority of cases, are not capable of becoming professional revolutionaries), the more difficult will it be for the police to "catch" all these "detail workers," and the more difficult will it be for them to frame up, out of an arrest for some petty affair, a "case" that would justify the government's expenditure on the "secret service." As for the number ready to help us, we have already referred in the previous chapter to the gigantic change that has taken place in this respect in the last five years or so. On the other hand, in order to unite all these tiny fractions into one whole, in order, in breaking up functions, to avoid breaking up the movement, and in order to imbue those who carry out these minute functions with the conviction that their work is necessary and important, for without this they will never do the work,[1] it is necessary to have a strong organisation of tried revolutionaries. The more secret such an organisation would be, the stronger and more widespread would be the confidence of the masses in the Party, and, as we know, in time of war, it is not only of great importance to imbue one's own army with confidence in its own strength, it is important also to convince the enemy and all *neutral* elements of this strength; friendly neutrality may sometimes decide the issue. If such an organisation existed on a firm theoretical basis, and possessed a Social-Democratic journal, we would have no reason to fear that the movement would be diverted from its path by the numerous "outside" elements that are attracted to it. (On the contrary, it is precisely at the present time, when primitive methods prevail among us, that many Social-Democrats are observed to gravitate towards the *Credo,* and only imagine that they are Social-Democrats.) In a word, specialisation necessarily presupposes centralisation, and in its turn imperatively calls for it. . . .

Not only are revolutionaries lagging behind the spontaneous awakening of the masses generally, but even working class revolutionaries are lagging behind the spontaneous awakening of the working class masses. And this *fact* most strikingly confirms, even from the "practical" point of view, not only the absurdity but even the *political reactionariness* of the "pedagogics" to which we are so often treated when discussing our duties to the workers. This fact proves that our very first and most imperative duty is to help to train working class revolutionaries who will be on the same level *in regard to Party activity* as intellectual revolutionaries (we emphasise the words "in regard to Party activity," because although it is necessary, it is not so easy and not so imperative to bring the workers up to the level of intellectuals in other respects). Therefore, attention must be devoted *principally* to the task of *raising* the workers to the level of revolutionaries, and not to *degrading* ourselves to the level of the "labour masses" as the Economists wish to do, or necessarily to the level of the average worker, as *Svoboda* desires to do (and by this raises itself to the second grade of Economist "pedagogics"). I am far from denying the necessity for popular literature for the workers, and especially popular (but, of course, not vulgar) literature for the especially backward workers. But what annoys me is that pedagogics are constantly con-

---

[1] *I recall the story a comrade related to me of a factory inspector, who, desiring to help, and while in fact helping Social-Democracy, bitterly complained that he did not know whether the "information" he sent reached the proper revolutionary quarter; he did not know how much his help was really required, and what possibilities there were for utilising his small services. Every practical worker, of course, knows of more than one case, similar to this, of our primitiveness depriving us of allies. And these services, each "small" in itself, but incalculable when taken together, could be rendered to us by office employees and officials, not only in factories, but in the postal service, on the railways, in the Customs, among the nobility, among the clergy and every other walk of life, including even the police service and the Court! Had we a real party, a real militant organisation of revolutionaries, we would not put the question bluntly to every one of these "abettors," we would not hasten in every single case to bring them right into the very heart of our "illegality," but, on the contrary, we would husband them very carefully and would train people especially for such functions, bearing in mind the fact that many students could be of much greater service to the Party as "abettors"—officials—than as "short-term" revolutionaries. But, I repeat, only an organisation that is already established and has no lack of active forces would have the right to apply such tactics.*

fused with questions of politics and organisation. You, gentlemen, who are so much concerned about the "average worker," as a matter of fact, rather insult the workers by your desire to *talk down* to them when discussing labour politics and labour organisation. Talk about serious things in a serious manner; leave pedagogics to the pedagogues, and not to politicians and to organisers! Are there not advanced people, "average people," and "masses," among the intelligentsia? Does not everyone recognise that popular literature is required also for the intelligentsia and is not such literature written? Just imagine someone, in an article on organising college or high-school students, repeating over and over again, as if he had made a new discovery, that first of all we must have an organisation of "average students." The author of such an article would rightly be laughed at. He would be told: give us an organisational idea, if you have one, and we ourselves will settle the question as to which of us are "average," as to who is higher and who is lower. But if you have no organisational ideas *of your own,* then all your chatter about "masses" and "average" is simply boring. Try to understand that these questions about "politics" and "organisation" are so serious in themselves that they cannot be dealt with in any other but a serious way. We can and must *educate* workers (and university and high-school students) so as to enable them to understand us when we speak to them about these questions; and when you do come to us to talk about these questions, give us real replies to them, do not fall back on the "average," or on the "masses"; don't evade them by quoting adages or mere phrases.

In order to be fully prepared for his task, the working class revolutionary must also become a professional revolutionary. Hence B——v is wrong when he says that as the worker is engaged for eleven and a half hours a day in the factory, therefore, the brunt of all the other revolutionary functions (apart from agitation) *"must necessarily* fall mainly upon the shoulders of an extremely small intellectual force." It need not "necessarily" be so. It is so because we are backward, because we do not recognise our duty to assist every capable worker to become a *professional* agitator, organiser, propagandist, literature distributor, etc., etc. In this respect, we waste our strength in a positively shameful manner; we lack the ability to husband that which should be tended and reared with special care. Look at the Germans: they have a hundred times more forces than we have. But they understand perfectly well that the "average" does not too frequently promote really capable agitators, etc., from its ranks. Hence they immediately try to place every capable workingman in such conditions as will enable him to develop and apply his abilities to the utmost: he is made a professional agitator, he is encouraged to widen the field of his activity, to spread it from one factory to the whole of his trade, from one locality to the whole country. He acquires experience and dexterity in his profession, his outlook becomes wider, his knowledge increases, he observes the prominent political leaders from other localities and other parties, he strives to rise to their level and combine within himself the knowledge of working class environment and freshness of socialist convictions with professional skill, without which the proletariat *cannot* carry on a stubborn struggle with the excellently trained enemy. Only in this way can men of the stamp of Bebel and Auer be promoted from the ranks of the working class. But what takes place very largely automatically in a politically free country must in Russia be done deliberately and systematically by our organisations. A workingman agitator who is at all talented and "promising" *must not be left* to work eleven hours a day in a factory. We must arrange that he be maintained by the Party, that he may in due time go underground, that he change the place of his activity, otherwise he will not enlarge his experience, he will not widen his outlook, and will not be able to stay in the fight against the gendarmes for at least a few years. As the spontaneous rise of the working class masses becomes wider and deeper, they not only promote from their ranks an increasing number of talented agitators, but also of talented organisers, propagandists and "practical workers" in the best sense of the term (of whom there are so few among our intelligentsia who, in the majority of cases, are somewhat careless and sluggish in their habits, so characteristic of Russians). When we have detachments of specially trained working class revolutionaries who have gone through long years of preparation (and, of course, revolutionaries "of all arms"), no political police in the world will be able to contend against them, for these detachments of men absolutely devoted and loyal to the revolution will themselves enjoy the absolute confidence and devotion of the broad masses of the workers. The *sin* we commit is that we do not sufficiently "stimulate" the workers to take this path, "common" to them and to the "intellectuals," of professional revolutionary training, and that we too frequently drag them back by our silly speeches about what "can be understood" by the masses of the workers, by the "average workers," etc.

In this, as in other cases, the narrowness of our field of organisational work is without a doubt directly due (although the overwhelming majority of the Economists and the novices in practical work do not appreciate it) to the fact that we restrict our theories and our political tasks to a narrow field. Subservience to spontaneity seems to inspire a fear of taking even one step away from what "can be understood" by the masses, a fear of rising too high above mere subservience to the immediate requirements of the masses. Have no fear, gentlemen! Remember that we stand so low on the plane of organisation that the very idea that we could rise *too high* is absurd!

### "CONSPIRATIVE" ORGANISATION AND "DEMOCRACY"

. . . Many, including apparently B. Krichevsky (*Rabocheye Dyelo*, No. 10, p. 18), misunderstand the polemics that Social-Democrats have always waged against the "conspirative" view of the political struggle. We have always protested, and will, of course, continue to protest against *restricting* the political struggle to conspiracies. But this does not, of course, mean that we deny the need for a strong revolutionary organisation. And in the pamphlet mentioned in the preceding footnote, after the polemics against reducing the political struggle to a conspiracy, a description is given (as a Social-Democratic ideal) of an organisation so strong as to be able to "resort to rebellion" and to "every other form of attack," in order to "deliver a smashing blow against absolutism." According to its *form* a strong revolutionary organisation of that kind in an autocratic country may also be described as a "conspirative" organisation, because the French word *"conspiration"* means in Russian "conspiracy," and we must have the utmost conspiracy for an organisation of that kind. Secrecy is such a necessary condition for such an organisation that all the other conditions (number and selection of members, functions, etc.) must all be subordinated to it. It would be extremely naive indeed, therefore, to fear the accusation that we Social-Democrats desire to create a conspirative organisation. . . .

Against us it will be argued: such a powerful and strictly secret organisation, which concentrates in its hands all the threads of secret activities, an organisation which of necessity must be a centralised organisation, may too easily throw itself into a premature attack, may thoughtlessly intensify the movement before political discontent, the ferment and anger of the working class, etc., are sufficiently ripe for it. To this we reply: speaking abstractly, it cannot be denied, of course, that a militant organisation *may* thoughtlessly commence a battle, which *may* end in defeat, which might have been avoided under other circumstances. But we cannot confine ourselves to abstract reasoning on such a question, because every battle bears within itself the abstract possibility of defeat, and there is no other way of *reducing this possibility* than by organised preparation for battle. If, however, we base our argument on the concrete conditions prevailing in Russia at the present time, we must come to the positive conclusion that a strong revolutionary organisation is absolutely necessary precisely for the purpose of giving firmness to the movement, and of *safeguarding* it against the possibility of its making premature attacks. It is precisely at the present time, when no such organisation exists yet, and when the revolutionary movement is rapidly and spontaneously growing, that we *already observe* two opposite extremes (which, as is to be expected, "meet"), *i.e.*, absolutely unsound Economism and the preaching of moderation, and equally unsound "excitative terror," which strives artificially to "call forth symptoms of its end in a movement which is developing and becoming strong, but which is as yet nearer to its beginning than to its end." (V. Zasulich, in *Zarya*, No. 2–3, p. 353.) And the example of *Rabocheye Dyelo* shows that *there are already* Social-Democrats who give way to both these extremes. This is not surprising because, apart from other reasons, the "economic struggle against the employers and the government" *can never* satisfy revolutionaries, and because opposite extremes will always arise here and there. Only a centralised, militant organisation that consistently carries out a Social-Democratic policy, that satisfies, so to speak, all revolutionary instincts and strivings, can safeguard the movement against making thoughtless attacks and prepare it for attacks that hold out the promise of success.

It will be further argued against us that the views on organisation here expounded contradict the "principles of democracy." Now while the first-mentioned accusation was of purely Russian origin, this one is of *purely foreign* origin. And only an organisation abroad (the League of Russian Social-Democrats) would be capable of giving its editorial board instructions like the following:

> "*Principles of Organisation*. In order to secure the successful development and unification of Social-Democracy, broad democratic principles of Party organisation must be emphasised, developed and fought for; and this is particularly necessary in view of the anti-democratic tendencies that have become revealed in the ranks of our Party." (*Two Congresses*, p. 18.)

We shall see how *Rabocheye Dyelo* fights against *Iskra's* "anti-democratic tendencies" in the next chapter. Here we shall examine more closely the "principle" that the Economists advance. Everyone will probably agree that "broad democratic principles" presuppose the two following conditions: first, full publicity, and second, election to all functions. It would be absurd to speak about democracy without publicity, that is, a publicity that extends beyond the circle of the membership of the organisation. We call the German Socialist Party a democratic organisation because all it does is done publicly; even its Party congresses are held in public. But no one would call an organisation that is hidden from every one but its members by a veil of secrecy, a democratic organisation. What is the use of advancing *"broad* democratic principles" when the fundamental condition for these principles *cannot be fulfilled* by a secret organisation? "Broad principles" turns out to be a resonant but hollow phrase. More than that, this phrase proves that the urgent tasks in regard to organisation are totally misunderstood. Everyone knows how great is the lack of secrecy among the "broad" masses of revolutionaries. We have heard the bitter complaints of B——v on this score, and his absolutely just demand for a "strict selection of members." (*Rabocheye Dyelo*, No. 6, p. 42.) And people who boast about their "sensitiveness to life" come forward in a situation like this, and *urge*, not strict secrecy and a strict (and therefore more restricted) selection of members but *"broad* democratic principles"! This is what we call being absolutely wide of the mark.

Nor is the situation with regard to the second attribute of democracy, namely, the principle of election, any better. In politically free countries, this condition is taken for granted. "Membership of the Party is open to those who accept the principles of the Party programme, and render all the support they can to the Party"—says point 1 of the rules of the German Social-Democratic Party. And as the political arena is as open to the public view as is the stage in a theatre, this acceptance or non-acceptance, support or opposition, is known to all from the press and public meetings. Everyone knows that a certain political worker commenced in a certain way, passed through a certain evolution, behaved in difficult periods in a certain way and possesses certain qualities and, consequently, knowing all the facts of the case, *every* Party member can decide for himself whether or not to elect this person for a certain Party office. The general control (in the literal sense of the term) that the Party exercises over every act this person commits in the political field brings into existence an automatically operating mechanism which brings about what in biology is called "survival of the fittest." "Natural selection" of full publicity, the principle of election and general control provide the guarantee that, in the last analysis, every political worker will be "in his proper place," will do the work for which he is best fitted by his strength and abilities, will feel the effects of his mistakes on himself, and prove before all the world his ability to recognise mistakes and to avoid them.

Try to put this picture in the frame of our autocracy! Is it possible in Russia for all those "who accept the principles of the Party programme and render all the support they can to the Party" to control every action of the revolutionary working in secret? Is it possible for all the revolutionaries to elect one of their number to any particular office, when, in the very interests of the work, he *must* conceal his identity from nine out of ten of these "all"? Ponder a little over the real meaning of the high-sounding phrases that *Rabocheye Dyelo* gives utterance to, and you will realise that "broad democracy" in Party organisation, amidst the gloom of autocracy and the domination of gendarme selection, is nothing more than a *useless and harmful toy*. It is a useless toy because, as a matter of fact, no revolutionary organisation has ever practised *broad* democracy, nor could it, however much it desired to do so. It is a harmful toy because any attempt to practise the "broad democratic principles" will simply facilitate the work of the police in making big raids, it will perpetuate the prevailing primitiveness, divert the thoughts of the practical workers from the serious and imperative task of training themselves to become professional revolutionaries to that of drawing up detailed "paper" rules for election systems. Only abroad, where very often people who have no opportunity of doing real live work gather together, can the "game of democracy" be played here and there, especially in small groups. . . .

## ◆§ THESES AND REPORT ON BOURGEOIS DEMOCRACY AND THE DICTATORSHIP OF THE PROLETARIAT

*Nicolai Lenin*

*Marxism originally was an egalitarian philosophy designed to create a perfect democracy, one free of all personal exploitation and social-class dominance. Yet the first establishment of Marxism, in Russia, was under the leadership of Bolsheviks who had explicitly rejected democratic methods. After the Bolshevik revolution, observers, including Socialists and non-Socialist liberals otherwise sympathetic to a popular revolution in Russia, felt that the Bolshevik regime was in fact perpetuating its antidemocratic tactics contrary to Socialist principles, to the great misfortune of the Russian people, who seemed to have gone from one despotism to another.*

*Lenin was far from insensitive to these criticisms, especially when they came from his old enemies, the moderate democratic Socialists. He thought he could defend the continuation of antidemocratic methods in the early years of the new regime as well as demolish Western claims to perfect democracy. In February, 1919, the (Democratic) Socialist International condemned the "dictatorship" of the Bolsheviks and called for at least minimal democratic liberties for the Russian people. Lenin answered (in the document which follows) with a statement which continues to have relevance for the current cold war between Communist and non-Communist countries, a controversy which frequently revolves around the very important distinctions between necessary despotism and false democracy.*

*Submitted to the First Congress of the Communist International, March 4, 1919*

1 The growth of the revolutionary movement of the proletariat in all countries has called forth the convulsive efforts of the bourgeoisie and of its agents in the working class organisations to find ideological political arguments in defence of the rule of the exploiters. Of these arguments, the condemnation of dictatorship and defence of democracy are put in the forefront. The sham and hypocrisy of this argument, reiterated in a thousand sharps and flats in the capitalist press and at the Berne Conference of the yellow International in February 1919, are obvious to all those who desire to remain loyal to the fundamental principles of socialism.

2 First of all this argument operates with the concepts "democracy in general" and "dictatorship in general" without putting the question as to which class is concerned. This non-class or above-class, alleged several democratic presentation of the question is a downright mockery of the fundamental tenet of socialism, *viz.*, the tenet of the class struggle, which the Socialists who have deserted to the side of the bourgeoisie recognise in words, but actually forget. There is not a single civilised capitalist country in the world in which "democracy in general" exists; what exists is bourgeois democracy, and what we are discussing is not "dictatorship in general," but the dictatorship of the oppressed class, *i.e.*, of the proletariat, over the oppressors and exploiters, *i.e.*, the bourgeoisie, with the object of overcoming the resistance of the exploiters in their struggle to preserve their rule.

3 History teaches that not a single oppressed class has ever come into power, or could come into power, without passing through the period of dictatorship, *i.e.*, the conquest of political power and the violent suppression of the desperate, furious and unscrupulous resistance which the exploiters always put up. The bourgeoisie, whose rule the Socialists who oppose "dictatorship in general" and who bow down before "democracy in general" now defend, achieved power in the advanced countries by means of a number of rebellions, by civil wars, by the violent suppression of kings, feudal barons and slave owners, and their attempts at restoration. In their books and pamphlets, in the resolutions of their congresses and in their agitational speeches, the Socialists of all countries have explained to the people the class character of these bourgeois revolutions, of this bourgeois dictatorship, a thousand and a million times. Hence, the present defence of bourgeois democracy cloaked in speeches about "democracy in general" and the present howling and shouting against the dictatorship of the proletariat cloaked by cries about "dictatorship in general" are a downright betrayal of socialism, the practical desertion to the side of the bourgeoisie, the denial of the right of the proletariat to make its own, proletarian revolution, and defence of bourgeois reformism at the very historical moment when bourgeois reformism is bankrupt all over the world, and when the war has created a revolutionary situation.

4 In explaining the class character of bourgeois civilisation, of bourgeois democracy and of bourgeois parliamentarism, all Socialists express the idea which was most scientifically expressed by Marx and Engels when they said that even the most democratic bourgeois republic is nothing more than a machine for the suppression of the working class by the bourgeoisie, of the masses of the toilers by a handful

V. I. Lenin, *Selected Works* (London: Lawrence and Wishart, Ltd., 1937), VII, 223–233.

of capitalists. Every one of the revolutionaries, every one of the Marxists who is now shouting against dictatorship and for democracy has sworn and assured the workers that he recognises this fundamental truth of socialism; but now, when the revolutionary proletariat is in a state of ferment and motion, which are directed towards the destruction of this machine of oppression and towards the achievement of the proletarian dictatorship, these traitors to socialism try to make it appear that the bourgeoisie granted the toilers "pure democracy," that the bourgeoisie has ceased to resist and is prepared to submit to the majority of the toilers, and that no state machine for the suppression of labour by capital exists, or has ever existed, in a democratic republic.

5   The Paris Commune*—which all the would-be Socialists honour in words, because they know that the masses of the workers warmly and sincerely sympathise with it—most strikingly illustrated the historical conventionality and limited value of bourgeois parliamentarism and of bourgeois democracy—institutions which are extremely progressive compared with mediævalism, but which inevitably require fundamental transformation in the epoch of proletarian revolution. It was Marx who best of all appraised the historical significance of the Paris Commune, and in analysing it revealed the exploiting character of bourgeois democracy and of bourgeois parliamentarism under which the oppressed classes receive the right once every few years to decide which of the representatives of the propertied classes shall "misrepresent" the people in parliament. It is precisely at the present time, when the Soviet movement, having spread to the whole world, is in the sight of all continuing the cause of the Paris Commune, that the traitors to socialism forget the concrete experience and the concrete lessons of the Paris Commune and repeat the old bourgeois piffle about "democracy in general." The Paris Commune was not a parliamentary institution.

6   Furthermore, the significance of the Paris Commune lies in the fact that it made an attempt to smash, to destroy the bourgeois state, bureaucratic, juridical, military and police apparatus to its foundations and to substitute for it self-governing mass organisations of the workers in which there would be no division between legislative and executive authority. All modern bourgeois-democratic republics, including the German Republic, which the traitors to socialism, in mockery of the truth, describe as a proletarian republic, preserve this state apparatus. Thus, again and again we get striking confirmation of the fact that cries in defence of "democracy in general" are really cries in defence of the bourgeoisie and of its exploiting privileges.

7   "The right of assembly" may be taken as an example of the demands of "pure democracy." Every class conscious worker who has not broken connections with his class will understand at once that it would be absurd to promise the right of assembly to the exploiters in the period and in the circumstances in which the exploiters are resisting their overthrow and are defending their privileges. Neither in England in 1649 nor in France in 1793 did the bourgeoisie, when it was revolutionary, grant "the right of assembly" to the monarchists and nobles who called for

* [A revolt of the citizenry of Paris against the newly formed republican government created at the end of the Franco-Prussian War (1871). Socialists—especially Marxists—considered it the first proletarian revolution of modern times, an exaggerated claim. Marx's essay "The Civil War in France" portrays and analyzes the Commune as an advanced social conception. (*Ed.*)]

the intervention of foreign troops and who "assembled" for the purpose of organising attempts at restoration. If the modern bourgeoisie which became reactionary long ago, demands that the proletariat give it guarantees beforehand that it will give "the right of assembly" to the exploiters—irrespective of the resistance the capitalists put up to their appropriation—the proletariat will only laugh at the hypocrisy of the bourgeoisie.

On the other hand, the workers know perfectly well that even in the most democratic bourgeois republics "the right of assembly" is but an empty phrase, because the rich own all the best public and private buildings and sufficient leisure to attend meetings, which are protected by the bourgeois state apparatus. The proletarians of town and country and the small peasants, *i.e.*, the overwhelming majority of the population, do not enjoy either the first, the second or the third of these privileges. As long as this situation prevails, "equality," *i.e.*, "pure democracy" is a sham. In order to achieve real equality, in order to realise democracy for the toilers in fact, it is first of all necessary to deprive the exploiters of all public and luxurious private buildings, it is first of all necessary to give leisure to the toilers, and to have the freedom of their assemblies protected by the armed workers and not by the sons of the aristocracy or capitalist officers commanding browbeaten soldiers.

Only after this change has taken place will it be possible, without mocking at the workers, the toilers and the poor, to speak of freedom of assembly, of equality. And nobody but the vanguard of the toilers, *viz.*, the proletariat, which overthrows the exploiters, the bourgeoisie, can bring about this change.

8   "Freedom of the press" is another of the principal slogans of "pure democracy." Here, too, the workers know, and the Socialists of all countries have admitted a million times, that this freedom is a sham as long as the best printing plants and the huge stocks of paper are in the possession of the capitalists, and as long as the press is ruled by capital—which rule manifests itself the more strikingly, more sharply and more cynically, the more democracy and the republican system are developed, as for example in America. In order to achieve real equality and real democracy for the toilers, for the workers and peasants, it is first of all necessary to deprive capital of the opportunity of hiring writers, of buying up publishing houses and bribing newspapers, and it is necessary to overthrow the yoke of capital, to overthrow the exploiters and to suppress their resistance. By "freedom" the capitalists have always meant the freedom of the rich to accumulate profits, and the freedom of the workers to die of starvation. By freedom of the press the capitalists mean the freedom of the rich to bribe the press, freedom to utilise wealth for the purposes of fabricating and manipulating so-called public opinion. Here, too, the champions of "pure democracy" prove in fact to be champions of the filthy and venal system by which the rich control the means for the education of the masses, they prove to be deceivers of the people, who, by means of plausible, eloquent and absolutely false phrases, turn the people away from the concrete historical tasks of liberating the press from its bondage to capital. Real freedom and equality will exist under the system which the Communists are building and under which it will be impossible for anyone to enrich himself at another's expense, under which it will be objectively impossible, either directly or indirectly, to subject the press to the power of money, and under which there will be nothing to prevent every toiler

(or group of toilers in any number) from having and exercising an equal right to use the public printing plants and public stocks of paper.

9  The history of the nineteenth and twentieth centuries, even before the war, showed what this notorious "pure democracy" really is under capitalism. The Marxists have always said that the more developed, the "purer" democracy is, the more naked, sharp and ruthless becomes the class struggle, the more "purely" the oppression of capital and the dictatorship of the bourgeoisie stand forth. The Dreyfus case in republican France, the sanguinary shooting down of strikers by mercenaries armed by the capitalists in the free and democratic republic of America—these and thousands of similar facts reveal the truth which the bourgeoisie vainly tries to conceal, *viz.*, that even in the most democratic republics it is the terror and dictatorship of the bourgeoisie which rule and which openly manifest themselves as soon as it begins to seem to the exploiters that the power of capital is tottering.

10  The imperialist war of 1914–18 finally revealed even to the backward workers the true character of bourgeois democracy even in the freest republics as the dictatorship of the bourgeoisie. For the sake of the enrichment of the German or the English group of millionaires or billionaires, tens of millions were killed, and the military dictatorship of the bourgeoisie was set up even in the freest republics. This military dictatorship continues to exist in the Entente countries even after the rout of Germany. It was precisely the war that most of all opened the eyes of the toilers, tore down the garlands of artificial flowers which decorated bourgeois democracy and revealed to the people the enormous speculation and profiteering that was going on during the war and in connection with the war. The bourgeoisie waged this war in the name of "liberty and equality," and in the name of "liberty and equality" war contractors amassed incalculable wealth. No efforts of the yellow Berne International will succeed in concealing from the masses the exploiting character of now utterly exposed bourgeois freedom, bourgeois equality and bourgeois democracy.

11  In Germany, in the most developed capitalist country on the Continent of Europe, the very first months of complete republican liberty brought about by the rout of imperialist Germany showed to the German workers and to the whole world the real class nature of the bourgeois democratic republic. The murder of Karl Liebknecht and Rosa Luxemburg* is an event of world-historical importance, not only because two of the best people and best leaders of the truly proletarian Communist International met with a tragic fate, but also because it utterly revealed the class nature of an advanced European state, one can say without exggeration, one of the most advanced in the world. If arrested persons, *i.e.*, persons taken under the protection of the state authorities, could be murdered with impunity by officers and capitalists under a government of social-patriots, it shows that a democratic republic in which such a thing could happen is the dictatorship of the bourgeoisie. Those who express horror at the murder of Karl Liebknecht and Rosa Luxemburg, but who fail to understand this truth, betray either stupidity or hypocrisy. "Freedom" in one of the freest and most advanced republics of the world, in the German Republic, is freedom to murder the arrested leaders of the proletariat with impunity. Nor can it be otherwise as long as capitalism exists, because the development of

* [Leaders in the abortive German Communist uprising of January, 1919, killed by panicky soldiers. (*Ed.*)]

democracy does not blunt but sharpens the class struggle, which has been brought to boiling point by the results and influences of the war and its consequences.

Throughout the civilised world Bolsheviks are being deported, persecuted and imprisoned; for example, in one of the freest bourgeois republics, Switzerland, the pogroms against the Bolsheviks in America, etc. From the point of view of "democracy in general" or of "pure democracy" it is positively ridiculous for advanced, civilised, democratic countries, which are armed to the teeth, to fear the presence of a few score of people from backward, starving, ruined Russia, which the bourgeois newspapers in tens of millions of copies describe as savage, criminal, etc., Russia. Clearly, the social conditions that could give rise to such a crying contradiction are, in fact, the dictatorship of the bourgeoisie.

12   Under such circumstances, the dictatorship of the proletariat is not only a fully legitimate means of overthrowing the exploiters and suppressing their resistance, but it is also absolutely necessary for the whole mass of the toilers as the sole means of protection against the dictatorship of the bourgeoisie, which brought about the war and is preparing for new wars.

The main thing the Socialists fail to understand and what constitutes their theoretical shortsightedness, their captivity to bourgeois prejudices and their political treachery to the proletariat, is that in capitalist society, as soon as there is any serious intensification of the class struggle on which it is based, there cannot be any middle course between the dictatorship of the bourgeoisie and the dictatorship of the proletariat. All dreams about some third course are merely the reactionary lamentations of the petty bourgeois. This is confirmed by the experience of more than a hundred years of development of bourgeois democracy and of the labour movement in all the advanced countries, and particularly by the experience of the past five years. It is also confirmed by the whole science of political economy by the whole content of Marxism, which explains that under any system of commodity production the dictatorship of the bourgeoisie is economically inevitable and that nothing can take the place of the latter except the class that is developed, multiplied, organised and consolidated by the very development of capitalism, *viz.*, the proletarian class.

13   The other theoretical and political mistake Socialists commit is their failure to understand that for thousands of years, from the embryonic form of the age of antiquity, the forms of democracy underwent inevitable change as one ruling class took the place of another. In the ancient republics of Greece, in the cities of the Middle Ages and in the advanced capitalist countries, democracy has different forms and different degrees of application. It would be very absurd to think that the most profound revolution in the history of mankind, that the first transference of power from the exploiting minority to the exploited majority that has ever occurred in the world, could proceed within the old framework of the old bourgeois parliamentary democracy, that it could proceed without extremely sharp changes, without creating new forms of democracy, new institutions embodying the new conditions for its application, etc.

14   The dictatorship of the proletariat is similar to the dictatorship of other classes in that, like all dictatorships, it was called forth by the necessity of suppressing the violent resistance of the class that was being deprived of political rule. The fundamental difference between the dictatorship of other classes—the dictatorship

of the landlords in the Middle Ages, the dictatorship of the bourgeoisie in all civilised capitalist countries—is that the dictatorship of the landlords and of the bourgeoisie meant the violent suppression of the resistance of the overwhelming majority of the population, *viz.*, the toilers. The dictatorship of the proletariat, on the contrary, means the violent suppression of the resistance of the exploiters, *i.e.*, the insignificant minority of the population, the landlords and capitalists.

Hence, it follows from this that the dictatorship of the proletariat must inevitably lead, not only to a change in the forms and institutions of democracy, speaking generally, but to such a change as will lead to the extension of the actual enjoyment of democracy to those who are oppressed by capitalism, to the toiling classes, to a degree hitherto unprecedented in world history.

And indeed, the form of the dictatorship of the proletariat which has been already devised, *i.e.*, the Soviet system in Russia, the Räte system in Germany,* the Shop Stewards' Committees, and analogous Soviet institutions in other countries, all imply and secure precisely for the toiling classes, *i.e.*, for the overwhelming majority of the population, such actual opportunities for enjoying democratic rights and liberties that nothing even approximating to them has ever existed even in the best and most democratic bourgeois republics.

The quintessence of the Soviet system lies in that the permanent and sole basis of the whole state system, the whole state apparatus, is the mass organisation of precisely those classes that were oppressed by capitalism, *i.e.*, the workers and semi-proletarians (peasants who do not exploit the labour of others, and who constantly have to sell at least part of their labour power). It is precisely those masses which, even in the most democratic bourgeois republics, while being equal in law, are in fact prevented by thousands of tricks and devices from taking part in political life and from enjoying democratic rights and liberties, who are now drawn unfailingly into constant and, moreover, decisive participation in the democratic administration of the state.

15     The equality of citizens irrespective of sex, religion, race or nationality, which bourgeois democracy always and everywhere promised but never carried out, and because of the rule of capitalism could not carry out, is carried out by the Soviet government, or the dictatorship of the proletariat immediately and to the full, because only the government of the workers, who are not interested in the private ownership of the means of production and in the struggle for their division and redivision, is able to carry this out.

16     The old, *i.e.*, bourgeois, democracy and parliamentarism were organised in such a manner that it was precisely the toiling masses who were mostly alienated from the apparatus of administration. The Soviet government, *i.e.*, the dictatorship of the proletariat, on the contrary, is organised in such a way as to bring the masses of the toilers closer to the apparatus of administration. The same aim is pursued by the unification of the legislative and executive authorities under the Soviet organisation of the state and by the substitution of production units, like the factories and works, for the territorial electoral constituencies.

17     The army was an apparatus of oppression not only under monarchies. It remains such in all bourgeois republics, even the most democratic. The Soviet govern-

* [An attempt to organize a socialist state based on local workers' councils (Räte). (*Ed.*)]

ment alone, as the permanent state organisation of precisely the classes that were oppressed by capitalism, is able to abolish the subordination of the army to bourgeois command and really merge the proletariat with the army, really arm the proletariat and disarm the bourgeoisie, without which the victory of socialism is impossible.

**18**   The Soviet organisation of the state is adapted to the leading role of the proletariat as the class which has been most concentrated and educated by capitalism. The experience of all revolutions and of all movements of oppressed classes, the experience of the world Socialist movement teaches that the proletariat alone is able to unite and lead the scattered and backward strata of the toiling and exploited population.

**19**   The Soviet organisation of the state alone is capable of effectively and immediately smashing and finally destroying the old, *i.e.*, bourgeois, bureaucratic and juridical apparatus which was preserved, and inevitably had to be preserved, under capitalist, even in the most democratic republics, for it was actually the greatest obstacle to the application of democracy for the benefit of the workers and the toilers. The Paris Commune took the first world-historical step in this direction. The Soviet government took the second.

**20**   The abolition of the state is the aim pursued by all Socialists, including, and particularly, Marx. Until this aim has been achieved, true democracy, *i.e.*, equality and liberty, will be impossible. And it is only Soviet or proletarian democracy that is leading to this goal practically, because, by unfailingly drawing the mass organisations of the toilers into constant participation in the administration of the state, it is beginning immediately to prepare the way for the complete withering away of the state. . . .

## ☙ SPEECHES ON COLLECTIVISATION AND INDUSTRIALISATION

*Josef Stalin*

> *The twin policies of planned industrialization and the collectivization of Russian agriculture were decided upon in 1927 at the Fifteenth Congress of the Communist Party, a convention which also ratified Stalin's political control by expelling his opponents, among whom Trotsky was the most important. Soviet industrialization involved elaborate machinery for central economic planning—the Gosplan—and a program —the Five Year Plan (ultimately condensed into four years)—covering every aspect of industrial activity. The plan from its inception favored the creation of heavy industry over industries catering directly to the consumer, such as textiles and residential building. Despite some quantitative and qualitative shortcomings, the first Five Year Plan was largely successful in providing Russia with a solid base for further industrial expansion as well as in training a whole new generation of industrial workers.*

*Unlike the planned industrialization, the "revolution" in the countryside was largely improvised as it went along and led to the extermination, planned and accidental, of millions of peasants who stood in the way of collectivization. As late as 1928, collectivization was still viewed by the Communist party leadership as a grass-roots movement to be encouraged from above through party agitation and government tax policies, but one which would not be completed for many years. During the following year, this gradualist policy was abandoned in favor of large-scale coercion and the extermination of the wealthier peasants, the kulaks. This phase was succeeded in turn by a somewhat less repressive policy, late in 1930, to stave off complete chaos. By 1932 Russian agriculture had been largely collectivized, though with mediocre economic results.*

*The selections which follow are taken from several speeches delivered by Stalin in the course of the year 1928, the opening year of the planned industrial expansion and of the new agrarian order. Note the intermeshing of industrialization and collectivization and of political and economic objectives in Stalin's justification of his policy. The constant underlying awareness of the advanced conditions in capitalist countries continues to be characteristic of Communist propaganda, especially in the more underdeveloped countries.*

I. GRAIN PROCUREMENTS AND THE PROSPECTS
FOR THE DEVELOPMENT OF AGRICULTURE; JANUARY, 1928

. . . Today the Soviet system rests upon two heterogeneous foundations: upon united *socialised* industry and upon *individual* small-peasant economy based on *private* ownership of the means of production. Can the Soviet system persist for long on these heterogeneous foundations? No, it cannot.

Lenin says that so long as individual peasant economy, which engenders capitalists and capitalism, predominates in the country, the danger of a restoration of capitalism will exist. Clearly, so long as this danger exists there can be no serious talk of the victory of socialist construction in our country.

Hence, for the consolidation of the Soviet system and for the victory of socialist construction in our country, the socialisation of industry alone is quite insufficient. What is required for that is to pass from the socialisation of industry to the socialisation of the whole of agriculture.

And what does that imply?

It implies, firstly, that we must gradually, but unswervingly, unite the individual

J. V. Stalin, *Works* (Moscow: Foreign Language Publishing House, 1954), XI, 8–11, 86–88, 92–94, 96–101, 165–169, 256–263.

peasant farms, which produce the smallest, marketable surpluses, into collective farms, kolkhozes, which produce the largest marketable surpluses.

It implies, secondly, that all areas of our country, without exception, must be covered with collective farms (and state farms) capable of replacing not only the kulaks, but the individual peasants as well, as suppliers of grain to the state.

It implies, thirdly, doing away with all sources that engender capitalists and capitalism, and putting an end to the possibility of the restoration of capitalism.

It implies, fourthly, creating a firm basis for the systematic and abundant supply of the whole country not only with grain, but also with other foodstuffs, while ensuring the necessary reserves for the state.

It implies, fifthly, creating a single and firm socialist basis for the Soviet system, for Soviet power.

It implies, lastly, ensuring the victory of socialist construction in our country.

Such are the prospects for the development of our agriculture.

Such is the task of victoriously building socialism in our country.

It is a complex and difficult task, but one that is quite possible to fulfil; for difficulties exist in order to be surmounted and vanquished.

We must realise that we can no longer make progress on the basis of small individual peasant economy, that what we need in agriculture is large farms capable of employing machines and producing the maximum marketable surpluses. There are two ways of creating large farms in agriculture: the *capitalist* way—through the wholesale ruin of the peasants and the organisation of big capitalist estates exploiting labour; and the *socialist* way—through the union of the small peasant farms into large collective farms, without ruining the peasants and without exploitation of labour. Our Party has chosen the socialist way of creating large farms in agriculture.

Even before the victory of the October Revolution, and then, immediately after that victory, Lenin set the Party the task of uniting the small peasant farms into large collective farms as the prospect for the development of our agriculture, and as the decisive means of securing the victory of socialism in the countryside, in agriculture. . . .

In pursuance of these [Lenin's] directives, the Fifteenth Congress of our Party stated in its resolution on "Work in the Countryside":

> "In the present period, the task of uniting and transforming the small individual peasant farms into large collective farms must be made the Party's *principal task* in the countryside."

That, comrades, is how matters stand in regard to the socialisation of agriculture in our country.

Our duty is to carry out these directives.


II. ON THE GRAIN FRONT; MAY 28, 1928

And so, what is the basis of our difficulties on the grain front?

The basis of our grain difficulties lies in the fact that the increase in the production of marketable grain is not keeping pace with the increase in the demand for grain.

Industry is growing. The number of workers is growing. Towns are growing. And, lastly, the areas producing industrial crops (cotton, flax, sugar beet, etc.) are growing, creating a demand for grain. All this leads to a rapid increase in the demand for grain —grain available for the market. But the production of marketable grain is increasing at a disastrously slow rate.

It cannot be said that the grain stocks at the disposal of the state have been smaller this year than last, or the year before. On the contrary, we have had far more grain in the hands of the state this year than in previous years. Nevertheless, we are faced with difficulties as regards the grain supply. . . .

I have already said in one of my reports that the capitalist elements in the countryside, and primarily the kulaks, took advantage of these difficulties in order to disrupt Soviet economic policy. You know that the Soviet Government adopted a number of measures aimed at putting a stop to the anti-Soviet action of the kulaks. I shall not therefore dwell on this matter here. In the present case it is another question that interests me. I have in mind the reasons for the slow increase in the production of marketable grain, the question why the increase in the production of marketable grain in our country is slower than the increase in the demand for grain, in spite of the fact that our crop area and the gross production of grain have already reached the pre-war level.

. . . How, then, is it to be explained that, in spite of these circumstances, the amount of marketable grain we are producing is only one half, and the amount we are exporting is only about one-twentieth, of the pre-war figure.

The reason is primarily and chiefly the change in the structure of our agriculture brought about by the October Revolution, the passing from large-scale landlord and large-scale kulak farming, which provided the largest amount of marketable grain, to small- and middle-peasant farming, which provides the smallest amount of marketable grain. The mere fact that before the war there were 15,000,000 to 16,000,000 individual peasant farms, whereas at present there are 24,000,000 to 25,000,000 peasant farms, shows that now the basis of our agriculture is essentially small-peasant farming, which provides the least amount of marketable grain.

The strength of large-scale farming, irrespective of whether it is landlord, kulak or collective farming, lies in the fact that large farms are able to employ machines, scientific methods, fertilisers, to increase the productivity of labour, and thus to produce the maximum quantity of marketable grain. On the other hand, the weakness of small-peasant farming lies in the fact that it lacks, or almost lacks, these opportunities, and as a result it is semi-consuming farming, yielding little marketable grain.

Take, for instance, the collective farms and the state farms. They market 47.2 per cent of their gross output of grain. In other words, they yield relatively more marketable grain than did landlord farming in pre-war days. But what about the small- and middle-peasant farms? They market only 11.2 per cent of their total output of grain. The difference, as you see, is quite striking. . . .

What, then, is the way out of the situation?

1   The way out lies, above all, in passing from small, backward and scattered peasant farms to united, large socially-conducted farms, equipped with machinery, armed with scientific knowledge and capable of producing the maximum amount of marketable grain. The way out lies in the transition from individual peasant farming to collective, socially-conducted economy in agriculture.

Lenin called on the Party to organise collective farms from the very first days of the October Revolution. From that time onwards the propaganda of the idea of collective farming has not ceased in our Party. However, it is only recently that the call for the formation of collective farms has met with a mass response. This is to be explained primarily by the fact that the widespread development of a co-operative communal life in the countryside paved the way for a radical change in the attitude of the peasants in favour of collective farms, while the existence of a number of collective farms already harvesting from 150 to 200 poods per dessiatin, of which from 30 to 40 per cent represents a marketable surplus, is strongly attracting the poor peasants and the lower strata of the middle peasants towards the collective farms.

. . . The widespread movement at the beginning of this year for the formation of new collective farms and for the expansion of the old ones should considerably increase the grain output of the collective farms by the end of the year. The task is to maintain the present rate of development of the collective-farm movement, to enlarge the collective farms, to get rid of sham collective farms, replacing them by genuine ones, and to establish a system whereby the collective farms will deliver to the state and co-operative organisations the whole of their marketable grain under penalty of being deprived of state subsidies and credits. I think that, if these conditions are adhered to, within three or four years we shall be able to obtain from the collective farms as much as 100,000,000 poods of marketable grain. . . .

Thus, if all these tasks are fulfilled, the state can in three or four years' time have at its disposal 250,000,000 to 300,000,000 additional poods of marketable grain— a supply more or less sufficient to enable us to manoeuvre properly within the country as well as abroad.

Such, in the main, are the measures which must be taken in order to solve the difficulties on the grain front.

Our task at present is to combine these basic measures with current measures to improve planning in the sphere of supplying the countryside with goods, relieving our trading organisations of the duty of supplying grain to a number of small and middle-sized towns.

Should not, in addition to these measures, a number of other measures be adopted —measures, say, to reduce the rate of development of our industry, the growth of which is causing a considerable increase in the demand for grain, which at present is outstripping the increase in the production of marketable grain? No, not under any circumstances! To reduce the rate of development of industry would mean to weaken the working class; for every step forward in the development of industry, every new factory, every new works, is, as Lenin expressed it, "a new stronghold" of the working class, one which strengthens the latter's position in the fight against the petty-bourgeois elemental forces, in the fight against the capitalist elements in our economy. On the contrary, we must maintain the present rate of development of industry; we must at the first opportunity speed it up in order to pour goods into the rural areas and obtain more grain from them, in order to supply agriculture, and primarily the collective farms and state farms, with machines, in order to industrialise agriculture and to increase the proportion of its output for the market.

Should we, perhaps, for the sake of greater "caution," retard the development of heavy industry so as to make light industry, which produces chiefly for the peasant

market, the basis of our industry? Not under any circumstances! That would be suicidal; it would undermine our whole industry, including light industry. It would mean
abandoning the slogan of industrialising our country, it would mean transforming our
country into an appendage of the world capitalist system of economy.

In this respect we proceed from the well-known guiding principles which Lenin
set forth at the Fourth Congress of the Comintern, and which are absolutely binding
for the whole of our Party. Here is what Lenin said on this subject at the Fourth
Congress of the Comintern:

> "The  salvation of Russia lies not only in a good harvest on the peasant farms
> —that is not enough: and not only in the good condition of light industry, which
> provides the peasantry with consumer goods—that, too, is not enough; we also
> need *heavy* industry."

Or again:

> "We are exercising economy in all things, even in schools. This must be so,
> because we know that unless we save heavy industry, unless we restore it, we
> shall not be able to build up any industry; and without that we shall be doomed
> as an independent country" (Vol. XXVII, p. 349).

These directives given by Lenin must never be forgotten.

How will the measures proposed affect the alliance between the workers and the
peasants? I think that these measures can only help to strengthen the alliance between
the workers and the peasants.

Indeed, if the collective farms and the state farms develop at increased speed; if,
as a result of direct assistance given to the small and middle peasants, the yield of
their farms increases and the cooperatives embrace wider and wider masses of the
peasantry; if the state obtains the hundreds of millions of poods of additional marketable grain required for manoeuvring; if, as a result of these and similar measures, the
kulaks are curbed and gradually overcome—is it not clear that the contradictions between the working class and the peasantry within the alliance of the workers and
peasants will thereby be smoothed out more and more; that the need for emergency
measures in the procurement of grain will disappear; that wide masses of the peasantry will turn more and more to collective forms of farming and that the fight to
overcome the capitalist elements in the countryside will assume an increasingly mass
and organised character?

Is it not clear that the cause of the alliance between the workers and the peasants
can only benefit by such measures?

It must only be borne in mind that the alliance of the workers and peasants under
the conditions of the dictatorship of the proletariat should not be viewed as an ordinary alliance. It is a special form of class alliance between the working class and the
labouring masses of the peasantry, which sets itself the object: (*a*) of strengthening
the position of the working class; (*b*) of ensuring the leading role of the working
class within this alliance; (*c*) of abolishing classes and class society. Any other conception of the alliance of the workers and peasants is opportunism, Menshevism, S.-R.-
ism—anything you like, but not Marxism, not Leninism.

. . . The alliance of the proletariat with the peasantry under the conditions of the dictatorship of the proletariat should not be regarded as an alliance with the whole of the peasantry. The alliance of the proletariat with the peasantry is an alliance of the working class with the labouring masses of the peasantry. Such an alliance cannot be effected without a struggle against the capitalist elements of the peasantry, against the kulaks. Such an alliance cannot be a stable one unless the poor peasants are organised as the bulwark of the working class in the countryside. That is why the alliance between the workers and the peasants under the present conditions of the dictatorship of the proletariat can be effected only in accordance with Lenin's well-known slogan: Rely on the poor peasant, build a stable alliance with the middle peasant, never for a moment cease fighting against the kulaks. For only by applying this slogan can the main mass of the peasantry be drawn into the channel of socialist construction.

\*     \*     \*

### III. INDUSTRIALISATION AND THE GRAIN PROBLEM; JULY 9, 1928

Comrades, . . . allow me to deal with some general questions of theoretical interest which arose here during the discussion at the plenum.

First of all, the general question *of the chief sources of development of our industry*, the means of guaranteeing our present rate of industrialisation. . . .

I think that there are two chief sources nourishing our industry: firstly, the working class; secondly, the peasantry.

In the capitalist countries industrialisation was usually effected, in the main, by robbing other countries, by robbing colonies or defeated countries, or with the help of substantial and more or less enslaving loans from abroad.

You know that for hundreds of years Britain collected capital from all her colonies and from all parts of the world, and was able in this way to make additional investments in her industry. This, incidentally, explains why Britain at one time became the "workshop of the world."

You know also that Germany developed her industry with the help, among other things, of the 5,000 million francs she levied as an indemnity on France after the Franco-Prussian war.

One respect in which our country differs from the capitalist countries is that it cannot and must not engage in colonial robbery, or the plundering of other countries in general. That way, therefore, is closed to us.

Neither, however, does our country have or want to have enslaving loans from abroad. Consequently, that way, too, is closed to us.

What then remains? Only one thing, and that is to develop industry, to industrialise the country with the help of *internal* accumulations.

Under the bourgeois system in our country, industry, transport, etc., were usually developed with the help of loans. Whether you take the building of new factories or the re-equipment of old ones, whether you take the laying of new railways or the erection of big electric power stations—not one of these undertakings was able to dispense with foreign loans. But they were enslaving loans.

Quite different is the situation in our country under the Soviet system. We are building the Turkestan Railway, with a length of 1,400 versts, which requires hundreds of millions of rubles. We are erecting the Dnieper Hydro-Electric Power Station, which also requires hundreds of millions of rubles. But have they involved us in any enslaving loans? No, they have not. All this is being done with the help of internal accumulations.

But what are the chief sources of these accumulations? As I have said, there are two such sources: firstly, the working class, which creates values and advances our industry; secondly, the peasantry.

The way matters stand with the peasantry in this respect is as follows: it not only pays the state the usual taxes, direct and indirect; it also *overpays* in the relatively high prices for manufactured goods—that is in the first place, and it is more less *underpaid* in the prices for agricultural produce—that is in the second place.

This is an additional tax levied on the peasantry for the sake of promoting industry, which caters for the whole country, the peasantry included. It is something in the nature of a "tribute," of a supertax, which we are compelled to levy for the time being in order to preserve and accelerate our present rate of industrial development, in order to ensure an industry for the whole country, in order to raise further the standard of life of the rural population and then to abolish altogether this additional tax, these "scissors" between town and country.

It is an unpalatable business, there is no denying. But we should not be Bolsheviks if we slurred over it and closed our eyes to the fact that, unfortunately, our industry and our country cannot *at present* dispense with this additional tax on the peasantry.

Why do I speak of this? Because some comrades, apparently, do not understand this indisputable truth. They based their speeches on the fact that the peasants are overpaying for manufactured goods, which is absolutely true, and are being underpaid for agricultural produce, which is also true. But what do they demand? They demand the establishment of replacement prices for grain, so that these "scissors," these underpayments and overpayments, would be done away with *at once*. But what would be the effect of doing away with the "scissors" this year or next year, say? The effect would be to retard the industrialisation of the country, including the industrialisation of agriculture, to undermine our young industry which is not yet firmly on its feet, and thus to strike at our entire national economy. Can we agree to this? Obviously, we cannot. Should the "scissors" between town and country, should all these underpayments and overpayments be done away with? Yes, they certainly should. Can we do away with them at once without weakening our industry, and hence our national economy? No, we cannot.

What, then, should our policy be? It should be gradually to close the "scissors," to diminish the gap from year to year, by lowering the prices for manufactured goods and improving agricultural technique—which cannot but result in reducing the cost of producing grain—and then, within the space of a number of years, to do away completely with this additional tax on the peasantry.

Are the peasants capable of bearing this burden? They undoubtedly are: firstly, because this burden will grow lighter from year to year, and secondly, because this additional tax is being levied not under conditions of capitalist development, where the masses of the peasantry are condemned to poverty and exploitation, but under

Soviet conditions, where exploitation of the peasants by the socialist state is out of the question, and where this additional tax is being paid in a situation in which the living standards of the peasantry are steadily rising.

That is how matters stand with regard to the basic sources of the industrialisation of our country at the present time.

## IV. INDUSTRIALISATION OF THE COUNTRY AND THE RIGHT DEVIATION IN THE CPSU (B) ; NOVEMBER 19, 1928

Our theses proceed from the premise that a fast rate of development of industry in general, and of the production of the means of production in particular, is the underlying principle of, and the key to, the industrialisation of the country, the underlying principle of, and the key to, the transformation of our entire national economy along the lines of socialist development.

But what does a fast rate of development of industry involve? It involves the maximum capital investment in industry. And that leads to a state of tension in all our plans, budgetary and non-budgetary. And, indeed, the characteristic feature of our control figures in the past three years, in the period of reconstruction, is that they have been compiled and carried out at a high tension. Take our control figures, examine our budget estimates, talk with our Party comrades—both those who work in the Party organisations and those who direct our Soviet, economic and co-operative affairs—and you will invariably find this one characteristic feature everywhere, namely, the state of tension in our plans.

The question arises: is this state of tension in our plans really necessary for us? Cannot we do without it? Is it not possible to conduct the work at a slower pace, in a more "restful" atmosphere? Is not the fast rate of industrial development that we have adopted due to the restless character of the members of the Political Bureau and the Council of People's Commissars?

Of course not! The members of the Political Bureau and the Council of People's Commissars are calm and sober people. Abstractly speaking, that is, if we disregarded the external and internal situation, we could, of course, conduct the work at a slower speed. But the point is that, firstly, we cannot disregard the external and internal situation, and, secondly, if we take the surrounding situation as our starting-point, it has to be admitted that it is precisely this situation that dictates a fast rate of development of our industry.

Permit me to pass to an examination of this situation, of these conditions of an external and internal order that dictate a fast rate of industrial development.

*External conditions.* We have assumed power in a country whose technical equipment is terribly backward. Along with a few big industrial units more or less based upon modern technology, we have hundreds and thousands of mills and factories the technical equipment of which is beneath all criticism from the point of view of modern achievements. At the same time we have around us a number of capitalist countries whose industrial technique is far more developed and up-to-date than that of our country. Look at the capitalist countries and you will see that their technology is not only advancing, but advancing by leaps and bounds, outstripping the old forms of industrial technique. And so we find that, on the one hand, we in our country have the most advanced system, the Soviet system, and the most advanced type of state power in the world, Soviet power, while, on the other hand, our industry, which should be the basis of socialism and of Soviet power, is extremely backward technically. Do you think that we can achieve the final victory of socialism in our country so long as this contradiction exists?

What has to be done to end this contradiction? To end it, we must overtake and outstrip the advanced technology of the developed capitalist countries. We have overtaken and outstripped the advanced capitalist countries in the sense of establishing a new political system, the Soviet system. That is good. But it is not enough. In order to secure the final victory of socialism in our country, we must also overtake and outstrip these countries technically and economically. Either we do this, or we shall be forced to the wall.

This applies not only to the building of socialism. It applies also to upholding the independence of our country in the circumstances of the capitalist encirclement. The independence of our country cannot be upheld unless we have an adequate industrial basis for defence. And such an industrial basis cannot be created if our industry is not more highly developed technically.

That is why a fast rate of development of our industry is necessary and imperative.

The technical and economic backwardness of our country was not invented by us. This backwardness is age-old and was bequeathed to us by the whole history of our country. This backwardness was felt to be an evil both earlier, before the revolution, and later, after the revolution. When Peter the Great, having to deal with the more highly developed countries of the West, feverishly built mills and factories to supply the army and strengthen the country's defences, that was in its way an attempt to break out of the grip of this backwardness. It is quite understandable, however, that none of the old classes, neither the feudal aristocracy nor the bourgeoisie, could solve the problem of putting an end to the backwardness of our country. More than that, not only were these classes unable to solve this problem, they were not even able to formulate the task in any satisfactory way. The age-old backwardness of our country can be ended only on the lines of successful socialist construction. And it can be ended only by the proletariat, which has established its dictatorship and has charge of the direction of the country.

It would be foolish to console ourselves with the thought that, since the backwardness of our country was not invented by us and was bequeathed to us by the whole history of our country, we cannot be, and do not have to be, responsible for it. That is not true, comrades. Since we have come to power and taken upon ourselves the task of transforming the country on the basis of socialism, we are responsible, and have to be responsible, for everything, the bad as well as the good. And just because we are responsible for everything, we must put an end to our technical and economic backwardness. We must do so without fail if we really want to overtake and outstrip the advanced capitalist countries. And only we Bolsheviks can do it. But precisely in order to accomplish this task, we must systematically achieve a fast rate of development of our industry. And that we are already achieving a fast rate of industrial development is now clear to everyone.

The question of overtaking and outstripping the advanced capitalist countries technically and economically is for us Bolsheviks neither new nor unexpected. It was raised in our country as early as in 1917, before the October Revolution. It was raised by Lenin as early as in September 1917, on the eve of the October Revolution, during the imperialist war, in his pamphlet *The Impending Catastrophe and How to Combat It. . . .*

Lenin wrote . . . on the eve of the October Revolution, in the period before the proletariat had taken power, when the Bolsheviks had as yet neither state power, nor a socialised industry, nor a widely ramified co-operative network embracing millions of peasants, nor collective farms, nor state farms. Today, when we already have something substantial with which to end completely our technical and economic backwardness, we might paraphrase Lenin's words roughly as follows:

"We have overtaken and *outstripped* the advanced capitalist countries *politically* by establishing the dictatorship of the proletariat. But that is not enough. We must utilise the dictatorship of the proletariat, our socialised industry, transport, credit system, etc., the co-operatives, collective farms, state farms, etc., in order to overtake and *outstrip* the advanced capitalist countries *economically* as well."

The question of a fast rate of development of industry would not face us so acutely as it does now if we had such a highly developed industry and such a highly developed technology as Germany, say, and if the relative importance of industry in the entire national economy were as high in our country as it is in Germany, for example. *If that were the case,* we could develop our industry at a slower rate without fearing to fall behind the capitalist countries and knowing that we could outstrip them at one stroke. But then we should not be so seriously backward technically and economically as we are now. The whole point is that we are behind Germany in this respect and are still far from having overtaken her technically and economically.

The question of a fast rate of development of industry would not face us so acutely if we were not the *only* country but *one of the countries* of the dictatorship of the proletariat, if there were a proletarian dictatorship not only in our country but in other, more advanced countries as well, Germany and France, say.

*If that were the case,* the capitalist encirclement could not be so serious a danger as it is now, the question of the economic independence of our country would naturally recede into the background, we could integrate ourselves into the system of more developed proletarian states, we could receive from them machines for making our industry and agriculture more productive, supplying them in turn with raw materials and foodstuffs, and we could, consequently, expand our industry at a slower rate. But you know very well that that is not yet the case and that we are still the *only* country of the proletarian dictatorship and are surrounded by capitalist countries, many of which are far in advance of us technically and economically.

That is why Lenin raised the question of overtaking and outstripping the economically advanced countries as one of life and death for our development.

Such are the *external* conditions dictating a fast rate of development of our industry. *Internal conditions.* But besides the external conditions, there are also internal conditions which dictate a fast rate of development of our industry as the main foundation of our entire national economy. I am referring to the extreme backwardness of our agriculture, of its technical and cultural level. I am referring to the existence in our country of an overwhelming preponderance of small commodity producers, with their scattered and utterly backward production, compared with which our large-scale socialist industry is like an island in the midst of the sea, an island whose base is expanding daily, but which is nevertheless an island in the midst of the sea.

We are in the habit of saying that industry is the main foundation of our entire national economy, including agriculture, that it is the key to the reconstruction of our backward and scattered system of agriculture on a collectivist basis. That is perfectly true. From that position we must not retreat for a single moment. But it must also be remembered that, while industry is the main foundation, agriculture constitutes the basis for industrial development, both as a market which absorbs the products of industry and as a supplier of raw materials and foodstuffs, as well as a source of the export reserves essential in order to import machinery for the needs of our national economy. Can we advance industry while leaving agriculture in a state of complete technical backwardness, without providing an agricultural base for industry, without reconstructing agriculture and bringing it up to the level of industry? No, we cannot.

Hence the task of supplying agriculture with the maximum amount of instruments and means of production essential in order to accelerate and promote its reconstruction on a new technical basis. But for the accomplishment of this task a fast rate of development of our industry is necessary. Of course, the reconstruction of a disunited and scattered agriculture is an incomparably more difficult matter than the reconstruction of a united and centralised socialist industry. But that is the task that confronts us, and we must accomplish it. And it cannot be accomplished except by a fast rate of industrial development.

We cannot go on indefinitely, that is, for too long a period, basing the Soviet regime and socialist construction on two *different* foundations, the foundation of the most large-scale and united socialist industry and the foundation of the most scattered and backward, small commodity economy of the peasants. We must gradually, but systematically and persistently, place our agriculture on a new technical basis, the basis of large-scale production, and bring it up to the level of socialist industry. Either we accomplish this task—in which case the final victory of socialism in our country will be assured, or we turn away from it and do not accomplish it—in which case a return to capitalism may become inevitable.

# ✒ THE GOD THAT FAILED

*Ignazio Silone*

The God That Failed *(1949) is a collection of six autobiographical essays, written by distinguished European and American men of letters, all of whom had, in the years between the Russian Revolution of 1917 and the Stalin-Hitler pact of 1939, joined the Communist party (or sympathized with it) only to be disillusioned. Conceived and edited by Richard Crossman (b. 1907), Labour Member of Parliament, British socialist, and an editor of the left-wing journal of opinion* New Statesman and Nation *of London, the book was first published in America in 1950. The careers and experiences of the six contributors—Arthur Koestler, Hungarian-born British subject and novelist; Ignazio Silone, Italian novelist, essayist, and critic; Richard Wright, American Negro novelist; André Gide, French novelist, essayist, and critic; Louis Fischer, American journalist; and Stephen Spender, British poet—display little in common except that all are imaginative writers who took the journey into communism and returned. It was in order that there might be a clearer understanding of the circumstances of their conversion and, perhaps even more pertinently, of their final abjuration, that these men were asked to write their political-psychological autobiographies.*

*Of the six essays that make up* The God That Failed, *the one by Ignazio Silone has been chosen to appear here. Silone was born in 1900 at Peschina dei Marsi, a village in the Abruzzi Apennines in Italy. His father was a small peasant landowner and his mother a cottage weaver. During World War I, at the age of seventeen, he was appointed secretary of land workers for the Abruzzi district and had to appear in court to face charges in connection with a violent demonstration against the war, a demonstration which he had organized. In 1921 he participated in the formation of the Italian Communist party and became editor of the weekly* Avanguardia *of Rome and of the* Lavoratore, *a daily published in Trieste. Even after the seizure of power by the Fascists and the proscription of the Communist party in Italy, Silone remained in his native country, printing illegal newspapers in the underground. He was arrested, imprisoned, and then exiled. During his exile he came to distrust, and finally to hate, the party which he had adopted so early in life. Finally, in 1930—just at the moment when so many writers were joining the Communists—Silone severed his connections with the organization. But he did not, as so many ex-Communists have done, abjure his faith in socialism. On the contrary, he became a leading figure in the Italian Socialist party, for which he formulated the political program known as the "Third Front." He returned from exile only in 1944, with the defeat and collapse of the Fascist regime, which he had passionately despised. In addition to his political activity Silone is one of Italy's most distinguished novelists. Among his works are* Fontamara (1934), Bread and Wine (1936), The School for Dictators (1938), The Seed Beneath the Snow (1942), *and the play* And He Hid Himself (1946).

I grew up in a mountainous district of southern Italy. The phenomenon which most impressed me, when I arrived at the age of reason, was the violent contrast, the incomprehensible, absurd, monstrous contrast between family and private life—in the main decent, honest, and well-conducted—and social relations, which were very often crude and full of hatred and deceit. Many terrifying stories are known of the misery and desperation of the southern provinces (I have told some myself), but I do not intend to refer now to events that caused a stir, so much as to the little occurrences of daily life. It was these commonplace minor events that showed up the strange double existence of the people among whom I grew up, the observation of which was one of the agonizing secrets of my adolescence.

I was a child just five years old when, one Sunday, while crossing the little square of my native village with my mother leading me by the hand, I witnessed the cruel, stupid spectacle of one of the local gentry setting his great dog at a poor woman, a seamstress, who was just coming out of church. The wretched woman was flung to the ground, badly mauled, and her dress was torn to ribbons. Indignation in the village was general, but silent. I have never understood how the poor woman ever got the unhappy idea of taking proceedings against the squire; but the only result was to add a mockery of justice to the harm already done. Although, I must repeat, everybody pitied her and many people helped her secretly, the unfortunate woman could not find a single witness prepared to give evidence before the magistrate, nor a lawyer to conduct the prosecution. On the other hand, the squire's supposedly Left-Wing lawyer turned up punctually, and so did a number of bribed witnesses who perjured themselves by giving a grotesque version of what had happened, and accusing the woman of having provoked the dog. The magistrate—a most worthy, honest person in private life—acquitted the squire and condemned the poor woman to pay the costs.

"It went very much against the grain with me," he excused himself a few days later at our house. "On my word of honor, I do assure you, I was very sorry about it. But even if I had been present at the disgusting incident as a private citizen and couldn't have avoided blaming him, still as a judge I had to go by the evidence of the case, and unfortunately it was in favor of the dog." "A real judge," he used to love to say, sententiously, "must be able to conceal his own egoistic feelings, and be impartial." "Really, we know," my mother used to comment, "it's a horrible profession. Better to keep ourselves to ourselves at home. My son," she used to say to me, "when you're grown up, be whatever you like, but not a judge."

I can remember other typical little incidents like that of the squire, the dog, and the seamstress. But I should not like to suggest, by quoting such episodes, that we were ignorant of the sacred concepts of Justice and Truth or that we held them in contempt. On the contrary; at school, in church, and at public celebrations they were often discussed with eloquence and veneration, but in rather abstract terms. To define our curious situation more exactly, I should add that it was based on a deception of which all of us, even the children, were aware; and yet it still persisted, being built on something quite apart from the ignorance and stupidity of individuals.

I remember a lively discussion one day in my catechism class between the boys who

Richard Crossman, ed., *The God That Failed* (New York: Harper's, 1950), pp. 73–84, 87–102.

were being prepared for confirmation and the parish priest. The subject was a marionette show at which we boys had been present with the priest the day before. It was about the dramatic adventures of a child who was persecuted by the devil. At one point the child-marionette had appeared on the stage trembling with fear and, to escape the devil who was searching for him, had hidden under a bed in a corner of the stage; shortly afterward the devil-marionette arrived and looked for him in vain. "But he *must* be here," said the devil-marionette. "I can smell him. Now I'll ask these good people in the audience." And he turned to us and asked: "My dear children, have you by any chance seen that naughty child I'm looking for, hiding anywhere?" "No, no, no," we all chorused at once, as energetically as possible. "Where is he then? I can't see him," the devil insisted. "He's left, he's gone away," we all shouted. "He's gone to Lisbon." (In our part of Italy, Lisbon is still the furthermost point of the globe, even today.) I should add that none of us, when we went to the theater, had expected to be questioned by a devil-marionette; our behavior was therefore entirely instinctive and spontaneous. And I imagine that children in any other part of the world would have reacted in the same way. But our parish priest, a most worthy, cultured and pious person, was not altogether pleased. We had told a lie, he warned us with a worried look. We had told it for good ends, of course, but still it remained a lie. One must never tell lies. "Not even to the devil?" we asked in surprise. "A lie is always a sin," the priest replied. "Even to the magistrate?" asked one of the boys. The priest rebuked him severely. "I'm here to teach you Christian doctrine and not to talk nonsense. What happens outside the church is no concern of mine." And he began to explain the doctrine about truth and lies in general in the most eloquent language. But that day the question of lies *in general* was of no interest to us children; we wanted to know, "Ought we to have told the devil where the child was hiding, yes or no?" "That's not the point," the poor priest kept repeating to us rather uneasily. "A lie is always a lie. It might be a big sin, a medium sin, an average sort of sin, or a little tiny sin, but it's always a sin. Truth must be honored."

"The truth is," we said, "that there was the devil on one side and the child on the other. We wanted to help the child, that's the real truth." "But you've told a lie," the parish priest kept on repeating. "For good ends, I know, but still a lie." To end it, I put forward an objection of unheard-of perfidy, and, considering my age, considerable precocity: "If it'd been a priest instead of a child," I asked, "what ought we to have replied to the devil?" The parish priest blushed, avoided a reply, and, as a punishment for my impertinence, made me spend the rest of the lesson on my knees beside him. "Are you sorry?" he asked me at the end of the lesson. "Of course," I replied. "If the devil asks me for your address, I'll give it to him at once."

It was certainly unusual for a discussion in such terms to take place in a catechism class, although free discussion was quite frequent in our family circle and among our friends. But this intellectual liveliness did not even create a stir in the humiliating and primitive stagnation of our social life.

\*       \*       \*

Some time earlier the so-called democratic system had, however, introduced a new technical detail into the relations between citizen and State. This was the secret vote, which though not in itself enough to change things radically, sometimes produced results which were surprising, and, as far as public order was concerned, scandalous. Though these incidents were isolated and had no immediate sequel, they were none the less disturbing.

I was seven years old when the first election campaign, which I can remember, took place in my district. At that time we still had no political parties, so the announcement of this campaign was received with very little interest. But popular feeling ran high when it was disclosed that one of the candidates was "the Prince." There was no need to add Christian and surname to realize which Prince was meant. He was the owner of the great estate formed by the arbitrary occupation of the vast tracts of land reclaimed in the previous century from the Lake of Fucino. About eight thousand families (that is, the majority of the local population) are still employed today in cultivating the estate's fourteen thousand hectares. The Prince was deigning to solicit "his" families for their vote so that he could become their deputy in parliament. The agents of the estate, who were working for the Prince, talked in impeccably liberal phrases: "Naturally," said they, "naturally, no one will be forced to vote for the Prince, that's understood; in the same way that no one, naturally, can force the Prince to allow people who don't vote for him to work on his land. This is the period of real liberty for everybody; you're free, and so is the Prince." The announcement of these "liberal" principles produced general and understandable consternation among the peasants. For, as may easily be guessed, the Prince was the most hated person in our part of the country. As long as he remained in the invisible Olympus of the great feudal proprietor (none of the eight thousand tenants had seen him, up to then, even from afar) public hatred for him was allowed, and belonged to the same category as curses against hostile deities; such curses, though useless, are satisfying. But now the clouds were being rent, and the Prince was coming down within reach of mortal men. From now on, consequently, they would have to keep their expressions of hatred within the narrow circle of private life and get ready to welcome him with due honors in the village streets.

My father seemed reluctant to accept this kind of logic. He was the youngest of several brothers, all of them peasant proprietors; the youngest, the most restless, and the only one with any inclinations toward insubordination. One evening his older brothers came and urged him, in the common interest, to be prudent and careful. For me (to whom no one paid any attention, for grown-ups think that children don't understand such things) it was a most instructive evening. "The Prince being a candidate is a real farce," the eldest brother admitted. "Political candidatures should be reserved for lawyers and other such windbags. But as the Prince is a candidate, all we can do is support him." "If the Prince's candidature is a farce," replied my father, "I don't understand why we should support him." "Because we're his dependents, as you know perfectly well." "Not in politics," said my father. "In politics we're free." "We don't cultivate politics, we cultivate the land," they answered him. "As cultivators of the land we depend on the Prince." "There's no mention of politics in our contracts for the land, only of potatoes and beetroots. As voters we're free." "The Prince's bailiff will also be free not to renew our contracts," they answered him. "That's why we're forced to be on his side." "I can't vote for someone merely because I'm forced to," said my father. "I'd feel humiliated." "No one will know how you vote," they answered him. "In the secrecy of the polling booth you can vote as you like, freely. But during the electioneering campaign we must be on the Prince's side, all of us together." "I'd be pleased to do it if I wasn't ashamed to," said my father, "but, do believe me, I'd be too much ashamed." To settle it, my uncles and my father reached this compromise: he would not come out either on the Prince's side or against him.

The Prince's election tour was prepared by the civil authorities, the police, the carabineers, and the agents of the estate. One Sunday, the Prince deigned to pass through the principal villages in the constituency, without stopping and without making any speeches. This tour of his was remembered for a long time in our district, mainly because he made it in a motorcar, and it was the first time we had seen one. The word "motorcar" itself had not yet found a place in our everyday language, and the peasants called it a "horseless carriage." Strange legends were current among the people about the invisible motive force which took the place of the horses, about the diabolical speed which the new vehicle could reach, and about the ruinous effect, particularly on the vines, of the stink it left behind it. That Sunday the entire population of the village had gone to meet the Prince on the road by which he was due to arrive. There were numerous visible signs of the collective admiration and affection for the Prince. The crowds were dressed up in their best, and were in a perfectly understandable state of excitement. The "horseless carriage" arrived late, and roared through the crowd and the village, without stopping and without even slowing down, leaving a thick white dust cloud behind it. The Prince's agents then explained, to anyone who cared to listen, that the "horseless carriage" went by "petrol vapor" and could only stop when the petrol had finished. "It isn't like horses," they explained, "where all one need do is to pull on the reins. There aren't any reins at all. Did you notice any reins?"

Two days later a strange little old man arrived from Rome; he wore glasses, and had a black stick and a small suitcase. Nobody knew him. He said he was an oculist and had put himself up as candidate against the Prince. A few people gathered round him out of curiosity, mainly children and women, who had not the right to vote. I was among the children, in my short trousers and with my schoolbooks under my arm. We begged the old man to make a speech. He said to us: "Remind your parents that the vote is secret. Nothing else." Then he said, "I am poor; I live by being an oculist; but if any of you have anything wrong with your eyes I'm willing to treat them for nothing." So we brought him an old woman who sold vegetables. She had bad eyes, and he cleaned them up and gave her a little phial with drops in it and explained how to use it. Then he said to us (we were only a group of children): "Remind your parents that the vote is secret," and he went away. But the Prince's election was so certain, to judge by the festive throngs which had welcomed him during his electioneering tour, that the authorities and the agents of the estate had announced in advance a whole program for the celebration of the inevitable victory. My father, according to the agreement with his brothers, did not side with either candidate, but managed to get himself included among the scrutineers of the ballot-papers. Great was everybody's surprise when it became known that in the secrecy of the polling booths an enormous majority had voted against the Prince and for the unknown oculist. It was a great scandal; the authorities called it sheer treachery. But the treachery was of such proportions that the agents of the estate could not take any reprisals against anyone. were broken open; the carabineers fled across the orchards and fields under cover of

will of the people only express itself sporadically? Why can it not become a permanent and stable basis for the reorganization of public life? And yet, it would be in-
correct to conclude, from a false interpretation of the episode I have just recorded,
that the major obstacle was fear. Our people have never been cowardly or spineless
or weak. On the contrary the rigors of the climate, the heaviness of the work, the
harsh conditions of the struggle for existence, have made them into one of the tough-
est, hardest, and most enduring peoples in the whole of Italy. So much so, that there
are fewer references in our local annals to political surprises resulting from the secret
vote than there are to revolts, localized and shortlived, but violent, destructive and
almost savage. These humiliated and downtrodden people could endure the worst
abuses without complaint, but then they would break out on unforeseen occasions.

My native village, at the period to which I am now referring, had some five thousand inhabitants, and public order was in the keeping of about twenty carabineers,
commanded by a lieutenant. This excessive number of police is in itself revealing.
There was not much sympathy between the soldiers and the carabineers during the
First World War, because the latter were on duty in the rear areas, and some of them,
it was said, took too much interest in the wives and fiancées of the men at the front.
In small places, rumors of this kind are immediately given a very exact personal application. So it happened one evening that three soldiers, home from the front on
short leave, had a quarrel with some carabineers and were arrested by them. This
action was ridiculous and ungallant to begin with, but it became absolutely monstrous
when the commanding officer of the carabineers canceled the three soldiers' leave and
sent them back to the front. I was a close friend of one of them (he was killed in
the war afterward), and his old mother came sobbing to me to tell me about the
affair. I begged the mayor, the magistrate and the parish priest to intervene, but they
all declared it was outside their province. "If that's the way things are," I said,
"there's nothing for it but *revolution*!" We have always used this fateful historical
term, in our dialect, in order to describe a mere violent demonstration. In those wartime years, for example, two "revolutions" had already taken place in my native village, the first against the town council because of bread rationing, the second against
the church because the seat of the bishopric had been transferred to another township. The third, which I am about to describe, went down in history as "the revolution of the three soldiers." The men were to be escorted to the train at five o'clock,
so the revolution was arranged for half an hour earlier, in front of the barracks. Unfortunately it took a more serious turn than had been intended. It began as a joke,
which three of us boys were bold enough to start. One of us, at the agreed moment,
went up the bell-tower and began hammering away at the great bell, the signal in
our part of the country denoting a serious fire or other public danger. The other two
went off to meet the peasants to explain what was happening. Alarmed by the ringing
of the tocsin, they had at once stopped working in the fields, and were hurrying
anxiously toward the village.

In a few minutes a threatening and tumultuous crowd had collected in front of the
barracks. They began by shouting abuse, then they threw stones, and finally shots
were fired. The siege of the barracks lasted until late at night. Rage had made my
fellow-villagers unrecognizable. In the end, the windows and gates of the barracks
were broken open; the carabineers fled across the orchards and fields under cover of

darkness; and the three soldiers, whom everyone had forgotten, went back to their homes unobserved. So we boys found ourselves absolute masters of the place for an entire night. "Now what are we going to do?" the other boys asked me. (My authority came, mainly, from the fact that I knew Latin.) "Tomorrow morning," I said, "the village is sure to be reoccupied by hundreds and hundreds of armed men, carabineers and police, who'll arrive from Avezzano, Sulmona, Aquila, and perhaps even from Rome." "But what are we going to do tonight, before they arrive?" the other boys insisted. "Obviously one night is not enough to create a new order of things," I said, thinking I had guessed what they were after. "Couldn't we take advantage of the fact that the whole village is asleep, to make Socialism?"

That was what the other boys wanted me to suggest. Perhaps they were still overexcited from their riotous evening; perhaps they really believed that anything was possible now. "I don't think," I said, "I honestly don't think that, even if the whole village is asleep, one can make Socialism in a single night." I must mention in my own justification that at that time the theory of Socialism overnight had not yet been propounded. "One night, though, might be enough to sleep in one's own bed before going to prison," one of the others finally suggested. And as we were tired, we all found this advice both sensible and acceptable.

Such episodes of violence—with their inevitable sequel of mass arrests, trials, legal expenses, and prison sentences—reinforced distrust, diffidence, and skepticism in the peasants' minds. For them, the State became the irremediable creation of the devil. A good Christian, if he wanted to save his soul, should avoid, as far as possible, all contact with the State. The State always stands for swindling, intrigue and privilege, and could not stand for anything else. Neither law nor force can change it. If retribution occasionally catches up with it, this can only be by the dispensation of God.

In 1915 an earthquake of exceptional violence destroyed a large part of our province and killed, in thirty seconds, about fifty thousand people. I was surprised to see how much my fellow-villagers took this appalling catastrophe as a matter of course. The geologists' complicated explanations, reported in the newspapers, aroused their contempt. In a district like ours, where so many injustices go unpunished, people regarded the recurrent earthquakes as a phenomenon requiring no further explanation. In fact, it was astonishing that earthquakes were not more frequent. An earthquake buries rich and poor, learned and illiterate, authorities and subjects alike beneath its ruined houses. Here lies, moreover, the real explanation of the Italians' well-known powers of endurance when faced with the cataclysms of nature. An earthquake achieves what the law promises but does not in practice maintain—the equality of all men. A neighbor of ours, a woman who kept a bakery, lay buried, but not hurt, for several days after the earthquake, when her house was completely destroyed. Not realizing that the disaster was general, and imagining that it was only her own house which had fallen down, either because of some defect in its construction or because someone had put a curse on it, the poor woman was greatly distressed; so much so that when a rescue party wanted to drag her out of the ruins she absolutely refused. She calmed down, however, and quickly regained her strength and her wish to live and to rebuild her house, the moment she was told there had been an earthquake and that an enormous number of other houses had collapsed as well.

What seemed to the poor people of our part of the world a much more serious calamity than any natural cataclysm was what happened *after* the earthquake. The State reconstruction program was carried out to the accompaniment of innumerable intrigues, frauds, thefts, swindles, embezzlements, and dishonesty of every kind. An acquaintance of mine, who had been sacked by one of the government departments concerned, gave me some information of this sort about certain criminal acts which were being committed by the head engineers of the department. Impressed rather than surprised, I hastened to pass on the facts to some persons in authority, whom I knew to be upright and honest, so that they could denounce the criminals. Far from denying the truth of what I told them, my honorable friends were in a position to confirm it. But, even then, they advised me not to get mixed up in it or to get worked up, in my simplicity, about things of that kind. "You're young," they said to me affectionately, "you must finish your studies, you've got your career to think of, you shouldn't compromise yourself with things that don't concern you." "Of course," I said, "it would be better for the denunciation to come from grown-up people like yourselves, people with authority, rather than from a boy of seventeen."

They were horrified. "We are not madmen," they answered. "We shall mind our own business and nobody else's."

I then talked the matter over with some reverend priests, and then with some of my more courageous relations. All of them, while admitting that they were already aware of the shameful things that were happening, begged me not to get mixed up in that hornets' nest, but to think of my studies, of my career, and of my future. "With pleasure," I replied, "but isn't one of you ready to denounce the thieves?" "We are not madmen," they replied, scandalized, "these things have nothing to do with us."

I then began to wonder seriously whether it mightn't be a good thing to organize, together with some other boys, a new "revolution" that would end up with a good bonfire of the corrupt engineers' offices; but I was dissuaded by the acquaintance who had given me the proof of their crooked dealings: a bonfire, he pointed out, would destroy the proofs of the crimes. He was older and more experienced than myself; he suggested I should get the denunciation printed in some newspaper. But which newspaper? "There's only one," he explained, "which could have any interest in publishing your denunciation, and that's the Socialist paper." So I set to work and wrote three articles, the first of my life, giving a detailed exposure of the corrupt behavior of State engineers in my part of the country, and sent them off to *Avanti*. The first two were printed at once and aroused much comment among the readers of the paper, but none at all among the authorities. The third article did not appear, because, as I learned later, a leading Socialist intervened with the editorial staff. This showed me that the system of deception and fraud oppressing us was much vaster than at first appeared, and that its invisible ramifications extended even into Socialism. However, the partial denunciation which had appeared unexpectedly in the press contained enough material for a number of law-suits, or at least for a board of enquiry; but nothing happened. The engineers, whom I had denounced as thieves and bandits and against whom quite specific charges had been leveled, did not even attempt to justify themselves or to issue a general denial. There was a short period of expectancy, and then everyone went back to his own affairs. . . .

For me to join the Party of Proletarian Revolution was not just a simple matter of signing up with a political organization; it meant a conversion, a complete dedication. Those were still the days when to declare oneself a Socialist or a Communist was equivalent to throwing oneself to the winds, and meant breaking with one's parents and not finding a job. If the material consequences were harsh and hard, the difficulties of spiritual adaptation were no less painful. My own internal world, the "Middle Ages," which I had inherited and which were rooted in my soul, and from which, in the last analysis, I had derived my initial aspiration to revolt, were shaken to their foundations, as though by an earthquake. Everything was thrown into the melting-pot, everything became a problem. Life, death, love, good, evil, truth, all changed their meaning or lost it altogether. It is easy enough to court danger when one is no longer alone; but who can describe the dismay of once and for all renouncing one's faith in the individual immortality of the soul? It was too serious for me to be able to discuss it with anyone; my Party comrades would have found it a subject for mockery, and I no longer had any other friends. So, unknown to anyone, the whole world took on a different aspect. How men are to be pitied!

The conditions of life imposed on the Communists by the Fascist conquest of the State were very hard. But they also served to confirm some of the Communists' political theses, and provided an opportunity to create a type of organization which was in no way incompatible with Communist mentality. So I too had to adapt myself, for a number of years, to living like a foreigner in my own country. One had to change one's name, abandon every former link with family and friends, and live a false life to remove any suspicion of conspirational activity. The Party became family, school, church, barracks; the world that lay beyond it was to be destroyed and built anew. The psychological mechanism whereby each single militant becomes progressively identified with the collective organization is the same as that used in certain religious orders and military colleges, with almost identical results. Every sacrifice was welcomed as a personal contribution to the "price of collective redemption"; and it should be emphasized that the links which bound us to the Party grew steadily firmer, not in spite of the dangers and sacrifices involved, but because of them. This explains the attraction exercised by Communism on certain categories of young men and of women, on intellectuals, and on the highly sensitive and generous people who suffer most from the wastefulness of bourgeois society. Anyone who thinks he can wean the best and most serious-minded young people away from Communism by enticing them into a well-warmed hall to play billiards, starts from an extremely limited and unintelligent conception of mankind.

*       *       *

It is not surprising that the first internal crises which shook the Communist International left me more or less indifferent. These crises originated from the fact that the main parties which had adhered to the new International, even after the formal acceptance of the twenty-one conditions laid down by Lenin to govern admission, were far from homogeneous. They had in common a hatred of imperialist war and of its results; they united in criticizing the reformist ideas of the Second International; but, as to the rest, for good or ill, each reflected its own country's unequal degree of historical development. That is why there were notable differences of opinion between Russian Bolshevism, formed in an atmosphere in which political liberty and a differentiated social structure were both alien concepts, and the Left-Wing Socialist groups of the Western countries. The history of the Communist International was therefore a history of schisms, a history of intrigues and of arrogance on the part of the directing Russian group toward every independent expression of opinion by the other affiliated parties. One after another, they were forced to break with the Communist International: the currents most attached to democratic and parliamentary forms . . ., the groups most attached to legality and most opposed to attempts at *coups d'état* . . ., the libertarian elements who deluded themselves about Soviet Democracy . . ., the revolutionary trade-unionists who opposed the bureaucratic submission of the trade unions to the Communist Party . . ., the groups most reluctant to break off all collaboration with Social Democracy . . ., and the extreme Left Wing which was intolerant of any opportunist move. . . .

These internal crises took place in a sphere far removed from my own and so I was not involved. I do not say this boastfully; on the contrary, I am merely trying to explain the situation. The increasing degeneration of the Communist International into a tyranny and a bureaucracy filled me with repulsion and disgust, but there were some compelling reasons which made me hesitate to break with it: solidarity with comrades who were dead or in prison, the nonexistence at that time of any other organized anti-Fascist force in Italy, the rapid political, and in some cases also moral, degeneration of many who had already left Communism, and finally the illusion that the International might be made healthy again by the proletariat of the West, in the event of some crisis occurring within the Soviet regime.

Between 1921 and 1927, I had repeated occasion to go to Moscow and take part, as a member of Italian Communist delegations, in a number of congresses and meetings of the Executive. What struck me most about the Russian Communists, even in such really exceptional personalities as Lenin and Trotsky, was their utter incapacity to be fair in discussing opinions that conflicted with their own. The adversary simply for daring to contradict, at once became a traitor, an opportunist, a hireling. *An adversary in good faith* is inconceivable to the Russian Communists. What an aberration of conscience this is, for so-called materialists and rationalists absolutely in their polemics to uphold the primacy of morals over intelligence! To find a comparable infatuation one has to go back to the Inquisition.

Just as I was leaving Moscow, in 1922, Alexandra Kollontaj said to me: "If you happen to read in the papers that Lenin has had me arrested for stealing the silver spoons in the Kremlin, that simply means that I'm not entirely in agreement with him about some little problem of agricultural or industrial policy." Kollontaj had acquired her sense of irony in the West and so only used it with people from the West. But even then, in those feverish years of building the new regime, when the new orthodoxy had not yet taken complete possession of cultural life, how difficult it was to reach an understanding with a Russian Communist on the simplest, and for us most obvious, questions; how difficult, I don't say to agree, but at least to understand each other, when talking of what liberty means for a man of the West, even for a worker. I spent hours one day trying to explain to one of the directors of the State publishing house, why she ought at least to be ashamed of the atmosphere of discouragement and intimidation in which Soviet writers lived. She could not understand what I was trying to tell her.

"Liberty"—I had to give examples—"is the possibility of doubting, the possibility of making a mistake, the possibility of searching and experimenting, the possibility of saying 'no' to any authority—literary, artistic, philosophic, religious, social, and even political." "But that," murmured this eminent functionary of Soviet culture in horror, "that is counter-revolution." Then she added, to get a little of her own back, "We're glad we haven't got your liberty, but we've got the sanatoria in exchange." When I observed that the expression "in exchange" had no meaning, "liberty not being merchandise that could be exchanged," and that I had seen sanatoria in other countries, she laughed in my face. "You're in the mood for joking with me today," she said to me. And I was so taken aback by her candor that I no longer dared to contradict her.

The spectacle of the enthusiasm of Russian youth in those first years of the creation of a new world, which we all hoped would be more humane than the old one, was utterly convincing. And what a bitter disillusionment it was, as the years went by and the new regime strengthened itself and its economic system got into shape and the armed attacks from abroad ceased, to see the long-promised ultimate democratization failing to come, and, instead, the dictatorship accentuating its repressive character.

One of my best friends, the head of the Russian Communist Youth, Lazar Schatzky, one evening confided to me how sad he was to have been born too late, and not to have taken part either in the 1905 or the 1917 Revolutions. "But there'll still be revolutions," I said to console him, "there'll always be need of revolutions, even in Russia." We were in the Red Square, not far from the tomb of Lenin. "What kind?" he wanted to know. "And how long have we got to wait?" Then I pointed to the tomb, which was still made of wood at that time, and before which we used every day to see an interminable procession of poor ragged peasants slowly filing.

"I presume you love Lenin," I said to him. "I knew him too and have a very vivid recollection of him. You must admit with me that this superstitious cult of his mummy is an insult to his memory and a disgrace to a revolutionary city like Moscow." I suggested to him, in short, that we should get hold of a tin or two of petrol and make a "little revolution" on our own, by burning the totem-hut. I did not, to be frank, expect him to accept my proposal there and then, but at least I thought he would laugh about it; instead of which my poor friend went very pale and began to tremble violently. Then he begged me not to say dreadful things of that kind, either to him or still less to others. (Ten years later, when he was being searched for as an accomplice of Zinoviev, he committed suicide by throwing himself from the fifth floor of the house he lived in.) I have been present at the march post of immense parades of people and armies in the Red Square, but, in my mind, the recollection of that young friend's emotion and of his frightened and affectionate voice, has remained stronger than any other image. It may be that that memory is "objectively" more important.

It is not easy to trace the history of the Communist International, and it would be undoubtedly premature. How can one separate the fatuous from the essential in the interminable discussions at its congresses and meetings? What speeches should be left to the mice in the archives to criticize, and which should be recommended to intelligent people anxious to understand? I do not know. What my memory prefers to recall may to some people seem only bizarre. They were discussing one day, in a special commission of the Executive, the ultimatum issued by the central committee of the British trade unions, ordering its local branches not to support the Communist-led minority movement, on pain of expulsion. After the representative of the English Communist Party had explained the serious disadvantages of both solutions—because one meant the liquidation of the minority movement and the other the exit of the minority from the Trades Unions—the Russian delegate Piatnisky put forward a suggestion which seemed as obvious to him as Columbus' egg. "The branches," he suggested, "should declare that they submit to the discipline demanded, and then, in practice, should do exactly the contrary." The English Communist interrupted, "But that would be a lie." Loud laughter greeted this ingenuous objection, frank, cordial, interminable laughter, the like of which the gloomy offices of the Communist International had perhaps never heard before. The joke quickly spread all over Moscow, for the Englishman's entertaining and incredible reply was telephoned at once to Stalin and to the most important offices of State, provoking new waves of mirth everywhere. The general hilarity gave the English Communist's timid, ingenuous objection its true meaning. And that is why, in my memory, the storm of laughter aroused by that short, almost childishly simple little expression—"But that would be a lie"—outweighs all the long, heavy oppressive speeches I heard during sittings of the Communist International, and has become a kind of symbol for me.

My visits to Moscow, as I have already said, were few, and limited to my functions as a member of the Italian Communist delegations. I have never been part of the organization of the Communist International, but I could follow its rapid corruption by observing a few acquaintances of mine who belonged to it. Among them, an outstanding example was the Frenchman Jacques Doriot. I had met him for the first time in Moscow in 1921; he was then a modest, willing and sentimental young workingman, and it was for his obvious docility and easy-going nature that he was chosen for the international organization in preference to other young French Communists, who were more intelligent and better educated than himself, but also less conventional. He lived up fully to expectation. Year by year, he became an increasingly important figure in the hierarchy of International Communism, and, year by year, each time I came across him, I found him changed for the worse, skeptical, cynical, unscrupulous, and rapidly becoming Fascist in his political attitude toward men and the State. If I could triumph over my natural repugnance and write a biography of Jacques Doriot, my theme would be: "Militant Communist into Fascist."

Once I met Doriot in Moscow, just after his return from a political mission in China. He gave a few friends and myself a disturbing account of the mistakes of the Communist International in the Far East. The next day, however, speaking before the Executive in full session, he affirmed the exact opposite. "It was an act of political wisdom," he confided to me after the meeting with a slight and superior smile. His case is worth mentioning because it was not isolated. Internal changes in French Communism later led Jacques Doriot to leave the Communist International, and gave him a chance to show himself openly in what had already been, for a long time, his true colors; but many others, who basically are no different from Doriot, have remained at the head of Communist Parties. Palmiro Togliatti, the Italian, referred to this phenomenon of duplicity and demoralization among the personnel of the Communist International in his speech before its Sixth Congress, and asked permission to repeat the words of the dying Goethe: "Light, more light."

In a certain sense, that speech was Togliatti's swan-song; for another year or two he kept up the effort to follow his inmost promptings and to reconcile being a Communist with speaking his mind frankly, but, in the end, even he had to capitulate and submit.

Besides internal differences resulting from its own heterogeneous composition, the Communist International felt the repercussions of every difficulty of the Soviet State. After Lenin's death, it was clear that the Soviet State could not avoid what seems to be the destiny of every dictatorship: the gradual and inexorable narrowing of its political pyramid. The Russian Communist Party, which had suppressed all rival parties and abolished any possibility of general political discussion in the Soviet assemblies, itself suffered a similar fate, and its members' political views were rapidly ousted by the policy of the Party machine. From that moment, every difference of opinion in the controlling body was destined to end in the physical extinction of the minority. The Revolution, which had extinguished its enemies, began to devour its favorite sons. The thirsty gods gave no more truce.

In May, 1927, as a representative of the Italian Communist Party, I took part with Togliatti in an extraordinary session of the enlarged Executive of the Communist International. Togliatti had come from Paris, where he was running the political secretariat of the Party, and I from Italy, where I was in charge of the underground organization. We met in Berlin and went on to Moscow together. The meeting— ostensibly summoned for an urgent discussion of what direction should be given to the Communist Parties in the struggle "against the imminent imperialist war"—was actually designed to begin the "liquidation" of Trotsky and Zinoviev, who were still members of the International Executive. As usual, to avoid surprises, the full session had been preceded and every detail prepared by the so-called Senior-convent, consisting of the heads of the most important delegations. Togliatti, on that occasion, insisted that I should accompany him to these restricted sittings. According to the rules, only he had a right to attend on behalf of the Italian delegation; but, rightly foreseeing what complications were about to arise, he preferred to have the support of the representative of the clandestine organization. At the first sitting which we attended, I had the impression that we had arrived too late. We were in a small office in the Communist International Headquarters. The German Thälmann was presiding, and immediately began reading out a proposed resolution against Trotsky, to be presented at the full session. This resolution condemned, in the most violent terms, a document which Trotsky had addressed to the Political Office of the Russian Communist Party. The Russian delegation at that day's session of the Senior-convent was an exceptional one: Stalin, Rikov, Bukharin and Manuilsky. At the end of the reading Thälmann asked if we were in agreement with the proposed resolution. The Finn Ottomar Kuusinen found that it was not strong enough. "It should be said openly," he suggested, "that the document sent by Trotsky to the Political Office of the Russian Communist Party is of an entirely counter-revolutionary character and constitutes clear proof that the man who wrote it no longer has anything in common with the working class." As no one else asked to speak, after consulting Togliatti, I made my apologies for having arrived late and so not having been able to see the document which was to be condemned. "To tell the truth," Thälmann declared candidly, "we haven't seen the document either."

Preferring not to believe my ears, I repeated my objection in other words: "It may very well be true," I said, "that Trotsky's document should be condemned, but obviously I cannot condemn it before I've read it."

"Neither have we," repeated Thälmann, "neither have the majority of the delegates present here, except for the Russians, read the document." Thälmann spoke in German and his words were translated into Russian for Stalin, and into French for two or three of us. The reply given to me was so incredible that I rounded on the translator. "It's impossible," I said, "that Thälmann should have said that. I must ask you to repeat his answer word for word."

At this point Stalin intervened. He was standing over at one side of the room, and seemed the only person present who was calm and unruffled.

"The Political Office of the Party," said Stalin, "has considered that it would not be expedient to translate and distribute Trotsky's document to the delegates of the International Executive, because there are various allusions in it to the policy of the Soviet State." (The mysterious document was later published abroad by Trotsky himself, in a booklet entitled *Problems of the Chinese Revolution,* and as anyone can today still see for himself, it contains no mention of the policy of the Soviet State, but a closely reasoned attack on the policy practiced in China by Stalin and the Communist International.

In a speech of April 15, 1927, in the presence of the Moscow Soviets, Stalin had sung the praises of Chiang Kai-shek, and confirmed his personal confidence in the Kuomintang; this was barely a week before the famous anti-Communist *volte face* of the Chinese Nationalist leader and of his party; the Communists were expelled from the Kuomintang overnight, tens of thousands of workers were massacred in Shanghai and, a month later, in Wuhan. It was natural therefore that Stalin should have been anxious to avoid a debate on these matters, seeking to protect himself behind a screen of *raison d'état.*)

Ernst Thälmann asked me if I were satisfied with Stalin's explanation. "I do not contest the right of the Political Office of the Russian Communist Party to keep any document secret," I said. "But I do not understand how others can be asked to condemn an unknown document." At this, indignation against myself and Togliatti, who appeared to agree with what I had said, knew no bounds; it was especially violent on the part of the Finn, whom I have already mentioned, a Bulgarian and one or two Hungarians.

"It's unheard-of," cried Kuusinen, very red in the face, "that we still have such petty bourgeois in the fortress of the World Revolution." He pronounced the words petty bourgeois with an extremely comical expression of contempt and disgust. The only person who remained calm and imperturbable was Stalin. He said, "If a single delegate is against the proposed resolution, it should not be presented." Then he added, "Perhaps our Italian comrades are not fully aware of our internal situation. I propose that the sitting be suspended until tomorrow and that one of those present should be assigned the task of spending the evening with our Italian comrades and explaining our internal situation to them." The Bulgarian Vasil Kolarov was given this ungrateful task.

He carried it out with tact and good humor. He invited us to have a glass of tea that evening in his room at the Hotel Lux. And he faced up to the thorny subject without much preamble. "Let's be frank," he said to us with a smile. "Do you think I've read that document? No, I haven't. To tell you the whole truth, I can add that that document doesn't even interest me. Shall I go further? Even if Trotsky sent me a copy here, secretly, I'd refuse to read it. My dear Italian friends, this isn't a question of documents. I know that Italy is the classic country of academies, but we aren't in an academy here. Here we are in the thick of a struggle for power between two rival groups of the Russian Central Directorate. Which of the two groups do we want to line up with? That's the point. Documents don't come into it. It's not a question of finding the historic truth about an unsuccessful Chinese revolution. It's a question of a struggle for power between two hostile, irreconcilable groups. One's got to choose. I, for my part, have already chosen, I'm for the majority group. Whatever the minority says or does, whatever document it draws up against the majority, I repeat to you that I'm for the majority. Documents don't interest me. We aren't in an academy here." He refilled our glasses with tea and scrutinized us with the air of a schoolmaster obliged to deal with two unruly youngsters. "Do I make myself clear?" he asked, addressing me specifically.

"Certainly," I replied, "very clear indeed." "Have I persuaded you?" he asked again. "No," I said. "And why not?" he wanted to know. "I should have to explain to you," I said, "why I'm against Fascism." Kolarov pretended to be indignant, while Togliatti expressed his opinion in more moderate, but no less succinct, terms. "One can't just declare oneself for the majority or for the minority in advance," he said. "One can't ignore the political basis of the question."

Kolarov listened to us with a benevolent smile of pity. "You're still too young," he explained, as he accompanied us to the door. "You haven't yet understood what politics are all about."

Next morning, in the Senior-convent, the scene of the day before was repeated. An unusual atmosphere of nervousness pervaded the little room into which a dozen of us were packed. "Have you explained the situation to our Italian comrades?" Stalin asked Kolarov. "Fully," the Bulgarian assured him. "If a single delegate," Stalin repeated, "is against the proposed resolution, it cannot be presented in the full session. A resolution against Trotsky can only be taken unanimously. Are our Italian comrades," he added turning to us, "favorable to the proposed resolution?"

After consulting Togliatti, I declared: "Before taking the resolution into consideration, we must see the document concerned." The Frenchman Albert Treint and the Swiss Jules Humbert-Droz made identical declarations. (Both of them, a few years later, also ended outside the Communist International.)

"The proposed resolution is withdrawn," said Stalin. After which, we had the same hysterical scene as the day before, with the indignant, angry protests of Kuusinen, Rakosi, Pepper and the others. Thälmann argued from our "scandalous" attitude that the whole trend of our anti-Fascist activity in Italy was most probably wrong, and that if Fascism was still so firmly entrenched in Italy it must be our fault. He asked because of this that the policy of the Italian Communist Party should be subjected to a thorough sifting. This was done; and as a reprisal for our "impertinent" conduct those fanatical censors discovered that the fundamental guiding lines of our activity, traced in the course of the previous years by Antonio Gramoci, were seriously contaminated by a petty-bourgeois spirit. Togliatti decided that it would be prudent for us both to address a letter to the Political Office of the Russian Communist Party explaining the reason for our attitude at the meeting of the Executive. No Communist, the letter said in effect, would presume to question the historical pre-eminence of our Russian comrades in the leadership of the International, but this pre-eminence imposed special duties on our Russian comrades; they could not apply the rights it gave them in a mechanical and authoritarian way. The letter was received by Bukharin, who sent for us at once and advised us to withdraw it so as not to worsen our already appalling political situation.

Days of somber discouragement followed for me. I asked myself: Have we sunk to this? Those who are dead, those who are dying in prison, have sacrificed themselves for this? The vagabond, lonely, perilous lives that we ourselves are leading, strangers in our own countries—is it all for this? My depression soon reached that extreme stage when the will is paralyzed and physical resistance suddenly gives way.

Before I left Moscow an Italian working-man came to see me. He had been a refugee in Russia for some years to avoid the long term of imprisonment to which a Fascist tribunal had sentenced him. (He is still, I believe, a Communist today.) He came to complain of the humiliating conditions of the workers in the Moscow factory to which he was attached. He was ready to put up with the material shortages of every kind, since to remedy them was clearly beyond the power of individuals, but he could not understand why the workmen were entirely at the mercy of the factory directorate and had no effective organization to protect their interests; why, in this respect also, they should be much worse off than in capitalist countries. Most of the much-vaunted rights of the working class were purely theoretical.

In Berlin, on my way back, I read in the paper that the Executive of the Communist International had severely rebuked Trotsky for a document he had prepared about recent events in China. I went to the offices of the German Communist Party and asked Thälmann for an explanation. "This is untrue," I said to him sharply.

But he explained that the statutes of the International authorized the Presidium, in case of urgency, to adopt any resolution in the name of the Executive. During the few days I had to stay in Berlin, while waiting for my false documents to be put in order, I read in the papers that the American, Hungarian and Czechoslovakian Communist Parties had energetically deplored Trotsky's letter. "Has the mysterious document finally been produced, then?" "No," he answered me. "But I hope the example set by the American, Hungarian and Czechoslovakian Communists has shown you what Communist discipline means." These things were said with no hint of irony, but indeed with dismal seriousness that befitted the nightmare reality to which they referred.

*     *     *

For reasons of health I had to go straight into a Swiss sanatorium, and all political decisions were suspended. One day, in a village not far from where I was taking my cure, I had a meeting with Togliatti. He explained to me at great length, clearly and frankly, the reasons for the line of conduct he had chosen. The present state of the International, he said in brief, was certainly neither satisfactory nor agreeable. But all our good intentions were powerless to change it; objective historical conditions were involved and must be taken into account. The forms of the Proletarian Revolution were not arbitrary. If they did not accord with our preferences, so much the worse for us. And besides, what alternative remained? Other Communists who had broken with the Party, how had they ended up? Consider, he said, the appalling condition of Social Democracy.

My objections to these arguments were not very coherent, mainly because Togliatti's arguments were purely political, whereas the agitation which my recent experiences had aroused in me went far beyond politics. These "inexcusable historical forms" to which we must bow down—what were they but a new version of the inhuman reality against which, in declaring ourselves Socialists, we had rebelled? I felt at that time like someone who has had a tremendous blow on the head and keeps on his feet, walking, talking and gesticulating, but without fully realizing what has happened.

Realization came, however, slowly and with difficulty during the course of the succeeding years. And to this day I go on thinking it over, trying to understand better. If I have written books, it has been to try and understand and to make others understand. I am not at all certain that I have reached the end of my efforts. The truth is this: the day I left the Communist Party was a very sad one for me, it was like a day of deep mourning, the mourning for my lost youth. And I come from a district where mourning is worn longer than elsewhere. It is not easy to free oneself from an experience as intense as that of the underground organization of the Communist Party. Something of it remains and leaves a mark on the character which lasts all one's life. One can, in fact, notice how recognizable the ex-Communists are. They constitute a category apart, like ex-priests and ex-regular officers. The number of ex-Communists is legion today. "The final struggle," I said jokingly to Togliatti recently, "will be between the Communists and the ex-Communists."

However, I carefully avoided, after I had left the Communist Party, ending up in one of the many groups and splinter-groups of ex-Communists; and I have never regretted this in any way, as I know well the kind of fate which rules over these groups and splinter-groups, and makes little sects of them which have all the defects of official Communism—the fanaticism, the centralization, the abstraction—without the qualities and advantages which the latter derives from its vast working-class following. The logic of opposition at all costs has carried many ex-Communists far from their starting-points, in some cases as far as Fascism.

Consideration of the experience I have been through has led me to a deepening of the motives for my separation which go very much further than the circumstantial ones by which it was produced. But my faith in Socialism (to which I think I can say my entire life bears testimony) has remained more alive than ever in me. In its essence, it has gone back to what it was when I first revolted against the old social order; a refusal to admit the existence of destiny, an extension of the ethical impulse from the restricted individual and family sphere to the whole domain of human activity, a need for effective brotherhood, an affirmation of the superiority of the human person over all the economic and social mechanisms which oppress him. As the years have gone by, there has been added to this an intuition of man's dignity and a feeling of reverence for that which in man is always trying to outdistance itself, and lies at the root of his eternal disquiet. But I do not think that this kind of Socialism is in any way peculiar to me. The "mad truths" recorded above are older than Marxism; toward the second half of the last century they took refuge in the workers' movement born of industrial capitalism, and continue to remain one of its most enduring founts of inspiration. I have repeatedly expressed my opinion on the relations between the Socialist Movement and the theories of Socialism; these relations are by no means rigid or immutable. With the development of new studies, the theories may go out of fashion or be discarded, but the movement goes on. It would be inaccurate, however, with regard to the old quarrel between the doctrinaires and the empiricists of the workers' movement, to include me among the latter. I do not conceive Socialist policy as tied to any particular theory, but to a faith. The more Socialist theories claim to be "scientific," the more transitory they are; but Socialist values are permanent. The distinction between theories and values is not sufficiently recognized, but it is fundamental. On a group of theories one can found a school; but on a group of values one can found a culture, a civilization, a new way of living together among men.

## ⌦ MEIN KAMPF

*Adolf Hitler*

*Had Adolf Hitler (1889–1945) never written* Mein Kampf *("My Struggle"), in all likelihood his own career, the history of Germany, and the history of the West during the crucial ten years from 1935 to 1945 would not have been affected. Yet the book does illuminate the outlook and mental processes of the Nazi leader and his followers long before they were taken very seriously. In the mid-1920s, when* Mein Kampf *appeared, Hitler was but one of a number of nationalist and anti-Semitic demagogues; his German National Socialist Workers' Party competed with other right-wing organizations for the loyalties of a limited and seemingly declining fraction of the German electorate. Few observers could have predicted then that Hitler and his party would gain national power by 1933 or that, at its climax, the totalitarian Nazi Germany constructed by them would control an empire dwarfing that of Napoleon or Rome.*

*Hitler was forced to retire from politics in 1924 for his part in the attempted overthrow of the government of the south German state of Bavaria. He wrote* Mein Kampf *while he was detained in the fortress prison of Landsberg. Despite its title, the book was only incidentally autobiographical. Hitler was chiefly interested in setting off his movement and his particular vision of the German future from that of competing right-wing groups. The book itself is formless, a collection of more or less developed random observations on a variety of topics. It is doubtful, moreover, that Mein Kampf should be regarded as a firm and definitive statement of its author's plans after his achievement of power, even though it does illustrate his ideology and direction.*

*For several years following its publication in 1925, Mein Kampf was only moderately successful, selling as few as 3,015 copies in 1928. Only with the rise to prominence of the Nazi party in 1930 did the book, by this time extensively revised, become a best seller. During Hitler's dictatorship, Mein Kampf became a kind of secular bible, obligatory wedding present, and, incidentally, the foundation of Hitler's private fortune.*

*The following selections sound most of the major themes found in the work but necessarily distort its flavor by omitting the innumerable tangents, digressions, and repetitions that are equally characteristic of Mein Kampf.*

One day I received orders from my headquarters to find out what was behind an apparently political organization which was planning to hold a meeting within the next few days under the name of "German Workers' Party"—with Gottfried Feder as one of the speakers. I was told to go and take a look at the organization and then make a report.

The curiosity of the army toward political parties in those days was more than understandable. The revolution had given the soldiers the right of political activity, and it was just the most inexperienced among them who made the most ample use of it. Not until the moment when the Center and the Social Democracy were forced to recognize, to their own grief, that the sympathies of the soldiers were beginning to turn away from the revolutionary parties toward the national movement and reawakening, did they see fit to deprive the troops of suffrage again and prohibit their political activity. . . .

And so I decided to attend the above-mentioned meeting of this party which up till then had been entirely unknown to me too.

In the evening when I entered the "Leiber Room" of the former Sterneckerbräu in Munich, I found some twenty to twenty-five people present, chiefly from the lower classes of the population.

Feder's lecture was known to me from the sources, so I was able to devote myself to an inspection of the organization itself.

Adolf Hitler, *Mein Kampf*, trans. R. Manheim (Boston: Houghton Mifflin Company, 1943), pp. 217–224, 579–583, 290–292, 294–296, 300–302, 305–308, 312, 314–320, 323–327, 448–451, 649–655.

My impression was neither good nor bad; a new organization like so many others. This was a time in which anyone who was not satisfied with developments and no longer had any confidence in the existing parties felt called upon to found a new party. Everywhere these organizations sprang out of the ground, only to vanish silently after a time. The founders for the most part had no idea what it means to make a party— let alone a movement—out of a club. And so these organizations nearly always stifle automatically in their absurd philistinism.

I judged the "German Workers' Party" no differently. When Feder finally stopped talking, I was happy. I had seen enough and wanted to leave when the free discussion period, which was now announced, moved me to remain, after all. But here, too, everything seemed to run along insignificantly until suddenly a "professor" took the floor; he first questioned the soundness of Feder's arguments and then—after Feder replied very well—suddenly appealed to "the facts," but not without recommending most urgently that the young party take up the "separation" of Bavaria from "Prussia" as a particularly important programmatic point. With bold effrontery the man maintained that in this case German-Austria would at once join Bavaria, that the peace would then become much better, and more similar nonsense. At this point I could not help demanding the floor and giving the learned gentleman my opinion on this point—with the result that the previous speaker, even before I was finished, left the hall like a wet poodle. As I spoke, the audience had listened with astonished faces, and only as I was beginning to say good night to the assemblage and go away did a man come leaping after me, introduce himself (I had not quite understood his name), and press a little booklet into my hand, apparently a political pamphlet, with the urgent request that I read it.

This was very agreeable to me, for now I had reason to hope that I might become acquainted with this dull organization in a simpler way, without having to attend any more such interesting meetings. Incidentally this apparent worker had made a good impression on me. And with this I left the hall.

At that time I was still living in the barracks of the Second Infantry Regiment in a little room that still very distinctly bore the traces of the revolution. During the day I was out, mostly with the Forty-First Rifle Regiment, or at meetings, or lectures in some other army unit, etc. Only at night did I sleep in my quarters. Since I regularly woke up before five o'clock in the morning, I had gotten in the habit of putting a few left-overs or crusts of bread on the floor for the mice which amused themselves in my little room, and watching the droll little beasts chasing around after these choice morsels. I had known so much poverty in my life that I was well able to imagine the hunger, and hence also the pleasure, of the little creatures.

At about five o'clock in the morning after this meeting, I thus lay awake in my cot, watching the chase and bustle. Since I could no longer fall asleep, I suddenly remembered the past evening and my mind fell on the booklet which the worker had given me. I began to read. It was a little pamphlet in which the author, this same worker, described how he had returned to national thinking out of the Babel of Marxist and trade-unionist phrases; hence also the title: *My Political Awakening*. Once I had begun, I read the little book through with interest; for it reflected a process similar to the one which I myself had gone through twelve years before. Involuntarily I saw my own development come to life before my eyes. In the course of the day I reflected a few times on the matter and was finally about to put it aside when, less than a week later, much to my surprise, I received a postcard saying that I had been accepted in the German Workers' Party; I was requested to express myself on the subject and for this purpose to attend a committee meeting of this party on the following Wednesday.

I must admit that I was astonished at this way of "winning" members and I didn't know whether to be angry or to laugh. I had no intention of joining a ready-made party, but wanted to found one of my own. What they asked of me was presumptuous and out of the question.

I was about to send the gentlemen my answer in writing when curiosity won out and I decided to appear on the appointed day to explain my reasons by word of mouth.

Wednesday came. The tavern in which the said meeting was to take place was the "Altes Rosenbad" in the Herrenstrasse, a very run-down place that no one seemed to stray into more than once in a blue moon. No wonder, in the year 1919 when the menu of even the larger restaurants could offer only the scantiest and most modest allurements. Up to this time this tavern had been totally unknown to me.

I went through the ill-lit dining room in which not a soul was sitting, opened the door to the back room, and the "session" was before me. In the dim light of a broken-down gas lamp four young people sat at a table, among them the author of the little pamphlet, who at once greeted me most joyfully and bade me welcome as a new member of the German Workers' Party.

Really, I was somewhat taken aback. As I was now informed that the actual "national chairman" had not yet arrived, I decided to wait with my declaration. This gentleman finally appeared. It was the same who had presided at the meeting in the Sterneckerbräu on the occasion of Feder's lecture.

Meanwhile, I had again become very curious, and waited expectantly for what was to come. Now at least I came to know the names of the individual gentlemen. The chairman of the "national organization" was a Herr Harrer, that of the Munich District, Anton Drexler.

The minutes of the last meeting were read and the secretary was given a vote of confidence. Next came the treasury report—all in all the association possessed seven marks and fifty pfennigs—for which the treasurer received a vote of general confidence. This, too, was entered in the minutes. Then the first chairman read the answers to a letter from Kiel, one from Düsseldorf, and one from Berlin, and everyone expressed approval. Next a report was given on the incoming mail: a letter from Berlin, one from Düsseldorf and one from Kiel, whose arrival seemed to be received with great satisfaction. This growing correspondence was interpreted as the best and most visible sign of the spreading importance of the German Workers' Party, and then—then there was a long deliberation with regard to the answers to be made.

Terrible, terrible! This was club life of the worst manner and sort. Was I to join this organization?

Next, new memberships were discussed; in other words, my capture was taken up.

I now began to ask questions—but, aside from a few directives, there was nothing, no program, no leaflet, no printed matter at all, no membership cards, not even a miserable rubber stamp, only obvious good faith and good intentions.

I had stopped smiling, for what was this if not a typical sign of the complete helplessness and total despair of all existing parties, their programs, their purposes, and their activity? The thing that drove these few young people to activity that was outwardly so absurd was only the emanation of their inner voice, which more instinctively than consciously showed them that all parties up till then were suited neither for raising up the German nation nor for curing its inner wounds. I quickly read the typed "directives" and in them I saw more seeking than knowledge. Much was vague or unclear, much was missing, but nothing was present which could not have passed as a sign of a struggling realization.

I knew what these men felt: it was the longing for a new movement which should be more than a party in the previous sense of the word.

That evening when I returned to the barracks I had formed my judgment of this association.

I was facing the hardest question of my life: should I join or should I decline?

Reason could advise me only to decline, but my feeling left me no rest, and as often as I tried to remember the absurdity of this whole club, my feeling argued for it.

I was restless in the days that followed.

I began to ponder back and forth. I had long been resolved to engage in political activity; that this could be done only in a new movement was likewise clear to me; only the impetus to act had hitherto been lacking. I am not one of those people who begin something today and lay it down tomorrow, if possible taking up something else again. This very conviction among others was the main reason why it was so hard for me to make up my mind to join such a new organization. I knew that for me a decision would be for good, with no turning back. For me it was no passing game, but grim earnest. Even then I had an instinctive revulsion toward men who start everything and never carry anything out. These jacks-of-all-trades were loathsome to me. I regarded the activity of such people as worse than doing nothing.

And this way of thinking constituted one of the main reasons why I could not make up my mind as easily as some others do to found a cause which either had to become everything or else would do better not to exist at all.

Fate itself now seemed to give me a hint. I should never have gone into one of the existing large parties, and later on I shall go into the reasons for this more closely. This absurd little organization with its few members seemed to me to possess the one advantage that it had not frozen into an "organization," but left the individual an opportunity for real personal activity. Here it was still possible to work, and the smaller the movement, the more readily it could be put into the proper form. Here the content, the goal, and the road could still be determined, which in the existing great parties was impossible from the outset.

The longer I tried to think it over, the more the conviction grew in me that through just such a little movement the rise of the nation could some day be organized, but never through the political parliamentary parties which clung far too greatly to the old conceptions or even shared in the profits of the new régime. For it was a new philosophy and not a new election slogan that had to be proclaimed.

Truly a very grave decision—to begin transforming this intention into reality!

What prerequisites did I myself bring to this task?

That I was poor and without means seemed to me the most bearable part of it, but it was harder that I was numbered among the nameless, that I was one of the millions whom chance permits to live or summons out of existence without even their closest neighbors condescending to take any notice of it. In addition, there was the difficulty which inevitably arose from my lack of schooling.

The so-called "intelligentsia" always looks down with a really limitless condescension on anyone who has not been dragged through the obligatory schools and had the necessary knowledge pumped into him. The question has never been: What are the man's abilities? but: What has he learned? To these "educated" people the biggest empty-head, if he is wrapped in enough diplomas, is worth more than the brightest boy who happens to lack these costly envelopes. And so it was easy for me to imagine how this "educated" world would confront me, and in this I erred only in so far as even then I still regarded people as better than in cold reality they for the most part unfortunately are. As they are, to be sure, the exceptions, as everywhere else, shine all the more brightly. Thereby, however, I learned always to distinguish between the eternal students and the men of real ability.

After two days of agonized pondering and reflection, I finally came to the conviction that I had to take this step.

It was the most decisive resolve of my life. From here there was and could be no turning back.

And so I registered as a member of the German Workers' Party and received a provisional membership card with the number 7.

\*        \*        \*

After my entrance into the German Workers' Party, I at once took over the management of propaganda. I regarded this department as by far the most important. For the present, it was less important to rack one's brains over organizational questions than to transmit the idea itself to a larger number of people. Propaganda had to run far in advance of organization and provide it with the human material to be worked on. Moreover, I am an enemy of too rapid and too pedantic organizing. It usually produces nothing but a dead mechanism, seldom a living organization. For organization is a thing that owes its existence to organic life, organic development. Ideas which have gripped a certain number of people will always strive for a greater order, and a great value must be attributed to this inner molding. Here, too, we must reckon with the weakness of men, which leads the individual, at first at least, instinctively to resist a superior mind. If an organization is mechanically ordered from above, there exists a great danger that a once appointed leader, not yet accurately evaluated and perhaps none too capable, will from jealousy strive to prevent the rise of abler elements within the movement. The harm that arises in such a case can, especially in a young movement, be of catastrophic significance.

For this reason it is more expedient for a time to disseminate an idea by propaganda from a central point and then carefully to search and examine the gradually gathering human material for leading minds. Sometimes it will turn out that men inconspicuous in themselves must nevertheless be regarded as born leaders.

*But it would be absolutely mistaken to regard a wealth of theoretical knowledge as characteristic proof for the qualities and abilities of a leader.*

The opposite is often the case.

The great *theoreticians* are only in the rarest cases great *organizers*, since the greatness of the *theoretician* and *program-maker* lies primarily in the *recognition* and *establishment of abstractly correct laws*, while the *organizer* must primarily be a *psychologist*. He must take people as they are and must therefore know them. He must not overestimate them, any more than he must underestimate them in the mass. On the contrary, he must endeavor to take weakness and bestiality equally into account, in order, considering all factors, to create a formation which will be a living organism, imbued with strong and stable power, and thus suited to upholding an idea and paving the way for its success.

Even more seldom, however, is a great theoretician a great leader. Much more readily will an *agitator* be one, something which many who only work scientifically on the question do not want to hear. And yet that is understandable. An agitator who demonstrates the ability to transmit an idea to the broad masses must always be a psychologist, even if he were only a demagogue. Then he will still be more suited for leadership than the unworldly theoretician, who is ignorant of people. *For leading means: being able to move masses.* The gift of shaping ideas has nothing to do with ability as a leader. And it is quite useless to argue which is of greater importance, to set up ideals and aims for mankind, or to realize them. Here, as so often in life: one would be utterly meaningless without the other. The finest theoretical insight remains without purpose and value if the leader does not set the masses in motion toward it. And conversely, of what avail would be all the genius and energy of a leader, if the brilliant theoretician did not set up aims for the human struggle? However, the combination of theoretician, organizer, and leader in one person is the rarest thing that can be found on this earth; this combination makes the great man.

As I have already remarked, I devoted myself to propaganda in the first period of my activity in the movement. What it had to do was gradually to fill a small nucleus of men with the new doctrine, and so prepare the material which could later furnish the first elements of an organization.

When a movement harbors the purpose of tearing down a world and building another in its place, complete clarity must reign in the ranks of its own leadership with regard to the following principles:

*Every movement will first have to sift the human material it wins into two large groups: supporters and members.*

*The function of propaganda is to attract supporters, the function of organization to win members.*

*A supporter of a movement is one who declares himself to be in agreement with its aims, a member is one who fights for them.*

*The supporter is made amenable to the movement by propaganda. The member is induced by the organization to participate personally in the recruiting of new supporters, from whom in turn members can be developed.*

*Since being a supporter requires only a passive recognition of an idea, while membership demands active advocacy and defense, to ten supporters there will at most be one or two members.*

*Being a supporter is rooted only in understanding, membership in the courage personally to advocate and disseminate what has been understood.*

*Understanding in its passive form corresponds to the majority of mankind which is lazy and cowardly. Membership requires an activistic frame of mind and thus corresponds only to the minority of men.*

*Propaganda will consequently have to see that an idea wins supporters, while the organization must take the greatest care only to make the most valuable elements among the supporters into members. Propaganda does not, therefore, need to rack its brains with regard to the importance of every individual instructed by it, with regard to his ability, capacity, and understanding, or character, while the organization must carefully gather from the mass of these elements those which really make possible the victory of the movement.*

*Propaganda tries to force a doctrine on the whole people; the organization embraces within its scope only those who do not threaten on psychological grounds to become a brake on the further dissemination of the idea.*

*Propaganda works on the general public from the standpoint of an idea and makes them ripe for the victory of this idea, while the organization achieves victory by the persistent, organic, and militant union of those supporters who seem willing and able to carry on the fight for victory.*

*The victory of an idea will be possible the sooner, the more comprehensively propaganda has prepared people as a whole and the more exclusive, rigid, and firm the organization which carries out the fight in practice.*

*From this it results that the number of supporters cannot be too large, but that the number of members can more readily be too large than too small.*

*If propaganda has imbued a whole people with an idea, the organization can draw the consequences with a handful of men. Propaganda and organization, in other words, supporters and members thus stand in a certain mutual relation. The better the propaganda has worked, the smaller the organization can be; and the larger the number of supporters, the more modest the number of members can be; and vice versa: the poorer the propaganda is, the larger the organization must be, and the smaller the host of followers of a movement remains, the more extensive the number of its members must be, if it still hopes to count on any success at all.*

*The first task of propaganda is to win people for subsequent organization; the first task of organization is to win men for the continuation of propaganda. The second task of propaganda is the disruption of the existing state of affairs and the permeation of this state of affairs with the new doctrine, while the second task of organization must be the struggle for power, thus to achieve the final success of the doctrine.*

If we were to divide mankind into three groups, the founders of culture, the bearers of culture, the destroyers of culture, only the Aryan could be considered as the representative of the first group. From him originate the foundations and walls of all human creation, and only the outward form and color are determined by the changing traits of character of the various peoples. He provides the mightiest building stones and plans for all human progress and only the execution corresponds to the nature of the varying men and races. In a few decades, for example, the entire east of Asia will possess a culture whose ultimate foundation will be Hellenic spirit and Germanic technology, just as much as in Europe. Only the *outward* form—in part at least—will bear the features of Asiatic character. It is not true, as some people think, that Japan adds European technology to its culture; no, European science and technology are trimmed with Japanese characteristics. The foundation of actual life is no longer the special Japanese culture, although it determines the color of life —because outwardly, in consequence of its inner difference, it is more conspicuous to the European—but the gigantic scientific-technical achievements of Europe and America; that is, of Aryan peoples. Only on the basis of these achievements can the Orient follow general human progress. They furnish the basis of the struggle for daily bread, create weapons and implements for it, and only the outward form is gradually adapted to Japanese character.

If beginning today all further Aryan influence on Japan should stop, assuming that Europe and America should perish, Japan's present rise in science and technology might continue for a short time; but even in a few years the well would dry up, the Japanese special character would gain, but the present culture would freeze and sink back into the slumber from which it was awakened seven decades ago by the wave of Aryan culture. . . . But if it is established that a people receives the most essential basic materials of its culture from foreign races, that it assimilates and adapts them, and that then, if further external influence is lacking, it rigidifies again and again, such a race may be designated as *"culture-bearing,"* but never as *"culture-creating."* An examination of the various peoples from this standpoint points to the fact that practically none of them were originally *culture-founding*, but almost always *culture-bearing*.

Approximately the following picture of their development always results:

Aryan races—often absurdly small numerically—subject foreign peoples, and then, stimulated by the special living conditions of the new territory (fertility, climatic conditions, etc.) and assisted by the multitude of lower-type beings standing at their disposal as helpers, develop the intellectual and organizational capacities dormant within them. Often in a few millenniums or even centuries they create cultures which originally bear all the inner characteristics of their nature, adapted to the above-indicated special qualities of the soil and subjected beings. In the end, however, the conquerors transgress against the principle of blood purity, to which they had first adhered; they begin to mix with the subjugated inhabitants and thus end their own existence; for the fall of man in paradise has always been followed by his expulsion. . . .

We see this most distinctly in connection with the race which has been and is the bearer of human cultural development—the Aryans. As soon as Fate leads them toward special conditions, their latent abilities begin to develop in a more and more rapid sequence and to mold themselves into tangible forms. The cultures which they found in such cases are nearly always decisively determined by the existing soil, the given climate, and—the subjected people. This last item, to be sure, is almost the most decisive. The more primitive the technical foundations for a cultural activity, the more necessary is the presence of human helpers who, organizationally assembled and employed, must replace the force of the machine. Without this possibility of using lower human beings, the Aryan would never have been able to take his first steps toward his future culture; just as without the help of various suitable beasts which he knew how to tame, he would not have arrived at a technology which is now gradually permitting him to do without these beasts. . . . For thousands of years the horse had to serve man and help him lay the foundations of a development which now, in consequence of the motor car, is making the horse superfluous. In a few years his activity will have ceased, but without his previous collaboration man might have had a hard time getting where he is today.

Thus, for the formation of higher cultures the existence of lower human types was one of the most essential preconditions, since they alone were able to compensate for the lack of technical aids without which a higher development is not conceivable. It is certain that the first culture of humanity was based less on the tamed animal than on the use of lower human beings.

Only after the enslavement of subjected races did the same fate strike beasts, and not the other way around, as some people would like to think. For first the conquered warrior drew the plow—and only after him the horse. Only pacifistic fools can regard this as a sign of human depravity, failing to realize that this development had to take place in order to reach the point where today these sky-pilots could force their drivel on the world.

The progress of humanity is like climbing an endless ladder; it is impossible to climb higher without first taking the lower steps. Thus, the Aryan had to take the road to which reality directed him and not the one that would appeal to the imagination of a modern pacifist. The road of reality is hard and difficult, but in the end it leads where our friend would like to bring humanity by dreaming, but unfortunately removes more than bringing it closer.

Hence it is no accident that the first cultures arose in places where the Aryan, in his encounters with lower peoples, subjugated them and bent them to his will. They then became the first technical instrument in the service of a developing culture.

Thus, the road which the Aryan had to take was clearly marked out. As a conqueror he subjected the lower beings and regulated their practical activity under his command, according to his will and for his aims. But in directing them to a useful, though arduous activity, he not only spared the life of those he subjected; perhaps he gave them a fate that was better than their previous so-called "freedom." As long as he ruthlessly upheld the master attitude, not only did he really remain master, but also the preserver and increaser of culture. For culture was based exclusively on his abilities and hence on his actual survival. As soon as the subjected people began to raise themselves up and probably approached the conqueror in language, the sharp dividing wall between master and servant fell. The Aryan gave up the purity of his blood and, therefore, lost his sojourn in the paradise which he had made for himself. He became submerged in the racial mixture, and gradually, more and more, lost his cutural capacity, until at last, not only mentally but also physically, he began to resemble the subjected aborigines more than his own ancestors. For a time he could live on the existing cultural benefits, but then petrifaction set in and he fell a prey to oblivion.

Thus cultures and empires collapsed to make place for new formations.

Blood mixture and the resultant drop in the racial level is the sole cause of the dying out of old cultures; for men do not perish as a result of lost wars, but by the loss of that force of resistance which is contained only in pure blood.

All who are not of good race in this world are chaff.

And all occurrences in world history are only the expression of the races' instinct of self-preservation, in the good or bad sense. . . .

The mightiest counterpart to the Aryan is represented by the Jew. In hardly any people in the world is the instinct of self-preservation developed more strongly than in the so-called "chosen." Of this, the mere fact of the survival of this race may be considered the best proof. Where is the people which in the last two thousand years has been exposed to so slight changes of inner disposition, character, etc., as the Jewish people? What people, finally, has gone through greater upheavals than this one—and nevertheless issued from the mightiest catastrophes of mankind unchanged? What an infinitely tough will to live and preserve the species speaks from these facts!

The mental qualities of the Jew have been schooled in the course of many centuries. Today he passes as "smart," and this in a certain sense he has been at all times. But his intelligence is not the result of his own development, but of visual instruction through foreigners. . . .

Since the Jew—for reasons which will at once become apparent—was never in possession of a culture of his own, the foundations of his intellectual work were always provided by others. His intellect at all times developed through the cultural world surrounding him.

The reverse process never took place.

For if the Jewish people's instinct of self-preservation is not smaller but larger than that of other peoples, if his intellectual faculties can easily arouse the impression that they are equal to the intellectual gifts of other races, he lacks completely the most essential requirement for a cultured people, the idealistic attitude.

In the Jewish people the will to self-sacrifice does not go beyond the individual's naked instinct of self-preservation. Their apparently great sense of solidarity is based on the very primitive herd instinct that is seen in many other living creatures in this world. It is a noteworthy fact that the herd instinct leads to mutual support only as long as a common danger makes this seem useful or inevitable. The same pack of wolves which has just fallen on its prey together disintegrates when hunger abates into its individual beasts. The same is true of horses which try to defend themselves against an assailant in a body, but scatter again as soon as the danger is past.

It is similar with the Jew. His sense of sacrifice is only apparent. . . .

Thus, the Jew of all times has lived in the states of other peoples, and there formed his own state, which, to be sure, habitually sailed under the disguise of "religious community" as long as outward circumstances made a complete revelation of his nature seem inadvisable. But as soon as he felt strong enough to do without the protective cloak, he always dropped the veil and suddenly became what so many of the others previously did not want to believe and see: the Jew.

The Jew's life as a parasite in the body of other nations and states explains a characteristic which once caused Schopenhauer, as has already been mentioned, to call him the "great master in lying." Existence impels the Jew to lie, and to lie perpetually, just as it compels the inhabitants of the northern countries to wear warm clothing.

His life within other peoples can only endure for any length of time if he succeeds in arousing the opinion that he is not a people but a "religious community," though of a special sort.

And this is the first great lie.

In order to carry on his existence as a parasite on other peoples, he is forced to deny his inner nature. The more intelligent the individual Jew is, the more he will succeed in this deception. Indeed, things can go so far that large parts of the host people will end by seriously believing that the Jew is really a Frenchman or an Englishman, a German or an Italian, though of a special religious faith. Especially state authorities, which always seem animated by the historical fraction of wisdom, most easily fall a victim to this infinite deception. Independent thinking sometimes seems to these circles a true sin against holy advancement, so that we may not be surprised if even today a Bavarian state ministry, for example, still has not the faintest idea that the Jews are members of a *people* and not of a *"religion"* though a glance at the Jew's own newspapers should indicate this even to the most modest mind. The *Jewish Echo* is not yet an official organ, of course, and consequently is unauthoritative as far as the intelligence of one of these government potentates is concerned.

The Jew has always been a people with definite racial characteristics and never a religion; only in order to get ahead he early sought for a means which could distract unpleasant attention from his person. And what would have been more expedient and at the same time more innocent than the "embezzled" concept of a religious community? For here, too, everything is borrowed or rather stolen. Due to his own original special nature, the Jew cannot possess a religious institution, if for no other reason because he lacks idealism in any form, and hence belief in a hereafter is absolutely foreign to him. And a religion in the Aryan sense cannot be imagined which lacks the conviction of survival after death in some form. Indeed, the Talmud is not a book to prepare a man for the hereafter, but only for a practical and profitable life in this world.

The Jewish religious doctrine consists primarily in prescriptions for keeping the blood of Jewry pure and for regulating the relation of Jews among themselves, but even more with the rest of the world; in other words, with non-Jews. But even here it is by no means ethical problems that are involved, but extremely modest economic ones. Concerning the moral value of Jewish religious instruction, there are today and have been at all times rather exhaustive studies (not by Jews; the drivel of the Jews themselves on the subject is, of course, adapted to its purpose) which make this kind of religion seem positively monstrous according to Aryan conceptions. The best characterization is provided by the product of this religious education, the Jew himself. His life is only of this world, and his spirit is inwardly as alien to true Christianity as his nature two thousand years previous was to the great founder of the new doctrine. Of course, the latter made no secret of his attitude toward the Jewish people, and when necessary he even took to the whip to drive from the temple of the Lord this adversary of all humanity, who then as always saw in religion nothing but an instrument for his business existence. In return, Christ was nailed to the cross, while our present-day party Christians debase themselves to begging for Jewish votes at elections and later try to arrange political swindles with atheistic Jewish parties—and this against their own nation.

On this first and greatest lie, that the Jews are not a race but a religion, more and more lies are based in necessary consequence. Among them is the lie with regard to the language of the Jew. For him it is not a means for expressing his thoughts, but a means for concealing them. When he speaks French, he thinks Jewish, and while he turns out German verses, in his life he only expresses the nature of his nationality. As long as the Jew has not become the master of the other peoples, he must speak their languages whether he likes it or not, but as soon as they became his slaves, they would all have to learn a universal language (Esperanto, for instance!), so that by this additional means the Jews could more easily dominate them!

To what an extent the whole existence of this people is based on a continuous lie is shown incomparably by the *Protocols of the Wise Men of Zion*, so infinitely hated by the Jews. They are based on a forgery, the *Frankfurter Zeitung* moans and screams once every week: the best proof that they are authentic. What many Jews may do unconsciously is here consciously exposed. And that is what matters. It is completely indifferent from what Jewish brain these disclosures originate; the important thing is that with positively terrifying certainty they reveal the nature and activity of the Jewish people and expose their inner contexts as well as their ultimate final aims. The best criticism applied to them, however, is reality. Anyone who examines the historical development of the last hundred years from the standpoint of this book will at once understand the screaming of the Jewish press. For once this book has become the common property of a people, the Jewish menace may be considered as broken. . . .

But now all this was to change. In the course of more than a thousand years he has learned the language of the host people to such an extent that he now thinks he can venture in future to emphasize his Judaism less and place his "Germanism" more in the foreground; for ridiculous, nay, insane, as it may seem at first, he nevertheless has the effrontery to turn "Germanic," in this case a "German." With this begins one of the most infamous deceptions that anyone could conceive of. Since of Germanism he possesses really nothing but the art of stammering its language—and in the most frightful way—but apart from this has never mixed with the Germans, his whole Germanism rests on the language alone. Race, however, does not lie in the language, but exclusively in the blood, which no one knows better than the Jew, who attaches very little importance to the preservation of his language, but all importance to keeping his blood pure. A man can change his language without any trouble—that is, he can use another language; but in his new language he will express the old ideas; his inner nature is not changed. This is best shown by the Jew who can speak a thousand languages and nevertheless remains a Jew. His traits of character have remained the same, whether two thousand years ago as a grain dealer in Ostia, speaking Roman, or whether as a flour profiteer of today, jabbering German with a Jewish accent. It is always the same Jew. That this obvious fact is not understood by a ministerial secretary or higher police official is also self-evident, for there is scarcely any creature with less instinct and intelligence running around in the world today than these servants of our present model state authority. . . .

But even more: all at once the Jew also becomes liberal and begins to rave about the necessary progress of mankind.

Slowly he makes himself the spokesman of a new era.

Also, of course, he destroys more and more thoroughly the foundations of any economy that will really benefit the people. By way of stock shares he pushes his way into the circuit of national production which he turns into a purchasable or rather tradeable object, thus robbing the enterprises of the foundations of a personal ownership. Between employer and employee there arises that inner estrangement which later leads to political class division.

Finally, the Jewish influence on economic affairs grows with terrifying speed through the stock exchange. He becomes the owner, or at least the controller, of the national labor force.

To strengthen his political position he tries to tear down the racial and civil barriers which for a time continue to restrain him at every step. To this end he fights with all the tenacity innate in him for religious tolerance—and in Freemasonry, which has succumbed to him completely, he has an excellent instrument with which to fight for his aims and put them across. The governing circles and the higher strata of the political and economic bourgeoisie are brought into his nets by the strings of Freemasonry, and never need to suspect what is happening.

Only the deeper and broader strata of the people as such, or rather that class which is beginning to wake up and fight for its rights and freedom, cannot yet be sufficiently taken in by these methods. But this is more necessary than anything else; for the Jew feels that the possibility of his rising to a dominant rôle exists only if there is some-one ahead of him to clear the way; and this someone he thinks he can recognize in the bourgeoisie, in their broadest strata in fact. The glovemakers and linen weavers, however, cannot be caught in the fine net of Freemasonry; no, for them coarser but no less drastic means must be employed. Thus, Freemasonry is joined by a second weapon in the service of the Jews: the *press*. With all his perseverance and dexterity he seizes possession of it. With it he slowly begins to grip and ensnare, to guide and to push all public life, since he is in a position to create and direct that power which, under the name of "public opinion," is better known today than a few decades ago.

In this he always represents himself personally as having an infinite thirst for knowledge, praises all progress, mostly, to be sure, the progress that leads to the ruin of others; for he judges all knowledge and all development only according to its possibilities for advancing his nation, and where this is lacking, he is the inexorable mortal enemy of all light, a hater of all true culture. He uses all the knowledge he acquires in the schools of other peoples, exclusively for the benefit of his race.

And this nationality he guards as never before. While he seems to overflow with "enlightenment," "progress," "freedom," "humanity," etc., he himself practices the severest segregation of his race. To be sure, he sometimes palms off his women on influential Christians, but as a matter of principle he always keeps his male line pure. He poisons the blood of others, but preserves his own. The Jew almost never marries a Christian woman; it is the Christian who marries a Jewess. The bastards, however, take after the Jewish side. Especially a part of the high nobility degenerates completely. The Jew is perfectly aware of this, and therefore systematically carries on this mode of "disarming" the intellectual leader class of his racial adversaries. In order to mask his activity and lull his victims, however, he talks more and more of the equality of all men without regard to race and color. The fools begin to believe him.

Since, however, his whole being still has too strong a smell of the foreign for the broad masses of the people in particular to fall readily into his nets, he has his press give a picture of him which is as little in keeping with reality as conversely it serves his desired purpose. His comic papers especially strive to represent the Jews as a harmless little people, with their own peculiarities, of course—like other peoples as well— but even in their gestures, which seem a little strange, perhaps, giving signs of a possibly ludicrous, but always thoroughly honest and benevolent, soul. And the constant effort is to make him seem almost more "insignificant" than *dangerous*.

His ultimate goal in this stage is the victory of "democracy," or, as he understands it: the rule of parliamentarianism. It is most compatible with his requirements; for it excludes the personality—and puts in its place the majority characterized by stupidity, incompetence, and last but not least, cowardice.

The final result will be the overthrow of the monarchy, which is now sooner or later bound to occur.

The tremendous economic development leads to a change in the social stratification of the people. The small craftsman slowly dies out, and as a result the worker's possibility of achieving an independent existence becomes rarer and rarer; in consequence the worker becomes visibly proletarianized. There arises the industrial "factory worker" whose most essential characteristic is to be sought in the fact that he hardly ever is in a position to found an existence of his own in later life. He is propertyless in the truest sense of the word. His old age is a torment and can scarcely be designated as living. . . .

The separation of worker and employer now seems complete in all fields of life. How far the inner Judaization of our people has progressed can be seen from the small respect, if not contempt, that is accorded to manual labor. This is not German. It took the foreignization of our life, which was in truth a Jewification, to transform the old respect for manual work into a certain contempt for all physical labor.

Thus, there actually comes into being a new class enjoying very little respect, and one day the question must arise whether the nation would possess the strength to articulate the new class into general society, or whether the social difference would broaden into a classlike cleavage. . . .

Scarcely has the new class grown out of the general economic shift than the Jew, clearly and distinctly, realizes that it can open the way for his own further advancement. First, he used the bourgeoisie as a battering-ram against the feudal world, then the worker against the bourgeois world. If formerly he knew how to swindle his way to civil rights in the shadow of the bourgeoisie, now he hopes to find the road to his own domination in the worker's struggle for existence.

From now on the worker has no other task but to fight for the future of the Jewish people. Unconsciously he is harnessed to the service of the power which he thinks he is combating. He is seemingly allowed to attack capital, and this is the easiest way of making him fight for it. In this the Jew keeps up an outcry against international capital and in truth he means the national economy which must be demolished in order that the international stock exchange can triumph over its dead body.

Here the Jew's procedure is as follows:

He approaches the worker, simulates pity with his fate, or even indignation at his lot of misery and poverty, thus gaining his confidence. He takes pains to study all the various real or imaginary hardships of his life—and to arouse his longing for a change in such an existence. With infinite shrewdness he fans the need for social justice, somehow slumbering in every Aryan man, into hatred against those who have been better favored by fortune, and thus gives the struggle for the elimination of social evils a very definite philosophical stamp. He establishes the Marxist doctrine.

By presenting it as inseparably bound up with a number of socially just demands, he promotes its spread and conversely the aversion of decent people to fulfill demands which, advanced in such form and company, seem from the outset unjust and impossible to fulfill. For under this cloak of purely social ideas truly diabolic purposes are hidden, yes, they are publicly proclaimed with the most insolent frankness. This theory represents an inseparable mixture of reason and human madness, but always in such a way that only the lunacy can become reality and never the reason. By the categorical rejection of the personality and hence of the nation and its racial content, it destroys the elementary foundations of all human culture which is dependent on just these factors. This is the true inner kernel of the Marxist philosophy in so far as this figment of a criminal brain can be designated as a "philosophy." With the shattering of the personality and the race, the essential obstacle is removed to the domination of the inferior being—and this is the Jew.

Precisely in political and economic madness lies the sense of this doctrine. For this prevents all truly intelligent people from entering its service, while those who are intellectually less active and poorly educated in economics hasten to it with flying colors. The intellectuals for this movement—for even this movement needs intellectuals for its existence—are "sacrificed" by the Jew from his own ranks.

Thus there arises a pure movement entirely of manual workers under Jewish leadership, apparently aiming to improve the situation of the worker, but in truth planning the enslavement and with it the destruction of all non-Jewish peoples. . . .

By the creation of a press whose content is adapted to the intellectual horizon of the least educated people, the political and trade-union organization finally obtains the agitational institution by which the lowest strata of the nation are made ripe for the most reckless acts. Its function is not to lead people out of the swamp of a base mentality to a higher stage, but to cater to their lowest instincts. Since the masses are as mentally lazy as they are sometimes presumptuous, this is a business as speculative as it is profitable.

It is this press, above all, which wages a positively fanatical and slanderous struggle, tearing down everything which can be regarded as a support of national independence, cultural elevation, and the economic independence of the nation.

Above all, it hammers away at the characters of all those who will not bow down to the Jewish presumption to dominate, or whose ability and genius in themselves seem a danger to the Jew. For to be hated by the Jew it is not necessary to combat him; no, it suffices if he suspects that someone might even conceive the idea of combating him some time or that on the strength of his superior genius he is an augmenter of the power and greatness of a nationality hostile to the Jew.

His unfailing instinct in such things scents the original soul[1] in everyone, and his hostility is assured to anyone who is not spirit of his spirit. Since the Jew is not the attacked but the attacker, not only anyone who attacks passes as his enemy, but also anyone who resists him. But the means with which he seeks to break such reckless but upright souls is not honest warfare, but lies and slander.

Here he stops at nothing, and in his vileness he becomes so gigantic that no one

[1] "Die ursprüngliche Seele."

need be surprised if among our people the personification of the devil as the symbol of all evil assumes the living shape of the Jew.

The ignorance of the broad masses about the inner nature of the Jew, the lack of instinct and narrow-mindedness of our upper classes, make the people an easy victim for this Jewish campaign of lies.

While from innate cowardice the upper classes turn away from a man whom the Jew attacks with lies and slander, the broad masses from stupidity or simplicity believe everything. The state authorities either cloak themselves in silence or, what usually happens, in order to put an end to the Jewish press campaign, they persecute the unjustly attacked, which, in the eyes of such an official ass, passes as the preservation of state authority and the safeguarding of law and order.

Slowly fear of the Marxist weapon of Jewry descends like a nightmare on the mind and soul of decent people.

They begin to tremble before the terrible enemy and thus have become his final victim.

The Jew's domination in the state seems so assured that now not only can he call himself a Jew again, but he ruthlessly admits his ultimate national and political designs. A section of his race openly owns itself to be a foreign people, yet even here they lie. For while the Zionists try to make the rest of the world believe that the national consciousness of the Jew finds its satisfaction in the creation of a Palestinian state, the Jews again slyly dupe the dumb *Goyim.*[2] It doesn't even enter their heads to build up a Jewish state in Palestine for the purpose of living there; all they want is a central organization for their international world swindle, endowed with its own sovereign rights and removed from the intervention of other states: a haven for convicted scoundrels and a university for budding crooks.

It is a sign of their rising confidence and sense of security that at a time when one section is still playing the German, Frenchman, or Englishman, the other with open effrontery comes out as the Jewish race.

How close they see approaching victory can be seen by the hideous aspect which their relations with the members of other peoples takes on.

With satanic joy in his face, the black-haired Jewish youth lurks in wait for the unsuspecting girl whom he defiles with his blood, thus stealing her from her people. With every means he tries to destroy the racial foundations of the people he has set out to subjugate. Just as he himself systematically ruins women and girls, he does not shrink back from pulling down the blood barriers for others, even on a large scale. It was and it is Jews who bring the Negroes into the Rhineland, always with the same secret thought and clear aim of ruining the hated white race by the necessarily resulting bastardization, throwing it down from its cultural and political height, and himself rising to be its master.

For a racially pure people which is conscious of its blood can never be enslaved by the Jew. In this world he will forever be master over bastards and bastards alone.

And so he tries systematically to lower the racial level by a continuous poisoning of individuals.

And in politics he begins to replace the idea of democracy by the dictatorship of the proletariat.

[2] *Yiddish for Gentiles.*

In the organized mass of Marxism he has found the weapon which lets him dispense with democracy and in its stead allows him to subjugate and govern the peoples with a dictatorial and brutal fist.

He works systematically for revolutionization in a twofold sense: economic and political.

Around peoples who offer too violent a resistance to attack from within he weaves a net of enemies, thanks to his international influence, incites them to war, and finally, if necessary, plants the flag of revolution on the very battlefields.

In economics he undermines the states until the social enterprises which have become unprofitable are taken from the state and subjected to his financial control.

In the political field he refuses the state the means for its self-preservation, destroys the foundations of all national self-maintenance and defense, destroys faith in the leadership, scoffs at its history and past, and drags everything that is truly great into the gutter.

Culturally he contaminates art, literature, the theater, makes a mockery of natural feeling, overthrows all concepts of beauty and sublimity, of the noble and the good, and instead drags men down into the sphere of his own base nature.

Religion is ridiculed, ethics and morality represented as outmoded, until the last props of a nation in its struggle for existence in this world have fallen.

Now begins the great last revolution. In gaining political power the Jew casts off the few cloaks that he still wears. The democratic people's Jew becomes the blood-Jew and tyrant over peoples. In a few years he tries to exterminate the national intelligentsia and by robbing the peoples of their natural intellectual leadership makes them ripe for the slave's lot of permanent subjugation.

The most frightful example of this kind is offered by Russia, where he killed or starved about thirty million people with positively fanatical savagery, in part amid inhuman tortures, in order to give a gang of Jewish journalists and stock exchange bandits domination over a great people.

The end is not only the end of the freedom of the peoples oppressed by the Jew, but also the end of this parasite upon the nations. After the death of his victim, the vampire sooner or later dies too. . . .

*The folkish\* philosophy is basically distinguished from the Marxist philosophy by the fact that it not only recognizes the value of race, but with it the importance of the personality, which it therefore makes one of the pillars of its entire edifice.* These are the factors which sustain its view of life.

If the National Socialist movement did not understand the fundamental importance of this basic realization, but instead were merely to perform superficial patchwork on the present-day state, or even adopt the mass standpoint as its own—then it would really constitute nothing but a party in competition with the Marxists; in that case, it would not possess the right to call itself a philosophy of life. If the social program of the movement consisted only in pushing aside the personality and replacing it by the masses, National Socialism itself would be corroded by the poison of Marxism, as is the case with our bourgeois parties.

The folkish state must care for the welfare of its citizens by recognizing in all and everything the importance of the value of personality, thus in all fields preparing the

\* [Combines the connotations of race, nation and tribe. (*Ed.*)]

way for that highest measure of productive performance which grants to the individual the highest measure of participation.

And accordingly, the folkish state must free all leadership and especially the highest—that is, the political leadership—entirely from the parliamentary principle of majority rule—in other words, mass rule—and instead absolutely guarantee the right of the personality.

From this the following realization results:

*The best state constitution and state form is that which, with the most unquestioned certainty, raises the best minds in the national community to leading position and leading influence.*

But as, in economic life, the able men cannot be appointed from above, but must struggle through for themselves, and just as here the endless schooling, ranging from the smallest business to the largest enterprise, occurs spontaneously, with life alone giving the examinations, obviously political minds cannot be "discovered." Extraordinary geniuses permit of no consideration for normal mankind.

From the smallest community cell to the highest leadership of the entire Reich, the state must have the personality principle anchored in its organization.

There must be no majority decisions, but only responsible persons, and the word "council" must be restored to its original meaning. Surely every man will have advisers by his side, but *the decision will be made by one man.*

The principle which made the Prussian army in its time into the most wonderful instrument of the German people must some day, in a transferred sense, become the principle of the construction of our whole state conception: *authority of every leader downward and responsibility upward.*

Even then it will not be possible to dispense with those corporations which today we designate as parliaments. But their councillors will then actually give counsel; responsibility, however, can and may be borne only by *one* man, and therefore only he alone may possess the authority and right to command.

Parliaments as such are necessary, because in them, above all, personalities to which special responsible tasks can later be entrusted have an opportunity gradually to rise up.

This gives the following picture:

The folkish state, from the township up to the Reich leadership, has no representative body which decides anything by the majority, but only *advisory bodies* which stand at the side of the elected leader, receiving their share of work from him, and in turn if necessary assuming unlimited responsibility in certain fields, just as on a larger scale the leader or chairman of the various corporations himself possesses.

As a matter of principle, the folkish state does not tolerate asking advice or opinions in special matters—say, of an economic nature—of men who, on the basis of their education and activity, can understand nothing of the subject. It, therefore, divides its representative bodies from the start into *political and professional chambers.*

In order to guarantee a profitable cooperation between the two, a special *senate* of the élite always stands over them.

In no chamber and in no senate does a vote ever take place. They are working institutions and not voting machines. The individual member has an advisory, but never a determining, voice. The latter is the exclusive privilege of the responsible chairman.

This principle—absolute responsibility unconditionally combined with absolute authority—will gradually breed an élite of leaders such as today, in this era of irresponsible parliamentarianism, is utterly inconceivable.

Thus, the political form of the nation will be brought into agreement with that law to which it owes its greatness in the cultural and economic field. . . .

I still wish briefly to take a position on the question as to what extent the demand for soil and territory seems ethically and morally justified. This is necessary, since unfortunately, even in so-called folkish circles, all sorts of unctuous big-mouths step forward, endeavoring to set the rectification of the injustice of 1918 as the aim of the German nation's endeavors in the field of foreign affairs, but at the same time find it necessary to assure the whole world of folkish brotherhood and sympathy.

I should like to make the following preliminary remarks: *The demand for restoration of the frontiers of 1914 is a political absurdity of such proportions and consequences as to make it seem a crime. Quite aside from the fact that the Reich's frontiers in 1914 were anything but logical. For in reality they were neither complete in the sense of embracing the people of German nationality, nor sensible with regard to geomilitary expediency. They were not the result of a considered political action, but momentary frontiers in a political struggle that was by no means concluded; partly, in fact, they were the results of chance.* With equal right and in many cases with more right, some other sample year of German history could be picked out, and the restoration of the conditions at that time declared to be the aim of an activity in foreign affairs. The above demand is entirely suited to our bourgeois society, which here as elsewhere does not possess a single creative political idea for the future, but lives only in the past, in fact, in the most immediate past; for even their backward gaze does not extend beyond their own times. The law of inertia binds them to a given situation and causes them to resist any change in it, but without ever increasing the activity of this opposition beyond the mere power of perseverance. So it is obvious that the political horizon of these people does not extend beyond the year 1914. By proclaiming the restoration of those borders as the political aim of their activity, they keep mending the crumbling league of our adversaries. Only in this way can it be explained that eight years after a world struggle in which states, some of which had the most heterogeneous desires, took part, the coalition of the victors of those days can still maintain itself in a more or less unbroken form.

All these states were at one time beneficiaries of the German collapse. Fear of our strength caused the greed and envy of the individual great powers among themselves to recede. By grabbing as much of the Reich as they could, they found the best guard against a future uprising. A bad conscience and fear of our people's strength is still the most enduring cement to hold together the various members of this alliance.

And we do not disappoint them. By setting up the restoration of the borders of 1914 as a political program for Germany, our bourgeoisie frighten away every partner who might desire to leave the league of our enemies, since he must inevitably fear to be attacked singly and thereby lose the protection of his individual fellow allies. Each single state feels concerned and threatened by this slogan.

Moreover, it is senseless in two respects:

(1) because the instruments of power are lacking to remove it from the vapors of club evenings into reality; and

(2) because, if it could actually be realized, the outcome would again be so pitiful that, by God, it would not be worth while to risk the blood of our people for *this*.

For it should scarcely seem questionable to anyone that even the restoration of the frontiers of 1914 could be achieved only by blood. Only childish and naïve minds can lull themselves in the idea that they can bring about a . correction of Versailles by wheedling and begging. Quite aside from the fact that such an attempt would pre-suppose a man of Talleyrand's talents, which we do not possess. One half of our political figures consist of extremely sly, but equally spineless elements which are hostile toward our nation to begin with, while the other is composed of good-natured, harmless, and easy-going soft-heads. Moreover, the times have changed since the Congress of Vienna: *Today it is not princes and princes' mistresses who haggle and bargain over state borders; it is the inexorable Jew who struggles for his domination over the nations.* No nation can remove this hand from its throat except by the sword. Only the assembled and concentrated might of a national passion rearing up in its strength can defy the international enslavement of peoples. Such a process is and remains a bloody one.

If, however, we harbor the conviction that the German future, regardless what happens, demands the supreme sacrifice, quite aside from all considerations of political expediency as such, we must set up an aim worthy of this sacrifice and fight for it.

The boundaries of the year 1914 mean nothing at all for the German future. Neither did they provide a defense of the past, nor would they contain any strength for the future. Through them the German nation will neither achieve its inner integrity, nor will its sustenance be safeguarded by them, nor do these boundaries, viewed from the military standpoint, seem expedient or even satisfactory, nor finally can they improve the relation in which we at present find ourselves toward the other world powers, or, better expressed, the real world powers. The lag behind England will not be caught up, the magnitude of the Union will not be achieved; not even France would experience a material diminution of her world-political importance.

Only one thing would be certain: even with a favorable outcome, such an attempt to restore the borders of 1914 would lead to a further bleeding of our national body, so much so that there would be no worth-while blood left to stake for the decisions and actions really to secure the nation's future. On the contrary, drunk with such a shallow success, we should renounce any further goals, all the more readily as "national honor" would be repaired and, for the moment at least, a few doors would have been reopened to commercial development.

As opposed to this, we National Socialists must hold unflinchingly to our aim in foreign policy, namely, *to secure for the German people the land and soil to which they are entitled on this earth.* And this action is the only one which, before God and our German posterity, would make any sacrifice of blood seem justified: before God, since we have been put on this earth with the mission of eternal struggle for our daily bread, beings who receive nothing as a gift, and who owe their position as lords of the earth only to the genius and the courage with which they can conquer and defend it; and before our German posterity in so far as we have shed no citizen's blood out of which a thousand others are not bequeathed to posterity. The soil on which some day German generations of peasants can beget powerful sons will sanction the investment of the sons of today, and will some day acquit the responsible statesmen of blood-guilt and sacrifice of the people, even if they are persecuted by their contemporaries.

And I must sharply attack those folkish pen-pushers who claim to regard such an acquisition of soil as a "breach of sacred human rights" and attack it as such in their scribblings. One never knows who stands behind these fellows. But one thing is certain, that the confusion they can create is desirable and convenient to our national enemies. By such an attitude they help to weaken and destroy from within our people's will for the only correct way of defending their vital needs. For no people on this earth possesses so much as a square yard of territory on the strength of a higher will or superior right. Just as Germany's frontiers are fortuitous frontiers, momentary frontiers in the current political struggle of any period, so are the boundaries of other nations' living space. And just as the shape of our earth's surface can seem immutable as granite only to the thoughtless soft-head, but in reality only represents at each period an apparent pause in a continuous development, created by the mighty forces of Nature in a process of continuous growth, only to be transformed or destroyed tomorrow by greater forces, likewise the boundaries of living spaces in the life of nations.

*State boundaries are made by man and changed by man.*

The fact that a nation has succeeded in acquiring an undue amount of soil constitutes no higher obligation that it should be recognized eternally. At most it proves the strength of the conquerors and the weakness of the nations. And in this case, right lies in this strength alone. If the German nation today, penned into an impossible area, faces a lamentable future, this is no more a commandment of Fate than revolt against this state of affairs constitutes an affront to Fate. No more than any higher power has promised another nation more territory than the German nation, or is offended by the fact of this unjust distribution of the soil. Just as our ancestors did not receive the soil on which we live today as a gift from Heaven, but had to fight for it at the risk of their lives, in the future no folkish grace will win soil for us and hence life for our people, but only the might of a victorious sword.

Much as all of us today recognize the necessity of a reckoning with France, it would remain ineffectual in the long run if it represented the whole of our aim in foreign policy. It can and will achieve meaning only if it offers the rear cover for an enlargement of our people's living space in Europe. For it is not in colonial acquisitions that we must see the solution of this problem, but exclusively in the acquisition of a territory for settlement, which will enhance the area of the mother country, and hence not only keep the new settlers in the most intimate community with the land of their origin, but secure for the total area those advantages which lie in its unified magnitude.

The folkish movement must not be the champion of other peoples, but the vanguard fighter of its own. Otherwise it is superfluous and above all has no right to sulk about the past. For in that case it is behaving in exactly the same way. The old German policy was wrongly determined by dynastic considerations, and the future policy must not be directed by cosmopolitan folkish drivel. In particular, we are not constables guarding the well-known "poor little nations," but soldiers of our own nation.

But we National Socialists must go further. *The right to possess soil can become a duty if without extension of its soil a great nation seems doomed to destruction.* And most especially when not some little nigger nation or other is involved, but the Germanic mother of life, which has given the present-day world its cultural picture. *Germany will either be a world power or there will be no Germany.* And for world power she needs that magnitude which will give her the position she needs in the present period, and life to her citizens.

*       *       *

*And so we National Socialists consciously draw a line beneath the foreign policy tendency of our pre-War period. We take up where we broke off six hundred years ago. We stop the endless German movement to the south and west, and turn our gaze toward the land in the east. At long last we break off the colonial and commercial policy of the pre-War period and shift to the soil policy of the future.*

If we speak of soil in Europe today, we can primarily have in mind only *Russia* and her vassal border states.

Here Fate itself seems desirous of giving us a sign. By handing Russia to Bolshevism, it robbed the Russian nation of that intelligentsia which previously brought about and guaranteed its existence as a state. For the organization of a Russian state formation was not the result of the political abilities of the Slavs in Russia, but only a wonderful example of the state-forming efficacity of the German element in an inferior race. Numerous mighty empires on earth have been created in this way. Lower nations led by Germanic organizers and overlords have more than once grown to be mighty state formations and have endured as long as the racial nucleus of the creative state race maintained itself. For centuries Russia drew nourishment from this Germanic nucleus of its upper leading strata. Today it can be regarded as almost totally exterminated and extinguished. It has been replaced by the Jew. Impossible as it is for the Russian by himself to shake off the yoke of the Jew by his own resources, it is equally impossible for the Jew to maintain the mighty empire forever. He himself is no element of organization, but a ferment of decomposition. The Persian empire in the east is ripe for collapse. And the end of Jewish rule in Russia will also be the end of Russia as a state. We have been chosen by Fate as witnesses of a catastrophe which will be the mightiest confirmation of the soundness of the folkish theory.

*Our task, the mission of the National Socialist movement, is to bring our own people to such political insight that they will not see their goal for the future in the breath-taking sensation of a new Alexander's conquest, but in the industrious work of the German plow, to which the sword need only give soil.*

# ✑ THE ORIGINS OF TOTALITARIANISM

*Hannah Arendt*

*As early as the 1920s, most Europeans were aware that Western civilization had entered a new era—an age of unprecedented subordination of individual rights to the wishes of all-powerful coercive states. Bolshevism in Russia and fascism in Italy soon found their imitators, and, with the onset of the Great Depression, countless other ideologies followed, sometimes attaining power but more often merely forming political parties or movements aiming at its acquisition. Such movements appeared from England to the Balkans, from the Iberian Peninsula to the Baltic, with the German Nazi state the most horrendous of all in its rejection of restraint and humanitarianism. The attempt to understand this phenomenon was bound to become a major concern for social scientists, historians, and even theologians.*

*One of the books which has become a classic in this area of analysis is Hannah Arendt's* The Origins of Totalitarianism, *first published in 1951, which traces the subject from late nineteenth-century anti-Semitic and antidemocratic movements and which tries to relate such developments in Germany, Italy, and Russia. The chapter we have included is concerned with an attempt to make sense out of the concentration camp as a characteristic totalitarian institution. Remember that the concentration camp was not a forced-labor camp, a death camp, or merely a location for political prisoners; all these, however repugnant, may be construed as being of political use. The concentration camp is distinguished from these, as Miss Arendt points out, precisely in that it has no real function except to "concentrate" people. It should be pointed out, with reference to the factual detail, that Hannah Arendt has not in the slightest exaggerated the terror of the Nazi camps. Other observers, however, have seen this terror less as the result of deliberate policy than—which is as frightening—as the result of the almost total chaos of totalitarian systems.*

## III: TOTAL DOMINATION

The concentration and extermination camps of totalitarian regimes serve as the laboratories in which the fundamental belief of totalitarianism that everything is possible is being verified. Compared with this, all other experiments are secondary in impor-

Hannah Arendt, *The Origins of Totalitarianism* (2d ed.; New York: Meridian Books, Inc., 1958), pp. 437–459.

tance—including those in the field of medicine whose horrors are recorded in detail in the trials against the physicians of the Third Reich—although it is characteristic that these laboratories were used for experiments of every kind.

Total domination, which strives to organize the infinite plurality and differentiation of human beings as if all of humanity were just one individual, is possible only if each and every person can be reduced to a never-changing identity of reactions, so that each of these bundles of reactions can be exchanged at random for any other. The problem is to fabricate something that does not exist, namely, a kind of human species resembling other animal species whose only "freedom" would consist in "preserving the species." Totalitarian domination attempts to achieve this goal both through ideological indoctrination of the elite formations and through absolute terror in the camps; and the atrocities for which the elite formations are ruthlessly used become, as it were, the practical application of the ideological indoctrination—the testing ground in which the latter must prove itself—while the appalling spectacle of the camps themselves is supposed to furnish the "theoretical" verification of the ideology.

The camps are meant not only to exterminate people and degrade human beings, but also serve the ghastly experiment of eliminating, under scientifically controlled conditions, spontaneity itself as an expression of human behavior and of transforming the human personality into a mere thing, into something that even animals are not; for Pavlov's dog, which, as we know, was trained to eat not when it was hungry but when a bell rang, was a perverted animal.

Under normal circumstances this can never be accomplished, because spontaneity can never be entirely eliminated insofar as it is connected not only with human freedom but with life itself, in the sense of simply keeping alive. It is only in the concentration camps that such an experiment is at all possible, and therefore they are not only *"la société la plus totalitaire encore réalisée"* (David Rousset) but the guiding social ideal of total domination in general. Just as the stability of the totalitarian regime depends on the isolation of the fictitious world of the movement from the outside world, so the experiment of total domination in the concentration camps depends on sealing off the latter against the world of all others, the world of the living in general, even against the outside world of a country under totalitarian rule. This isolation explains the peculiar unreality and lack of credibility that characterize all reports from the concentration camps and constitute one of the main difficulties for the true understanding of totalitarian domination, which stands or falls with the existence of these concentration and extermination camps; for, unlikely as it may sound, these camps are the true central institution of totalitarian organizational power.

There are numerous reports by survivors. The more authentic they are, the less they attempt to communicate things that evade human understanding and human experience —sufferings, that is, that transform men into "uncomplaining animals." None of these reports inspires those passions of outrage and sympathy through which men have always been mobilized for justice. On the contrary, anyone speaking or writing about concentration camps is still regarded as suspect; and if the speaker has resolutely returned to the world of the living, he himself is often assailed by doubts with regard to his own truthfulness, as though he had mistaken a nightmare for reality.[1]

---

[1] *See especially Bruno Bettelheim*, op. cit. *"It seemed as if I had become convinced that these horrible and degrading experiences somehow did not happen to 'me' as subject but to 'me' as an object.*

This doubt of people concerning themselves and the reality of their own experience only reveals what the Nazis have always known: that men determined to commit crimes will find it expedient to organize them on the vastest, most improbable scale. Not only because this renders all punishments provided by the legal system inadequate and absurd; but because the very immensity of the crimes guarantees that the murderers who proclaim their innocence with all manner of lies will be more readily believed than the victims who tell the truth. The Nazis did not even consider it necessary to keep this discovery to themselves. Hitler circulated millions of copies of his book in which he stated that to be successful, a lie must be enormous—which did not prevent people from believing him as, similarly, the Nazis' proclamations, repeated *ad nauseam*, that the Jews would be exterminated like bedbugs (*i.e.*, with poison gas), prevented anybody from *not* believing them.

There is a great temptation to explain away the intrinsically incredible by means of liberal rationalizations. In each one of us, there lurks such a liberal, wheedling us with the voice of common sense. The road to totalitarian domination leads through many intermediate stages for which we can find numerous analogies and precedents. The extraordinarily bloody terror during the initial stage of totalitarian rule serves indeed the exclusive purpose of defeating the opponent and rendering all further opposition impossible; but total terror is launched only after this initial stage has been overcome and the regime no longer has anything to fear from the opposition. In this context it has been frequently remarked that in such a case the means have become the end, but this is after all only an admission, in paradoxical disguise, that the category "the end justifies the means" no longer applies, that terror has lost its "purpose," that it is no longer the means to frighten people. Nor does the explanation suffice that the revolution, as in the case of the French Revolution, was devouring its own children, for the terror continues even after everybody who might be described as a child of the revolution in one capacity or another—the Russian factions, the power centers of party, the army, the bureaucracy—has long since been devoured. Many things that nowadays have become the specialty of totalitarian government are only too well known from the study of history. There have almost always been wars of aggression; the massacre of hostile populations after a victory went unchecked until the Romans mitigated it by introducing the *parcere subjectis*; through centuries the extermination of native peoples went hand in hand with the colonization of the Americas, Australia and Africa; slavery is one of the oldest institutions of mankind and all empires of antiquity were based on the labor of state-owned slaves who erected their public buildings. Not even concentration camps are an invention of totalitarian movements. They emerge for

---

*This experience was corroborated by the statements of other prisoners. . . . It was as if I watched things happening in which I only vaguely participated. . . . 'This cannot be true, such things just do not happen.' . . . The prisoners had to convince themselves that this was real, was really happening and not just a nightmare. They were never wholly successful."*

*See also Rousset, op. cit., p. 213. ". . . Those who haven't seen it with their own eyes can't believe it. Did you yourself, before you came here, take the rumors about the gas chambers seriously?*

*"No," I said.*

*". . . You see? Well, they're all like you. The lot of them in Paris, London, New York, even at Birkenau right outside the crematoriums . . . still incredulous, five minutes before they were sent down into the cellar of the crematorium. . . ."*

the first time during the Boer War, at the beginning of the century, and continued to be used in South Africa as well as India for "undesirable elements"; here, too, we first find the term "protective custody" which was later adopted by the Third Reich. These camps correspond in many respects to the concentration camps at the beginning of totalitarian rule; they were used for "suspects" whose offenses could not be proved and who could not be sentenced by ordinary process of law. All this clearly points to totalitarian methods of domination; all these are elements they utilize, develop and crystallize on the basis of the nihilistic principle that "everything is permitted," which they inherited and already take for granted. But wherever these new forms of domination assume their authentically totalitarian structure they transcend this principle, which is still tied to the utilitarian motives and self-interest of the rulers, and try their hand in a realm that up to now has been completely unknown to us: the realm where "everything is possible." And, characteristically enough, this is precisely the realm that cannot be limited by either utilitarian motives or self-interest, regardless of the latter's content.

What runs counter to common sense is not the nihilistic principle that "everything is permitted," which was already contained in the nineteenth-century utilitarian conception of common sense. What common sense and "normal people" refuse to believe is that everything is possible. We attempt to understand elements in present or recollected experience that simply surpass our powers of understanding. We attempt to classify as criminal a thing which, as we all feel, no such category was ever intended to cover. What meaning has the concept of murder when we are confronted with the mass production of corpses? We attempt to understand the behavior of concentration-camp inmates and SS-men psychologically, when the very thing that must be realized is that the psyche *can* be destroyed even without the destruction of the physical man; that, indeed, psyche, character, and individuality seem under certain circumstances to express themselves only through the rapidity or slowness with which they disintegrate. The end result in any case is inanimate men, *i.e.*, men who can no longer be psychologically understood, whose return to the psychologically or otherwise intelligibly human world closely resembles the resurrection of Lazarus. All statements of common sense, whether of a psychological or sociological nature, serve only to encourage those who think it "superficial" to "dwell on horrors."

If it is true that the concentration camps are the most consequential institution of totalitarian rule, "dwelling on horrors" would seem to be indispensable for the understanding of totalitarianism. But recollection can no more do this than can the uncommunicative eyewitness report. In both these genres there is an inherent tendency to run away from the experience; instinctively or rationally, both types of writer are so much aware of the terrible abyss that separates the world of the living from that of the living dead, that they cannot supply anything more than a series of remembered occurrences that must seem just as incredible to those who relate them as to their audience. Only the fearful imagination of those who have been aroused by such reports but have not actually been smitten in their own flesh, of those who are consequently free from the bestial, desperate terror which, when confronted by real, present horror, inexorably paralyzes everything that is not mere reaction, can afford to keep thinking about horrors. Such thoughts are useful only for the perception of political contexts and the mobilization of political passions. A change of personality of any sort whatever can no more be induced by thinking about horrors than by the real experience of horror. The reduction of a man to a bundle of reactions separates him as radically as mental disease from everything within him that is personality or character. When, like Lazarus, he rises from the dead, he finds his personality or character unchanged, just as he had left it.

Just as the horror, or the dwelling on it, cannot affect a change of character in him, cannot make men better or worse, thus it cannot become the basis of a political community or party in a narrower sense. The attempts to build up a European elite with a program of intra-European understanding based on the common European experience of the concentration camps have foundered in much the same manner as the attempts following the first World War to draw political conclusions from the international experience of the front generation. In both cases it turned out that the experiences themselves can communicate no more than nihilistic banalities. Political consequences such as postwar pacifism, for example, derived from the general fear of war, not from the experiences in war. Instead of producing a pacifism devoid of reality, the insight into the structure of modern wars, guided and mobilized by fear, might have led to the realization that the only standard for a necessary war is the fight against conditions under which people no longer wish to live—and our experiences with the tormenting hell of the totalitarian camps have enlightened us only too well about the possibility of such conditions. Thus the fear of concentration camps and the resulting insight into the nature of total domination might serve to invalidate all obsolete political differentiations from right to left and to introduce beside and above them the politically most important yardstick for judging events in our time, namely: whether they serve totalitarian domination or not.

In any event, the fearful imagination has the great advantage to dissolve the sophistic-dialectical interpretations of politics which are all based on the superstition that something good might result from evil. Such dialectical acrobatics had at least a semblance of justification so long as the worst that man could inflict upon man was murder. But, as we know today, murder is only a limited evil. The murderer who kills a man—a man who has to die anyway—still moves within the realm of life and death familiar to us; both have indeed a necessary connection on which the dialectic is founded, even if it is not always conscious of it. The murderer leaves a corpse behind and does not pretend that his victim has never existed; if he wipes out any traces, they are those of his own identity, and not the memory and grief of the persons who loved his victim; he destroys a life, but he does not destroy the fact of existence itself.

The Nazis, with the precision peculiar to them, used to register their operations in the concentration camps under the heading "under cover of the night (*Nacht und Nebel*)." The radicalism of measures to treat people as if they had never existed and to make them disappear in the literal sense of the word is frequently not apparent at first glance, because both the German and the Russian system are not uniform but consist of a series of categories in which people are treated very differently. In the case of Germany, these different categories used to exist in the same camp, but without coming into contact with each other; frequently, the isolation between the categories was even stricter than the isolation from the outside world. Thus, out of racial considerations, Scandinavian nationals during the war were quite differently treated by the Germans than the members of other peoples, although the former were outspoken enemies of the Nazis. The latter in turn were divided into those whose "extermination" was immediately on the agenda, as in the case of the Jews, or could be expected in the predictable future, as in the case of the Poles, Russians and Ukrainians, and into those who were not yet covered by instructions about such an over-all "final solution," as in the case of the French and Belgians. In Russia, on the other hand, we must distinguish three more or less independent systems. First, there are the authentic forced-labor groups that live in relative freedom and are sentenced for limited periods. Secondly, there are the concentration camps in which the human material is ruthlessly exploited and the mortality rate is extremely high, but which are essentially organized for labor purposes. And, thirdly, there are the annihilation camps in which the inmates are systematically wiped out through starvation and neglect.

The real horror of the concentration and extermination camps lies in the fact that the inmates, even if they happen to keep alive, are more effectively cut off from the world of the living than if they had died, because terror enforces oblivion. Here, murder is as impersonal as the squashing of a gnat. Someone may die as the result of systematic torture or starvation, or because the camp is overcrowded and superfluous human material must be liquidated. Conversely, it may happen that due to a shortage of new human shipments the danger arises that the camps become depopulated and that the order is now given to reduce the death rate at any price. David Rousset called his report on the period in a German concentration camp *"Les Jours de Notre Mort,"* and it is indeed as if there were a possibility to give permanence to the process of dying itself and to enforce a condition in which both death and life are obstructed equally effectively.

It is the appearance of some radical evil, previously unknown to us, that puts an end to the notion of developments and transformations of qualities. Here, there are neither political nor historical nor simply moral standards but, at the most, the realization that something seems to be involved in modern politics that actually should never be involved in politics as we used to understand it, namely all or nothing —all, and that is an undetermined infinity of forms of human living-together, or nothing, for a victory of the concentration-camp system would mean the same inexorable doom for human beings as the use of the hydrogen bomb would mean the doom of the human race.

There are no parallels to the life in the concentration camps. Its horror can never be fully embraced by the imagination for the very reason that it stands outside of life and death. It can never be fully reported for the very reason that the survivor returns to the world of the living, which makes it impossible for him to believe fully in his own past experiences. It is as though he had a story to tell of another planet, for the status of the inmates in the world of the living, where nobody is supposed to know if they are alive or dead, is such that it is as though they had never been born. Therefore all parallels create confusion and distract attention from what is essential. Forced labor in prisons and penal colonies, banishment, slavery, all seem for a moment to offer helpful comparisons, but on closer examination lead nowhere.

Forced labor as a punishment is limited as to time and intensity. The convict retains his rights over his body; he is not absolutely tortured and he is not absolutely dominated. Banishment banishes only from one part of the world to another part of the world, also inhabited by human beings; it does not exclude from the human world altogether. Throughout history slavery has been an institution within a social order; slaves were not, like concentration-camp inmates, withdrawn from the sight and hence the protection of their fellow-men; as instruments of labor they had a definite price and as property a definite value. The concentration-camp inmate has no price, because he can always be replaced; nobody knows to whom he belongs, because he is never seen. From the point of view of normal society he is absolutely superfluous, although in times of acute labor shortage, as in Russia and in Germany during the war, he is used for work.

The concentration camp as an institution was not established for the sake of any possible labor yield; the only permanent economic function of the camps has been the financing of their own supervisory apparatus; thus from the economic point of view the concentration camps exist mostly for their own sake. Any work that has been performed could have been done much better and more cheaply under different conditions. Especially Russia, whose concentration camps are mostly described as forced-labor camps because Soviet bureaucracy has chosen to dignify them with this name, reveals most clearly that forced labor is not the primary issue; forced labor is the normal condition of all Russian workers, who have no freedom of movement and can be arbitrarily drafted for work to any place at any time. The incredibility of the horrors is closely bound up with their economic uselessness. The Nazis carried this uselessness to the point of open anti-utility when in the midst of the war, despite the shortage of building material and rolling stock, they set up enormous, costly extermination factories and transported millions of people back and forth. In the eyes of a strictly utilitarian world the obvious contradiction between these acts and military expediency gave the whole enterprise an air of mad unreality.

This atmosphere of madness and unreality, created by an apparent lack of purpose, is the real iron curtain which hides all forms of concentration camps from the eyes of the world. Seen from outside, they and the things that happen in them can be described only in images drawn from a life after death, that is, a life removed from earthly purposes. Concentration camps can very aptly be divided into three types corresponding to three basic Western conceptions of a life after death: Hades, Purgatory, and Hell. To Hades correspond those relatively mild forms, once popular even in non-totalitarian countries, for getting undesirable elements of all sorts—refugees, stateless persons, the asocial and the unemployed—out of the way; as DP camps, which are nothing other than camps for persons who have become superfluous and bothersome, they have survived the war. Purgatory is represented by the Soviet Union's labor camps, where neglect is combined with chaotic forced labor. Hell in the most literal sense was embodied by those types of camp perfected by the Nazis, in which the whole of life was thoroughly and systematically organized with a view to the greatest possible torment.

All three types have one thing in common: the human masses sealed off in them are treated as if they no longer existed, as if what happened to them were no longer of any interest to anybody, as if they were already dead and some evil spirit gone mad were amusing himself by stopping them for a while between life and death before admitting them to eternal peace.

It is not so much the barbed wire as the skillfully manufactured unreality of those whom it fences in that provokes such enormous cruelties and ultimately makes extermination look like a perfectly normal measure. Everything that was done in the camps is known to us from the world of perverse, malignant fantasies. The difficult thing to understand is that, like such fantasies, these gruesome crimes took place in a phantom world, which, however, has materialized, as it were, into a world which is complete with all sensual data of reality but lacks that structure of consequence and responsibility without which reality remains for us a mass of incomprehensible data. The result is that a place has been established where men can be tortured and slaughtered, and yet neither the tormentors nor the tormented, and least of all the outsider, can be aware that what is happening is anything more than a cruel game or an absurd dream.

The films which the Allies circulated in Germany and elsewhere after the war showed clearly that this atmosphere of insanity and unreality is not dispelled by pure reportage. To the unprejudiced observer these pictures are just about as convincing as snapshots of mysterious substances taken at spiritualist séances.[1] Common sense reacted to the horrors of Buchenwald and Auschwitz with the plausible argument: "What crime must these people have committed that such things were done to them!"; or, in Germany and Austria, in the midst of starvation, overpopulation, and general hatred: "Too bad that they've stopped gassing the Jews"; and everywhere with the skeptical shrug that greets ineffectual propaganda.

If the propaganda of truth fails to convince the average person because it is too monstrous, it is positively dangerous to those who know from their own imaginings what they themselves are capable of doing and who are therefore perfectly willing to believe in the reality of what they have seen. Suddenly it becomes evident that things which for thousands of years the human imagination had banished to a realm beyond human competence can be manufactured right here on earth, that Hell and Purgatory, and even a shadow of their perpetual duration, can be established by the most modern methods of destruction and therapy. To these people (and they are more numerous in any large city than we like to admit) the totalitarian hell proves only that the power of man is greater than they ever dared to think, and that man can realize hellish fantasies without making the sky fall or the earth open.

These analogies, repeated in many reports from the world of the dying, seem to express more than a desperate attempt at saying what is outside the realm of human speech. Nothing perhaps distinguishes modern masses as radically from those of previous centuries as the loss of faith in a Last Judgment: the worst have lost their fear and the best have lost their hope. Unable as yet to live without fear and hope, these masses are attracted by every effort which seems to promise a man-made fabrication of the Paradise they had longed for and of the Hell they had feared. Just as

---

[1] It is of some importance to realize that all pictures of concentration camps are misleading insofar as they show the camps in their last stages, at the moment the Allied troops marched in. There were no death camps in Germany proper, and at that point all extermination equipment had already been dismantled. On the other hand, what provoked the outrage of the Allies most and what gives the films their special horror—namely, the sight of the human skeletons—was not at all typical for the German concentration camps; extermination was handled systematically by gas, not by starvation. The condition of the camps was a result of the war events during the final months: Himmler had ordered the evacuation of all extermination camps in the East, the German camps were consequently vastly overcrowded, and he was no longer in a position to assure the food supply in Germany.

the popularized features of Marx's classless society have a queer resemblance to the Messianic Age, so the reality of concentration camps resembles nothing so much as medieval pictures of Hell.

The one thing that cannot be reproduced is what made the traditional conceptions of Hell tolerable to man: the Last Judgment, the idea of an absolute standard of justice combined with the infinite possibility of grace. For in the human estimation there is no crime and no sin commensurable with the everlasting torments of Hell. Hence the discomfiture of common sense, which asks: What crime must these people have committed in order to suffer so inhumanly? Hence also the absolute innocence of the victims: no man ever deserved this. Hence finally the grotesque haphazardness with which concentration-camp victims were chosen in the perfected terror state: such "punishment" can, with equal justice and injustice, be inflicted on anyone.

In comparison with the insane end-result—concentration-camp society—the process by which men are prepared for this end, and the methods by which individuals are adapted to these conditions, are transparent and logical. The insane mass manufacture of corpses is preceded by the historically and politically intelligible preparation of living corpses. The impetus and what is more important, the silent consent to such unprecedented conditions are the products of those events which in a period of political disintegration suddenly and unexpectedly made hundreds of thousands of human beings homeless, stateless, outlawed and unwanted, while millions of human beings were made economically superfluous and socially burdensome by unemployment. This in turn could only happen because the Rights of Man, which had never been philosophically established but merely formulated, which had never been politically secured but merely proclaimed, have, in their traditional form, lost all validity.

The first essential step on the road to total domination is to kill the juridical person in man. This was done, on the one hand, by putting certain categories of people outside the protection of the law and forcing at the same time, through the instrument of denationalization, the nontotalitarian world into recognition of lawlessness; it was done, on the other, by placing the concentration camp outside the normal penal system, and by selecting its inmates outside the normal judicial procedure in which a definite crime entails a predictable penalty. Thus criminals, who for other reasons are an essential element in concentration-camp society, are ordinarily sent to a camp only on completion of their prison sentence. Under all circumstances totalitarian domination sees to it that the categories gathered in the camps—Jews, carriers of diseases, representatives of dying classes—have already lost their capacity for both normal or criminal action. Propagandistically this means that the "protective custody" is handled as a "preventive police measure," that is, a measure that deprives people of the ability to act. Deviations from this rule in Russia must be attributed to the catastrophic shortage of prisons and to a desire, so far unrealized, to transform the whole penal system into a system of concentration camps.

The inclusion of criminals is necessary in order to make plausible the propagandistic claim of the movement that the institution exists for asocial elements. Criminals do not properly belong in the concentration camps, if only because it is harder to kill the juridical person in a man who is guilty of some crime than in a totally innocent person. If they constitute a permanent category among the inmates, it is a concession of the totalitarian state to the prejudices of society, which can in this way most readily be accustomed to the existence of the camps. In order, on the other hand, to keep the camp system itself intact, it is essential as long as there is a penal system in the country that criminals should be sent to the camps only on completion of their sentence, that is when they are actually entitled to their freedom. Under no circumstances must the concentration camp become a calculable punishment for definite offenses.

The amalgamation of criminals with all other categories has moreover the advantage of making it shockingly evident to all other arrivals that they have landed on the lowest level of society. It soon turns out, to be sure, that they have every reason to envy the lowest thief and murderer; but meanwhile the lowest level is a good beginning. Moreover it is an effective means of camouflage: this happens only to criminals and nothing worse is happening than that what deservedly happens to criminals.

The criminals everywhere constitute the aristocracy of the camps. (In Germany, during the war, they were replaced in the leadership by the Communists, because not even a minimum of rational work could be performed under the chaotic conditions created by a criminal administration. This was merely a temporary transformation of concentration camps into forced-labor camps, a thoroughly atypical phenomenon of limited duration.) What places the criminals in the leadership is not so much the affinity between supervisory personnel and criminal elements—in the Soviet Union apparently the supervisors are not, like the SS, a special elite trained to commit crimes —as the fact that only criminals have been sent to the camp in connection with some definite activity. They at least know why they are in a concentration camp and therefore have kept a remnant of their juridical person. For the politicals this is only subjectively true; their actions, insofar as they were actions and not mere opinions or someone else's vague suspicions, or accidental membership in a politically disapproved group, are as a rule not covered by the normal legal system of the country and not juridically defined.

To the amalgam of politicals and criminals with which concentration camps in Russia and Germany started out, was added at an early date a third element which was soon to constitute the majority of all concentration-camp inmates. This largest group has consisted ever since of people who had done nothing whatsoever that, either in their own consciousness or the consciousness of their tormenters, had any rational connection with their arrest. In Germany, after 1938, this element was represented by masses of Jews, in Russia by any groups which, for any reason having nothing to do with their actions, had incurred the disfavor of the authorities. These groups, innocent in every sense, are the most suitable for thorough experimentation in disfranchisement and destruction of the juridical person, and therefore they are both qualitatively and quantitatively the most essential category of the camp population. This principle was most fully realized in the gas chambers which, if only because of their enormous capacity, could not be intended for individual cases but only for people in general. In this connection, the following dialogue sums up the situation of the individual: "For what purpose, may I ask, do the gas chambers exist?"—"For what purpose were you born?" It is this third group of the totally innocent who in every case fare the worst in the camps. Criminals and politicals are assimilated to this category; thus deprived of the protective distinction that comes of their having done something, they are utterly exposed to the arbitrary. The ultimate goal, partly achieved in the Soviet Union and clearly indicated in the last phases of Nazi terror, is to have the whole camp population composed of this category of innocent people.

Contrasting with the complete haphazardness with which the inmates are selected are the categories, meaningless in themselves but useful from the standpoint of organization, into which they are usually divided on their arrival. In the German camps there were criminals, politicals, asocial elements, religious offenders, and Jews, all distinguished by insignia. When the French set up concentration camps after the Spanish Civil War, they immediately introduced the typical totalitarian amalgam of politicals with criminals and the innocent (in this case the stateless), and despite their inexperience proved remarkably inventive in creating meaningless categories of inmates. Originally devised in order to prevent any growth of solidarity among the inmates, this technique proved particularly valuable because no one could know whether his own category was better or worse than someone else's. In Germany this eternally shifting though pedantically organized edifice was given an appearance of solidity by the fact that under any and all circumstances the Jews were the lowest category. The gruesome and grotesque part of it was that the inmates identified themselves with these categories, as though they represented a last authentic remnant of their juridical person. Even if we disregard all other circumstances, it is no wonder that a Communist of 1933 should have come out of the camps more Communistic than he went in, a Jew more Jewish, and, in France, the wife of a Foreign Legionary more convinced of the value of the Foreign Legion; it would seem as though these categories promised some last shred of predictable treatment, as though they embodied some last and hence most fundamental juridical identity.

While the classification of inmates by categories is only a tactical, organizational measure, the arbitrary selection of victims indicates the essential principle of the institution. If the concentration camps had been dependent on the existence of political adversaries, they would scarcely have survived the first years of the totalitarian regimes. One only has to take a look at the number of inmates at Buchenwald in the years after 1936 in order to understand how absolutely necessary the element of the innocent was for the continued existence of the camps. "The camps would have died out if in making its arrests the Gestapo had considered only the principle of opposition," and toward the end of 1937 Buchenwald, with less than 1,000 inmates, was close to dying out until the November pogroms brought more than 20,000 new arrivals. In Germany, this element of the innocent was furnished in vast numbers by the Jews since 1938; in Russia, it consisted of random groups of the population which for some reason entirely unconnected with their actions had fallen into disgrace. But if in Germany the really totalitarian type of concentration camp with its enormous majority of completely "innocent" inmates was not established until 1938, in Russia it goes back to the early thirties, since up to 1930 the majority of the concentration-camp population still consisted of criminals, counterrevolutionaries and "politicals" (meaning, in this case, members of deviationist factions). Since then there have been so many innocent people in the camps that it is difficult to classify them—persons who had some sort of contact with a foreign country, Russians of Polish origin (particularly in the years 1936 to 1938), peasants whose villages for some economic reason were liquidated, deported nationalities, demobilized soldiers of the Red Army who happened to belong to regiments that stayed too long abroad as occupation forces or had become prisoners of war in Germany, etc. But the existence of a political opposition is for a concentration-camp system only a pretext, and the purpose of the system is not achieved even when, under the most monstrous terror, the population becomes more or less voluntarily co-ordinated, *i.e.*, relinquishes its political rights. The aim of an arbitrary system is to destroy the civil rights of the whole population, who ultimately become just as outlawed in their own country as the stateless and homeless. The destruction of a man's rights, the killing of the juridical person in him, is a prerequisite for dominating him entirely. And this applies not only to special categories such as criminals, political opponents, Jews, homosexuals, on whom the early experiments were made, but to every inhabitant of a totalitarian state. Free consent is as much an obstacle to total domination as free opposition. The arbitrary arrest which chooses among innocent people destroys the validity of free consent, just as torture—as distinguished from death—destroys the possibility of opposition.

Any, even the most tyrannical, restriction of this arbitrary persecution to certain opinions of a religious or political nature, to certain modes of intellectual or erotic social behavior, to certain freshly invented "crimes," would render the camps superfluous, because in the long run no attitude and no opinion can withstand the threat of so much horror; and above all it would make for a new system of justice, which, given any stability at all, could not fail to produce a new juridical person in man, that would elude the totalitarian domination. The so-called *"Volksnutzen"* of the Nazis, constantly fluctuating (because what is useful today can be injurious tomorrow) and the eternally shifting party line of the Soviet Union which, being retroactive, almost daily makes new groups of people available for the concentration camps, are the only guaranty for the continued existence of the concentration camps, and hence for the continued total disfranchisement of man.

The next decisive step in the preparation of living corpses is the murder of the moral person in man. This is done in the main by making martyrdom, for the first time in history, impossible: "How many people here still believe that a protest has even historic importance? This skepticism is the real masterpiece of the SS. Their great accomplishment. They have corrupted all human solidarity. Here the night has fallen on the future. When no witnesses are left, there can be no testimony. To demonstrate when death can no longer be postponed is an attempt to give death a meaning, to act beyond one's own death. In order to be successful, a gesture must have social meaning. There are hundreds of thousands of us here, all living in absolute solitude. That is why we are subdued no matter what happens."

The camps and the murder of political adversaries are only part of organized oblivion that not only embraces carriers of public opinion such as the spoken and the written word, but extends even to the families and friends of the victim. Grief and remembrance are forbidden. In the Soviet Union a woman will sue for divorce immediately after her husband's arrest in order to save the lives of her children; if her husband chances to come back, she will indignantly turn him out of the house. The Western world has hitherto, even in its darkest periods, granted the slain enemy the right to be remembered as a self-evident acknowledgment of the fact that we are all men (and *only* men). It is only because even Achilles set out for Hector's funeral, only because the most despotic governments honored the slain enemy, only because the Romans allowed the Christians to write their martyrologies, only because the

Church kept its heretics alive in the memory of men, that all was not lost and never could be lost. The concentration camps, by making death itself anonymous (making it impossible to find out whether a prisoner is dead or alive) robbed death of its meaning as the end of a fulfilled life. In a sense they took away the individual's own death, proving that henceforth nothing belonged to him and he belonged to no one. His death merely set a seal on the fact that he had never really existed.

This attack on the moral person might still have been opposed by man's conscience which tells him that it is better to die a victim than to live as a bureaucrat of murder. Totalitarian terror achieved its most terrible triumph when it succeeded in cutting the moral person off from the individualist escape and in making the decisions of conscience absolutely questionable and equivocal. When a man is faced with the alternative of betraying and thus murdering his friends or of sending his wife and children, for whom he is in every sense responsible, to their death; when even suicide would mean the immediate murder of his own family—how is he to decide? The alternative is no longer between good and evil, but between murder and murder. Who could solve the moral dilemma of the Greek mother, who was allowed by the Nazis to choose which of her three children should be killed?

Through the creation of conditions under which conscience ceases to be adequate and to do good becomes utterly impossible, the consciously organized complicity of all men in the crimes of totalitarian regimes is extended to the victims and thus made really total. The SS implicated concentration-camp inmates—criminals, politicals, Jews —in their crimes by making them responsible for a large part of the administration, thus confronting them with the hopeless dilemma whether to send their friends to their death, or to help murder other men who happened to be strangers, and forcing them, in any event, to behave like murderers. The point is not only that hatred is diverted from those who are guilty (the *capos* were more hated than the SS), but that the distinguishing line between persecutor and persecuted, between the murderer and his victim, is constantly blurred.

Once the moral person has been killed, the one thing that still prevents men from being made into living corpses is the differentiation of the individual, his unique identity. In a sterile form such individuality can be preserved through a persistent stoicism, and it is certain that many men under totalitarian rule have taken and are each day still taking refuge in this absolute isolation of a personality without rights or conscience. There is no doubt that this part of the human person, precisely because it depends so essentially on nature and on forces that cannot be controlled by the will, is the hardest to destroy (and when destroyed is most easily repaired).

The methods of dealing with this uniqueness of the human person are numerous and we shall not attempt to list them. They begin with the monstrous conditions in the transports to the camps, when hundreds of human beings are packed into a cattle-car stark naked, glued to each other, and shunted back and forth over the countryside for days on end; they continue upon arrival at the camp, the well-organized shock of the first hours, the shaving of the head, the grotesque camp clothing; and they end in the utterly unimaginable tortures so gauged as not to kill the body, at any event not quickly. The aim of all these methods, in any case, is to manipulate the human body —with its infinite possibilities of suffering—in such a way as to make it destroy the human person as inexorably as do certain mental diseases of organic origin.

It is here that the utter lunacy of the entire process becomes most apparent. Torture, to be sure, is an essential feature of the whole totalitarian police and judiciary apparatus; it is used every day to make people talk. This type of torture, since it pursues a definite, rational aim, has certain limitations: either the prisoner talks within a certain time, or he is killed. To this rationally conducted torture another, irrational, sadistic type was added in the first Nazi concentration camps and in the cellars of the Gestapo. Carried on for the most part by the SA, it pursued no aims and was not systematic, but depended on the initiative of largely abnormal elements. The mortality was so high that only a few concentration-camp inmates of 1933 survived these first years. This type of torture seemed to be not so much a calculated political institution as a concession of the regime to its criminal and abnormal elements, who were thus rewarded for services rendered. Behind the blind bestiality of the SA, there often lay a deep hatred and resentment against all those who were socially, intellectually, or physically better off than themselves, and who now, as if in fulfillment of their wildest dreams, were in their power. This resentment, which never died out entirely in the camps, strikes us as a last remnant of humanly understandable feeling.

The real horror began, however, when the SS took over the administration of the camps. The old spontaneous bestiality gave way to an absolutely cold and systematic destruction of human bodies, calculated to destroy human dignity; death was avoided or postponed indefinitely. The camps were no longer amusement parks for beasts in human form, that is, for men who really belonged in mental institutions and prisons; the reverse became true: they were turned into "drill grounds," on which perfectly normal men were trained to be full-fledged members of the SS.

The killing of man's individuality, of the uniqueness shaped in equal parts by nature, will, and destiny, which has become so self-evident a premise for all human relations that even identical twins inspire a certain uneasiness, creates a horror that vastly overshadows the outrage of the juridical-political person and the despair of the moral person. It is this horror that gives rise to the nihilistic generalizations which maintain plausibly enough that essentially all men alike are beasts. Actually the experience of the concentration camps does show that human beings can be transformed into specimens of the human animal, and that man's "nature" is only "human" insofar as it opens up to man the possibility of becoming something highly unnatural, that is, a man.

After murder of the moral person and annihilation of the juridical person, the destruction of the individuality is almost always successful. Conceivably some laws of mass psychology may be found to explain why millions of human beings allowed themselves to be marched unresistingly into the gas chambers, although these laws would explain nothing else but the destruction of individuality. It is more significant that those individually condemned to death very seldom attempted to take one of their executioners with them, that there were scarcely any serious revolts, and that even in the moment of liberation there were very few spontaneous massacres of SS men. For to destroy individuality is to destroy spontaneity, man's power to begin something new out of his own resources, something that cannot be explained on the basis of reactions to environment and events. Nothing then remains but ghastly marionettes with human faces, which all behave like the dog in Pavlov's experiments, which all react with perfect reliability even when going to their own death, and which do nothing but react. This is the real triumph of the system: "The triumph of the SS demands that the tortured victim allow himself to be led to the noose without protesting, that he renounce and abandon himself to the point of ceasing to affirm his identity. And it is not for nothing. It is not gratuitously, out of sheer sadism, that the SS men desire his defeat. They know that the system which succeeds in destroying its victim before he mounts the scaffold . . . is incomparably the best for keeping a whole people in slavery. In submission. Nothing is more terrible than these processions of human beings going like dummies to their death. The man who sees this says to himself: 'For them to be thus reduced, what power must be concealed in the hands of the masters,' and he turns away, full of bitterness but defeated."

If we take totalitarian aspirations seriously and refuse to be misled by the common-sense assertion that they are utopian and unrealizable, it develops that the society of the dying established in the camps is the only form of society in which it is possible to dominate man entirely. Those who aspire to total domination must liquidate all spontaneity, such as the mere existence of individuality will always engender, and track it down in its most private forms, regardless of how unpolitical and harmless these may seem. Pavlov's dog, the human specimen reduced to the most elementary reactions, the bundle of reactions that can always be liquidated and replaced by other bundles of reactions that behave in exactly the same way, is the model "citizen" of a totalitarian state; and such a citizen can be produced only imperfectly outside of the camps.

The uselessness of the camps, their cynically admitted anti-utility, is only apparent. In reality they are most essential to the preservation of the regime's power than any of its other institutions. Without concentration camps, without the undefined fear they inspire and the very well-defined training they offer in totalitarian domination, which can nowhere else be fully tested with all of its most radical possibilities, a totalitarian state can neither inspire its nuclear troops with fanaticism nor maintain a whole people in complete apathy. The dominating and the dominated would only too quickly sink back into the "old bourgeois routine"; after early "excesses," they would succumb to everyday life with its human laws; in short, they would develop in the direction which all observers counseled by common sense were so prone to predict. The tragic fallacy of all these prophecies, originating in a world that was still safe, was to suppose that there was such a thing as one human nature established for all time, to identify this human nature with history, and thus to declare that the idea of total domination was not only inhuman but also unrealistic. Meanwhile we have learned that the power of man is so great that he really can be what he wishes to be.

It is in the very nature of totalitarian regimes to demand unlimited power. Such power can only be secured if literally all men, without a single exception, are reliably dominated in every aspect of their life. In the realm of foreign affairs new neutral territories must constantly be subjugated, while at home ever-new human groups must be mastered in expanding concentration camps, or, when circumstances require liquidated to make room for others. The question of opposition is unimportant both in foreign and domestic affairs. Any neutrality, indeed any spontaneously given friendship, is from the standpoint of totalitarian domination just as dangerous as open hostility, precisely because spontaneity as such, with its incalculability, is the greatest of all obstacles to total domination over man. The Communists of non-Communist countries, who fled or were called to Moscow, learned by bitter experience that they constituted a menace to the Soviet Union. Convinced Communists are in this sense, which alone has any reality today, just as ridiculous and just as menacing to the regime in Russia, as, for example, the convinced Nazis of the Röhm faction were to the Nazis.

What makes conviction and opinion of any sort so ridiculous and dangerous under totalitarian conditions is that totalitarian regimes take the greatest pride in having no need of them, or of any human help of any kind. Men insofar as they are more than animal reaction and fulfillment of functions are entirely superfluous to totalitarian regimes. Totalitarianism strives not toward despotic rule over men, but toward a system in which men are superfluous. Total power can be achieved and safeguarded only in a world of conditioned reflexes, of marionettes without the slightest trace of spontaneity. Precisely because man's resources are so great, he can be fully dominated only when he becomes a specimen of the animal-species man.

Therefore character is a threat and even the most unjust legel rules are an obstacle; but individuality, anything indeed that distinguishes one man from another, is intolerable. As long as all men have not been made equally superfluous—and this has been accomplished only in concentration camps—the ideal of totalitarian domination has not been achieved. Totalitarian states strive constantly, though never with complete success, to establish the superfluity of man—by the arbitrary selection of various groups for concentration camps, by constant purges of the ruling apparatus, by mass liquidations. Common sense protests desperately that the masses are submissive and that all this gigantic apparatus of terror is therefore superfluous; if they were capable of telling the truth, the totalitarian rulers would reply: The apparatus seems superfluous to you only because it serves to make men superfluous.

The totalitarian attempt to make men superfluous reflects the experience of modern masses of their superfluity on an overcrowded earth. The world of the dying, in which men are taught they are superfluous through a way of life in which punishment is meted out without connection with crime, in which exploitation is practiced without profit, and where work is performed without product, is a place where senselessness is daily produced anew. Yet, within the framework of the totalitarian ideology, nothing could be more sensible and logical; if the inmates are vermin, it is logical that they should be killed by poison gas; if they are degenerate, they should not be allowed to contaminate the population; if they have "slave-like souls" (Himmler), no one should waste his time trying to re-educate them. Seen through the eyes of the ideology, the trouble with the camps is almost that they make too much sense, that the execution of the doctrine is too consistent.

While the totalitarian regimes are thus resolutely and cynically emptying the world of the only thing that makes sense to the utilitarian expectations of common sense, they impose upon it at the same time a kind of supersense which the ideologies actually always meant when they pretended to have found the key to history or the solution to the riddles of the universe. Over and above the senselessness of totalitarian society is enthroned the ridiculous supersense of its ideological superstition. Ideologies are harmless, uncritical, and arbitrary opinions only as long as they are not believed in seriously. Once their claim to total validity is taken literally they become the nuclei of logical systems in which, as in the systems of paranoiacs, everything follows comprehensibly and even compulsorily once the first premise is accepted. The insanity of such systems lies not only in their first premise but in the very logicality with which they are constructed. The curious logicality of all isms, their simple-minded trust in the salvation value of stubborn devotion without regard for specific, varying factors, already harbors the first germs of totalitarian contempt for reality and factuality.

Common sense trained in utilitarian thinking is helpless against this ideological supersense, since totalitarian regimes establish a functioning world of no-sense. The ideological contempt for factuality still contained the proud assumption of human mastery over the world; it is, after all, contempt for reality which makes possible changing the world, the erection of the human artifice. What destroys the element of pride in the totalitarian contempt for reality (and thereby distinguishes it radically from revolutionary theories and attitudes) is the supersense which gives the contempt for reality its cogency, logicality, and consistency. What makes a truly totalitarian device out of the Bolshevik claim that the present Russian system is superior to all others is the fact that the totalitarian ruler draws from this claim the logically impeccable conclusion that without this system people never could have built such a wonderful thing as, let us say, a subway; from this, he again draws the logical conclusions that anyone who knows of the existence of the Paris subway is a suspect because he may cause people to doubt that one can do things only in the Bolshevik way. This leads to the final conclusion that in order to remain a loyal Bolshevik, you have to destroy the Paris subway. Nothing matters but consistency.

With these new structures, built on the strength of supersense and driven by the motor of logicality, we are indeed at the end of the bourgeois era of profits and power, as well as at the end of imperialism and expansion. The aggressiveness of totalitarianism springs not from lust for power, and if it feverishly seeks to expand, it does so neither for expansion's sake nor for profit, but only for ideological reasons: to make the world consistent, to prove that its respective supersense has been right.

It is chiefly for the sake of this supersense, for the sake of complete consistency, that it is necessary for totalitarianism to destroy every trace of what we commonly call human dignity. For respect for human dignity implies the recognition of my fellow-men or our fellow-nations as subjects, as builders of worlds or cobuilders of a common world. No ideology which aims at the explanation of all historical events of the past and at mapping out the course of all events of the future can bear the unpredictability which springs from the fact that men are creative, that they can bring forward something so new that nobody ever foresaw it.

What totalitarian ideologies therefore aim at is not the transformation of the outside world or the revolutionizing transmutation of society, but the transformation of human nature itself. The concentration camps are the laboratories where changes in human nature are tested, and their shamefulness therefore is not just the business of their inmates and those who run them according to strictly "scientific" standards; it is the concern of all men. Suffering, of which there has been always too much on earth, is not the issue, nor is the number of victims. Human nature as such is at stake, and even though it seems that these experiments succeed not in changing man but only in destroying him, by creating a society in which the nihilistic banality of *homo homini lupus* is consistently realized, one should bear in mind the necessary limitations to an experiment which requires global control in order to show conclusive results.

Until now the totalitarian belief that everything is possible seems to have proved only that everything can be destroyed. Yet, in their effort to prove that everything is possible, totalitarian regimes have discovered without knowing it that there are crimes which men can neither punish nor forgive. When the impossible was made possible it became the unpunishable, unforgivable absolute evil which could no longer be understood and explained by the evil motives of self-interest, greed, covetousness, resentment, lust for power, and cowardice; and which therefore anger could not revenge, love could not endure, friendship could not forgive. Just as the victims in the death factories or the holes of oblivion are no longer "human" in the eyes of their executioners, so this newest species of criminals is beyond the pale even of solidarity in human sinfulness.

It is inherent in our entire philosophical tradition that we cannot conceive of a "radical evil," and this is true both for Christian theology, which conceded even to the Devil himself a celestial origin, as well as for Kant, the only philosopher who, in the word he coined for it, at least must have suspected the existence of this evil even though he immediately rationalized it in the concept of a "perverted ill will" that could be explained by comprehensible motives. Therefore, we actually have nothing to fall back on in order to understand a phenomenon that nevertheless confronts us with its overpowering reality and breaks down all standards we know. There is only one thing that seems to be discernible: we may say that radical evil has emerged in connection with a system in which all men have become equally superfluous. The manipulators of this system believe in their own superfluousness as much as in that of all others, and the totalitarian murderers are all the more dangerous because they do not care if they themselves are alive or dead, if they ever lived or never were born. The danger of the corpse factories and holes of oblivion is that today, with populations and homelessness everywhere on the increase, masses of people are continuously rendered superfluous if we continue to think of our world in utilitarian terms. Political, social, and economic events everywhere are in a silent conspiracy with totalitarian instruments devised for making men superfluous. The implied temptation is well understood by the utilitarian common sense of the masses, who in most countries are too desperate to retain much fear of death. The Nazis and the Bolsheviks can be sure that their factories of annihilation which demonstrate the swiftest solution to the problem of overpopulation, of economically superfluous and socially rootless human masses, are as much of an attraction as a warning. Totalitarian solutions may well survive the fall of totalitarian regimes in the form of strong temptations which will come up whenever it seems impossible to alleviate political, social, or economic misery in a manner worthy of man.

# International Organization for Peace

*German tanks still roamed the Caucasus, the recovery of the Pacific from Japan by costly island-hopping was far from complete, Sicily was barely secured, and Italy was still crawling with German troops when the Allies met at Teheran in December, 1943, to plan for the eventual peace. It was the first meeting at which the three major powers (the United States,*

*Great Britain, and Russia) were present, Stalin having been persuaded
to join his capitalist colleagues, Winston Churchill and Franklin D.
Roosevelt. Roosevelt had worked for and secured a commitment that, as
military conquests were completed, there should be a general gathering
of the victors to establish a successor to the ill-fated League of Nations.
It was essential to the Western powers that Russia be brought out of her
self-imposed isolation; otherwise the new organization could by no means
be considered a world forum.*

*Accordingly, at San Francisco in 1945, the United Nations Charter was
drawn up. It created a General Assembly initially made up of the former
wartime allies, a permanent Security Council of the five Great Powers
(the United States, Great Britain, France, Russia, and China) which
further included six delegates from the Assembly who were elected by
the Assembly for two-year terms. In the first twenty years of the United
Nations, membership was extended even to the former Axis partners
and went beyond the 100 mark as newly independent nations received
recognition. The UN has not only played a major role in settling disputes
by concerted action against aggression (notably in Korea in 1950), but
has gathered information and provided aid in such related areas as world
health, education, crime, and poverty. Above all, it seems to many the
hope for world peace through negotiation and the basis for world
federation, a fulfillment of the dreams of unification envisioned by Kant
in the eighteenth century and Dante in the thirteenth.*

*Since its inception the UN has achieved immeasurable stature by the
actions of those who have risen from domestic political status to the
isolated grandeur of the General Secretariat—Trygve Lie, Dag
Hammarskjöld, and U Thant, all from smaller, traditionally neutralist,
countries. The Secretary General is charged with the execution of the
UN's decisions, including mediation in current disputes, a role which
inevitably creates a side automatically hostile to his interference. Yet,
considering the hostility generated in areas like Korea, Indonesia,
Kashmir, the Suez Canal, the Congo, and Israel, the record of negotiated
truces has been quite miraculous. Dag Hammarskjöld (1905–1961),
whose apologia for the UN follows, was its leader from 1953 until he
died in an air crash on September 18, 1961, while flying to Northern
Rhodesia to negotiate a cease-fire with rebel forces in the Congo.*

*But the UN has been extremely unpopular with some individuals and
nations. In parts of the United States road signs urge, "Get the U.S. out
of the UN." There is some fear of the organization's "supersovereignty."
The earlier use of the Soviet veto has familiarized English-speaking people*

*with the Russian word "nyet," and suggestions for Russia's expulsion from the UN have been frequent.*

*Lord Cherwell, former director of Britain's atomic energy program, cabinet member in Churchill's Conservative second ministry, summarized many objections to the UN in a speech delivered in the House of Lords in 1956, which is reprinted here as a contrast to Hammarskjöld's positive assessment.*

# ∾§ THE POSITIVE ROLE OF THE U.N. IN A SPLIT WORLD

## Dag Hammarskjöld

. . . Fundamental though the differences splitting our world are, the areas which are not committed in the major conflicts are still considerable. Whether the countries concerned call themselves non-committed, neutral, neutralist or something else, they have all found it not to be in harmony with their role and interests in world politics to tie their policies, in a general sense, to any one of the blocs or to any specific line of action supported by one of the sides in the major conflict. The reasons for such attitudes vary. That, however, is less important in this special context than the fact that conflicts arising within the non-committed areas offer opportunities for solutions which avoid an aggravation of big-power differences and can remain uninfluenced by them. There is thus a field within which international conflicts may be faced and solved with such harmony between the power blocs as was anticipated as a condition for Security Council action in San Francisco. Agreement may be achieved because of a mutual interest among the big powers to avoid having a regional or local conflict drawn into the sphere of bloc politics.

With its constitution and structure, it is extremely difficult for the United Nations to exercise an influence on problems which are clearly and definitely within the orbit of present-day conflicts between power blocs. If a specific conflict is within that orbit, it can be assumed that the Security Council is rendered inactive, and it may be feared that even positions taken by the General Assembly would follow lines strongly influenced by considerations only indirectly related to the concrete difficulty under consideration. Whatever the attitude of the General Assembly and the Security Council, it is in such cases also practically impossible for the Secretary-General to operate effectively with the means put at his disposal, short of risking seriously to impair the usefulness of his office for the Organization in all the other cases for which the services of the United Nations Secretariat are needed.

This clearly defines the main field of useful activity of the United Nations in its

Dag Hammarskjöld, "The Positive Role of the U.N. in a Split World," *United Nations Review*, VII (October 1960), 24–28.

efforts to prevent conflicts or to solve conflicts. Those efforts must aim at keeping newly arising conflicts outside the sphere of bloc differences. Further, in the case of conflicts on the margin of, or inside, the sphere of bloc differences, the United Nations should seek to bring such conflicts out of this sphere through solutions aiming, in the first instance, at their strict localization. In doing so, the Organization and its agents have to lay down a policy line, but this will then not be for one party against another, but for the general purpose of avoiding an extension or achieving a reduction of the area into which the bloc conflicts penetrate.

Experience indicates that the preventive diplomacy, to which the efforts of the United Nations must thus to a large extent be directed, is of special significance in cases where the original conflict may be said either to be the result of, or to imply risks for, the creation of a power vacuum between the main blocs. Preventive action in such cases must in the first place aim at filling the vacuum so that it will not provoke action from any of the major parties, the initiative for which might be taken for preventive purposes but might in turn lead to counteraction from the other side. The ways in which a vacuum can be filled by the United Nations so as to forestall such initiatives differ from case to case, but they have this in common: temporarily, and pending the filling of a vacuum by normal means, the United Nations enters the picture on the basis of its non-commitment to any power bloc, so as to provide to the extent possible a guarantee in relation to all parties against initiatives from others.

The special need and the special possibilities for what I here call preventive United Nations diplomacy have been demonstrated in several recent cases, such as Suez and Gaza, Lebanon and Jordan, Laos and the Congo.

A study of the records of the conflicts to which I have just referred shows how it has been possible to use the means and methods of the United Nations for the purposes I have indicated. In all cases, whatever the immediate reason for the United Nations initiative, the Organization has moved so as to forestall developments which might draw the specific conflict, openly or actively, into the sphere of power bloc differences. It has done so by introducing itself into the picture, sometimes with very modest means, sometimes in strength, so as to eliminate a political, economic and social, or military vacuum.

The view expressed here as to the special possibilities and responsibilities of the Organization in situations of a vacuum has reached an unusually clear expression in the case of the Congo. There, the main argument presented for United Nations intervention was the breakdown of law and order, the rejection of the attempt to maintain order by foreign troops, and the introduction of the United Nations Force so as to create the basis for the withdrawal of the foreign troops and for the forestalling of initiatives to introduce any other foreign troops into the territory with the obvious risks for widening international conflict which would ensue.

Whether the Congo operation is characterized as a case of preventive diplomacy, or as a move in order to fill a vacuum and to forestall the international risks created by the development of such a vacuum, or as a policy aimed at the localization of a conflict with potentially wide international repercussions, is not essential. Whatever the description, the political reality remains. It is a policy which is justified by the wish of the international community to avoid this important area being split by bloc conflicts. It is a policy rendered possible by the fact that both blocs have an interest in avoiding such an extension of the area of conflict because of the threatening conse-quences, were the localization of the conflict to fail.

Those who look with impatience at present-day efforts by the United Nations to resolve major international problems are inclined to neglect, or to misread, the signifi-cance of the efforts which can be made by the United Nations in the field of practical politics in order to guide the international community in a direction of growing stability. They see the incapacity of the United Nations to resolve the major bloc conflicts as an argument against the very form of international cooperation which the Organization represents. In doing so, they forget what the Organization has achieved and can achieve, through its activities regarding conflicts which are initially only on the margin of, or outside, the bloc conflicts, but which, unless solved or localized, might widen the bloc conflicts and seriously aggravate them. Thus the Organization in fact also exercises a most important, though indirect, influence on the conflicts be-tween the power blocs by preventing the widening of the geographical and political area covered by these conflicts and by providing for solutions whenever the interests of all parties in a localization of conflict can be mobilized in favor of its efforts.

The Organization in this way also makes a significant contribution in the direction of an ultimate solution of the differences between the power blocs, as it is obvious that it is a condition for an improvement in the situation that the area to which those differences apply, as a minimum requirement, is not permitted to expand and, so far as possible, is reduced.

It is with this background that the initiative for United Nations intervention in the Congo conflict was taken under Article 99 of the Charter, for the first time applied fully, according to its letter and in the spirit in which it must have been drafted. It is also in this light that one has to view the fact that not only the first but also the subsequent decisions in the Security Council regarding the Congo have been taken by votes in which the power-bloc conflicts have not been reflected.

These observations are of special interest when we turn to the consideration of questions regarding which the power-bloc interests openly clash. I have in mind espe-cially disarmament. In general terms, it is not surprising that, in the case of problems so deeply related to the security of many nations and to the predominant powers within the different blocs, negotiations have presented extraordinary difficulties. On the other hand, it is also evident that there is a latitude within which a shared interest in avoiding an aggravation of the situation overrides the specific security interests of any one party and within which, for that reason, agreement may be possible.

*De facto*, we have seen such an agreement developing in the field of nuclear tests. I believe that there are also other questions within the field of disarmament regarding which success is possible for new efforts to reach agreement, on at least so much of a common *de facto* policy as is indicated by the mutual interest to avoid a widening of the substantive basis for the present-day race toward a world crisis. Approached in this way, disarmament seems to offer important possibilities, still incompletely ex-plored, of a gradual reduction of the area in which clashing security interests so far have rendered formal agreement impossible.

There is no contradiction between this application to the disarmament problem of the philosophy and practices successfully tried by the United Nations in specific con-flicts and the view that there can be no solution to the disarmament problem short of the acceptance of total disarmament under satisfactory control by both sides. The pragmatic approach and the, so to say, global one are not a variance, for it is obvious that efforts to avoid a widening of the field of conflict and to reduce the area in which concrete agreement for the moment is impossible should at all events be integrated into a wider, more far-reaching plan under which the security interests of the parties can be balanced out against each other in ways that will make it possible for the parties to reach the ideal target of total disarmament.

It is certainly not productive to approach the disarmament problem solely on a pragmatic basis, without integration of the steps taken into a plan ultimately aiming at full disarmament. Likewise, however, it seems unrealistic to approach the total problem oblivious of the fact that all political experience and all previous negotiation show that the road to progress lies in the direction of efforts to contain and reduce the area of disagreement by mobilizing such common interests as may exist and as may override other and special interests tending in the opposite direction.

The members of the General Assembly will excuse me for presenting these general observations on a problem to which the Assembly has devoted so much attention. I have done so only because it seems to me that the experiences from other political fields in which the United Nations has acted with success have a bearing also on a field like this one where, so far, the Organization has failed to achieve results.

The responsibilities and possibilities of the Organization in the exercise of preventive diplomacy apply also to the economic sphere. Far less dramatic in their impact as the economic activities must be, they are of decisive long-term significance for the welfare of the international community. In the end, the United Nations is likely to be judged not so much by the criterion of how successfully it has overcome this or that crisis as by the significance of its total contribution toward building the kind of world community in which such crises will no longer be inevitable.

This aim, naturally, cannot be reached overnight, nor can it be considerably furthered by any institutional or constitutional reforms of the United Nations. It cannot even be achieved by the political resolution of the conflicts which today divide the major powers. Essential though such a political resolution would be, it would not by itself ensure stability and peace in the face of the dangerous economic and social vacuum created and maintained by the enormous gap which separates countries at different stages of development.

In the enduring task of bridging the gulf between countries, all member nations, whether developed or underdeveloped, whether in the East or the West, have a common interest. This common interest is recognized by everyone. It is clearly stated in the Charter of the United Nations, in which countries pledge themselves to take joint and separate action in cooperation with the Organization to promote "higher standards of living, full employment and conditions of economic and social progress and development." It is reflected in all of the debates of the Economic and Social Council as well as of the General Assembly on the relevant items. It has borne fruit in a host of activities within the United Nations and its sister institutions. And yet, in considering the rate of progress that has been made in relation to the task that remains to be achieved, it is difficult to escape a feeling of disappointment.

It is true that the mere recognition of the community of interest in the economic development of underdeveloped countries itself represents a major step forward. And the expressions of common interest in economic development are no lip service. The achievements of the United Nations family in the economic and social field, as generously supported by member governments, demonstrates their seriousness. However, it must, in the context of a newly emerging Africa, be registered, in a spirit of candid realism, that the rate of achievement is not at all commensurate with the needs.

The coincidence of interest in the economic field stems from the economic interdependence of the world community. The degree of interdependence has been increasing rapidly, partly as the inevitable outcome of an accelerating rate of advance in science and technology, partly owing to the emergence of the countries of the continents of Asia and of Africa to independence and full participation in the affairs of the world at large, but, to a significant degree, also as a result of economic forces making for a growing integration of the world community.

For the first time in history, the concept of a world economy has come to take on a significant meaning not only for the student of economics but also for the statesman and the layman.

Unfortunately, this growing interdependence has recently been reflected much less in efforts and activities within the United Nations than outside it. The United Nations can welcome regional arrangements among neighboring or like-minded countries; as long as such arrangements are so designed as to reinforce rather than to supplant the common effort toward establishing conditions of economic and social progress, they have an important role to play. A real danger arises, however, when such regional arrangements are so envisaged as to make them fall within the sphere of bloc conflict. In that case, efforts which properly should embody and be supported by a common interest may instead lead to a weakening of the uniting force of that interest and aggravate the split. This, obviously, is the reverse of the major purpose and function of the United Nations in its efforts to provide for a growing measure of political stability.

Just as it is clearly within the interests of the entire world community to prevent the widening of the area of conflict in cases of political crises, so it must be in the interests of all constantly to seek to widen rather than to restrict the area of coincidence of economic interest within the United Nations. Unless this is done, the entire world, and not just one or the other side, is bound to lose. As I noted in my statement to the Economic and Social Council at its thirtieth session, "the United Nations Organization remains the only universal agency in which countries with widely differing political institutions and at different stages of economic development may exchange views, share their problems and experiences, probe each other's reactions to policies of mutual interest, and initiate collective action."

It was this recognition of the growing area of coincidence of economic interest which was at the basis of my proposal and of the Council's decision that it hold its thirtieth session at the ministerial level in order to undertake, at the beginning of a new decade, a broad examination of the direction to be taken by the United Nations to meet the challenge of both national and collective responsibility for economic growth and development.

At its thirteenth session, the General Assembly adopted resolution 1316 (XIII) calling upon member states to undertake a review of accomplishments to date and to chart their future courses of cooperative action for the purpose of giving further impetus to the economic development of the less developed countries. At the national level also, many countries, both developed and underdeveloped, have found it useful to establish long-term plans for economic growth as guide-lines for economic policy, and others have established national commissions on economic and social goals and policies.

In the light of these events, and in the light of the changes that have taken place in the national economic and political landscape since the Charter was first signed, it was my belief that the Economic and Social Council might usefully explore the question of the desirability and feasibility of some United Nations undertaking to chart the future course of cooperative action to implement the economic and social objectives of the Charter.

A common stand has not yet been reached on the possibility or advisability of harmonizing and coordinating national economic policies. Even the idea of regular and systematic consultation with a view to achieving fuller knowledge of the facts and the issues is new. In view of the very modest and very recent progress in harmonization of national economic policies, even within regional grouping of like-minded countries, it is not surprising that no consensus on the possibility or desirability of harmonizing or coordinating national economic policies within the framework of the United Nations should as yet exist.

And yet, though the objective is not within immediate reach, and though I do not wish to underestimate the obstacles, the importance of a harmonization of national economic development policies within the United Nations must be stressed. Even though the session at the ministerial level did not produce the results that some may have hoped, it did represent a beginning. It did lead to a useful exchange of views. It did provide an opportunity for contacts between ministers in charge of economic questions, some of whom have only limited alternative possibilities of making such direct contacts. It did lead to at least one important step looking toward better coordination in the future of policies of economic projections. Thus, this meeting, with its achievements—and its shortcomings—may be regarded as opening the door to new efforts to explore and utilize for common ends the wide area of common economic interests, at the same time as it demonstrates the difficulties we encounter and the early stage of evolution at which we still find ourselves.

Until now, the economic analyses undertaken by the Secretariat and consequently the debates within the Economic and Social Council and the General Assembly have been concerned essentially with past and present trends. Now, with the program of work in economic projections initiated by the Council, we may hope that, as we succeed in ascertaining the constituent elements of policies of economic growth, the Organization will be able to make an important contribution toward widening the bounds of the area of coincidence of interest within the United Nations, thus helping to harmonize decisions of governments in the field of national policy and in the promotion of rapid and stable economic development for all.

In the introduction to my report to the General Assembly at its fourteenth session I discussed the role of the United Nations. In that context I said:

"The work of today within and for the United Nations is a work through which the basis may be laid for increasingly satisfactory forms of international cooperation and for a future international system of law and order, for which the world is not yet ripe."

I continued:

"It has so often been said that the world of today is one which requires organized international cooperation on a basis of universality that one repeats it with hesitation. However, there are reasons to do so. It still seems sometimes to be forgotten that— whatever views may be held about the United Nations as an institution—the principle of organized international cooperation on a basis of universality which is at present reflected in this Organization is one which has emerged from bitter experiences and should now be considered as firmly established."

In the previous parts of this introduction I have tried to outline my views on some specific problems arising for the Organization at the present juncture, which may well, in the perspective of history, come to be regarded as a turning point. Especially, I have wished to draw the attention of the members to the scope for possible diplomatic and political action by the Organization in a split world and to the desirability of the widening of that scope by patient and persistent action, using as the lever the community of interests which is created by the desire of everybody to limit the area of conflict, to reduce the risk of conflicts and to create a basis for joint action for solution, or at least localization, of conflicts.

Recent developments—reflected in a revolutionary technical evolution of arms for destruction, in the entry of new major regions of the world in full strength into international politics and in new and worldwide economic interdependence—have given to the Organization, and what it represents as an instrument in the hands of member governments, greatly increased responsibilities, but also increased usefulness.

The Organization and its activities can be viewed on different levels. It provides member governments with a highly developed, continuously operating conference and negotiation machinery. However, to a growing extent it has provided them also with an effective executive organ for joint action. In this latter respect, the evolution has taken a course somewhat different from the one envisaged in San Francisco, but, as recent developments have shown, the departure as to methods is not considerable and the conformity as to aims is complete. Finally, the Organization is also the embodiment of an ideal and the symbol of an approach to international life which recognizes the common interest of all in the rejection of the use of force, in any form, as a means for settling international disputes and in adherence to the principles of law, justice, and human rights.

The Organization has often in the past been faced, and is likely in its continued work again and again to be faced, with situations in which a compromise with these last-mentioned principles might seem to facilitate the achievement of results in negotiations or to promise an easier success for the Organization in its executive efforts to resolve a problem. It is for the members themselves to judge to what extent the Organization, in particular cases, has accepted such compromises and to what extent it has remained faithful to the principles and ideals which it embodies.

It is my firm conviction that any result bought at the price of a compromise with the principles and ideals of the Organization, either by yielding to force, by disregard of justice, by neglect of common interests or by contempt for human rights, is bought at too high a price. That is so because a compromise with its principles and purposes weakens the Organization in a way representing a definite loss for the future that cannot be balanced by an immediate advantage achieved.

The United Nations has increasingly become the main platform—and the main protector of the interests—of those many nations who feel themselves strong as members of the international family but who are weak in isolation. Thus, an increasing number of nations have come to look to the United Nations for leadership and support in ways somewhat different from those natural in the light of traditional international diplomacy. They look to the Organization as a spokesman and as an agent for principles which give them strength in an international concert in which other voices can mobilize all the weight of armed force, wealth, an historical role and that influence which is the other side of a special responsibility for peace and security. Therefore, a weakening of the Organization, resulting from an attempt to achieve results at the cost of principles, is a loss not only for the future but also immediately in respect of the significance of the Organization for the vast majority of nations and in respect of their confidence in the Organization on which its strength in our present-day world ultimately depends.

There are in the Charter elements of a thinking which, I believe, belongs to an earlier period in the development of the world community. I have in mind especially the concept that the permanent members of the Security Council should not only, as is natural, be recognized as carrying special responsibility for peace and security, but that, further, these permanent members, working together, should represent a kind of "built-in" directing group for the world community as organized in the United Nations.

The fifteen years which have passed since the founding of the United Nations have witnessed a different development. In the first place, we have seen a split among the permanent members which, in fact, has created the major war risk of today and considerably hampered the development of the Organization. But, further, we have experienced a growth into independence of a majority of states of two great continents, with other interests, other traditions, and other concepts of international politics than those of the countries of Europe and the Americas. Who can deny that today the countries of Asia or the countries of Africa, acting in a common spirit, represent powerful elements in the international community, in their ways as important as any of the big powers, although lacking in their military and economic potential?

The United Nations is an organic creation of the political situation facing our generation. At the same time, however, the international community has, so to say, come to political self-consciousness in the Organization and, therefore, can use it in a meaningful way in order to influence those very circumstances of which the Organization is a creation.

It is impossible for anyone to say where the international community is heading and how the United Nations will change in the further course of the evolution of international politics. But it can safely be said that international cooperation will become increasingly essential for the maintenance of peace, progress and international justice. It can also safely be said that if the United Nations firmly adheres to its principles and purposes, with flexibility and intelligent adjustment to needs as regards procedure, members engaged in this cooperation will increasingly turn to the Organization for assistance. Therefore, they will find it increasingly necessary to maintain its strength as an instrument for the world community in their efforts to reduce those areas of major conflict where the Organization so far has been powerless, as well as in efforts to resolve problems, arising outside or on the margin of these areas, in a spirit reflecting the overriding common interest.

This concept of the role and of the future of the United Nations may go beyond the conventional thinking which sees in the Organization only, or mainly, a machinery for negotiation, but I am convinced of its realism and I am convinced also that the Organization and its member nations would act rightly and wisely if they acted consistently with this concept in mind, even if temporarily it may seem to point out a road full of risks and of difficulties which they may doubt that the Organization is yet strong enough to overcome.

# ✍ THE UNITED NATIONS ORGANIZATION: IN ITS PRESENT FORM IT CANNOT WORK

*Lord Cherwell*

I intend to deal mainly with one particular matter, the United Nations Organization, which I think ought to be analyzed, and at which I shall not be able to throw quite so many bouquets as most speakers seemed to do. Like the noble Viscount, Lord Bruce of Melbourne, I hate living in a fool's paradise, and though, like everyone else, I wish UNO [United Nations Organization] could work, I have come reluctantly to the view that, in its present form, it cannot. It is composed, of course, of men full of the best intentions, and its admirers are equally well meaning. But I cannot help feeling that people tend to overestimate its power for good and to underrate its potentialities for evil. We know all too well nowadays how easy it is for people to fall victims to phrases, to be hypnotized by slogans, and I am afraid that that is what is happening in the case of U.N. "Send it to U.N." is becoming a sort of incantation. In so many quarters it seems to be treated as a shibboleth. You have only to mouth the words and go through the ceremonial, and all will be well.

There are obvious psychological reasons for this curious attitude of mind. During the war many men in the forces positively reveled in the fact that they did not have to think out the consequences of their actions and that all they had to do was obey. It seems to me that something similar is happening on a bigger scale. People in authority—and in a democracy we are all involved—have to take decisions, and some-

Lord Cherwell, "The United Nations Organization: In Its Present Form It Cannot Work," *The United Nations: The Continuing Debate*, ed. C. A. McClelland (San Francisco: Chandler Publishing House, 1960), pp. 23–31.

times terrible decisions. How tempting to unload this burden. If slavish obedience to U.N. is regarded not merely as respectable but positively meritorious, what a splendid way of escaping from these awful responsibilities. I cannot help feeling that some sort of subconscious longing of this sort may be at work in many minds.

We are often told that U.N. is the only hope of the world for avoiding war, and therefore that we ought to believe that it must and will succeed in this laudable object. I wish I could see the logic of this. One might just as well say that, if a man's only hope of avoiding bankruptcy is in winning a football pool, all right-thinking people ought to believe that he will do so.

Somehow the proponents of U.N.'s infallibility have managed to persuade themselves that anyone who does not put his complete faith in the organization is not anxious to maintain peace—in fact, is almost a warmonger. Some of them have reached a hysterical state of mind in which merely to question whether U.N. will succeed in establishing peace in the world is considered wicked. No doubt I shall incur their severe displeasure, for what I intend to do is to attempt to analyze dispassionately the utility and value of this important—I said "important," not "impotent"—organization.

First, what is this superbody to which we are to confide our fate? U.N. consists of some 79 nations supposed to be sovereign and independent, though in some cases this is a somewhat dubious claim. They range from the giant powers, Soviet Russia and the United States, to tiny entities like Panama and Iceland. The population of the biggest is more than 1,000 times greater than that of the smallest. The discrepancy in wealth and power is far more than ten-thousandfold.

Yet in the Assembly, which is the ultimate governing body of U.N., each has an equal vote. Thus barely 5 percent of the world's population could claim a two-thirds majority in the Assembly. Or, to put it another way, half the population of the world is represented by 4 delegates and the other half by 75 delegates. What is more, these nations are represented in the Assembly by any group or body or individual which may succeed in seizing power.

There is, it is true, a so-called Credentials Committee. But it does not appear to be at all strict in making the delegates show that they represent the views of the majority or of any properly elected or selected government. Anybody who has seized power—I believe, for instance, Mr. Kadar in Hungary—can, and does, send a delegate to vote on his behalf. In fact it is even worse than I have said, for these sovereign, independent nations vary enormously in their standards of education and outlook. Some are the most highly civilized and educated countries on the planet. The inhabitants of others can scarcely read or write. Yet no attention is paid to this fact. Only recently, there was a close vote for the vice presidency of the Assembly, between (I think it was) Italy and Liberia—Italy, one of the oldest and most civilized cultures in history; Liberia, a small artificial state which has been in existence barely a hundred years, and very few of whose inhabitants have any conception of the outside world.

This is the Assembly, as I have said, the ultimate governing body of U.N. We were recently told that it is "the highest tribunal in the world," whose decisions all must obey without hesitation or question. As I have said, and, I hope, shown, the constitution of this body is utterly indefensible. If the vote of each nation were weighted in accordance with its population, there might be some semblance—though a very poor semblance—of logic in it. But this is not so, for the vote of 400 million Indians or 160 million Americans is equated to the vote of 4 million Bolivians or 100,000 Icelanders. Icelanders are admirable people, but I do not think the discrepancy between their culture and ours is as great as all that. And, of course, the 600 million inhabitants of Communist China have no vote at all. I do not suggest that weighting votes by populations would turn the Assembly into a tribunal. The long and short of it is that justice cannot be found by counting the votes, however weighted, of interested parties.

This brings me to the word "tribunal," in the phrase "the highest tribunal in the world." Nothing could be more inept as a description of the Assembly. There is no pretense that it is a judicial body. No sworn evidence is taken or is obtainable; there is no judicial summing up, or any recognized body of law to which nations have an obligation to conform. The Assembly is split into a number of blocs. There are the Afro-Asian block, the South American bloc, and the Iron Curtain bloc, the members of which tend to vote together on their likes and dislikes, in accordance with instructions from their home governments.

No one pretends they are influenced by the evidence or the speeches. Judicial impartiality is the last thing that seems to matter. To describe a majority vote of such a body as a decision of the highest tribunal in the world is simply laughable. To pillory as criminal any nation which hesitates to comply with its decisions is monstrous. A judicial decision is one thing; a vote by a number of interested parties, without pretense of impartiality, without evidence or a body of laws to guide them, is totally different.

Yet it is to this body that the leader of the opposition, only a few days ago, told us to say, "We obey you. We accept whatever you say." The absurdity of the constitution of the Assembly was, of course, recognized from the start by those framing the Charter of U.N. No nation could be expected to submit unquestioningly to such a body. Only if the great powers were in agreement would there be any chance of its decisions being respected or enforced. If they were, it was hoped they could prevent small local wars among the minor powers. If they were not, it was realized that it would be useless to expect the machine to operate.

To ensure this a sort of executive body, the Security Council, was instituted, on which the five great powers had permanent seats. Six more seats were allocated for 2 years at a time to other nations, selected by the Assembly. It is perhaps typical that, at the recent moment of crisis, apparently Siam presided over the meetings of the Security Council.

According to the charter, whilst the Assembly can recommend, only the Council can act. All the signatories of the charter undertook to accept and carry out the decisions of the Council, but not those of the Assembly. Since what were at that time regarded as the five great powers had a veto in the Council, obviously action could never be taken against one of them, because no nation was under obligation to obey resolutions of the Assembly. This sensible intention appears now to be cast aside.

When the charter was concocted, the great powers, with the exception of Germany, were allies, and it was hoped that their mutual good feeling and their common objectives would ensure that they would, in general, be in agreement. Unhappily, this idealistic hope was not fulfilled. Every time any controversial question arose, Russia interposed her veto. Often she was alone, but usually any Iron Curtain country which had managed to get elected to the Security Council by the Assembly, voting in the curious manner I have described, supported her.

Russia applied her veto, as I have said, on scores of occasions in the Security Council. No one seemed at all shocked. Our left-wingers regarded it as a more or less amiable idiosyncrasy, unfortunate but not to be taken amiss. England and France used the veto on only one occasion. There is a great deal that one could say about that special case, but that would carry me too far.

In view of the persistent use of the veto by Russia, a procedure was introduced which was not originally contained in the charter of the United Nations. This consisted in convoking a special meeting of the Assembly and obtaining a recommendation in the desired sense by a two-thirds majority. Though no nation was, or is, under obligation to obey such a resolution this procedure could give a veneer of U.N. respectability to action which America or other nations desired to take against Russia's wishes. Now it has been invoked against us and, of course, the considerable, and very vocal, body of people who always think England must be wrong have been howling about her delay in coming immediately to heel. . . .

The Assembly's activities in recent months raise a broad question which the Government spokesmen will no doubt be able to clear up. So far as I can see, this procedural change, namely, the agreement to call the Assembly together out of season, on the demand of seven nations, has been used to insinuate *sub silentio* a very vital change in the constitution of the United Nations as laid down in the charter. As I have said, according to the charter, the Assembly is purely and simply a deliberative body. Provided that the Council is not dealing with it, the Assembly can discuss any matter and make recommendations. But if action is required, it must be referred to the Security Council.

According to the charter, executive functions are the province of the Security Council. So far as I know, the charter has not been amended, and any executive powers which the Assembly claims seem to have been assigned to it by itself. Indeed, in recent months it seems to have usurped functions that it was never intended to exercise. It has instructed the Secretary General, so far as I can see, to raise a military force, to negotiate with Nasser, to clear the Suez Canal, and generally to take executive action. I can find no warrant, in the charter to which we all subscribe, for such action by the Assembly. It is as though the House of Commons were to instruct the clerk of the Parliaments to raise a private army, to negotiate with the Mau Mau leaders, and to settle the dispute with the Argentine about the Falkland Islands.

I now turn to the question whether U.N. ever could work except if the great powers are unanimous in enforcing their will on the smaller nations. We are told that the intention is to substitute law for war; that this is, in essence, the whole object of the United Nations. It is another of those comfortable slogans expressing a desire felt by all of us in rhyming monosyllables, which seem to have an almost hypnotic effect. Of course, we all want the rule of law amongst nations, but what are the laws which we wish to rule? Evidently, it is not the laws accepted in principle for thousands years—the fulfillment of contracts and the sanctity of treaties. Rather, it seems to be commandments promulgated *ad hoc* by the Assembly whenever differences arise. That is submission to an arbitrary body. It is not law.

But even if this monstrous interpretation of the word "law" were taken, how is it to be enforced? As everybody knows, law is useless unless it is backed by a police force. It is no use magistrates' finding a man guilty; they cannot compel him to make restitution or send him to prison if he refuses. Thus, even if we accepted this weird U.N. body, with its odd form of voting, as the ultimate tribunal, it would be no good whatever unless it had some way of enforcing its decisions. We are told that in that case all we have to do is to endow U.N. with a police force. Indeed, my noble leader seems to be greatly encouraged because a beginning has been made in doing this in the last few weeks. I think, on analysis, that this also is a case of wishful thinking.

A police force can operate because, on the whole, people are more or less equally strong, so that one policeman can arrest one man, and, again, because the proportion of criminals in the country is comparatively small, so that a police force of reasonable strength can cope with any gang it is likely to have to deal with. A U.N. police force would have a very different situation to confront. What sort of police force would be required to turn Russia out of Hungary, or America out of Formosa, should the Afro-Asian bloc, voting with the Latin-American or the Iron Curtain countries, secure a vote to this effect in the Assembly? . . .

A police force, to be of any use, would have to be stronger than any nation or combination of nations. In fact it would have to be more powerful than the Russian and American armies combined. How, otherwise, could it impose the will of U.N. in case those powers happened to be on the same side? To contemplate such a huge force, is of course, simply absurd. It would cost at least 10,000 million pounds [$28 billion] a year to maintain; it would have to be backed by shipyards, and factories capable of producing the fleets and aircraft, the arms and ammunitions it required, which would cost thousands of millions more; and it would have to recruit many millions of men and train and officer them.

On top of all this, nobody has explained where these gigantic armies, navies, and air forces would be stationed, or how they would be transported. Once the facts are faced, I do not think anybody will seriously maintain that a police force capable of imposing U.N.'s will on the great powers, should they object, can be contemplated seriously. Nor, for my part, should I like to see it. For who would care to put an overwhelming military force at the disposal of an Assembly constituted and voting as I have described?

A new factor has come into the picture with the development of nuclear weapons. Any nation today which possesses hydrogen bombs can impose its will on any nation which has none. Though in the future there will be others, at present only two nations have a reasonable supply of these weapons—the United States and Russia. As long as they are on opposite sides, peace between them may be maintained because each of them knows that a nuclear war would spell complete annihilation to one side or the other or probably to both. But if one of the two is uninterested or even lukewarm, the other can impose its will on any of the other nations of the world. For it is little use hoping the opposing possessor of H-bombs, whatever his initial attitude, will come to the rescue in due course. There will not be any due course. In the last two world wars, it was possible for America to hover for years before coming to a decision. Next time, the whole thing will be settled in a matter of days, perhaps even of hours.

Thus, all the other nations, whatever they deem to be their status, must attach themselves to one or another of the H-bomb powers. Unless they can get support from their protector, they will just have to give way. I do not think there is any means of escaping this painful conclusion. Nor is there any end in sight to this situation— nations glaring at one another and bluffing more or less about their power and readiness to annihilate one another.

If force is ruled out, what about economic sanctions? The objection to these is that they can be applied only against some nations while others are immune. What is the use of enactments which can be enforced against one part of the community but not against the other? We, unhappily, are one of the nations most vulnerable to economic sanctions. But what would be the use of trying to impose them on Russia?

Only nations which have built up an artificial economy, which depends upon the rule of law and on the observance of the sanctity of treaties as it existed throughout the nineteenth century, are vulnerable to such sanctions. Autarchic systems are immune. Cutting off their imports or exports scarcely affects them. Napoleon discovered that 150 years ago.

Finally, we are told that no nation can stand out against world opinion; that we can rely upon the moral forces of the Assembly's resolution. Surely this is more wishful thinking. What is more, it is flatly contradicted by experience. For several years now, U.N. has condemned Egypt for refusing to allow the passage of Israel's ships through the Suez Canal in direct conflict with its obligations under the 1888 treaty. Has the moral force of this condemnation had any effect on the Egyptians? None whatever. By a huge majority, U.N. has called upon Russia to withdraw its troops from Hungary. Has the moral force of this resolution had any effect? Ask the Hungarians. If the Russians do not comply, we are told, they will be branded by the Assembly. The trouble is that they have been branded already, and they do not seem to mind.

But, we are told, "Look at the great triumph of U.N. in stopping the North Koreans overrunning the South Koreans." Nothing could be more misleading. America was able to obtain U.N.'s blessing for warlike action on that occasion simply owing to the fluke that the Russian delegate had retired from the Security Council in a sulk, so that he could not interpose his veto in time. What would have happened if he had been present? The use of armed forced would have been vetoed. Does anybody believe that the United States would simply have let events take their course and abandoned millions who had put their trust in them to be massacred? Of course not. With or without U.N.'s approval, they would have taken action, and quite right, too. We should have thought less of them if they had flinched.

If all the nations in the world adopted Christian principles, of which there does not seem any immediate prospect, moral force might become effective. But this would happen only if nations had the feeling that they were being treated with justice. How can anyone talk of justice without sworn evidence and penalties for perjury, without the possibility of testing witnesses' statements by cross examination? Even more important is that nations would have to be convinced that their case has been heard before an impartial tribunal and that the judges had given their verdict without fear or favor. Finally, it would be essential for the nations to be convinced that they were equal before the law and that judgment would be enforced upon everybody, great or small.

As I have explained, none of these vital conditions is fulfilled by U.N. in its present form, and I question whether, in the state of mind obtaining in almost all the countries of the world today, with their inflamed ideas of national sovereignty and dignity, any system can be invented which would fulfill these essential conditions. My view is that it is nonsense to demand that nations should submit their vital interests to the decision of a body constituted in such an absurd manner as the General Assembly of U.N. Any government which did so would be neglecting its duty. Civilization is built upon the basis that contracts and treaties must be, and will be, observed. As I have said, the United Kingdom relies for its very existence on this principle. . . .

They say that all we should do is to chant in unison the magic syllables "U.N., U.N.," although they know perfectly well that it never has availed, and never will avail, to compel a nation protected by a powerful friend, preferably with a veto, to honor its obligations. As things have developed, U.N. is used as a device behind whose gimcrack façade a thief can shelter as long as he contents himself with stealing from nations which can be prevented from retaliating by one of the two great powers.

## ∝§ THE ORGANIZATION MAN

*William H. Whyte, Jr.*

*During World War I alert social observers noted a phenomenon which had hitherto escaped detection. The needs of total war prompted study of the power of governments and industries to deploy millions of people into essential jobs, interlock their labors, pool their talents, and coordinate their decisions on an unprecedented scale. Armies had been bureaucratically maneuvered since the days of Frederick the Great, but this had never been the case with whole civilian populations. Eighteenth-century industrialists employed hundreds of textile operatives, the automotive industry hired tens of thousands, and French, Austrian, and Prussian governmental bureaus had maintained huge numbers of civil servants for over two hundred years; but only in the mid-twentieth century has monolithic management become a dominant institutional feature of Western civilization. As automation subsequently reduced the number of blue-collar workers and a service-centered economy emerged, management personnel has proliferated. By 1960 more than 50 percent of the employed were in the white-collar category.*

*The "organization man"—the epitome of the administrative class—has come into his own; suburbia owes its being to him, and his ethical, social, and economic standards control the entire culture. But his moral problems multiply. He senses that he has become a cog in a complex administrative machine, that the day of individualism is doomed. At stake are the classic concepts of free will versus consumer indoctrination, conscience versus business ethics, and creativity and the inviolability of the personality versus the standardization and conformity of mass-produced art and ideas.*

*The literary artist has used his vehicle to alert and, hopefully, to change the possibly horrendous course of organization conformity: Huxley and Orwell and their followers have set before us the appalling image of anti-Utopia. More recently sociologists and psychologists, many having themselves facilitated organizational control in such fields as personnel management and advertising, have conducted astute studies of the puzzling nature of the new society. The findings of William H. Whyte, Jr., an assistant managing editor of* Fortune *magazine, follow, presenting surprising, sometimes shocking, analyses of two aspects of modern social control.*

## SCIENTISM

. . . [Scientism] is the practical part of the Social Ethic, for it is the promise that with the same techniques that have worked in the physical sciences we can eventually create an exact science of man. In one form or another, it has had a long and dismal record of achievement; even its proponents readily admit that the bugs are appalling. But this has not shaken the faith in scientism, for it is essentially a utopian rather than a technical idea.

The preamble of the believers is always the same. We are in a terrible fix and it is almost too late. We have applied science to things, and only now have we begun applying it to man himself. Already we have learned some useful social techniques; we can measure personality, can spot the obstacles to good group dynamics, and predict communication response. But these are merely the beginning; if only we provide the time and money, before long we can unwrap the whole enigma with a unified science of man.

Here, extracted from the proceedings of several conferences, is a fair composite of the message:

*If we draw into our group increasing numbers of hardheaded students, some of whom are not afraid of mathematics, and if we have faith and daring, we*

William H. Whyte, Jr., *The Organization Man* (Garden City, N.Y.: Anchor Books, Double-day & Company, Inc., 1956), pp. 26–51.

*can build a science of man. . . . The conditions which determine human happi-*
*ness are discoverable scientific methods and are to a major extent capable of*
*realization. . . . More than ever, the world's greatest need is a science of human*
*relationships and an art of human engineering based upon the laws of such*
*science. We should, to put it brutally, pay more attention, first to the scientific*
*aspects of our problems rather than to the philosophical ones. . . . Although*
*human relationship problems are extremely complicated, science is gradually*
*reducing them to simple fundamentals through which these complexities are*
*reduced to factors that respond to direct and simple treatment.*

Inevitably, there is the atom-bomb analogy:

*It is trite but true to say that if social science had been given early enough*
*the four billion dollars that have been spent on the atomic bomb and on chem-*
*ical and germ warfare—say, half for research and the other half for popular*
*education—perhaps then the first release of atomic energy would have been for*
*peaceful purposes.*

And how very ancient it all is! Most of the people who hearken to the vision of
a unified science of man believe theirs is a fresh new vision, but in reality it is a
cliché that has been kicked around for centuries. Ever since Newton, scores of natural
scientists have stepped out of their area of competence to suggest the possibilities
of a science of man, and Erasmus's *Praise of Folly* suggests that even before this some
savants had much the same idea. It was an understandable dream for a natural scientist to have. Even Descartes himself was seized with the idea that the discipline of
mathematics could be extended to the affairs of man. Eventually, he thought, a "Universal Mathematical Science" would solve the problem of society—if only there were
sufficient funds and time for the job.

Later others tried the geometric tack: Thomas Hobbes worked out a complete set
of algebraic equations to explain ethics. As Laurence Sterne remarked, his equations
"plussed or minussed you to heaven or hell . . . so that none but the expert mathema-
tician would ever be able to settle his accounts with Saint Peter." In 1725 one Francis
Hutchison devised an even more elaborate mathematical calculation on morality, and
without the advantages of modern technocracy, he was able to produce formulas fully
as intricate as any being worked out today.

With the founding of the École Polytechnique in Paris at the end of the eighteenth
century scientism was given another forward push; Saint-Simon and Auguste Comte
energized a formidable school with the promise of positivism. If man would only
apply the discipline of the natural sciences to the study of man, then only a sufficient
expenditure of time, money, and thought would separate him from the good society.

If only . . . In a hundred variations, this promise has been phrased and rephrased.
Yet one would gather from current exhortations that we are just about starting from
scratch just the same. Current literature is full of dawn-of-discovery analogies—Balboa
discovering the Pacific, Newton and the apple, etc. But it is precisely this figure of
thought, this sense of being on the frontier that gives scientism so tremendous an
appeal.

And for people in the commercial as well as the academic world. " 'SECOND IN-

DUSTRIAL REVOLUTION' TO FORCE MAJOR CHANGES IN PRODUCTION, MERCHANDISING, AND SELLING" headlined *Advertising Age* (October 5, 1953). E. B. Weiss, perhaps the best-known consultant in the merchandising field, explained to readers that it isn't simply that such advances as electronic calculators and automatic factories are going to make for more efficiency. A whole new science, he says, is abuilding, and with the confusion between control of the physical and control of the mental which is characteristic of believers in scientism, he proclaims that "The Second Industrial Revolution will substitute the machine for the common, and for some fairly uncommon functions of the human *mind*." It is not his contention, he says in qualification, "that the robot will replace *all* human endeavor." But almost all. After initial successes, such as cutting out the personal element in retail selling, making inventory-taking automatic, the machine will advance into hitherto sacrosanct areas, and with what seems unwonted relish, he cites a scientist's prophecy that in time the machine will replace man in the realm of reasoning and logical deduction. "NEXT WEEK: No. 2 in this series—How Cybernetic Principles Are Being and Will Be Applied in Factory, Office, and Warehouse."

The field of public relations is particularly susceptible. Here, for example, the *Public Relations Journal* editorializes on the subject:

> *Now, whether he knows it or not, every practicing public-relations man is an engineer too—a* social *engineer. He develops new relationships and operations in society, designs new organizations and institutions, sets up and lubricates the human machinery for getting things done. The challenge of social engineering in our time is like the challenge of technical engineering fifty years ago. If the first half of the twentieth century was the era of the technical engineers, the second half may well be the era of the social engineers.*

Dip into personnel journals, advertising trade journals, and you will find the same refrain. A lot of it is sheer malarkey, of course, but I think most of it is evidence of a genuine longing to be related to a faith.

We talk much about the alienation of the worker from the satisfaction of the whole job, but the same longing for a sense of continuity and purpose affects managerial people every bit as much. As our organizations have grown larger and more bureaucratic, they have created great layers of staff functions and the people in them often feel neither fish nor fowl—intellectuals, yet not of the intellectual world; managerial, yet without authority or prestige. Scientism, with its implications of the specialist as eventual savior, can give the frustrated a sense of purpose that cuts across organization and occupational lines. I do not believe I read into scientism a coherence that they themselves do not feel. No matter what branch of social engineering a man is engaged in—"mass" communication, "the engineering of consent," public relations, advertising, personnel counseling—he can feel himself part of a larger movement.

Their good will is overpowering. Thoreau once said if you see a man approach you with the obvious intent of doing you good, you should run for your life; it is hard to restrain the impulse in talking with social engineers. Theirs is not a mere limited desire to help out a bit with the scientific method; the vision that energizes them is total—and exclusive. Science is not merely a tool; it is the only path to salvation in a world where the laymen have gone mad. There is no justification, one angry social engineer writes, "in inflicting wounds on social scientists who might conceivably be blazing trails toward solutions of an otherwise hopeless crisis in civilization." If the techniques are faulty, and this they admit, that is a matter of unfinished detail and insufficient funds, not principles, and no one should criticize until he offers a counter-utopia himself.

One should not fall into the trap of equating social engineering with social science. Some social scientists do believe in social engineering but a great many do not, and the claims some make in the name of social science are a serious embarrassment to them. A pretty good case could be made that the field would be more productive were it now called social *studies*. The study of man and society is quite worthy enough an occupation without being saddled with the task of hammering out a finite, embracing science, and the ultimate test of a social scientist's particular way of looking at people cannot be absolute truth; only the arrogant—or the stupid—can so aspire.

Part of the trouble lies in our new-found ability to measure more precisely, and the idea that the successes of natural science were due in large measure to the objectiveness of the phenomena studied eludes social engineers. There are, of course, aspects of man's behavior that we can properly measure and we learn much by doing so. But how fascinating, alas, it all is! Here, it would seem, we can at last be rid of the bugbear of values. The median income level of a hundred selected families in an urban industrial universe correlates .76 with population density—not .78 or .61 but .76, and that's a fact. The next step beckons: having measured this far, it seems that there is nothing that can't be measured. We are purged of bias, and somehow by the sheer accumulation of such bias-free findings, we will have the basis of a theoretical formula that describes all. Just like physics.

In a pure example of scientism, psychologist James G. Miller has described how an institute could make this final integration.

> *In constructing theory, we can employ models from the physical sciences. All psychological phenomena are essentially naturalistic—that is, ultimately they can be translated into principles of physics. . . . By having individuals from different disciplines working closely together on both theory and research, communication between disciplines can be greatly improved. . . . If there are general principles running through them all, these are more likely to be discovered by groups from different fields working together, and in close communication, than by individuals working alone. . . . Another related possibility is the use throughout all theoretical work of what Bertalanffy has called "general system theory." This is the contention, developing from the unity of science movement, that every system—whether it be a strictly physical system like a dry cell, or an automobile; a biological system like a single nerve cell or organ; a total organism; or a society—has certain formal characteristics which make possible comparison of it with all others. Hence, generalizations about all systems are feasible. . . . Perhaps an over-all theory of behavior is too near the end of the rainbow to be reached; perhaps it is a will-o'-the-wisp. If so, our efforts may still be rewarded by the salvage of microtheories about limited areas.*

Let us assume, for the moment, that a precise science of man is not a will-o'-the-wisp and that we are on our way to achieving it. We are left with a knotty problem.

What do we do about good and evil, right and wrong? Believers in scientism confess that the question requires hard thinking. They are glad that ethical relativism has freed us from the narrow view that our own group's given values are the only correct ones. Obviously, then, a science of man could not freeze on one scheme of ethics. If we are to be governed by it, however, it would need some sort of ethics. How are we to determine just what they should be?

Social engineers have emboldened themselves to seek the final solution. Now, they say, we will *scientifically determine ethics*. This is to be done, in part, through the concept of "equilibrium." "How can we hope . . . to fix with assurity a particular class of behavior as right or good?" asks anthropologist Elliot Chapple. "From our point of view, this can be done by the use of the concept of equilibrium . . . hence good or bad, right or wrong, are comparable to the concept of health and medicine."

I have read definitions of many equilibrium concepts but I am still not sure just what they mean and I am not sure their creators do either; as far as can be determined, it is one of those mushy words so serviceable to obscuring contradictions. As Gunnar Myrdal, in explaining his own theoretical model in *An American Dilemma*, has pointed out, in borrowing the equilibrium notion from physics most social scientists have thought of only one kind of equilibrium, the *stable* equilibrium. This generally can lead to an acceptance of social harmony—either that of the status quo or some future one—and the companion terms such as disharmony, disequilibrium, maladjustment, disorganization, are by implication "bad" things.

This helps explain the bias against conflict that is so prevalent in most social-science literature. Where the by-products of harmony are the good things, the by-products of conflict—such as tension, frustration—are the bad things. Without taking the equally wrong position of saying that tension and frustration per se are good, one can point out that it takes a rather firm set of values to classify them as bad. Few social engineers would state categorically that they classify conflict as bad; nevertheless the practical gist of the ethics-of-equilibrium notion is that good values are values that allow groups to interact benevolently on one another and the individuals in them.

If we grant the concept of equilibrium we are still left with a formidable task in getting down to cases. How do we find what an organization's equilibrium is? If it isn't in it, how is it to be gotten there? If ethics is to be scientized, some specific people will have to do it, and some specific people are going to have to see to it the ethics are applied to society. Who, then, is to be in charge?

Being most of them democratically inclined, the new utopians take this question very seriously. If manipulating people is bad—and manipulation is one of the dirtiest words in the new lexicon—how can one justify the manipulation of people for good ends? At every convocation of believers the matter is dialectically treated, and the result of this soul-searching has been a new enrichment of the vocabulary. Though social engineers love to analyze semantic folly, no group has searched more arduously for the magic term which will combine manipulation with moral sanction. Thus we hear that the wielder of the new social techniques will be a "peace planner," a "group therapist," and "integrative leader," a "social diagnostician"—a person empowered to dominate society, but disciplined by a scientific code of ethics from using his knowledge in any but good ways.

In spelling this out social engineers characteristically shield themselves from the implication of their doctrine by describing how social engineering could be applied to a worthy cause. In a typical example, psychiatrist William Borberg explains how social engineering would be applied to the United Nations.

> *Now, the knowledge accumulated in the social sciences and the understanding of its possible value to the United Nations must of necessity be greater among the scientists themselves than among policy-making leaders and diplomats. I therefore wonder whether the social scientists might not consider the desirability of creating themselves an organ for the purpose of that relationship. . . . This would be one of the means by which we may gradually introduce into the thinking of policy-making leaders more and more scientific knowledge, scientific methods, and scientific mentality, and thus gradually substitute the present, essentially emotional basis for peace by a much better and much more reliable one, the scientific view of peace.*

As in other such suggested projects, the scientific elite is not supposed to give orders. Yet there runs through all of them a clear notion that questions of policy can be made somewhat nonpartisan by the application of science. There seems little recognition that the contributions of social science to policy-making can never go beyond staff work. Policy can never be scientific, and any social scientist who has risen to an administrative position has learned this quickly enough. Opinion, values, and debate are the heart of policy, and while fact can narrow down the realm of debate, it can do no more.

And what a terrible world it would be! Hell is no less hell for being antiseptic. In the 1984 of Big Brother one would at least know who the enemy was—a bunch of bad men who wanted power because they liked power. But in the other kind of 1984 one would be disarmed for not knowing who the enemy was, and when the day of reckoning came the people on the other side of the table wouldn't be Big Brother's bad henchmen; they would be a mild-looking group of therapists who, like the Grand Inquisitor, would be doing what they did to help you.

But such a specter is not the consequence of scientism that should preoccupy us. It's not merely that social engineers have no such vision in mind—they don't; the point is that they couldn't pull it off if they did. Curiously, many who have warned most urgently of the horrors of a scientific utopia are themselves awed by scientism; their fears are based on the premise that it can work. Science-fiction writers, perhaps our most vigorous moralists, often seem to say that what would be wrong would be *too much* scientism, and even those dead set against it appear impressed with the possibility of its dominance. Some European critics of America have gone them one better. They say it has already happened. If anybody wants to see man crushed by science and mechanization, it appears he has only to take a trip to the U.S. The latest such critic, Robert Jungk, draws a picture of white-coated men around UNIVAC, and docile robots listening to piped music. *Tomorrow*, he warns, *is already here.*

That kind of tomorrow isn't here and it probably never will be. The implied choice between science and humanity is a false one. The danger is not in science dominating man, and the fears of this rest on a false personalization of the inanimate, not to mention a romantic, if retrograde, longing for a past utopia. Nor need the specter of a scientific elite worry us. It need not worry us because a "science of man" cannot work in the way it believers think it can, and in subsequent chapters I hope to demonstrate how naïve some of the current techniques are.

But the gospel of scientism is no less important for that reason. To stretch a point, the trouble is not so much that these techniques work, but that they *do not* work. Schemes that don't work can have as much effect on society as schemes that do. Machiavellian rules ask one to compromise, in this case, on one's ethics. But at least they can work, and if we sell our souls we get some satisfying sin in recompense. Scientism asks that we make a compromise, but it can't deliver anything really in return. The scientific formulas for "mass communication," for example: using them we manage to debase our prose, assault our instincts, and insult our listeners—but never do we get that sure-fire communion promised for our surrender. A poor bargain.

What I am arguing is that the real impact of scientism is upon our values. The danger, to put it another way, is not man being dominated but man surrendering. At the present writing there is not one section of American life that has not drunk deeply of the promise of scientism. It appears in many forms—pedagogy, aptitude tests, that monstrous nonentity called "mass communication"—and there are few readers who have not had a personal collision with it.

## BELONGINGNESS

What kind of society is to be engineered? Some critics of social engineering are sure that what is being cooked up for us is a socialistic paradise, a radically new, if not brave, world, alien to every tradition of man. This is wrong. Lump together the social engineers' prescriptions for the new society and you find they are anything but radical. Boiled down, what they ask for is an environment in which everyone is tightly knit into a belongingness with one another; one in which there is no restless wandering but rather the deep emotional security that comes from total integration with the group. Radical? It is like nothing so much as the Middle Ages.

And what, some have been asking, was so wrong with the Middle Ages anyway? They had excellent human relations. They didn't have the self-consciousness about their society to make them rationalize it or the scientific approach with which to do it. But belongingness they had. They knew where they stood—peasant and noble alike. They saw the fruit of their labor, and the tiny world about them protected as well as demanded. Psychologically, they had a home.

Not that we should go back to all this, mind you. The job, to paraphrase, is to *re-create* the belongingness of the Middle Ages. What with the Enlightenment, the Industrial Revolution, and other calamities, the job is immensely more difficult than it was in those simpler days. But with new scientific techniques we can solve the problem. What we must do is to learn consciously to achieve what once came naturally. We must form an elite of skilled leaders who will guide men back, benevolently, to group belongingness.

An unfair paraphrase? The young men who enthuse so unqualifiedly about human relations as the last best hope would be shocked to be accused of holding so reactionary a view. The people who have been the intellectual founders of the human-relations gospel, however, have not been so muddy-minded. They were not the cheery optimists their latter-day followers seem to be; they were rather pessimistic about the capacities of man, and the society they prescribed was by no means a utopia which would be all things to all men. A man would have to make sacrifices to enjoy it, and the prophets of belongingness stated this with admirable toughness of mind.

The father of the human-relations school is Elton Mayo. Mayo, professor of industrial research at the Harvard Business School, was concerned with the anomie, or rootlessness, of the industrial worker. Ever since he first started studying industry in Australia in 1903 he had been looking for a way to reconcile the worker's need for belongingness with the conflicting allegiances of the complex would he now finds himself in.

For Mayo, and his colleagues, the great turning point came as the result of what started to be a very modest experiment. In 1927 some of Mayo's colleagues began the now celebrated study at the Hawthorne, Illinois, plant of Western Electric. The company had a challenging problem for them. For several years it had been trying to measure how much more telephone equipment the workers would produce as lighting was improved in the rooms they worked in. The researchers chose three rooms and progressively increased the illumination in each, at the same time keeping a careful record of the work output. To their surprise, there seemed no clear relation between production and better illumination. They tried a more careful experiment: this time they would use only two rooms, one a "control" group where conditions would be left the same and the experimental room where the changes would be introduced. Again, mixed results: output went up in the experimental room—but so did it go up in the control room.

At this point the Harvard group entered the picture and collaborated with the company on a more elaborate experiment: in a "relay assembly" test room they isolated a group of women operators from others doing the same work and one by one introduced changes—not only lighting, but changes in rest periods, hours, and economic incentives. According to the commonly accepted "scientific management principles" earlier advanced by Frederick Taylor, these changes in physical conditions and, most particularly, incentives would make the test group more productive than the other. But they didn't. As experiment followed experiment (the research was to continue until 1932) it became abundantly clear that physical changes were not the key. As in the earlier experiments, output did shoot ahead where conditions were changed, but so did output shoot ahead where no changes had been made.

How come? The researchers came to the conclusion that output shot up in both groups because in both groups the workers' participation had been solicited and this involvement, clearly, was more important than physical perquisites. The workers were a social system; the system was informal but it was what really determined the worker's attitude toward his job. This social system could work against management, but if the managers troubled themselves to understand the system and its functions for the worker, the system could work for management.

In the literature of human relations the Hawthorne experiment is customarily regarded as a discovery. In large part it was; more than any other event, it dramatized the inadequacy of the purely economic view of man. The conclusions that flowed from the experiment, however, were a good bit more than a statement of objective fact, for Mayo and his group were evangelists as well as researchers. He had come to quite similar conclusions many years before, and for him the Hawthorne experiment did not reveal so much as confirm.

The two slim books Mayo published since Hawthorne have proved to be an immensely powerful manifesto. Mayo never pretended that he was free from values and he frankly presents an argument as well as a diagnosis. In *The Social Problems of an Industrial Civilization,* he opens his case by picturing man's happiness in more primitive times. "Historically and traditionally our fathers worked for social cooperation—and achieved it. This is true also of any primitive society. But we, for at least a century of the most amazing scientific and material progress, have abandoned the effort—by inadvertence, it is true—and we are now reaping the consequences."

In the Middle Ages people had been disciplined by social codes into working well together. The Industrial Revolution, as Mayo described the consequences, had split society into a whole host of conflicting groups. Part of a man belonged to one group, part to another, and he was bewildered; no longer was there *one* group in which he could sublimate himself. The liberal philosophers, who were quite happy to see an end to feudal belongingness, interpreted this release from the group as freedom. Mayo does not see it this way. To him, the dominant urge of mankind is to belong: "Man's desire to be continuously associated in work with his fellows," he states, "is a strong, if not the strongest, human characteristic."

Whether the urge to co-operate is in fact man's most dominant drive, it does not follow that the co-operation is necessarily good. What is he going to co-operate *about*? What ends is the group working toward? But these questions do not greatly interest Mayo, and he seems to feel that the sheer fact of "spontaneous" co-operation carries its own ethic. "For *all* of us," Mayo states, "the feeling of security and certainty derives *always* from assured membership of a group." (Italics mine.)

Suppose there is a conflict between the individual and the group? Mayo sees conflict primarily as a breakdown in communication. If a man is unhappy or dissatisfied in his work, it is not that there is a conflict to be resolved so much as a misunderstanding to be cleared up. The worker might not see it this way, and most certainly the unions do not, but we have already been told that the individual is a nonlogical animal incapable of rationally solving his own problems or, in fact, of recognizing what the problem is.

At this point the human relations doctrine comes perilously close to demanding that the individual sacrifice his own beliefs that he may belong. The only way to escape this trap would be through the notion that by the process of equilibrium, a clarification of which never seems to detain anyone very long, what's good for the group is good for the individual. In speaking of the primitive group Mayo writes, "The situation is not simply that the society exercises a forceful compulsion on the individual; on the contrary, the social code and the desire of the individual are, for all practical purposes, identical. Every member of the group participates in all social activities because it is his chief desire to do so."

How to get back to this idyllic state? Mayo does not recommend a return to the Middle Ages. Too much water—and damn muddy water too, if you ask Mayo—has flowed under the bridge for that. The goal must be "an *adaptive* society"—a society in which we can once again enjoy the belongingness of primitive times but without the disadvantages of them.

This won't come about naturally. What with the mischief caused by the philosophers of individualism, most contemporary leaders are untrained in the necessary social skill to bring the adaptive society to pass. What is needed is an administrative elite, people trained to recognize that what man really wants most is group solidarity even if he does not realize it himself. They won't push him around; they won't even argue with him—unfettered as they will be of "prejudice and emotion," they won't have any philosophy, other than co-operation, to argue about. They will adjust him. Through the scientific application of human relations, these neutralist technicians will guide him into satisfying solidarity with the group so skillfully and unobtrusively that he will scarcely realize how the benefaction has been accomplished.

When Mayo got down to cases he was entirely consistent with his philosophy. His advocacy of "nondirective counseling" is a good case in point. In the course of their interviewing at Hawthorne, Mayo and his colleagues became impressed with the therapeutic effects the interviews had on the workers and went on to make the interview a management tool. The idea was to have a group of counselors who would be paid by management but who would not report to management what the workers said to them when they spilled their troubles. Since the workers knew this they could feel free to talk out their problems.

Implicit in this technique is the assumption that the worker's problems can indeed be *talked out*. He is to adjust to the group rather than vice versa; and the alternative of actually changing reality is hardly considered. If a worker is sore at his foreman the chances are good that he is not really sore at the foreman because of some rational gripe but is merely venting on the foreman certain repressed feelings. By listening patiently, like a psychiatrist, the counselor helps such persons understand that what they are really sore about flows from inner, subjective conflict. Characteristically, Mayo cites a woman worker who "discovered for herself during an interview that her dislike of a certain supervisor was based upon a fancied resemblance to a detested stepfather."

In similar cases it is possible the worker might not be maladjusted at all. The foreman might have been dividing up the work load problem badly, and maybe he had a few syndromes himself. The nondirective counseling idea, however, pooh-poohs the possibility: if there is a conflict of values that can't be talked out the interview has no provision in it for action to be taken—the setup itself, in short, is a value judgment that adjustment, rather than change, is the desideratum.

For a number of reasons, one being the hostility of the unions to it, the nondirective counseling system as such has never taken hold of the American industry. But the basic idea has. As I hope to demonstrate in later chapters, many of the more popular techniques—such as psychological "personality" testing, conference techniques—are all manifestations of the same principle. The rock is the group and maladjustment is disharmony with it.

Ironically, the primary target of this adjustment has become the managers themselves. While Mayo intended human relations to apply to the workers and managers both, the managers first seized on it as an excellent tool for manipulating the workers into a chronic contentment that would turn them away from the unions. But manipulation is a two-edged weapon; having learned how illogical workers were, managerial pioneers of human relations soon began to ponder the fact that their colleagues weren't so logical either. They needed to belong too—and even more than the worker, for more of their life was involved in the organization. Looking at the neuroses about him, many a progressive young organization man resolved that here, not on the shop floor, was the place that needed human relations most.

The use of psychological tests, if I may get a bit ahead of my story, is symptomatic. Originally, they were introduced by the managers as a tool for weeding out unqualified workers. As time went on, and personality tests were added to aptitude tests, the managers began using them on other managers, present and prospective, and today most personality testing is directed not at the worker, but at the organization man. If he is being hoist, it is by his own philosophy.

Not so long after Mayo and his colleagues documented the importance of the group at Hawthorne, a former student of Mayo's, anthropologist Lloyd Warner, began coming to remarkably similar conclusions in a study of a New England town. This study, which has had a tremendous impact on social science, was an impressively large-scale undertaking in which some twenty researchers spent three years making a study of Newburyport, Massachusetts. Every conceivable fact about Newburyport was to be dug up, and through scientific evaluations, some objective conclusions were to be arrived at.

Several years before, Warner had studied a tribe of Australian aborigines and had been immensely impressed by the way in which the tribal customs and the unwritten laws kept the individual in harmony with the group. The rituals and sanctions seemed illogical at times, but they shielded man from the kind of individual decisions which a fast-changing industrial society could overwhelm him with.

When Warner began poking around Newburyport, he discovered strong parallels. It was a venerable old New England town rich in tradition and full of people with a strong attachment to the past. There were Memorial Day celebrations instead of the Nurngin totem rites, but in many ways it seemed much the same, and Warner drew the same moral. Of the many conclusions that came out of the study, by all odds the most important finding was the function of social structure in fixing the individual in a satisfying relation to the society. Newburyport did not present altogether as happy a picture of stability as a medieval or primitive society would have. Even though it had been touched by the Industrial Revolution, however, it did provide excellent grist for Warner's argument that the happiness of man depended on the rootedness in a stable group. Like several other old communities, it had lost the economic basis of its early prosperity and thus was frozen somewhat in the mold of previous times.

Warner saw, and charted, seven class divisions in Newburyport, and from these generalized a concept of class and status for the country as a whole. The concept has long since been subjected to a thoroughgoing critical analysis by many social scientists; suffice it to say here that Warner's description carried with it a strong note of advocacy. Warner did believe that there should be some mobility between classes and he thought it healthy that a number of people could move up from, say, the upper-middle to the lower-upper. But not *too* many. The class structure would become meaningless in that case, and people would become bewildered for lack of a firm group to relate themselves to.

Conflict, change, fluidity—these are the evils from which man should be insulated. To Warner, the unconscious yearning for belongingness was all-important. During the time he and his associates were at Newburyport, the workers in the shoe factory there went on strike. Ostensibly, the strike was over economic matters; the workers thought they wanted more money. But Warner and his colleagues saw it another way. They saw so many other factors that they produced a book on the subject (called, somewhat flatly, *The Social System of the Modern Factory*). The real cause of the strike, the book implies, was not so much the economic plight of the workers as the social one. Back in the eighteen-hundreds they had enjoyed the status that comes from a firm hierarchy of skills and there had been the steadying hand of the paternal local capitalists. But now increased mechanization, while not rampant in the shoe industry, had down-graded the old high-status jobs; equally unfortunate, the absentee ownership of "Big City capitalism" had supplanted the local oligarcy. Whether they knew it or not, in short, the workers struck because the cohesive society of old had broken down.

Someday someone is going to create a stir by proposing a radical new tool for the study of people. It will be called the face-value technique. It will be based on the premise that people often do what they do for the reasons they think they do. The use of this technique would lead to many pitfalls, for it is undeniably true that people do not always act logically or say what they mean. But I wonder if it would produce findings any more unscientific than the opposite course.

That strike at Newburyport, for example. Warner did devote a couple of sentences to the logical, economic factors, but it's clear in reading the other three hundred pages that he feels that the real cause lay in the fact that there was no longer any "hierarchy of skills" that used to give workers a sense of satisfaction and status. Well, maybe so, but most of the workers who struck didn't happen to have been around to remember the idyllic days of old described by Warner, and it is somewhat debatable if they would have liked them quite as much as Warner seems to believe they would. As far as I can gather from a careful reading of Warner's account of it, the workers acted with eminent logic. They wanted more money; the employers didn't want to give it to them; the workers banded together in strike, and the employers gave in. Is it so very naïve, then, to explain this strike as very much of an economic matter? Any more naïve than to attribute it to a nostalgia for ancient paternalism? Who has the nostalgia?

In fairness to Warner, it should be pointed out that he has subsequently been coming to the view that there is more mobility than Newburyport would suggest. His followers, however, have not been so flexible, and the Warner thesis, for all the defections of its author, remains a very powerful force. Among educators in particular it is one of the principal ideological bases for the belief that only a segment of society should be schooled in the humanities. The majority, goes the idea, should be taught lesser skills; rather than tantalize themselves with aspirations, they should adjust to the fact of a fairly fixed social system.

Neither Warner nor Mayo had much enthusiasm for the union as a social group;

in Mayo's case it split loyalties in the factory scheme of things; in Warner's case it split the loyalties of the stable, fixed, small community. It could be argued, however, that if workers needed an embracing group the union had as much right to be it as any other group. Which brings us to the third variation on belongingness—the proposition of Frank Tannenbaum. Unlike Mayo, he is the father of no school; he is an historian rather than a labor leader. But his views are well worth examining all the same; they may not be symptomatic of labor thought but they are symptomatic of the growing quest for belongingness.

In the opening pages of Tannenbaum's *A Philosophy of Labor* (New York: Knopf, 1951) there is the customary salute to the Middle Ages.

> *Membership in a guild, manorial estate, or village protected man throughout his life and gave him the peace and serenity from which could flow the medieval art and craft. The life of man was a nearly unified whole. Being a member of an integrated society protected and raised the dignity of the individual and gave each person his own special role. Each man, each act, was part of a total life drama, the plot of which was known and in which the part allotted to each was prescribed. No one was isolated or abandoned. His individuality and his ambitions were fulfilled within the customary law that ruled the community to which he belonged.*

Then came the Industrial Revolution and paradise lost.

> *The Industrial Revolution destroyed the solid moorings of an older way of life and cast the helpless workers adrift in a strange and difficult world. The peasant who had been reared in the intimacy of a small village . . . now found himself isolated and bewildered in a city crowded with strangers and indifferent to a common rule. The symbolic universe that had patterned the ways of men across the ages in village, manor, or guild had disappeared. This is the great moral tragedy of the industrial system.*

To make matters worse, Tannenbaum continues, the philosophers of the enlightenment rationalized this breakdown of the old society in terms of individualism. "This doctrine gave the social disintegration then taking place a moral purpose. . . . In its extreme form the theory seemed to advance the idea that the best society was that in which organized human relations and responsibilities were least."

As Tannenbaum rightly points out, this doctrine of self-sufficiency was all very fine for the *bourgeoisie*, but for the workers, self-sufficiency was an illusion. In learning this, however, the workers were taking the first steps to recreating a community. In making them recognize their individual helplessness, the employers made them recognize their common strength. "The trade-union," as Tannenbaum says, "was the visible evidence that man is not a commodity, and that he is not sufficient unto himself."

The kind of sufficiency Tannenbalm is most concerned with is social rather than economic, and thus to him the real promise of the unions lay in their potential as a social unit. But the workers, no less affected by the Protestant Ethic than their employers, had too pressing an agenda to be diverted from bread-and-butter economic matters. Thus, in fighting the unions, the employers were diverting the unions' ener-gies from the ultimate goal. And the employers didn't do it just to save money; they resisted unionization "because a society tends to become an all-embracing way of life."

Now, however, Tannenbaum argues that the unions are at last in a position to be-come instruments of "governance" rather than instruments of war. "Only when the battle for recognition is finished can the institutional role come into its own. If the trade-union could not fulfill its larger responsibilities, it would have no reason for existence, would not be a true society, would have no moral role, and would dis-integrate." The true end, then, is for a society in which the worker, like his ancestors in the Middle Ages, will be firmly rooted in a group with customs, laws, and guides. He will lose his mobility—not for him the upward—and individual—path to the managerial world; the "fluidity," both geographic and social, that we will see in sub-urbia is precisely the thing Tannenbaum wants to insulate man from. And the trend away from fluidity is not to be denied. "Institutionally the trade-union movement is an unconscious effort to harness the drift of our time and reorganize it around the cohesive identity that men working together always achieve. That is why the trade-union is a repudiation of the individualism of the French Revolution and the liberal-ism of English utilitarian philosophers."

Tannenbaum seems to be working the other side of the street from Mayo and Warner. But while they are truer to the medieval spirit in wanting the nobility rather than the serfs to be in charge, the outlook is the same. Any dispute is merely juris-dictional; they don't agree on *which* group should do the embracing but they are all of a piece on the idea the embracing should be done—although not by the state, for that would be totalitarian.

I do not mean to deprecate study of the function of groups. One can study some-thing without deifying it, and a recognition that a society can be all embracing doesn't require belief that it should be. The most vigorous criticism of the human-relations doctrine has come from social scientists, and most of them have by no means been uninterested in the power of the group or its value. However one differs with the findings of particular studies, the point at issue should be the findings, not the fact of the studies. An obvious point perhaps, but there does seem too little middle ground between the near-evangelical acceptance of social-science research on the one hand, and the damnation of it as the improper study of mankind because its particulars are found wanting.

Nor do values mar it; the point is to recognize the values that we may judge them. Mayo made his quite explicit, and in fairness to him and the other pioneers of human relations, we must remember the prevailing climate of opinion at the time; as John Dewey was to authoritarian education, so they were to authoritarian indus-try. Mayo emphasized group cohesiveness and administrative social skill so much be-cause he felt—with considerable justification—that Americans had been slighting these matters. At a time when the people in charge of big organizations clung to the mechanistic views of the efficiency experts, Mayo brought a badly needed shift in perspective; he helped sensitize a steady stream of influential management people to the importance of the whole vast informal network beneath them and the necessity of comprehending it. One does not have to go along with Mayo's philosophy of the adaptive society to recognize the benefits in better management that he helped bring about.

But what was once counter-cyclical is now orthodoxy. Already human relations is a standard part of the curriculum of the business schools and it will not be very long before it is standard in the high schools too. Human relations can mean a lot of things—as one critic defines it, it is any study called human relations to escape the discipline of established theory in the appropriate field. But, generally speaking, most human-relations doctrine is pointed toward the vision of Mayo, and this reinforces what many people are already very well prepared to believe.

Particularly, the organization man. Who is the hero in human relations? In the older ideology, it was the top leader who was venerated. In human relations it is the organization man, and thus the quasi-religious overtones with which he gratefully endows it. The older ideology provided an unsatisfactory view of the system for the large and growing bureaucratic slice of management. The human-relations doctrine, however, not only tells them that they are important, but that they are the key figures. As sociologist Reinhard Bendix has observed, in the new managerial ideology, it is not the leaders of industry that are idealized—if anything, they are scolded—but the lieutenants. The people that the workers are to co-operate with are not the top employers but enlightened bureaucrats.

At times it almost seems that human relations is a revolutionary tool the organization man is to use *against* the bosses. Listen to an unreconstructed boss give a speech castigating unreconstructed bosses for not being more enlightened about human relations, and you get the feeling the speech is a subtle form of revenge on the part of the harried underling who wrote it. For reasons of protocol, organization men publicly extol human relations for the beneficial effects it casts downward, but privately they spend most of their time talking about using it upward. Whenever there is responsible criticism of human relations, there is a hurt response from middle management staff people, and, invariably, the complaint boils down to something like this: Why, why hurt us? Many of the criticisms are true all right—some people have gone haywire on this—but we progressives have a tough enough fight converting the reactionaries on top, and any criticism at this time only gives aid and comfort to them.

It is not an easy complaint to answer—many older executives are indeed reactionary and many are against human relations for strange reasons. What makes the complaint particularly tough to answer, however, is the trusting way organization men assume that only techniques are subject for criticism and that surely the goals must be noncontroversial. They thought that battle was won long ago. So it was. If I do not dwell more in this book on the beneficial aspects of human relations, it is because they have been reiterated quite enough already.

In practice, of course, corporations have not changed their ways quite so much as their self-congratulations on human relations suggest, and many a highly publicized program is only a sugar-coating of the mixture as before. Because there remains a divergence between precept and practice, however, does not mean that precept is any the less important. While older men may appropriate the vocabulary of human relations without the underlying philosophy, the younger men believe. They have had an indoctrination their superiors did not, and though experience may disillusion them somewhat they view the day of their ascension with genuine missionary zeal.

The point I am trying to make is not that the corporation, or any other specific kind of organization, is going to be *the* citadel of belongingness. The union of Frank Tannenbaum, the community of Lloyd Warner, the corporation of Elton Mayo —each is in conflict as to which group is going to furnish the vital belongingness, and these three by no means exhaust the roster of groups proposed. Spokesmen in other areas have similarly bewailed the lack of an encompassing, integrated life, and in an excess of good will have asked that their group take over the whole messy job. Many a contemporary prescription for utopia can be summarized if you cross out the name of one group and substitute another in the following charge: Society has broken down; the family, the church, the community, the schools, business—each has failed to give the individual the belongingness he needs and thus it is now the task of——group to do the job. It is fortunate there are so many groups; with such competition for the individual psyche it is difficult for any one of them to land the franchise.

But ideologically these pleas do not cancel each other out. For there is always the common thread that a man must belong and that he must be unhappy if he does not belong rather completely. The idea that conflicting allegiances safeguard him as well as abrade him is sloughed over, and for the people who must endure the tensions of independence there is no condolence; only the message that the tensions are sickness—either in themselves or in society. It does not make any difference whether the Good Society is to be represented by a union or by a corporation or by a church; it is to be a society unified and purged of conflict.

To turn about and preach that conflicting allegiances are absolute virtues is not justified either. But at this particular time the function they perform in the maintenance of individual freedom is worthy of more respect. Clark Kerr, Chancellor of the University of California, at Berkeley, has put it well:

> *The danger is not that loyalties are divided today but that they may be undivided tomorrow. . . . I would urge each individual to avoid total involvement in any organization; to seek to whatever extent lies within his power to limit each group to the minimum control necessary for performance of essential functions; to struggle against the effort to absorb; to lend his energies to many organizations and give himself completely to none; to teach children, in the home and in the school, "to be laws to themselves and to depend on themselves," as Walt Whitman urged us many years ago—for that is the well source of the independent spirit.*

## ᵉ§ THE HIDDEN PERSUADERS

*Vance Packard*

*The problem raised by this selection will be only too familiar to every
reader. The economy of every industrial nation in the world, whether
capitalist or socialist, is becoming increasingly dependent upon advertising
in some form or other. And advertisers in turn can hardly be expected
to ignore the rapidly expanding body of knowledge about the workings
of the human mind. Clearly, the implications for politics and social life
in general are profound, so much so, in fact, that no one today even
claims to see bottom.*

*One result is that, ever since David Riesman's* The Lonely Crowd *(1950),
Americans—who in this as in other respects seem only one step ahead
of the rest of the world—have become a nation of amateur sociologists,
eagerly drinking in each new revelation of some aspect of our collective
psyche. Since the publication of* The Hidden Persuaders *in 1957, Vance
Packard has written three more successful books in the same genre:* The
Status Seekers *(1959),* The Waste Makers *(1960), and* The Pyramid
Climbers *(1962).*

### 1. THE DEPTH APPROACH

This book is an attempt to explore a strange and rather exotic new area of American
life. It is about the way many of us are being influenced and manipulated—far more
than we realize—in the patterns of our everyday lives. Large-scale efforts are being
made, often with impressive success, to channel our unthinking habits, our purchasing decisions, and our thought processes by the use of insights gleaned from psychiatry and the social sciences. Typically these efforts take place beneath our level
of awareness; so that the appeals which move us are often, in a sense, "hidden."

Some of the manipulating being attempted is simply amusing. Some of it is disquieting, particularly when viewed as a portent of what may be ahead on a more intensive and effective scale for us all. Co-operative scientists have come along providentially to furnish some awesome tools.

The use of mass psychoanalysis to guide campaigns of persuasion has become

*The Hidden Persuaders* (New York: David McKay Company, Inc., 1957), pp. 3–7, 13–23,
255–266.

the basis of a multimillion-dollar industry. Professional persuaders have seized upon it in their groping for more effective ways to sell us their wares—whether products, ideas, attitudes, candidates, goals, or states of mind.

This depth approach to influencing our behavior is being used in many fields and is employing a variety of ingenious techniques. It is being used most extensively to affect our daily acts of consumption. The sale to us of billions of dollars' worth of United States products is being significantly affected, if not revolutionized, by this approach, which is still only barely out of its infancy. Two thirds of America's hundred largest advertisers have geared campaigns to this depth approach by using strategies inspired by what marketers call "motivation analysis."

Meanwhile, many of the nation's leading public-relations experts have been indoctrinating themselves in the lore of psychiatry and the social sciences in order to increase their skill at "engineering" our consent to their propositions. Fund raisers are turning to the depth approach to wring more money from us. A considerable and growing number of our industrial concerns (including some of the largest) are seeking to sift and mold the behavior of their personnel—particularly their own executives—by using psychiatric and psychological techniques. Finally, this depth approach is showing up nationally in the professional politicians' intensive use of symbol manipulation and reiteration on the voter, who more and more is treated like Pavlov's conditioned dog.

The efforts of the persuaders to probe our everyday habits for hidden meanings are often interesting purely for the flashes of revelation they offer us of ourselves. We are frequently revealed, in their findings, as comical actors in a genial if twitchy Thurberian world. The findings of the depth probers provide startling explanations for many of our daily habits and perversities. It seems that our subconscious can be pretty wild and unruly.

What the probers are looking for, of course, are the *whys* of our behavior, so that they can more effectively manipulate our habits and choices in their favor. This has led them to probe why we are afraid of banks; why we love those big fat cars; why we really buy homes; why men smoke cigars; why the kind of car we draw reveals the brand of gasoline we will buy; why housewives typically fall into a hypnoidal trance when they get into a supermarket; why men are drawn into auto showrooms by convertibles but end up buying sedans; why junior loves cereal that pops, snaps, and crackles.

We move from the genial world of James Thurber into the chilling world of George Orwell and his Big Brother, however, as we explore some of the extreme attempts at probing and manipulating now going on.

Certain of the probers, for example, are systematically feeling out our hidden weaknesses and frailties in the hope that they can more efficiently influence our behavior. At one of the largest advertising agencies in America psychologists on the staff are probing sample humans in an attempt to find how to identify, and beam messages to, people of high anxiety, body consciousness, hostility, passiveness, and so on. A Chicago advertising agency has been studying the housewife's menstrual cycle and its psychological concomitants in order to find the appeals that will be more effective in selling her certain food products.

Seemingly, in the probing and manipulating nothing is immune or sacred. The same Chicago ad agency has used psychiatric probing techniques on little girls. Public-relations experts are advising churchmen how they can become more effective manipulators of their congregations. In some cases these persuaders even choose our friends for us, as at a large "community of tomorrow" in Florida. Friends are furnished along with the linen by the management in offering the homes for sale. Everything comes in one big, glossy package.

Somber examples of the new persuaders in action are appearing not only in merchandising but in politics and industrial relations. The national chairman of a political party indicated his merchandising approach to the election of 1956 by talking of his candidates as products to sell. In many industrial concerns now the administrative personnel are psychoanalyzed, and their futures all charted, by trained outside experts. And then there is the trade school in California that boasts to employers that it socially engineers its graduates so that they are, to use the phrase of an admiring trade journal, "custom-built men" guaranteed to have the right attitudes from the employer's standpoint.

What the persuaders are trying to do in many cases was well summed up by one of their leaders, the president of the Public Relations Society of America, when he said in an address to members: "The stuff with which we work is the fabric of men's minds." In many of their attempts to work over the fabric of our minds the professional persuaders are receiving direct help and guidance from respected social scientists. Several social-science professors at Columbia University, for example, took part in a seminar at the university attended by dozens of New York public-relations experts. In the seminar one professor, in a sort of chalk talk, showed these manipulators precisely the types of mental manipulation they could attempt with most likelihood of success.

All this probing and manipulation has its constructive and its amusing aspects; but also, I think it fair to say, it has seriously antihumanistic implications. Much of it seems to represent regress rather than progress for man in his long struggle to become a rational and self-guiding being. Something new, in fact, appears to be entering the pattern of American life with the growing power of our persuaders.

In the imagery of print, film, and air wave the typical American citizen is commonly depicted as an uncommonly shrewd person. He or she is dramatized as a thoughtful voter, rugged individualist, and, above all, as a careful, hardheaded consumer of the wondrous products of American enterprise. He is, in short, the flowering of twentieth-century progress and enlightenment.

Most of us like to fit ourselves into this picture, and some of us surely are justified in doing so. The men and women who hold up these glowing images, particularly the professional persuaders, typically do so, however, with tongue in cheek. The way these persuaders—who often refer to themselves good-naturedly as "symbol manipulators"—see us in the quiet of their interoffice memos, trade journals, and shop talk is frequently far less flattering, if more interesting. Typically they see us as bundles of daydreams, misty hidden yearnings, guilt complexes, irrational emotional blockages. We are image lovers given to impulsive and compulsive acts. We annoy them with our seemingly senseless quirks, but we please them with our growing docility in responding to their manipulation of symbols that stir us to action. They have found the supporting evidence for this view persuasive enough to encourage them to turn to depth channels on a large scale in their efforts to influence our behavior. . . .

## 2. THE TROUBLE WITH PEOPLE

The trend in marketing to the depth approach was largely impelled by difficulties the marketers kept encountering in trying to persuade Americans to buy all the products their companies could fabricate.

One particularly disturbing difficulty was the apparent perversity and unpredictability of the prospective customers. Marketers repeatedly suffered grievous losses in campaigns that by all the rules of logic should have succeeded. The marketers felt increasing dissatisfaction with their conventional methods for sizing up a market. These methods were known in the trade most commonly as "nose-counting." Under nose-counting, statistic-minded interviewers would determine the percentage of married women, ages twenty-one to thirty-five, in Omaha, Nebraska, who said they wanted, and would buy, a three-legged stove if it cost no more than $249.

The trouble with this approach, they found, was that what people might tell interviewers had only a remote bearing on how the people would actually behave in a buying situation when confronted with a three-legged stove or almost anything else.

Gradually many perceptive marketers began becoming suspicious of three basic assumptions they had made, in their efforts to be logical, concerning the predictable behavior of human beings, especially customers.

First, they decided, you can't assume that people know what they want.

A major ketchup maker kept getting complaints about its bottle, so it made a survey. Most of the people interviewed said they would prefer another type the company was considering. When the company went to the expense of bringing out this other bottle in test markets, it was overwhelmingly rejected in favor of the old bottle, even by people who had favored it in interviews. In a survey of male beer drinkers the men expressed a strong preference for a "nice dry beer." Whey they were then asked how a beer could be dry they were stumped. Those who were able to offer any answers at all revealed widely different notions.

Second, some marketers concluded, you can't assume people will tell you the truth about their wants and dislikes even if they know them. What you are more likely to get, they decided, are answers that will protect the informants in their steadfast endeavor to appear to the world as really sensible, intelligent, rational beings. One management consulting firm has concluded that accepting the word of a customer as to what he wants is "the least reliable index the manufacturer can have on what he ought to do to win customers."

The Advertising Research Foundation took magazines to task for asking people what magazines they read frequently, and naïvely accepting the answers given as valid. The people, it contended, are likely to admit reading only magazines of high prestige value. One investigator suggests that if you seriously accepted people's answers you might assume that *Atlantic Monthly* is America's most-read magazine and some of the confession magazines the least read; whereas actually the confession magazines in question may have twenty times the readership of *Atlantic Monthly.*

A brewery making two kinds of beer made a survey to find what kind of people drank each beer, as a guide to its merchandisers. It asked people known to favor its general brand name: "Do you drink the light or the regular?" To its astonishment it found people reporting they drank light over the regular by better than three to one. The truth of the matter was that for years the company, to meet consumer demand, had been brewing nine times as much regular beer as light beer. It decided that in asking people that question it was in effect asking: Do you drink the kind preferred by people of refinement and discriminating taste, or do you just drink the regular stuff?

The Color Research Institute conducted an experiment after it began suspecting the reliability of people's comments. Women while waiting for a lecture had the choice of two waiting rooms. One was a functional modern chamber with gentle tones. It had been carefully designed for eye ease and to promote a relaxed feeling. The other room was a traditional room filled with period furniture, oriental rugs, expensive-looking wallpaper.

It was found that virtually all the women instinctively went into the Swedish modern room to do their waiting. Only when every chair was filled did the women start to overflow into the more ornate room. After the lecture the ladies were asked "Which of those two rooms do you like the better?" They looked thoughtfully at the two rooms, and then 84 per cent of them said the period room was the nicer room.

In another case the institute asked a group of people if they borrowed money from personal-loan companies. Every person said no. Some of them virtually shouted their answer. The truth was that all those selected for interviewing were people who were listed in the records of a local loan company as borrowers.

Psychologists at the McCann-Erickson advertising agency asked a sampling of people why they didn't buy one client's product—kippered herring. The main reason the people gave under direct questioning was that they just didn't like the taste of kippers. More persistent probing however uncovered the fact that 40 per cent of the people who said they didn't like the taste of kippers had never, in their entire lives, tasted kippers!

Finally, the marketers decided it is dangerous to assume that people can be trusted to behave in a rational way.

The Color Research Institute had what it felt was a startling encounter with this proneness to irrationality when it tested package designs for a new detergent. It was testing to see if a woman is influenced more than she realizes, in her opinion of a product, by the package. It gave the housewives three different boxes filled with detergent and requested that they try them all out for a few weeks and then report which was the best for delicate clothing. The wives were given the impression that they had been given three different types of detergent. Actually only the boxes were different; the detergents inside were identical.

The design for one was predominantly yellow. The yellow in the test was used because some merchandisers were convinced that yellow was the best color for store shelves because it has very strong visual impact. Another box was predominently blue without any yellow in it; and the third box was blue but with splashes of yellow.

In their reports the housewives stated that the detergent in the brilliant yellow box was too strong; it even allegedly ruined their clothes in some cases. As for the detergent in the predominantly blue box, the wives complained in many cases that it left their clothes dirty looking. The third box, which contained what the institute felt was an ideal balance of colors in the package design, overwhelmingly received favorable responses. The women used such words as "fine" and "wonderful" in describing the effect the detergent in that box had on their clothes.

A department store that had become skeptical of the rationality of its customers tried an experiment. One of its slowest-moving items was priced at fourteen cents. It changed the price to two for twenty-nine cents. Sales promptly increased 30 per cent when the item was offered at this "bargain" price.

One of the most costly blunders in the history of merchandising was the Chrysler Corporation's assumption that people buy automobiles on a rational basis. It decided back in the early 1950's, on the basis of direct consumer surveys and the reasoning of its eminently sensible and engineering-minded executives, that people wanted a car in tune with the times, a car without frills that would be sturdy and easy to park. With streets and parking spaces becoming increasingly packed with cars the times seemed obviously to call for a more compact car, a car with a shorter wheel base.

In 1953 *Tide*, a leading trade journal of marketing-management men, asked "Is This the End of the 'Big Fat Car'?" and told of Chrysler's decision that such was the case, and its planned style revolution for all its makes. The company's styling director was quoted as saying, "The people no longer want to buy a big fat car. The public wants a slim car." The article also mentioned that Chrysler had recently mailed stockholders a pamphlet entitled "Leadership in Engines," an area where it felt it was supreme.

What happened? Chrysler's share of the auto market dropped from 26 per cent in 1952 to about 13 per cent in 1954. The company was desperate. It looked more deeply into what sells cars and completely overhauled its styling. The result is shown in another article in *Tide* two years later. It reported:

> Chrysler, going downhill in 1954, makes a marketing comeback. Whole line suffered mostly from styling. One look at this year's products tells the story. People want long, low cars today. So some of the new cars by Chrysler are as much as 16 inches longer and 3 inches lower. Plymouth is now the longest car in the low-price field. The Dodge is the first car with 3-color exteriors.

The happy result (for Chrysler) was that its share of the market bounced back very substantially in 1955. *Tide* called it one of the most remarkable turnabouts in marketing history.

Our toothbrushing habits offer a prime example of behavior that is at least seemingly irrational. If you ask people why they brush their teeth, most of them will tell you that their main purpose in doing so is to get particles of food out of the crevices of their teeth and thus combat decay germs. Tooth-paste producers accepted this explanation for many years and based their sales campaigns on it. Advertising men who made a study of our toothbrushing habits, however, came upon a puzzle. They found that most people brushed their teeth once a day, and at the most pointless moment possible in the entire twenty-four-hour day, from the dental hygiene standpoint. That was in the morning just before breakfast, after decay germs had had a whole night to work on their teeth from particles left from supper—and just before the consumption of breakfast would bring in a new host of bacteria.

One advertising agency puzzling over this seemingly irrational behavior made a more thorough study of the reasons why we brush our teeth. It concluded that we are motivated by differing reasons, based on our personality. Some people, particularly hypochondriacs, are really concerned about those germs and are swayed by a "decay" appeal. (The hammering in recent years on all the wondrous anti-decay pastes has swollen the size of this group.) Another group, mostly extroverts, brush their teeth in the hope they will be bright and shiny. The majority of people, however, brush their teeth primarily for a reason that has little to do with dental hygiene or even their teeth. They put the brush and paste into their mouth in order to give their mouth a thorough purging, to get rid of the bad taste that has accumulated overnight. In short, they are looking for a taste sensation, as a part of their ritual of starting the day afresh. At least two of the major paste merchandisers began hitting hard at this appeal in 1955 and 1956. One promised a "clean mouth taste" and the other proclaimed that its paste "cleans your breath while it guards your teeth." (More recently one of these products got itself a new ad agency, as often happens, and the new mentor began appealing to the extrovert in us through the slogan, "You'll wonder where the yellow went. . . ." Good results are reported, which simply proves there is always more than one way to catch a customer.)

*Business Week*, in commenting on the often seemingly irrational behavior of consumers, said: "People don't seem to be reasonable." However, it made this further point: "But people do act with purpose. Their behavior makes sense if you think about it in terms of its goals, of people's needs and their motives. That seems to be the secret of understanding or manipulating people."

Another aspect of people's behavior that troubled marketers is that they are too easily satisfied with what they already have. Most of the marketers' factories have ever-larger warehouses full of goods to move.

By the mid-fifties American goods producers were achieving a fabulous output, and the output with automation promised to keep getting more fabulous. Since 1940, gross national product had soared more than 400 per cent; and man-hour productivity was doubling about every quarter century.

One way of viewing this rich, full life the people were achieving was the glowing one that everyone could enjoy an ever-higher standard of living. That view was thoroughly publicized. But there was another way of viewing it: that we must consume more and more, whether we want to or not, for the good of our economy.

In late 1955 the church publication *Christianity and Crisis* commented grimly on America's "ever-expanding economy." It observed that the pressure was on Americans to "consume, consume and consume, whether we need or even desire the products almost forced upon us." It added that the dynamics of an ever-expanding system require that we be "persuaded to consume to meet the needs of the productive process."

With growing productivity and prosperity the average American had five times as many discretionary dollars as he had in 1940. (These are dollars we have after we take care of our basic, immediate needs.) But discretionary dollars are also deferrable dollars—we can defer spending them if we are satisfied with what we already have. This hazard posed by so many optional dollars in our pockets was summed up quite eloquently in the October 24, 1955, issue of *Advertising Age* by an executive of the publishing firm of McGraw-Hill. He stated:

> As a nation we are already so rich that consumers are under no pressure of immediate necessity to buy a very large share—perhaps as much as 40%—of what is produced, and the pressure will get progressively less in the years ahead. But if consumers exercise their option not to buy a large share of what is produced, a great depression is not far behind.

The view virtually all goods producers choose to take when confronted with a threat of overproduction was voiced in what might seem a comical way to nonnatives of his state by Senator Alexander Wiley, of Wisconsin, sometimes known as "the cheese Senator." In the mid-fifties when America had such a glut of cheese that cheese was even being stored in old World War II vessels, thanks largely to the great outpouring of the product from his section, he said: "Our problem is not too much cheese produced, but rather too little cheese consumed."

In the early fifties, with overproduction threatening on many fronts, a fundamental shift occurred in the preoccupation of people in executive suites. Production now became a relatively secondary concern. Executive planners changed from being maker-minded to market-minded. The president of the National Sales Executives in fact exclaimed: "Capitalism is dead—consumerism is king!"

There was talk at management conventions of "the marketing revolution" and considerable pondering on how best to "stimulate" consumer buying, by creating wants in people that they still didn't realize existed. An auto maker talked of increasing his car sales by selling to "those who do not yet know what they need."

This urgently felt need to "stimulate" people brought new power, glory, and prosperity to the professional stimulators or persuaders of American industry, particularly the skilled gray-flanneled suiters of New York's Madison Avenue, known as "ad alley." In 1955, $9,000,000,000 was poured into United States advertising, up a billion from 1954 and up three billion from 1950. For each man, woman, and child in America in 1955 roughly $53 was spent to persuade him or her to buy products of industry. Some cosmetics firms began spending a fourth of all their income from sales on advertising and promotion. A cosmetics tycoon, probably mythical, was quoted as saying: "We don't sell lipstick, we buy customers."

One big and intimidating obstacle confronting the stimulators was the fact that most Americans already possessed perfectly usable stoves, cars, TV sets, clothes, etc. Waiting for those products to wear out or become physically obsolete before urging replacements upon the owner was intolerable. More and more, ad men began talking of the desirability of creating "psychological obsolescence."

At a conference of gas-range people the conferees were exhorted to emulate the more up-to-date car makers in this business of creating psychological obsolescence. They were reminded that auto merchandisers strive to make everyone ashamed to drive a car more than two or three years. The gas-range people were told bluntly by the director of American Color Trends: "Ladies and gentlemen, you know and I know that too many housekeepers have the attitude that 'any old piece of equipment will do so long as it works at all.'" He described the recent trend to change the color of many products and explained: "All of these trends have a definite bearing on what you can do to step up the obsolescence of gas appliances."

By the mid-fifties merchandisers of many different products were being urged by psychological counselors to become "merchants of discontent." One ad executive exclaimed with fervor: "What makes this country great is the creation of wants and desires, the creation of dissatisfaction with the old and outmoded."

A third major dilemma that was forcing marketers to search for more powerful tools of persuasion was the growing sameness of their products, with increased standardization. Too many people were complacently saying that the gasoline brands were "all the same" and equally good. Pierre Martineau, director of research at *The Chicago Tribune*, frankly asked a group of ad men: "What difference really is there between brands of gasoline, tires, cigarette tobacco, orange juice, milk, and what have you? . . . What is the advertising direction going to be when the differences become trivial or nonexistent?"

How can you make a logical sales talk to a prospect to persuade him to swear by your brand when in truth the brands are essentially alike in physical characteristics? That was a real dilemma for ad men. Ad agency president David Ogilvy commented on this problem by stating: "I am astonished to find how many advertising men even among the new generation, believe that women can be persuaded by logic and argument to buy one brand in preference to another, even when the two brands concerned are technically identical. . . . The greater the similarity between products, the less part reason really plays in brand selection. There really isn't any significant difference between the various brands of whisky or the various cigarettes or the various brands of beer. They are all about the same. And so are the cake mixes and the detergents and the automobiles." (This was not to imply, of course, that *all* brands of a product are the same. In some lines substantial differentiations exist. And it is also true that most companies strive mightily to develop product differences.)

An annual conference of advertising-agency men heard an appeal for more "gifted artists" in persuasion to cope with this problem of the "rapidly diminishing product differences."

Thus it was that for several compelling reasons marketers began groping for new and more penetrating persuasion techniques, for deeper approaches, better hooks. They needed customer-catching techniques that would be powerful and still not get them in trouble with the Federal Trade Commission, which has been taking a sternly righteous and disapproving attitude toward overextravagant claims and promises, such as had often characterized some of the ad copy of yesteryear.

The search for more persuasive ways to sell was summed up colorfully by a car salesman in Atlanta who said of his problem in selling cars in a then-slack market: "If buyer shopping gets any worse, we'll have to hit the customer over the head and get him to sign while he's unconscious."

His use of the word unconscious, as we shall see, was unwittingly prophetic.

## 23. THE QUESTION OF MORALITY

What are the implications of all this persuasion in terms of our existing morality? What does it mean for the national morality to have so many powerfully influential people taking a manipulative attitude toward our society? Some of these persuaders, in their energetic endeavors to sway our actions, seem to fall unwittingly into the attitude that man exists to be manipulated.

While some of the persuaders brood occasionally about the implications of their endeavors, others feel that what is progress for them is progress for the nation. Some of the depth marketers, for example, seem to assume that anything that results in raising the gross national product is automatically good for America. An ad executive from Milwaukee related in *Printer's Ink* that America was growing great by the systematic creation of dissatisfaction. He talked specifically of the triumph of the cosmetics industry in reaching the billion-dollar class by the sale of hope and by making women more anxious and critical about their appearance. Triumphantly he concluded: "And everybody is happy."

Others contend that the public has become so skeptical of advertising appeals that its psyche is not being damaged by all the assaults on it from the various media. (On the other hand, it can be pointed out that this growing skepticism was a major reason ad men turned to subconscious appeals. They wanted to bypass our conscious guard.)

*Business Week*, in dismissing the charge that the science of behavior was spawning some monster of human engineering who was "manipulating a population of puppets from behind the scenes," contended: "It is hard to find anything very sinister about a science whose principal conclusion is that you get along with people by giving them what they want."

But is "everybody happy?" And should we all be "given" whatever our ids "want"?

Certainly a good deal can be said on the positive side for the socially constructive results that have come from the explorations into human behavior arising from the persuaders' endeavors. The merchandisers in their sales appeals to us have gotten away from some of their crude excesses of old and are more considerate of our wants and needs, even if those needs are often subconscious. Edward Weiss, the ad executive, made this point when he said that social knowledge was helping ad men to "forget about the gimmicks and to concentrate on the *real reasons* why people buy goods." We've seen how the merchandisers of beer and other predominantly middle-class products have become more realistic in the messages.

Likewise a food packer became more sensible in his selling as a result of a depth study. He had been offering a free trip to Hollywood as a prize to persons who sent in the best fifty-word statement "Why I like. . . ." This brought in lots of statements but very little stimulation of sales. A depth study of housewives showed why. Married women with two children and a husband working weren't interested in going to Hollywood, free or otherwise. Who'd take care of the children and cook for the husband? An analysis of people sending in the statements showed they were mostly teen-agers who had never done any food shopping in their lives!

The use of the insights of the social sciences in dealing with company personnel has likewise—where not accompanied by "social engineering"—brought some enlightened policies and constructive changes. *Advanced Management* reported that one large company now carefully interviews researchers and other responsible newcomers to find the conditions under which they feel they work best. Do they like to work alone, or with a group? Do they like their desk in a corner or in the middle of the cubicle? Do they like to work on one project at a time or have several going simultaneously? This management, in short, tries to manipulate the environment to suit the individual, not vice versa.

On the other hand, a good many of the people-manipulating activities of persuaders raise profoundly disturbing questions about the kind of society they are seeking to build for us. Their ability to contact millions of us simultaneously through newspapers, TV, etc., gives them the power, as one persuader put it, to do good or evil "on a scale never before possible in a very short time." Are they warranted in justifying the manipulation on the ground that anything that increases the gross national product is "good" for America; or on the ground that the old doctrine "Let the Buyer Beware" absolves them of responsibility for results that may seem to some antisocial?

Perhaps the supporters of optimism-generation in both business and government can make an impressive case for the need to preserve public confidence if we are to have peace and prosperity. But where is it leading us? What happens, actually, to public confidence when the public becomes aware (as it gradually must) that the leaders of industry and government are resolutely committed to a confidence-inspiring viewpoint, come hell or high water?

How can you know what to believe?

It is my feeling that a number of the practices and techniques I've cited here very definitely raise questions of a moral nature that should be faced by the persuaders and the public. For example:

What is the morality of the practice of encouraging housewives to be nonrational and impulsive in buying the family food?

What is the morality of playing upon hidden weaknesses and frailties—such as our anxieties, aggressive feelings, dread of nonconformity, and infantile hang-overs—to sell products? Specifically, what are the ethics of businesses that shape campaigns designed to thrive on these weaknesses they have diagnosed?

What is the morality of manipulating small children even before they reach the age where they are legally responsible for their actions?

What is the morality of treating voters like customers, and child customers seeking father images at that?

What is the morality of exploiting our deepest sexual sensitivities and yearnings for commercial purposes?

What is the morality of appealing for our charity by playing upon our secret desires for self-enhancement?

What is the morality of developing in the public an attitude of wastefulness toward national resources by encouraging the "psychological obsolescence" of products already in use?

What is the morality of subordinating truth to cheerfulness in keeping the citizen posted on the state of his nation?

The persuaders themselves, in their soul-searching, are at times exceptionally articulate in expressing their apprehensions and in admitting some of their practices are a "little cold-blooded." One of them, Nicholas Samstag, confessed in *The Engineering of Consent*: "It may be said that to take advantage of a man's credulity, to exploit his misapprehensions, to capitalize on his ignorance is morally reprehensible—and this may well be the case. . . . I do not quite know."

The June, 1954, issue of *The Public Relations Journal* contained a remarkable venture into soul-searching by a Hawaiian public-relations man, Kleber R. Miller. He said, "What I wish to pose here is . . . whether the public-relations practitioner realizes the depths of the moral considerations involved," in some of his activities. He said the principal assumption is that the public-relations practitioner will be able to create on any desired scale "a climate of opinion and emotion that is most favorable to the cause of the client he represents. . . . The public-relations man is continually faced with the question whether the end justifies the means." Mr. Miller went on, "What degree of intensity is proper in seeking to arouse desire, hatred, envy, cupidity, hope, or any of the great gamut of human emotions on which he must play." He made this penetrating point:

"One of the fundamental considerations involved here is the right to manipulate human personality."

Such a manipulation, he went on to say, inherently involves a disrespect for the individual personality.

It seems to me that both the Advertising Research Foundation and the Public Relations Society of America might well concern themselves with drawing up realistic up-to-date codes defining the behavior of ethically responsible persuaders. Such codes might set up ground rules that would safeguard the public against being manipulated in ways that might be irresponsible and socially dangerous.

The social scientists and psychiatrists co-operating with the persuaders in their manipulative endeavors face some uncomfortable moral questions, too. Their questions perhaps are more perplexing. They have a workable rationale for explaining their co-operation with, say, the merchandisers. After all, they are, in their depth probing, broadening the world's available knowledge concerning human behavior, and they can explain that knowledge which is not put to use is lost. In this they could quote Alfred North Whitehead, who pointed out that knowledge doesn't keep any better than fish.

Still, there was the disturbing fact that some of them were being *used* by the manipulators. *Printer's Ink* devoted a special feature to the way social scientists "can be used" in merchandising problems. One point it made: "Use mostly those social scientists who demonstrate a knowledge and appreciation of business problems. Beware of those who don't. Many can be exceedingly naïve and unscientific in their approach to advertising."

Perhaps the most uncomfortable aspect of the situation for the scientists was stated by an ad executive writing under a pseudonym for *The Nation*. He said: "Social scientists in the past have paid attention to the irrational patterns of human behavior because they wish to locate their social origins and thus be able to suggest changes that would result in more rational conduct. They now study irrationality—and other aspects of human behavior—to gather data that may be used by salesmen to manipulate consumers."

In their efforts to be co-operative with the persuaders the scientists also showed some tendency to accept assumptions that definitely were dubious. In 1953 a leading advertising researcher concluded that Americans would have to learn to live a third better if they were to keep pace with growing production and permit the United States economy to hit a "$400,000,000,000 gross national product in 1958." (Actually it shot past the $400,000,000,000 mark in 1956.) To find how Americans could be persuaded to live a third better *Tide* put the question to "quite a few of the leading U.S. sociologists." The response of Professor Philip J. Allen, of the University of Virginia, was particularly interesting. He mapped out a "systematic program" by which it could be achieved, and stressed that his scheme would require:

> Sufficient financial backing for regular utilization of mass media, constantly to communicate the desired objectives to the "common man." New values can be deliberately created, disseminated, and adopted as personal and collective goals highly desirable of achievement. But the concerted effort of the major social institutions—particularly the educational, recreational, and religious—must be enlisted with the ready co-operation of those in control of the mass media on the one hand and the large creators of goods and services who buy up time and space for advertising their "wares" on the other. . . . By utilizing the various tested devices, our modern genius in advertising may alight upon simple phrases well organized in sequence and timing, and co-ordinated with other efforts geared to realize the "grand design." But there are required a host of laborers with plenty of financial backing.

In mapping out his "grand design" for making us all more dutiful consumers he accepted, without any question that I could note, the basic assumption that achieving the one-third-better goal was worth any manipulating that might be necessary to achieve it.

One of the experts consulted, Bernice Allen, of Ohio University, did question the assumption. She said: "We have no proof that more material goods such as more cars or more gadgets has made anyone happier—in fact the evidence seems to point in the opposite direction."

It strikes me that it would be appropriate for the Social Science Research Council and such affiliates as the American Psychological Association to develop codes of ethics that would cover the kind of co-operation that can be condoned and not condoned in working with the people-manipulators. The American Psychological Association has a guidebook running 171 pages (*Ethical Standards of Psychologists*) that covers more than a hundred problems and cites hundreds of examples of dubious behavior, but there is barely a mention in the entire manual of the kind of co-operation with depth manipulators I have detailed. The A.P.A. does state: "The most widely shared pattern of values among psychologists appears to be a respect for evidence combined with a respect for the dignity and integrity of the human individual." That is an admirable statement and might well be spelled out in terms of permissible and nonpermissible behavior in the field of commerce.

Beyond the question of specific practices of the persuaders and their associated scientists is the larger question of where our economy is taking us under the pressures of consumerism. That, too, is a moral question. In fact I suspect it is destined to become one of the great moral issues of our times.

Industrialists such as General David Sarnoff contend that trying to hold back, or argue about, the direction our automated factories are taking us is like trying to hold back the tides and seasons. He feels it is pointless even to talk about the desirability of the trend. Some demur. The advertising director of a major soup company commented: "If we create a society just to satisfy automation's production, we will destroy the finest value in our society." There were also signs that some segments of the public itself might be less than grateful for the outpouring of goods our economy was bestowing upon us. In the mid-fifties *Harper's* published two articles taking a dim view of our worldly riches. One by economist Robert Lekachman, entitled "If We're So Rich, What's Eating Us?" recounted the outpouring of goods and said: "All these good things, worthy of universal exultation, have caused instead a chronic case of economic hypochondria." And Russell Lynes, in his bitter-funny article "Take Back Your Sable!" put in a good word for depressions, not the evils they produce but the climate: "A climate in many respects more productive than prosperity—more interesting, more lively, more thoughtful, and even, in a wry sort of way, more fun."

Dr. Dichter has been quick to realize the essentially moral question posed by the across-the-board drive to persuade us to step up our consumption. His publication *Motivations* stated in April, 1956:

> We now are confronted with the problem of permitting the average American to feel moral even when he is flirting, even when he is spending, even when he is not saving, even when he is taking two vacations a year and buying a second or third car. One of the basic problems of this prosperity, then, is to give people the sanction and justification to enjoy it and to demonstrate the hedonistic approach to his life is a moral, not an immoral, one. This permission given to the consumer to enjoy his life freely, the demonstration that he is right in surrounding himself with products that enrich his life and give him pleasure must be one of the central themes of every advertising display and sales promotion plan.

On another occasion Dr. Dichter pointed out that the public's shift away from its "puritan complex" was enhancing the power of three major sales appeals: desire for comfort, for luxury, and for prestige.

The moral nature of the issue posed by the pressures on us to consume is pointed up by the fact religious spokesmen have been among the first to speak out in criticism of the trend. The minister of my own church, Loring Chase (Congregational in New Canaan, Conn.), devoted his Lenten sermon in 1956 to the problem of prosperity. The self-denial pattern of Lent, he said, "stands in vivid contrast to the prevailing pattern of our society, which keeps itself going economically by saying to us, 'You really owe it to yourself to buy this or that.' " He described the national picture provided by our economy of abundance and stated: "Over against this . . . one feels a certain embarrassment of Jesus' reminder that 'a man's life does not consist of the abundance of his possessions. . . .' " He concluded that "the issue is not one of few or many possessions. The issue is whether we recognize that possessions were meant to serve life, and that life comes first." The Protestant publication *Christianity and Crisis* contended that the next great moral dilemma confronting America would be the threat to the "quality of life" created by abundance of worldly goods. It conceded that if we are to have an expanding economy based on mass production we cannot deny the necessity of mass consumption of new goods, and "for this advertising is obviously essential. Yet there is a dilemma," it explained. "We are being carried along by a process that is becoming an end in itself and which threatens to overwhelm us. . . . There is a loss of a sense of proportion in living when we become so quickly dissatisfied with last year's models."

The profound nature of the dilemma was clearly drawn, however, when it added: "This is not to criticize those who make the products in question or those who promote and sell them. They and all of us who consume them are caught up in the same whirl. This whirl is so much the substance of our life that it is difficult to get outside it long enough to look at it and ask where it all leads us."

Theologian Reinhold Niebuhr likewise took note of the dilemma by pointing out that the problem of achieving "a measure of grace" in an economy of abundance was very perplexing. And he added that "we are in danger . . . of developing a culture that is enslaved to its productive process, thus reversing the normal relation of production and consumption."

This larger moral problem of working out a spiritually tolerable relationship between a free people and an economy capable of greater and greater productivity may take decades to resolve. Meanwhile, we can address ourselves to the more specific problem of dealing with those more devious and aggressive manipulators who would play upon our irrationalities and weaknesses in order to channel our behavior. I concede that some pushing and hauling of the citizenry is probably necessary to make our $400,000,000,000-a-year economy work, with lures such as premiums and thirty-six-months-to-pay. But certainly our expanding economy can manage to thrive without the necessity of psychoanalyzing children or mind-molding men or playing upon the anxieties we strive to keep to ourselves. America is too great a nation —and Americans too fine a people—to have to tolerate such corrosive practices.

We still have a strong defense available against such persuaders: we can choose not to be persuaded. In virtually all situations we still have the choice, and we cannot be too seriously manipulated if we know what is going on. It is my hope that this book may contribute to the general awareness. As Clyde Miller pointed out in *The Process of Persuasion,* when we learn to recognize the devices of the persuaders, we build up a "recognition reflex." Such a recognition reflex, he said, "can protect us against the petty trickery of small-time persuaders operating in the commonplace affairs of everyday life, but also against the mistaken or false persuasion of powerful leaders. . . ."

Some persons we've encountered who are thoroughly acquainted with the operations of the merchandising manipulators, I should add, still persist in acts that may be highly tinged with illogicality. They admit to buying long, colorful cars they really don't need and sailboats that they concede probably appeal to them because of childhood memories (if the Dichter thesis applies). Furthermore, they confess they continue brushing their teeth once a day at the most illogical time conceivable from a dental-health standpoint—just before breakfast. But they do all these things with full knowledge that they are being self-indulgent or irrational. When irrational acts are committed knowingly they become a sort of delicious luxury.

It is no solution to suggest we should all defend ourselves against the depth manipulators by becoming carefully rational in all our acts. Such a course not only is visionary but unattractive. It would be a dreary world if we all had to be rational, right-thinking, nonneurotic people all the time, even though we may hope we are making general gains in that direction.

At times it is pleasanter or easier to be nonlogical. But I prefer being nonlogical by my own free will and impulse rather than to find myself manipulated into such acts.

The most serious offense many of the depth manipulators commit, it seems to me, is that they try to invade the privacy of our minds. It is this right to privacy in our minds—privacy to be either rational or irrational—that I believe we must strive to protect.

# Part Five

# Retrospect and Prospect

## ✑ THE DECLINE OF THE WEST

*Oswald Spengler*

> *Men have always been fascinated by the attempt to orient themselves
> and their societies in time, to determine a pattern for human history
> which would put into perspective the distinctive qualities of one's own
> culture as well as emphasizing the constant factors running through all
> human affairs. One of the most intriguing of such attempts is Oswald
> Spengler's book* The Decline of the West, *which appeared in Germany
> immediately after World War I. Spengler especially wanted to explain
> the late nineteenth-century cultural malaise which was already being widely
> interpreted as part of a pattern of sociological, economic, political, and
> spiritual degeneration. He wished to predict the way the tide was turning
> in order to allow Europeans to ride it: overcoming it he considered out
> of the question.*
>
> *Spengler (1880–1936) was not a professional historian, and many of
> his interpretations are considered questionable by those who are. But
> his book has managed to hold considerable respect even on the part of
> academics who question his credentials. He was a man of immense
> learning, and few historians are competent to evaluate the enormous
> detail about the many societies he discusses. His book, furthermore, is
> strikingly original in method: Spengler, who has been followed in this
> by such men as Arnold Toynbee, Pitirim Sorokin, Amaury de Riencourt,
> and Herbert Muller, made use of a comparative approach, treating great
> cultures as units, putting them side by side for investigation, and
> discovering a common cyclical pattern through which each one passes.
> From this perspective, he felt he could predict the coming doom of
> modern Western civilization, now nearing the end of its cycle.*
>
> *The book has appealed largely to those who share Spengler's pessimism.
> In the 1920s it was part of the same depressing German cultural
> environment which bred expressionism in art and in the theater and
> which led to the irrationalism of the Nazi regime. But the work survived
> the Weimar regime of the 1920s and appears to be capable of surviving
> the more sober assessments of other philosophers of history.*

## I. Scope of the Work

In this book is attempted for the first time the venture of predetermining history, of
following the still untravelled stages in the destiny of a Culture, and specifically

Oswald Spengler, *The Decline of the West* (New York: Alfred A. Knopf, Inc., 1926), I,
3–4, 25–27, 31–41.

of the only Culture of our time and on our planet which is actually in the phase of fulfilment—the West-European-American.

Hitherto the possibility of solving a problem so far-reaching has evidently never been envisaged, and even if it had been so, the means of dealing with it were either altogether unsuspected or, at best, inadequately used.

Is there a logic of history? Is there, beyond all the casual and incalculable elements of the separate events, something that we may call a metaphysical structure of historic humanity, something that is essentially independent of the outward forms—social, spiritual and political—which we see so clearly? Are not these actualities indeed secondary or derived from that something? Does world-history present to the seeing eye certain grand traits, again and again, with sufficient constancy to justify certain conclusions? And if so, what are the limits to which reasoning from such premisses may be pushed?

Is it possible to find in life itself—for human history is the sum of mighty life-courses which already have had to be endowed with ego and personality, in customary thought and expression, by predicating entities of a higher order like "the Classical" or "the Chinese Culture," "Modern Civilization"—a series of stages which must be traversed, and traversed moreover in an ordered and obligatory sequence? For everything organic the notions of birth, death, youth, age, lifetime are fundamentals—may not these notions, in this sphere also, possess a rigorous meaning which no one has as yet extracted? In short, is all history founded upon general biographic archetypes?

The decline of the West, which at first sight may appear, like the corresponding decline of the Classical Culture, a phenomenon limited in time and space, we now perceive to be a philosophical problem that, when comprehended in all its gravity, includes within every great question of Being.

If therefore we are to discover in what form the destiny of the Western Culture will be accomplished, we must first be clear as to what culture *is*, what its relations are to visible history, to life, to soul, to nature, to intellect, what the forms of its manifestations are and how far these forms—peoples, tongues and epochs, battles and ideas, states and gods, arts and craft-works, sciences, laws, economic types and world-idea, great men and great events—may be accepted and pointed to as symbols.

## IX. The Only Historical Method Is Goethe's

In opposition to all these arbitrary and narrow schemes, derived from tradition or personal choice, into which history is forced, I put forward the natural, the "Copernican," form of the historical process which lies deep in the essence of that process and reveals itself only to an eye perfectly free from prepossessions.

Such an eye was Goethe's. That which Goethe called *Living Nature* is exactly that which we are calling here world-history, *world-as-history*. Goethe, who as artist portrayed the life and development, always the life and development, of his figures, the thing-becoming and not the thing-become ("Wilhelm Meister" and "Wahrheit und Dichtung"), hated Mathematics. For him, the world-as-mechanism stood opposed to the world-as-organism, dead nature to living nature, law to form. As naturalist, every line he wrote was meant to display the image of a thing-becoming, the "impressed form" living and developing. Sympathy, observation, comparison, immediate and inward certainty, intellectual *flair*—these were the means whereby he was enabled to approach the secrets of the phenomenal world in motion. *Now these are the means of historical research*—precisely these and no others. It was this *god-like* insight that prompted him to say at the bivouac fire on the evening of the Battle of Valmy: "Here and now begins a new epoch of world history, and you, gentlemen, can say that you 'were there.' " No general, no diplomat, let alone the philosophers, ever so directly felt history "becoming." It is the deepest judgment that any man ever uttered about a great historical act in the moment of its accomplishment.

And just as he followed out the development of the plant-form from the leaf, the birth of the vertebrate type, the process of the geological strata—*the Destiny in nature and not the Causality*—so here we shall develop the form-language of human history, its periodic structure, its *organic logic* out of the profusion of all the challenging details.

In other aspects, mankind is habitually, and rightly, reckoned as one of the organisms of the earth's surface. Its physical structure, its natural functions, the whole phenomenal conception of it, all belong to a more comprehensive unity. Only in *this* aspect is it treated otherwise, despite that deeply-felt relationship of plant destiny and human destiny which is an eternal theme of all lyrical poetry, and despite that similarity of human history to that of any other of the higher life-groups which is the refrain of endless beast-legends, sagas and fables.

But only bring analogy to bear on this aspect as on the rest, letting the world of human Cultures intimately and unreservedly work upon the imagination instead of forcing it into a ready-made scheme. Let the words youth, growth, maturity, decay—hitherto, and to-day more than ever, used to express subjective valuations and entirely personal preferences in sociology, ethics and aesthetics—be taken at last as objective descriptions of organic states. Set forth the Classical Culture as a self-contained phenomenon embodying and expressing the Classical soul, put it beside the Egyptian, the Indian, the Babylonian, the Chinese and the Western, and determine for each of these higher individuals what is typical in their surgings and what is necessary in the riot of incident. And then at last will unfold itself the picture of world-history that is natural to us, men of the West, and to us alone.

## X. *Ourselves and the Romans*

Our narrower task, then, is primarily to determine, from such a world-survey, the state of West Europe and America as at the epoch of 1800–2000—to establish the chronological position of this period in the ensemble of Western culture-history, its significance as a chapter that is in one or other guise necessarily found in the biography of every Culture, and the organic and symbolic meaning of its political, artistic, intellectual and social expression-forms.

Considered in the spirit of analogy, this period appears as chronologically parallel —"contemporary" in our special sense—with the phase of Hellenism, and its present culmination, marked by the World-War, corresponds with the transition from the Hellenistic to the Roman age. *Rome*, with its rigorous realism—uninspired, barbaric, disciplined, practical, Protestant, *Prussian*—will always give us, working as we must by analogies, the key to understanding our own future. The *break of destiny that we express by hyphening the words "Greeks-Romans" is occurring for us also, separating that which is already fulfilled from that which is to come.* Long ago we might and should have seen in the "classical" world a development which is the complete counterpart of our own Western development, differing indeed from it in every detail of the surface but entirely similar as regards the inward power driving the great organism towards its end. We might have found the constant *alter ego* of our own actuality in establishing the correspondence, item by item, from the "Trojan War" and the Crusades, Homer and the Nibelungenlied, through Doric and Gothic, Dionysian movement and Renaissance, Polycletus and John Sebastian Bach, Athens and Paris, Aristotle and Kant, Alexander and Napoleon, to the world-city and the imperialism common to both Cultures. . . .

## XII. The Problem of Civilization

Looked at in this way, the "Decline of the West" comprises nothing less than the problem of *Civilization*. We have before us one of the fundamental questions of all higher history. What is Civilization, understood as the organic-logical sequel, fulfilment and finale of a culture?

For every Culture has *its own* Civilization. In this work, for the first time the two words, hitherto used to express an indefinite, more or less ethical, distinction, are used in a *periodic* sense, to express a strict and necessary *organic succession*. The Civilization is the inevitable *destiny* of the Culture, and in this principle we obtain the viewpoint from which the deepest and gravest problems of historical morphology become capable of solution. Civilizations are the most external and artificial states of which a species of developed humanity is capable. They are a conclusion, the thing-become succeeding the thing-becoming, death following life, rigidity following expansion, intellectual age and the stone-built, petrifying world-city following mother-earth and the spiritual childhood of Doric and Gothic. They are an end, irrevocable, yet by inward necessity reached again and again.

So, for the first time, we are enabled to understand the Romans as the *successors* of the Greeks, and light is projected into the deepest secrets of the late-Classical period. What, but this, can be the meaning of the fact—which can only be disputed by vain phrases—that the Romans were barbarians who did not *precede* but *closed* a great development? Unspiritual, unphilosophical, devoid of art, clannish to the point of brutality, aiming relentlessly at tangible successes, they stand between the Hellenic Culture and nothingness. An imagination directed purely to practical objects —they had religious laws governing godward relations as they had other laws governing human relations, but there was no specifically Roman saga of gods—was something which is not found at all in Athens. In a word, Greek *soul*—Roman *intellect*; and this antithesis is the differentia between Culture and Civilization. Nor is it only to the Classical that it applies. Again and again there appears this type of strong-minded, completely non-metaphysical man, and in the hands of this type lies the intellectual and material destiny of each and every "late" period. Such are the men who carried through the Babylonian, the Egyptian, the Indian, the Chinese, the Roman Civilizations, and in such periods do Buddhism, Stoicism, Socialism ripen into definitive world-conceptions which enable a moribund humanity to be attacked and re-formed in its intimate structure. *Pure* Civilization, as a historical process, consists in a progressive *taking-down* of forms that have become inorganic or dead.

The transition from Culture to Civilization was accomplished for the Classical world in the 4th, for the Western in the 19th Century. From these periods onward the great intellectual decisions take place, not as in the days of the Orpheus-movement or the Reformation in the "whole world" where not a hamlet is too small to be unimportant, but in three or four world-cities that have absorbed into themselves the whole content of History, while the old wide landscape of the Culture, become merely provincial, serves only to feed the cities with what remains of its higher mankind.

*World-city and province*—the two basic ideas of every civilization—bring up a wholly new form-problem of History, the very problem that we are living through to-day with hardly the remotest conception of its immensity. In place of a world, there is *a city, a point,* in which the whole life of broad regions is collecting while the rest dries up. In place of a type-true people, born of and grown on the soil, there is a new sort of noman, cohering unstably in fluid masses, the parasitical city dweller, tradition-less, utterly matter-of-fact, religionless, clever, unfruitful, deeply contemptuous of the countryman and especially that highest form of countryman, the country gentleman. This is a very great stride towards the inorganic, towards the end—what does it signify? France and England have already taken the step and Germany is beginning to do so. After Syracuse, Athens, and Alexandria comes Rome. After Madrid, Paris, London come Berlin and New York. It is the destiny of whole regions that lie outside the radiation-circle of one of these cities—of old Crete and Macedon and to-day the Scandinavian North—to become "provinces."

Of old, the field on which the opposed conception of an epoch came to battle was some world-problem of a metaphysical, religious or dogmatic kind, and the battle was between the soil-genius of the countryman (noble, priest) and the "worldly" patrician genius of the famous old small towns of Doric or Gothic springtime. Of such a character were the conflicts over the Dionysus religion—as in the tyranny of Kleisthenes of Sikyon—and those of the Reformation in the German free cities and the Huguenot wars. But just as these cities overcame the countryside (already it is a purely civic world-outlook that appears in even Parmenides and Descartes), so in turn the world-city overcame them. It is the common intellectual process of later periods such as the Ionic and the Baroque, and to-day—as in the Hellenistic age which at its outset saw the foundation of artificial, land-alien Alexandria—Culture-cities like Florence, Nürn-berg, Salamanca, Bruges and Prag, have become provincial towns and fight inwardly a lost battle against the world-cities. The world-city means cosmopolitanism in place of "home," a cold matter-of-fact in place of reverence for tradition and age, scientific irreligion as a fossil representative of the older religion of the heart, "society" in place of the state, natural instead of hard-earned rights. It was in the conception of *money* as an inorganic and abstract magnitude, entirely disconnected from the notion of the fruitful earth and the primitive values, that the Romans had the advantage of the Greeks. Thenceforward any high ideal of life becomes largely a question of money. Unlike the Greek stoicism of Chrysippus, the Roman stoicism of Cato and Seneca pre-supposes a private income; and, unlike that of the 18th Century, the social-ethical sentiment of the 20th, if it is to be realized at a higher level than that of professional (and lucrative) agitation, is a matter for millionaires. To the world-city belongs not a folk but a mass. Its uncomprehending hostility to all the traditions representative of the Culture (nobility, church, privileges, dynasties, convention in art and limits of knowledge in science), the keen and cold intelligence that confounds the wisdom of the peasant, the new-fashioned naturalism that in relation to all matters of sex and society goes back far beyond Rousseau and Socrates to quite primitive instincts and conditions, the reappearance of the *panem et circenses* in the form of wage-disputes and football-grounds—all of these things betoken the definite closing-down of the Culture and the opening of a quite new phase of human existence—anti-provincial, late, futureless, but quite inevitable.

This is what has to be *viewed,* and viewed not with the eyes of the partisan, the ideologue, the up-to-date novelist, not from this or that "standpoint," but in a high, time-free perspective embracing the whole millenniums of historical world-forms, if we are really to comprehend the great crisis of the present.

To me it is a symbol of the first importance that in the Rome of Crassus—triumvir and all-powerful building-site speculator—the Roman people with its proud inscriptions, the people before whom Gauls, Greeks, Parthians, Syrians afar trembled, lived in appalling misery in the many-storied lodging-houses of dark suburbs, accepting with indifference or even with a sort of sporting interest the consequences of the military expansion: that many famous old-noble families, descendants of the men who defeated the Celts and the Samnites, lost their ancestral homes through standing apart from the wild rush of speculation and were reduced to renting wretched apartments; that, while along the Appian Way there arose the splendid and still wonderful tombs of the financial magnates, the corpses of the people were thrown along with animal carcases and town refuse into a monstrous common grave—till in Augustus's time it was banked over for the avoidance of pestilence and so became the site of Maecenas's renowned park; that in depopulated Athens, which lived on visitors and on the bounty of rich foreigners, the mob of parvenu tourists from Rome gaped at the works of the Periclean age with as little understanding as the American globe-trotter in the Sistine Chapel at those of Michelangelo, every removable art-piece having ere this been taken away or bought at fancy prices to be replaced by the Roman buildings which grew up, colossal and arrogant, by the side of the low and modest structures of the old time. In such things—which it is the historian's business not to praise or to blame but to consider morphologically—there lies, plain and immediate enough for one who has learnt to see, an *idea.*

For it will become manifest that, from this moment on, all great conflicts of world-outlook, of politics, of art, of science, of feeling will be under the influence of this one opposition. What is the hallmark of a politic of Civilization to-day, in contrast to a politic of Culture yesterday? It is, for the Classical rhetoric, and for the Western journalism, both serving that abstract which represents the power of Civilization— *money.* It is the money-spirit which penetrates unremarked the historical forms of the people's existence, often without destroying or even in the least disturbing these forms— the form of the Roman state, for instance, underwent very much less alteration between the elder Scipio and Augustus than is usually imagined. Though forms subsist, the great political parties nevertheless cease to be more than reputed centres of decision. The decisions in fact lie elsewhere. A small number of superior heads, whose names are very likely not the best-known, settle everything, while below them are the great mass of second-rate politicians—rhetors, tribunes, deputies, journalists—selected through a provincially-conceived franchise to keep alive the illusion of popular self-determination. And art? Philosophy? The ideals of a Platonic or those of a Kantian age had for the higher mankind concerned a general validity. But those of a Hellenistic age, or those of our own, are valid exclusively for the brain of the Megalopolitan. For the villager's or, generally, the nature-man's world-feeling our Socialism—like its near relation Darwinism (how utterly un-Goethian are the formulae of "struggle for existence" and "natural selection"!) like its other relative the woman-and-marriage problem of Ibsen, Strindberg, and Shaw, like the impressionistic tendencies of anarchic sensuousness and the whole bundle of modern longings, temptations and pains expressed in Baudelaire's verse and Wagner's music—are simply non-existent. The smaller the town, the more unmeaning it becomes to busy oneself with painting or with music of these kinds. To the Culture belong gymnastics, the tournament, the agon, and to the Civilization belongs Sport. This is the true distinction between the Hellenic palaestra and the Roman circus. Art itself becomes a sport (hence the phrase "art for art's sake") to be played before a highly-intelligent audience of connoisseurs and buyers, whether the feat consist in mastering absurd instrumental tone-masses and taking harmonic fences, or in some *tour de force* of colouring. Then a new fact-philosophy appears, which can only spare a smile for metaphysical speculation, and a new literature that is a necessity of life for the megalopolitan palate and nerves and both unintelligible and ugly to the provincials. Neither Alexandrine poetry nor *plein-air* painting is anything to the "people." And, then as now, the phase of transition is marked by a series of scandals only to be found at such moments. The anger evoked in the Athenian populace by Euripides and by the "Revolutionary" painting of Apollodorus, for example, is repeated in the opposition to Wagner, Manet, Ibsen, and Nietzsche.

It is possible to understand the Greeks without mentioning their economic relations; the Romans, on the other hand, can *only* be understood through these. Chaeronea and Leipzig were the last battles fought about an idea. In the First Punic War and in 1870 economic motives are no longer to be overlooked. Not till the Romans came with their practical energy was slave-holding given that big collective character which many students regard as the die-stamp of Classical economics, legislation and way of life, and which in any event vastly lowered both the value and the inner worthiness of such free labour as continued to exist side by side with gang-labour. And it was not the Latin, but the Germanic peoples of the West and America who developed out of the steam-engine a big industry that transformed the face of the land. The relation of these phenomena to Stoicism and to Socialism is unmistakable. Not till the Roman Caesarism—foreshadowed by C. Flaminius, shaped first by Marius, handled by strong-minded, large-scale men of fact—did the Classical World learn the *pre-eminence of money*. Without this fact neither Caesar, nor "Rome" generally, is understandable. In every Greek is a Don Quixote, in every Roman a Sancho Panza factor, and these factors are dominants.

## XIII. Imperialism the Last Phase

Considered in itself, the Roman world-dominion was a negative phenomenon, being the result not of a surplus of energy on the one side—that the Romans had never had since Zama—but of a deficiency of resistance on the other. That the Romans did *not* conquer the world is certain; they merely took possession of a booty that lay open to everyone. The *Imperium Romanum* came into existence not as the result of such an extremity of military and financial effort as had characterized the Punic Wars, but because the old East forwent all external self-determination. We must not be deluded by the appearance of brilliant military successes. With a few ill-trained, ill-led, and sullen legions, Lucullus and Pompey conquered whole realms—a phenomenon that in the period of the battle of Ipsus would have been unthinkable. The Mithradatic danger, serious enough for a system of material force which had never been put to any real test, would have been nothing to the conquerors of Hannibal. After Zama, the Romans never again either waged or were capable of waging a war against a great military Power. Their classic wars were those against the Samnites, Pyrrhus and Carthage. Their grand hour was Cannae. To maintain the heroic posture for centuries on end is beyond the power of any people. The Prussian-German people have had three great moments (1813, 1870 and 1914), and that is more than others have had.

Here, then, I lay it down that *Imperialism,* of which petrifacts such as the Egyptian empire, the Roman, the Chinese, the Indian may continue to exist for hundreds or thousands of years—dead bodies, amorphous and dispirited masses of men, scrap-material from a great history—is to be taken as the typical symbol of the passing away. Imperialism is Civilization unadulterated. In this phenomenal form the destiny of the West is now irrevocably set. The energy of culture-man is directed inwards, that of civilization-man outwards. And thus I see in Cecil Rhodes* the first man of a new age. He stands for the political style of a far-ranging, Western, Teutonic and especially German future, and his phrase "expansion is everything" is the Napoleonic reasser-tion of the indwelling tendency of *every* Civilization that has fully ripened—Roman, Arab or Chinese. It is not a matter of choice—it is not the conscious will of individuals, or even that of whole classes or peoples that decides. The expansive tendency is a doom, something daemonic and immense, which grips, forces into service, and uses up the late mankind of the world-city stage, willy-nilly, aware or unaware. Life is the process of effecting possibilities, and for the brain-man there are *only extensive* possi-bilities. Hard as the half-developed Socialism of to-day is fighting against expansion, one day it will become arch-expansionist with all the vehemence of destiny. Here the form-language of politics, as the direct intellectual expression of a certain type of humanity, touches on a deep metaphysical problem—on the fact, affirmed in the grant of unconditional validity to the causality-principle, that *the soul is the complement of its extension. . . .*

Rhodes is to be regarded as the first precursor of a Western type of Caesars, whose day is to come though yet distant. He stands midway between Napoleon and the force-men of the next centuries, just as Flaminius, who from 232 B.C. onward pressed the Romans to undertake the subjugation of Cisalpine Gaul and so initiated the policy of colonial expansion, stands between Alexander and Caesar. Strictly speaking, Flamin-ius was a private person—for his real power was of a kind not embodied in any con-stitutional office—who exercised a dominant influence in the state at a time when the state-idea was giving way to the pressure of economic factors. So far as Rome is con-cerned, he was the archetype of opposition Caesarism; with him there came to an end the *idea of state-service* and there began the "will to power" which ignored traditions and reckoned only with forces. Alexander and Napoleon were romantics; though they

* [Cecil Rhodes was the imperialist-adventurer who was chiefly responsible for the British economic and political conquests in Africa in the late nineteenth century. (*Ed.*)]

stood on the threshold of Civilization and in its cold clear air, the one fancied himself an Achilles and the other read Werther. Caesar, on the contrary, was a pure man of fact gifted with immense understanding.

But even for Rhodes political success means territorial and financial success, and only that. Of this Roman-ness within himself he was fully aware. But Western Civilization has not yet taken shape in such strength and purity as this. It was only before his maps that he could fall into a sort of poetic trance, this son of the parsonage who, sent out to South Africa without means, made a gigantic fortune and employed it as the engine of political aims. His idea of a trans-African railway from the Cape to Cairo, his project of a South African empire, his intellectual hold on the hard metal souls of the mining magnates whose wealth he forced into the service of his schemes, his capital Bulawayo, royally planned as a future Residence by a statesman who was all-powerful yet stood in no definite relation to the State, his wars, his diplomatic deals, his road-systems, his syndicates, his armies, his conception of the "great duty to civilization" of the man of brain—all this, broad and imposing, is the prelude of a future which is still in store for us and with which the history of West-European mankind will be definitely *closed*.

He who does not understand that this outcome is obligatory and insusceptible of modification, that our choice is between *this* and willing nothing at all, between cleaving to *this* destiny or despairing of the future and of life itself; he who cannot feel that there is grandeur also in the realizations of powerful intelligences, in the energy and discipline of metal-hard natures, in battles fought with the coldest and most abstract means; he who is obsessed with the idealism of a provincial and would pursue the ways of life of past ages—must forgo all desire to comprehend history, to live through history or to make history.

Thus regarded, the Imperium Romanum appears no longer as an isolated phenomenon, but as the normal product of a strict and energetic, megalopolitan, predominantly practical spirituality, as typical of a final and irreversible condition which has occurred often enough though it has only been identified as such in this instance.

Let it be realized, then:

That the secret of historical form does not lie on the surface, that it cannot be grasped by means of similarities of costume and setting, and that in the history of men as in that of animals and plants there occur phenomena showing deceptive similarity but inwardly without any connexion—e.g., Charlemagne and Haroun-al-Raschid, Alexander and Caesar, the German wars upon Rome and the Mongol onslaughts upon West Europe—and other phenomena of extreme outward dissimilarity but of identical import—e.g., Trajan and Rameses II, the Bourbons and the Attic Demos, Mohammed and Pythagoras.

That the 19th and 20th centuries, hitherto looked on as the highest point of an ascending straight line of world-history, are in reality a stage of life which may be observed in every Culture that has ripened to its limit—a stage of life characterized not by Socialists, Impressionists, electric railways, torpedoes and differential equations (for these are only body-constituents of the time), but by a civilized spirituality which possesses not only these but also quite other creative possibilities.

That, as our own time represents a transitional phase which occurs with certainty under particular conditions, there are perfectly well-defined states (such as have occurred more than once in the history of the past) *later* than the present-day state of West Europe, and therefore that

The future of the West is not a limitless tending upwards and onwards for all time towards our present ideals, but a single phenomenon of history, strictly limited and defined as to form and duration, which covers a few centuries and can be viewed and, in essentials, calculated from available precedents.

## XIV. The Necessity and Range of Our Basic Idea

This high plane of contemplation once attained, the rest is easy. To this *single* idea one can refer, and by it one can solve, without straining or forcing, all those separate problems of religion, art-history, epistemology, ethics, politics, economics with which the modern intellect has so passionately—and so vainly—busied itself for decades.

This idea is one of those truths that have only to be expressed with full clarity to become indisputable. It is one of the inward necessities of the Western Culture and of its world-feeling. It is capable of entirely transforming the world-outlook of one who fully understands it, i.e., makes it intimately his own. It immensely deepens the world-picture natural and necessary to us in that, already trained to regard world-historical evolution as an organic unit seen backwards from our standpoint in the present, we are enabled by its aid to follow the broad lines into the future—a privilege of dream-calculation till now permitted only to the physicist. It is, I repeat, in effect the sub-stitution of a Copernican for a Ptolemaic aspect of history, that is, an immeasurable widening of horizon.

Up to now everyone has been at liberty to hope what he pleased about the future. Where there are no facts, sentiment rules. But henceforward it will be every man's business to inform himself of what *can* happen and therefore of what with the un-alterable necessity of destiny and irrespective of personal ideals, hopes or desires, *will* happen. When we use the risky word "freedom" we shall mean freedom to do, not this or that, but the necessary or nothing. The feeling that this is "just as it should be" is the hall-mark of the man of fact. To lament it and blame it is not to alter it. To birth belongs death, to youth age, to life generally its form and its allotted span. The present is a civilized, emphatically not a cultured time, and *ipso facto* a great number of life-capacities fall out as impossible. This may be deplorable, and may be and will be deplored in pessimist philosophy and poetry, but it is not in our power to make otherwise. It will not be—already it is not—permissible to defy clear historical experi-ence and to expect, merely because we hope, that this will spring or that will flourish.

It will no doubt be objected that such a world-outlook, which in giving this cer-tainty as to the outlines and tendency of the future cuts off all far-reaching hopes, would be unhealthy for all and fatal for many, once it ceased to be a mere theory and was adopted as a practical scheme of life by the group of personalities effectively moulding the future.

Such is not my opinion. We are civilized, not Gothic or Rococo, people; we have to reckon with the hard cold facts of a *late* life, to which the parallel is to be found not in Pericles's Athens but in Caesar's Rome. Of great painting or great music there can no longer be, for Western people, any question. Their architectural possibilities have been exhausted these hundred years. Only *extensive* possibilities are left to them. Yet, for a sound and vigorous generation that is filled with unlimited hopes,

I fail to see that it is any disadvantage to discover betimes that some of these hopes must come to nothing. And if the hopes thus doomed should be those most dear, well, a man who is worth anything will not be dismayed. It is true that the issue may be a tragic one for some individuals who in their decisive years are overpowered by the conviction that in the spheres of architecture, drama, painting, there is nothing left for *them* to conquer. What matter if they do go under! It has been the convention hitherto to admit no limits of any sort in these matters, and to believe that each period had its own task to do in each sphere. Tasks therefore were found by hook or by crook, leaving it to be settled posthumously whether or not the artist's faith was justified and his life-work necessary. Now, nobody but a pure romantic would take this way out. Such a pride is not the pride of a Roman. What are we to think of the individual who, standing before an exhausted quarry, would rather be told that a new vein will be struck to-morrow—the bait offered by the radically false and mannerized art of the moment—than be shown a rich and virgin claybed near by? The lesson, I think, would be of benefit to the coming generations, as showing them what is possible—and therefore necessary—and what is excluded from the inward potentialities of their time. Hitherto an incredible total of intellect and power has been squandered in false directions. The West-European, however historically he may think and feel, is at a certain stage of life invariably uncertain of his own direction; he gropes and feels his way and, if unlucky in environment, he loses it. But now at last the work of centuries enables him to view the disposition of his own life in relation to the general culture-scheme and to test his own powers and purposes. And I can only hope that men of the new generation may be moved by this book to devote themselves to technics instead of lyrics, the sea instead of the paintbrush, and politics instead of epistemology. Better they could not do.

## ᥕᥱ THE REVOLT OF THE MASSES

*José Ortega y Gasset*

> *José Ortega y Gasset (1883–1955) was the leading Spanish intellectual of the twentieth century, and almost singlehandedly he succeeded in bringing his nation into the mainstream of modern European thought. As a young man he studied in German universities and became an advocate of* Lebensphilosophie *(life-philosophy), a movement which stressed the idea that man's reason is not absolute but embedded in specific historical and "vital" contexts. Accordingly, when Ortega became a professor of metaphysics at the University of Madrid in 1910, metaphysics ceased to be an abstract and forbidding discipline and became an exciting confrontation with Spain's most pressing social and intellectual problems. Soon the brightest young men in the country were flocking to his lectures. An outspoken liberal and antimonarchist, Ortega was elected to the*

*republican* Cortes *(legislature) from 1931 to 1936; but he left the country in disgust when it became a battlefield between fascism and communism, and did not return until 1949.*

The Revolt of the Masses *(1930) is Ortega's best-known book and a twentieth-century classic. In it he discusses a problem which pervades all modern societies in one form or another: the rise of the common man to power and the threat thereby posed to traditional values. Just as Christianity has been discredited in the eyes of many Europeans by its involvement with the old regime, Ortega is afraid that such fragile ideals as truth, beauty, freedom, and nobility of character may not survive the disappearance of the aristocrats who conceived them and kept them alive through the centuries. If anything, the years since 1930 would have substantiated his fears: the barbarism of Nazism and Stalinism may well represent the triumph of the mass man in his sense.*

*Ortega's aristocratic beliefs did not make him an upholder of the status quo in Spain or Latin America where wealthy oligarchs still strive to keep the masses in subjection; but he was no democratic revolutionary either. Rather, he was a humanist and a conservative in the best sense: anxious to conserve the values of civilization in a time of troubles.*

## 1. THE COMING OF THE MASSES

There is one fact which, whether for good or ill, is of utmost importance in the public life of Europe at the present moment. This fact is the accession of the masses to complete social power. As the masses, by definition, neither should nor can direct their own personal existence, and still less rule society in general, this fact means that actually Europe is suffering from the greatest crisis that can afflict peoples, nations, and civilisation. Such a crisis has occurred more than once in history. Its characteristics and its consequences are well known. So also is its name. It is called the rebellion of the masses. In order to understand this formidable fact, it is important from the start to avoid giving to the words "rebellion," "masses," and "social power" a meaning exclusively or primarily political. Public life is not solely political, but equally, and even primarily, intellectual, moral, economic, religious; it comprises all our collective habits, including our fashions both of dress and of amusement.

Perhaps the best line of approach to this historical phenomenon may be found by turning our attention to a visual experience, stressing one aspect of our epoch which is plain to our very eyes. This fact is quite simple to enunciate, though not so to analyse. I shall call it the fact of agglomeration, of "plenitude." Towns are full of

*The Revolt of the Masses* (authorized transl.; New York: W. W. Norton & Company, Inc., 1932), pp. 11–18, 54–60, 68–77, 187–190.

people, houses full of tenants, hotels full of guests, trains full of travellers, cafés full of customers, parks full of promenaders, consulting-rooms of famous doctors full of patients, theatres full of spectators, and beaches full of bathers. What previously was, in general, no problem, now begins to be an everyday one, namely, to find room.

That is all. Can there be any fact simpler, more patent, more constant in actual life? Let us now pierce the plain surface of this observation and we shall be surprised to see how there wells forth an unexpected spring in which the white light of day, of our actual day, is broken up into its rich chromatic content. What is it that we see, and the sight of which causes us so much surprise? We see the multitude, as such, in possession of the places and the instruments created by civilisation. The slightest reflection will then make us surprised at our own surprise. What about it? Is this not the ideal state of things? The theatre has seats to be occupied—in other words, so that the house may be full—and now they are overflowing; people anxious to use them are left standing outside. Though the fact be quite logical and natural, we cannot but recognise that this did not happen before and that now it does; consequently, there has been a change, an innovation, which justifies, at least for the first moment, our surprise.

To be surprised, to wonder, is to begin to understand. This is the sport, the luxury, special to the intellectual man. The gesture characteristic of his tribe consists in looking at the world with eyes wide open in wonder. Everything in the world is strange and marvellous to well-open eyes. This faculty of wonder is the delight refused to your football "fan," and, on the other hand, is the one which leads the intellectual man through life in the perpetual ecstasy of the visionary. His special attribute is the wonder of the eyes. Hence it was that the ancients gave Minerva her owl, the bird with ever-dazzled eyes.

Agglomeration, fullness, was not frequent before. Why then is it now? The components of the multitudes around us have not sprung from nothing. Approximately the same number of people existed fifteen years ago. Indeed, after the war it might seem natural that their number should be less. Nevertheless, it is here we come up against the first important point. The individuals who made up these multitudes existed, but not *qua* multitude. Scattered about the world in small groups, or solitary, they lived a life, to all appearances, divergent, dissociate, apart. Each individual or small group occupied a place, its own, in country, village, town, or quarter of the great city. Now, suddenly, they appear as an agglomeration, and looking in any direction our eyes meet with the multitudes. Not only in any direction, but precisely in the best places, the relatively refined creation of human culture, previously reserved to lesser groups, in a word, to minorities. The multitude has suddenly become visible, installing itself in the preferential positions in society. Before, if it existed, it passed unnoticed, occupying the background of the social stage; now it has advanced to the footlights and is the principal character. There are no longer protagonists; there is only the chorus.

The concept of the multitude is quantitative and visual. Without changing its nature, let us translate it into terms of sociology. We then meet with the notion of the "social mass." Society is always a dynamic unity of two component factors: minorities and masses. The minorities are individuals or groups of individuals which are specially qualified. The mass is the assemblage of persons not specially qualified.

By masses, then, is not to be understood, solely or mainly, "the working masses." The mass is the average man. In this way what was mere quantity—the multitude— is converted into a qualitative determination: it becomes the common social quality, man as undifferentiated from other men, but as repeating in himself a generic type. What have we gained by this conversion of quantity into quality? Simply this: by means of the latter we understand the genesis of the former. It is evident to the verge of platitude that the normal formation of a multitude implies the coincidence of desires, ideas, ways of life, in the individuals who constitute it. It will be objected that this is just what happens with every social group, however select it may strive to be. This is true; but there is an essential difference. In those groups which are characterised by not being multitude and mass, the effective coincidence of its members is based on some desire, idea, or ideal, which of itself excludes the great number. To form a minority, of whatever kind, it is necessary beforehand that each member separate himself from the multitude for *special*, relatively personal, reasons. Their coincidence with the others who form the minority is, then, secondary, posterior to their having each adopted an attitude of singularity, and is consequently, to a large extent, a coincidence in not coinciding. There are cases in which this singularising character of the group appears in the light of day: those English groups, which style themselves "nonconformists," where we have the grouping together of those who agree only in their disagreement in regard to the limitless multitude. This coming together of the minority precisely in order to separate themselves from the majority is a necessary ingredient in the formation of every minority. Speaking of the limited public which listened to a musician of refinement, Mallarmé wittily says that this public by its presence in small numbers stressed the absence of the multitude.

Strictly speaking, the mass, as a psychological fact, can be defined without waiting for individuals to appear in mass formation. In the presence of one individual we can decide whether he is "mass" or not. The mass is all that which sets no value on itself—good or ill—based on specific grounds, but which feels itself "just like every- body," and nevertheless is not concerned about it; is, in fact, quite happy to feel itself as one with everybody else. Imagine a humble-minded man who, having tried to estimate his own worth on specific grounds—asking himself if he has any talent for this or that, if he excels in any direction—realises that he possesses no quality of excellence. Such a man will feel that he is mediocre and commonplace, ill-gifted, but will not feel himself "mass."

When one speaks of "select minorities" it is usual for the evil-minded to twist the sense of this expression, pretending to be unaware that the select man is not the petulant person who thinks himself superior to the rest, but the man who demands more of himself than the rest, even though he may not fulfil in his person those higher exigencies. For there is no doubt that the most radical division that it is possible to make of humanity is that which splits it into two classes of creatures: those who make great demands on themselves, piling up difficulties and duties; and those who demand nothing special of themselves, but for whom to live is to be every moment what they already are, without imposing on themselves any effort towards perfection; mere buoys that float on the waves. This reminds me that orthodox Buddhism is composed of two distinct religions: one, more rigorous and difficult, the other easier and more trivial: the Mahayana—"great vehicle" or "great path"—and the Hinayana—"lesser vehicle" or "lesser path." The decisive matter is whether we attach our life to one or the other vehicle, to a maximum or a minimum of demands upon ourselves.

The division of society into masses and select minorities is, then, not a division into social classes, but into classes of men, and cannot coincide with the hierarchic separation of "upper" and "lower" classes. It is, of course, plain that in these "upper" classes, when and as long as they really are so, there is much more likelihood of finding men who adopt the "great vehicle," whereas the "lower" classes normally comprise individuals of minus quality. But, strictly speaking, within both these social classes, there are to be found mass and genuine minority. As we shall see, a characteristic of our times is the predominance, even in groups traditionally selective, of the mass and the vulgar. Thus, in the intellectual life, which of its essence requires and pre-supposes qualification, one can note the progressive triumph of the pseudo-intellectual, unqualified, unqualifiable, and, by their very mental texture, disqualified. Similarly, in the surviving groups of the "nobility," male and female. On the other hand, it is not rare to find to-day amongst working men, who before might be taken as the best example of what we are calling "mass," nobly disciplined minds.

There exist, then, in society, operations, activities, and functions of the most diverse order, which are of their very nature special, and which consequently cannot be properly carried out without special gifts. For example: certain pleasures of an artistic and refined character, or again the functions of government and of political judgment in public affairs. Previously these special activities were exercised by quali-fied minorities, or at least by those who claimed such qualification. The mass asserted no right to intervene in them; they realised that if they wished to intervene they would necessarily have to acquire those special qualities and cease being mere mass. They recognised their place in a healthy dynamic social system.

If we now revert to the facts indicated at the start, they will appear clearly as the heralds of a changed attitude in the mass. They all indicate that the mass has decided to advance to the foreground of social life, to occupy the places, to use the instruments and to enjoy the pleasures hitherto reserved to the few. It is evident, for example, that the places were never intended for the multitude, for their dimensions are too limited, and the crowd is continuously overflowing; thus manifesting to our eyes and in the clearest manner the new phenomenon: the mass, without ceasing to be mass, is supplanting the minorities.

No one, I believe, will regret that people are to-day enjoying themselves in greater measure and numbers than before, since they have now both the desire and the means of satisfying it. The evil lies in the fact that this decision taken by the masses to assume the activities proper to the minorities is not, and cannot be, manifested solely in the domain of pleasure, but that it is a general feature of our time. Thus —to anticipate what we shall see later—I believe that the political innovations of recent times signify nothing less than the political domination of the masses. The old democracy was tempered by a generous dose of liberalism and of enthusiasm for law. By serving these principles the individual bound himself to maintain a severe dis-cipline over himself. Under the shelter of liberal principles and the rule of law, minorities could live and act. Democracy and law—life in common under the law— were synonymous. To-day we are witnessing the triumphs of a hyperdemocracy in which the mass acts directly, outside the law, imposing its aspirations and its desires by means of material pressure. It is a false interpretation of the new situation to say that the mass has grown tired of politics and handed over the exercise of it to specialised persons. Quite the contrary. That was what happened previously; that was democracy. The mass took it for granted that after all, in spite of their defects and weaknesses, the minorities understood a little more of public problems than it did itself. Now, on the other hand, the mass believes that it has the right to impose and to give force of law to notions born in the café. I doubt whether there have been other periods of history in which the multitude has come to govern more directly than in our own. That is why I speak of hyperdemocracy.

The same thing is happening in other orders, particularly in the intellectual. I may be mistaken, but the present-day writer, when he takes his pen in hand to treat a subject which he has studied deeply, has to bear in mind that the average reader, who has never concerned himself with this subject, if he reads does so with the view, not of learning something from the writer, but rather, of pronouncing judgment on him when he is not in agreement with the commonplaces that the said reader carries in his head. If the individuals who make up the mass believed themselves specially qualified, it would be a case merely of personal error, not a sociological subversion. *The characteristic of the hour is that the commonplace mind, knowing itself to be commonplace, has the assurance to proclaim the rights of the commonplace and to impose them wherever it will.* As they say in the United States: "to be different is to be indecent." The mass crushes beneath it everything that is different, everything that is excellent, individual, qualified and select. Anybody who is not like everybody, who does not think like everybody, runs the risk of being eliminated. And it is clear, of course, that this "everybody" is not "everybody." "Everybody" was normally the complex unity of the mass and the divergent, specialised minorities. Nowadays, "everybody" is the mass alone. Here we have the formidable fact of our times, described without any concealment of the brutality of its features.

\*    \*    \*

## 6. THE DISSECTION OF THE MASS-MAN BEGINS

What is he like, this mass-man who to-day dominates public life, political and non-political, and why is he like it, that is, how has he been produced?

It will be well to answer both questions together, for they throw light on one another. The man who to-day is attempting to take the lead in European existence is very different from the man who directed the XIXth Century, but he was produced and prepared by the XIXth Century. Any keen mind of the years 1820, 1850, and 1880 could by simple *a priori* reasoning, foresee the gravity of the present historical situation, and in fact nothing is happening now which was not foreseen a hundred years ago. "The masses are advancing," said Hegel in apocalyptic fashion. "Without some new spiritual influence, our age, which is a revolutionary age, will produce a catastrophe," was the pronouncement of Comte. "I see the flood-tide of nihilism rising," shrieked Nietzsche from a crag of the Engadine. It is false to say that history cannot be foretold. Numberless times this has been done. If the future offered no opening to prophecy, it could not be understood when fulfilled in the present and on the point of falling back into the past. The idea that the historian is on the reverse side of a prophet, sums up the whole philosophy of history. It is true that it is only possible to anticipate the general structure of the future, but that is all that we in truth understand of the past or of the present. Accordingly, if you want a good view of your own age, look at it from far off. From what distance? The answer is simple. Just far enough to prevent you seeing Cleopatra's nose.

What appearance did life present to that multitudinous man who in ever-increasing abundance in the XIXth Century kept producing? To start with, an appearance of universal material ease. Never had the average man been able to solve his economic problem with greater facility. Whilst there was a proportionate decrease of great fortunes and life became harder for the individual worker, the middle classes found their economic horizon widened every day. Every day added a new luxury to their standard of life. Every day their position was more secure and more independent of another's will. What before would have been considered one of fortune's gifts, inspiring humble gratitude towards destiny, was converted into a right, not to be grateful for, but to be insisted on.

From 1900 on, the worker likewise begins to extend and assure his existence. Nevertheless, he has to struggle to obtain his end. He does not, like the middle class, find the benefit attentively served up to him by a society and a state which are a marvel of organisation. To this ease and security of economic conditions are to be added the physical ones, comfort and public order. Life runs on smooth rails, and there is no likelihood of anything violent or dangerous breaking in on it. Such a free, untrammeled situation was bound to instil into the depths of such souls an idea of existence which might be expressed in the witty and penetrating phrase of an old country like ours: "Wide is Castile." That is to say, in all its primary and decisive aspects, life presented itself to the new man as *exempt from restrictions*. The realisation of this fact and of its importance becomes immediate when we remember that such a freedom of existence was entirely lacking to the common men of the past. On the contrary, for them life was a burdensome destiny, economically and physically. From birth, existence meant to them an accumulation of impediments which they were obliged to suffer, without possible solution other than to adapt themselves to them, to settle down in the narrow space they left available.

But still more evident is the contrast of situations, if we pass from the material to the civil and moral. The average man, from the second half of the XIXth Century on, finds no social barriers raised against him. That is to say, that as regards the forms of public life he no longer finds himself from birth confronted with obstacles and limitations. There is nothing to force him to limit his existence. Here again, "Wide is Castile." There are no "estates" or "castes." There are no civil privileges. The ordinary man learns that all men are equal before the law.

Never in the course of history had man been placed in vital surroundings even remotely familiar to those set up by the conditions just mentioned. We are, in fact, confronted with a radical innovation in human destiny, implanted by the XIXth Century. A new stage has been mounted for human existence, new both in the physical and the social aspects. Three principles have made possible this new world: liberal democracy, scientific experiment, and industrialism. The two latter may be summed up in one word: technicism. Not one of those principles was invented by the XIXth Century; they proceed from the two previous centuries. The glory of the XIXth Century lies not in their discovery, but in their implantation. No one but recognises that fact. But it is not sufficient to recognise it in the abstract, it is necessary to realise its inevitable consequences.

The XIXth Century was of its essence revolutionary. This aspect is not to be looked for in the scenes of the barricades, which are mere incidents, but in the fact that it placed the average man—the great social mass—in conditions of life radically opposed to those by which he had always been surrounded. It turned his public existence upside down. Revolution is not the uprising against pre-existing order, but the setting up of a new order contradictory to the traditional one. Hence there is no exaggeration in saying that the man who is the product of the XIXth Century is, for the effects of public life, a man apart from all other men. The XVIIIth-Century man differs, of course, from the XVIIth-Century man, and this one in turn from his fellow of the XVIth Century, but they are all related, similar, even identical in essentials when confronted with this new man. For the "common" man of all periods "life" had principally meant limitation, obligation, dependence; in a word, pressure. Say oppression, if you like, provided it be understood not only in the juridical and social sense, but also in the cosmic. For it is this latter which has never been lacking up to a hundred years ago, the date at which starts the practically limitless expansion of scientific technique—physical and administrative. Previously, even for the rich and powerful, the world was a place of poverty, difficulty and danger.[1]

The world which surrounds the new man from his birth does not compel him to limit himself in any fashion, it sets up no veto in opposition to him; on the contrary, it incites his appetite, which in principle can increase indefinitely. Now it turns out—and this is most important—that this world of the XIXth and early XXth Centuries not only has the perfections and the completeness which it actually possesses, but furthermore suggests to those who dwell in it the radical assurance that to-morrow it will be still richer, ampler, more perfect, as if it enjoyed a spontaneous, inexhaustible power of increase. Even to-day, in spite of some signs which are making a tiny breach in that sturdy faith, even to-day, there are few men who doubt that motorcars will in five years' time be more comfortable and cheaper than to-day. They believe in this as they believe that the sun will rise in the morning. The metaphor is an exact one. For, in fact, the common man, finding himself in a world so excellent, technically and socially, believes that it has been produced by nature, and never thinks of the personal efforts of highly-endowed individuals which the creation of this new world presupposed. Still less will he admit the notion that all these facilities still require the support of

---

[1] *However rich an individual might be in relation to his fellows, as the world in its totality was poor, the sphere of conveniences and commodities with which his wealth furnished him was very limited. The life of the average man to-day is easier, more convenient and safer than that of the most powerful of another age. What difference does it make to him not to be richer than others if the world is richer and furnishes him with magnificent roads, railways, telegraphs, hotels, personal safety and aspirin?*

certain difficult human virtues, the least failure of which would cause the rapid disappearance of the whole magnificent edifice.

This leads us to note down in our psychological chart of the mass-man of to-day
two fundamental traits: the free expansion of his vital desires, and therefore, of his
personality; and his radical ingratitude towards all that has made possible the ease
of his existence. These traits together make up the well-known psychology of the
spoilt child. And in fact it would entail no error to use this psychology as a "sight"
through which to observe the soul of the masses of to-day. Heir to an ample and
generous past—generous both in ideals and in activities—the new commonalty has
been spoiled by the world around it. To spoil means to put no limit on caprice, to
give one the impression that everything is permitted to him and that he has no
obligations. The young child exposed to this regime has no experience of its own
limits. By reason of the removal of all external restraint, all clashing with other
things, he comes actually to believe that he is the only one that exists, and gets used
to not considering others, especially not considering them as superior to himself.
This feeling of another's superiority could only be instilled into him by someone
who, being stronger than he is, should force him to give up some desire, to restrict
himself, to restrain himself. He would then have learned this fundamental discipline:
"Here I end and here begins another more powerful than I am. In the world, apparently, there are two people: I myself and another superior to me." The ordinary
man of past times was daily taught this elemental wisdom by the world about him,
because it was a world so rudely organised, that catastrophes were frequent, and
there was nothing in it certain, abundant, stable. But the new masses find themselves
in the presence of a prospect full of possibilities, and furthermore, quite secure,
with everything ready to their hands, independent of any previous efforts on their
part, just as we find the sun in the heavens without our hoisting it up on our
shoulders. No human being thanks another for the air he breathes, for no one has
produced the air for him; it belongs to the sum-total of what "is there," of which
we say "it is natural," because it never fails. And these spoiled masses are unintelligent enough to believe that the material and social organisation, placed at their
disposition like the air, is of the same origin, since apparently it never fails them,
and is almost as perfect as the natural scheme of things.

My thesis, therefore, is this: the very perfection with which the XIXth Century
gave an organisation to certain orders of existence has caused the masses benefited
thereby to consider it, not as an organised, but as a natural system. Thus is explained
and defined the absurd state of mind revealed by these masses; they are only concerned with their own well-being, and at the same time they remain alien to the
cause of that well-being. As they do not see, behind the benefits of civilisation, marvels
of invention and construction which can only be maintained by great effort and
foresight, they imagine that their role is limited to demanding these benefits peremp-
torily, as if they were natural rights. In the disturbances caused by scarcity of food,
the mob goes in search of bread, and the means it employs is generally to wreck the
bakeries. This may serve as a symbol of the attitude adopted, on a greater and more
complicated scale, by the masses of to-day towards the civilisation by which they are
supported.

8. WHY THE MASSES INTERVENE IN EVERYTHING,
AND WHY THEIR INTERVENTION IS SOLELY BY VIOLENCE

We take it, then, that there has happened something supremely paradoxical, but which was in truth most natural; from the very opening-out of the world and of life for the average man, his soul has shut up within him. Well, then, I maintain that it is in this obliteration of the average soul that the rebellion of the masses consists, and in this in its turn lies the gigantic problem set before humanity to-day.

I know well that many of my readers do not think as I do. This also is most natural and confirms the theorem. For although my opinion turn out erroneous, there will always remain the fact that many of those dissentient readers have never given five minutes' thought to this complex matter. How are they going to think as I do? But by believing that they have a right to an opinion on the matter without previous effort to work one out for themselves, they prove patently that they belong to that absurd type of human being which I have called the "rebel mass." It is precisely what I mean by having one's soul obliterated, hermetically closed. Here it would be the special case of intellectual hermetism. The individual finds himself already with a stock of ideas. He decides to content himself with them and to consider himself intellectually complete. As he feels the lack of nothing outside himself, he settles down definitely amid his mental furniture. Such is the mechanism of self-obliteration.

The mass-man regards himself as perfect. The select man, in order to regard himself so, needs to be specially vain, and the belief in his perfection is not united with him consubstantially, it is not ingenuous, but arises from his vanity, and even for himself has a fictitious, imaginary, problematic character. Hence the vain man stands in need of others, he seeks in them support for the idea that he wishes to have of himself. So that not even in this diseased state, not even when blinded by vanity, does the "noble" man succeed in feeling himself as in truth complete. Contrariwise, it never occurs to the mediocre man of our days, to the New Adam, to doubt of his own plenitude. His self-confidence is, like Adam's, paradisiacal. The innate hermetism of his soul is an obstacle to the necessary condition for his discovery of his insufficiency, namely: a comparison of himself with other beings. To compare himself would mean to go out of himself for a moment and to transfer himself to his neighbour. But the mediocre soul is incapable of transmigrations—the supreme form of sport.

We find ourselves, then, met with the same difference that eternally exists between the fool and the man of sense. The latter is constantly catching himself within an inch of being a fool; hence he makes an effort to escape from the imminent folly, and in that effort lies his intelligence. The fool, on the other hand, does not suspect himself; he thinks himself the most prudent of men, hence the enviable tranquillity with which the fool settles down, instals himself in his own folly. Like those insects which it is impossible to extract from the orifice they inhabit, there is no way of dislodging the fool from his folly, to take him away for a while from his blind state and to force him to contrast his own dull vision with other keener forms of sight. The fool is a fool for life; he is devoid of pores. This is why Anatole France said that the fool is much worse than the knave, for the knave does take a rest sometimes, the fool never.

It is not a question of the mass-man being a fool. On the contrary, to-day he is more clever, has more capacity of understanding than his fellow of any previous period. But that capacity is of no use to him; in reality, the vague feeling that he possesses it seems only to shut him up more within himself and keep him from using it. Once for all, he accepts the stock of commonplaces, prejudices, fag-ends of ideas or simply empty words which chance has piled up within his mind, and with a boldness only explicable by his ingenuousness, is prepared to impose them everywhere. This is what in my first chapter I laid down as the characteristic of our time; not that the vulgar believes itself super-excellent and not vulgar, but that the vulgar proclaims and imposes the rights of vulgarity, or vulgarity as a right.

The command over public life exercised to-day by the intellectually vulgar is perhaps the factor of the present situation which is most novel, least assimilable to anything in the past. At least in European history up to the present, the vulgar had never believed itself to have "ideas" on things. It had beliefs, traditions, experiences, proverbs, mental habits, but it never imagined itself in possession of theoretical opinions on what things are or ought to be—for example, on politics or literature. What the politician planned or carried out seemed good or bad to it, it granted or withheld its support, but its action was limited to being an echo, positive or negative, of the creative activity of others. It never occurred to it to oppose to the "ideas" of the politician others of its own, nor even to judge the politician's "ideas" from the tribunal of other "ideas" which it believed itself to possess. Similarly in art and in other aspects of public life. An innate consciousness of its limitation, of its not being qualified to theorise, effectively prevented it doing so. The necessary consequence of this was that the vulgar never thought, even remotely, of making a decision on any one of the public activities, which in their greater part are theoretical in character. To-day, on the other hand, the average man has the most mathematical "ideas" on all that happens or ought to happen in the universe. Hence he has lost the use of his hearing. Why should he listen if he has within him all that is necessary? There is no reason now for listening, but rather for judging, pronouncing, deciding. There is no question concerning public life, in which he does not intervene, blind and deaf as he is, imposing his "opinions."

But, is this not an advantage? Is it not a sign of immense progress that the masses should have "ideas," that is to say, should be cultured? By no means. The "ideas" of the average man are not genuine ideas, nor is their possession culture. An idea is a putting truth in checkmate. Whoever wishes to have ideas must first prepare himself to desire truth and to accept the rules of the game imposed by it. It is no use speaking of ideas when there is no acceptance of a higher authority to regulate them, a series of standards to which it is possible to appeal in a discussion. These standards are the principles on which culture rests. I am not concerned with the form they take. What I affirm is that there is no culture where there are no standards to which our fellow-men can have recourse. There is no culture where there are no principles of legality to which to appeal. There is no culture where there is no acceptance of certain final intellectual positions to which a dispute may be referred.[1] There is no culture where economic relations are not subject to a regulating principle to protect interests involved. There is no culture where aesthetic controversy does not recognise the necessity of justifying the work of art.

When all these things are lacking there is no culture; there is in the strictest sense of the word, barbarism. And let us not deceive ourselves, this is what is beginning to appear in Europe under the progressive rebellion of the masses. The traveller who arrives in a barbarous country knows that in that territory there are no ruling principles to which it is possible to appeal. Properly speaking, there are no barbarian standards. Barbarism is the absence of standards to which appeal can be made.

The varying degrees of culture are measured by the greater or less precision of the standards. Where there is little such precision, these standards rule existence only *grosso modo;* where there is much they penetrate in detail into the exercise of all the activities.

Anyone can observe that in Europe, for some years past, "strange things" have begun to happen. To give a concrete example of these "strange things" I shall name certain political movements, such as Syndicalism and Fascism. We must not think that they seem strange simply because they are new. The enthusiasm for novelty is so innate in the European that it has resulted in his producing the most unsettled history of all known to us. The element of strangeness in these new facts is not to be attributed to the element of novelty, but to the extraordinary form taken by these new things. Under the species of Syndicalism and Fascism there appears for the first time in Europe a type of man who does not want to give reasons or to be right, but simply shows himself resolved to impose his opinions. This is the new thing: the right not to be reasonable, the "reason of unreason." Here I see the most palpable manifestation of the new mentality of the masses, due to their having decided to rule society without the capacity for doing so. In their political conduct the structure of the new mentality is revealed in the rawest, most convincing manner; but the key to it lies in intellectual hermetism. The average man finds himself with "ideas" in his head, but he lacks the faculty of ideation. He has no conception even of the rare atmosphere in which ideas live. He wishes to have opinions, but is unwilling to accept the conditions and presuppositions that underlie all opinion. Hence his ideas are in effect nothing more than appetites in words, something like musical romanzas.

To have an idea means believing one is in possession of the reasons for having it, and consequently means believing that there is such a thing as reason, a world of intelligible truths. To have ideas, to form opinions, is identical with appealing to such an authority, submitting oneself to it, accepting its code and its decisions, and therefore believing that the highest form of intercommunion is the dialogue in which the reasons for our ideas are discussed. But the mass-man would feel himself lost if he accepted discussion, and instinctively repudiates the obligation of accepting that supreme authority lying outside himself. Hence the "new thing" in Europe is "to have done with discussions," and detestation is expressed for all forms of intercommunion which imply acceptance of objective standards, ranging from conversation to Parliament, and taking

---

[1] *If anyone in a discussion with us is not concerned with adjusting himself to truth, if he has no wish to find the truth, he is intellectually a barbarian. That, in fact, is the position of the mass-man when he speaks, lectures, or writes.*

in science. This means that there is a renunciation of the common life based on culture, which is subject to standards, and a return to the common life of barbarism. All the normal processes are suppressed in order to arrive directly at the imposition of what is desired. The hermetism of the soul which, as we have seen before, urges the mass to intervene in the whole of public life, also inevitably leads it to one single process of intervention: direct action.

When the reconstruction of the origins of our epoch is undertaken, it will be observed that the first notes of its special harmony were sounded in those groups of French syndicalists and realists of about 1900, inventors of the method and the name of "direct action." Man has always had recourse to violence; sometimes this recourse was a mere crime, and does not interest us here. But at other times violence was the means resorted to by him who had previously exhausted all others in defence of the rights of justice which he thought he possessed. It may be regrettable that human nature tends on occasion to this form of violence, but it is undeniable that it implies the greatest tribute to reason and justice. For this form of violence is none other than reason exasperated. Force was, in fact, the *ultima ratio*. Rather stupidly it had been the custom to take ironically this expression, which clearly indicates the previous submission of force to methods of reason. Civilisation is nothing else than the attempt to reduce force to being the *ultima ratio*. We are now beginning to realise this with startling clearness, because "direct action" consists in inverting the order and proclaiming violence as *prima ratio*, or strictly as *unica ratio*. It is the norm which proposes the annulment of all norms, which suppresses all intermediate process between our purpose and its execution. It is the Magna Charta of barbarism.

It is well to recall that at every epoch when the mass, for one purpose or another, has taken a part in public life, it has been in the form of "direct action." This was, then, the natural *modus operandi* of the masses. And the thesis of this essay is strongly confirmed by the patent fact that at present when the overruling intervention in public life of the masses has passed from casual and infrequent to being the normal, it is "direct action" which appears officially as the recognized method.

All our communal life is coming under this regime in which appeal to "indirect" authority is suppressed. In social relations "good manners" no longer hold sway. Literature as "direct action" appears in the form of insult. The restrictions of sexual relations are reduced.

Restrictions, standards, courtesy, indirect methods, justice, reason! Why were all these invented, why all these complications created? They are all summed up in the word civilisation, which, through the underlying notion of *civis*, the citizen, reveals its real origin. By means of all these there is an attempt to make possible the city, the community, common life. Hence, if we look into all these constituents of civilisation just enumerated, we shall find the same common basis. All, in fact, presuppose the radical progressive desire on the part of each individual to take others into consideration. Civilisation is before all, the will to live in common. A man is uncivilised, barbarian in the degree in which he does not take others in account. Barbarism is the tendency to disassociation. Accordingly, all barbarous epochs have been times of human scattering, of the pullulation of tiny groups, separate from and hostile to one another.

The political doctrine which has represented the loftiest endeavour towards common

life is liberal democracy. It carries to the extreme the determination to have consideration for one's neighbour and is the prototype of "indirect action." Liberalism is that
principle of political rights, according to which the public authority, in spite of being
all-powerful, limits itself and attempts, even at its own expense, to leave room in the
State over which it rules for those to live who neither think nor feel as it does, that is
to say as do the stronger, the majority. Liberalism—it is well to recall this to-day—is
the supreme form of generosity; it is the right which the majority concedes to minorities and hence it is the noblest cry that has ever resounded in this planet. It announces
the determination to share existence with the enemy; more than that, with an enemy
which is weak. It was incredible that the human species should have arrived at so noble
an attitude, so paradoxical, so refined, so acrobatic, so antinatural. Hence, it is not to
be wondered at that this same humanity should soon appear anxious to get rid of it.
It is a discipline too difficult and complex to take firm root on earth.

Share our existence with the enemy! Govern with the opposition! Is not such a
form of tenderness beginning to seem incomprehensible? Nothing indicates more
clearly the characteristics of the day than the fact that there are so few countries where
an opposition exists. In almost all, a homogeneous mass weighs on public authority
and crushes down, annihilates every opposing group. The mass—who would credit
it as one sees its compact, multitudinous appearance?—does not wish to share life
with those who are not of it. It has a deadly hatred of all that is not itself.

## 15.  WE ARRIVE AT THE REAL QUESTION

This is the question: Europe has been left without a moral code. It is not that the
mass-man has thrown over an antiquated one in exchange for a new one, but that at
the centre of his scheme of life there is precisely the aspiration to live without con-
forming to any moral code. Do not believe a word you hear from the young when they
talk about the "new morality." I absolutely deny that there exists to-day in any corner
of the Continent a group inspired by a new *ethos* which shows signs of being a moral
code. When people talk of the "new morality" they are merely committing a new
immorality and looking for a way of introducing contraband goods. Hence it would
be a piece of ingenuousness to accuse the man of to-day of his lack of moral code.
The accusation would leave him cold, or rather, would flatter him. Immoralism has
become a commonplace, and anybody and everybody boasts of practising it.

If we leave out of question, as has been done in this essay, all those groups which
imply survivals from the past—Christians, Idealists, the old Liberals—there will not
be found amongst all the representatives of the actual period, a single group whose
attitude to life is not limited to believing that it has all the rights and none of the
obligations. It is indifferent whether it disguises itself as reactionary or revolutionary;
actively or passively, after one or two twists, its state of mind will consist, decisively,
in ignoring all obligations, and in feeling itself, without the slightest notion why, possessed of unlimited rights. Whatever be the substance which takes possession of such
a soul, it will produce the same result, and will change into a pretext for not con-
forming to any concrete purpose. If it appears as reactionary or anti-liberal it will be

in order to affirm that the salvation of the State gives a right to level down all other standards, and to manhandle one's neighbour, above all if one's neighbour is an outstanding personality. But the same happens if it decides to act the revolutionary; the apparent enthusiasm for the manual worker, for the afflicted and for social justice, serves as a mask to facilitate the refusal of all obligations, such as courtesy, truthfulness and, above all, respect or esteem for superior individuals. I know of quite a few who have entered the ranks of some labour organisation or other merely in order to win for themselves the right to despise intelligence and to avoid paying it any tribute. As regards other kinds of Dictatorship, we have seen only too well how they flatter the mass-man, by trampling on everything that appeared to be above the common level.

This fighting-shy of every obligation partly explains the phenomenon, half ridiculous, half disgraceful, of the setting-up in our days of the platform of "youth" as youth. Perhaps there is no more grotesque spectacle offered by our times. In comic fashion people call themselves "young," because they have heard that youth has more rights than obligations, since it can put off the fulfilment of these latter to the Greek Kalends of maturity. The youth, as such, has always been considered exempt from *doing* or *having done* actions of importance. He has always lived on credit. It was a sort of false right, half ironic, half affectionate, which the no-longer young conceded to their juniors. But the astounding thing at present is that these take it as an effective right precisely in order to claim for themselves all those other rights which only belong to the man who has already done something.

Though it may appear incredible, "youth" has become a *chantage*; we are in truth living in a time when this adopts two complementary attitudes, violence and caricature. One way or the other, the purpose is always the same; that the inferior, the man of the crowd, may feel himself exempt from all submission to superiors.

It will not do, then, to dignify the actual crisis by presenting it as the conflict between two moralities, two civilisations, one in decay, the other at its dawn. The mass-man is simply without morality, which is always, in essence, a sentiment of submission to something, a consciousness of service and obligation. But perhaps it is a mistake to say "simply." For it is not merely a question of this type of creature doing without morality. No, we must not make his task too easy. Morality cannot be eliminated without more ado. What, by a word lacking even in grammar, is called *amorality* is a thing that does not exist. If you are unwilling to submit to any norm, you have, *nolens volens,* to submit to the norm of denying all morality, and this is not amoral, but immoral. It is a negative morality which preserves the empty form of the other. How has it been possible to believe in the amorality of life? Doubtless, because all modern culture and civilisation tend to that conviction. Europe is now reaping the painful results of her spiritual conduct. She has adopted blindly a culture which is magnificent, but has no roots.

In this essay an attempt has been made to sketch a certain type of European, mainly by analysing his behaviour as regards the very civilization into which he was born. This had to be done because that individual does not represent a new civilization struggling with a previous one, but a mere negation. Hence it did not serve our purpose to mix up the portrayal of his mind with the great question: What are the radical defects from which modern European culture suffers? For it is evident that in the long run the form of humanity dominant at the present day has its origin in these defects.

This great question must remain outside these pages. Its treatment would require of us to unfold in detail the doctrine of human existence which, like a *leitmotiv*, is interwoven, insinuated, whispered in them. Perhaps, before long, it may be cried aloud.

## ᴥᔆ THE FUTURE AS HISTORY

### Robert L. Heilbroner

*If in this country we have had our share of utopian prophets and more than our share of science-fiction writers, historian-prophets like Spengler (see page 525) or Toynbee have been alien to the American tradition. Perhaps to survey the vast sweep of human experience, viewing past and future in the same plane, runs counter to our preoccupation with the practical and the tangible. Perhaps it is also true that nothing in our experience as a nation forced us to accept our past as a straitjacket or our history as a mortgage on our future. America's increasing involvement in a complex and intractable world during this century may indeed be undermining our traditional dream of a future of unlimited possibilities. In any case, it is to this problem of the historical relevance of American optimism that the contemporary economist and historian Robert L. Heilbroner addresses himself in the selection that follows.*

### 1. A Recapitulation

. . . In the past, as we know, we have approached the future with the sustaining beliefs of a philosophy of optimism. That is, we always conceived of the future in terms of its benignity, its malleability, its compatibility with our hopes and desires. But if our preceding pages have had any purpose, it has been to demonstrate the inadequacy of this belief today. It is no longer possible for America to commit itself trustingly into the hands of a deity of history whose agent forces are comfortably circumscribed and comfortingly familiar. If one thing is certain it is that history's forces have reached a power utterly unlike that of our sheltered past, and that the changes those forces portend are very different from the propitious historic transformations they brought about in our past.

Robert L. Heilbroner, *The Future as History* (New York: Grove Press, Inc., 1959), pp. 175–209.

Let us briefly recapitulate what some of those changes are likely to be:

1 As a consequence of the new weapons technology we have not only lost our accustomed military security, but also any possibility of enforcing a military "solution" to the problem of communism. The weapons stalemate has thus magnified the influence of the non-military determinants of the central struggle of our times. The "historic forces" of politics and economics, of technologies and ideologies, are therefore of crucial importance in the resolution of this contest.

2 The trend of these forces is not an encouraging one. In the huge continents to the East and South we have witnessed an explosive awakening of hitherto ignored or abused peoples, who now seek a rapid redress of their age-old grievances. This has led the underdeveloped nations into a desperate effort for economic development—an effort which, in the environment of underdevelopment, turns naturally in the direction of economic collectivism. There are strong possibilities that this collectivism will veer far to the left, whether or not it falls directly under communist hegemony. It is likely as well to discard the frail structures of democracy, and to maintain its morale by an exaggerated nationalism. Finally, we must not ignore the possibility that American economic growth, by widening the gap between the underdeveloped peoples and ourselves, may place America at the focus of the frustration and resentments which economic development is likely at first to generate.

3 At the same time, the drift of Western society is itself away from the traditional forms of capitalism. In all nations, including our own, a framework of "socialist" planning is replacing the unregulated market mechanism. In Europe this drift into planning is made more significant by the fact that European capitalism, unlike American, is not a self-assured and unchallenged social order.

4 However, within our own nation there are strong tendencies which move us away from the traditional, and now perhaps nostalgic idea of American society. One of these is the rampant technological and scientific development which marks our time. This development manifests itself in a proliferation of institutions needed to "support" the increasingly dependent individual, and in the rise of bureaucratic apparatuses needed to control the technological machinery itself. The rise of the welfare state, on the one hand, and of the military bureaucracy, on the other, are instances of the manner in which technology is enforcing a socialization of life.

5 There are also visible other tendencies which are transforming our society, particularly in its economic aspect. There is a strong likelihood that a radical redefinition of the limits of public economic activity will be enforced by the pressure of events. Over the near future this is likely to be provided in disguised form by the enlarging military sector, but in the longer run we shall probably be forced to find civilian outlets to replace the military. Somewhat further ahead lies the still more difficult problem of providing internal economic discipline in a society in which the usual market control mechanisms are increasingly weakened by widespread social abundance.

6 All these collectivist trends are accelerated by our main historic movement—our growth. The problem then is the degree to which our blind economic momentum makes it impossible to respond effectively to the technological, political, and

economic forces which are bringing about a closing-in of our historic future. This is a question to which dogmatic answers cannot be given. But it must be pointed out that an effective control over the historic forces of our times would require changes not only in the structure of power but in the common denominator of values, which do not seem likely to occur, at least for a considerable period.

The probabilities, in other words, are that "history" will go against us for a long time, and that the trend of events, both at home and abroad, will persist in directions which we find inimical and uncongenial. It would be foolish to pretend to a degree of prescience about the future which no amount of analysis can provide, or to be doctrinaire about the evolution of events. Yet surely, to hope for the best in a situation where every indication leads us to expect a worsening, is hardly the way to fortify ourselves against the future. Optimism as a philosophy of historic expectations can no longer be considered a national virtue. It has become a dangerous national delusion.

But if our optimism fails and misleads us, what shall we put in its place? How shall we prepare ourselves for the oncoming challenges of the future? What might be the character of a philosophy suited to our times? These are the deeply meaningful questions to which we now turn.

## 2. The Failures of Optimism

It may help us to formulate answers to these questions if we ask ourselves what it has been about the recent past for which optimism as a philosophy of historic expectations has failed to prepare us. The answer is explicit in the theme of this book. It is an outlook on the future *as history.*

This is not to say that optimism does not contain—albeit tacitly—an estimate of the future "as history." We have already endeavored to show its roots in the technological, political, and economic forces that have generated modern history, and its unconscious assumptions about the automatic progress which those forces effect. But what is missing from the philosophy of optimism is a conscious recognition of the special circumstances of history from which it arose and about which it generalizes. It is a failure to see itself as the product of a unique and sheltered historic experience which could not be enlarged into a model for all historic experience irrespective of its setting.

As a result, optimism has misled us in two particulars. First, it has caused us to overestimate the degree of our freedom in history. Because it mirrors an historic experience in which our conscious efforts to "make" history coincided with and were aided by the movement *of* history, optimism has given us the notion that history is only, or largely, the product of our volitions. Thus it has deluded us as to our power when the forces of history run not with, but counter to, our designs. It has filled us with a belief that everything is possible, and has made it not a sign of wisdom but a suspicion of weakness to think in terms of what is impossible.

Secondly, optimism has given us a simplistic idea of the forces of history. Assessing those forces in terms of their eighteenth- and nineteenth-century manifestations, it has failed to alert us to the possibility that the identical basic forces, in another environment, might lead to very different results from those which we assume to be their natural outcome. Thus the philosophy of optimism has presented the idea of technical progress solely in terms of the enhancement of man's productive powers—which was

indeed its outstanding attribute in the past—rather than in terms of the social repercussions of technology which may well be its principal impact upon us in the present
and future. Similarly, the optimistic outlook has taught us that the impetus of popular
political aspiration leads naturally to the development of democratic governments, as
it did in the cradle of history in which it was nurtured, but has failed to alert us as
to the turning which those self-same aspirations can take—and have already taken—
in an environment in which the preconditions for Western parliamentary democracy
are totally absent. Finally, in the terms of the optimistic philosophy, the consequences
of economic progress have been perhaps the most artlessly conceived of all. Quite aside
from whether it correctly judged the outcome of the internal mechanics of capitalism,
the optimistic outlook made economic advancement itself an unambiguous and self-
evident social goal—a point of view which, however justified by the conditions of
insufficiency of the nineteenth century, entirely obscures the new problems, both of
organization and of values, which the achievement of abundance itself brings into
being.

Thus if we are to suggest the attributes of a philosophy of expectations better
adapted to our times than that of optimism, we shall have to explore more fully the
two main areas in which optimism is deficient. First we shall have to ask: What is
possible at this moment in our history? What are the limits of intervention into, what
are the "necessities" of the historic process? Secondly, we shall have to inquire: What
attributes of the forces of history are neglected by the philosophy of optimism? How
can we prepare for their unexpected and often unwelcome repercussions? In a word,
how can we think about the future as history?

## 3. The Limits of the Possible

Everyone who considers the first of these questions—what is "possible" and "impossible" in history—soon comes up against a classic dilemma. This is the dilemma
of "free will"—or in terms of the historic process, of determinism versus historic
freedom. It is the dilemma of choosing between a world where everything is "possible"
and therefore where nothing can be counted on, including the most basic necessities
for the continuance of the human community; and a world where nothing is possible,
and therefore where nothing can be hoped for except that which is inevitably and
immutably fixed and beyond alteration. It is a choice between history as chaos and
history as a prison. . . .

Once we approach the matter in this direct and pragmatic fashion, the idea of what
is "possible" in history presents itself intelligibly enough before us. We then find ourselves confronted, as a condition of life, with a situation which may be logically awkward but which is not at all awkward as a fact. This is the coexistence of freedom and
necessity in history—the simultaneous existence of its glacial imperturbability, its
"laws," its "necessities" on the one hand, and its "freedom," its openness, its amen-
ability to our wills on the other.

The point at which we can divide freedom from necessity also comes to us with
reasonable clarity. We all know that there are some historic events—such as, for instance, the internal politics of Soviet rule—which it is virtually impossible for us to
affect. We recognize another class of events that lie directly—or at least to an important
degree—within the scope of our control and responsibility. The "possibility" of war,

for instance, is a matter in which we are quite sure that our free decisions play an immense and probably determinative role—all the more so, since so many aspects of the "historic" situation clearly set the stage for war.

This is, however, only one way of assessing what is historically possible for us. For what we deem to be "historic events" by no means exhausts the aspects of change and development in history. As Karl Popper reminds us, "There is no history of mankind, there is only an indefinite number of histories of all kinds of aspects of human life"; and when we turn to those aspects of history with which this book has been primarily concerned—the aspects of social change rather than of immediate political conflict— we find our possibilities of history-making sharply curtailed. In our society, the "history" of technological progress and penetration, or the "history" of political belief and economic development are not facets of human life which we normally subject to "history-making" decisions. In general we allow these aspects of history to follow their autonomous courses, and to evolve by their unguided interactions. Thus we limit our idea of what is possible in history by excluding from our control the forces of history themselves.

This is a very different situation from that which obtains in a more collectivistic society. The enormous national effort of Russian growth or the wholesale alterations in the social structure of China are instances of historic change whose possibility was initially discounted by observers who had in mind the limitations of historic intervention in our own kind of society. The point, then, is that there are no fixed and immutable limits to what is historically possible. Rather, different organizations of society define for themselves the limits of what is and what is not within reach of conscious history-making choice. Authoritarian societies, as a generality, have a much more comprehensive direction of the "forces" of history than open societies. On the other hand, open societies, through their democratic apparatus, retain a wider degree of control over the course of their "heroic" history, i.e., over the policies of their leaders.

## 4. The Possibilities before America

What does this imply for the "possibility" of altering the historic outlook that lies before us?

To the extent that we are concerned with those aspects of the future which will be molded by the anonymous forces of technology, political ideology, and economic evolution, we must accept the conclusion that the possibilities of major intervention are not great. For the portents of the future spring, in the main, from underlying pressures of ideologies and from the fixed structures of institutions whose conscious manipulation does not now lie within the reach of our accepted "history-making" powers. Of course we can make small changes in the superstructure of our institutions. But if, for example, we really want to undo the "creeping socialism" of our time, we should have to do more than legislate away our institutions of social welfare and economic control. To remove these institutions without removing the massive technology and the economic instability which have produced them would only be to open the way for a social explosion which would probably swing even further leftward. Essentially, the only way to halt the creep of "socialism" is to return to an atomistic economy with small-scale technical and economic units, and with a wholly different climate of political and social beliefs. This it is obviously impossible for us to attempt, without a degree of historic intervention which is entirely alien to our social philosophy.

It may even be that with the most violent assault upon "history," with the most revolutionary intervention into institutions and ideologies, it would still not be possible to reverse the basic direction of our historic momentum. In our time, we have seen extraordinary attempts to reshape the social forces of history, and extraordinary results in imposing a heroic, revolutionary will upon social history. Yet the changes which were inaugurated were in nearly every instance in accord with the drift and temper of world history as a whole. There has been no successful revolution against the forces of technology, of popular political aspiration, and of socialism, although it is obvious that the slogans of "democracy" and "socialism" have been put to cruel use. No revolutionary has been able to preach anti-industrialism, or the inequality of classes, or the ideals of capitalism. Gandhi, who came closest to being an exception insofar as his dislike of technology was concerned, was nonetheless unable to keep India closed off from modern technology. The few nations which have sought to stand against the political trend—like Spain—have been in a state of exhaustion and have had no subsequent important historic development. There have been few major revolutions since 1945 which have not flown the banners of socialism.

Thus there seems indeed to be a basic character to world civilization in our times from which no vital historic effort can depart very far in its essentials, and the fact that even revolutions have had to conform to this pattern makes it unlikely in the extreme that a non-revolutionary society, such as our own, will succeed in resisting it. To what ultimate ends this "inevitable" direction of historic forces may carry society we do not know, for such questions take us far beyond the horizon of the "given" historic situation. What may be the final impact of science and technology on civilization, the end effect of our egalitarian political ideals, or the ultimate organization of collectivism, we do not know. All that we do know is that, for the moment, these general historic tendencies are firmly in the saddle, and that short of the profoundest change in the character of our civilization, or an incalculable redirection of events, they bid fair to dominate the social environment of the future.

But the fact that the *main direction* of historic movement is too deeply rooted to be turned aside does not mean that our future is therefore caught in a deterministic vise. It is not just necessity, but a mixture of necessity and freedom which, as always, confronts us as a condition of historic existence. If the idea of the future as history tells us what it is not "possible" for our kind of society to do, it also makes clear what *is* possible.

For example, the spreading hegemony of scientific technology may be an inescapable general tendency of our times, but the social consequences which we have previously discussed do not follow as an inescapable corollary. They are largely the result of *non-intervention* before the historic closing-in of science and technology. But non-intervention is not the only possible response to this historic force. It is rather a kind of abdication before the problem itself. It leads us to ignore the very thought that there may exist other controls over the technological revolution than the economic calculus which is at present our main device for regulating its admission into our lives. One need hardly say that a society which consistently ignored considerations of economics would seriously jeopardize its own well-being. But this does not mean that a society cannot, however imperfectly, attempt to weigh the non-economic advantages and disadvantages, the non-economic costs and benefits that seem likely to accrue from major alterations in its technological apparatus, and allow these considerations to balance, offset—and on occasion, even to veto—the guide of profitability. Thus the actual impact of science and technology on our social existence will depend not merely on the presence of these overriding forces in our age, but on the influence which we *unavoidably* exert on their social application—including the passive influence of permitting economic criteria to exert their sway largely unchallenged.

The same general conclusion is true with respect to the possibilities of influencing the other main forces which affect our future. There is little doubt, for instance, of the overwhelming power of popular aspirations in the underdeveloped nations, or of the likelihood that those aspirations, in the frustrating conditions of underdevelopment, will lead toward economic collectivism and political dictatorship. But the fact that there is very little we can do about this is very different from saying that we therefore have no control over this aspect of the future. On the contrary, it is only by understanding the "inevitable" outlook that we can hope to devise policies which have some chance of exerting a lasting and positive effect on the course of economic development. Similar alternatives confront us in dealing with the trend of all industrialized nations, ourselves included, toward some form of economic collectivism. To continue to set ourselves adamantly against this trend is to minimize rather than maximize our possible historic influence. The possibility poised by history is not that of denying the advent of planning, but of seizing control of it to assure the kind of collective economic responsibility we want.

Thus the outlook on the future as history does not pave the way for an attitude of passivity and still less for defeatism. Those who would reject the idea of the "inevitable" future for these reasons are in fact more likely to object to the bold measures to which it points as the only means of rescuing our future from the category of "inevitable fate." It is unquestionably true that the exercise of such historic control is fraught with risk. *But so is the exercise of non-control.* The issue is not the simple and clear-cut one of a greater or lesser freedom. It is the difficult and clouded choice of a subservience to the necessities imposed by the forces visibly at work in our midst, or the perilous freedom of an exercise of historic control over ourselves.

How we shall behave in the face of this difficult choice of historic paths, it is not easy to say. Whether in the end we shall remain passive before the enveloping changes of history, or attempt to adapt our institutions so as to minimize their impact, is a question whose answer inevitably involves subjective biases. The degree to which the "common sense," the "basic instincts" of the people can be relied upon, the flexibility and farsightedness of the powers that be—these are matters about which purely objective judgments are impossible. All that one can say is that the challenges are very subtle; that the requisite changes in institutions, while not revolutionary, are nonetheless very great; and that the required degree of farsightedness is correspondingly high. Thus it is not difficult to conclude that the possibilities of historic intervention will not, in fact, be put to use. A critic who assesses the American scene in terms of its alertness to the underlying challenges of our times can scarcely fail to be struck by the general poverty of the prevailing outlook: the men of wealth and power, mentally locked within their corporate privileges; the middle classes, more Bourbon than the

Bourbons; the working classes, unable to formulate any social program or purpose beyond "getting theirs"; the academicians, blind to the irrationalities of the society they seek to rationalize.

Yet it is one of the disconcerting facts of an open society that it offers so many opportunities for facile generalizations and so little sure ground for generally valid ones. As long as there is still visible in American society a continuing evidence of new thought and dissent, a self-control with respect to the use of political power, and above all, a nagging awareness that all is not right, it would be arrogant and unjust to shrug away our future as a hopeless cause. There are, after all, great traditions of responsibility and social flexibility in America. In them there may yet reside the impetus to seize the historic possibilities before us, and to make those changes which may be necessary if the forces of history are not to sweep over us in an uncontrolled and destructive fashion. But it is useless to hope that this will happen so long as we persist in believing that in the future toward which we are blindly careering everything is "possible," or that we can escape the ultimate responsibility of defining our limits of possibility for ourselves.

## 5. The Idea of Progress

In our last section we have been concerned with the problems of historic possibility and impossibility, of freedom and necessity, which a philosophy of optimism tends to obscure. Now we must turn to a second shortcoming of our traditional outlook on history. This is the tendency of our philosophy to present the workings of the forces of history in an overly simplified manner—a manner which has entirely failed to prepare us for the actual turnings which history has taken. If we are to sum up the shortcoming in a phrase it would be this: *The optimistic philosophy equates the movement of history's forces with the idea of progress.*

Whether there is such a thing as "progress" in history depends, of course, on what we mean by the word. It is clear enough that there has been, particularly in the last three centuries, a steady and cumulative accretion of technical virtuosity and scientific knowledge which permits us to speak of "progress" in these fields in a fairly specific sense. One particularly important aspect of this progress has been the measurable lengthening of the longevity of man and the improvement of his capacity to alleviate his bodily ills. A second instance of definable progress has been in the rise of the level of well-being of the masses in the West—although this can be said to be more than offset by an actual decline, over the last century, of the "well-being" of the teeming masses of the East. A third instance, less easily indexed, but no less demonstrable in the large, is the historic progress from a society in which man is born into his status toward a society in which he is able to define his status for himself.

It is with these aspects of the forces of history that optimism identifies progress, and so long as the meaning of "progress" is restricted to such reasonably definable movements, there can be no objection to the word. But it is also apparent that we cannot generalize from these specific concepts of progress to the larger idea of an all-embracing progress of "society." There is no reason to believe that today's private morality, level of social ethics, and general nobility of public ideals are in any sense superior to much of the recorded past, if indeed they are equal to the best of American Revolutionary times or to the heights reached in the golden ages of Greece and Rome.

Our cultural and aesthetic public existence is hardly at an historic high point. And if, with all his gains in health, well-being, or status, the average person is "happier," more serenely or creatively engaged in life than in the past, this is not apparent in the happiness, serenity, or creativity of our age. We often imagine that "life" is much better today than, say, in the Dark Ages, but this depends very much on whose lives we conjure up in these two periods. After all, we live at a time when German brutality reached what may be, statistically, a record for the systematic extermination of life, and when Russian despotism at its worst took us back to the level of morality of the crueler Biblical kings.

Yet these somber considerations do not dispose of the idea of progress. Rather they raise the question: Why is it that the forces of history, which are indisputably the carriers of potentially beneficial political and economic and technological change, have not resulted in a corresponding improvement in the human condition? What are the attributes of these forces, as agents of change, which the optimistic philosophy glosses over? Let us try to identify some of these attributes which are omitted in the optimistic notion of progress.

## 6. The Inertia of History

Because we live in a time of great change, and because our philosophy of optimism makes us expectant of and receptive to change, we may easily overlook a deeply important aspect of historic development. This is its quality of inertia. It is a quality which is manifest not only in resistance to change—although that is one of its more important aspects—but in the viscosity which is imparted to history because people tend to repeat and continue their ways of life as long as it is possible for them to do so.

We do not usually call inertia to mind when we seek the great molding forces of history. And yet this humble characteristic is responsible for more of "history" than all the campaigns, the movements, the revolutions we readily call to mind. The simple, but quintessential fact that human beings persist in living their lives in familiar ways, which are the only ways they know how, is the very lifeline of social continuity itself.

This inertia which exerts so powerful a drag on history undoubtedly has its biological and psychological roots. But it is more than just an "innate" human characteristic. It is also the outcome of the historic social condition of man. For the persistence of habit acts as a protective reflex for the overwhelming majority of men who know very little except that life is a fragile possession, and that tried and true ways, however onerous, have at least proved capable of sustaining it. A mulish perseverance in old ways is not without reason when life is lived at the brink of existence where a small error may spell disaster. An instance in point was provided some years ago when a team of United Nations agricultural experts sought in vain to persuade Turkish farmers to improve their crops by removing the stones from their fields. Finally a few of the younger ones consented—whereupon, to the chagrin of the experts, their yields promptly *declined*. In the arid climate of Turkey, the stones had served the function of helping to retain the scanty moisture in the soil.

Inertia shows itself as well in a general reluctance to embrace new social ideas. Reformers throughout history have deplored the tenacity with which the privileged classes have clung to their prerogatives—even when it was no longer in their "best interests" to do so. This is not so surprising when we view the enormous gulf which has normally separated the privileged and the unprivileged. What is far more striking is the difficulty which reformers have had in making even the most miserable and oppressed classes "see" the inequity of their lot, and in persuading them to rise in protest. The fact that our historic glance is easily caught by a few *jacqueries* obscures the fact that revolutions are remarkable in history not for their frequency but for their rarity, even though the "normal" condition of man has always been harsh enough to warrant revolutionary sentiments. We must conclude that whenever it has been possible the human being has *wished* to believe in the rightness and fixity of the situation in which he has found himself.

The inertia of ideologies as well as of institutions is often taken as a lamentable fact. It is the despair of the social engineer, the *bête noir* of the utopian planner. Nonetheless we must remember that there is a constructive role which this inertia also plays. A society without ideological inertia would live from instant to instant in peril of a fatal turning. The fixity of our voting habits, our customary beliefs, our stubbornly held ideas, even when these are wrong, serves a purpose in protecting and stabilizing the community. The reformer who despairs because people will not listen to reason forgets that it is this same suspicion of change which helps to prevent people from heeding the Pied Pipers for whom society never lacks. We may make progress only by freeing ourselves from the rut of the past, but without this rut an orderly society would hardly be possible in the first place.

This historic undertow of inertia warns us against facile conceptions of "progress" in two respects. In the first place it disabuses us of the notion of the "ease" of social change. For most of the world's peoples, who have known only the changelessness of history, such a stress on the difficulty of change would not be necessary. But for ourselves, whose outlook is conditioned by the extraordinary dynamism of our unique historic experience, it is a needed caution. Contrary to our generally accepted belief, change is not the rule but the exception in life. Whether it is imposed from above or imposes itself from below, change must reckon with the reluctance of humankind to relinquish habits not only of a lifetime, but of life itself. This is the reason why even such enormous transformations as those we have dealt with in this book are slow, stretched out over generations, invisible from one day to the next.

Second, the drag of inertia warns us against the overestimation of the effects of change. The optimistic conception of progress calls our attention to the sweeping improvements which can be brought about by technology or democracy or economic advance. All that is certainly true as far as it goes. No one can doubt the capacity of history's forces to legislate beneficial changes in society. But there is a level of social existence to which these forces penetrate last and least. This is the level at which "society" is visible only as the personal and private encounters of each of us with his fellow man. It is the level at which life is *lived,* rather than the level at which it is abstractly conceived.

Here, at this final level of personal experience, the inertia of history is most apparently manifest. It is here that the revolutionary, having brought about tremendous changes in "society," comes to grips with the petty irritations of inefficient colleagues and apathetic clerks, of the "human factor" which like sand in a machine, has wrecked so many well-planned enterprises. It is not that revolutions, or the more gradual changes of historic evolution, make these daily frictions of life any worse. It is rather that so much of life remains the same, regardless of the new boundaries in which it is contained.

In this grinding persistence of the "human factor" lies the reason for much of the disillusion which so frequently follows a passionate attempt to bring about social progress. As Ignazio Silone has written: "Political regimes come and go; bad habits remain." The underlying sameness of life, the reassertion of old established ways, of "bad habits," is an aspect of history which must not be lost to sight amid the more dramatic changes of the superstructure of society. An appreciation of the fact of human inertia must not lead us to understate the extent to which change is possible in society, We have seen that optimism misleads us with respect to the possibilities of "progress" of human life at a fundamental level.

## 7. The Heritage of the Human Condition

We have seen that optimism misleads us with respect to the possibilities of "progress" because it tends to underestimate the difficulty and to overestimate the consequences of historic change. But it compounds that shortcoming with a second and perhaps even more important failure. This is its lack of realism as to our starting point in the making of history. It is its failure to confront truthfully and unflinchingly the condition of the human being as it now exists.

Optimism tacitly views that condition in a favorable light. The very assumption that the growth of technical skill, political equality, or economic well-being will automatically lead to "progress"—rather than to increased destructiveness, heightened social disorder, or vulgar opulence—already takes for granted an environment in which rationality, self-control, and dignity are paramount social attributes.

But this is hardly the impression one gets from an examination of the panorama of human existence. If there is such a thing as an average human being, he is to be found among the majority of mankind which lives in the continents of the East and South. The chasm which divides the average life on these continents from our own is so wide that we can barely imagine existence on the other side. To be an Indian villager, a Chinese peasant, an African mine-worker is to be in a human condition whose dark and narrow confines cannot be penetrated by a Western mind.

But life on our side of the chasm is also very far from presenting a heartening vista. In the United States, for example, preventable disease and even deformity are still widespread. Mental aberration identifiably touches a tenth of the population. Criminality, in various social forms from murder to tax evasion, is prevalent among all classes. The urban environment in which life is mainly lived is crowded, often unspeakably ugly, and in its spreading slums, vicious. The average education is barely adequate to allow the population to cope with the technological complexities of the age, and insufficient to allow all but a few to understand them. Large numbers of families do not know or care how to raise their children, as witness the epidemic incidence of juvenile disorders.

The list could be extended without difficulty. But what characterizes many, if not all of these degradations of life, is that they are unnecessary. Most of them could be vastly alleviated by a sustained and wholehearted effort. Yet such an effort—as to whose immense "value" all would agree—seems impossible to undertake. Indeed, the very suggestion that these areas of need should carry an absolutely overriding priority, taking precedence over any and all more "profitable" activities, smacks of a suspicious radicalism. We are simply not concerned, beyond a mild lip-service, with mounting an all-out effort to raise the level of national health or civic virtue, or mass living conditions or average education or upbringing. Looking at some of the institutions we nourish and defend, it would not be difficult to maintain that our society is an immense stamping press for the careless production of underdeveloped and malformed human beings, and that, whatever it may claim to be, it is not a society fundamentally concerned with moral issues, with serious purposes, or with human dignity.

The point, however, is not to berate ourselves for our obvious failure to produce anything like a "good society." The point is rather that, with all its glaring and inexcusable failures, the United States is still probably the most favored and favorable place on earth for a child to be born and to grow up.

These melancholy facts must assume their rightful place in any evaluation of the prospects for "social progress." For in such a social atmosphere the forces of history do not lead automatically in the direction which optimism assumes. In an atmosphere of neglect of and indifference to human capabilities, it is not at all surprising that technology should result in the trivialization of life and the stultification of work. It is certainly not remarkable that, in the harsh and primitive setting of underdevelopment, popular political aspirations press toward extreme and violent "solutions" to the problems of underdevelopment; nor that, in the more advanced societies, they mold society in the image of the mediocrity of mind and sentiment they represent. Nor, given the prevalence of physical poverty in the backward nations and of psychological poverty in all nations, is the pre-eminence of materialistic drives and goals to be wondered at. In sum, today as in the past, the half-educated, half-emancipated state of human society assures that there will be a long continuation of the violence, the instability, the blatant injustice, which are the most grievous aspects of the human tragedy. This is the true heritage of the human condition, and its bitter legacy.

What is perhaps the most sorrowful aspect of this tragedy is that its victims are chosen arbitrarily and at random. There is no guilt or innocence, no measure of culpability or responsibility in the fate meted out by a world which is still more brute than man. Those who fall in wars do not "start" the wars. The victims of Hitler or Stalin were not those who raised these dictators to power. Nor will there be a fine balancing of accounts when the crimes of South Africa eventually exact their terrible retribution, or when the indignities of the American South work their full damage to the American social fabric. In a world in which conscious morality can be regarded with derision, and reason with suspicion, this random toll of social tragedy cannot be avoided. It is the consequence of a situation in which, as Albert Camus writes in *The Fall:* "We cannot assert the innocence of anyone, whereas we can state with certainty the guilt of all."

To raise these dark thoughts is not to sermonize that man is "wicked" or to avoid the conclusion that some men are much more guilty than others. Neither is it to maintain that there is no hope for a betterment of the human condition. On the contrary, there is today a greater long-term prospect for such betterment than humanity has ever known before. But the heritage of the past is too deep to be overcome in a matter of a few generations. It will be a long while until the human condition has been substantially improved. Not to face up to this fact with compassion and concern is only to cringe before reality. And while this should urge us on with all the strength at our command to support every effort to improve the condition of man, it cannot but chasten us as to the reasonable expectations of the "progress" which that condition will permit.

## 8. *The Ambiguity of Events*

In the very idea of progress, as we commonly accept it, is contained the notion of goals. We strive for specific objectives, located in the future, and imagine that each objective gained is a recognizable step toward "progress." As a result we find ourselves confounded when, having reached an objective, what we encounter is not the "progress" we anticipated but a new set of problems stemming from the very advance itself.

This disconcerting aspect of experience can be described as the ambiguity of events. By this we mean that every event in history has a Januslike quality—one face which regards the past, and one which looks ahead; one aspect which is the culmination of what has gone before, and another which is the point of departure for what is to follow.

Simplistic ideas of progress see only the near face of events when they look to the future. Hence such views of the future typically underrate its complexities. They do not consider that the solution of one problem is only the formulation of the next. What an awareness of the ambiguity of events thus subtracts from the optimistic view of progress is the luxury of believing that progress is a simple pyramiding of success. The two-sided nature of future events does not deny that our problems may be our opportunities but it asserts with equal conviction that our opportunities may become our problems.

There is no more dramatic example of this than the impact on world history of that most "unambiguous" of all evidences of progress: the development of modern medicine. It is not necessary to spell out the enormous benefits which medical science has brought to mankind. Yet no assessment of the over-all impact of modern medicine on our age can ignore the fact that it has also been the "cause" of an immense amount of additional suffering in the world. By its success in reducing the scourges of mass disease and infant mortality, the "progress" of medical science has crowded the already overpopulated villages and cities of Asia and South America with still more mouths, and has thus aggravated the very human suffering it set out to relieve.

Needless to say, not every instance of progress cancels itself out in so direct and distressing a fashion as this. The point, rather, is that progress does not merely consist in the surmounting of a previous problem, but inherently consists in the emergence of a new problem which, although different, may be quite as grave as the old. In the course of this book, for example, we have seen such new problems emerging from the advance of technology or from the achievement of abundance in our own society. These new problems do not gainsay the advances which technology or economic growth bring us. But it may well be that the consequences of our technological captivity, or the control problems of economic abundance will be just as humanly crushing as the problems of insufficiency or technical inadequacy from whose solution they emerged. There is no reason to believe that the successive problems of "progress" pose easier challenges; indeed it is probable that the overcoming of the "simpler" problems of poverty and disease opens the doors on progressively more profound, elusive, and insoluble human dilemmas.

Marx and Hegel called this ambiguous aspect of progress the dialectic of history. Marx, however, brought his dialectical analysis to a halt with the achievement of communism as the "terminus" of the history of class struggle. Ironically enough, it is probable that there is no aspect of future history which today more desperately needs dialectical clarification than the achievement of the communist—or for the West, the socialist—goal. It is clear that as the "near side" of socialism approaches, it is the "far side" which becomes of ever greater interest and importance. To consider socialism as a "goal" of social history is to fall prey to the optimistic delusion that goals are milestones in history from which the next stage of development promises to be "easier" or unambiguously "better" than the past. To rid oneself of this comforting notion is not to lessen one's ardor to resolve the difficulties of the present, but to arm oneself realistically for the continuance of the human struggle in the future.

## 9. The Grand Dynamic of History

Is there then no possibility for progress?

As it must by now be clear, much depends on what one means by the question. If by "progress" we mean a fundamental elevation in the human estate, a noticeable movement of society in the direction of the ideals of Western humanism, a qualitative as well as a quantitative betterment of the condition of man, it is plain that we must put away our ideas of progress over the foreseeable vista of the historic future. For whereas there is no question but that the forces of our time are bringing about momentous and profound changes, it is only optimistic self-deception to anticipate, or even to wish for, the near advent of a perceptibly "better" world as a result. Taking into account the human condition as it now exists, the laggard slowness with which improvements in institutions are followed by improvements in "life," the blurred and ambiguous fashion in which history passes from problem to problem, it is certain enough that the tenor of world history will remain much as it is for a long while to come.

Indeed, from the point of view of the West and especially of America, it may seem to be deteriorating. As we have seen thorough the pages of this book, many of the tendencies of world history are likely to manifest themselves to us as a worsening of the outlook. We may well be tempted to interpret this growing intractability of the environment as the metamorphosis of progress into retrogression.

Against this dark horizon it is hardly possible to cling to the sanguine hopes and complacent expectations of the past. And yet if we can lift our gaze beyond the confines of our own situation, it is possible to see that every one of these changes is essential and inescapable if the present condition of humankind is to be surpassed. Until the avoidable evils of society have been redressed, or at least made the target of the wholehearted effort of the organized human community, it is not only premature but presumptuous to talk of "the dignity of the individual." The ugly, obvious, and terrible wounds of mankind must be dressed and allowed to heal before we can begin to know the capacities, much less enlarge the vision, of the human race as a whole.

In the present state of world history the transformations which are everywhere at work are performing this massive and crude surgery. We have dwelt sufficiently in the preceding pages on the violence and cruelty, the humanly deforming aspects of the changes about us. Now we must see that in their ultimate impact on history it is the positive side of these great transformations which must be stressed. However unruly the revolution of the underdeveloped nations, it is nonetheless the commencement of a movement away from the squalor and apathy which three-quarters of the human race still consider to be life. With all its disregard for Western standards of justice and liberty, the forced march of communism is nevertheless retreading the essential, but now forgotten path of early industrial development of the West. Whatever its capacity for the destruction or the diminution of man, the perfection and application of industrial technology is withal the only possible escape from the historic indenture of man. And no matter what its difficulties, the painful evolution beyond present-day capitalism is indispensable if those nations which have gained the benefits of material wealth are now to cope rationally with its administration.

Thus the blind and often brutal impact of the historic forces of our day can still be said to point in the direction of optimism and of progress. Only in our present situation, the West is no longer the spearhead of those forces, but their target. What is at bottom a movement of hope and well-being for the inarticulate and inadequate masses of mankind is a fearful threat to the delicate and now gravely exposed civilization of the articulate and advanced few.

No member of the Western community who loves its great achievements and who has enjoyed the inestimable value of its liberties and values can confront this outlook of history without anguish. Of all those who will feel the blows of the future, none will suffer more than the heirs of the long tradition of Western humanism, and none will more acutely feel the delays and the recession of "progress" as the world endures its protracted ordeal.

More aware than the rising masses of the world of the destination to which their inchoate revolution may hopefully carry them, it is the humanist spirits of the West who will feel most betrayed by the violence and excess which will likely accompany its course. Ever hopeful of the re-entry of the communist nations into the Western community of thought, it is the Western intellectuals and idealists who will bear the full agony of watching for and waiting for signs of change which may be very long in coming. Alive to the immense potential benefits of the technical virtuosity of their age, it is again the guardians of the humanist tradition who will most despair at its continued misapplication; just as it will be they rather than the masses who will wish for a more responsible form of economic society and who will chafe at the continuance of the old order.

This prospect of disappointment and delay may give rise to a tragedy greater than the tragic events of history itself. This would be the disillusion of Western thought and the abandonment of its hopes for and its distant vision of progress. It would be the surrender of the very ideals of the West before the crushing advent of history, and the adoption of an indifference, or worse, a cynicism before the march of events.

If this tragedy is to be avoided, the West will have need of two qualities: fortitude and understanding. It must come to see that because this is not a time of fulfillment does not mean that it is a time of waste. It is rather a time when the West must take upon itself a new and more difficult role in history than in the past: not that of leading in the van of history's forces under the banner of progress, but that of preserving from the ruthless onslaught of history's forces the integrity of the very idea of progress itself.

Particularly for Americans will this long period of abeyance provide a test of the spirit. Accustomed by our historic training to expect a mastery over events which is no longer possible, we are apt to interpret the intransigence of history as a kind of personal betrayal rather then as a vast and impersonal process of worldwide evolution. Thus there is the danger that we may abandon our optimism for a black and bitter pessimism, or for a kind of "heroic" defiance.

But neither pessimism nor defiance, any more than optimism, will give us the fortitude and understanding we require. For this we need an attitude which accepts the outlook of the historic future without succumbing to false hopes or to an equally false despair; a point of view which sees in the juggernaut of history's forces both the means by which progress painfully made in the past may be trampled underfoot, and the means by which a broader and stronger base for progress in the future may be brought into being.

Such an attitude may retain its kernel of optimism. But more is needed for the display of stoic fortitude than a residual faith in the idea of progress. Above all there is required an understanding of the grand dynamic of history's forces in preparing the way for eventual progress. There is needed a broad and compassionate comprehension of the history-shaking transformations now in mid-career, of their combined work of demolition and construction, of the hope they embody and the price they will exact. Only from such a sense of historic understanding can come the strength to pass through the gauntlet with an integrity of mind and spirit.

What is tragically characteristic of our lives today is an absence of just such an understanding. It is very difficult while America and the West are at bay to feel a sense of positive identification with the forces that are preparing the environment of the future. Less and less are we able to locate our lives meaningfully in the pageant of history. More and more do we find ourselves retreating to the sanctuary of an insulated individualism, sealed off in our private concerns from the larger events which surround us.

Such an historic disorientation and disengagement is a terrible private as well as public deprivation. In an age which no longer waits patiently through this life for the rewards of the next, it is a crushing spiritual blow to lose one's sense of participation in mankind's journey, and to see only a huge milling-around, a collective living-out of lives with no larger purpose than the days which each accumulates. When we estrange ourselves from history we do not enlarge, we diminish ourselves, even as individuals. We subtract from our lives one meaning which they do in fact possess, whether we recognize it or not. We cannot help living in history. We can only fail to be aware of it. If we are to meet, endure, and transcend the trials and defeats of the future—for trials and defeats there are certain to be—it can only be from a point of view which, seeing the future as part of the sweep of history, enables us to establish our place in that immense procession in which is incorporated whatever hope humankind may have.

## POST-CIVILIZATION

*Kenneth E. Boulding*

*"Philosophy of history," the attempt to place one's own society in the overall pattern of human history, has been with us certainly since Genesis and Herodotus, with such thinkers as Augustine and Hegel making major contributions to it. Much of this activity in the past (much in the present, too) has been of a speculative and metaphysical nature, claiming to offer insights into the very nature of things. It was inevitable in the mid-twentieth century that sober social scientists should take up the task, leaving elaborate metaphysical constructions behind and cautiously concentrating on the cold hard facts of technology and their implications for economics and politics. Among these men have been Kenneth Boulding, Daniel Bell (*The End of Ideology, 1959*), and Roderick Seidenberg (*Post-Historic Man, 1957*).*

*Just as their scope is narrower and their methods more down-to-earth than were those of the older speculators, so are their conclusions more cautious. Leaving behind both stark pessimism and facile optimism, these writers are more likely to strike a balance, emphasizing the constant human tendency to adapt social institutions to inevitable changes as well as the inescapable breakdown of the* status quo *in an era of rapid development in all areas of life.*

*Finally, in contrast to many earlier philosophers of history who, like Hegel or Spengler, were political conservatives or, like Nietzsche, politically isolated, Boulding and his colleagues are much more likely to be men actively interested in politics and social change, usually from the standpoint of the left, either moderate or extreme. The following essay, reprinted in its entirety, originally appeared in* Liberation, *a publication at the heart of what has frequently been called the "New American Left." We have taken it from an anthology edited by Paul Goodman, a leading American radical.*

*Professor Boulding, originally from England, came to the United States
in 1937 and has had a distinguished career as an economist and student
of contemporary world problems, including the question of disarmament.
He has been at the University of Michigan since 1949.*

We are living in what I call the second great change in the state of man. The first
is the change from pre-civilized to civilized societies. The first five hundred thousand
years or so of man's existence on earth were relatively uneventful. Compared with his
present condition, he puttered along in an astonishingly stationary state. There may
have been changes in language and culture which are not reflected in the artifacts,
but if there were, these changes are lost to us. The evidence of the artifacts, however,
is conclusive. Whatever changes they were, they were almost unbelievably slow. About
ten thousand years ago, we begin to perceive an acceleration in the rate of change.
This becomes very noticeable five thousand years ago with the development of the
first civilization. The details of this first great change are probably beyond our recovery. However, we do know that it depended on two phenomena: the development
of agriculture and the development of exploitation. Agriculture, that is the domesti-
cation of crops and livestock and the planting of crops in fields, gave man a secure
surplus of food from the food producer. In a hunting and fishing economy it seems
to take the food producer all his time to produce enough food for himself and his
family. The moment we have agriculture, with its superior productivity of this form
of employment of human resources, the food producer can produce more food than
he and his family can eat. In some societies in these happy conditions, the food
producer has simply relaxed and indulged himself with leisure. As soon, however,
as we get politics, that is exploitation, we begin to get cities and civilization. Civilization, it is clear from the origin of the word, is what happens in cities, and the city is
dependent (in its early stages, at any rate) on the existence of a food surplus from
the food producer and some organization which can take it away from him. With
this food surplus, the political organization feeds kings, priests, armies, architects,
and builders, and the city comes into being. Political science in its earliest form is
the knowledge of how to take the food surplus away from the food producer without
giving him very much in return.

Now I argue that we are in the middle of the second great change in the state of
man, which is as drastic and as dramatic, and certainly as large as, if not larger than,
the change from pre-civilized to civilized society. This I call the change from civilization to post-civilization. It is a strange irony that just at the moment when civilization
has almost completed the conquest of pre-civilized societies, post-civilization has been
treading heavily upon its heels. The student of civilization may soon find himself
in the unfortunate position of the anthropologist who studies pre-civilized societies.

Paul Goodman, ed., *Seeds of Liberation* (New York: George Brazillier, Inc., 1964), pp.
12–23.

Both are like the student of ice on a hot day—the subject matter melts away almost before he can study it.

These great changes can be thought of as a change of gear in the evolutionary process, resulting in progressive acceleration of the rate of evolutionary change. Even before the appearance of man on the earth, we can detect earlier evolutionary gear-shiftings. The formation of life obviously represented one such transition, the movement from the water to the land another, the development of the vertebrates another, and so on. Man himself represents a very large acceleration of the evolutionary process. Whether he evolved from pre-existing forms or landed from a space ship and was not able to get back to where he came from, is immaterial. Once he had arrived on earth, the process of evolution could go on within the confines of the human nervous system at a greatly accelerated rate. The human mind is an enormous muta-tion-selection process. Instead of the mutation-selection process being confined, as it were, to the flesh, it can take place within the image, and hence, very rapid changes are possible. Man seems to have been pretty slow to exploit this potentiality, but one suspects that even with primitive man, the rate of change in the biosphere was much larger than it had been before, because of the appearance of what Teilhard de Chardin calls the noosphere, or sphere of knowledge.

Civilization represents a further acceleration of the rate of change, mainly because one of the main products of civilization is history. With the food surplus from agri-culture it became possible to feed specialized scribes. With the development of writing, man did not have to depend on the uncertain memories of the aged for his records, and a great process of accumulation of social knowledge began. The past could now communicate, at least in one direction, with the present, and this enor-mously increased the range and possibility of enlargements of the contents of the human mind.

Out of civilization, however, comes science, which is a superior way of organizing the evolution of knowledge. We trace the first beginnings of science, of course, almost as far back as the beginning of civilization itself. Beginning about 1650, however, we begin to see the organization of science into a community of knowledge, and this leads again to an enormous acceleration of the rate of change. The world of 1650 is more remote to us than the world of ancient Egypt or Samaria would have been to the man of 1650. Already in the United States and Western Europe, in a smaller degree in Russia and in some other parts of the world, we see the beginnings of post-civilized society—a state of man as different from civilization as civilization is from savagery. What we really mean, therefore, by the anemic term "economic development" is the second great transition in the state of man. It is the movement from civilized to post-civilized society. It is nothing short of a major revolution in the human condition, and it does not represent a mere continuance and development of the old patterns of civilization.

As a dramatic illustration of the magnitude of the change, we can contemplate Indonesia. This is a country which has about the same extent, population and per capita income as the Roman Empire at its height. For all I know it is producing a literature and an art at least comparable to that of the Augustan age. It is, therefore, a very good example of a country of high civilization. Because of this fact, it is one of the poorest countries in the world. It is desperately anxious to break out of its present condition. Jakarta is a city about the size of ancient Rome, though perhaps a little less splendid. All this points up the fact that the Roman Empire was a desperately poor and under-developed society. The Roman cities seem to have been always about three weeks away from starvation, and even at its height it is doubtful whether the Roman Empire ever had less than seventy-five to eighty per cent of its population in agriculture.

Civilization, that is, is a state of society in which techniques are so poor that it takes about eighty per cent of the population to feed the hundred per cent. But we do have about twenty per cent of the people who can be spared from food-producing to build Parthenons and cathedrals, to write literature and poetry, and fight wars. By contrast, in the United States today we are rapidly getting to the point where we can produce all our food with only ten per cent of the population and still have large agricultural surpluses. But for the blessings of agricultural policy, we might soon be able to produce all our food with five per cent of the population. It may even be that agriculture is on its way out altogether and that within another generation or so we will produce our food in a totally different way. Perhaps both fields and cows are merely relics of civilization, the vestiges of a vanishing age. This means, however, that even in our society, which is at a very early stage of post-civilization, we can now spare about ninety per cent of the people to produce bathtubs, automobiles, H-bombs and all the other conveniences of life. Western Europe and Japan are coming along behind the United States very fast. The Russians, likewise, are advancing toward post-civilization, although by a very different road. At the moment their ideology is a handicap to them in some places—especially in agriculture, which still occupies forty-five per cent of the people. And, if the Russians ever discover that super-peasants are a good deal more efficient than collective farms, they may cut away some of the ideology that hangs around their neck and move even more rapidly toward post-civilized society.

I'm not at all sure what post-civilization will look like but it will certainly be a world-wide society. Until very recently, each civilized society was a little island in a sea of barbarism which constantly threatened to overwhelm it. Civilization is haunted by the spectre of decline and fall, though it is noteworthy that in spite of the rise and fall of particular civilizations, civilization itself expanded steadily in geographical coverage, from its very beginnings. We must face the fact, however, that post-civilized society will be world-wide, if only because of its ease of communication and transportation. I flew last year from Idlewild to Brussels, and on glimpsing the new Brussels Airport out of the corner of my eye, I thought for a moment that we had come back and landed at Idlewild again.

The characteristic institutions of civilization are, as we have seen, first agriculture, then the city, then war, in the sense of clash of organized armed forces, and finally, inequality, the sharp contrast between the rich and the poor, between the city and the country, between the urbane and the rustic. The state is based very fundamentally on violence and exploitation, and the culture tends to be spiritually monolithic.

In post-civilization all these institutions suffer radical change. Agriculture, as we have seen, diminishes until it is a small proportion of the society; the city, likewise, in the classical sense, disintegrates. Los Angeles is perhaps the first example of the post-civilization, post-urban agglomeration—under no stretch of the imagination could it be called a city. War, likewise, is an institution in process of disintegration. National defense as a social system has quite fundamentally broken down on a world scale. The ICBM and the nuclear warhead have made the nation-state as militarily obsolete as the city-state, for in no country now can the armed forces preserve an area of internal peace by pushing violence to the outskirts. Poverty and inequality, likewise, are tending to disappear, at least on their traditional scale. In civilized societies the king or the emperor could live in a Versailles and the peasant in a hovel. In post-civilized society, it is almost impossible for the rich to consume on a scale which is more, let us say, than ten times that of the poor. There is no sense in having more than ten automobiles!

Another profound change in the passage from civilization to post-civilization is the change in the expectation of life. In civilized society, birth and death rates tend to be about forty per thousand and the expectation of life at birth is twenty-five years. In post-civilized society, the expectation of life at birth rises at least to seventy and perhaps beyond. It may be that we are on the edge of a biological revolution, just as dramatic and far-reaching as the discovery of atomic energy and that we may crack the problem of aging and prolong human life much beyond its present span. Whether or not, however, we go forward to Methuselah, the mere increase of the average age of death to seventy is a startling and far-reaching change. It means, for instance, that in an equilibrium population, the birth and death rate cannot be more than about fourteen per thousand. This unquestionably implies some form of conscious control of births. It means also a much larger proportion of the population in later years.

It is perfectly possible to paint an anti-utopia in which a post-civilized society appears as universally vulgar or dull. On the whole, however, I welcome post-civilization and I have really very little affection for civilization. In most pre-civilized societies the fact that the life of man is for the most part nasty, brutish and short, does not prevent the poets and philosophers from sentimentalizing the noble savage. Similarly, we may expect the same kind of sentimentalizing of the noble Romans and civilized survivals like Winston Churchill. On the whole, though, I will not shed any tears over the grave of civilization any more than I will over pre-civilized society. The credit balance of post-civilization is large. It at least gives us a chance of a modest utopia, in which slavery, poverty, exploitation, gross inequality, war and disease—these prime costs of civilization—will fall to the vanishing point.

What we have at the moment is a chance to make a transition to this modest utopia —a chance which is probably unique in the history of this planet. If we fail, the chance will probably not be repeated in this part of the universe. Whatever experiments may be going on elsewhere, the present moment indeed is unique in the whole four billion years of the history of the planet. In my more pessimistic moments, I think the chance is a slim one, and it may be that man will be written off as an unsuccessful experiment. We must look at the traps which lie along the path of the transition, which might prevent us from making it altogether.

The most urgent trap is, of course, the trap of war. War, as I have suggested, is an institution peculiarly characteristic of civilization. Pre-civilized societies have sporadic feuding and raiding, but they do not generally have permanent organized armed forces, and they do not generally develop conquest and empire; or if they do, they soon pass into a civilized form. An armed force is essentially a mobile city designed to throw things at another mobile or stationary city with presumably evil intent. As far as I know, not more than two or three civilizations have existed without war. The Mayans and the people of Mohenjodaro seem to have lived for fairly long periods without war, but this was an accident of their monopolistic situation and they unquestionably occupied themselves with other kinds of foolishness. If pre-civilized society, however, cannot afford war, post-civilized society can afford far too much of it, and hence will be forced to get rid of the institution because it is simply inappropriate to the technological age. The breakdown in the world social system of national defense really dates from about 1949, when the United States lost its monopoly of nuclear weapons. A system of national defense is only feasible if each nation is stronger at home than its enemies, so that it can preserve a relatively large area of peace within its critical boundaries. Such a system is only possible, however, if the range of the deadly missile is short and if the armed forces of each nation lose power rapidly as they move away from home. The technological developments of the twentieth century have destroyed these foundations of national defense, and have replaced it with another social system altogether, which is "deterrence."

"Deterrence" is a social system with properties very different from that of national defense, which it replaced. Under national defense, for instance, it is possible to use the armed forces; under "deterrence" it is not—that is, if the deterring forces are ever used, the system will have broken down. We live in a society with a positive possibility of irretrievable disaster—a probability which grows every year. Herman Kahn recently said: "All we are doing is buying time, and we are doing nothing with the time that we buy." The armed forces of the world are caught in a technological process which not only destroys their own function, but threatens all of us. Even if a few of us do crawl out of the fallout shelters, it is by no means clear that we can put the world back together again. Even if the human race could survive one nuclear war, it is very doubtful that it could survive a second; and as the purpose of the first nuclear war would be to set up a political system which would produce the second, unless there is a radical change in attitude towards national defense, the prospects of the human race seem to be dim. Fortunately, "there is still time, brother" and evolution can still go on in the minds of men. The critical question is whether it can go on rapidly enough. The abolition of national defense, which is what we must face, is going to be a painful process, as we have come to rely on it to preserve many of the values which we hold dear. If the task can be perceived, however, by a sufficient number of people, there is at least a chance that we may avoid this trap before it is too late.

Even if we avoid the war trap, we may still fall into the population trap. Population control is an unsolved problem even for the developed areas of the world, which have moved the furthest toward post-civilization. An equilibrium of population in a stable post-civilized society may represent a fairly radical interference with ancient human institutions and freedoms. In a stable post-civilized society, as I have suggested, the birth and death rates must be of the order of fourteen per thousand, and the average number of children per family cannot much exceed two. There are many social institutions which might accomplish this end. So far, however, the only really sure-fire method of controlling population is starvation and misery.

In many parts of the world—indeed, for most of the human race for the moment —the impact on certain post-civilized techniques of civilized society has produced a crisis of growth, which may easily be fatal. In the tropics especially, with DDT and a few simple public-health measures, it is easy to reduce the death rate to nine or ten per thousand while the birth rate stays at forty per thousand. This means an annual increase of population of three per cent *per annum*, almost all of it concentrated in the lower age groups. We see dramatic examples of this phenomenon in places like the West Indies, Ceylon, and Formosa; but thanks to the activity of the World Health Organization, it is taking place rapidly all over the tropical world. Perhaps the most important key to the transition to post-civilization is heavy investment in human resources—that is, in education. The conquest of disease and infant mortality, however, before the corresponding adjustment to the birth rate, produces enormous numbers of children in societies which do not have the resources to educate them—especially as those in the middle-age groups, who after all must do all the work of a society, come from the much smaller population of the pre-DDT era.

Even in the developed countries, population control presents a very serious problem. The United States, for instance, at the moment is increasing in population even more rapidly than India. The time when we thought that the mere increase in income would automatically solve the population problem has gone by. In the United States, and certain other societies, in the early stages of post-civilization, the child has become an object of conspicuous domestic consumption. The consumption patterns of the American spending unit seem to follow a certain *"gestalt"* in which household capital accumulates in a certain order, such as the first car, the first child, the washer and dryer, the second child, the deep freeze, the third child, the second car, the fourth child, and so on. The richer we get, the more children we can afford to have and the more children we do have. We now seem to be able to afford an average of something like four children per family, and as, in a post-civilized society, these four children all survive, the population doubles every generation. A hundred years of this and even the United States is going to find itself uncomfortably crowded. It can be argued, indeed, that from the point of view of the amenities of life we are already well beyond the optimum population.

The third trap on the road to post-civilization is the technological trap. Our present technology is fundamentally suicidal. It is based on the extraction of concentrated deposits of fossil fuels and ores, which in the nature of things are exhaustible. Even at present rates of consumption, they will be exhausted in a time span which is not very long measured against human history and which is infinitesimally small on the geological time scale. If the rest of the world advances to American standards of consumption, these resources will disappear almost overnight. On this view economic development is the process of bringing closer the evil day when everything will be gone—all the oil, the coal, the ores—and we will have to go back to primitive agriculture and scratching in the woods.

There are indications, however, that suicidal technology is not absolutely necessary and that a permanent high-level technology is possible. Beginning in the early part of the twentieth century, it is possible to detect an anti-entropic movement in technology. This begins perhaps with the Haber process for the fixation of nitrogen from the air. A development of similar significance is the Dow process for the extraction of magnesium from the sea. Both these processes take the diffuse and concentrate it, instead of taking the concentrated and diffusing it, as do most processes of mining and economic production. These anti-entropic processes foreshadow a technology in which we shall draw all the materials we need from the virtually inexhaustible reservoirs of the sea and the air and draw our energy from controlled fusion—either artificially produced on the earth or from the sun.

This is why I so much resent spending half the world's income on armaments—because the more we do this, the less chance we have of making the transition to a stable, high-level society. The human race is in a precarious position on its planet and it should act accordingly. It has a chance, never to be repeated, of making its great transition, and if it fails, at least one good experiment in intelligence will have gone to waste. I suppose there are similar experiments of this nature going on in other parts of the universe; but I must confess to a hopelessly anthropocentric prejudice in favor of planet earth. It's a nice planet, and I'm in favor of it and I have no desire to see its principal inhabitant blow it up or starve it out.

When we look at the nature of possible remedies for our immediate problems, it seems clear that we are all engulfed in a profound and appallingly dangerous misallocation of our intellectual resources. The misallocation lies in the fact that although all our major problems are in social systems, we persist in regarding them as if they were essentially problems in physical or biological systems. We persist in regarding agricultural problems, for instance, as one of crops, whereas it is clearly fundamentally a problem of farmers. We persist in regarding the flood-control problem as a problem of the river and we even turn it over to army engineers, who treat the river as an enemy. A flood, however, is no problem at all to a river. It is a perfectly normal part of its way of life. The flood, essentially, is a problem of people and of social institutions, of architecture and zoning. Professor Gilbert White, of the University of Chicago, suggests that after spending over four billion dollars on flood control in this country, we are more in danger of major disasters than we were before. What we really mean by flood control is the substitution of a major disaster every fifty or one hundred years for minor inconveniences every five or ten.

In national defense we have fallen into exactly the same trap. We regard this as a problem in physical systems and in hardware, whereas it is essentially a problem in social systems. Here again, we are building into our societies the eventual certainty of total disaster. In face of the fact that war and peace is the major problem of our age, we are putting practically nothing into peace research; even when we do put money into arms control and disarmament research we spend sixty million dollars for Project Vela, which deals wholly with physical systems, and one hundred and fifty thousand on Project Vulcan, which deals with social systems and with unanswerable questions at that. When we look at biological and medical research, and still more, research into population, the disparity is just as striking. We persist in regarding disease as a biological problem, whereas it is fundamentally a bio-social system. Yet the number of sociologists in our medical schools can be counted almost on the fingers of one hand.

Nevertheless, in spite of the dangers, it is a wonderful age to live in, and I would not wish to be born in any other time. The wonderful and precious thing about the present moment is that there is still time—the Bomb hasn't gone off, the population explosion may be caught, the technological problem can, perhaps, be solved. If the human race is to survive, however, it will have to change more in its ways of thinking in the next twenty-five years than it has done in the last twenty-five thousand. There is hope, however, in the fact that we are very far from having exhausted the capacity of this extraordinary organism that we call man. I once calculated the capacity of the human nervous system in terms of the number of different states it might assume, which is a very rough measure. This comes to two to the ten billionth power, assuming that each of our ten billion neurons is capable of only two states. This is a very large number. It would take you ninety years to write it down at the rate of one digit a second. If you want a standard of comparison, the total number of neutrinos, which are the smallest known particles, which could be packed into the known astronomical universe (this is the largest physical number I could think of) could easily be written down in three minutes. I find it hard to believe, therefore, that the capacity of the human organism has been exhausted.

What we have to do now, however, is to develop almost a new form of learning. We have to learn from rapidly changing systems. Ordinarily we learn from stable systems. It is because the world repeats itself that we catch on to the law of repetition. Learning from changing systems is perhaps another step in the acceleration of evolution that we have to take. I have been haunted by a remark which Norman Meier, the psychologist, made in a seminar a few months ago, when he said that a cat who jumps on a hot stove never jumps on a cold one. This seems precisely to describe the state we may be in today. We have jumped on a lot of hot stoves and now perhaps the cold stove is the only place on which to jump. In the rapidly changing system it is desperately easy to learn things which are no longer true. Perhaps the greatest task of applied social science at the moment is to study the conditions under which we learn from rapidly changing systems. If we can answer this question, there may still be hope for the human race.